Studies in Economic History

Aims and Scope

This series from Springer provides a platform for works in economic history that truly integrate economics and history. Books on a wide range of related topics are welcomed and encouraged, including those in macro-economic history, financial history, labor history, industrial history, agricultural history, the history of institutions and organizations, spatial economic history, law and economic history, political economic history, historical demography, and environmental history.

Economic history studies have greatly developed over the past several decades through application of economics and econometrics. Particularly in recent years, a variety of new economic theories and sophisticated econometric techniques—including game theory, spatial economics, and generalized method of moment (GMM)—have been introduced for the great benefit of economic historians and the research community.

At the same time, a good economic history study should contribute more than just an application of economics and econometrics to past data. It raises novel research questions, proposes a new view of history, and/or provides rich documentation. This series is intended to integrate data analysis, close examination of archival works, and application of theoretical frameworks to offer new insights and even provide opportunities to rethink theories.

The purview of this new Springer series is truly global, encompassing all nations and areas of the world as well as all eras from ancient times to the present. The editorial board, who are internationally renowned leaders among economic historians, carefully evaluate and judge each manuscript, referring to reports from expert reviewers. The series publishes contributions by university professors and others well established in the academic community, as well as work deemed to be of equivalent merit.

All books and chapters in the Studies in Economic History book series are indexed in Scopus.

Patrick Gray • Joshua Hall
Ruth Wallis Herndon • Javier Silvestre
Editors

Standard of Living

Essays on Economics, History, and Religion in Honor of John E. Murray

Springer

Editors
Patrick Gray
Religious Studies
Rhodes College
Memphis, TN, USA

Joshua Hall
College of Business and Economics
West Virginia University
Morgantown, WV, USA

Ruth Wallis Herndon
Department of History
Bowling Green State University
Bowling Green, OH, USA

Javier Silvestre
Applied Economics
Facultad de Economia y Empresa
Zaragoza, Spain

ISSN 2364-1797 ISSN 2364-1800 (electronic)
Studies in Economic History
ISBN 978-3-031-06476-0 ISBN 978-3-031-06477-7 (eBook)
https://doi.org/10.1007/978-3-031-06477-7

This Springer imprint is published by the registered company Springer Nature Switzerland AG
The registered company address is: Gewerbestrasse 11, 6330 Cham, Switzerland

Preface

John Edward Murray was the Joseph R. Hyde III Professor of Political Economy and Professor of Economics at Rhodes College in Memphis, Tennessee, when he passed away suddenly on March 27, 2018, at the age of 58.

He was born on April 9, 1959, in Cincinnati, and became the first member of his family to attend college. He worked at a variety of jobs to pay his tuition, including phlebotomist, house painter, roofer, and ice cream vendor, graduating in 1981 from Oberlin College with a degree in economics. He later added an MS in mathematics from the University of Cincinnati, and the MA and PhD in economics from The Ohio State University, where he wrote his dissertation under Rick Steckel.

John taught high school math before pursuing his graduate work in economics. After finishing at Ohio State, he accepted a position at the University of Toledo, where he remained for 18 years before accepting the Hyde Professorship at Rhodes College in 2011.

He had a lifelong penchant for learning, spending a summer studying the German language in Schwabish Hall in 1984, and summers as an NEH scholar in Munich in 1995 and at Duke in 2013.

Murray authored two books and co-edited a third. His first book, *Origins of American Health Insurance: A History of Industrial Sickness Funds* (Yale University Press, 2007) was named one of ten "Noteworthy Books in Industrial Relations and Labor Economics" in 2008 by the Industrial Relations Section, Princeton University. His second book was co-edited with Ruth Wallis Herndon and titled *Children Bound to Labor: The Pauper Apprentice System in Early America* (Cornell University Press, 2009). *Economic History Review* said it was "a model for both comparative and national studies" of childhood and labor in historical context. His third book, *The Charleston Orphan House: Children's Lives in the First Public Orphanage in America* (University of Chicago Press, 2013), received the George C. Rogers, Jr. Prize, awarded by the South Carolina Historical Society for the best book on South Carolina history.

He published book chapters, monographs, encyclopedia and handbook contributions, and numerous articles in refereed journals including the *Journal of Economic History*, *Explorations in Economic History*, *Economic History Review*, *Agricultural*

History, and many others. His clear, crisp writing style and ability to explain complicated economic concepts made him a frequent choice to write for the popular press as well.

John's scholarly interests were varied, which is reflected in the essays in this volume. His most recent work centered on coal mine safety, post bellum African-American labor supply, and families in nineteenth-century Charleston. He published extensively in the areas of the history of healthcare and health insurance, religion, and family-related issues from education to orphanages, fertility, and marriage, not to mention his work in anthropometrics, labor markets, and literacy. His intellectual work was often informed by his religious convictions, and he spent time studying Catholic theology at Sacred Heart Major Seminary in Detroit.

John had a deep commitment to his family. His first book was dedicated to his wife Lynn, and his second and third books to his children Rose and Sarah. He would share with delight information about his family with colleagues, and his office was filled with artwork by his children and family photos.

This anthology honors John E. Murray, whose scholarly interests and collegial network ranged well beyond the economics departments in which he worked throughout his professional life. His sudden death in March 2018 ended many ongoing conversations in economics, history, and religion. John considered himself a historian as well as an economist, and he held himself to the scholarly standards of both disciplines. He interpreted economic data and put it to work in the service of history. He read history and put it to work in the service of economics. His work was also informed by his lifelong study of religion, and he maintained lively and collegial friendships with scholars of religion. The essays in this volume reflect John's scholarly interests and were written with his interests in mind.

John Murray was a person who conversed with others. The following chapters continue conversations that John started, encouraged, or inspired. He read secondary literature voraciously and would quickly contact the author of an article or book that caught his interest. His gift for starting conversations brought many people into his network and led to wonderful collaborations. The four editors of this volume met him at different moments of his professional life and in very different circumstances.

1996: John started the conversation that brought Ruth Herndon into his scholarly community. In 1996, when Herndon was at the Philadelphia Center for Early American Studies at the University of Pennsylvania (now the McNeil Center), she published a brief "Research Note" in the *Journal of Social History* about the signature literacy of poor people warned out of New England towns in the latter eighteenth century. Literacy and poor people being two of John's interests, he naturally read the essay and promptly wrote Herndon at the Philadelphia Center, unaware that since the article's publication she had taken up a faculty position in the Department of History at the University of Toledo, where John was himself teaching in the Department of Economics. When Herndon received John's letter, forwarded from the Philadelphia Center, she picked up her office phone, and called her new UT colleague. After John got over the shock of this serendipity, he initiated a series of brown bag lunch conversations that gradually grew into co-authored conference papers, then a co-authored journal article, then a major research grant proposal supporting their co-edited anthology *Children Bound to Labor.* Although Herndon subsequently moved to Bowling Green State University and Murray moved to Rhodes College, they continued their conversation on childhood, parenting, education, and labor in historical context. Shortly before he died, they had proposed a conference session together.

2003: Josh Hall first met John when he was teaching at Capital University in Columbus Ohio. Economic history was what first got Josh interested in economics and he had heard that there was an Ohio economic history meeting that he might attend. Having been born in Toledo, he figured that was enough of a connection to reach out to John Murray by email. And so a correspondence began that touched on baseball, the Wright Brothers, graduate school in economics, and economic history. In 2004, John provided advice when Josh applied to doctoral programs in economics. In 2007, Josh was a finalist for a job at Rhodes College he didn't get. However, a year later they were searching for an endowed chair and he encouraged John to apply. The rest, as they say, is history. Josh greatly misses John's occasional email exchanges and is not surprised that so many were touched so deeply by John and his work.

2004: Javier Silvestre met John at the 2004 Cliometrics World Congress, in Venice, where the latter chaired the session in which the former presented a paper. Both shared a broad interest in workplace safety in different countries. Some time after the Congress, John proposed that Silvestre coauthor a paper on safety in European coal mining, using an almost unexploited source. However, it was not until several years later that the real work began. The resulting paper ended up with a strong focus on technology, to that point an almost entirely unexplored field for both authors. Once the paper was accepted for publication, in 2014, such an amount of information on technological change in nineteenth-century European coal mining had been gathered that John proposed that he and Silvestre embark on a project together. The premise was that, as far as technological change is concerned, perhaps different strands of the literature, economic history in particular, had been more focused on the eighteenth and twentieth centuries. Technology in nineteenth-century coalmining needed to be reassessed. John's enthusiasm was contagious. Over the years, regular emails were exchanged on the subject of improvements in mechanical fans, safety lamps, or explosives. He travelled to Spain a few times. In Zaragoza, intense work sessions on the "coal project," as John called it, were combined with long evening walks and talks. It was difficult not to share some of his many interests: from freedom of speech to sports, via blues music, as well as dogs, of course, to mention but a few. He was also a visiting scholar at the University of Barcelona. His *Origins of American Health Insurance* book came at a time when the study of the genesis of the Spanish welfare state was gathering strength among young economic historians.

2011: Patrick Gray met John through mutual acquaintances in the Department of Economics when he moved from Toledo to Memphis in 2011 to become the Joseph R. Hyde III Professor of Political Economy at Rhodes College. Lunch conversations regularly turned to such topics as baseball—especially John's beloved Cincinnati

Reds—and raising children. John was very well read, and he wore his learning lightly. This made him an outstanding scholar. John was not a member of the Austrian School, but he agreed with the remark attributed to Friedrich Hayek that "if you only understand economics, then you don't understand economics," and he exemplified the spirit it expressed. His wide-ranging publications attest to a boundless intellectual curiosity and a punctilious attention to detail. John's endowed chair came with a generous book budget, and he was not afraid to use it. Theology was a special interest. His home and office bookshelves groaned under the additional weight of volumes related to biblical studies, church history, and philosophy. Copious notes in the margins and underlined passages show that, far from being just for show, he had actually read them. How to read and teach Augustine and Luther in the interdisciplinary humanities sequence offered at Rhodes were frequent topics of conversation. His approach to these texts bespoke an admirable humility that comes with knowing the limits of one's knowledge and expertise. Along with his gentle spirit and hearty laugh, this is what his colleagues will miss.

Religious Studies
Rhodes College
Memphis, TN, USA
Patrick Gray

College of Business and Economics
West Virginia University
Morgantown, WV, USA
Joshua Hall

Department of History
Bowling Green State University
Bowling Green, OH, USA
Ruth Wallis Herndon

Applied Economics
Facultad de Economia y Empresa
Zaragoza, Spain
Javier Silvestre

Contents

1 **Urbanization, Sanitation, and Mortality in the Progressive Era, 1899–1929** 1
Louis P. Cain and Elyce J. Rotella

2 **The Continuing Puzzle of Hypertension Among African Americans: Developmental Origins and the Mid-century Socioeconomic Transformation** 19
Garrett T. Senney and Richard H. Steckel

3 **Health and Safety vs. Freedom of Contract: The Tortured Path of Wage and Hours Limits Through the State Legislatures and the Courts** 43
Price Fishback

4 **Sickness Experience in England, 1870–1949** 69
Andrew Hinde, Martin Gorsky, Aravinda Guntupalli, and Bernard Harris

5 **Friendly Societies and Sickness Coverage in the Absence of State Provision in Spain (1870–1935)** 97
Margarita Vilar-Rodríguez and Jerònia Pons-Pons

6 **A Difficult Consensus: The Making of the Spanish Welfare State** 119
Sergio Espuelas

7 **The Effect of the 1918 Influenza Pandemic on US Life Insurance Holdings** 141
Joanna Short

8 **"Theft of Oneself": Runaway Servants in Early Maryland: Deterrence, Punishment, and Apprehension** 167
Farley Grubb

9 **Adult Guardianship and Local Politics in Rhode Island, 1750–1800** 185
Ruth Wallis Herndon and Amílcar E. Challú

10 **Later-Life Realizations of Maryland's Mid-Nineteenth-Century Pauper Apprentices** 211
Howard Bodenhorn

11 **Family Allocation Strategy in the Late Nineteenth Century** 245
Trevon Logan

12 **Child Labor and Industrialization in Early Republican Turkey** 279
Semih Gokatalay

13 **Orphans, Widows, and the Economics of the Early Church** 297
Patrick Gray

14 **An Economic Approach to Religious Communes: The Shakers** 309
Metin Coşgel

15 **Religion, Human Capital, and Economic Diversity in Nineteenth-Century Hesse-Cassel** 323
Kristin Mammen and Simone A. Wegge

16 **Productivity, Mortality, and Technology in European and US Coal Mining, 1800–1913** 345
Javier Silvestre

17 **Breathing Apparatus for Mine Rescue in the UK, 1890s–1920s** 373
John Singleton

18 **Grain Market Integration in Late Colonial Mexico** 395
Amílcar E. Challú

19 **William McKinley, Optimal Reneging, and the Spanish-American War** 423
Joshua R. Hendrickson

20 **Capitalism and the Good Society: The Original Case for and Against Commerce** 451
Daniel Cullen

21 **Situating Southern Influences in James M. Buchanan and Modern Public Choice Economics** 465
Art Carden, Vincent Geloso, and Phillip W. Magness

22 **John Murray: A Teacher, a Mentor, and a Friend** 477
Joshua R. Hendrickson

Contributors

Howard Bodenhorn Clemson University, Clemson, SC, USA

Louis P. Cain Northwestern University, Evanston, IL, USA

Art Carden Samford University, Birmingham, AL, USA

Amílcar E. Challú Bowling Green State University, Bowling Green, OH, USA

Metin Coşgel University of Connecticut, Storrs, CT, USA

Daniel Cullen Rhodes College, Memphis, TN, USA

Sergio Espuelas Universitat de Barcelona, Barcelona, Spain

Price Fishback University of Arizona, Tucson, AZ, USA

Vincent Geloso George Mason University, Fairfax, VA, USA

Semih Gokatalay UC San Diego, La Jolla, CA, USA

Martin Gorsky London School of Hygiene and Tropical Medicine, London, UK

Patrick Gray Rhodes College, Memphis, TN, USA

Farley Grubb University of Delaware, Newark, DE, USA

Aravinda Guntupalli University of Aberdeen, King's College, Aberdeen, Scotland

Joshua Hall West Virginia University, Morgantown, WV, USA

Bernard Harris University of Strathclyde, Glasgow, UK

Joshua R. Hendrickson University of Mississippi, Oxford, MS, USA

Ruth Wallis Herndon Bowling Green State University, Bowling Green, OH, USA

Andrew Hinde University of Southampton, Alton, Hampshire, UK

Trevon Logan Ohio State University, Columbus, OH, USA

Phillip W. Magness American Institute for Economic Research, Great Barrington, MA, USA

Kristin Mammen College of Staten Island –CUNY, Staten Island, NY, USA

Jerònia Pons-Pons Universidad de Sevilla, Sevilla, Spain

Elyce J. Rotella University of Michigan, Ann Arbor, MI, USA

Garrett T. Senney Office of the Comptroller of the Currency, Washington, DC, USA

Joanna Short Augustana College, Rock Island, IL, USA

Javier Silvestre Universidad de Zaragoza, Zaragoza, Spain

John Singleton Sheffield Hallam University, Sheffield, UK

Richard H. Steckel Ohio State University, Columbus, OH, USA

Margarita Vilar-Rodríguez University of A Coruña, Coruña, Spain

Simone A. Wegge College of Staten Island and the Graduate Center, City University of New York, New York, NY, USA

Chapter 1
Urbanization, Sanitation, and Mortality in the Progressive Era, 1899–1929

Louis P. Cain and Elyce J. Rotella

Abstract Between 1899 and 1929, deaths from waterborne diseases declined dramatically in American cities. The major cause of such declines was spending on sanitation systems (water, sewers, and refuse collection). Cities spent enormous amounts to build and maintain water and sewer systems, and to collect and dispose of refuse. We first estimate the size of the payoff to cities of such expenditures, where the payoff is measured in averted deaths. Using a panel of annual mortality and municipal expenditure data from 152 cities, we estimate that a 1% increase in sanitation expenditures was associated with a 3% decline in the mortality rate. In the second section of the paper, we ask whether the mortality reducing effects of sanitation expenditures differed by the type of water resources available to the city (ocean, lake, river). The answer is unambiguously yes, with cities located on lakes facing the most difficult sanitary situation.

Keywords Urbanization · Mortality · Sanitation · Water · Sewers · Refuse

1.1 Introduction

As the nineteenth century drew to a close, the demand for public sanitation works in American cities began to accelerate. No city can exist without a supply of freshwater, but the widespread acceptance of the germ theory made it clear that the water should be clean – and not just clean to the senses of taste, smell, and sight, but clean

L. P. Cain
Northwestern University, Evanston, IL, USA

Loyola University Chicago, Chicago, IL, USA
e-mail: lcain@northwestern.edu

E. J. Rotella (✉)
University of Michigan, Ann Arbor, MI, USA
e-mail: rotella@umich.edu

P. Gray et al. (eds.), *Standard of Living*, Studies in Economic History,
https://doi.org/10.1007/978-3-031-06477-7_1

according to accepted biological standards. Especially after the adoption of the flush toilet, it became necessary to help the water that made its way into homes and businesses find its way back out. And, it became imperative that both wastewater and solid waste be removed as potential breeding grounds for diseases that plagued cities. In the early years of the nineteenth century, water for firefighting was a principal driving force behind the demand for improved urban water supplies. In the later years of that century, citizens' demand for urban water supplies became more complex. In the middle of the century, sanitarians such as Edwin Chadwick (1842) in London and Lemuel Shattuck (1850, 1948) in Massachusetts demonstrated the correlation between bad water and disease. Once the germ theory was promulgated, there was an explanation for the relationship. Cities with existing sanitary facilities were now pressed to improve them; cities which lacked facilities were now pressed to build them. Disease prevention required that the water be treated, and both filtration and chlorination were adopted in a wide variety of cities. Similarly, wastewater required treatment, and a variety of sewage treatment technologies were invented and adopted in the first decades of the twentieth century. The question that motivates this study is: what kind of return did cities realize from the investments they made in sanitary infrastructure?

In *Constructing Urban Culture*, Stanley Schultz (1989) explores the relationship between American cities and city planning. Public health problems as they emerged in rapidly growing metropolises at the end of the nineteenth century led to technological solutions. As part of his examination of the effect of sewering the cities, Schultz presents data on death rates and miles of sewer constructed and concludes: "Filtration of water and sewage brought a dramatic drop in typhoid mortality rates, a drop that averaged 65 percent in selected major cities" (174). In Schultz's analysis, the cause of the drop in typhoid deaths is simply asserted. Earlier studies by economic historians of public health determinants of mortality include Edward Meeker (1972, 1974) and Gretchen A. Condran and Eileen M. Crimmins-Gardner (1978, 1983).

The goal of our study is to estimate the direction and magnitude of the relationship between the public works improvements of the Progressive era and the decline in mortality from waterborne diseases. Did cities' expenditures on water, sewers, and refuse "pay off" by reducing the death rate from typhoid, diarrhea, and dysentery? If yes, how big was the payoff?

Among economic historians who have scrutinized other dimensions of the Progressive movement is John Murray. In his *Origins of American Health Insurance* (2007), he examined sickness funds which would have mitigated the expenses of getting sick. We do not have as good data on morbidity as there are for mortality, but it seems reasonable to believe that a reduction in mortality attributable to waterborne diseases is consistent with a reduction in morbidity as well. Consequently, we argue that sanitation works which reduced morbidity and mortality thereby ameliorated a portion of the risks that sickness insurance would have covered. Murray's project is complementary to this paper. Our results help explain Murray's finding of little popular support for compulsory health insurance. People preferred to push municipalities to spend money on avoiding illness by reducing waterborne diseases as opposed to mitigating through insurance the expenses incurred as a result of getting sick.

David Cutler and Grant Miller (2005) studied the effectiveness of urban water supplies in the early twentieth century by using what they argue is exogenous variation in both the timing and location of the new technologies to identify the effects of water improvements. They conclude that the causal influence of water purification (specifically filtration and chlorination) on mortality was large. They find that clean water was responsible for nearly half the total mortality reduction in those cities, as well as for three-quarters of the reduction in infant mortality and nearly two-thirds of the reduction in child mortality. In a later paper (2006), they argue that this improvement was not limited to the largest cities. Similarly, Joseph Ferrie and Werner Troesken (2008) estimate that 35–56% of the decrease in Chicago's crude death rate up to 1925 can be attributed to water purification and the eradication of waterborne diseases. Marcella Alsan and Claudia Goldin (2019) examine the development of clean water and effective sewerage systems in Boston between 1880 and 1920 and estimate that those works were responsible for much of the first sustained decrease in child (under 5) mortality.

In this study, we expand the list of expenditures to include sewage works and refuse collection as well as waterworks. If such expenditures were effective in reducing the death rate from waterborne diseases, did they pay off by reducing the total death rate as well? A decline in the total death rate could have resulted because deaths from waterborne causes were a large share of total deaths, and the factors that were responsible for the decline in waterborne deaths determined the decline in total deaths. Secondly, improvements in water, sewers, and refuse could have led to reductions in deaths from causes other than waterborne diseases because such diseases were spread by the same vectors, or because declines in morbidity from the causes responsible for waterborne diseases reduce the likelihood of deaths from other causes. To paraphrase demographers, people accumulated fewer insults when these waterborne diseases were averted, and, therefore, they were less likely to succumb to other diseases. For example, Preston and Van de Walle (1978) argue that, in the case of intestinal diseases, public health changes led to this effect (see also Szreter 1988; Wohl 1984; Woods 2000).

This paper examines relationships between US municipal expenditures and death rates from 1899 to 1929. Urban historians (Glaab and Brown 1967; Mohl 1985) consider this to be an era of reform, the first awakening of the environmental movement leading to a dramatic expansion in budgetary expenditures on such works. By 1907, virtually every American city had installed sewers, and most big cities were using filtration and chlorination to assure the safety of their water supplies (Galishoff 1980; Tarr et al. 1980).

From the very late 1890s to the very early 1930s (with a few missing years), the federal government published compilations of both financial and mortality statistics for cities.[1] This paper stops in 1929 before the onset of the Great Depression and the

[1] Data on both finances and mortality are contained in *Bureau of Labor Statistics Bulletin*, #24, 30, 36, and 42, for the years 1899–1902, and *Census Bulletin* #20 for 1902–1903. The Bureau of the Census published *Mortality Statistics of Cities* annually between 1900 and 1936 and *Financial Statistics of Cities* more or less annually between 1905 and 1931.

availability of federal funds for municipal improvements. Its main focus is to link statistically both the total death rate and the death rate from diarrhea, dysentery, and typhoid (diseases spread by impure water and filth) to the expenditures on sanitation (water supply, wastewater, and refuse works).

A second question addressed in this paper derives from Cain's (1977) argument that there are four distinct urban sanitary histories. The differentiating feature is the type of water resource on which a city is located. Cities located on *salt water* cannot draw their water supply from the abundant water close at hand and often have to rely on sources hundreds of miles removed from the city. On the other hand, these cities can dispose of their wastes in the adjacent salt water. Cities located on *freshwater lakes* have historically used the lake for both water supplies and waste disposal. Such cities are forced to geographically separate the water intake and sewer outfall as far as possible to avoid befouling their drinking water with their wastes. This interdependency creates what are arguably the most difficult sanitation problems faced by any type of city. Cities located on *major rivers* simply have drawn their water upstream from the city and disposed of their wastes downstream, taking care that the potential sewage backwash cannot reach the water intake. Cities located on smaller, *minor rivers* often have had to look elsewhere for an adequate water supply; they utilize distant lakes and rivers or rely on well water. Such small river cities still dispose their wastes in the river, but they may have to build sewers to a downstream point where the river can receive a large volume of wastewater.

Each of the cities in our sample has been identified as belonging to one of these groups. We will examine whether the effects of the water, sewer, and refuse variables differed by city type. Since the different city types faced different costs and constraints in attempting to reduce mortality by investing in water, sewage, and refuse works, we expect that the payoff to such investments varied between cities. Therefore, cities facing different costs and constraints had incentives to invest in sanitation strategies involving different mixes of these variables.

1.2 Data

Annual data on mortality and municipal expenditures were collected for 152 cities for the period 1899–1929. The sample was defined to include all cities with populations over 25,000 in the 1910 Census. A few smaller freshwater lake cities were added in order to increase the number of observations in that group. While some cities had to be dropped from the sample because of insufficient data, the pooled sample used in the reported regressions includes data from 87 cities in 1902 and 125 cities in 1929.

1.2.1 Mortality Data and Variables

The mortality data used in this study were collected from the *Mortality Statistics of Cities* which annually published death-by-cause statistics. Data were collected on deaths from typhoid fever, dysentery, and diarrhea as well as all causes taken together. While historical evidence on death-by-cause is notoriously problematic because of changing definitions of diseases and changes in diagnoses, the diseases studied in this paper were well identified in this period.

Typhoid, dysentery, and diarrheal diseases were spread by impure water and food, and by contact with feces and other filth. In this paper, we follow the convention of referring to this group of diseases as "waterborne," even though water is not the exclusive means of transmission. We expect, as did contemporaries, that these diseases were controlled by programs to deliver clean water, remove and treat sewage, and collect and dispose of refuse.

Deaths from all causes and deaths from waterborne diseases were used together with population data to calculate the total death rates (TDR) and waterborne disease death rates (WDR) used as dependent variables in the regressions reported in Sect. 1.4.

1.2.2 Financial Data and Variables

This study makes use of data on annual operating costs and capital acquisition costs of waterworks, sewage works, and refuse collection and disposal systems. These data were published in various bulletins up to 1903 and in *Financial Statistics of Cities* beginning in 1905. There are few direct figures available for 1904. Not every series was reported every year, and no *Financial Statistics* were published in 1913, 1914, or 1920. For 1921 and 1922, information on sewers and refuse were reported together under the heading "Sanitation." Interpolation based on expenditures in the same city in adjacent years was used to apportion the 1921 and 1922 reported figures between refuse and sewers.

Financial data were used to construct two kinds of variables employed in the regression analysis: capital variables and current operating cost variables. Expenditures on capital were aggregated over all years up to the year of observation and then divided by the population in the year of observation thereby producing an estimate of the per capita value of the works. The per capita value of sewage facilities (SEWKALL) and refuse collection and disposal facilities (REFKALL) were constructed in this manner. The accumulated value of capital in waterworks (WATKALL) includes the value of the waterworks at the beginning of the period. This value was reported in the Census bulletins, and, for most cities, this is the value in 1899. Galishoff (1980, 52) includes a graph based on US Public Health Service data indicating that most cities had selected the source they used and constructed municipal works before the turn of the twentieth century. Treatment, principally filtration, and disinfection, principally chlorination, were adopted after the turn of the century. A small minority of cities in the sample did not have municipal waterworks and were not included in the main regressions reported in Sect. 1.4.

Information on annual operating expenditures for water, sewers, and refuse were used to create the variables WATERAV3, SEWERAV3, and REFUSEAV3 which are the average operating expenditures per capita for the year under observation and the previous 2 years.

1.2.3 Control Variables

Six variables were collected for control purposes. These include each city's land area (LANDAREA) and assessed valuation (ASSDPC) for each year. Land area provides a measure of geographical size and change within the study period, while the assessed valuation measures the city's ability to pay. Since the Progressive era was a period of annexation and consolidation, the inclusion of these variables controls for this type of city size growth.[2]

Two series were collected from the historical weather records to control for climatological differences in time and space. The total rainfall in inches measures the wetness of a particular year, while the length of the growing season in days measures for how much of the year climactic conditions (temperature, altitude, and rainfall) permitted normal plant growth.[3]

Finally, two dummy variables were employed. The first, WAR, includes the period of the First World War and its aftermath, which included a vigorous inflation and a virulent outbreak of influenza. The other, LATE20, controls for 3 years in the late 1920s when many cities overestimated their populations, the figure used to make per capita calculations.

1.3 The Regression Model

Annual statistics from 1899 through 1929 were pooled to create a panel data set. The data used in the regressions cover the period 1902–1929 with data on 1899–1901 used to create variables based on averages and aggregates of past expenditures. The effects of capital and operating costs on death rates were estimated using a one-way fixed effects regression model. This technique runs an ordinary least squares regression on the entire panel, estimating a separate intercept term for each city.

---

[2] Data on Allegheny, Pennsylvania, were collected and added to those of Pittsburgh to incorporate that annexation explicitly in the sample.

[3] Unfortunately, the weather bureau did not collect information for all the cities in the sample, so in some cases what has been included comes from a city which is a climatological clone of a sample city.

Chi-squared tests confirm the superiority of this specification over the simple OLS model without fixed effects.

The simple OLS model was estimated with the full set of control variables discussed above plus variables for population density (population/land area), population growth (the population this year/the average population in the three previous years), and the year. The weather variables proved to be very powerful with mortality substantially higher in the wetter and warmer cities. All the control variables had the expected signs. While they were important for explaining the urban mortality experience, all but YEAR, LANDAREA, ASSDPC, and the two dummy variables (WAR and LATE20) were dropped from the regressions reported in the next section because their impacts are included in the fixed effects.[4]

1.4 Results

The first three decades of the twentieth century were years of considerable improvement in medical practice, food delivery and preparation, and urban sanitation. Also, living standards were rising as personal income was rising throughout the period. The widespread acceptance of the germ theory of disease led to the adoption of procedures designed to reduce the spread of many common nineteenth-century diseases. As Mokyr (1983) emphasizes, the evolutionary diffusion of public health techniques over the twentieth century explains much of the decline in mortality rates and the emergence of a new demographic regime. As life expectancy increased, other diseases came to be more common causes of death. The "Second Industrial Revolution" based on electricity and automobiles introduced potentially more deadly technologies, while accelerated urbanization increased the potential for violence.[5] The overall pattern of change in urban mortality can be seen in Table 1.1.

In 1902, the 15.124 per 10,000 population deaths attributable to waterborne diseases were 8.9% of all deaths. By 1929, the 1.857 per 10,000 deaths from waterborne diseases were only 1.4% of the total. The total death rate dropped by 20% over the period (16.713/1000 to 13.409/1000), but death rates from waterborne disease dropped by almost 90%. We can get some idea of the importance of this rapid decline in waterborne diseases by engaging in a simple counterfactual exercise. If, beginning in 1902, there had been no decline in the death rate from waterborne diseases, and if the death rate from all other causes had declined at its actual rate, then the total death rate in 1929 would have been 14.836 instead of 13.323. That is, instead of falling nearly 20% from 1902 to 1929, the death rate would have fallen by only 12.2%. From this, we can conclude that 43.2% of the actual decline in the

[4] A one-way random effects model was also estimated allowing for city-specific heteroscedasticity correction using a generalized least squares technique. The results were almost identical to the OLS specification, and, therefore, only the OLS fixed effects results are reported.

[5] The proportion of total deaths from accidents, suicides, and other acts of violence does not appear to have increased over the study period.

Table 1.1 Average urban death rates

Year	Total deaths	Deaths from Waterborne diseases	Deaths from Waterborne diseases as a Percentage of all deaths
1902	16.713	15.124	8.9%
1903	16.868	15.064	8.8
1904	16.686	15.377	9.1
1905	16.826	15.673	9.2
1906	17.136	16.455	9.5
1907	17.682	16.749	9.3
1908	16.370	15.171	9.1
1909	15.545	14.105	9.0
1910	16.657	14.232	8.5
1911	15.776	11.824	7.4
1912	15.234	10.072	6.6
1913	n.a.	n.a.	
1914	n.a.	n.a.	
1915	15.197	8.691	5.6
1916	15.503	9.131	5.7
1917	15.861	8.780	5.4
1918	20.691	8.279	3.9
1919	14.489	5.838	4.0
1920	14.721	5.751	3.9
1921	12.958	5.054	3.9
1922	13.272	4.080	3.0
1923	13.661	4.028	2.9
1924	13.128	3.502	2.6
1925	13.367	3.668	2.7
1926	13.774	3.240	2.3
1927	12.660	2.410	1.9
1928	13.715	2.213	1.6
1929	13.409	1.857	1.4
1929/1902	67.828	12.278	
Percentage change			
1902–1929	19.769	87.722	

Total death rates are per 1000 inhabitants; waterborne disease death rates are per 10,000 inhabitants These rates are averages for the cities included in the pooled sample. Waterborne diseases include diarrhea, dysentery, and typhoid

total death rate between 1902 and 1929 can be attributed to the decline in deaths from waterborne diseases.

The variables included in the regressions are described in Table 1.2; the results with the total death rate as the dependent variable are reported in Table 1.3. The variable WATKALL captures improvements in water quality that resulted from filtration, the construction of filter beds and plants. In each case reported in Table 1.3,

Table 1.2 Definitions of independent variables included in regressions

WATKALL	Sum of all capital expenditures on waterworks prior to the year under observation plus the value of municipal waterworks in 1899 (or in the year acquired) in per capita terms
WATERAV3	Average operating expenditures on waterworks and water treatment over the two preceding years and the year under observation in per capita terms
SEWKALL	Sum of all capital expenditures on sewage facilities up to the year under observation in per capita terms
SEWERAV3	Average operating expenditures on the sewer system over the two previous years and the year under observation in per capita terms
REFKALL	Sum of all capital expenditures on refuse collection and disposal up to the year under observation in per capita terms
REFUSEAV3	Average operating expenditures on refuse collection and disposal over the two preceding years and the year under observation in per capita terms
YEAR	A trend variable, the year under observation
WAR	A dummy variable equal to 1, if year = 1917–1920
LATE20	A dummy variable equal to 1, if year = 1925–1927
ASSDPC	Assessed valuation in hundreds of dollars per person
LANDAREA	Square miles in hundreds of square miles

this coefficient is positive, quite the opposite of what would be expected if there were a spillover to deaths from other causes from the factors one anticipates would reduce waterborne diseases. For all the cities in the sample, and in three of the four city types, the positive coefficient is statistically significant suggesting that an additional dollar spent on waterworks was associated with higher overall death rates, after controlling for sewer and refuse expenditures. The variable WATERAV3 captures improvements in water quality resulting from disinfection, expenditures for chlorination. In only one case, freshwater lake cities, is this variable negative. Similar difficulties are present in the sewer and refuse variables.

We conclude from Table 1.3 that a consideration of expenditures on urban sanitation in the years 1899–1929 produces little understanding of what determined the *total* death rate. Even though the decline in waterborne diseases was a very large part of the decline in total urban mortality in this period, the results do not show that the total death rate responded as one might expect from the expenditures on water, sewers, and refuse. Hereafter, consideration of the effects of urban sanitation expenditures will focus on their impact on the *waterborne disease* death rate. These results are reported in Table 1.4.

For all cities taken together, the existence of a waterworks and the addition of filtration works during this period (WATKALL) had an important effect on reducing waterborne deaths. On the other hand when we examine the impact of operating expenditures (WATERAV3), we see that cities with higher waterborne disease death rates either spent more on disinfection or the addition of disinfection marginally increased deaths. Examining these results by the various city types puts the findings into sharper relief. The negative coefficient on the water capital variable is significant only for saltwater cities that must travel the greatest distance to find a source of

Table 1.3 Total death rate regression results

Fresh water					
Variable	All	Salt water	Lake	Major river	Minor river
WATKALL	0.00205[a]	0.00047	0.00515[a]	0.00297[a]	0.00260[a]
WATERAV3	0.01193[a]	0.01190	−0.04553[a]	0.00888	0.01692
SEWKALL	0.00115[b]	0.00144	0.00174	0.00219[b]	0.00126
SEWERAV3	0.01842[b]	0.03447[a]	−0.00999	0.00009	−0.00884
REFKALL	0.00495	−0.01396	−0.06731[a]	−0.00965	0.06949[a]
REFUSEAV3	−0.03913[a]	−0.04246[a]	−0.01679	−0.06290[a]	−0.02534
YEAR	−0.01301[a]	−0.01583[a]	−0.00268	−0.00902[a]	−0.01488[a]
WAR	0.15811[a]	0.11243[a]	0.13657[a]	0.16132[a]	0.18510[a]
LATE20	−0.02067[a]	−0.01242	−0.03640[b]	−0.02714	−0.03270[b]
ASSDPC	0.00177[a]	−0.00231[b]	0.00123	0.00188[a]	0.00310[b]
LANDAREA	0.00008[a]	0.00003	−0.00107[a]	−0.00036[a]	−0.00095[a]
R^2	0.657	0.760	0.737	0.568	0.680
n	2609	716	291	883	723

Dependent variable is the log of the total death rate
[a]Statistically significant at the 95% confidence level
[b]Statistically significant at the 90% confidence level

Table 1.4 Waterborne disease death rate regression results

Fresh water					
Variable	All	Salt water	Lake	Major river	Minor river
WATKALL	−0.00349[a]	−0.00818[a]	0.00653	−0.00075	−0.00028
WATERAV3	0.00945	−0.01690	−0.09220[b]	−0.01414	0.02982
SEWKALL	−0.01332[a]	−0.00951[a]	−0.00119	−0.01201[a]	−0.02099[a]
SEWERAV3	−0.04766[b]	0.00126	−0.10747	0.09388	−0.37971[a]
REFKALL	−0.07875[a]	−0.13693[a]	−0.64572[a]	−0.08444[a]	0.01024
REFUSEAV3	−0.05264[a]	−0.05707[b]	0.17879[a]	−0.07358[a]	−0.11522[a]
YEAR	−0.07369[a]	−0.08113[a]	−0.05024[a]	−0.06788[a]	−0.06652[a]
WAR	0.21762[a]	0.16005[a]	0.11556	0.20325[a]	0.25446[a]
LATE20	0.00264	−0.08883[a]	0.01338	0.10020[a]	−0.04403
ASSDPC	0.00408[a]	0.00338	−0.02260[a]	0.00393[b]	−0.00235
LANDAREA	0.00029[a]	0.00042[a]	−0.00326[a]	0.00002	0.00018
R^2	0.840	0.897	0.825	0.824	0.829
n	2609	716	291	883	723

Dependent variable is log of the waterborne disease death rate.
[a]Statistically significant at the 95% confidence level
[b]Statistically significant at the 90% confidence level

fresh water. The expected negative effect is present in both types of river cities, but the coefficient is in fact positive for freshwater lake cities. While this coefficient is not statistically different from zero, the positive sign may be interpreted as a consequence of these cities customarily drawing water from the same water source into which they deposit their wastes. The differences in the size of the coefficients are also worthy of note. An additional dollar spent on water capital in saltwater cities has ten times the impact as in major river cities, and expenditures in major river cities have three times the impact as in minor river cities.

The only city type in which annual expenditures for the water department show a positive coefficient is minor river cities, those which rely most heavily on groundwater supplies.[6] Since this city type is the only one for which refuse capital expenditures do not have a significant negative effect, where the effect is in fact positive, one might conclude that refuse could be leeching into groundwater supplies. It is only in freshwater lake cities where disinfection has a significant negative effect, and it seems likely chlorination was important in combatting impurities in the wastewater that was discharged into these cities' water supply sources.

The two sewage variables both have a statistically significant negative effect on the waterborne disease death rate in the regression for all cities taken together. In each type of city, the expenditure on sewer construction and sewage treatment works has a negative effect. It is significant for all but the freshwater lake cities, who, given the interdependency between water supply and wastewater disposal, have to spend a great deal more to get the same effect on death rates as the other city types. The variable means reported in Table 1.5 do not indicate, however, that these freshwater lake cities spent a great deal more for sewage capital than did the other city types.[7]

Annual expenditures on sewers have a more complex pattern across city types. While the all city regression has a significant negative coefficient, the same is true only for the minor river cities. Lake cities also have the expected negative coefficient, but those for saltwater cities and major river cities are in fact positive. None of these latter three coefficients is statistically significant. In almost every case, minor river cities use the river as their disposal source, but they may have to convey their wastewater several miles downstream to a point where the river is sufficiently large to handle the city's volume. It is a simple matter of disposal strategy, which is less of a problem for the other three types. Both saltwater cities and major river cities locate their water supply sources in such a way as to minimize the cost of wastewater disposal. They have located their sewage works such that sewage services have an effect on the death rate, but the annual expenditures on sewer maintenance get short shrift relative to the need to maintain the purity of their water supplies.

The solid waste variables, which involve many fewer dollars than the other two as the table of variable means (Table 1.5) documents, prove to have a statistically significant negative effect in almost every city type and for all cities taken together. Given the close connection between waterborne and foodborne diseases, the regular removal and disposal of food wastes in such a way as to remove them from water supply sources has important consequences. The only exception to the significant

[6] Some, such as Denver, constructed systems reminiscent of saltwater cities to tap distant sources.

[7] In the case of the Sanitary District of Chicago, more than 10 years of capital expense led to a large decrease in cholera deaths in the first year after the Main Channel was opened. Unfortunately, the District is a supra-governmental body and, therefore, not included in the *Financial Statistics of Cities*. When the North Side Treatment Works opened in the mid-1920s, Chicago had spent more on sewage treatment than the expenditures in the next ten largest cities combined.

Table 1.5 Means of variables included in regressions

Fresh water					
Variable	All	Salt water	Lake	Major river	Minor river
WATKALL	29.057	34.323	26.706	27.367	26.726
WATERAV3	1.5753	1.7403	1.4698	1.6647	1.3472
SEWKALL	10.900	11.223	11.987	10.369	10.830
SEWERAV3	0.30401	0.44751	0.23902	0.22481	0.28773
REFKALL	0.29401	0.23173	0.29952	0.29795	0.36411
REFUSEAV3	0.79976	0.95536	0.88345	0.72686	0.71077
YEAR	1916.4	1916.2	1916.5	1916.3	1916.7
WAR	0.13147	0.12989	0.12371	0.13137	0.13555
LATE20	0.13952	0.13128	0.15120	0.13930	0.14523
ASSDPC	10.873	11.851	8.7395	12.275	9.1335
LANDAREA	195.11	233.61	256.80	191.35	137.42
TDR	15.208	15.083	13.579	16.008	15.001
WDR	8.6698	8.4624	8.1803	8.8118	8.8762

negative effect for outlays of refuse disposal capital is minor river cities, where the potential that decomposing refuse may pollute groundwater supplies is a possible explanation for the (statistically insignificant) positive effect observed for those cities. The only exception for annual expenditures on refuse disposal is freshwater lake cities, which had a significant positive effect. This coefficient is a puzzle.

Inasmuch as the fixed effects model controls for variation between cities, and since the regressions are estimated on a pooled cross-section, time-series basis, three variables are used to control for variation across time in all the regressions. The first such variable is YEAR, which has the expected negative coefficient and is statistically significant in all cases. These years saw tremendous increases in medical knowledge and education, as well as important changes in food preparation with canning, dehydration, and refrigeration producing large changes in the way the typical household confronted meal planning and preparation.

WAR is a dummy variable for the years 1917–1920 during which three major events may have had a positive effect on waterborne death rates. The first is the effect that wartime controls and postwar inflation might have on expenditure levels, conceivably postponing some sanitation expenditures to postwar years when inflation caused deferred expenditures to be more expensive. The second is rapid population growth in some urban areas, much of it due to the migration of agricultural workers from the south to urban industrial jobs in the north, and to the growth of cities with large military installations. The crowding this created, both during and after the war, put pressure on existing sanitation systems and may have led to increases in waterborne death rates. In fact, there is a marked slowing in the rate of decrease in these diseases revealed in Table 1.1, followed by an acceleration in the early 1920s. The third effect, the influenza pandemic of 1918–1919, may have increased the disease environment so that low levels of waterborne contamination affected more people. The coefficients on WAR are all positive and statistically significant for all cities other than lake cities.

The third of the variables controlling for variation across time is LATE20, a dummy for the period 1925–1927 during which many cities consistently overestimated their population given the levels reported in the 1930 Census. Thus, the death rates would tend to be underestimated.

Finally, ASSDPC and LANDAREA are included to control for the fact that, during these years, many cities grew by annexation and consolidation, although the great age of annexation was ending just as the study period begins (Cain 1983). Since annexed areas could be either healthy or unhealthy, either well-endowed with sanitation capital or not, the diverse pattern of coefficients should not be surprising. Their inclusion in these regressions is attributable to the fact annexation is not considered to be a fixed effect ex ante.[8]

These regression results only pertain to cities with municipal water supplies. In an attempt to assess whether the results of Tables 1.3 and 1.4 might also apply to cities with private water supplies, two additional regressions were run. The results are reported in Table 1.6. Because the number of cities without municipal supplies is relatively small, it is not possible to run regressions by city type. The first regression simply reruns the sample for all cities reported in the earlier tables without the water variables. The second regression repeats this specification for the cities with private supplies.[9] The final column of Table 1.6 reports the results of a simple

Table 1.6 Municipal vs. private water supplies

Variable	Municipal	Private	Test result
SEWKALL	−0.01376[a]	−0.00951[a]	Same
SEWERAV3	−0.05106[b]	0.00246	Same
REFKALL	−0.08150[a]	−0.22241[a]	Differ
REFUSEAV3	−0.04310[a]	0.00941	Same
YEAR	−0.07514[a]	−0.07448[a]	Same
WAR	0.21399[a]	0.19256[a]	Same
LATE20	0.00457	0.09407[a]	Differ
ASSDPC	0.00402[a]	−0.00014	Differ
LANDAREA	0.00028[a]	0.00019	Same
R^2	0.840	0.831	
n	2609	933	

Dependent variable is the log of the waterborne disease death rate

[a]Statistically significant at the 95% confidence level

[b] Statistically significant at the 90% confidence level

[8] Regressions excluding these two variables indicate that the loss of what in the all cities case are two statistically significant coefficients does not affect the overall results reported here.

[9] It should be noted that the distribution of cities by type for these two cases is approximately equal. It should also be noted that the cities included in the private regression are those that had no municipal works at the start of the study period. Inasmuch as several of these cities shifted to municipally owned works during the period, they are also included in the other regression for those years.

statistical test as to whether the coefficients of the first equation are in the confidence intervals of the second equation. By this test, three of the four coefficients for the sewage and refuse variables in the cities with municipal waterworks are in the confidence intervals for the cities with private works. Six of the nine variables included in the equation meet this test. This provides support for a conclusion that the effects of sanitation expenditures on the waterborne disease death rate are similar in cities with municipal and private waterworks.

1.5 Summary and Conclusion

This paper seeks to answer two questions. First, was there a payoff to cities' expenditure on sanitation works, and how big was that payoff? As Table 1.7 documents, cities received a big payoff to expenditures on waterworks, sewer systems, and refuse collection and disposal in the form of reduced deaths from waterborne diseases.[10] The second question is whether there were observable differences in the four city types. As Table 1.7 illustrates, the answer to that question is yes. This study further demonstrates that the mechanisms which do a good job of explaining the decline in waterborne disease death rates (Table 1.4) do not perform anywhere near as well in explaining the decline in the total death rate (Table 1.3). Indeed, the correlation between the two grows smaller over time, suggesting that additional study is needed to explain the decline in overall urban mortality in the early twentieth century.

The total per capita expenditures that appear in the first row of Table 1.7 are the sum of the variable mean expenditures listed in Table 1.5. The greater expenditures for saltwater cities are attributable to the high expenditure on water capital in those cities. The rest of Table 1.7 lists the annual decrease in the number of deaths attributable to waterborne diseases that would result from a one-percent increase in per capita expenditures on each of the six categories. Over all the cities in the pooled sample, a one-percent increase in each of the six categories would have saved 27 lives annually in a city of average size.

In Table 1.7, we see substantial differences between the types of cities. A one-percent increase in expenditures on water capital in saltwater cities would have averted almost 24 deaths, a much greater effect than elsewhere. A one-percent increase in annual expenditures on water, interpreted as expenditures on disinfection, would have had its greatest effect in freshwater lake cities, averting over 11 deaths. Increased expenditures on sewer capital had their greatest potential impact

[10] In 1902, typhoid deaths were, on average, 26% of all deaths from waterborne diseases; by 1929, this had fallen to 16%. Thus, deaths from typhoid had fallen faster than those from intestinal/diarrheal diseases.

Table 1.7 Reduced waterborne disease deaths from increased expenditures

Fresh water					
	All	Salt water	Lake	Major river	Minor river
Total expenditure per capita	$42.93	$48.92	$41.58	$40.65	$40.27
Averted deaths associated with a 1% increase in expenditures per capita					
Variable					
WATKALL	−8.79	−23.73	14.28	−1.81	−0.66
WATERAV	31.29	−2.49	−11.08	−2.07	3.57
SEWKALL	−12.58	−9.03	−1.17	−10.97	−20.15
SEWERAV3	−1.26	0.05	−2.10	1.86	−9.69
REFKALL	−2.01	−2.68	−15.81	−2.22	0.33
REFUSEAV	−3.65	−4.61	12.93	−4.71	−7.27
TOTAL	−26.99	−42.49	−2.94	−19.92	−33.88

in river cities, particularly minor river cities, where the number of deaths attributable to waterborne diseases would have been reduced by an annual average of more than 20. An additional one-percent increase on annual operating expenditures for sewers in minor river cities would have saved an additional ten lives. The 16 reduced deaths in freshwater lake cities that would have resulted from a one-percent increase in expenditures on refuse capital could have been countered by 13 more deaths from increased annual expenditures on refuse collection and disposal, which worked to reduce mortality in the other three city types.

The differences we see in Table 1.7 are consistent with the sketch of each city type appearing in the first section of this essay. To reiterate with the broadest brush-strokes, the capital expenditures of saltwater cities on water supply and wastewater works helped reduce waterborne disease deaths. While most cities adopted disinfection of their water supplies during this period, disinfection proved to have a significant effect only in the freshwater lake cities. The intelligent location of sewage works was important to both major and minor river cities, and the annual operating expenditures of the sewer system were of additional importance to minor river cities. This study incorporates refuse collection and disposal as part of sanitation, and the effects are as we expected with the exception of the positive effect of annual operating expenditures in freshwater lake cities. Finally, and tentatively, the comparison of cities with municipal versus private waterworks presented in Table 1.6 suggests the analysis of cities with municipal waterworks derived from Tables 1.3, 1.4, and 1.7 applies generally.

Acknowledgments We are grateful for the research assistance of Ashish Aggarwal, Supriya Mathew, and Stacey Tevlin and for the financial assistance of the Center for Economic History, the Balzan Foundation, and Loyola University Chicago. We thank George Alter; John Brown; Stanley Engerman; Joel Mokyr; Tom Weiss; participants in the International Economic History Congress in Leuven, Belgium; and participants in seminars at the University of Illinois, Indiana University, and Northwestern University.

Appendix: Murray Reminiscences

Louis Cain: I first met John at an academic conference, perhaps he was still in grad school. In any event, it was about a quarter century ago when our friendship began. We got to spend an extended time talking about our work when John came to give a seminar at Northwestern in 2000. In the Fall of 2005, I joined Bob Fogel's Center for Population Economics at the University of Chicago and began lobbying to have John come and give a seminar there. Six years later, he came. By then, Bob's health was failing, and we often didn't know until an hour or so before the seminar began whether he would appear. I knew Bob would enjoy John's topic, but Bob's assistant called just before lunch to say that he was not going to make it. I apologized for Bob's absence, but John was just happy to have been invited. He had booked a flight that left several hours after the seminar so we had a lot of time to talk about the books each of us was finishing. As luck would have it, those books were both the subject of an "author-meets-critics" session at the 2012 Social Science History Association meetings in Vancouver. I was grateful and appreciative that one of our critics was John Murray. His comments were always to the point but delivered with the kindness that was the hallmark of this gentle and generous scholar.

Elyce Rotella: I got to know John at meetings of the Economic History Association and the Social Science History Association but did not come to know him well until after I relocated to the University of Michigan in 2007. Because John was at the University of Toledo – less than an hour away from Ann Arbor – he came regularly to our weekly Economic History Seminar. He was an active seminar participant with valuable comments to offer for every paper. It was a pleasure to see him regularly which gave me the opportunity to develop a personal relationship that typically involved sharing stories of our musical daughters. We had many research interests in common. One of my treasured possessions is an autographed copy of his book on health insurance that he gave to me.

In addition to being a highly productive scholar, John was the very definition of a good citizen. He was a stalwart of the Economic History Association, the Social Science History Association, and the Cliometric Society – serving in leadership and service positions for these groups and their journals. When a colleague was elected President of the Social Science History Association, he immediately approached John for the big job of chairing the Program Committee. John had to turn down the offer because he had already done that job a few years earlier.

References

Alsan M, Goldin C (2019) Watersheds in child mortality: the role of effective water and sewerage infrastructure, 1880–1920. J Polit Econ 127(2):586–638

Cain LP (1977) An economic history of urban location and sanitation. Res Econ Hist 3:337–389

Cain LP (1983) To annex or not? A tale of two towns: Hyde Park and Evanston. Exp Econ Hist 20(1):58–72
Chadwick E (1842) Report of the sanitary condition of the labouring population of Great Britain, reprinted in Flinn, MW (ed) (1965) University Press. Edinburgh
Condran GA, Crimmins-Gardner EM (1978) Public health measures and mortality in US cities in the late nineteenth century. Hum Ecol 6(1):27–54
Condran GA, Crimmins-Gardner EM (1983) Mortality variation in US cities in 1900. Soc Sci Hist 7(1):31–59
Cutler D, Miller G (2005) The role of public health improvements in health advances: the twentieth-century United States. Demography 42(1):1–22
Cutler D, Miller G (2006) Water, water everywhere: municipal finance and water supply in American cities. In: Glaeser E, Goldin C (eds) Corruption and reform: lessons from America's history. University of Chicago Press, Chicago, pp 153–184
Ferrie JP, Troesken W (2008) Water and Chicago's mortality transition, 1850–1925. Exp Econ Hist 45(1):1–16
Galishoff S (1980) Triumph and failure: the American response to the urban water supply problem, 1860-1923. In: Melosi MY (ed) Pollution and reform in American cities, 1870–1930. University of Texas Press, Austin, pp 35–57
Glaab CN, Brown T (1967) A history of urban America. Macmillan, New York
Meeker E (1972) The improving health of the United States, 1850-1915. Exp Econ Hist 9(3):353–373
Meeker E (1974) The social rate of return on investment in public health, 1880-1910. J Econ Hist 34(3):392–421
Mohl R (1985) The new city: urban America in the industrial age, 1860–1920. Harlan Davidson, Arlington Heights, IL
Mokyr J (1983) Technological progress and the decline of European mortality. Am Econ Rev 83(2):324–330
Murray J (2007) Origins of American health insurance. Yale University Press, New Haven
Preston SH, Van de Walle E (1978) Urban French mortality in the nineteenth century. Pop Stud 32(2):27–297
Schultz SK (1989) Constructing urban culture. Temple University Press, Philadelphia
Shattuck L (1850, 1948) Report of the sanitary commission of Massachusetts, 1850. Harvard University Press, Cambridge
Szreter S (1988) The importance of social intervention in Britain's mortality, c, 1850-1944: a reinterpretation of the role of public health. Soc Hist Med 1(1):1–38
Tarr J, McCurley J, Yosie TF (1980) The development and impact of urban wastewater technology: changing concepts of water quality control, 1850-1930. In: Melosi MY (ed) Pollution and reform in American cities, 1870–1930. University of Texas Press, Austin, pp 59–62
U.S, Bureau of Labor Statistics (1899–1902) Bureau of labor statistics bulletin #24, 30, 36, 42
U.S. Bureau of the Census (1900–1929) Mortality statistics of cities
U.S. Bureau of the Census (1904) Census bulletin #20
U.S. Bureau of the Census (1905–1929) Financial statistics of cities
U.S. Bureau of the Census (1910, 1916) General statistics of cities, 1909, 1915
Wohl A (1984) Endangered lives: public health in Victorian Britain. Methuen, London
Woods R (2000) The demography of Victorian England and Wales. Cambridge University Press, Cambridge

Chapter 2
The Continuing Puzzle of Hypertension Among African Americans: Developmental Origins and the Mid-century Socioeconomic Transformation

Garrett T. Senney and Richard H. Steckel

Abstract African Americans have an excessive prevalence of hypertension relative to whites, particularly in the South. We seek to understand this puzzle by applying the developmental origins hypothesis to the rapid socioeconomic improvement that occurred after World War II. The long experience of pre-World War II poverty prepared African Americans born around the 1950s for survival in a lean world of poor nutrition and hard work, but created vulnerabilities for chronic diseases when conditions improved later in life. We analyze individual-level evidence from the CDC's Behavioral Risk Factor Surveillance System with household income data, finding results consistent with the developmental origins hypothesis, that accelerated income growth from poverty strongly indicates an increased prevalence of hypertension. This strongly suggests that the collection of individual-level, intergenerational data is necessary to further evaluate this puzzle.

Keywords Developmental origins · Hypertension · Health · Behavioral Risk Factor Surveillance System · Cardiovascular disease

G. T. Senney (✉)
Office of the Comptroller of the Currency, Washington, DC, USA
e-mail: Garrett.Senney@occ.treas.gov

R. H. Steckel
Ohio State University, Columbus, OH, USA
e-mail: Steckel.1@osu.edu

P. Gray et al. (eds.), *Standard of Living*, Studies in Economic History,
https://doi.org/10.1007/978-3-031-06477-7_2

2.1 Introduction

African Americans have a high prevalence of hypertension, an important precursor of cardiovascular disease and stroke, which is a major contributor to the racial disparities in health observed in America (Lackland and Keil 1996; Sowers et al. 2002; Wong et al. 2002; Hertz et al. 2005). In 2007–2014, the age-adjusted hypertension prevalence rates were 41.6% for African Americans and 29.0% for whites (Mozaffarian et al. 2016, chart 9.2). An extensive literature documents that the disparity in hypertension prevalence persists even after adjustment for a wide range of socioeconomic and behavioral factors (Redmond et al. 2011). Figure 2.1 shows that the prevalence of hypertension for African Americans in 2011 varied widely across the country. It is important to note that hypertension is particularly pronounced in the South. The highest rates exist in the swath of states from Texas to West Virginia. Notably, this region roughly coincides with the stroke and the diabetes belts identified by the CDC, conditions that are recognized as correlates or precursors of cardiovascular disease (Lackland et al. 2016).[1]

The prevalence of hypertension is also elevated in other states adjacent to this block. However, that elevated prevalence for African Americans living in the South contrasts with the lower rates among blacks living in Africa or in the Caribbean (Cooper et al. 1997). Given this evidence, unique aspects of the American environment likely contribute to the pattern of hypertension prevalence. The previous literature discusses numerous possible explanations for the high prevalence of hypertension among African Americans, but there is no scientific consensus on its

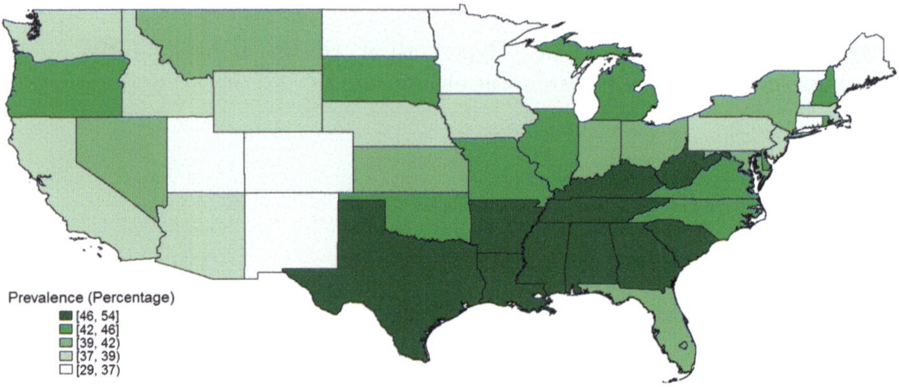

Fig. 2.1 Hypertension prevalence in 2011 of African Americans 18 years and older. (Source: BRFSS, CDC. Note: Prevalence denotes the share of individuals who are being treated for hypertension or who have been told by a physician, nurse, or healthcare professional that they have hypertension. Because some individuals have not been examined for hypertension, this measure underestimates the true rate)

[1] www.cdc.gov/dhdsp/maps/national_maps/stroke_all.htm and www.cdc.gov/diabetes/pdfs/data/diabetesbelt.pdf.

underlying cause. Therefore, the situation of higher prevalence of hypertension among African Americans in the South is a unique and interesting public health puzzle.

One approach worth further study, the developmental origins hypothesis, relates changes in the intergenerational socioeconomic conditions to increases in the prevalence of chronic adult diseases. Medical studies have shown that young children respond to poor nutrition and stress by compromising organ integrity and degrading biological processes that regulate physiological systems in later life (Gluckman et al. 2008; Barker and Thornburg 2013). If people rendered vulnerable then face an energy-rich diet or elevated stress in later life, pathophysiological processes are set into motion that might significantly increase their likelihood to have hypertension.

The developmental origins hypothesis views rapid socioeconomic improvement near the middle of the twentieth century as a possible latent factor that has elevated hypertension among African Americans who had an intergenerational history of poverty. Beginning in the 1950s, the South underwent an economic, social, technological, and political revolution that had profound effects for African Americans, creating a sudden improvement in living conditions broadly defined. Being guided by the literature on hypertension and the developmental origins hypothesis, we empirically examine the claim that this major socioeconomic change created unbalanced physical growth for cohorts born on the cusp of change, which made them particularly vulnerable to hypertension as adults.

We investigate the connection between socioeconomic change and hypertension using individual-level data gathered by the Behavioral Risk Factor Surveillance System (BRFSS) and by state-level, household income data for African Americans. As discussed below, two factors allow us to identify and measure the impact of the changing socioeconomic environment on hypertension among African Americans. First, conditions in utero are crucial for the development of major organs such as the cardiovascular system. At this age, the growth process adapts the design of these organs to the type of nutritional conditions the child is expected to inhabit in later life. Once fully formed, these organs have limited capacity to adapt to changing environmental conditions. Second, a sudden improvement in conditions between birth and adulthood places these cohorts at greater risk of hypertension. Successive generations of poverty and hard work, for example, led to low birth weight and limited the functional capacity of these organ systems. By dividing the BRFSS data into birth cohorts that experienced contrasting rates of socioeconomic change, we can measure the effects of rapid socioeconomic improvement on adult hypertension.

We consider how rapid socioeconomic change operated on biological processes known to affect hypertension. In this regard, income acts as a portmanteau variable that captures several effects associated with improving socioeconomic status. The others include diet, work effort or physical activity, leisure, and obesity, all of which accompanied the mid-century industrialization and modernization of the South. Specifically, we consider how the diffusion of new technology, especially the tractor and the cotton picker after 1950, eased work effort and calories expended in agriculture. Higher incomes enabled the purchases of automobiles that reduced the need for walking as a primary source of transportation. Other activities that would expend calories, such as recreational exercise, made limited headway in the South. With industrialization women increasingly worked outside the home, and while beneficial for income, led to unsupervised eating habits of children who consumed more snack foods, perhaps while watching television after school, and to greater purchase of less-nutritious prepared foods for family meals. In the context of the southern diet, which featured starch, fat, and salt, these behavior patterns contributed to obesity, which is a major risk factor for hypertension (Hall et al. 2015; Jiang et al. 2016; Leggio et al. 2017).

Because our data and methods lead to conclusions that are only suggestive, an important goal is to motivate the collection of intergenerational household-level data for African Americans that could provide a rigorous evaluation of this methodology. Most useful would be intergenerational evidence on household income and socioeconomic status combined with measures of lifestyle behaviors and hypertension.

2.2 Background

The literature discusses numerous possible explanations for the disparity in hypertension prevalence, including obesity, diet, quality of medical care, stress related to socioeconomic change, poor access to health insurance, socioeconomic status, salt retention, and substance abuse (Centers for Disease Control and Prevention 2010). Several studies report, however, that the disparity in hypertension prevalence persists even after adjustment for a wide range of socioeconomic, behavioral, and biomedical risk factors (Redmond et al. 2011). Despite large interventions to eliminate hypertension disparities, evidence such as that shown in Table 2.2 indicates that these differences have actually grown over the past few decades (Geronimus et al. 2007), suggesting that unrecognized factors are important in driving inequalities in hypertension (Fuchs 2011).

The developmental origins hypothesis provides a mechanism for understanding the origins of hypertension and other noncommunicable diseases found in later adult life. Some 30 years ago, David Barker and colleagues proposed the developmental origins approach (Barker and Osmond 1986; Barker 1990), after Barker noticed that older adult deaths from heart disease in England were correlated with infant mortality rates and birth sizes in their cohorts and geographic locations of birth. Although there were many skeptics, discovery of the relationship stimulated a search for possible mechanisms built around the idea that early life conditions influence adult susceptibility to cardiovascular disease (Lackland 2004). Subsequently, medical researchers proposed and refined ideas (see, e.g., discussions in Kuzawa and Pike (2005) and Kuzawa and Sweet (2009)), and a strong following developed among economists, demographers, and numerous medical researchers (Lackland et al. 1999, 2003; Hanson and Gluckman 2008; Skogen and Overland 2012; Barker and Thornburg 2013; Steckel 2013; Lackland 2014). This type of work also engages economic history (Fogel and Costa 1997; Bleakley 2007), environmental economics (Deschenes et al. 2009), and family decision-making (Del Bono and Ermisch

2009; Del Bono et al. 2012). The approach also has the advantage of providing a mechanism for understanding the interconnection with stroke and diabetes.

Mounting evidence suggests that fetuses and infants respond to poor nutrition and stress by compromising organ integrity and degrading biological processes that regulate physiological systems in later life (Gluckman et al. 2008; Barker and Thornburg 2013). Evidence shows that individuals are predisposed to hypertension if the heart, vascular tree, kidneys, and pancreas are modified in the womb in response to maternal social stress and poor nutrition. If people rendered vulnerable face an energy-rich diet or elevated stress in later life, pathophysiological processes are set into motion that might significantly increase their likelihood of hypertension.

During their developmental stages, humans are able to accommodate stresses and environmental changes by pleiotropic gene expression patterns that promote survival. The adaptations made to the stressful environment change the structure and function of organs before birth and might be passed on to future generations through epigenetic mechanisms (Aiken and Ozanne 2014). When the fetus is optimized for a lean world, but instead must process a lush load of net nutrition as an adult, there is a mismatch between expectations and reality. This unexpectedly rich nutrition actually proves harmful in certain ways to the individual in the longer term (De Boo and Harding 2006; Swanson et al. 2009). Given this mounting evidence, there is a need for determining the mechanisms that underlie the observation and the generality of the finding for other noncommunicable diseases (Jasienska 2009; Kuzawa and Sweet 2009).

Study of the Helsinki birth cohort, a longitudinal study of 13,517 men and women who were born in Helsinki University Hospital from 1924 to 1944, shows that low birth weight, especially when followed by obesity in early adolescence, is associated with later life hypertension (Barker et al. 2002). Figure 2.2 shows the excess burden of hypertension as a function of these factors. All births of low weight (<3000 g) had elevated odds ratios of adult hypertension, but the risks were greatest (odds = 2.5) for individuals born with weights under 3000 g and a BMI at 11 that exceeded 17.6.

Our goal is not to test or evaluate all of the suggested explanations for elevated hypertension among African Americans, which would be a considerable task, but rather to integrate social science research with medical knowledge to advance the understanding of this puzzle. Our efforts are warranted by the persistence of the puzzle and the lack of generally accepted explanations. With our data and methods, we cannot "prove" that the mechanism of the hypothesis operated through rapidly changing socioeconomic conditions, but we can achieve the important goal of making a plausible case for additional study.

2.3 Creating a Vulnerable Population

The Socioeconomic Transformation Figure 2.3 shows that the American South was relatively poor for several decades following the Civil War. Regional income per capita in New England was roughly three times that of the South (Kim and Margo 2003). Conditions drastically improved in the middle of the twentieth cen-

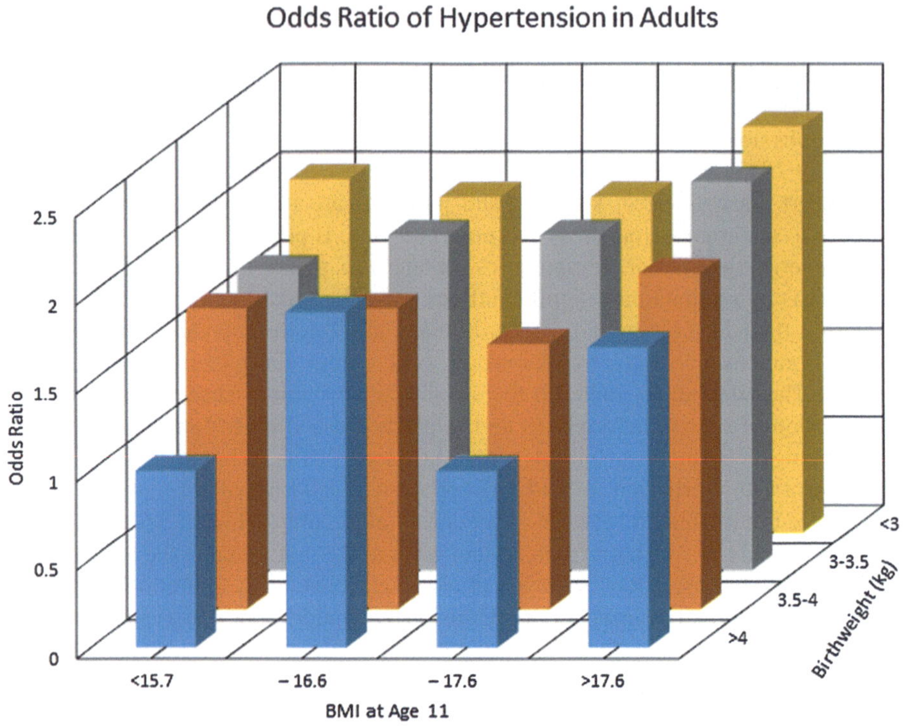

Fig. 2.2 Odds ratios of hypertension in adults as a function of birth weight and BMI at age 11. (Source: Barker et al. 2002)

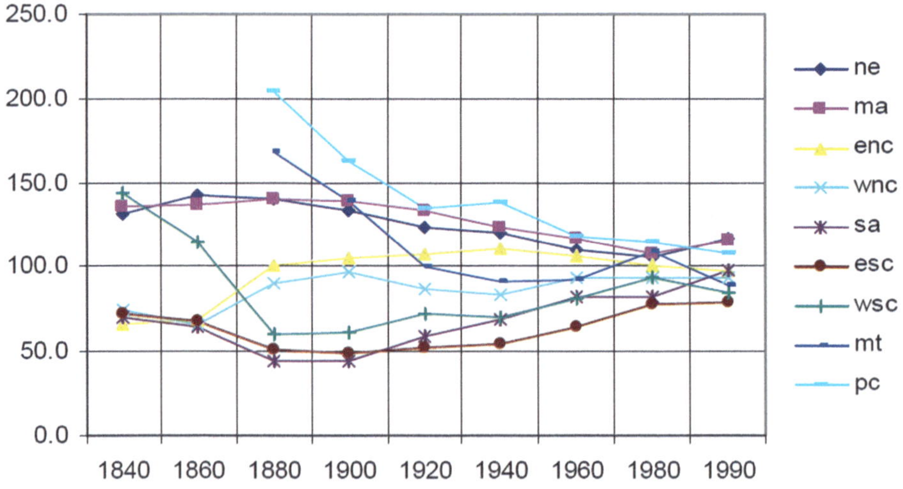

Fig. 2.3 Relative regional income per capita, 1840–1990 (USA = 100). Legend: *ne* New England, *ma* Middle Atlantic, *enc* East North Central, *wnc* West North Central, *sa* South Atlantic, *esc* East South Central, *wsc* West South Central, *mt* Mountain, *pc* Pacific. (Source: Kim and Margo 2003)

tury, as regional industrial structures as well as income per capita converged dramatically. Southern per capita incomes grew significantly faster than the national average (Kim and Margo 2003). This was a remarkable achievement because the quarter century following 1950 was the strongest period for economic growth in the twentieth century. Not only did the South gain relative to the rest of the country in mid-century, but African Americans gained relative to whites. Between 1940 and 1980, the real incomes of white men grew 2.5 times, while that for African Americans grew fourfold (Smith and Welch 1989). As a percentage of white male wages, those for African Americans averaged 43.3 in 1940 and 72.6 in 1980. Opinions differ on the sources of this progress, but schooling, civil rights legislation, and south-north migration were all part of the mix (Heckman 1990; Donohue and Heckman 1991; Margo 1993).

Pointing toward the importance of civil rights legislation in creating new labor market opportunities, the median income of African American men in the South relative to the 25th percentile of southern white men grew by 34% points between 1960 and 1990 (Card and Krueger 1993). Therefore, we argue that southern African American adolescents of the 1960s and 1970s were particularly vulnerable to hypertension as adults because their parents and older ancestors were poor, and this generation realized dramatic improvements in net nutrition beyond an age when biological adaptation to rapidly improving circumstances was limited or impossible. Income growth per se created vulnerabilities, but as discussed below, this variable is also a proxy for many changes affecting the diet, work effort, and lifestyles of the African American population, especially those living in the South. Among these factors was desegregation of hospitals and fair housing laws, which may have had independent, beneficial effects on hypertension.

In our analysis, the developmental origins hypothesis predicts that the children of generationally poor parents who were born under rapidly improving conditions would have higher rates of hypertension as adults. This paper considers how these changes translated into greater prevalence of hypertension for African Americans by relying on the timing of socioeconomic change and its differential impact across states to identify forces that influence this disease. The empirical strategy has acknowledged limitations, but if the hypothesis is powerful, one would expect to find elevated prevalence rates in states and among ethnic groups with this dynamic environmental history.

Earlier work using state-level data has found that long-term poverty followed by rapid economic improvement increased the risk for type 2 diabetes at the state level (Steckel 2013). Given the aforementioned related study and following the developmental origins hypothesis, we suspect that African American families, especially in the South, who were persistently and severely poor until undergoing significant income growth after the middle of the twentieth century will have suffered high rates of hypertension.

Circumstantial evidence suggests an association between income growth and prevalence. Figures 2.4 and 2.5 provide data on the socioeconomic transformation in the South and its relationship to the geographic prevalence of hypertension.

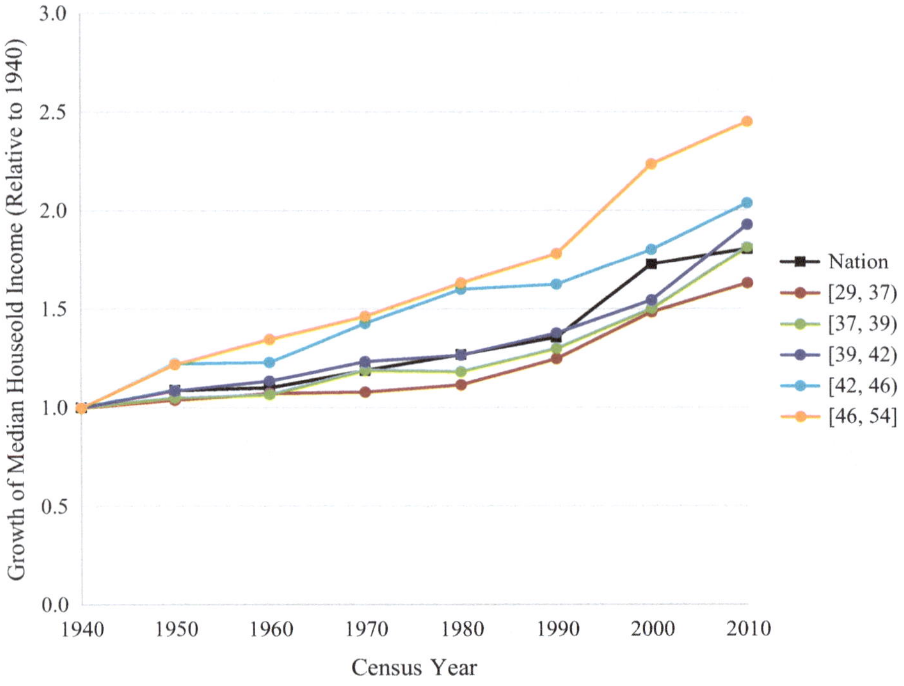

Fig. 2.4 Growth of black median household income by hypertension region (population weighted). (Sources: Census 1940, Census 1950 V2 Detailed Characteristics Table 87 and 56 for AL and HI, Census 1960 V1 Chapter D: Detailed Characteristics Table 133, Census 1970 V1 Chapter D: Detailed Characteristics Table 192, Census 1980 V1 Chapter D: Detailed Characteristics Table 243 and 244 for AL, Census 1990 V1 CP-2 Table 53, Census 2000 Summary File 4, Census 2010 ACS)

Figure 2.4 shows the growth of median African American household income from 1940 to 2010 ranked by the prevalence of hypertension in 2011 and organized by clusters of states having similar levels of prevalence. The group of states having the highest prevalence of hypertension in 2011 were also the states in which income growth was most rapid. For example, in the cluster of states where prevalence was in the range of 46%–54%, median household income grew the fastest, by a factor of 2.45 from 1940 to 2010. Figure 2.5 shows that the states with the highest prevalence rates in 2011 were also the poorest in 1940. These results indicate that rapid growth out of poverty may have triggered the rise in the prevalence of hypertension.

2.4 Controls

We recognize that many variables other than those associated with fetal origins are linked to hypertension, and they must be recognized in the empirical analysis. Among these are smoking, educational attainment, current income, and exercise.

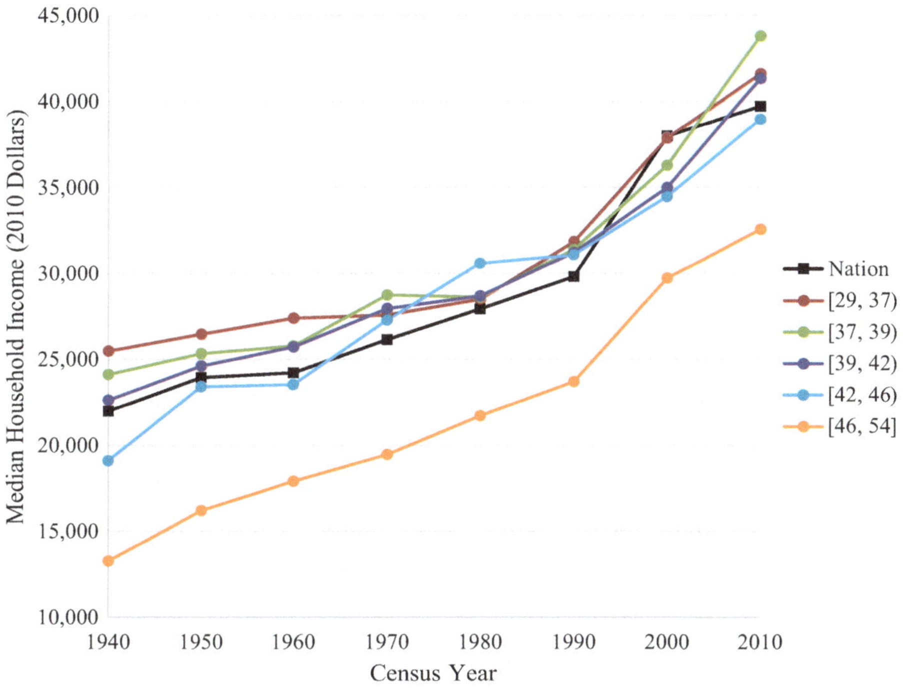

Fig. 2.5 Black median household income by hypertension region (population weighted). (Sources: Census 1940, Census 1950 V2 Detailed Characteristics Table 87 and 56 for AL and HI, Census 1960 V1 Chapter D: Detailed Characteristics Table 133, Census 1970 V1 Chapter D: Detailed Characteristics Table 192, Census 1980 V1 Chapter D: Detailed Characteristics Table 243 and 244 for AL, Census 1990 V1 CP-2 Table 53, Census 2000 Summary File 4, Census 2010 ACS)

Numerous studies identify smoking as a risk factor in cardiovascular disease, although there is some disagreement on the biological pathways (Rhee et al. 2007; Virdis et al. 2010; Gao et al. 2017). Likely suspects are impaired endothelial function, arterial stiffness, inflammation, and lipid modification.

Education and current income may operate through several pathways to lower hypertension (Leng et al. 2015). First, high-income, well-educated people were better informed about the risks and causes of hypertension, and therefore more likely to pursue a healthy lifestyle. Second, the poor and less educated have less knowledge of healthcare facilities, and a greater feeling of helplessness or lack of control over their health situation (Xu et al. 2013).

Exercise obviously affects obesity, but studies show that it has an independent beneficial effect on hypertension (Dimeo et al. 2012; Pescatello et al. 2015; Naci et al. 2018). A meta-analysis of major exercise and drug trials showed that exercise and drug interventions were similarly effective in reducing mortality outcomes for coronary heart disease, and physical activity interventions were actually more effective for the secondary prevention of stroke mortality (Naci and Ioannidis 2013).

2.5 Testing the Hypothesis: Data and Methods

We investigate the strength of the developmental origins hypothesis by analyzing data on individuals collected by the 2011 BRFSS, a cross-sectional telephone survey conducted by state health departments with technical assistance from the CDC. In addition to age and race, this source provides data on education, poverty, smoking, obesity, and patterns of exercise. These variables are defined by answers to the following questions:

- Hypertension: Have you ever been told by a doctor, nurse, or other health professional that you have high blood pressure?
- Smoking: Do you now smoke cigarettes every day, some days, or not at all?
- Education: What is the highest grade or year of school you completed?
- Exercise: During the past month, other than your regular job, did you participate in any physical activities or exercises such as running, calisthenics, golf, gardening, or walking for exercise?
- Obesity: About how much do you weigh without shoes? About how tall are you without shoes? Data used to calculate BMI.

According to the developmental origins hypothesis, one would expect rapid socioeconomic change to have had its greatest impact on adult disease for African Americans when the individuals were children or young adults. Development in utero and early childhood created a thrifty phenotype for them, and rich net nutrition would have challenged their cardiovascular system as adults. To match periods of vulnerability to chronological patterns of economic growth, we divide the BRFSS sample into five cohorts defined by these age groups: 18–34, 35–44, 45–54, 55–64, and 65+. The group aged 65+ in 2011 would have been children or young adults between roughly 1940 and 1970, so for this cohort, we measure economic growth between these 2 years.[2] Similarly, for the group aged 55–64 in 2011, the corresponding years are 1950–1980, and so forth. There is nothing compelling about a 30-year interval, and so we also conduct sensitivity tests for other windows. For a 20-year interval, the oldest age group would have spent birth to early adulthood from roughly 1940 to 1960.

The BRFSS questionnaire provides information on income and poverty, but unfortunately, the data cannot be linked longitudinally because the survey participants differ over time. As an alternative, we use the median income of African American households at the state level, which has limitations because there is heterogeneity within states. Competitive labor markets within states ameliorate the problem but migration complicates it. We adjust nominal income using the Federal Reserve Bank of Minneapolis' Chained-weighted CPI with 1982–1984 as the base year. The variable we use is the ratio of median household income in period 2 to that in period 1.

---

[2] We would consider measuring growth from an earlier period, say 1930, but unfortunately the median household income data are unavailable prior to 1940.

Our interpretation of the developmental origins hypothesis accepts that rapidly improving socioeconomic conditions that follow persistent poverty create non-harmonious growth and elevate the risk of adult hypertension. Individuals whose families lived in poverty for generations would have been prone to have children whose cardiovascular system would be stressed by rich net nutrition later in life. Under this theory, sudden prosperity would have created nutritional abundance and weight gain, exposing these cohorts of children to greater risk of hypertension. Maternal income has been shown to have a significant impact on birth weight for those infants who are already at high risk hereditarily. However, it is not clear whether income acts as a developmental buffer for low-birth-weight infants as their lives progress. These findings suggest the existence of biosocial interactions between hereditary predisposition and socioeconomic environment matter (Conley and Bennett 2001). The developmental origins concept connects non-harmonious growth trajectories in early life with chronic illnesses of adulthood. As noted in Barker (2002), per capita income can be a proxy for nutritional conditions as discussed below.

We employ a probit regression to model the presence or absence of hypertension of individuals in 2011. In this statistical formulation, the dependent variable takes on the value of 0 or 1 depending upon the hypertensive condition of the individual, with 1 (present) and 0 (absent). The model estimates the probability that an observation with particular characteristics will fall into either the present or the absent category.

Among the explanatory variables, economic change is measured by the ratio of median household income at the state level in period 2 compared to period 1. Period 1 is defined by the approximate year of birth and period 2 by the approximate year in which the individual reached early adulthood. The times can be only approximate because income is measured every decade.

Under the proposed hypothesis, the coefficient on the ratio of income should be positive, large, and statistically significant, but the size of the coefficient would depend upon the timing of the birth cohorts relative to the rate of economic growth. Specifically, the impact would have been greater on individuals who were older when rapid growth occurred because they had less opportunity to adjust.

2.6 Results

The coefficients in the table of results denote the marginal effect of each independent variable on the dependent variable, holding other variables constant. As indicated earlier, the value of the variable rMedian income used in the regression depends upon the age group in which the individual is located. To capture the effect of changing socioeconomic circumstances on hypertension, we measure income growth from the time period of birth to young adulthood.

It is well-known that hypertension increases with age, and for this reason, we include age dummies as regressors that identify birth cohorts. As the age of the groups declined relative to the period of rapid growth, individuals had greater opportunity to adapt to change, and consistent with this observation, the coefficients on the dummy variables for age declined. Notably the coefficient for the age group 65+ (1.536) was 4.1 times greater than that for the age group 35–44. This result is consistent with our expectation, derived from the developmental origins hypothesis, that individuals who were younger during a time of great change had more opportunity to adapt.

The results for the other coefficients are as expected. Higher median household income in 2010 lowers the prevalence of hypertension because richer households are better able to afford medical care. A related income measure, living in poverty, raises it. Many studies have noted that health improves with the level of education and in our specification people with lower education (high school or less) have a greater prevalence. Several studies also report that the prevalence of hypertension increases with smoking, obesity, and lack of exercise, all of which are confirmed in Table 2.2.

It is reasonable to ask whether this number is large or small. In making this determination, we note that reported hypertension underestimates actual hypertension prevalence, especially among minority groups. A recent study found that fewer than 50% of adults with hypertension controlled their blood pressure in 2007–2008, which approximately doubles the impact on health of the income coefficient in Table 2.2. The coefficient on median income in 2010 is negative and significant in two specifications and is marginally significant in a third one. The direction of the effect (negative) is intuitive because larger current income enables households to better provide healthcare for their children.

The regression results suggest that intergenerational poverty followed by rapid socioeconomic improvement elevates the risk of hypertension, which describes the experience of African American adults born after World War II. This analysis is consistent with developmental origins hypothesis as states with the larger income growth, controlling for other factors, tended to have larger prevalence of hypertension. Below we offer interpretations of the variables that control for current conditions.

Lower education suggests that the individual is less informed about the importance of regular health maintenance or less able to locate resources to assist in obtaining healthcare. In line with established research, we find that the coefficient is positive and statistically significant. Stress associated with poverty can cause hypertension. It is well documented that potential stresses include job, financial, and family distress (Kulkarni et al. 1998). The coefficient is positive and significant; our result is well in line with the documented fact that low-income families tend to have generally poorer health than wealthier families (Marmot 2002).

Medical research has shown that excess body fat is associated with higher levels of hypertension and mortality (Faeh et al. 2011; Zheng et al. 2013). Consistent with this pattern, obese individuals were significantly more likely to be hypertensive in all cohorts. Similarly, exercise reduced the chances of hypertension, although the variable is marginally significant in only one specification.

2.7 Discussion

In recent decades, social scientists and medical researchers have studied the upward trend in obesity rates, and collectively they have put forward several explanations. All begin, however, with some type of energy accounting, i.e., that the growth of calorie consumption outpaces the growth of physical activity. Among the ideas put forward are a rise in the cost of time-intensive, home-prepared meals associated with women working outside the home (Cutler et al. 2003; Hamrick and Okrent 2015), technological change that made work less demanding (Philipson and Posner 2003; Lakdawalla and Philipson 2009), changes in diet featuring processed foods that replaced home-prepared meals (Devine et al. 2006), stress-induced eating created by managing the challenges of socioeconomic change (Torres and Nowson 2007), and the proliferation of fast-food restaurants that conveniently provided calories at low cost (Chou et al. 2004; Schlosser 2012). Many of these arguments apply to African Americans, especially those who lived in the South.

Table 2.1 shows the trend in obesity by race from 1959–1962 to 2015–2016. In all years, obesity rates of blacks exceeded those of whites, and on average were 39% higher. Here we discuss pathways by which the transformation of African American socioeconomic conditions, particularly in the South, ultimately promoted obesity, which in turn contributed to hypertension in a vulnerable population by reducing the physical activity of daily life in an environment of a rich diet and little recreational exercise. The major components of our analysis are the mechanization of agriculture, lack of recreational exercise, the spread of automobiles, women's employment outside the home, and the continuation of a rich diet.

The Mechanization of Agriculture Based on the 1950 Census, agriculture was the dominant industry in the South (U.S. Bureau of the Census 1952). In the swath of states that extend from Texas and Oklahoma to North Carolina, the average share of African Americans employed in agriculture was 31.8%. It exceeded 35% in North Carolina, South Carolina, Arkansas, and Georgia. By 1980, however, the average share in the 11 states had declined to 3.4% and slightly exceeded 5% in only three states—Florida, Arkansas, and Mississippi (U.S. Bureau of the Census 1983).

Relief from field labor came late to the South relative to other regions (Hurt 1989). Mechanization of the harvest was difficult to accomplish in the region's most important crops of cotton and tobacco. Even today, the latter requires extensive hand labor and thus mechanization contributed little to productivity in this crop. Therefore, we focus on the predominant crop, cotton.

A 1939 study of man-hours per acre in cotton production in the Mississippi Delta showed that that vast majority of time (62.9%) was devoted to the harvest, while cultivating, thinning, and weeding the crop absorbed an additional 30.9% (Holley 2000, p.134). Picking cotton by traditional methods required long hours of stoop labor, and unlike grain for which mechanical harvesters had existed for over a century, cotton harvesting faced two challenges: irregularly spaced bolls and bolls that ripened at different times on the same plant (Holley 2000). Development of new

Table 2.1 Trend in obesity rates, white and African Americans

Year	Freq.	% obese AA	% obese white
1959–1962	6672	20.82	13.21
1971–1974	16,730	22.28	13.73
1976–1980	12,520	30.91	20.62
1988–1994	17,752	28.57	21.41
1999–2000	5448	37.77	27.60
2005–2006	5563	43.60	32.04
2009–2010	6527	48.63	33.87
2015–2016	5992	44.77	37.21

Source: CDC. National Health and Nutrition Examination Survey

Table 2.2 Explaining the prevalence of hypertension across individuals within age cohorts with 30-year income gap after birth

	80/50	30 Year Gap
rMedian Income	0.015***	0.022***
	(0.007)	(0.007)
Income 2010	-0.004***	-0.004***
	(0.001)	(0.001)
HS or Less	0.085***	0.086***
	(0.019)	(0.019)
Poverty	0.163***	0.163***
	(0.023)	(0.023)
Smoking	0.072***	0.072***
	(0.019)	(0.019)
Obesity	0.483***	0.483***
	(0.001)	(0.002)
Exercise	-0.004***	-0.004***
	(0.001)	(0.002)
Age 35-44	0.396***	0.374***
	(0.037)	(0.039)
Age 45-54	0.893***	0.862***
	(0.032)	(0.036)
Age 55-64	1.340***	1.302***
	(0.032)	(0.038)
Age 65+	1.589***	1.536***
	(0.034)	(0.043)
N	21,718	21,718
Pseudo R^2	0.2472	0.2473

Notes: Age group 18–34 is the omitted group. rMedian income for the 30-year gap column: 65+ (70/40), 55–64 (80/50), 45–54 (90/60), 35–44 (00/70), and 18–34 (10/80)

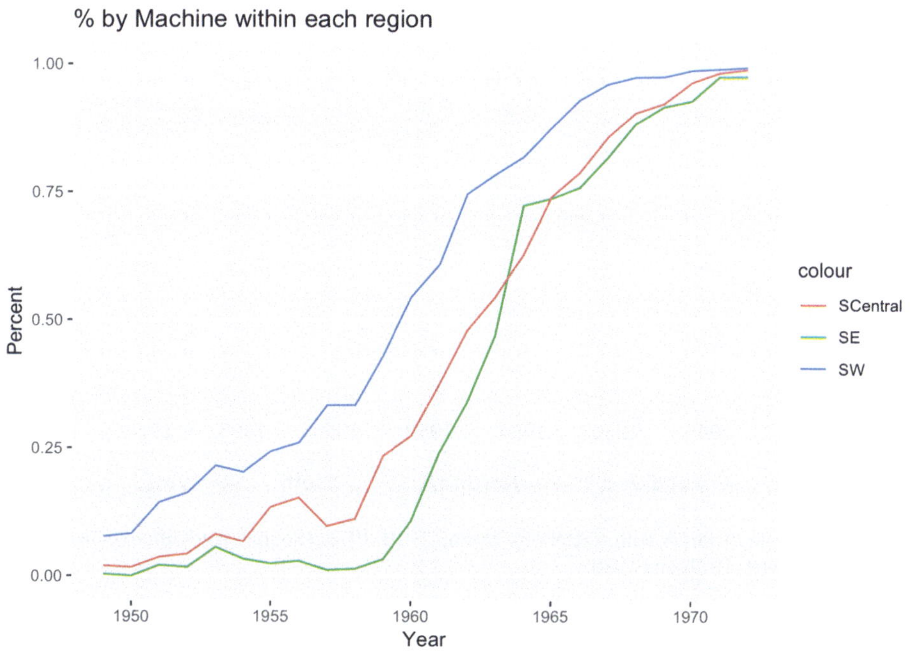

Fig. 2.6 Diffusion of the cotton picker: percent of the crop picked by machine within regions. (Source: US Department of Agriculture (1974), Table 185)

varieties that ripened bolls at about the same time solved the latter, but it took some engineering to build a machine that was effective at removing bolls with little destruction of fibers while also eliminating plant debris.

The diffusion of the cotton-picking machine during the 1950s and 1960s nearly eliminated hand labor in picking by the early 1970s. Figure 2.6 demonstrates the extent of change. In 1950, approximately 5% of the crop was picked by machine and by 1970 the figure had risen to virtually 100%. Although mechanical cotton pickers largely replaced hand labor between the late 1940s and the 1960s, hand methods persisted on small farms for a decade or more (Heinicke and Grove 2008; Logan 2015).

The diffusion of the tractor was a second important change that eased the burden of physical labor in the South (Fig. 2.7). Relative to other regions, farmers were slow to adopt this machine, and mules lingered on small farms operated by older farmers until the 1960s (Ellenberg 2007). Southern customs were fashioned by a long history of physical labor in the fields that welcomed rest at the end of the work-day and discouraged work on Sunday. These habits persisted after diffusion of the tractor and the mechanical cotton harvester, thereby adding to weight gain in an environment where people maintained a rich diet and eschewed recreational exercise (Church et al. 2011)

The South was not a region where habits of recreational exercise and health club memberships readily replaced a decline in caloric expenditure associated with a

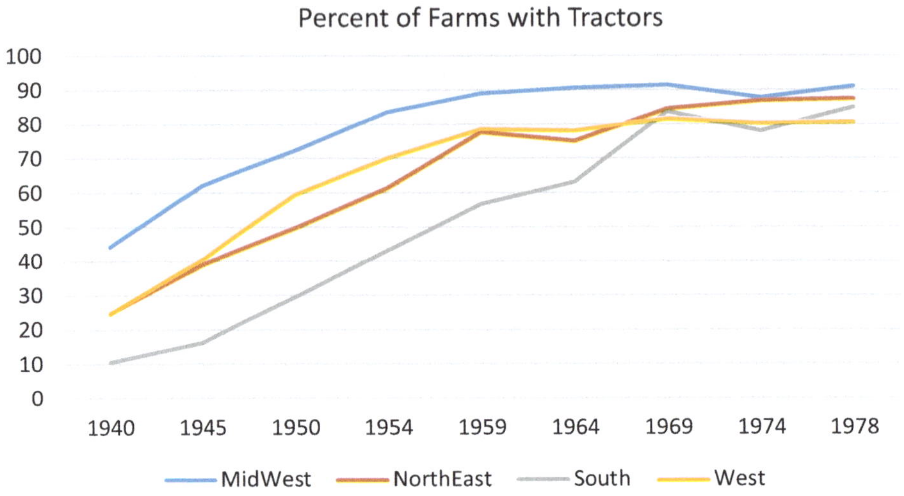

Fig. 2.7 Percent of farms with tractors by region, 1940–1978. (Source: Agriculture censuses of 1945, 1959, 1964, 1974, and 1979)

reduction in physical labor. In 2007, the share of the population belonging to health clubs ranged from a low of 6.3% in West Virginia to a high of 21.8% in Colorado (Active Marketing Group 2007). In every state in the high hypertension region of the South, the share of the population belonging to a health club was below the national average of 15.5%.

Diffusion of Automobiles Rising incomes enabled families to replace walking with a less taxing form of transportation and hauling, the automobile. According to the Federal Highway Administration's National Household Travel Survey, from 1950 to 1980, the number of miles traveled in a personal vehicle per capita increased by more than 2.3 times, while the number of vehicle registrations per capita increased by about 2.5 times for the South. That was by far the biggest increase of any region in the country. Table 2.3 shows that in the mid-1930s, whites were nearly four times more likely than African Americans to own automobiles (59% vs. 15%). With the relatively larger income growth for African Americans, they experienced significantly more growth in car ownership rates as well. By 1970 the ratio was 1.57 and by 1989 it had fallen to 1.25 as nearly 70% of African Americans owned automobiles (Lebergott 2014).

Women's employment outside the home Table 2.4 shows the growing labor force employment of black women with children from 1950 to 1980. The first column gives the ratio of the percent in 1980 to that in 1950 for all industries in each region. In the South, for example, the share employed grew by 43%. All regions registered gains in women's employment from 1950 to 1980.

All regions but the West showed declines in women's employment in agriculture, a sector that featured great strides in mechanization. Important crops in the Pacific

Table 2.3 Percent of US families with automobiles by race

	Race	
Year	White	Black
1935–1936	59	15
1970	83	53
1989	86	69

Source: Lebergott (2014), p. 130

Table 2.4 Trend in employment of black women with children, by region and industry

	Ratio of female labor force participation rate, 1980/1950		
Region	Total 8050	Agriculture 8050	Manufacturing 8050
Northeast	1.32	0.64	4.25
Midwest	1.72	0.83	8.98
South	1.43	0.38	17.66
Southwest	1.80	0.26	22.33
West	1.52	1.13	17.44

Source: US Census

states such as grapes, fruit, and vegetables mechanized somewhat but continued to employ considerable hand labor. Notably, the South in 1980 employed only 38% of the black female labor it did in 1950.

Economic historians know that rapid economic change created many new opportunities but also disrupted family life, as studies of industrialization make clear (Hareven 1982; Tilly and Scott 1989). As southern agriculture mechanized and food became cheaper, farm women joined the labor force, often taking jobs in manufacturing, food processing plants, the service sector, and government installations (McMillen 1989). To realize these opportunities, families may have relocated and members may have acquired new skills, adopted new communing patterns, and so forth, all of which were stressful. By far the largest gains in the employment of women with children occurred in manufacturing. The Southwest led the pack with a gain of over 2,000%, but the South was second at 1,766%. The great shift of women's employment to manufacturing had profound implications for the home economy.

First, consider the growth in the value of employed women's time, which is a key ingredient in the explanation for substitution of restaurant or premade meals from home cooking. The latter was very time-intensive and the switch created a less nutritious diet but was significantly less time demanding. Second, families that had both parents employed outside the home had less opportunity to supervise the eating and leisure habits of their children. These children, whose after-school time was once occupied by field labor or chores around the home, were now free to enjoy more leisure time. Ownership rates of TVs increased over 30-fold for southerners from 1950 to 1970 (Census 1950 and 1970).

The Rich Southern Diet The traditional southern diet was rich in starch, fat, and salt. The food ways of southerners had roots in the nineteenth century, when pioneer farmers planted corn and created swine herds (Taylor 1989). For most of the year, the hogs foraged on acorns and other products of the forest and then early in the fall they were assembled for fattening on corn. Meat processing occurred after the first cold spell, and a massive increase of pork consumption followed. According to USDA Nationwide Food Surveys from 1955, 1965, and 1977, southerners on average consumed 4% more meat, 5% more fats and oils, and 18% more sugar and sweets (by weight) weekly than the national average.

Fat was rendered into lard and the hams and shoulders were salted, smoked, and stored. As long as pork was available, these farmers ate it daily, accompanied by various forms of corn processed into bread, grits, or hominy. When available, vegetables were usually fried or boiled with pork lard. Sweet potatoes were also common fare in the diet because they required minimal cultivation and they could be stored for months in underground cellars. By the twentieth century, the price of wheat began to decline, and new methods of milling and distribution enabled even poor southern farmers to buy flour in bulk to make into biscuits that were eaten with syrup or red-eye gravy. According to USDA Nationwide Food Surveys in 1977, southerners consumed about 12% less fresh fruits by weight than the national average. This lower consumption pattern still holds. Southern states currently have the highest proportions of adults who self-report consuming one or less fruit and one or less vegetable in any form per day (Centers for Disease Control and Prevention 2013).

The traditional southern diet was a disaster for heart disease when accompanied by a decline in physical labor combined with habits that eschewed recreational exercise. The southern diet is gradually changing, but fried foods such as chicken, catfish, and hushpuppies remain popular to this day. Pockets of strong dietary tradition linger in many rural regions, a pattern that offers an opportunity to study hypertension prevalence at the county level.

2.8 Conclusions

Heart disease is a major public health problem that causes disabilities and premature death. In an effort to design remedies, numerous studies have investigated causes, leading to recommendations on diet, exercise, cessation of smoking, weight control, careful monitoring of blood pressure and so forth (De Backer 2008). Our goal has not been to displace but to supplement such studies with investigating an early warning to future potential severe cardiovascular problems. While beneficial, such research does not harness intergenerational information that would be quite useful if guided by developmental origins concepts. Heart attacks and strokes often appear after the disease is well-advanced, but this problem could be lessened by knowledge of a person's proclivity based on socioeconomic information that many patients could readily provide, such as occupations of the parents and grandparents and their counties of birth (counties in the USA vary widely in their economic prosperity). Individuals thought to be vulnerable, for example, could be encouraged to engage in healthy behaviors at younger ages and to have regular medical exams.

Our analysis confirms or is at least consistent with the developmental origins hypothesis as applied to heart disease in explaining regional differences in hypertension among African Americans within the USA in 2011. Income growth substantially increased the prevalence of actual (as opposed to undiagnosed or untreated) hypertension. The traditional southern diet was a disaster for heart disease when accompanied by a decline in physical labor and habits that eschewed recreational exercise. The southern diet is gradually changing but pockets of strong dietary tradition linger in many rural regions, a pattern that offers an opportunity to study hypertension at the county level.

A topic untouched by the evidence analyzed here is the consequence of duration of relative poverty and affluence on hypertension. One might reasonably hypothesize that for a given increase in income, children of those women having had longer intergenerational experiences of poverty may have had greater susceptibility. Similarly, for a given duration of poverty, children of women having had greater increases in income would also be more susceptible. Individual-level intergenerational evidence is needed to investigate these interesting questions.

The developmental origins hypothesis has especially relevant implications for the developing world, where vast numbers of poor families are on the verge of experiencing rapid income growth. Chronic adult illnesses, like heart disease, are likely to increase dramatically in the once-poor but now rapidly growing countries (Lopez et al. 2006; Kinsella and He 2009).

We acknowledge that our evidence cannot "prove" that fetal origins mechanisms, working through socioeconomic channels, explain high rates of hypertension among African Americans in the American South. Preferably, we would have panel data on birth cohorts that link family socioeconomic histories with adult health outcomes, but to our knowledge, this evidence is currently unavailable. One of our goals is to stimulate research to acquire such evidence by showing that, despite its flaws, our state-level data are consistent with the hypothesis, and therefore deserves more study.

Acknowledgments The views in this paper are those of the authors and do not reflect those of the Office of the Comptroller of the Currency or the Department of the Treasury.

Appendix: Murray Reflections by Richard Steckel

John Murray entered my graduate economic history class in 1989 and we soon became friends. We had a common educational ancestor in Oberlin College and like me, he came late to the field of economic history as an older student. It was greatly rewarding to see him flourish under the freedom economic history offered for research topics. Virtually, every subfield of economics has a history, and soon he was exploring interdisciplinary topics as well, writing a term paper on the Shakers, which later turned into a dissertation on the relationship of their living standards to their rise and decline in the century after 1780. John had an important qualification for a good economic historian, a nose for data and delight in discovering useful evidence in the archives. In fact, he and his wife, the epidemiologist Lynn Wellage, spent part of their honeymoon at the restored Pleasant Hill Shaker site. His intellectual curiosity propelled him into research on many topics from anthropometric history, literacy, fertility, the origins of American health insurance, and the Charleston Orphan House. Beyond his substantial research output, John was truly a good citizen, winning teaching awards, serving on editorial boards, helping as referee and book review editor, being trustee of the Cliometric Society, and performing various tasks for the Social Science History Association. As his dissertation advisor, I sometimes wondered if I pushed him too hard as a graduate student, urging him to gather more evidence, conduct additional analyses, and rewrite his work. One day, frustrated with the lack of light at the end of the tunnel, he came into my office and said he had enough. I told him to finish writing and he would be ready to graduate in a few weeks. Several years later, he thanked me for pressing him so hard because it expedited publishing and tenure.

John Murray was one of the good guys in the economic history profession. Friendly, gregarious, approachable, and eager to offer comments and suggestions on research in progress, he had many friends and admirers. I am proud to be among them.

References

Active Marketing Group (2007) Health club industry review, San Diego

Aiken CE, Ozanne SE (2014) Transgenerational developmental programming. Hum Reprod Update 20(1):63–75

Barker D (1990) The fetal and infant origins of adult disease: the womb may be more important than the home. BMJ Brit Med J 301(6761):1111

Barker D (2002) Fetal programming of coronary heart disease. Trends Endocrin Met 13(9):364–368

Barker D, Osmond C (1986) Infant mortality, childhood nutrition, and ischaemic heart disease in England and Wales. Lancet 1(8489):1077–1081

Barker D, Thornburg K (2013) The obstetric origins of health for a lifetime. Clin Obstet Gynecol 56(3):511–519

Barker D, Eriksson JG, Forsen T, Osmond C (2002) Fetal origins of adult disease: strength of effects and biological basis. Int J Epidemiol 31(6):1235–1239

Bleakley H (2007) Disease and development: evidence from Hookworm eradication in the South. Q J Econ 122(1):73–117

Card D, Krueger AB (1993) Trends in relative black-white earnings revisited. Amer Econ Rev 83(2):85–91

Centers for Disease Control and Prevention (2010) A closer look at African American men and high blood pressure control: a review of psychosocial factors and systems-level interventions. US Dept of Health and Human Services, USGPO

Centers for Disease Control and Prevention (2013) State indicator report on fruits and vegetables. US Dept of Health and Human Services, USGPO

Chou SY, Grossman M, Saffer M (2004) An economic analysis of adult obesity: results from the behavioral risk factor surveillance system. J Health Econ 23(3):565–587

Church TS, Thomas DM, Tudor-Locke C, Katzmarzyk PT, Earnest CP, Rodarte RQ, Martin CK, Blair SN, Bouchard C (2011) Trends over 5 decades in US occupation-related physical activity and their associations with obesity. PloS One 6(5):e19657–e19657

Conley D, Bennett NG (2001) Birth weight and income: interactions across generations. J Health Soc Behavior 42(4):450–465

Cooper R, Rotimi C, Ataman S, McGee D, Osotimehin B, Kadiri S, Muna W, Kingue S, Fraser H, Forrester T, Bennett F, Wilks R (1997) The prevalence of hypertension in seven populations of west African origin. Am J Public Health 87(2):160–168

Cutler DM, Glaeser EL, Shapiro JM (2003) Why have Americans become more obese? J Econ Perspect 17(3):93–118

De Backer G (2008) Risk factors and prevention of cardiovascular disease: a review. Dialogues 13(2):83–90

De Boo HA, Harding JE (2006) The developmental origins of adult disease (Barker) hypothesis. Aust NZ J Obstet Gynecol 46(1):4–14

Del Bono E, Ermisch J (2009) Birth weight and the dynamics of early cognitive and behavioural development. IZA Discussion Papers. Bonn, Institute for the Study of Labor, pp 1–30

Del Bono E, Ermisch J, Francesconi M (2012) Intrafamily resource allocations: a dynamic structural model of birth weight. J Labor Econ 30(3):657–706

Deschenes O, Greenstone M, Guryan J (2009) Climate change and birth weight. Am Econ Rev 99(2):211–217

Devine CM, Jastran M, Jabs J, Wethington E, Farell TJ, Bisogni CA (2006) A lot of sacrifices: workfamily spillover and the food choice coping strategies of low-wage employed parents. Soc Sci Med 63(10):2591–2603

Dimeo F, Pagonas N, Seibert F, Arndt R, Zidek W, Westhoff Timm H (2012) Aerobic exercise reduces blood pressure in resistant hypertension. Hypertension 60(3):653–658

Donohue JJ, Heckman J (1991) Continuous versus episodic change: the impact of civil rights policy on the economic status of blacks. J Econ Lit 29(4):1603–1643

Ellenberg G (2007) Mule South to tractor South mules, machines, agriculture, and culture in the cotton South, 1850-1950. University of Alabama, Tuscaloosa

Faeh D, Braun J, Tarnutzer S, Bopp M (2011) Obesity but not overweight is associated with increased mortality risk. Eur J Epidemiol 26(8):647–655

Fogel R, Costa D (1997) A theory of technophysio evolution, with some implications for forecasting population, health care costs, and pension costs. Demography 34(1):49–66

Fuchs FD (2011) Why do Black Americans have higher prevalence of hypertension? An enigma still unsolved. Hypertension 57(3):379–380

Gao K, Shi X, Wang W (2017) The life-course impact of smoking on hypertension, myocardial infarction and respiratory diseases. Sci Rep 7(1):4330

Geronimus AT, Bound J, Keene D, Hicken M (2007) Black-white differences in age trajectories of hypertension prevalence among adult women and men, 1999-2002. Ethn Dis 17(1):40–48

Gluckman PD, Hanson MA, Cooper C, Thornburg KL (2008) Effect of in utero and early-life conditions on adult health and disease. New Engl J Med 359(1):61–73

Hall JE, do Carmo JM, da Silva AA, Wang Z, Hall ME (2015) Obesity-induced hypertension. Circ Res 116(6):991–1006

Hamrick KS, Okrent AM (2015) The role of time in fast-food purchasing behavior in the United States. In: Evans R (ed) Purchasing food away from home: demand patterns for fast food and full-service. Nova Science Publishers, New York

Hanson MA, Gluckman PD (2008) Developmental origins of health and disease: new insights. Basic Clin Pharmacol 102(2):90–93

Hareven TK (1982) Family time and industrial time: the relationship between the family and work in a New England industrial community. Cambridge University Press, Cambridge

Heckman JJ (1990) The central role of the South in accounting for the economic progress of black Americans. Am Econ Rev 80(2):242–246

Heinicke C, Grove WA (2008) Machinery has completely taken over: the diffusion of the mechanical cotton picker, 1949 1964. J Interdiscipl Hist 39(1):65–96
Hertz RP, Unger AN, Cornell JA, Saunders E (2005) Racial disparities in hypertension prevalence, awareness, and management. Arch Intern Med 165(18):2098–2104
Holley D (2000) The second great emancipation: the mechanical cotton picker, Black migration, and how they shaped the modern South. University of Arkansas, Fayetteville
Hurt RD (1989) Mechanization. In: Wilson C, Ferris W (eds) Encyclopedia of southern culture. University of North Carolina Press, Chapel Hill, pp 26–27
Jasienska G (2009) Low birth weight of contemporary African Americans: an intergenerational effect of slavery? Am J Hum Bio 21(1):16–24
Jiang SZ, Lu W, Zong XF, Ruan HY, Liu Y (2016) Obesity and hypertension. Exp Ther Med 12(4):2395–2399
Kim S, Margo R (2003) Historical perspectives on US economic geography. National Bureau of Economic Research, Cambridge
Kinsella K, He W (2009) An aging world: 2008. National Institute of Aging, Washington DC
Kulkarni S, O'Farrell I, Erasi M, Kochar MS (1998) Stress and hypertension. Wisc Med J 97(11):34–38
Kuzawa C, Pike IL (2005) Introduction. Am J Hum Bio 17(1):1–4
Kuzawa C, Sweet E (2009) Epigenetics and the embodiment of race: developmental origins of US racial disparities in cardiovascular health. Am J Hum Bio 21(1):2–15
Lackland DT (2004) Fetal and early life determinants of hypertension in adults: implications for study. Hypertension 44(6):811–812
Lackland DT (2014) Racial differences in hypertension: implications for high blood pressure Management. Am J Med Sci 348(2):135–138
Lackland DT, Keil JE (1996) Epidemiology of hypertension in African Americans. Semin Nephrol 16(2):63–70
Lackland DT, Egan BM, Jones PJ (1999) Impact of nativity and race on 'Stroke Belt' mortality. Hypertension 34(1):57–62
Lackland DT, Egan BM, Ferguson PL (2003) Low birth weight as a risk factor for hypertension. J Clin Hypertens 5(2):133–136
Lackland DT, Voeks JH, Boan AD (2016) Hypertension and stroke: an appraisal of the evidence and implications for clinical management. Exp Rev Cardio Ther 14(5):609–616
Lakdawalla D, Philipson T (2009) The growth of obesity and technological change. Econ Hum Bio 7(3):283–293
Lebergott S (2014) Pursuing happiness: American consumers in the twentieth century. Princeton University Press, Princeton
Leggio M, Lombardi M, Caldarone E, Severi P, D'Emidio S, Armeni M, Bravi V, Bendini MG, Mazza A (2017) The relationship between obesity and hypertension: an updated comprehensive overview on vicious twins. Hypertens Res 40:947
Leng B, Jin Y, Li G, Chen L, Jin N (2015) Socioeconomic status and hypertension: a meta-analysis. J Hypertens 33(2):221–229
Logan TD (2015) A time (not) apart: a lesson in economic history from cotton picking books. Rev Black Pol Econ 42(4):301–322
Lopez AD, Mathers CD, Ezzati M, Jamison DT, Murray CJL (2006) Global and regional burden of disease and risk factors, 2001: systematic analysis of population health data. Lancet 367(9524)
Margo RA (1993) What is the key to black progress? second thoughts. In: McCloskey DN (ed) Myths and morals of US economic history. Oxford University Press, New York, pp 65–69
Marmot M (2002) The influence of income on health: views of an epidemiologist. Health Aff 21(2):31–46
McMillen S (1989) No easy time: rural southern women, 1940-1990. In: Hurt RD (ed) The rural South since World War II. Louisiana State University Press, Baton Rouge, pp 59–94
Mozaffarian D, Benjamin EJ, Go AS et al (2016) Executive summary: heart disease and stroke statistics—2016 update. Circulation 133(4):447

Naci H, Ioannidis JPA (2013) Comparative effectiveness of exercise and drug interventions on mortality outcomes: metaepidemiological study. Brit Med J 347:f5577–f5577
Naci H, Salcher-Konrad M, Dias S et al (2018) How does exercise treatment compare with antihypertensive medications? a network meta-analysis of 391 randomised controlled trials assessing exercise and medication effects on systolic blood pressure. British J Sport Med 53(13):859–869
Pescatello LS, MacDonald HV, Lamberti L, Johnson BT (2015) Exercise for hypertension: a prescription update integrating existing recommendations with emerging research. Curr Hypertens Rep 17(11):87
Philipson TJ, Posner RA (2003) The long-run growth in obesity as a function of technological change. Perspect Biol Med 46(3 Suppl):S87–107
Redmond N, Baer HJ, Hicks LS (2011) Health behaviors and racial disparity in blood pressure control in the National Health and Nutrition Examination Survey. Hypertension 57(3):383–389
Rhee MY, Na SH, Kim YK et al (2007) Acute effects of cigarette smoking on arterial stiffness and blood pressure in male smokers with hypertension. Am J Hypertens 20(6):637–641
Schlosser E (2012) Fast food nation: the dark side of the all-American meal. Mariner Books/ Houghton Mifflin Harcourt, Boston
Skogen JC, Overland S (2012) The fetal origins of adult disease: a narrative review of the epidemiological literature. JRSM Short Rep 3(8):59
Smith JP, Welch FR (1989) Black economic progress after Myrdal. J Econ Lit 27(2):519–564
Sowers J, Ferdinand KC, Bakris GL, Douglas JG (2002) Hypertension-related disease in African Americans: factors underlying disparities in illness and its outcome. Postgrad Med 112(4):24–26, 29–30, 33–24 passim
Steckel RH (2013) The hidden cost of moving up: type 2 diabetes and the escape from persistent poverty in the American South. Am J Hum Bio 25(4):508–515
Swanson JM, Entringer S, Buss C, Wadhwa PD (2009) Developmental origins of health and disease: environmental exposures. Semin Reprod Med 27(5):391–402
Taylor JG (1989) Foodways. In: Wilson CR, Ferris W (eds) Encyclopedia of southern culture. University of North Carolina Press, Chapel Hill, pp 613–616
Tilly L, Scott JW (1989) Women, work, and family. Routledge, New York
Torres SJ, Nowson CA (2007) Relationship between stress, eating behavior, and obesity. Nutrition 23(11-12):887–894
U.S. Bureau of the Census (1952) Characteristics of the population, number of inhabitants, general and detailed characteristics of the population. US Government Printing Office, Washington DC
U.S. Bureau of the Census (1983) Characteristics of the population. US Government Printing Office, Washington DC
US Department of Agriculture (1974) Statistics on cotton and related data 1920-1972. US Department of Agriculture, Washington DC
Virdis A, Giannarelli C, Neves MF et al (2010) Cigarette smoking and hypertension. Curr Pharm Des 16(23):2518–2525
Wong MD, Shapiro MF, Boscardin WJ, Ettner SL (2002) Contribution of major diseases to disparities in mortality. New Eng J Med 347(20):1585–1592
Xu LJ, Meng Q, He SW et al (2013) The effects of health education on patients with hypertension in China: a meta-analysis. Health Educ J 73(2):137–149
Zheng H, Tumin D, Qian Z (2013) Obesity and mortality risk: new findings from body mass index trajectories. Am J of Epidemiol 178(11):1591–1599

Chapter 3
Health and Safety vs. Freedom of Contract: The Tortured Path of Wage and Hours Limits Through the State Legislatures and the Courts

Price Fishback

Abstract The paper examines changes in wage and hour labor regulation between 1898 and 1938. Many see the 1905 *Lochner* Supreme Court decision striking down hours limits for men as the beginning of 30 years in which labor regulation was stymied by the doctrine of "freedom of contract." That issue played a role but judges often weighed it against safety issues. As a result, hours limits for men in dangerous industries were found to be constitutional. The debates over minimum wages for women also centered on these issues. These laws passed muster in state supreme courts and initially at the US Supreme Court. In 1923, a majority of Supreme Court judges emphasized freedom of contract in declaring a female minimum wage unconstitutional. Seeing close votes and substantial turnover of judges on the Supreme Court, many states continued promulgating advisory minimums and passed new laws. Ultimately, turnover on the Court and a renewed emphasis on the role of minimum wages in ensuring health and safety of women and children during the Depression led the Court to declare minimums for women constitutional. This opened the door for federal minimum wage legislation for all workers.

Keywords Lochner · Freedom of contract · Labor regulations · Minimum wage · Hour limits

---

P. Fishback (✉)
Department of Economics, University of Arizona, Tucson, AZ, USA
e-mail: fishback@arizona.edu

P. Gray et al. (eds.), *Standard of Living*, Studies in Economic History,
https://doi.org/10.1007/978-3-031-06477-7_3

3.1 Introduction

During the early 1900s, the worker-employer relationship was defined by implicit contracts in which some of the parameters of the contracts were determined by labor regulations. Most of the prescriptive regulations were targeted at safety issues, and the courts appear to have supported them as constitutional. The controversial regulations were hours maximums for men and wage minimums for women. With respect to hours and wage limits, the judges' decisions identified tensions between the freedom to contract and the protection of health and safety of workers. Where the judges drew the line on which regulations were constitutional or not often was determined by their beliefs about the workers' outside options when negotiating with employers and how much health and safety was affected by hours and wages. A large number of judges ruled on these issues, and the constitutionality of the wage and hours restrictions appeared to be in flux as various state laws were addressed by the courts over four decades. On the US Supreme Court, there was quite a bit of turnover and many of the decisions in this area were close. As a result, many states shifted their existing laws to become advisory rules that they continued to update. Since the enforcement of laws had never been well funded, the states continued to rely on publicity and the employers' own willingness to follow rules as their means of "enforcement." Seeing close votes and substantial turnover of judges on the Supreme Court, a number of states began passing new minimum wage laws in the early 1930s when the Depression began threatening the standard of living of many working families. Ultimately, turnover on the Court and a renewed emphasis on the role of minimum wages in ensuring health and safety of women and children during the Depression led the Court to declare minimums for women constitutional. This opened the door for federal minimum wage legislation for all workers.

3.2 Shifting Restrictions for Labor Contracts

Circa 1900 the relationship between worker and employer was an "at will contract" in which both sides could end the agreement. Most of these "contracts" were unwritten, as each worker had continuous negotiations with the employer about wages, hours, and working conditions. State governments enacted nearly all workplace regulations with an exception for railroad workers on interstate trains. The state laws typically passed constitutional muster if they related to safety and health conditions in the workplace because these areas were thought to fit within the police power of the state government.

There was significant uncertainty about the survival and thus enforceability of laws that set maximum hours and minimum wages or and dealt with workers signing nonunion pledges. This uncertainty came from the back and forth of rulings by state courts and ultimately the US Supreme Court. Legal scholars often argue that the 5–4 decision by the Supreme Court in *Lochner v. New York* in 1905, which struck down a maximum hours law for bakers, was the beginning of a 30-year period in which judges routinely made decisions to preserve "freedom of contract" for employers.

A closer study of the interactions between state laws and court decisions suggests that the situation was more complex. The Supreme Court decisions often involved close votes, there was significant turnover of judge during the period, and the court sometimes ruled in favor of maximum hours for men and minimum wages for women, as seen in Tables 3.1 and 3.2. When a Supreme Court decision struck down a law, a number of states passed new laws that they thought might avoid the feature found unconstitutional. Meanwhile, a number of states just continued enforcing their existing laws. As one example, the 1937 *West Coast Hotel v. Parrish* decision that affirmed the constitutionality of the women's minimum law addressed a Washington law that had been in place since 1913, 10 years before the Supreme Court's *Adkins* decision that had ostensibly determined a minimum wage was unconstitutional.

The possibility that interpretations might shift was heightened by the roughly even division of Justices with different attitudes on the highest court. "Freedom of contract" Justices (FC Justices) believed that employers and workers both had bargaining power. In economic terms, they seemed to believe that workers were mobile and had a choice of employers and could use their outside options effectively when negotiating. "Health and safety" Justices (HS Justices) often agreed that freedom of contract was important but believed that workers had few options and employers had such an advantage in bargaining that workers needed regulatory protection or collective bargaining to protect them from accepting wages that were too low and hours that were too long to be healthy. These views drew increasing strength in the 1930s as the Great Depression deepened.

3.2.1 The Rules and How They Varied Across States

In 1900 except for union contracts, the relationship between worker and employer typically involved an unwritten "at will" contract that allowed either side to terminate the relationship at any time. The states and the common law were the primary regulators of these relationships and set rulings or enacted laws that set restrictions on the contracts. For example, they set the parameters for how workers would be compensated when the worker was injured at work. Over the course of the nineteenth century, the common law evolved to a position that called for the employer to compensate injured workers for damages from workplace accidents when the accident was caused by employer negligence, as long as the employer could not invoke one of three defenses. The employer did not have to compensate the injured worker when the worker had agreed to assume the risk (assumption of risk), when a fellow worker had caused the accident (fellow-servant), or when the worker's own actions had contributed to causing the accident (contributory negligence). By 1900, however, 30 states had enacted laws that eliminated at least one of the defenses for

Table 3.1 Votes of Supreme Court Justices on constitutionality of statute in major labor law cases, 1898–1917

	1898	1905	1905	1908	1908	1915	1917	1917	1917	1917		
Case	Holden v. Hardy	Cantwell v. Missouri	Lochner v. New York	Adair v. U.S.	Muller v. Oregon	Coppage v. Kansas	Bunting v. Oregon	Wilson v. New	Stettler v. O'Hara	Hitchman Coal & Coke v. Mitchell	Start	End
Issue	Men's hours	Men's hours	Men's hours	Prevent firing of RR union workers	Women's hours	Stop yellow dog contracts	Men/women hours overtime pay	RR men hours, wages, overtime	Women's wage	stop yellow dog contract		
Vote (For-Against) Justice	7–2	?-?	4–5	2–6	9–0	3–6	6–3	5–4	4–4 affirmed	3–6		
John Marshall Harlan	Yes		Yes	No-op	Yes						1877	1911
Horace Gray	Yes										1882	1902
Melville Fuller	Yes		No	No	Yes						1888	1910
David Brewer	No		No	No	Yes						1890	1910
Henry Billings Brown	Yes		No								1891	1906
George Shiras	Yes		Yes								1892	1903
Edward Douglas White	Yes			No	Yes	No					1894	1910
Rufus Peckham	No		No-op	No	Yes						1896	1909
Joseph McKenna	Yes		No	Yes	Yes	No	Yes	Yes	Yes	No	1898	1925

Vote (For-Against) Justice	7–2	?-?	4–5	2–6	9–0	3–6	6–3	5–4	4–4 affirmed	3–6		
Oliver Wendell Holmes				Yes	Yes	Yes	Yes	Yes	Yes	Yes	1902	1932
William Day			Yes		Yes	Yes	Yes	No	Yes	No	1903	1922
William Moody				Not. Part	Yes						1906	1910
Charles Evan Hughes						Yes					1910	1916
Edward Douglas White							No	Yes-op	No	No	1910	1921
Willis van Devanter						No	No	No	No	No	1911	1937
Joseph Lamar						No					1911	1916
Mahlon Pitney						No-op	Yes	No	No	No-op	1912	1922

(continued)

Table 3.1 (continued)

	1898	1905	1905	1908	1908	1915	1917	1917	1917	1917		
Case	Holden v. Hardy	Cantwell v. Missouri	Lochner v. New York	Adair v. U.S.	Muller v. Oregon	Coppage v. Kansas	Bunting v. Oregon	Wilson v. New	Stettler v. O'Hara	Hitchman Coal & Coke v. Mitchell	Start	End
Issue	Men's hours	Men's hours	Men's hours	Prevent firing of RR union workers	Women's hours	Stop yellow dog contracts	Men/women hours overtime pay	RR men hours, wages, overtime	Women's wage	stop yellow dog contract		
Vote (For-Against) Justice	7–2	?-?	4–5	2–6	9–0	3–6	6–3	5–4	4–4 affirmed	3–6		
James McReynolds						No	No	No	No	No	1914	1941
Louis Brandeis							Recused	Yes	Recused	Yes	1916	1939
John Clarke							Yes	Yes	Yes	Yes	1916	1922

Table 3.2 Votes of Supreme Court Justices on constitutionality of statute in major labor law cases, 1917–1937

	1917	1917	1917	1923	1930	1931	1934	1935	1936	1936	1937	1937
	Bunting v. Oregon	Wilson v. New	Stettler v. O'Hara	Adkins v. Children's Hospital	Tagg Bros & Moorhead v. U.S.	O'Gorman & Young v. Hartford Fire Ins.	Nebbia v. New York	Schechter Poultry	Carter v. Carter Coal Co.	Morehead v. New York ex. Rel. Tipaldo	West Coast Hotel v. Parrish	Jones & Laughlin Steel v. U.S.
	Men/women hours overtime pay	RR men hours, wages, overtime	Women's wage	Women's wage	Ag interstate reg. of commission rates	Regulate insurance broker commission rates	Milk min. Price	NRA	Code like NRA in coal	Women's minimum wage	Women's min. Wage	Nat'l Labor Relations Act
Vote (for-against) justice	6–3	5–4	4–4 affirmed	3–5	9–0	5–4	5–4	0–9	4–5	4–5	5–4	5–4
Joseph McKenna	Yes	Yes	Yes	No								
Oliver Wendell Holmes	Yes	Yes	Yes	Yes								
William day	Yes	No	Yes									
Edward Douglas white	No	Yes-op	No									
Willis van Devanter	No	No	No	No	Yes	No	No	No	No	No	No	No
Mahlon Pitney	Yes	No	No									
James McReynolds	No	No	No	No	Yes	No	No	No	No	No	No	No

(continued)

Table 3.2 (continued)

	1917	1917	1917	1923	1930	1931	1934	1935	1936	1936	1937	1937
	Bunting v. Oregon	Wilson v. New	Stettler v. O'Hara	Adkins v. Children's Hospital	Tagg Bros & Moorhead v. U.S.	O'Gorman & Young v. Hartford Fire Ins.	Nebbia v. New York	Schechter Poultry	Carter v. Carter Coal Co.	Morehead v. New York ex. Rel. Tipaldo	West Coast Hotel v. Parrish	Jones & Laughlin Steel v. U.S.
	Men/women hours overtime pay	RR men hours, wages, overtime	Women's wage	Women's wage	Ag interstate reg. of commission rates	Regulate insurance broker commission rates	Milk min. Price	NRA	Code like NRA in coal	Women's minimum wage	Women's min. Wage	Nat'l Labor Relations Act
Vote (for-against) justice	6–3	5–4	4–4 affirmed	3–5	9–0	5–4	5–4	0–9	4–5	4–5	5–4	5–4
Louis Brandeis	Recused	Yes	Recused	Recused	Yes-op	Yes-op	Yes	No	Yes	Yes	Yes	Yes
John Clarke	Yes	Yes	Yes									
William Howard Taft				Yes								
George Sutherland				No-op	Yes	No	No	No	No-op	No	No	No
Pierce Butler				No	Yes	No	No	No	No	No-op	No-op	No
Edward Sanford				Yes								
Harlan Fiske stone					Yes	Yes	Yes	No	Yes	Yes	Yes	Yes

Vote (for-against) justice	6–3	5–4	4–4 affirmed	3–5	9–0	5–4	5–4	0–9	4–5	4–5	5–4	5–4
Charles Evan Hughes					Yes	Yes	Yes	No-op	Yes	Yes	Yes	Yes-op
Owen Roberts					Yes	Yes	Yes-op	No	No	No	Yes	Yes
Benjamin Cardozo					Yes	Yes	Yes	No	Yes	Yes	Yes	Yes

Notes. Horace Lurton was on the court from 1910 through 1914 but did not participate in these cases

workers in general and another 24 had done so for railroads or street railroads. By 1908 25 states prevented employers from signing contracts that waived suits for negligence damages prior to the accident occurring, often after a number of court decisions had struck them down. Richard Epstein (1982) described these contracts as private ways of structuring the equivalent of workers' compensation contracts. Between 1911 and 1940, every state except Mississippi had enacted a workers' compensation law that required employers to cover medical costs and up to two-thirds of wage losses for all workers injured in accidents arising out of or in the course of employment.

Most of the state regulations dealt specifically with safety or health in the workplace. Before the Civil War, the states began establishing restrictions to promote railroad safety, as much to require the railroads to protect passengers as to protect their workers. By 1924 45 states and the federal government had established a series of safety regulations concerning railroad equipment and practices, and 30 had them for street railroads. Between 1869 and 1880, mining states adopted regulations requiring the filing of mine maps and basic ventilation. Nearly all mining states had safety regulations that expanded in scope during the early twentieth century (Fishback 1992, 2006). Meanwhile, at the behest of the nascent union movement, many states established bureaus to collect labor statistics in the 1880s; 28 had them by 1894 and 44 were in place by 1924.[1] By the 1880s, some states had begun to establish specific regulations of workplace conditions, typically with respect to safety, and access to bathrooms and time off for lunch. Between 1895 and 1924, sanitation/bathroom regulations spread from 11 to 35 states, and the number of states with ventilation laws rose from 10 to 26, for machine guards from 12 to 35, for fire escape access from 23 to 37 states, and from 5 to 24 states for building regulations. The building, fire escape, and boiler regulations were also established at the city or county levels. By 1924 14 states had regulations banning sweatshops, while 32 states had enacted bakery regulations, 20 of those were enacted after the Lochner decision struck down bakery hours regulations. Teeth were added to these laws by the establishment of inspectors for factories (rising from 15 in 1895 to 41 in 1924), child labor inspectors (13 to 41), mine inspectors (23 to 33, largely matching the number with significant mining), and boiler inspectors (15 to 17). Reporting of accidents for mines was required in 1924 by 32 states, for railroads by 39, and for factories by 23.

[1] The information on state laws throughout the paper was compiled by Rebecca Holmes (2003, 2005) for her award-winning dissertation on the development of state labor legislation. Holmes et al. (2008) and Fishback et al. (2009) have developed summary indices and explored a number of correlations with various measures of labor markets during the period.

3.2.2 Hours Restrictions and Freedom to Contract

There was much greater uncertainty about what the state governments could do about restrictions on wages and hours. States set regulations that influenced the nature of wage payments. By 1924 30 states required wage payments in cash, and 37 required that wages be paid either fortnightly or monthly, while 12 put restrictions on repayments of advances made to the worker by the employer.[2] Setting minimum wages and maximum hours was another matter.

3.2.2.1 Hours Restrictions for Males

Weekly and daily hours were a constant source of negotiation between workers and employers in the early 1900s. Average hours per day in manufacturing fell from 10 around 1890 to around 9.7 by 1905 and 9.2 in 1914, while average weekly hours fell from 60 in 1890 to 57.7 by 1905 to 53.6 during World War I and to 50.3 by 1926 (Carter et al. 2006, series Ba4552, p. 2-302 and Ba4568, p. 2-303). These changes were determined to a limited degree by changes in hours legislation (Whaples 1990). By 1905 7 states had enacted hours limits for textiles, 9 for manufacturing, 16 for railroads, 11 for mines, 11 for street railroads, 22 for public work, and 4 for other types of workers (including a law for New York bakers).

The key to the constitutionality of hours regulations for males was whether judges considered the hours limits to be necessary to protect the health and safety of workers. In 1898 in *Holden v. Hardy* (169 US 366, 1898), the Supreme Court upheld a Utah mining law setting a maximum of 8 h per day for miners and ore smelting and refining as a valid exercise of police power because their safety was at risk if they worked more than 8 h. Seven years later, the court reaffirmed the *Holden* decision by upholding a similar Missouri law in *Cantwell v. Missouri* (199 US 385, 1905) on safety grounds (Cushman 1998, 247n58). Table 3.1 shows that only Rufus Peckham and David Brewer dissented in the *Holden* case, while I have been unable to find votes for the *Cantwell* case.

In contrast, the Supreme Court struck down a New York state law limiting the hours of male bakers in *Lochner v. New York* (198 US 45, 1905). Justice Rufus Peckham wrote for the 5–4 majority that the law was a violation of freedom of contract. The bakers were able enough "to assert their rights and care for themselves without the protecting arm of the State." He argued that the limits were not related to a public health issue that might have constituted a legitimate exercise of police power. The four dissenting justices made a health and safety argument in favor of the laws. They argued that the legislature was in a better position than the courts to assess whether there were sufficient threats to the bakers' health from long hours to use the police power to impose a limit to protect the bakers.

[2] Cushman (1998, 57–58) cites a series of Supreme Court decisions related to these issues and affirming the legislation.

The two types of decisions seem to have led to two different paths for hours legislation for men. In 1916 the federal government enacted the Adamson Act in 1916 setting a maximum of 8 h per day with added pay for overtime for interstate railway workers. It was upheld in another 5–4 Supreme Court decision in 1917 in *Wilson v. New* (243 US 332, 1917). By 1924 the number of states regulating hours for intrastate railroads had risen from 16 to 27. The number regulating hours for other types of workers had risen from 4 to 11. Most of these settings seem to have met the requirement that the workers' or their customers' safety were at risk. Meanwhile, the states were active in limiting hours when they were the employer, as the number of states regulating hours for public work rose from 8 in 1900 to 30 in 1924.

On the other path, the number of states with hours laws for textiles, manufacturing, and street railroads listed by the BLS as active in 1924 had not changed or had fallen. It might be that these also survived because they promoted safety, they had not been challenged, or they were not enforced. Alternatively, the state regulators may have taken heart in the Supreme Court's decision in *Bunting v. Oregon* (243 US 426, 1917) to uphold a 10-h day law for men and women in Oregon. As seen in Table 3.1, Justice McKenna had supported the hours limits in 1898 in *Holden* and in *Wilson* in 1917 for the Adamson Act but voted against the 1905 baker's law in *Lochner* (see Table 3.1). In *Bunting* he argued that the plaintiff had *not* met the burden of proof that there was *no* safety reason for the law.[3] Later, Chief Justice William Howard Taft suggested that the *Bunting* decision had implicitly overruled *Lochner* (Cushman 1998, 61).

3.2.2.2 Allowing Paternalistic Hours Restrictions for Women and Children

As part of the campaign to limit child labor and protect their safety in workplaces, the states generally imposed restrictions on child labor through minimum ages, as well as hours limits for the child workers above those ages. The number of states imposing minimum wages rose from 17 in 1894 to 42 in 1924. The number imposing general restrictions rose from 20 to 44. The hours restrictions on child labor varied across types of employment. The number imposing general restrictions on hours rose from 7 to 35, and restrictions on mechanical employments rose from 18 to 28, from 6 to 22 in mercantile jobs, and from 15 to 26 in textiles, where the whole family had often worked in southern mills. A number of studies have found weak effects of these laws on child labor activity. Fishback (1998) argues that many of the Progressive Era labor laws did not pass until after a group of employers joined reformers to pass laws that codified what those employers were already doing. The reformers still saw this as useful because the new laws brought the straggling employers into conformity.

[3] In an odd contrast in Table 1, Justice William Day voted against the railroad hours limits in *Wilson* even though he had supported the hours limits in *Lochner*, *Muller*, and *Bunting*, as well as the minimum wage in *Stettler*.

On similar paternalistic grounds, states imposed hours restrictions on women's labor. Between 1895 and 1924, the number of states with hours restrictions in general rose from 2 to 28, the number for mechanical female employment rose from 12 to 28, for textiles the rise was from 8 to 27, and for mercantile work the rise was from 3 to 27. The expansion was supported by a series of Supreme Court decisions, starting with *Muller v. Oregon* (208 US 412, 1908).[4] The court argued that women needed more protection than men against long hours of work and that it was important that they maintain their health so that they could have "vigorous" offspring; therefore, "the physical well-being of woman becomes an object of public interest and care in order to preserve the strength and vigor of the race" (quoted in Cushman (1998), 54). Goldin (1988) found that the laws had relatively small impacts on the hours worked by women, but the restrictions appear to have lowered the hours of work by men. This might have been why the women's hours laws continued to face challenges in the courts. Although six Justices had been replaced after the 2008 *Muller* decision, the US Supreme Court reaffirmed the women's hours maximums in a series of cases in 1914 and 1915.[5]

3.3 Minimum Wage Laws

The next major issue in the 1910s was minimum wages for women, and the FC and HS Justices disagreed about the impact of wages on health and safety. These disagreements led to a pair of close decisions in 1917 that allowed hours limits and requirements of overtime pay for *men and women* in dangerous work. Further, the initial decision on a women's minimum wage law affirmed the state court's support for the minimum in a split decision with new HS Judge Louis Brandeis recusing himself because he had represented the state in the lower court decisions. When the women's minimum wage came up again in 1923 in *Adkins v. Children's Hospital*, the regulation was struck down in a 5–3 decision with Brandeis again recusing himself. The majority argued that the minimum wage had a much more indirect effect on the health and safety of women than the maximum hours laws. During the Great Depression, attitudes toward minimum wages began to shift. A number of states passed new minimum wage laws. Hoover jawboned industry to maintain wage rates, and the New Deal introduced the National Recovery Administration (NRA), in which industry leaders negotiated wages, hours, and price agreements for codes that had the force of law. As seen in Table 3.2, four FC Justices who had voted

---

[4] Prior to *Muller*, state courts in Massachusetts, Nebraska, Oregon, and Washington had supported the constitutionality of the limits on women's hours, while in Illinois it was declared unconstitutional. See *Commonwealth v. Hamilton Mfg. Co.*, 120 Massachusetts 383; *Wenham v. State*, 65 Nebraska 394, 400, 406; *State v. Buchanan*, 29 Washington 602; *Commonwealth v. Beatty*, 15 Pa.Sup.Ct. 5, 17; against them is the case of *Ritchie v. People*, 155 Illinois 98.

[5] Cushman (1998, 247n59) cites *Bosley v. McLaughlin* (236 US 3851915), *Miller v. Wilson* (236 US 373, 1915), *Hawley v. Walker* (232 US 718, 1914), and *Riley v. Massachusetts* (232 US 671, 1914).

against the minimum wage law in *Adkins* in Willis Van Devanter, James McReynolds, George Sutherland, and Pierce Butler maintained their stance against minimum wages before retiring in the late 1930s. Meanwhile, HS Justice Louis Brandeis, who had recused himself from *Adkins*, was joined by new HS Justices Harlan Fiske Stone, Benjamin Cardozo, and Chief Justice Charles Evan Hughes. In 1936 Justice Owen Roberts opposed one version of the minimum wage that sought to circumvent the *Adkins* decision and then in 1937 supported a version that asked to overturn it on the grounds that wages that were too low created a health and safety risk. When the Court supported the constitutionality of the Fair Labor Standards Act of 1938 that limited hours and set minimum wages and rules for overtime pay for women and men in interstate commerce, the uncertainty surrounding the issue was largely settled.

3.3.1 The Initial Laws and Court Decisions

Between 1912 and 1919, 15 states and Washington, D.C., adopted minimum wage laws for women.[6] The laws were found to be constitutional in the state supreme courts in Arkansas, Massachusetts, Minnesota, and Oregon, and Washington (Clark 1921, 33), but there remained uncertainty until the Supreme Court ruled on minimum wages. At the national level, three Supreme Court rulings in 1917 seemed to support some wage regulation, although Cushman (1998, 60–65) argues that the Justices focused mostly on the hours issues and minimized the wage restrictions in their opinions. The *Bunting v. Oregon* (23 US 4261917) and *Wilson v. New* (243 US 332, 1917) hours law cases also involved paying overtime wages, and men were among the workers in both settings. In the *Bunting* case, the plaintiffs pressed an argument that the laws involved wage regulation and that "insufficiency of wage does not justify legislative regulation. The wage had no bearing on health." "The effect is to take money from the employer and give it to the laborer without due process or value in return," and thus was a "taking" that was not "neutral" (Cushman quoting the decision, 1998, 60). The judges treated the case as a case about hours and not about wages. FC Justice McKenna argued that the overtime pay acted like a fine designed to deter employers from having workers work beyond the hours maximum.

[6]The states were Massachusetts and Ohio in 1912; California, Colorado, Minnesota, Nebraska, North Dakota, Oregon, Utah, Washington, and Wisconsin in 1913; Arkansas in 1915; Arizona in 1917; D.C. in 1918; and Texas in 1919. Ohio passed a constitutional amendment but never enforced the law and Nebraska never put it into operation. All of the rest except Colorado set specific rates, generally through commissions. Violations were treated as misdemeanors in which the court could award back wages in most states. Massachusetts differed in that it reported the names of violators in newspapers instead. Nebraska in 1919 repealed the law but then adopted a constitutional amendment in 1920 that authorized legislation, while Texas in 1921 repealed its law. See Clark (1921, 10–12) and Smith (1932) for descriptions of the laws at various times.

In the *Wilson v. New* case, the Adamson Act had included overtime pay and also subject to a commission report planned to reduce the hours per day while requiring daily pay to stay the same. The Justice Department argued that the wage minimum was health-related because "physical efficiency is impossible without proper living conditions...which can not be secured without payment of an adequate wage. An adequate wage, therefore, is essential to safe, regular, and efficient service in interstate commerce" (quoted in Cushman 1998, 62). Chief Justice White wrote for the majority stating that railroads were involved in public service and could be regulated in ways not applicable to private business (Cushman, 62–64).

The most direct decision about minimum wages for adult women wage standards came when the Oregon Supreme Court ruling on the Oregon law was appealed to the Supreme Court. The Oregon court had used the same reasoning as in *Muller v. Oregon*. In *Stettler v. O'Hara* (243 US 6291917), the Court split 4–4 with HS Justices McKenna, Holmes, Day, and Clarke supporting the statute and FC Justices White, Van Devanter, Pitney, and McReynolds opposing. HS Justice Brandeis recused himself because he had been a lawyer for the state in the litigation. These apparent affirmations of wage regulation made it easier for Arizona in 1917, Washington D.C. in 1918, and Texas in 1919 to adopt minimum wage laws for women. However, Texas in 1921 later repealed its law (Clark 1921).[7]

The constitutionality of minimum wages for women was struck down in *Adkins v. Children's Hospital* (261 US 525, 1923). The decision declared unconstitutional the efforts by Congress to set up minimum wages for women in Washington, D.C., in 1918. In the ensuing court challenge, Justice Felix Frankfurter, who later joined the Supreme Court, defended the minimum as essential to protecting the health of women and their children and to prevent them from requiring poverty relief at the expense of taxpayers. The plaintiffs argued that the minimum was a taking and was similar to price-fixing, that the activities did not affect the public interest, and that "wages, unlike hours affected health only 'indirectly or remotely'" (Cushman 1998, 67). Justice Sutherland wrote for the 5–3 majority and accepted the hospital's argument while also affirming the "freedom of contract" doctrine. Chief Justice William Howard Taft dissented (with Edward Sanford joining) using arguments from dissents in the *Lochner* case and the majority in the *Bunting* case. He argued that it was not clear that wages had a more indirect impact on health than hours, and the legislature was in a better position than the judges to determine the issue (Cushman 1998, p. 69). Oliver Wendell Holmes dissented separately and expressed dissatisfaction with the "liberty of contract" doctrine while arguing that the legislation had the proper goal of removing conditions that led to "ill health, immorality, and the deterioration of the race" (quoted by Cushman (1998), p. 69).

[7] See Elizabeth Brandeis (1935, 499–539) for discussions of the application of the laws.

3.3.2 State Responses to the Adkins' Decision Over the Next Decade

After the 1923 decision, it might have seemed settled that laws limiting women's hours in general and men's hours in dangerous jobs were constitutional but that hours maximums for most males and minimum wages for men and women were not. Certainly, the initial decisions that followed appeared to confirm that belief. Over the next few years, the Supreme Court ruled the Arizona and Arkansas laws void in *Murphy v. Sardell* (169 US 366, 1925) and *Donham v. West-Nelson Mfg. Co.* (273 US 657, 1927). State supreme courts in Kansas in 1925 and Minnesota in 1925 declared their minimum wage laws unconstitutional. The Minnesota decision reversed several of their earlier decisions declaring the law constitutional.[8]

Contemporary interest groups and state legislators and governors, however, had seen a series of decisions on each law that had switched back and forth as they move up through the courts. At the Supreme Court level, the votes had often been close, and there was turnover on the court. Eight Justices had been appointed after 1920, and three of those had resigned by 1932. Only five of the Judges from the 1923 court that had decided *Adkins* were still on the court in 1933. Seeing this history, one can imagine that interest groups on both sides of the issues would be pressuring state governments to pass or oppose new laws.

Despite the *Adkins* ruling, a number of states continued to maintain minimum wage laws on an advisory basis. In North Dakota, Massachusetts, and Washington, the commissions seem to have carried on as before because their state supreme courts had declared their laws constitutional.[9] Wisconsin rewrote its law in 1925 and changed the basis of its legislation from requiring the "necessary cost of proper living" to a more negative idea that "no wage shall be oppressive, and it passed muster in federal court.[10] A Women's Bureau Study in 1932 reported that California, Colorado, Massachusetts, Minnesota, North Dakota, Oregon, South Dakota, Washington, and Wisconsin were still listed as having minimum wage laws. North Dakota set specific rates in the statutes, while commissions or agencies within the other states established rates, although Colorado had no appropriations to operate the law. Violations were generally treated as misdemeanors in which back under-

[8] See US Bureau of Labor Statistics, "Minimum Wage Legislation in the United States." *Monthly Labor Review* 37 (1933): 1344–1354. The Kansas case was *Topeka Laundry Col v. Court of Industrial Relations (119 Kans. 13)* and the Minnesota case was *Stevenson v. St. Clair (161 Minn. 444).*

[9] See US Bureau of Labor Statistics, "Minimum Wage Legislation in the United States." *Monthly Labor Review* 37 (1933): 1344–1354. In Washington see *Larsen v. Rice (100 Wash. 642 in 1918; Spokane Hotel v. Younger (113 Wash. 359 in 1920; Sports. v. Moritz (141 Wash. 417).* In North Dakota, it was *Northwestern T.E. Co. v. Workmen's Compensation Bureau (47 N.D. 397).* In Massachusetts the case was *Holcombe v. Creamer (231, Mass 99) in 1918.*

[10] See US Bureau of Labor Statistics. *Handbook of Labor Statistics, 1931, Edition. Bulletin No. 541, 1931, p.* 448. The ruling is *Folding Furniture Works v. Industrial Commission (300 Fed. 991, 1924, US District Court, W.D., Wisconsin).*

payments could be collected. Massachusetts had no fines, and instead published the names of violators in the newspaper (Smith 1932, 11 and supplemental charts), although a Massachusetts court ruling in 1924 stated that the Minimum Wage Commission *could not require* a newspaper to publish the list.[11] It is not clear from the study how well the laws were being enforced. The BLS (1931, 449) suggested that it was understood in California and Washington and likely also in North Dakota, Oregon, and South Dakota that public opinion would help enforce the rates they set.

In many ways, the situation for women's minimum wage laws was similar to the situation for most laws at the time period. For example, the fines for violating mine safety regulations were generally low, and enforcement was costly because inspectors in many states had to go to court to enforce the law in many states (see Fishback (2006) and Graebner (1976), 97–100). Thus, enforcement largely relied on public opinion and the mine owners' respect for the law.

The wage declines during the Depression and the election of Roosevelt appear to have emboldened seven states to pass new minimum wage laws for adult women between 1933 and 1935, including Connecticut, Illinois (1933), New Hampshire (1933), New Jersey (1933), New York (1933), Ohio (1933), and Utah (1933 after 1929 repeal).[12] Several of the laws were based on a standard bill sponsored by the National Consumers League. The BLS (1933b, 1346) stated they were "drawn by the legislatures in view of the objections raised in the *Adkins* case and it is evident that the laws were so worded as to overcome the major difficulties. During the recent period of economic depression it has become apparent that unfair wage standards not only undermine the health and well-being of the workers but threaten the stability of industry itself." "The experience of the past few years should add much force and weight to the reasoning in the opinion in *Stettler v. O'Hara* holding that the enactment of such laws is a valid exercise of the police power and that they are not only a valid but necessary means of protecting the public health, morals and welfare."

3.3.3 Restrictions Imposed by the National Recovery Administration

Worries about industry stability and declining wages led both the Hoover and Roosevelt administrations to try several ways to maintain higher wages during the Depression. President Hoover had tried "jawboning" leading manufacturers into volunteering for work-sharing arrangements in which they would reduce hours per week, increase the number employed, and hold hourly earnings roughly the same (Rose 2010; Neumann et al. 2013). The New Dealers promoted a similar idea as part of the National Industrial Recovery Act of June 16, 1933. In addition to allotting

[11] "Legislative Notes." *American Labor Legislation Review* 14 (1924), p. 203

[12] US Bureau of Labor Statistics (1933a, b)

money to hire workers to build large public works through the Public Works Administration, they called for employers, workers, and consumers to meet together and negotiate "Fair Codes of Competition." The Codes were to include agreements to set minimum wages and maximum hours in the industry and set prices and quality of goods and the codes were to be enforced through prosecutions by US district attorneys in US district court.[13]

Section 7a of the NIRA stated that every code gave employees collective bargaining rights, banned yellow dog contracts, and required that employers shall comply with maximum hours of labor, minimum rates of pay, and other conditions of employment "approved or *prescribed* by the President." The Codes were to include agreements to set minimum wages and maximum hours per week in the industry and set prices and quality of goods and the codes were to be enforced through prosecutions by US district attorneys in US district court.[14]

In the absence of a code, Section 7c gave the President, after hearings and investigations, the "authority to prescribe a limited code of fair competition fixing such maximum hours of labor, minimum rates of pay, and other conditions of employment…as he finds to be necessary," and the codes were to be enforced like a regular code.

Only a handful of industries had created codes by late July of 1933. As a stopgap measure, Roosevelt issued an Executive Order on July 27 allowing firms to display the Blue Eagle if they voluntarily signed President's Reemployment Agreements (PRAs). The stated goal was to limit weekly hours, "raise wages, create employment, and thus increase purchasing power and restore business" in a plan that "depends wholly on united action by all employers." The conditions of the PRAs included maximum hours of 40 per week for office workers and 35 per week for factory workers and minimum weekly earnings of $15 per week in cities with more than 500,000 people, $14.50 per week where population was between 250,000 and 500,000, and $14 hours per week in cities with 2500 to 250,000 people. In smaller towns, the firms were to increase all wages by not more than 20 percent with a target of $12 per week. The minimum hourly wage was set at 40 cents per hour unless the wage rate for the same class of work in 1929 was less than 40 cents, and then the minimum was to be the larger of $30 cents per hour or the prevailing hourly rate in July 1919. No compensation that was currently above the minimum was to be lowered. No children below 14 years of age were to be employed and those 14–16 were

[13] Section 3d of the NIRA gave the president the authority to hold hearings and set up codes of fair competition "if complaint is made to the President that abuses inimical to the public interest and contrary to the policy herein declared are prevalent in any trade or industry or subdivision thereof, and if no code of fair competition therefor has theretofore been approved by the President." Violations were misdemeanors with fines of up to $500 for each day an offense occurred. Section 3e gave the right to impose trade restrictions on foreign imports that violated the codes.

[14] Section 3d of the NIRA gave the president the authority to hold hearings and set up codes of fair competition "if complaint is made to the President that abuses inimical to the public interest and contrary to the policy herein declared are prevalent in any trade or industry or subdivision thereof, and if no code of fair competition therefor has theretofore been approved by the President." Violations were misdemeanors with fines of up to $500 for each day an offense occurred. Section 3e gave the right to impose trade restrictions on foreign imports that violated the codes.

to work no more than 3 h per day, and these were required to be between 7 a.m. and 7 p.m. Implicit was the expectation of an increase in employment, as employers were "not to use any subterfuge to frustrate the spirit and intent of this agreement which is, among other things, to increase employment by a universal covenant, to remove obstructions to commerce, and to shorten hours and to raise wages for the shorter week to a living basis." Price increases were allowed only based on actual costs, and firms were "to support and patronize establishments" that were also National Recovery Administration (NRA) members. Finally, they were "to cooperate to the fullest extent in having a Code of Fair Competition submitted by his industry at the earliest possible date" with an expectation that the Codes would be created by September 1, a date that few industries met.

The PRA and the industry Codes were not regulations per se because the firms were voluntarily signing the PRA or joining in the industry codes. If the firm/employer did not sign the code or agreement, however, they were not subject to the minimum wage or the maximum hours. Thus, the PRA and NRA minimums were based on bargaining, unlike a statutory minimum wage. The government made signing the PRAs attractive by developing a massive advertising campaign to get consumers to buy from firms that displayed the Blue Eagle symbol associated with the NRA. The campaign included parades in every major city as well as 20,000 canvassers going door-to-door to 20 million households to get people to sign pledges to support the NRA by buying only from firms displaying the Blue Eagle. A large number of firms signed the pledges, and average hours worked in manufacturing dropped from around 41 h per week in July 1933 to 33.8 h in November 1933 (Neumann et al. 2013, 108).

Jason Taylor (2019, chapter 4) and Royal Meeker (1933, 467–8) both suggested an undercurrent of coercion as well. The administration sought to make firms believe that noncompliance would cost them dearly with unspoken threats of boycotts. In August 1933, the mercurial NIRA head General Hugh Johnson announced: "the time is coming when someone is going to take one of those Blue Eagles off of someone's window in a clear cut case and that is going to be a sentence of economic death" (Anonymous 1933).

Codes were created in hundreds of industries, although the enforcement of the codes was relatively weak, and violations were not uncommon. The problems with violations followed the typical patterns found in settings related to cartel enforcement with more heterogeneous sectors and codes that were less precise being violated more often (Taylor 2011, 2019).

The NRA legislation was set to expire in June 1935, and Vittoz (1987) argues that there were a number of Congressmen who were inclined to allow them to expire. The issue became moot in May 1935 when the Supreme Court unanimously struck down the NRA codes on May 27, 1935, in *L. A. Schechter Poultry Corp. v. United States* (295 US 495, 1935). Chief Justice Hughes argued that the codes were not "voluntary" but had become the equivalent of regulations created by market participants although approved by the President and that the delegation of this power was unconstitutional. In his own words:

> Section 3 of the Recovery Act is without precedent. It supplies no standards for any trade, industry or activity. It does not undertake to prescribe rules of conduct to be applied to particular states of fact determined by appropriate administrative procedure. Instead, it authorizes the making of codes to prescribe them. For that legislative undertaking, it sets up no standards, aside from the statement of the general aims of rehabilitation, correction and expansion found in § 1. In view of the broad scope of that declaration, and of the nature of the few restrictions that are imposed, the discretion of the President in approving or prescribing codes, and thus enacting laws for the government of trade and industry throughout the country, is virtually unfettered. The code-making authority thus sought to be conferred is an unconstitutional delegation of legislative power.

3.3.4 The Path to a Constitutional Minimum Wages

Although the *Schechter* ruling supported freedom of contract, the decision was more about the improper delegation of regulatory authority by the legislature.[15] Cushman (1998, 71–83) argues that shifts in the composition of the court in the late 1920s and early 1930s led to a series of decisions that expanded the scope for public interest to be used to support the police power of the state and thus weaken the "freedom of contract" doctrine.[16] Further, he argued that "a bevy of contemporary Court watchers" anticipated that minimum wages would eventually be declared constitutional after the 5–4 Supreme Court decision on *Nebbia v. New York* (291 US 502, 1934). A number of contemporaries thought cutthroat price competition was driving firms out of business during the Depression. When New York law establishing a minimum price for milk reached the Supreme Court, Justice Roberts wrote for the majority that the law was constitutional because the minimum price law insured that the public had adequate access to milk, which was necessary for the health of

[15] Cushman (1998) suggests that a similar statement might be made about the 5–4 Supreme Court ruling in *Carter v. Carter Coal Co.* (298 US 238, 1936), which struck down the attempt in the Bituminous Coal Conservation Act of 1935 to reestablish a version of the NRA bituminous coal code that set prices, wages, and hours. The majority ruled that the excise tax in the act was a "penalty" designed to coerce compliance, and Congress did not have the power to control wages, hours, and working conditions because it has "no general power to regulate for the promotion of the general welfare" and cannot control production within a state before the coal is sold in interstate commerce (p. 298).

[16] Cushman (1998, 77) states that these included a unanimous decisions in *Tagg Brothers & Moorhead v. United States* (280 US 420, 1930) to allow the Secretary of Agriculture to set commissions for brokers in stockyards and a 5–4 majority decision on *O'Gorman & Young, Inc. v. Hartford Fire Ins. Co.*, 282 US 251 (1931), written by Brandeis to limit commissions for agents selling fire insurance in New Jersey. In the insurance case, the claim was that insurance rates were already regulated and that the commissions were a large enough share of insurance rates that they could be regulated as well to prevent insurers from being driven out of their public service business. Justice Van Devanter's dissent joined by McReynolds, Sutherland, and Butler argued that the state had the right to regulate the business but "it may not say what shall be paid to employees or interfere with the freedom of the parties to contract in respect of wages" (Cushman 1998, 77).Van Devanter did acknowledge that there might be special circumstances that would allow the freedom of contract to be abridged, but they had not occurred in the *O'Gorman* setting (Cushman 1998, 77).

the population. He argued that "the use of private property and the making of private contracts are, as a general rule free from government interference; but they are subject to public regulation when the public need requires" (p. 291).

When the court struck down a New York minimum wage law with a 5–4 vote in *Morehead v. New York ex. Rel. Tipaldo* (298 US 587, 1936), their predictions looked less accurate. The lawyers representing the state of New York went to great pains to identify differences between the D.C. law in *Adkins* and their own law to try to avoid asking the justices to overturn *Adkins*. Justice Butler wrote the majority opinion and still applied the freedom of contract doctrine in *Adkins*. Yet Chief Justice Hughes dissented saying that he could not agree that *Adkins* was a controlling case because the construction of the statutes in the two cases was different. "I can find nothing in the Federal Constitution which denies to the state the power to protect women from being exploited by overreaching employers through the refusal of a fair wage as defined in the New York statute and ascertained in a reasonable manner by competent authority" (p. 619). In his dissent, Justice Harlan Fiske Stone, joined by Brandeis and Cardozo, argued that since the *Adkins* decision, "we have had opportunity to learn that a wage is not always the result of free bargaining between employers and employees; that it may be one forced upon employees by their economic necessities and upon employers by the most ruthless of their competitors," further that insufficient wages place burdens on society as a whole (p. 635). "We should follow our decision in the *Nebbia* cases and leave...the solution of the problems to which the statute is addressed where it seems to me the Constitution has left them, to the legislative branch" (p. 636).

The minimum wage became constitutional when Owen Roberts switched sides and voted to uphold the Washington state minimum wage law for women in *West Coast Hotel v. Parrish* (300 US 379, 1937). The situation illustrates some of the uncertainties about the interactions between court decisions and statutes. Remember that the Washington state minimum wage law had been passed in 1913, long before the *Adkins* decision in 1923. The Washington Supreme Court had ruled it constitutional in three earlier cases and supported it again in the case appealed to the US Supreme Court. In a later memorandum, Roberts claimed that he had joined the majority in the *Morehead* decision that struck down the New York minimum wage because New York had specifically *not* asked the court to overrule *Adkins* on the grounds that the law in the two laws was very different. When Roberts could find no real difference in the laws, he decided to stick with the *Adkins* precedent and declare the New York law unconstitutional. In *West Coast Hotel*, he claimed he was asked directly to overrule *Adkins*; therefore, he applied his reasoning from the *Nebbia* case and agreed with the majority that the Washington minimum wage law was constitutional. Roberts believed that women were "especially liable to be overreached and exploited by unscrupulous employers," which, in turn, was "not only detrimental to the health and wellbeing of the women affected, but casts a direct burden for their support upon the community."[17] One can easily imagine how distraught the New York state lawyers who had worked so hard to avoid *Adkins* in their *Morehead* briefs were when they discovered Roberts' reasoning.

A common story about this process is that President Roosevelt tried to pack the Supreme Court with new justices after the 1936 election because he was dissatisfied with the court striking down the AAA and the NRA and worried about them continuing to find the other laws unconstitutional. Therefore, in 1937 he declared his court-packing plans to add a new justice for each justice over the age of 70 on the Supreme Courts and in lower courts. Seeing the 1937 dates on decisions to support the minimum wage, the National Labor Relations Act, and the Social Security Act, people have claimed that the Justices supported the decisions to prevent the court-packing plan. A popular phrase describing the change has become a "switch in time, saves nine" justices. Cushman (1998) and others since have argued that this is inaccurate. Roberts voted to support the minimum wage in December well before the court-packing plan was announced, Congress offered stiff opposition to the attempts to pack the court and many members of Congress talked with and corresponded with the Justices to let them know that there was little chance the court-packing plan would go through.

Soon after the ruling, Arizona, Nevada, New York, and Washington, D.C., passed new laws, and Colorado, Connecticut, Minnesota, and Wisconsin strengthened existing laws (Trafton 1937, 1938). The decision also opened the door for Congress to pass the Fair Labor Standards Act of 1938, which established a minimum wage, maximum hours, and overtime pay *for men* as well as for women while establishing federal regulation of child labor. By the time a challenge to the Act reached the Court in *United States v. Darby Lumber* (312 US 100, 1941), none of the FC Judges who had ruled against the minimum wage in *West Coast Hotel* in 1937 were still on the bench. Harlan Fiske Stone wrote the unanimous opinion supporting the constitutionality of the regulations for firms involved in interstate commerce.

3.4 Concluding Remarks

Prior to the New Deal, state governments had the primary responsibility for regulating labor markets. Congress occasionally stepped in with statutory regulation in clear cases of interstate commerce, as with the railroads. The federal courts also played a role by making decisions about the constitutionality of state labor laws. Between 1900 and 1940, there was a great deal of uncertainty as to whether the states could limit men's hours and establish a minimum wage for women. The US Supreme Court decisions on these issues were often close because the judges had

[17] See Cushman 1998, 94–95. When reading Cushman about the New York case, it can be confusing because he refers to the case as *Morehead* and as *Tipaldo*.

different opinions about how to balance freedom of contract and protection of health and safety of workers. Even though the identities of the judges changed in three waves, there was always close to an even split in the number of judges on each side of the issue. Meanwhile, some state governments continued with their existing laws or passed new ones with language designed to avoid the constitutional pitfalls found in prior statutes. The declines in wages and high unemployment during the Great Depression appear to have ultimately shifted the balance in favor of the health and safety arguments, as the federal government and some states enacted statutes that created wage regulations. The deciding vote on the Supreme Court was cast by Justice Owen Roberts in 1937 when he decided to overturn the 1923 *Adkins* decision and declare the Washington law from 1913 constitutional in *West Coast Hotel v. Parrish* in 1937. The decision paved the way for the Fair Labor Standards Act of 1938 that set minimum wages and applied overtime rules for both men and women.

Acknowledgments The author is also affiliated as Honorary Professor at Stellenbosch University. I would like to thank the Hoover Institution for funding to support the writing of this paper. Earlier drafts were presented at two conferences under the Regulation and Rule of Law Initiative at the Hoover Institution, the 2019 ASSA Meetings, and in seminars at UC-Davis, and UC-Irvine. I have received valuable comments from Lee Alston, Vellore Arthi, Will Baude, Dan Bogart, Charlie Calomiris, Greg Clark, Chris Demuth, Jesus Fernandez-Villaverde, Diana Furchtgott-Roth, Nicole Garnett, Gary Libecap, Christos Makridis, Mike McConnell, Alan Olmstead, Gary Richardson, Andy Seltzer, Bob Topel, and John Wallis. Special thanks go to Samuel Allen and Rebecca Holmes for all of their help in developing the data used in the paper.

Appendix: Fishback on Murray

John Murray was an exemplary scholar and a great colleague. His journal articles about the experiences of workers, social insurance, public assistance, health, heights, and safety were all well conceived and well executed. John wrote marvelous books on sickness insurance in the early 1900s and the safety net for children in the early 1800s that showed how narrative and quantitative evidence could be brought together to provide a deep and readable analysis. Better yet, John was one of the kindest and most thoughtful people I have known. Each time we met, it was a joyous occasion and I miss him deeply.

References

Allen S, Fishback P, Holmes R (2013) The impact of progressive era labor regulations on the manufacturing labor market. Unpublished working paper presented at the Economic History Association meetings in Arlington. Virginia, September

Brandeis E (1966) Labor legislation. In: Commons JR (ed) History of labor in the United States, Volume III. Augustus Kelley, New York. Reprint of 1935 edition

Carter SB, Gartner SS, Haines MR, Olmstead AL, Sutch R, Wright G (eds) (2006) Historical Statistics of the United States: Earliest Times to the Present, Five Volumes. New York: Cambridge University Press
Casebeer K (1989) Drafting Wagner's Act: Leon Keyserling and the Precommittee drafts of the Labor Disputes Act and the National Labor Relations Act. Berkeley J Employ Labor Law 11(1):73–131
Clark L (1921) Minimum wage laws of the United States: construction and operation, Bulletin of the bureau of labor statistics number 285. Government Printing Office, Washington, DC
Cushman B (1998) Rethinking the new deal court: the structure of a constitutional revolution. Oxford University Press, New York
Epstein R (1982) The historical origins of workers' compensation law. Ga L Rev 16:775
Fishback P (1998) Operations of 'unfettered' labor markets: exit and voice in American labor markets at the turn of the century. J Econ Lit 36(2):722–765
Fishback P, Holmes R, Allen S (2009) Lifting the curse of dimensionality: measures of the labor legislation climate in the states during the progressive era. Labor Hist 50(August):313–346
Fishback P, Kantor S (2000) Prelude to the welfare state: the origins of workers' compensation. University of Chicago Press, Chicago
Fishback P (2006) The irony of reform: did large employers subvert workplace safety reform, 1869 to 1930? In: Glaeser E, Goldin C (eds) Corruption and reform. University of Chicago Press, Chicago
Goldin C (1988) Maximum hours legislation and female employment: a quantitative reassessment. J Pol Econ 96(1):189–205
Graebner W (1976) Coal-mining safety in the progressive era. University of Kentucky Press, Lexington
Gregg R (1919) The National war Labor Board. Harv L Rev 33(1):39–63
Holmes R (2003) The impact of state labor regulations on manufacturing input demand during the progressive era. Unpublished Ph.D. dissertation, University of Arizona
Holmes R (2005) The impact of state labor regulations on manufacturing input demand during the progressive era, dissertation summary. J Econ Hist 65(2):531–532
Holmes R, Fishback P, Allen S (2008) Measuring the intensity of state labor regulation during the progressive era. In: Rosenbloom J (ed) Quantitative economic history: the good of counting. Routledge, New York, pp 119–145
Huberman M, Meissner C (2010) Riding the wave of trade: the rise of labor regulation in the golden age of globalization. J Econ Hist 70(3):657–685
Neumann T, Taylor J, Fishback P (2013) Comparisons of weekly hours over the past century and the importance of work sharing policies in the 1930s. Am Econ Rev PP 102(3):105–110
Roosevelt FD (1933) The President's reemployment agreement. July 27, 1933. Online by Gerhard Peters and John T. Woolley, The American Presidency Project. http://www.presidency.ucsb.edu/ws/?pid=14492
Rose J (2010) Hoover's truce: wage rigidity in the onset of the great depression. J Econ Hist 70(4):843–870
Smith F (1932) Labor laws for women in the states and territories, Bulletin of the women's bureau no. 98. Government Printing Office, Washington, DC
Taylor J (2019) Unpacking the NIRA monolith: the microeconomics of the National Industrial Recovery Act. University of Chicago Press, Chicago
Taylor J (2011) Work-sharing during the great depression: did the President's reemployment agreement promote reemployment? Economica 78(309):133–158
Trafton G (1937) New labor laws of 1937. Am Labor Legis Rev 27:181–188
Trafton G (1938) New labor laws of 1938. Am Labor Legis Rev 28:181–188
U.S. Bureau of Labor Statistics (1931) Handbook of labor statistics, 1931, Edition. Bulletin No. 541. Government Printing Office
U.S. Bureau of Labor Statistics (1933a) Minimum-wage laws of Connecticut and Ohio. Mon Labor Rev 37:57–65

U.S. Bureau of Labor Statistics (1933b) Minimum wage legislation in the United States. Mon Labor Rev 37:1344–1354

U.S. Bureau of Labor Statistics (1934a) Labor legislation during 1933. Mon Labor Rev 38:559–577

U.S. Bureau of Labor Statistics (1934b) Labor legislation during 1934. Mon Labor Rev 39:1376–1385

U.S. Bureau of Labor Statistics (1936) Labor legislation during 1935. Mon Labor Rev 42:121–139

Vittoz S (1987) New Deal labor policy and the American industrial economy. University of North Carolina Press, Chapel Hill

Whaples R (1990) The shortening of the American work week: an economic and historical analysis of its context, causes, and consequences. Ph.D. dissertation. University of Pennsylvania

Chapter 4
Sickness Experience in England, 1870–1949

Andrew Hinde, Martin Gorsky, Aravinda Guntupalli, and Bernard Harris

Abstract Using data from the Hampshire Friendly Society, a sickness insurance institution in southern England, we examine morbidity trends in England between 1870 and 1949. Morbidity prevalence increased between 1870 and around 1890, mainly because of a rise in the average duration of sickness episodes, but after 1890 average durations fell markedly even though the incidence of sickness rose. During the first two decades of the twentieth century, sickness prevalence increased gradually, but this rise was entirely due to the greatly increased duration of claims made by men aged 65 years and over. After the early 1920s, both the incidence and the average duration of sickness claims declined. These trends seem to be measuring 'objective morbidity': they vary closely with year-on-year changes in the mortality of men of working age, but do not show any clear relationship with real wages or unemployment. Our conclusions are different from those of earlier research using English sickness insurance data. We believe that one reason for this was a methodological problem with the analysis performed by nineteenth-century actuaries.

Keywords Hampshire Friendly Society · Sickness insurance · Health · Morbidity · Sickness

A. Hinde (✉)
University of Southampton, Southampton, England

M. Gorsky
London School of Hygiene and Tropical Medicine, London, England
e-mail: Martin.Gorsky@lshtm.ac.uk

A. Guntupalli
University of Aberdeen, Aberdeen, Scotland
e-mail: aravinda.guntupalli@abdn.ac.uk

B. Harris
University of Strathclyde, Glasgow, Scotland
e-mail: bernard.harris@strath.ac.uk

P. Gray et al. (eds.), *Standard of Living*, Studies in Economic History,
https://doi.org/10.1007/978-3-031-06477-7_4

4.1 Introduction

The question of how sickness, or morbidity, evolved during the period of mortality decline at the end of the nineteenth and the start of the twentieth centuries has been debated ever since Riley (1989, 1997) argued that sickness rates rose as mortality rates fell. Riley analysed aggregate data from sickness insurance schemes operated by the Ancient Order of Foresters (AOF) in Britain and concluded that there was a rise in reported morbidity between 1870 and 1910. This rise was not primarily attributable to changes in the age structure of the insured population, but represented an increase in age-specific sickness rates. Riley argued, following the nineteenth-century actuaries who had originally analysed similar data, that the increasing morbidity was due to the increased duration of periods of sickness: people were not ill more often, but they were ill for longer when they did succumb. He said this was a consequence of improved care of the sick, which meant, first, that a greater proportion of them recovered from their afflictions, but that those who recovered took longer to recover than their predecessors had taken to die; and, second, that those who still died took longer to do so. Both of these effects increased the average duration of sickness episodes and hence raised the prevalence of sickness at any time.

More recently Edwards et al. (2003) used individual-level sickness insurance data for the Hampshire Friendly Society (HFS) in southern England to examine morbidity trends. Contrary to Riley, they failed to find evidence of a rise in morbidity, except perhaps after the period spanned by Riley's data, and they discussed the possibility that this later rise might be associated with the advent of national insurance in England in the early twentieth century. Using a larger sample drawn from the same source, Harris et al. (2012) analysed the prevalence and incidence of sickness by age between 1870 and 1950. They also found little evidence of a rise in prevalence, except perhaps among those aged 50–65 years between the 1870s and the 1890s and again between the 1920s and the 1940s, though the prevalence in this age group fell back in the intervening period (Harris et al. 2012, pp. 733–4). Among those aged under 65 years, neither the incidence nor the average duration of episodes of sickness showed an overall trend. Among those aged over 65 years (whom they only analysed for the period after 1900), prevalence did not change greatly. There was, however, clear evidence of a rise in duration and a fall in incidence among those aged over 65 years during the first half of the twentieth century.

The data used by Riley (1997), Edwards et al. (2003) and Harris et al. (2012) come from sickness insurance schemes. Such data are indirect estimates of sickness in that they measure absence from work.[1] Morbidity trends reported from sickness insurance schemes may vary for many reasons. One reason is that morbidity 'objectively defined' changes. This 'objective morbidity' is unobservable in practice, but denotes some kind of measure of sickness which would be consistent over time and space, and which would be independent of the context in which the measurement was made. In practice, we observe derivatives of 'objective morbidity', such as the inability to work, or more accurately a declaration by an individual (subject to the

[1]Alternatively, they indicate that a person's health rendered him or her unable to carry out the duties of their normal employment (Harris et al. 2011, p. 644).

certification procedure, lay or medical, employed by the insurance scheme) that he or she is unable to work, this declaration being confirmed by those administering the scheme. How closely this measure captures 'objective morbidity' is not really a helpful question as we cannot observe the latter. What is important if we are to use sickness insurance data to infer morbidity trends is that the relationship between the measure of morbidity we use and 'objective morbidity' is, at least at the population level, consistent over time.

But this may not be so. Johansson (1991) suggested that whether or not a person is classified as too ill to work may depend on cultural views about how 'objectively' sick a person has to be in order to adopt the sick role. Reported sickness rates may thus rise or fall, even when morbidity 'objectively defined' is not changing. Specifically, she argued that the threshold for adopting the 'sick role' fell over time with economic and institutional development, and with the increased salience of scientific medicine, so that a rise in reported morbidity does not necessarily mean that morbidity 'objectively defined' also rose. In brief, people declared themselves (or were declared by the medical profession to be) unfit to work with increasingly minor ailments. She termed this the 'cultural inflation' of morbidity (Johansson 1991, 1992).

Whiteside (1987) argued that the sickness reported by sickness insurance schemes may be disguised unemployment, so that reported sickness rates might vary inversely with the health of the economy. The AOF (1928), p. 57) commented that the General Strike of 1926 was associated with higher 'benefit expenditure'. A few years later, the High Chief Ranger of the AOF commented that '[t[he year … 1931 is showing a decided increase [in sickness claims]. That increase is undoubtedly much more closely associated with economic stress and unemployment than with real incapacity to work, even after allowing fully for the ill-effects of unemployment on health' (AOF 1931, pp. 40–1). Macnicol (1998) suggested that changes in claim rates may have depended on the availability of alternative forms of insurance (e.g. statutory pensions) for underemployed older workers.

The trends exhibited by sickness insurance data may also vary with the nature of the insurance funds. Murray (2003) analysed what he referred to as 'sickness absence' from work using data from a series of large funds in continental Europe. Funds where membership was compulsory revealed different trends in sickness absence from those where membership was voluntary. Murray attributed this discrepancy to the changing financial health of the two types of fund over time and to the fact that they attracted different risk pools. The compulsory funds exhibited an increase in sickness absence between 1885 and 1905 which Murray interpreted as being due to their greater ability to pay benefits. The voluntary funds were always under pressure because their members were disproportionately drawn from persons who considered themselves to be less healthy than average. As the pressure increased, they sought to reduce the benefits paid, leading to a decline in the prevalence of sickness absence among their members.

Finally, reported levels of morbidity might be affected by changes and variations in members' attitudes to the use of insurance schemes and changes in institutions' preparedness to pay benefits (Harris 1999; Downing 2015). Such attitudes might vary *between* schemes, since they can arise from different procedures laid down in the constitutions of individual schemes, or the differential ability of schemes to monitor claims (Downing 2015). But they may also occur *within* the same scheme over time, especially if administrators' views of the financial health of the scheme are the driving force.

Gorsky et al. (2011) addressed each of the effects mentioned above in the context of the HFS data. This was possible because the HFS has left a comprehensive set of Annual Reports and other documents in which changes in the volume and nature of sickness claims were discussed and actions proposed to maintain consistency in the processing and monitoring of claims. Although the HFS introduced a number of changes in the arrangements used to monitor the veracity of sickness insurance claims, the authors concluded that 'most of the relative rise in morbidity seems to have been real, and not the result of cultural changes in the definition of the sick role or in the generosity or policing' of insurance benefits (Gorsky et al. 2011, p. 1,782). They suggested that sickness benefit might have been used from time to time as a substitute for other forms of benefit—mainly pensions—among a small number of older members (mostly aged over 65 years), thereby allowing some older workers to disguise their exit from the labour force by claiming long-term sickness benefit (Macnicol 1998). But they found little evidence of systematic variation in reported sickness rates with the state of the economy or of 'diagnostic creep' whereby claims were lodged for ever more trivial illnesses. The HFS's actuary also pointed out repeatedly that members who were insured for sickness benefit at a higher rate tended to claim more from the fund (Gorsky and Harris 2005).

In this paper, we present a reanalysis of the data used by Edwards et al. (2003) and Harris et al. (2012) using an approach different from theirs. We measure the trend in morbidity over time using annual age-standardised sickness prevalence ratios and age-standardised incidence ratios for the period 1870–1949. We then use regression models to examine the association between the trends in reported 'sickness absence' and a range of factors which might be plausibly related to the tendency to claim sickness benefit. These factors include a more objective measure of 'healthiness' (based on mortality rates) as well as measures describing economic trends and changes in social policy.

Section 4.2 of the paper briefly describes the HFS data. Section 4.3 presents trends in age-standardised morbidity. The regression models are examined in Sect. 4.4. Section 4.5 discusses the findings, focusing on the differences between the trends revealed by the HFS data and those from the AOF. This section also presents evidence that an analysis by contemporaries which purported to show that the rise in morbidity in the late-nineteenth century was duration-driven was flawed. In Sect. 4.6, we summarise our conclusions.

4.2 Data

The HFS data have been described in detail elsewhere (Edwards et al. 2003; Gorsky et al. 2006), so only a brief description is given here. The HFS was an autonomous institution set up in rural southern England in 1825 to provide benefits to working people. Its membership grew slowly until about 1850 but the rate of recruitment then accelerated (Harris et al. 2012, p. 725). It was administered by the local gentry and consequently had a paternalistic character. Initially, its members were drawn from rural and small-town Hampshire although, as time went on, it expanded to a limited extent outside the county boundaries. It provided three principal types of benefit: sick pay for members unable to work temporarily because of illness or injury, life insurance, and a pension. Most HFS members were men; women were allowed to be members in the early years but in 1850 were prohibited from subscribing for sick pay. Therefore, our data relate only to males. Members could choose to subscribe for all three benefits, or just one or two. Our data relate only to those who subscribed for sick pay, and comprise a sample of approximately 10% of members, the sample consisting of 5552 men born between 1790 and 1926. The sickness histories of these men are based on details of the number of days' sick pay each man received in each year from 1870 to 1894, and each quarter from 1895 onwards. Our analysis covers the period from 1870—the first year for which we have data on the number of sick-days each member experienced—to 1949. In all, there are 83,533 man-years of exposure in our data.

The data measure the length of time each man was (in any year or quarter) off work and claiming sickness benefit.[2] They provide direct estimates of sickness *prevalence*, but assumptions are required in order to estimate sickness *incidence*, since if a man received some sick pay in a given year (or quarter), we do not know whether the episode was a continuation of a previous sickness episode or how many separate sickness episodes this represented. Provided the same assumptions are made throughout, it is still possible to examine changes over time in the incidence of sickness. After experimenting with several algorithms, we settled on one which calculates the minimum number of distinct sickness episodes consistent with the observed data: the 'minimum incidence' assumption. In this case, any man who reported sickness in two successive quarters (or years before 1895) is assumed to have had only one period of sickness which started in the first quarter (or year) and ended in the second quarter (or year), unless this was incompatible with the pattern of sickness reported in adjacent quarters (or years).[3] The assumptions required to estimate the incidence of sickness from our data are less demanding after 1895, once the data become available quarterly rather than annually.[4]

[2] The rules of the Hampshire Friendly Society as set out in 1868 used the phrase 'rendered incapable of gaining his livelihood' to describe qualifying sickness (Hampshire Friendly Society 1846–77, p. 19).

[3] We did compare the trends in sickness incidence using different assumptions and found that they moved in parallel: the choice of assumption did not seem to affect our estimate of the trend.

[4] An advantage of the 'minimum incidence' assumption is that the difference between the estimates of incidence immediately before and after 1895 is also small.

4.3 Trends in Sickness in the Hampshire Friendly Society

Figure 4.1 shows the number of sick weeks reported each year between 1870 and 1949 together with the total number of insured men exposed to the risk of sickness in our sample in each year. The graph also shows the number of insured men aged 55 years and over. The threshold of 55 years was chosen because there is evidence that age-specific morbidity rises much more rapidly after that age than it does at younger ages (Harris et al. 2012, p. 730). The exposed to risk rose gradually from 1870 until around 1920, during which period the proportion of the membership aged over 55 years also increased. Then a recruitment drive raised the number of new members rapidly from 1925 onwards. Since most new joiners were young, this reduced the proportion of members aged over 55 years. The fall in the exposed to risk after 1938 is because we only collected data for men who joined up to 1939. The total number of sick weeks in the sample rose fairly steadily to a peak in 1940.

Because we know the date of birth of every member, we can work out the age composition of the members in all years from 1870 to 1949. This allows us to control for variations in the age structure over time using *standardised prevalence ratios*(SPRs). The SPR for year i, SPR_i, is given by the formula

$$SPR_i = \frac{P_i}{\sum_x p_x E_{x,i}} \tag{4.1}$$

where P_i is the total number of sick weeks (or sickness claims) reported in year i among those who were members of the society in that year and eligible for sick pay,

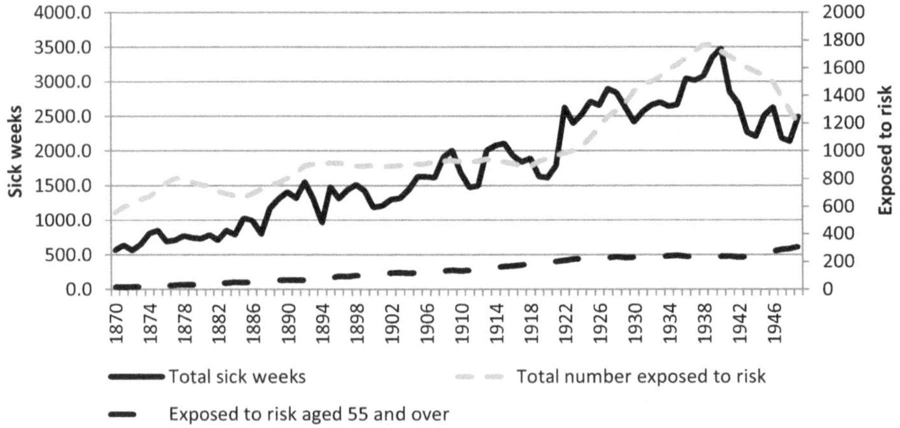

Fig. 4.1 Total sick weeks and number of insured men exposed to the risk of sickness in each year from 1870 to 1949
Source: Hampshire Friendly Society data

Table 4.1 Standard schedule of morbidity prevalence by age

Age group, x	p_x
Under 20 years	0.015
20–24 years	0.015
25–29 years	0.016
30–34 years	0.020
35–39 years	0.024
40–44 years	0.027
45–49 years	0.032
50–54 years	0.042
55–59 years	0.051
60–64 years	0.080
65 years and over	0.146

Source: Hampshire Friendly Society data

$E_{x,i}$ is the number of members in year i in age group x, and p_x is a standard age-specific morbidity prevalence for age group x. Table 4.1 gives details of the age groups and the standard age-specific morbidity prevalence, which was calculated as the average prevalence of morbidity in each age group over the whole period from 1870 to 1949. The rapid increase in p_x at older ages demonstrates the need for age-standardisation. We have also computed standardised incidence ratios (SIRs) for the period from 1895 onwards using the formula

$$SIR_i = \frac{C_i}{\sum_x c_x E_{x,i}}, \tag{4.2}$$

where C_i is the total number of claims estimated to have been made in year under the 'minimum incidence' assumption and c_x is a standard age-specific incidence schedule (based on the average estimated incidence over the whole period). The outcome of the standardisation exercise is shown in Fig. 4.2. Because the annual SPR_is and SIR_is are noisy, we have also drawn moving averages to help highlight the trends.[5]

The SPR_is increase by about 25% during the 1880s to peak in the early 1890s before falling back by the end of the century. They then rise gently and somewhat erratically to reach a second peak in the late 1920s before beginning a sustained fall, punctuated only by the morbid year of 1940. Comparing the SIR_is over the whole period is difficult because of the change to the data after 1 January 1895. Looking at the two periods separately, we can say that there seems to have been a gentle

[5] An 11-point moving average seemed to us to offer the best compromise between smoothness and fidelity to the original data. We use the moving averages solely to aid visual interpretation of the graphs.

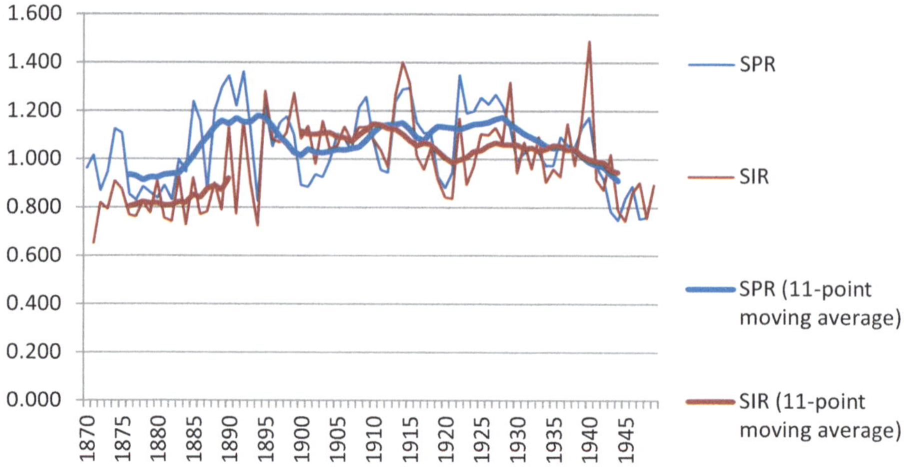

Fig. 4.2 Standardised morbidity ratios based on sick weeks (SPR) and estimated incidence (SIR), 1870–1949
Source: Hampshire Friendly Society data
Note: SPR, standardised prevalence ratio; SIR, standardised incidence ratio. The SIR values for the periods 1870–1894 and 1895–1949 are not exactly comparable because of the different units of time used in the data. Accordingly, we do not compute moving averages of the SIR across the time point 1 January 1895. The SPRs are comparable across the whole period. We have not estimated the SIR for 1870 as we cannot be sure how many episodes of sickness reported in 1870 actually began in earlier years

increase in the incidence between the mid-1870s and 1900, though the year-on-year variability is high in the early 1890s. Between 1895 and 1915, the SIR_is are roughly constant. There is a slight dip around 1920 followed by another period of roughly constant values. SIR_{1940} reveals the incidence of sickness in that year to have been exceptional. After 1940 there is a substantial decline.

Harris et al. (2012, p. 733) observed that the trend in the incidence and duration of sickness among those aged 65 years and over was different from that among younger men. Gorsky et al. (2011, p. 1,782) examined a belief by the HFS authorities that, during the early twentieth century, some men aged 65 years and over were using lengthy periods of sick pay as substitutes for pension payments (after an investigation, the Society concluded that this might have been happening in a handful of cases, but too few to be worth acting upon). We have repeated the analyses reported in Fig. 4.2 using only data for men aged under 65 years (Fig. 4.3). For the period to 1900, the trends for the under-65s are similar to those for all men (this is not surprising, as few members of the HFS were aged 65 years or over before 1900). After 1900, though, the SPR_is for the under 65s begin a slow, erratic decline. The peak in sickness prevalence in the 1920s vanishes, but the years of high morbidity just before World War I stand out more. Trends in the SIR_is for the under-65s are rather similar to those for all men. This is to be expected, as the over-65s tended to have lengthy sickness episodes, which would have a greater impact on prevalence than incidence.

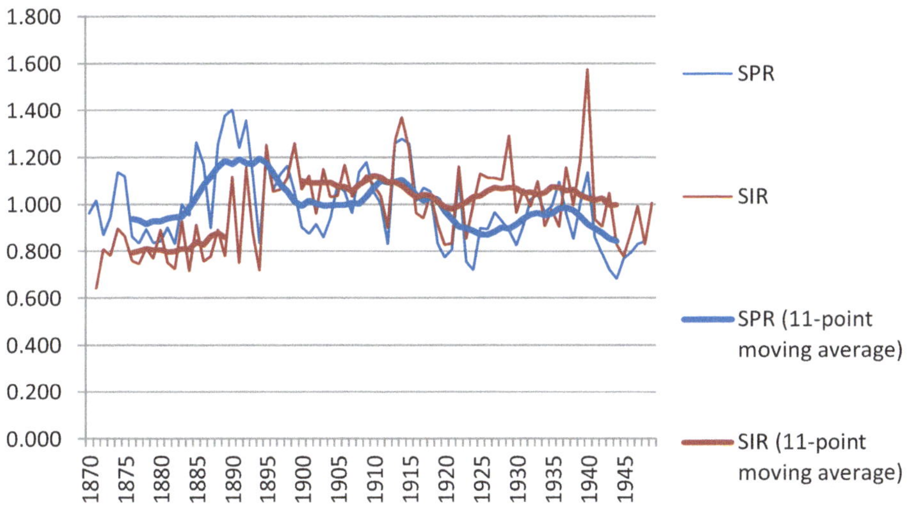

Fig. 4.3 Standardised morbidity ratios based on sick weeks (SPR) and estimated incidence (SIR), 1870–1949 excluding men aged 65 years and over
Source: Hampshire Friendly Society data
Note: SPR, standardised prevalence ratio; SIR, standardised incidence ratio. The SIR values for the periods 1870–1894 and 1895–1949 are not exactly comparable because of the different units of time used in the data. Accordingly, we do not compute moving averages of the SIR across the time point 1 January 1895. The SPRs are comparable across the whole period. We have not estimated the SIR for 1870 as we cannot be sure how many episodes of sickness reported in 1870 actually began in earlier years

The ratio between the prevalence of sickness and its incidence is the average duration of sickness episodes. This is plotted for the raw (unstandardised) data in Fig. 4.4. Looking first at Fig. 4.4(a) and taking all men together, the average duration of episodes of sickness rose during the 1880s. It also rose between around 1900 and the early 1920s before falling until the mid-1930s. Obvious trends in average duration among the under-65s are more difficult to discern, apart from the rise during the 1880s.

A limitation of Fig. 4.4(a) is that we cannot compare the periods before and after 1 January 1895. This is especially frustrating because a key conclusion of Riley's (1997) analysis of the AOF data was that sickness durations were rising between 1870 and around 1910. Figure 4.4(a) reveals a clear rise in durations during the 1880s and a rise after about 1900, the latter being a characteristic largely of those aged 65 years and over, but trends in the 1890s are not clear.

Figure 4.4(b) attempts a consistent comparison of average durations across the whole period by artificially reducing the level of detail in the data for the period from 1895 onwards so that it matches that for the earlier period. Doing this means that the reported *level* of the average durations is certainly overstated for the post-1895 period but that we can compare across the 1 January 1895 and try to

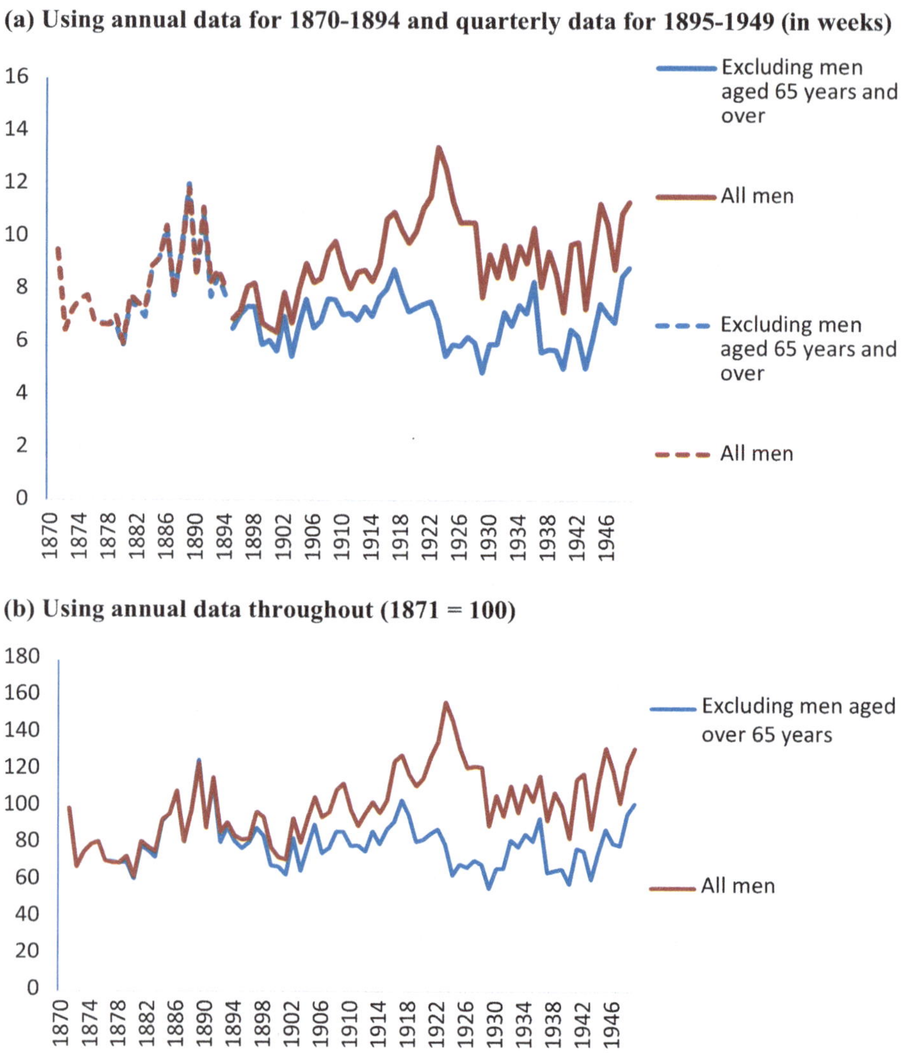

Fig. 4.4 Mean durations of sickness, 1895–1949. (**a**) Using annual data for 1870–1894 and quarterly data for 1895–1949 (in weeks). (**b**) Using annual data throughout (1871 = 100)
Source: Hampshire Friendly Society data
Note: The mean durations have been calculated by dividing the total number of sick weeks in each year by the total number of claims made. In graph (a), the series for the period before 1895 and that for the period from 1895 onwards are not strictly comparable. In graph (b), all years may be compared but the level is likely to be inaccurate, so the series has been indexed to 1871 = 100

establish the *trend* over the whole period.[6] The results do not differ greatly from those in Fig. 4.4(a).[7] There was a rise in mean durations during the 1880s and a fall in the 1890s. After 1900 average durations rose sharply among those aged 65 years and over to a peak around 1925 before falling back quickly; among those aged under 65, there were fluctuations in the mean duration, but no obvious secular trend. The difference between those aged 65 and over and those aged under 65 is partly associated with the different conditions giving rise to claims for sick pay. The most widespread causes of sickness among elderly men were diseases of the circulatory system, diseases of the nervous system and diseases of the skin, whereas among younger men, diseases of the respiratory system and injury were most commonly cited (Gorsky et al. 2006).

Our results thus confirm the observations of Harris et al. (2012) that there was a rise in the duration of claims after 1900 among those aged over 65 years. The magnitude of this rise is worth emphasising, however. The average duration of a claim in the age group 65 years and over in 1900 was 18 weeks; in 1925 it was 60 weeks.

Figure 4.4 is based on unstandardised data. In other words, it does not adjust for changes in the age structure of the HFS membership. Mean durations of sickness were much greater among older men than among younger men. Obtaining a standardised measure of the duration involves adjusting the quantity P_i / C_i to take account of the relative effect of age on the reported prevalence and incidence. One way of achieving this is to define a 'standardised duration ratio' (SDR_i) to be equal to SPR$_i$/SIR$_i$. It is straightforward to show that this implies that

$$SDR_i = \frac{P_i}{\sum_x E_{x,i} p_x} \cdot \frac{\sum_x E_{x,i} c_x}{C_i} = \frac{P_i}{C_i} \cdot \frac{\sum_x E_{x,i} c_x}{\sum_x E_{x,i} p_x}. \tag{4.3}$$

In other words, it involves adjusting the mean durations estimated from the 'raw' prevalence and incidence (the quantities plotted in Fig. 4.4) by a factor $\frac{\bullet_x E_{x,i} c_x}{\bullet_x E_{x,i} p_x}$, which reflects the expected average duration of sickness in a population with the age structure of the HFS in year i and the average age-specific incidence and prevalence rates.

Figure 4.5 plots the SDR$_i$s for all men, as well as the SIR$_i$s adjusted to render them comparable for the periods before and after 1 January 1895. The incidence of sickness rises by about 25% between the 1870s and the 1890s. Thereafter, it

[6] To achieve consistency, we deliberately ignore data for the years from 1895 onwards which indicate that a man had two or more spells of sickness in the same year, and count these as if they were a single spell. In effect, we are transforming the data for the period 1895 onwards so that they are reported in the same way as the data for the period 1870–1894.

[7] The effect of the coarser level of detail in the data before 1895 is that the incidence of sickness is underestimated by about 10% compared with the period from 1895 onwards.

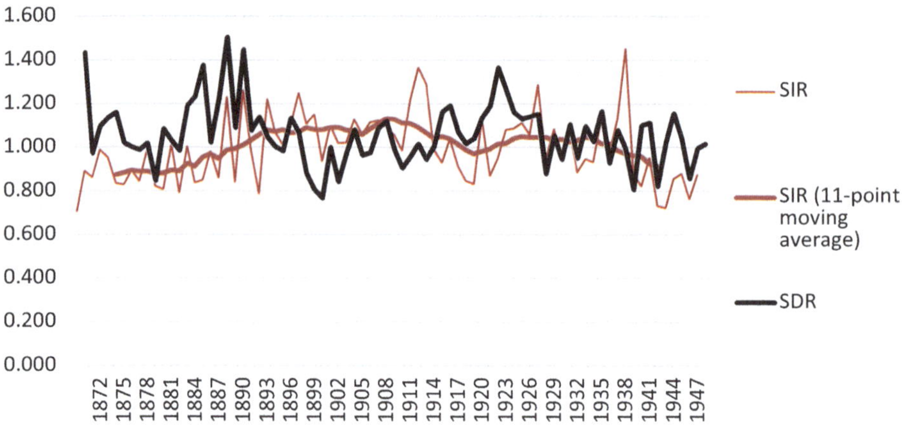

Fig. 4.5 Standardised incidence ratios (SIR_is) and 'standardised duration ratios' (SDR_is) adjusted to use annual data throughout
Source: Hampshire Friendly Society data
Note: Each SDR_i is computed as SPR_i/SIR_i, where SPR_i is the standardised prevalence ratio in year *i*

does not change appreciably in the long run, though there are year-on-year fluctuations. There is evidence of a decrease in incidence after 1940. The 'standardised duration ratios' rise in the 1880s, but fall rapidly during the 1890s and, although they rise a bit during the first two decades of the twentieth century, they never again reach the values they attained in the late 1880s. After the early 1920s, they once more subside.

Riley's analysis (1997) of data from the AOF found that '[b]etween the 1870s and the first decade of the twentieth century age-standardised sickness prevalence increased from about 9 to about 12.5 days per member per year (or by about 40%)' (Riley 1999a, p. 121). Our results suggest that, during the 1880s, there was an increase in sickness prevalence, after adjusting for changes in the age structure, of about 25%, but this was largely reversed during the 1890s. This rise and fall was associated with a rise and fall in the average duration of periods of sickness among all age groups. Although the difference in the nature of the data makes a comparison across 1 January 1895 awkward, Fig. 4.5 suggests that there was a rise in the incidence of sickness between 1880 and 1895. After 1900, though there were short-term fluctuations in both the incidence and prevalence of sickness, the main trend was a large increase in the average duration of claims among men aged 65 years and over. The prolongation of claims among these old men was driving almost all of the overall increase in sickness prevalence in the early twentieth century. Once this trend changed after the mid-1920s, and the duration of claims among the over-65s started to be curtailed, both the incidence and duration of sickness fell away.

4.4 Factors Associated with Morbidity Trends

In this section, we consider the association between a range of covariates and the sickness trend revealed by the HFS data by regressing the SPR_is on a set of covariates designed to measure aspects of the social and economic environment which have been considered relevant in accounting for variations in reported sickness. We capture economic conditions using the annual unemployment rate and real wages (Mitchell 1988, pp. 60–2, 124, 168–9).[8] We also include dummy variables for wartime years. Most of the members of the HFS were able-bodied males, and many of these would have been recruited by the armed forces during the World Wars. Those who were not serving in the forces are likely to have been in poorer health than the average, and may have been required to work harder and longer than their health could bear, so may have experienced increased morbidity rates. We included an interaction between wartime and unemployment, to examine whether the effect of unemployment was greater among those left behind during the period of conscription. We measure changes in the social policy environment with dummy variables distinguishing the pre-national insurance era from the later period, and the period after the introduction of the state contributory pension scheme.[9]

We include a measure of variations in the disease environment, or in the 'general healthiness' of each year. A rise in the mortality rate should indicate a more hostile disease environment. If reported sickness varies more closely with this proxy for the hostility of the disease environment than it does with unemployment or other economic indicators, it suggests that the morbidity trends we are capturing are 'real' in the sense that they reflect trends in 'objective morbidity'. We experimented with a range of different measures of mortality: the national death rate from all causes for males aged 35–44, 45–54 and 55–64 years, and the death rate in Hampshire for males at all ages from influenza and bronchitis.[10] All the mortality variables produced similar results, but we present only those using the national death rate from

[8] The real wage series was originally produced by Phelps-Brown and Hopkins (1956). We have preferred this series to more recent variants as it relates specifically to working class men in southern England, into which group most of the HFS members fell. The unemployment data were originally published by Feinstein (1972, pp. T126–T127) and refer to the whole of the United Kingdom (UK). Given the impact of both occupational and regional factors on UK unemployment rates during this period, these statistics may not be an accurate guide to fluctuations in the level of unemployment among members of the Hampshire Friendly Society.

[9] Although national insurance was introduced in 1911, the labour market was then severely disrupted by World War I. Our dummy variables assume national insurance started to take effect in 1919 (it was officially introduced earlier but World War I intervened before it could have a widespread impact), and the introduction of state contributory pensions (for workers over the age of 65) took effect in 1926 (Macnicol 1998, p. 214).

[10] These measures of mortality fall short of the ideal for our purposes, but in different respects. The Hampshire-specific mortality rate from influenza and bronchitis is geographically a better measure of changes in the disease environment faced by the men in our sample, but includes death rates for infants and children. The national death rates for adult males are a better age match to the men in the sample, but are less geographically focussed. For the mortality data for Hampshire, we only analyse the period 1870–1935 as population data for the late 1930s and early 1940s are likely to be unreliable because of World War II (which led to population movements which were not captured by official statistics as there was no population census in 1941).

Table 4.2 Results of models of standardised prevalence rate

	Using national death rate for males aged 45–54 years		Using death rate for males in Hampshire for males of all ages	
	All men	Excluding men aged 65 years and over	All men	Excluding men aged 65 years and over
Constant	1.056 [24.752]	1.043 [30.070]	1.043 [27.521]	1.030 [27.777]
Unemployment rate	−0.007 [−1.161]	−0.006 [−0.928]	−0.010 [−1.047]	−0.007 [−0.915]
Real wages	0.000 [0.315]	−0.001 [−0.604]	0.002 [0.919]	0.000 [0.212]
War year	−0.050 [−0.582]	−0.099 [−1.183]	0.073 [0.532]	−0.005 [−0.036]
War * unemployment rate	0.036 [1.042]	0.052 [1.418]	0.021 [0.393]	0.043 [0.738]
National insurance era	0.095 [0.986]	−0.104 [−1.156]	0.137 [1.424]	−0.102 [−1.036]
State pension scheme	−0.138 [−1.407]	−0.012 [−0.128]	−0.100 [−0.944]	0.016 [0.143]
National death rate among males aged 45–54 years	0.033 [3.204]	0.038 [3.333]		
Death rate from influenza and bronchitis among all males in Hampshire			0.059 [2.096]	0.062 [1.972]
Years covered	1870–1949	1870–1949	1870–1935	1870–1935
AR(1) φ	0.608 [6.572]	0.486 [4.631]	0.509 [4.457]	0.451 [3.746]

Notes: *t*-statistics in parentheses. All models were estimated using maximum likelihood with an AR(1) error term. Correlations between the residuals at lags greater than 1 were close to zero. Real wages, the unemployment rate and the death rate were differenced to remove the trend

Source: Hampshire Friendly Society data. Unemployment rate from Feinstein (1972, pp. T126–7; real wages from Mitchell (1988, pp. 168–9); all-cause death rates for males in England and Wales aged 45–54 years from Mitchell (1988, pp. 60–2); death rates from influenza and bronchitis for males in Hampshire taken from *Annual Reports* of the Registrar General for the years 1870–1920, and Registrar General's *Statistical Reviews* for the years 1921–1935

all causes for males aged 45–54 years and the death rate in Hampshire from influenza and bronchitis for males at all ages. We estimated models using SPR_i for all men and for those aged under 65 years only (Table 4.2).

The results are clear. In all four models, reported morbidity is associated consistently with our measures of the hostility of the disease environment, but does not seem to have been influenced as strongly by the economic outlook, wartime, or changes in social policy. War tended to reduce the prevalence of reported sickness, except among the unemployed. The fit of the models to the data is reasonably good in most years (Fig. 4.6). The effects of the introduction of national insurance and the state contributory pension scheme were not strong, but national insurance was associated with a reduction in claims among those aged under 65 years and an increase

(a) All men

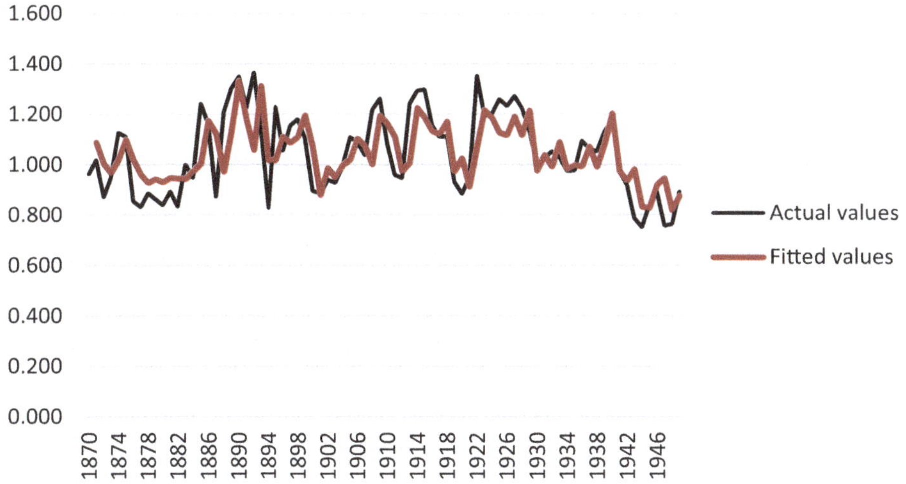

(b) Excluding men aged 65 years and over

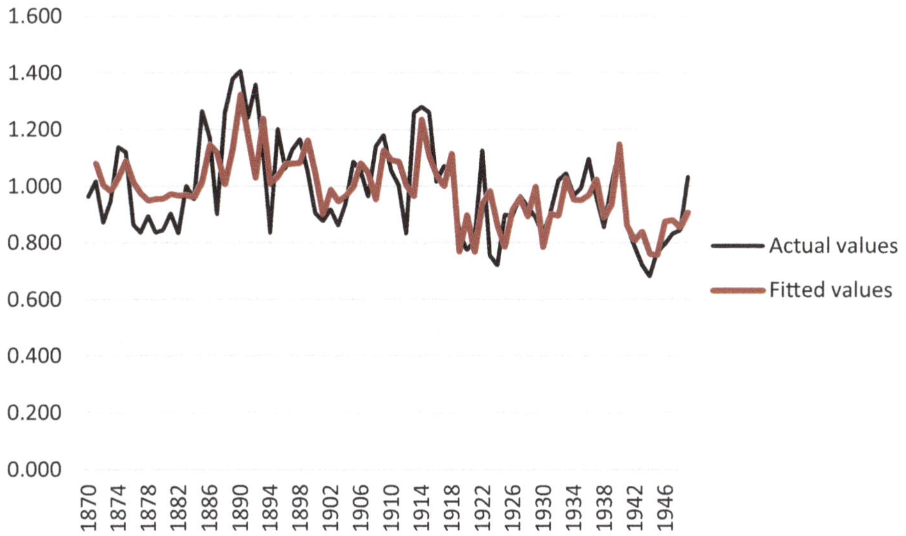

Fig. 4.6 Actual standardised prevalence ratios and those predicted from the model, 1870–1949. (**a**) All men. (**b**) Excluding men aged 65 years and over

Source: Hampshire Friendly Society data

Note: The fitted values are from models using the national death rate for males aged 45–54 years: see Table 4.2

in those aged 65 years and over, whereas the state contributory pension scheme was associated with a reduction in claims among men aged 65 years and over, as we might expect.[11]

The conclusion of this modelling exercise is that reported sickness prevalence in the HFS data, which is based on a medically certified inability to work, seems to be reflecting 'objective morbidity' reasonably closely. It adjusts in response to temporal changes in the general 'healthiness', and does not seem to respond closely to any behavioural factors which might be associated with changes in the economic environment. Among men aged under 65 years, there is some evidence of systematically lower sickness rates in the era following the introduction of national insurance. Thus, national insurance may, as Edwards et al. (2003) speculate, have had some effect on reported sickness levels, but its effect was in the opposite direction from the one they expected. The increased reported morbidity of the over 65s in the first decades of the twentieth century was not associated with short-run changes in unemployment rates or real wages, but the decreased morbidity among this group after the 1920s may have been influenced by the appearance of state contributory pensions.[12]

4.5 Prevalence, Incidence and Duration of Sickness

Our results broadly confirm those of Edwards et al. (2003) and Harris et al. (2012). However, we have been able to provide a more systematic history of the prevalence, incidence and duration of reported sickness among HFS members. Our results are different from those obtained by Riley using data on AOF members. Looking at the period between 1870 and 1910, Riley found an increase in morbidity of close to 40% among the AOF members, and he attributed this mainly to a rise in the duration of sickness episodes. During the same period, we observe an increase of about 25% in age-standardised sickness prevalence, almost all of which occurred during the

[11] It is possible that the weak effects of some social and economic covariates (notably unemployment) arise because unemployment rates in Hampshire did not reflect national rates. We have not been able to locate time series of local unemployment rates.

[12] Gorsky et al. (2011, pp. 1,781–2) noted that concern that HFS members were using sickness to disguise unemployment was only rarely mentioned in the annual reports of the Society. It might be argued that unemployment itself could lead to ill-health and thus we might expect sickness rates to rise at times of high unemployment. This may be true, but the effect is likely to be too weak to detect in our data, as even in the worst years of the early 1930s, the national unemployment rate did not rise above 16%. Ismay (2015) reminds us that friendly societies were able to exclude from membership individuals known to or suspected to be likely to try to take unfair advantage of being members. She also argues that they fostered a loyalty and a feeling among their members that did much to nullify the moral hazard associated with commercial insurance contracts (although others have suggested that such traditional loyalty became severely strained during the early twentieth century, and Downing (2015) argues that it varied both between societies and between different branches of the same society).

1880s and was associated with an increase in both the incidence and the duration of episodes of sickness. After 1890 this increase in prevalence was reversed, the reversal being almost entirely due to a *decline* in the average duration of sickness episodes. The only period during which there was a rise in age-standardised sickness prevalence which is accounted for mainly by duration was the first two decades of the twentieth century and, at this time, the rise in duration was concentrated among men aged over 65 years.

The idea that, as mortality declines, morbidity rises due to the increasing duration of spells of sickness has a plausibility derived from the well-known model of the epidemiologic transition (Omran 1971). This model posits that, as mortality declined, infectious diseases retreated and were replaced by 'degenerative and man-made' diseases as causes of death, a process which happened in England and Wales between 1860 and 1960 (Omran 1971, pp. 738, 740).[13] Infectious diseases tend to be of short duration and kill quickly or not at all, whereas degenerative disorders tend to be long-lasting, killing more slowly but more reliably. Assuming that the conditions which are the main causes of death are likely also to be significant causes of sickness, the movement of a population through the epidemiologic transition is, therefore, likely to be accompanied by a rise in the average duration of spells of sickness.

Some infectious diseases were declining rapidly as causes of death after 1870 in England and Wales. A good example is respiratory tuberculosis, or phthisis. No cure for phthisis existed at this time and, since recovery without treatment was rare once a person started to suffer serious ill health from the symptoms, we can suppose either that the incidence fell, or that improved medical care allowed patients to survive for longer before eventually succumbing, or both.[14] But other, normally acute, infections were on the increase. Russian influenza, which arrived in the UK in 1889, was epidemic from 1890 to 1892 (Registrar General 1907, p. lxxv; Parsons 1891). Between 1887 and 1891, there was an increase from 1483 to 2095 in the total number of claims made to the HFS. Of this increase of 612, 435 (71%) was due to influenza (Edwards et al. 2003, p. 152). Figure 4.2 shows that, around this time, the incidence starts to fluctuate quite wildly from year to year, with peaks higher than had been experienced since 1870. The HFS authorities became concerned about the financial health of the Society following an actuarial valuation in 1889, and set in place a more rigorous system for policing claims (Gorsky et al. 2011, p. 1,781). Our

[13] Omran's model has not gone unchallenged. Weisz and Olszynko-Gryn (2010), for example, argued that it is overdetermined by contemporary development theory. Here, however, we are not concerned with what drives the epidemiologic transition, simply with the fact that it involves a shift in the distribution of causes of death.

[14] The HFS data do provide information on the causes of episodes of sickness, but unfortunately for our purposes only from 1895 onwards. Although there is some uncertainty about the underlying causes of the decline in tuberculosis mortality, epidemiological thinking both in the early twentieth century and nowadays favours improved isolation of infected cases and hence reduced transmission rates (Newsholme 1908; Wilson 2005) which would lead to a reduced incidence of this disease. Since tuberculosis was a long-lasting condition, this is likely to have reduced the mean duration of sickness episodes as a whole.

analysis suggests that they were right to be concerned that claims in the late 1880s and early 1890s were running at unusually high levels. To what extent the subsequent return of the volume of claims to 'normal' levels was a response to the more stringent monitoring regime established in the 1890s and to what extent it derived simply from the natural waning of the Russian influenza pandemic we cannot say. However, influenza claims were still being made at a greater rate in 1910 than in they were during the 1870s (Edwards et al. 2003, p. 152). This reflects the continuing high mortality from influenza during the first decade of the twentieth century: the age-standardised national death rate for males from influenza was 22 per 100,000 in the 1880s, 385 per 100,000 in the 1890s, and still 221 per 100,000 in the decade 1901–1910 (Registrar General 1919, p. ccv).[15]

A duration-driven increase in sickness has not always been observed in British data. When Riley (1999a) looked at three local sickness insurance schemes for which he had individual-level—as opposed to aggregate-level—data, he found that morbidity trends were different in each. In Abthorpe, Northamptonshire, the average duration declined as well as the incidence; in Ashbourne in Derbyshire, incidence fell dramatically but duration was roughly constant; only in Morcott in Leicestershire was the pattern of increasing duration observed (Riley 1999a, p. 116). Even where morbidity was unambiguously rising, this rise seems to have been as much in the incidence of sickness as in its duration. The Guild of St George Friendly Society in Cheshire, for example, shows a 'rate of falling sick' which more than doubled between 1873 and 1913, whereas the average duration increased by about 40% between 1873 and 1903 and `by about 70% between 1871 and 1913 (Riley 1989, p. 187).

A key piece of evidence in support of increased durations comes from large surveys undertaken by nineteenth-century actuaries. Riley (1989, p. 164) wrote that '[t]he testimony from the actuaries is unambiguous. Sickness rates … increased … because the average sickness episode became more protracted'. In support of this statement, Riley cites two pieces of evidence: a survey by Samuel Hudson of the Ancient Order of Foresters in 1897 which 'concluded that sickness time exceeded the expected amount by 16.5% because of heavy demands from members who were not dying' (Riley 1997, p. 163) and the massive survey by Alfred Watson of the Independent Order of Oddfellows (IOOF) Manchester Unity between 1893 and 1897 (Watson 1903). Here we focus on the second of these, which was produced by a future Government Actuary, and the results of which are still used (with appropriate adjustments) today.[16] Is Watson's testimony really 'unambiguous'?

[15] Of course, the arrival of the Russian influenza may have resulted in greater awareness of the disease and an increased tendency to report it as a cause of death. Our main point, though, is that the Russian influenza heralded a step change in the incidence of mortality from the disease in England and Wales which lasted for at least two decades.

[16] They are, for example, included in the standard book of formulae and tables which all actuarial students of the Institute and Faculty of Actuaries use in the professional examinations (Institute and Faculty of Actuaries 2002).

Watson compared his results for 1893–1897 with those obtained in a survey of the IOOF by Henry Ratcliffe which covered the period 1866–1870. Riley (1997, p. 173) says that Ratcliffe and Watson's tables 'show very clearly that, among Oddfellows, the average duration of sickness episodes increased'.

However Watson's and Ratcliffe's investigations differed in how they treated spells of sickness already in progress at the start of the investigations. Watson asked for details of when these spells actually started, so that he could accurately assign them to the correct duration category. Ratcliffe assumed that all such spells started on the date which the investigation started. To see the difference this makes, consider a man who fell sick 24 months before the investigation started, and was sick for a period of 36 months, his spell ending 12 months after the investigation started. This spell contributes 12 person-months of sickness experience during the period of the investigation. Ratcliffe assigned these equally to the 0–6-month and 6–12-month duration categories, whereas Watson—armed with information as to when the spell really did begin—would correctly assign the 12-months to the 24–36-month duration category. The effect of this is that Ratcliffe underestimated the amount of sickness experience at longer durations compared with Watson.

Watson was aware of this difficulty. In his words:

> [t]he returns prepared for the investigation of the experience of 1866–70 did not supply the dates when sickness attacks began and ended, and it is understood that all attacks which were current on 1st January 1866 were scheduled as having begun on that day, thus overstating the first-period sickness and correspondingly under-stating that falling within the after-periods (Watson 1903, pp. 38–9).

However, he then asserted that:

> [w]hen ... all due allowance has been made for this circumstance, there must still remain a great percentage of excess, and the conclusion seems to be irresistible that the serious increase of sickness previously noted is in great measure to be traced to the increase of permanent cases; and that these cases are not only more numerous at the older ages—where excess was perhaps anticipated—but that at every period of life protracted sickness now represents a much heavier liability than it did in the period 1866–70 (Watson 1903, p. 39).

Watson did not attempt to evaluate the potential impact of the different methods used by Ratcliffe and himself. Neither could he explain why sickness at longer durations had increased at all ages: '[n]o satisfactory explanation for this phenomenon can be suggested' (Watson 1903, p. 39), although he did offer some tentative suggestions elsewhere (see Watson (1900) and Snow (1913)).

In the Appendix, we show that the different methods employed by the two investigations account for at least one third of the apparent increase in the durations reported by Watson, and may account for almost all of the increase. This explains why reported durations seem to have increased in the IOOF data at all ages, and not predominantly at older ages. The evidence from the two IOOF investigations of 1866–1870 and 1893–1897, therefore, does not necessarily imply a real increase in durations, but may be more closely associated with methodological differences.

In arguing that the increase in reported durations was much smaller than Riley or Watson supposed, we are not taking issue with the fact that the IOOF data reveal an increase in the prevalence of sickness. This being the case, then if spells of sickness only became protracted to a limited extent, there must have been more of them: in other words, the incidence of sickness must have risen.

4.6 Conclusion

In this paper, we have analysed the trend in morbidity in England between 1870 and 1949 using individual-level sickness data for several thousand members of a sickness insurance scheme in the southern county of Hampshire. Our conclusions may be summarised as follows.

First, age-standardised morbidity did rise between 1870 and 1890, and again towards the 1920s, but between 1870 and 1910, the magnitude of the increase was only just over half that observed by Riley (1997). Moreover, we find that the rise in morbidity was the result both of the increasing incidence of sickness and the increasing duration of sickness episodes. The view that the greater length of episodes of sickness led to the rise in reported morbidity derives, in part, from comparisons made between contemporary actuarial investigations that we have shown to be confounded by methodological differences. Riley explained his results as 'a transition from frequent but brief episodes of sickness to less frequent but notably protracted episodes' (Riley 1999b, p. 134). The HFS data show that only during the 1880s was a rise in morbidity being driven mainly by the increased duration of sickness episodes (Table 4.3). Before 1900 morbidity fluctuated. During the 1880s, it rose because the duration of sickness episodes increased but, during the 1890s, it fell (even though sickness incidence was rising) because the duration of episodes decreased markedly. Between 1900 and about 1920, there was a rise in morbidity among men aged 65 years and over because the duration of their sickness episodes

Table 4.3 Summary of trends in age-standardised morbidity in the Hampshire Friendly Society data

Period	Prevalence	Incidence	Duration
1870–c.1880	Roughly constant	Roughly constant	Roughly constant
c. 1880–c.1890	Increase	Slow increase	Rapid increase
c. 1890–c.1900	Decrease	Increase	Rapid decrease
c. 1900–c. 1923	Increase among over 65s, constant among under 65s	Roughly constant	Increase among over 65s; roughly constant among under 65s
c. 1923–c. 1928	Slow increase for under 65s Decrease for over 65s	Increase for under 65s	Decrease
c. 1928–1949	Decrease	Roughly constant	Decrease

Source: Hampshire Friendly Society data

increased. Among younger men, however, morbidity changed rather little. After the 1920s, a new phase dawned in which both morbidity and mortality declined, the decline in morbidity arising from a decrease in both the incidence and duration of periods of sickness.

Second, the trends we have reported based on the HFS data do seem to be measuring 'objective morbidity', in that our annual estimates of morbidity are associated more closely with independent measures of changes in the disease environment than they are with economic or social policy changes. Morbidity was not closely associated with the unemployment rate or real wages. The introduction of national insurance in 1911 seems to have had only a limited effect on the level of sickness benefit claimed. However, reported morbidity in the HFS data was associated with changes in the general health environment. To be sure, there are other elements of 'cultural inflation' (such as general attitudinal changes, increases in the number of doctors or diagnostic changes) which we have discussed elsewhere (e.g. Gorsky et al. 2011). Contemporaries also believed that the introduction of parallel or multiple insurance schemes would increase the propensity to claim (essentially, because it increased the benefit/wage ratio). It was also why they believed that the introduction of workmen's compensation in 1897 led to an increase in sickness prevalence, and it was why some of them were hostile to the introduction of national insurance (Harris et al. 2011, pp. 648–9). However, secular historical changes in the relationship between individual and medical treatment or in cultural attitudes towards morbidity are not required to account for the morbidity trends we have observed.

Acknowledgements An earlier version of parts of this paper was presented at the Social Science History Association's 38th Annual Conference held in Chicago in November 2013. The research on which this paper is based was funded by research grant #RES-062-23-0324 from the United Kingdom Economic and Social Research Council.

Appendix: Analysis of the Apparent Increase in the Duration of Sickness Among the Independent Order of Oddfellows Between 1866–1870 and 1893–1897

Where does the idea that the increase in morbidity in the second half of the nineteenth century arose because of the increasing duration of episodes of sickness come from? In this Appendix, we focus on Watson's report, since this is the weightiest piece of evidence.

Watson's analysis (Watson 1903, pp. 38–9 and 143–59) was based on person-years of sickness. He classified the person-years according to duration since the episode of sickness began using the duration categories 0–6 months, 6–12 months, 12–24 months and over 24 months. He then compared the actual amount of sickness recorded in each of the duration categories with the amount which would have been expected on the basis of Henry Ratcliffe's investigation of the Oddfellows' sickness experience in 1866–1870 (Table 4.4). There are two key observations from this table.

Table 4.4 Watson's results for standardised morbidity in 1893–1897 compared with 1866–1870

	Standardised morbidity ratio		
Duration category	16–44 years	45–64 years	65 years and over
0–6 months	112	100	81
6–12 months	123	113	92
12–24 months	129	105	96
Over 24 months	264	243	238

Source: Watson (1903, p. 159)

1. The increase in morbidity between 1866–1870 and 1893–1897 is very largely a consequence of the increase in the amount of sickness experience recorded at durations over 24 months.
2. This increase occurs in all age categories.

We need to explain both these observations.

Sickness Episodes in Progress at the Start of the Investigation

The increase in morbidity at longer durations between 1866–1870 and 1893–1897 was characteristic of all age groups: indeed, it was actually stronger among the younger members than among those aged over 65 years. This matters, because it means that whatever was causing it was affecting all age groups. Explanations such as a replacement of acute conditions by chronic degenerative conditions (Riley 1989, p. 172) are unlikely, as if they were the cause, we should expect the increase in morbidity at longer durations to be concentrated among older members. Riley (1989, p. 192) acknowledges that there was an increase in sickness at all ages and describes this as 'unsettling', presumably because it suggests that something other than the conventional epidemiological transition is at work. However, he does not suggest what this might be. Perhaps the same need to posit a cause which would affect all age groups stumped Watson?

It is possible to use Watson's data to obtain some idea as to the proportion of the apparent increase in the duration of sickness between Ratcliffe's investigation of 1866–1870 and Watson's investigation of 1893–1897 which might have been due to the different methods employed by the two men.

Watson provides overall data concerning the amount of sickness observed in his investigation. This was, to the nearest person-year, 52,718 at durations 0–3 months, 12,436 at durations 3–6 months, 11,923 at durations 6–12 months, 12,660 at durations 12–24 months and 45,310 at durations over 24 months, making a total of 135,048 person-years (Watson 1903, p. 141). Consider spells of sickness of durations 0–3, 3–6, 6–12, 12–24 months and 24 months and over. Let the number of spells which last for 24 months or more be l_{24}, and the numbers lasting at least 12, 6 and 3 months be l_{12}, l_6 and l_3, respectively. Let the total number of spells be l_0. Let the person-years of experience in each of Watson's duration categories be $p_{0\text{-}3}$, $p_{3\text{-}6}$,

$p_{6\text{-}12}$, $p_{12\text{-}24}$ and p_{24+}, respectively, and let the mean duration of the spells in each duration category be $m_{0\text{-}3}$, $m_{3\text{-}6}$, $m_{6\text{-}12}$, $m_{12\text{-}24}$ and m_{24+} years.

Using standard life table methods, we can show that the following relationships hold:

$$p_{24+} = (m_{24+} - 2)l_{24},$$

$$p_{12-24} = l_{24} + (m_{12-24} - 1)(l_{12} - l_{24}),$$

$$p_{6-12} = 0.5l_{12} + (m_{6-12} - 0.5)(l_6 - l_{12}),$$

$$p_{3-6} = 0.25l_6 + (m_{3-6} - 0.25)(l_3 - l_6)$$

$$p_{0-3} = 0.25l_3 + m_{0-3}(l_0 - l_3).$$

Thus, substituting the total number of person-years in each duration category calculated from Watson's data, we have

$$45{,}310 = (m_{24+} - 2)l_{24},$$

$$12{,}660 = l_{24} + (m_{12-24} - 1)(l_{12} - l_{24}),$$

$$11{,}923 = 0.5l_{12} + (m_{6-12} - 0.5)(l_6 - l_{12}),$$

$$12{,}436 = 0.25l_6 + (m_{3-6} - 0.25)(l_3 - l_6)$$

$$52{,}718 = 0.25l_3 + m_{0-3}(l_0 - l_3).$$

This set of five equations with ten unknowns has many solutions, but there are restrictions on the values of some of the unknowns. We know that there are restrictions on the mean durations of spells in each category. Let us assume that $m_{0\text{-}3} = 0.125$ $m_{3\text{-}6} = 0.375$ $m_{6\text{-}12} = 0.75$ and that $m_{12\text{-}24} = 1.5$ (i.e. that spells under 3 months long are, on average, 1.5 months long; those between 3 and 6 months long are, on average, 4.5 months long; that spells lasting between 6 and 12 months are, on average, 9 months long; and that spells lasting between 12 and 24 months are, on average, 18 months long). Then the five equations become

$$45{,}310 = (m_{24+} - 2)l_{24}, \tag{4.A1}$$

$$12{,}660 = 0.5(l_{12} + l_{24}), \tag{4.A2}$$

$$11{,}923 = 0.25(l_6 + l_{12}), \tag{4.A3}$$

$$12{,}436 = 0.125\left(l_3 + l_6\right) \tag{4.A4}$$

$$52{,}718 = 0.125\left(l_0 + l_3\right). \tag{4.A5}$$

Since $l_0 \geq l_3 \geq l_6 \geq l_{12} \geq l_{24} > 0$, then eq. (4.A2) implies that $l_{24} \leq 12,660$. Substituting this into eq. (4.A1) produces

$m_{24+} \geq 2 + \frac{45{,}310}{12{,}660} = 5.58$, or that the average duration of spells longer than 24 months' long is at least 5.58 years.

For simplicity, suppose it is 6 years. With $m_{24+} = 6$, we can solve eqs. (4.A1)–(4.A5) to give

$$\begin{aligned} l_{24} &= 11{,}328, \\ l_{12} &= 13{,}992, \\ l_6 &= 33{,}700, \\ l_3 &= 65{,}788, \\ l_0 &= 355{,}956. \end{aligned}$$

With other values of m_{24+} we obtain different solutions (Table 4.5).

We now need to consider the impact of the difference between Watson's and Ratcliffe's treatment of the spells ongoing at the start of the period of investigation. A Lexis chart showing the sickness for a set of spells of more than 2 years' duration illustrates the situation (Figure 4.7). Calendar time is on the horizontal axis, and duration of spell is on the vertical axis. Suppose these spells last m + 2 years and imagine that claims for these sickness spells are made at a rate which is constant over time. Then the person-years of sickness at durations over 2 years during the period of investigation are represented by the area of the rectangle ABDC. This is the person-years calculation used by Ratcliffe in his 1866–1870 investigation. However, the spells under way at the start of the investigation, which are

Table 4.5 Numbers of spells with durations greater than 0, 3, 6, 12 and 24 months according to mean length of spells over 24 months' long

m_{24+}	l_{24}	l_{12}	l_6	l_3	l_0
6	11,328	13,993	33,700	65,789	355,956
7	9062	16,258	31,434	68,054	353,690
8	7552	17,768	29,924	69,564	352,180
9	6473	18,847	28,845	70,643	351,101
10	5664	19,656	28,036	71,452	350,292
11	5034	20,286	27,406	72,082	349,662
12	4531	20,789	26,903	72,585	349,159
13	4119	21,201	26,491	72,997	348,747
14	3776	21,544	26,148	73,340	348,404
15	3485	21,835	25,857	73,631	348,113

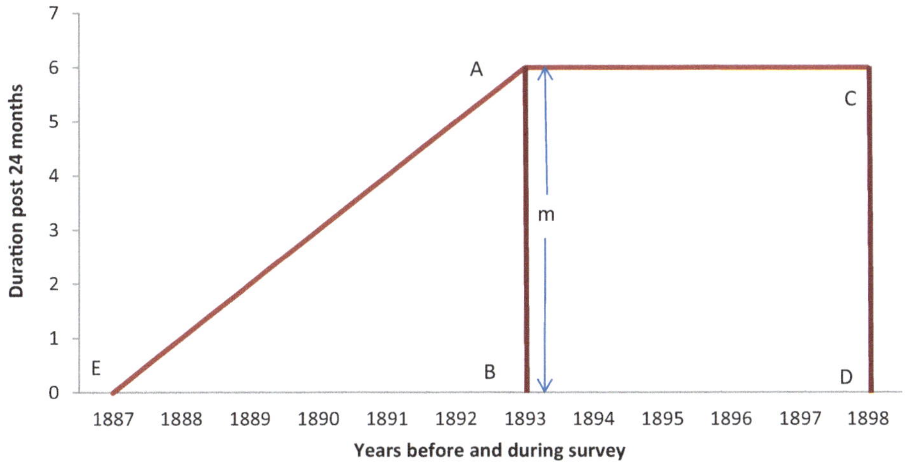

Fig. 4.7 Lexis chart to illustrate difference between Watson and Ratcliffe's treatment of spells under way at the start of the period of investigation
Note. This chart illustrates the case of $m = 6$ years

represented by the vertical line AB, will have durations at the start ranging from just above 0 to just under *m* years distributed uniformly between 0 and *m* (because of the constant rate of claims). The person-years of sickness before the start of the investigation which they encompass is represented by the area of the triangle ABE. It is this additional sickness which Watson's approach brings in.

The ratio between Watson's sickness prevalence and Ratcliffe's sickness prevalence is equal to $\frac{0.5m^2 + 5m}{5m} = \frac{0.5m + 5}{5} = \frac{m}{10} + 1$. So, if the average length of spells of over 2 years duration is 6 years (the minimum that Watson's own figures allow), then, relative to Ratcliffe, he has inflated the sickness in the 24 months and over duration segment by 1.4 times. If the average length is 10 years (by no means impossible given Watson's data), the inflation factor is 1.8 times., and if the average length is 14 years, it will be 2.2 times. Note also that this inflation factor is the same for all age groups provided *m* is the same for all age groups.

There will also be some inflation in the shorter duration segments, but since *m* is much smaller in these, the extent of the inflation will be much less: indeed, it cannot be more than 5% in the 12–24-month category and 2.5% in the 0–6- and 6–12-month categories.

Watson's 12-Month 'Off' Period

Watson also adopted a 12-month 'off' period when compiling his tables (Watson 1903, p. 15). This suggests that he treated a new sickness within 12 months of the previous one as a continuation of the previous one. According to Riley (1997, pp. 172–3), this was different from the treatment by Ratcliffe in earlier investigations. Riley points out, correctly, that this means that comparisons of the incidence of claims between Ratcliffe and Watson are therefore not possible (Watson will record a lower incidence than Ratcliffe). He fails to mention, however, that altering the definition of the 'off' period will also have an impact on the duration of claims, and confound the comparison of durations between the two surveys. Watson described this 12-month 'off' period as 'moderately long' (1903, p. 15). By comparison with shorter 'off' periods, it will tend to inflate the number of claims of long duration.

It therefore seems that the different treatment of spells in progress at the start of the investigation by Ratcliffe and Watson is likely to account for a substantial proportion of the apparent increase in morbidity at longer durations. Since Watson's data show a rise of some 2.4–2.6 times (Table 4.4), then the changed methods account for a minimum of 30% (using the minimum possible duration of sickness episodes over 2 years long which Watson's own data allow) and could account for close to 100% of the increase, especially if the rather extended 'off' period used by Watson is also factored into the calculations. Moreover, since the impact of this change in method is not necessarily age specific, the notable and 'unsettling' fact that the apparent increase was roughly the same for all age groups suggests that the changed methods might be the main reason.

Watson's Treatment of Sickness Claims Spanning More Than One Calendar Year

According to Riley, Watson treated a claim spanning more than one calendar year as several separate episodes, the second and subsequent episodes starting on each 1 January. This will artificially inflate the number of episodes and, when comparing the incidence of claims between Ratcliffe's and Watson's surveys, will act in the opposite direction to Watson's 12-month 'off' period.

It will, however, tend to change the distribution of claims by duration, as longer claims are more likely to cross the end of the calendar year and hence to be counted multiple times. Its effect is to increase the proportion of longer claims and, again, to make it look as if the mean duration of claims is rising faster than it actually is. Its effect, though, is likely to be fairly small. Assuming an exponential distribution of claim durations such that the mean claim duration is x years, then the impact on the longest duration claims involves multiplying the number of such claims by a factor which is less than or equal to $(1 + x)$. So if x is, say, 0.2 years, it will involve inflating the number of long claims by no more than 20%.

Conclusion

Table 4.4 reports standardised morbidity ratios of between 238 and 264 in 1893–1897 for claims of over 24 months duration compared with 1866–1870. It seems possible, and may be more likely than not, that the majority of this increase is accounted for by the different methods used by Watson and Ratcliffe in their computations. There are three specific differences, and all will tend to mean that Watson inflates the proportion of claims of longer duration compared with Ratcliffe. It is possible, therefore, that the increase in the average duration of claims reported by these actuaries is entirely artefactual.[17]

References

AOF [Ancient Order of Foresters] (1928) First quarterly report of the 94th executive council. Ancient Order of Foresters, Southampton

AOF [Ancient Order of Foresters] (1931) First quarterly report of the 97th executive council. Ancient Order of Foresters, Southampton

Downing A (2015) To claim or not to claim? Friendly societies in New Zealand 1879–1884. University of Oxford. Discussion Paper in Economic and Social History no. 138

Edwards C, Gorsky M, Harris B, Hinde A (2003) Sickness, insurance and health: assessing trends in morbidity through friendly society records. Annales de Demographie Historique 105:131–167

Feinstein C (1972) National income, expenditure and output of the United Kingdom, 1855–1965. Cambridge University Press, Cambridge

Gorsky M, Harris BJ (2005) The measurement of morbidity in inter-war Britain: evidence from the Hampshire Friendly Society. In: Borowy I, Gruner W (eds) Facing illness in troubled times: health in Europe in the interwar years 1918–1939. Peter Lang, Frankfurt-am-Main, pp 129–164

Gorsky M, Harris B, Hinde A (2006) Age, sickness and longevity in the late-nineteenth and twentieth centuries: evidence from the Hampshire Friendly Society. Soc Sci Hist 30:571–600

Gorsky M, Guntupalli AM, Harris BJ, Hinde A (2011) The 'cultural inflation' of morbidity during the English mortality decline: a new look. Soc Sci Med 73:1,775–1,783

Hampshire Friendly Society (1846–77) Rules and tables for the years 1846, 1852, 1855, 1857, 1868, 1875, 1877 including amendments (Hampshire Archives and Local Studies 18M89/4/3)

[17] We all knew John in different ways, as both friend and colleague, and are delighted to have this opportunity to express our appreciation of him.

This volume has demonstrated the enormous range of John's sympathies and research interests. Our own work overlapped with his in relation both the history of health and the history of social insurance. So far as health is concerned, we had common interests in relation both to anthropometric history and the history of morbidity. John was instrumental in providing us with an early platform for our work on the sickness records of the Hampshire Friendly Society when he edited a special issue of Social Science History, and our contribution to this volume arises directly from that. We hope it is a contribution which he would have welcomed and approved.

Over the years, we had the pleasure, individually and collectively, of meeting John at several academic gatherings, including meetings of the Economic History Society, the Society for the Social History of Medicine, and conferences on Economics and Human Biology. It was always a pleasure to hear his own work and he was a sympathetic and perceptive analyst of the work of others. He was also great company.

John was a great supporter of early-career researchers. He offered his support as research mentor and referee and was a source of great inspiration, both intellectually and personally. He had a brilliant mind and a very kind soul, and it was a privilege to have known him.

Harris B (1999) Morbidity and mortality during the health transition: a comment on James C. Riley 'Why sickness and death rates do not move parallel to one another over time'. Soc Hist Med 12:125–131

Harris BJ, Gorsky M, Guntupalli AM, Hinde A (2011) Ageing, sickness and health in England and Wales during the mortality transition'. Soc Hist Med 24:643–665

Harris BJ, Gorsky M, Guntupalli AM, Hinde A (2012) Long-term changes in sickness and health: further evidence from the Hampshire Friendly Society. Econ Hist Rev 65:719–745

Institute and Faculty of Actuaries (2002) Formulae and tables for actuarial examinations, 2nd edn. Institute and Faculty of Actuaries, London

Ismay P (2015) Between providence and risk: Odd Fellows, benevolence and the social limits of actuarial science, 1820s-1880s. Past and Present 226:115–147

Johansson SR (1991) The health transition: the cultural inflation of morbidity during the decline of mortality. Health Transit Rev 1:39–65

Johansson SR (1992) Measuring the cultural inflation of morbidity during the decline in mortality. Health Transit Rev 2:78–89

Macnicol J (1998) The politics of retirement in Britain, 1878–1948. Cambridge University Press, Cambridge

Mitchell BR (1988) British historical statistics. Cambridge University Press, Cambridge

Murray JE (2003) Social insurance claims as mortality estimates: sickness or absence. Soc Hist Med 16:225–245

Newsholme A (1908) The prevention of tuberculosis. Methuen, London

Omran A (1971) The epidemiologic transition: a theory of the epidemiology of population change. Milbank Mem Fund Q 49:509–538. (reprinted in Milbank Mem Fund Q 83 (2005): 731–757)

Parsons HF (1891) Report on the influenza epidemic of 1889–90. [British Parliamentary Papers 1890-91/XXXIV Cd. 6387]. Her Majesty's Stationery Office, London

Phelps-Brown H, Hopkins SV (1956) Seven centuries of the prices of consumables compared with builders' wage rates. Economica 23:296–314

Registrar General (1907) Supplement to the sixty-fifth annual report of the Registrar General of births, deaths and marriages in England and Wales 1891–1900, Part I. His Majesty's Stationery Office, London

Registrar General (1919) Supplement to the seventy-fifth annual report of the Registrar General of births, deaths and marriages in England and Wales 1901-1910, Part III: registration summary tables. His Majesty's Stationery Office, London

Riley J (1989) Sickness, recovery and death: a history and forecast of ill-health. Macmillan, Basingstoke

Riley J (1997) Sick not dead: the health of British workingmen during the mortality decline. Johns Hopkins University Press, Baltimore

Riley J (1999a) Why sickness and death rates do not move parallel to one another over time. Soc Hist Med 12:101–124

Riley J (1999b) Reply to Bernard Harris: morbidity and mortality during the health transition: a comment on James C. Riley. Soc Hist Med 12:133–137

Snow E (1913) Some statistical problems suggested by the sickness and mortality data of certain of the large friendly societies. J R Stat Soc 76:445–517

Watson AW (1900) The methods of analyzing and presenting the mortality, sickness and secession experience of friendly societies, with examples drawn from the experience of the Manchester Unity of Oddfellows. J Institute Actuaries 35:268–332

Watson AW (1903) An account of an investigation of the sickness and mortality experience of the I.O.O.F. Manchester Unity: during the five years 1893–1897. Independent Order of Oddfellows Manchester Unity, Manchester

Weisz G, Olszynko-Gryn J (2010) The theory of epidemiologic transition: the origins of a citation classic. J Hist Med Allied Sci 65:287–326

Whiteside N (1987) Counting the cost: sickness and disability among working people in an era of industrial recession, 1920–39. Econ Hist Rev 40:228–246

Wilson LG (2005) Commentary: medicine, population and tuberculosis. Int J Epidemiol 334:521–524

Chapter 5
Friendly Societies and Sickness Coverage in the Absence of State Provision in Spain (1870–1935)

Margarita Vilar-Rodríguez and Jerònia Pons-Pons

Abstract This paper stems from the book *Origins of American Health Insurance: A History of Industrial Sickness Funds*, published by John Murray in 2007, which has served as a basic reference point for our research work in recent years. In particular, this study aims to analyse the origin and development of friendly societies in Spain prior to the Spanish Civil War (1936–1939), taking their key economic role, especially in the sickness scheme, as study perspective. In this analysis, it can be seen how the initial pecuniary aid offered by friendly societies became a service of medical and pharmaceutical provision that drove their development in the country's more urban areas within a context where state sickness insurance was lacking.

Keywords Friendly societies · Sickness · Health · Voluntary associations · Sickness insurance

M. Vilar-Rodríguez (✉)
University of A Coruña, A Coruña, Spain
e-mail: mvilar@udc.es

J. Pons-Pons
Universidad de Sevilla, Sevilla, Spain
e-mail: jpons@us.es

P. Gray et al. (eds.), *Standard of Living*, Studies in Economic History,
https://doi.org/10.1007/978-3-031-06477-7_5

5.1 Introduction

The historiography has defined the concept of friendly society[1] as a voluntary association created for the purpose of offering members financial assistance in the event of situations such as sickness, industrial accidents, old age or unemployment, among others (Van Der Linden 1996: 11–38). Harris (2012: 1–2) qualified this concept by pointing out that this definition had its limitations, as in the case of Germany they were compulsory (Guinnane et al. 2012). Moreover, he emphasised that a very important part of the work of these societies in the countries where they flourished was the provision of more or less broad medical coverage. That is to say, he highlighted their economic function as the main role of friendly societies and their intrinsic nature, but he did not disregard the fact that as a supplementary aspect, many of them also provided access to social, cultural and recreational activities. An important contribution to the analysis of the economic and financial role of sickness coverage was John Murray's book *Origins of American Health Insurance: A History of Industrial Sickness Funds*, published in 2007. In this work, Murray examined the sickness funds for workers offered by different types of societies in the United States from the late nineteenth century to the 1940s. As a result of this analysis, Murray underlined three basic conclusions. First, he pointed out the important economic function of these funds in covering workers' risk of sickness. Second, he highlighted the high degree of satisfaction that these schemes entailed for members, which put a brake on initiatives promoting different state projects of compulsory sickness insurance. Third, he indicated the negative impact of technological changes in medicine and management, helping usher in the decline of these societies, which were unable to withstand the competition from private insurance companies. As part of this study, Murray also analysed the causes of the decline of sickness funds (known as friendly societies or mutual aid societies in Europe) in the United States in light of the success of insurance companies, above all from the 1940s. Relevant factors included the difficulties that these mutuals experienced to introduce new actuarial techniques in the calculation of risk or to address the increase in medical and pharmaceutical costs at a time of great technical advances in diagnosis and treatment. In general, Murray's work minimises the impact of institutional aspects on this process of decline, maybe because it was not a key factor in the case of the United States. However, the important role of these fraternal societies in offering social services in the United States is beyond all doubt, as other authors such as Beito (2000) have also affirmed.

The historiography also provides excellent research works that examine the strategic role and the process of expansion and decline of friendly societies in different European countries from different study perspectives. These range from the more general works of the above-mentioned Van der Linden (1996) or Brückweh et al. (2012) to case studies by country. Thus, Harris (2004, 2009), Harris and Bridgen

---

[1] Called friendly society in Great Britain, *mutualité* in France, *società di mutuo soccorso* in Italy and *sociedad de socorros mutuos* in Spain

(2007), Harris et al. (2006), Gorsky (1998) and Gorsky and Sheard (2006) address the British case. For the French case, the works of Radelet (1991) and Dreyfus (1996, 2009), for example, are noteworthy; for Italy there is the research of Marucco (1981), and for the Dutch case, the work of Van Leeuwen (2007) is notable.

As in the rest of Europe, in Spain friendly societies played an essential role in the coverage of sickness from 1850 to 1950, first providing cash benefits in the event of loss of wages[2] and, subsequently, primary medical care and even the provision of treatment in specialities such as gynaecology, ophthalmology and dentistry, as well as some surgery. However, a strange phenomenon has occurred in the Spanish historiography. For decades, friendly societies have been the focus of a huge number of studies (Castillo 1994; Castillo and Ortiz de Orruño 1997; Maza Zorrilla 2003; Castillo and Ruzafa 2009), but concentrating on sociability (Maza Zorrilla 1995, 2002; Guereña 1994; Duch Plana 2019) and on their typology within a supplementary function in the social and cultural sphere. Indeed, there are many works in the Spanish historiography that base their analysis on the typology of friendly societies, distinguishing between general societies, popular societies and others based on their territory, trade, profession, factory or company, or linked to political parties or religious organisations, etc., as indicated by Marín Casado (2015, 38 and 247). The fact is that this profusion of literature does not address the economic and financial purpose of friendly societies, or this is only considered as a marginal objective, with some exceptions (Vilar Rodríguez 2010; Pons and Vilar 2011; Vilar and Pons 2012; León-Sanz 2012; Pons and Vilar 2014). The profusion of analysis of their social capital and the issue of sociability may therefore lead lay readers to have a distorted picture of the functionality of these institutions, focused almost exclusively on their social role. The aim of this paper is to analyse the economic importance of friendly societies in Spain in the coverage of the risk of sickness before the outbreak of the Spanish Civil War (1936–1939) and the passage of compulsory sickness insurance (*seguro obligatorio de enfermedad*; *SOE*) in 1942.

5.2 The Origins of the Friendly Societies in Spain: A Historical Synthesis

With regard to their origin and long-term evolution, a recent contribution, Nieto Sánchez and Lopez Barahona (2020), makes it possible to link the friendly societies of the nineteenth and twentieth centuries with preceding entities. These authors analyse the creation of medieval religious confraternities on the part of guilds and their evolution in the eighteenth century, wherein the concept of mutual aid was established, and which would persist in the friendly societies of the contemporary period. The confraternities developed as from the Early Middle Ages under the Crown of Aragon, and in the Early Modern Period under the Crown of Castile. Their

[2] Hence, their name, mutual aid, in which the concept aid meant pecuniary assistance

functions included providing coverage of the risks of death, sickness, disability, work-related accidents, unemployment, captivity, widowhood and orphanhood. These entities provided aid for funeral costs, medical and healthcare costs and payment of dowries, pensions and ransoms. As the authors point out, one of the most remarkable aspects was their transformation in the second half of the eighteenth century. Specifically, as a result of the disturbances of 1766, the so-called Esquilache Riots, the state decided to ban, in some cases, or control these kinds of associations. In the wake of this incident, a national census of confraternities was undertaken. Subsequently, a law of 1784 prohibited them definitively and obliged them to transform into societies or associations known as *montepíos*, which were required to adopt this name, although the invocation of a religious figure was permitted, and to relax admission requirements and lower membership fees. With these changes, the state intended to erode the autonomy of professional associations and use mutual aid to supplement the system of charity, which at this time was both deficient and scarce. Very few of them survived in the following century.

This form of collective solidarity received a new boost with the belated Spanish industrialisation, and the liberal state had to accept these types of associations for the sake of, and extension of, the welfare and coverage of the popular and working classes. The legal changes that derived from the break-up of the Old Regime drove this process. These included the regulation of free employment contracts between workers and employers (1834), the abolition of guilds as the only regulating institutions of professional activity (1836) and the right of freedom of association (1839) which fostered professional associationism oriented towards mutual aid in the event of misfortune, sickness and future needs (Martín Valverde 1987: XXXII and XXXIX; Alarcón 1975: 35). The organisations that emerged in the following decades made it possible to alleviate the precariousness and insecurity of workers, and new popular societies were created (Maza Zorrilla 1991: 178 and Castillo 1994: 10). The law of associations of 1887 consolidated this process by recognising the free activity of non-profit associations, among which were included friendly societies, welfare societies and credit and consumer cooperatives (Vilar Rodríguez 2010).

In 1904, the statistics produced by the Institute of Social Reforms reflected the growth process of these new friendly societies and the stages of their expansion (Table 5.1). By this year, only a few of the societies created in the preindustrial period, 26, had survived, mainly *montepíos* constituted in the eighteenth century. These were the heirs to the transformation of medieval confraternities into *montepíos* in the eighteenth century and their subsequent evolution. Four of them were categorised as created in time immemorial and in most cases linked to fishermen (Asociación de Socorros Mutuos del Clero (Pontevedra), Cofradía de Mareantes (Zumaya-Guipúzcoa), Congregación y Hermandad de la Purísima Sangre de Nuestro Señor Jesucristo (Montblanc-Tarragona) and Sociedad de Pescadores Noble Cabildo de San Andrés (Castro Urdiales-Santander). These were joined by 1 founded in the sixteenth century, 2 in the seventeenth century and 19 in the eighteenth century (11 of them in the province of Barcelona and 6 in Guadalajara).

During the nineteenth century, on the basis of this inheritance and with the transformation of the manufacturing world and industrial growth, these associations assumed a crucial role in the coverage of sickness, old age and industrial accidents.

This was at a time when the nature of charity was changing and there was still no realistic plan for the construction of a state-led system of social insurances, which would not be developed until the early twentieth century. Initially, 130 friendly societies were created from 1801 to 1850, and then the pace quickened in the second half of the nineteenth century, along with industrial development, with the constitution of 241 entities of this type between 1851 and 1880. There was then a huge surge from 1881 to 1904 with the formation of 1048 societies. This final boom coincided with the acceleration of industrialisation in Catalonia and the Basque Country, the appearance in Spain of big business linked to the Second Industrial Revolution, the development of the labour movement and the freedom of association linked to the law of 1887. The concentration in Catalonia, and to a lesser extent in the Balearic Islands, increased during this period, and these were among the leading regions in terms of the number of societies and members.

The friendly society model spread unequally throughout Spanish territory, being more concentrated in the industrial zones of eastern Spain, Madrid and the Basque Country, where the working class suffered more uprooting of families and a greater dependence on wages in an urban environment. This unequal impact can be seen in Tables 5.1 and 5.2. In absolute terms, the highest numbers of friendly societies and members were concentrated in the provinces of the Spanish Levant, the coastal provinces of Catalonia (Barcelona, Gerona and Tarragona), the Balearic Islands, Alicante and Castellón. As well as this eastern sector, there was also concentration in the two other most industrialised areas in Spain, the province of Biscay and Madrid. This distribution is maintained if we consider the density of these societies in accordance with their number and the number of members per 100,000 inhabitants (Table 5.3). The high incidence in the regions of Cataluña and the Balearic Islands led to the creation of the Catalan Federation of Mutual Provident Societies (*Federación de Mutualidades de Catalunya*) in 1896 (the first in Spain) which, with successive transformations and a change of name, encompassed most of the friendly societies in this region. In its evolution, it went on from 51 mutuals in 1896, to embrace 106 in 1898, 554 in 190 and 747 in 1915 with 167,623 members (Moreta i Amat 1991; Solà i Gussinyer 1994, 2003; Duch Plana 2019).

Table 5.1 Year of foundation of the friendly societies existing in 1904

Foundation	Number of societies	Members
Hasta 1800	26	4469
1801–1850	65	13,609
1851–1860	65	17,916
1861–1870	71	15,918
1871–1880	105	23,365
1881–1890	300	72,561
1891–1900	502	103,004
1901–1904	548	98,536

Source: Instituto de Reformas Sociales (1908)

The data that appear in the table do not coincide with the statistical summary from p. 142 of the same source. The data have been checked and rectified

Table 5.2 Distribution of the number of friendly societies in Spain and their members in 1904

Province	Number	Members	Average number of members per society	Province	Number	Members	Average number of members per society
Álava	6	2786	464.33	Lérida	27	3356	124.30
Albacete	12	2569	214.08	Logroño	10	2555	255.50
Alicante	36	16,195	449.86	Lugo	3	474	158.00
Almería	0	0	0	Madrid	64	34,955	546.17
Ávila	3	464	154.67	Málaga	5	2153	430.60
Badajoz	25	4196	167.84	Murcia	16	3136	196.00
Balearics	66	14,379	217.86	Navarre	7	3536	505.14
Barcelona	572	124,254	217.23	Orense	1	790	790.00
Burgos	8	1089	136.13	Oviedo	23	7958	346.00
Cáceres	15	1799	119.93	Palencia	26	3322	127.77
Cádiz	19	3148	165.68	Pontevedra	3	303	101.00
Canaries	6	6952	1158.67	Salamanca	10	1685	168.50
Castellón	36	4101	113.92	Santander	32	4345	135.78
Ciudad Real	27	6452	238.96	Segovia	2	145	72.50
Córdoba	10	1238	123.08	Seville	29	3599	124.10
Coruña (La)	26	8365	321.73	Soria	2	637	318.50
Cuenca	11	2430	220.91	Tarragona	109	13,424	123.16
Gerona	192	26,059	135.72	Teruel	11	1752	159.27
Granada	6	584	97.33	Toledo	21	5666	269.81
Guadalajara	33	1879	56.94	Valencia	8	1067	133.38
Guipúzcoa	31	6442	207.81	Valladolid	31	3779	121.90
Huelva	18	3315	184.17	Biscay	40	5855	146.38
Huesca	14	1622	115.86	Zamora	3	522	174.00
Jaén	16	3688	230.50	Zaragoza	8	1402	175.25
León	10	1321	132.10	Total	1689	351,743	208.26

Source: See Table 5.1

The incidence of these societies was less in the regions of the centre and south of Spain, such as eastern Andalusia, Extremadura and Castile-La Mancha. In rural areas, the population preferred to protect their livelihoods, harvests and livestock through formulas of solidarity rather than seek sickness and old-age coverage. In the case of Navarre, for example, of the 12 institutions included in the statistics of 1904, only 6 correspond to friendly societies, the rest are credit cooperatives or mutual livestock societies. Anyway, the incidence of friendly societies could vary within the same agricultural world depending on the type of property, with little presence in the areas with large estates where powerful landowners exercised a strong paternalism and control, which impeded any form of association among workers, and a different story in the areas with smallholder farming. This is not a strict rule, as other factors could also have an influence, but it should be taken into account.

Table 5.3 Density of friendly societies per province in 1904

Province	Number of associations per 100,000 inhabitants	Number of members per 100,000 inhabitants	Province	Number of associations per 100,000 inhabitants	Number of members per 100,000 inhabitants
Barcelona	54	11,782	Granada	1	1018
Gerona	64	8707	Guadalajara	16	938
Castellón	11	6319	Jaén	3	777
Balearics	21	4613	Teruel	4	712
Madrid	8	4509	Cádiz	4	695
Badajoz	4	4196	Huesca	5	662
Tarragona	32	3974	Seville	5	648
Alicante	7	3444	Murcia	2	542
Guipúzcoa	15	3232	Salamanca	3	525
Álava	6	2890	Cáceres	4	496
Albacete	4	2569	Soria	1	423
Ciudad Real	8	2006	Málaga	0.9	420
Canaries	1	1938	León	2	342
Biscay	12	1880	Zaragoza	1	332
Palencia	12	1725	Burgos	2	321
Santander	11	1574	Córdoba	2	271
Toledo	5	1503	Ávila	1	231
Valladolid	7	1356	Orense	0.2	195
Logroño	5	1343	Zamora	1	189
Coruña	3	1279	Valencia	0.9	132
Huelva	6	1270	Lugo	0.6	101
Oviedo	3	1269	Segovia	1	91
Lérida	9	1222	Pontevedra	0.6	66
Navarre	2	1149			

Source: See Table 5.1

There were different social coverage goals among the societies created in the nineteenth century. A few were created by professional groups to cover old age. This was the case of the Sociedad Médica General de Socorros Mutuos, promoted by the contributors and editors of the Bulletin of Medicine, Surgery and Pharmacy in 1835, which covered old-age pensions for the doctors, surgeons and pharmacists who were members that had not reached the age of 38 when they joined.[3] However,

[3] Biblioteca Virtual del Patrimonio bibliográfico. *Estatutos de la Sociedad Médica General de socorros mutuos*, Madrid, 1847. In 1860, the *Sociedad Artístico-Musical de Socorros Mutuos* was created for the same purpose. Biblioteca Nacional de España M-15-163. *Anuario y estatutos de la Sociedad Artístico-Musical de Socorros Mutuos 1882–1883*, Madrid, 1983. This society granted lifelong pensions to members unable to perform or produce their art, but only until 1/4 of their social capital was reached. In any event, those affected in such cases could apply for exceptional, although limited, pensions.

in the great majority, the coverage offered was sickness provision. For most societies providing this coverage, the aim was cash benefits to make up for the lack of earnings from work during the time off due to these circumstances. This was the case of the Sociedad de Socorros Mutuos de Artesanos, founded in Vitoria in 1849 with 89 members and which had 1025 members, 945 active and 80 honorary, by 1898. During this period, 1849–1898, the society paid out 1,300,000 pesetas in aid to the sick and those unfit for work, and for funerals for the deceased.[4] This cash benefit, which predominated in the nineteenth century, was gradually modified with the introduction of medical and pharmaceutical provisions, which explains the growth and expansion of these services during the first decades of the twentieth century. In 1905, when a friendly society was created in Almácera, in the province of Valencia, cash benefits still comprised the main social purpose. In its regulations, aid of 2 pesetas a day for 40 days was established for sick members, to be reduced to 1 peseta for the following 20 days. A medical certificate from the society's doctor was always required. In these cases, the patient could resort to the charity hospital, specifically Santo Hospital de Valencia, and could continue to receive the cash benefit while in hospital.[5] In the societies where the primary objective was to provide monetary aid, the main job of the society's visiting doctor was to monitor the sick, helped by inspectors and auxiliary personnel.[6] Most societies, of course, made explicit exclusions for chronic illnesses, epidemics or infirmities related to bad social behaviour (alcoholism, venereal diseases, etc., including suicide).

A process of transition had begun in some societies in the late nineteenth century, with the increase of spending on doctors' fees, pharmaceutical expenses and doctors' assistants (*practicantes*).[7] This is what seems to occur with the *La Ovetense* friendly society founded in 1859, in whose balance sheet of 1881 medical (1500 reales per quarter), pharmaceutical and doctors' assistant expenses accounted for 43.23% of the society's expenditure, compared with 39.70% spent on pensions. The society's articles included the right to a pension in the event of sickness, which corresponded to 5 reales a day for the first 8 months, after which subscribers only had the right to medical care, medicines and travel expenses. As a result of this process in the first decade of the twentieth century, the friendly societies had strengthened their provision of medical services, which from then on would become the main enticement for new members to join. In 1904, the *Sociedad de Socorros*

[4] Repositorio Documental Universidad de Valladolid, LEG_22_1_n1702. *Sociedad de Socorros mutuos de Artesanos de Vitoria. Cuentas Generales del año 1898*. Vitoria, 1899. For a broader study on this society, see Marín Casado (2015: 243–262).

[5] Biblioteca Nacional de España C-2475-29. *Reglamento de la Sociedad de Socorros mutuos de Almácera bajo el patrocinio de Santo Tomás de Villanueva*, Valencia, 1905

[6] Biblioteca Nacional de España, C-2529-55. *Reglamento de la Sociedad de Socorros mutuos Destosense*, Tortosa, 1912. In this society, the doctor was appointed with the title of "Médico-fiscal" (literally a fiscal doctor), as well as appointing inspectors and visitors who took responsibility for supervising the sick.

[7] Biblioteca Virtual de Asturias. Memoria de la Ovetense. *Sociedad de socorros mutuos fundada en el año 1859. Estado de la Sociedad a 31 de diciembre de 1881*. Fondos Comisión PMH — Signatura 452 (12)

Mutuos de Dependencia Mercantil in Valencia included one or more licensed surgeons in its statutes, whose charges would be the appropriate percentage of the fees collected from full members as estimated by the Board. Moreover, treatment by an eye specialist, a dentist and a bloodletter was included.[8]

In 1910, *La Honradez*, a friendly society of doormen, office boys and clerks in Madrid, had established a complex organisation of medical services that was included in its statutes and regulations.[9] The society had a medical team, admitted by public tender, divided into four levels depending on years of seniority. Each step up the scale brought the doctor a salary increase of 250 pesetas. The members and their families enrolled in the social register could request medical care at home or visit the corresponding doctor's surgery in the area. In the first case, after notification, the doctor was to visit the patient within a deadline of 6 h. If another doctor was requested, this had to be justified and the time limit was not applied. The doctor in question had to treat the patient at home or in the surgery, including surgical operations if necessary, and also perform an initial check-up for members and inform the society of any chronic cases. The society included coverage of specialities: an obstetrician-gynaecologist for difficult births, an auxiliary obstetrician, childbirth teachers, an eye specialist and a dentist. This society had already been transformed from a traditional friendly society into a medical coverage society, although it maintained the original term in its denomination out of respect for tradition.

5.3 The Expansion of the Medical and Pharmaceutical Provision of Friendly Societies in Spain (1914–1936)

In the Spanish case, during the first decades of the twentieth century, friendly societies covered to some extent the state's passivity in matters of public health in general, and the shortcomings of charitable healthcare coverage in particular. It should be borne in mind that, unlike insurance against industrial accidents (1900/1933), old age (1909/1922), maternity (1923/1931) and unemployment (1932), the Spanish government did not legislate, regulate or finance the risk of sickness before the Civil War (1936–1939).[10] Consequently, healthcare coverage remained in the hands of

[8] Biblioteca Nacional de España, 47/412877. *Estatutos y Reglamento de la Sociedad de Socorros mutuos de la Dependencia mercantil de Valencia fundada en 1886*, Madrid, 1904

[9] Biblioteca Nacional de España, C-2618-4. *Estatutos y Reglamento de la Sociedad de Beneficencia y Socorros Mutuos de Porteros, ordenanzas y empleados de Madrid*, Madrid, 1910. Its main social purpose was to aid members in accordance with the regulations in the event of sickness, but it also covered funeral expenses and provided a retirement pension on reaching the statutory retirement age or in the event of physical disability. Another enticement for potential members was the establishment of primary or elementary classes for members' children.

[10] The first year refers to the approval of a voluntary system and the second to its transformation into compulsory insurance.

private initiative and under a legal regime of complete freedom before the coup d'état of 1936. During this period, the state's responsibility was limited to protecting the public against any abuses or fraud committed by the different funds or societies providing private insurance, whether in terms of healthcare provision or of an economic nature.[11] Meanwhile, the public authorities only took responsibility for financing charitable medical care, earmarked exclusively for those who possessed an official certificate of poverty. In this way, the welfare of a large part of the population depended on their capacity to access private medical services, an alternative that was beyond the means of most people.

In fact, the stance of Spanish governments during this stage was quite paradoxical from several points of view. On the one hand, they defended the introduction of a compulsory sickness insurance with broad coverage and substantial duration in the questionnaire prior to the International Conference on Sickness Insurance held in Geneva in 1927 (INP 1927: 47). However, they did not advocate or push through any legislative measure to implement state sickness insurance. This passivity was justified with the argument that the country's social needs in this respect were already met. In particular, the authorities emphasised the key work in healthcare coverage of thousands of Spanish workers employed by friendly societies and private insurance companies (INP 1927: 22) (Tables 5.4 and 5.5).

On the other hand, the mistrust between the friendly societies (mostly of worker origin) and governments prevented the creation of collaborative mechanisms to develop and implement state sickness coverage. As part of this impasse, the Spanish

Table 5.4 Distribution of insured according to risks covered (percentages)

Type of coverage	1915	1918	1921	1925
Sickness (1)	35.25	36.76	37.11	36.56
Funeral expenses	7.58	6.02	5.62	7.41
Maternity (2)	1.12	1.47	1.23	1.47
Disability	12.30	12.65	12.50	11.86
Old age	3.08	2.67	2.52	2.72
Death	19.02	20.98	22.63	22.65
Medical treatment (3)	9.73	9.21	8.28	7.80
Pharmaceutical treatment (4)	8.25	6.54	5.98	5.71
Widowhood	2.64	1.76	1.53	1.32
Orphanhood	0.31	0.20	0.23	0.20
Other risks	0.53	1.61	2.20	2.16
No data	0.20	0.13	0.16	0.13
Total of 1+2+3+4	54.36	53.98	52.61	51.54
Total	435,123	692,953	821,840	1,048,027

Source: INP (National Welfare Institute; *Instituto Nacional de Previsión*) (1927: 101)

[11] According to the National Welfare Institute (INP 1927: 80 and 98), there were three state inspection mechanisms: Civil Governors, the *Comisaría General de Seguros* and the *Comisaría Sanitaria Central*.

Table 5.5 Data sent to the International Labour Conference (1927) (totals in current pesetas)

	Funds or FSs		Fees			Cost of the FSs medical service provision		
	Number entities	Number members	Of members (%)	Of protectors and patrons (%)	Total	Medical care (%)	Pharmaceutical care (%)	Total
1915	1274	143,993	94.83	5.17	2,954,317.11	38.08	61.92	230,337.59
1916	1332	198,953	94.62	5.38	3,565,824.64	35.10	64.90	279,915.19
1917	1391	245,989	93.37	6.63	4,405,979.00	35.38	64.62	307,408.24
1918	1438	262,630	90.34	9.66	3,919,305.93	31.06	68.94	458,087.25
1919	1477	278,320	90.40	9.60	3,654,651.62	28.81	71.19	515,657.86
1920	1514	303,640	88.59	11.41	4,781,800.29	35.56	64.44	597,251.94
1921	1553	318,321	90.36	9.64	5,014,344.49	31.07	68.93	750,801.61
1922	1628	338,144	93.51	6.49	6,468,298.56	40.80	59.20	654,344.17
1923	1680	352,630	93.36	6.64	8,239,695.48	39.46	60.54	771,091.25
1924	1722	366,065	93.22	6.78	9,159,124.71	38.04	61.96	885,561.32
1925	1770	398,999	94.17	5.83	9,855,338.09	37.66	62.34	1,008,962.89

Source: INP (1927)

delegation at the Geneva Conference also showed itself to be against subsidising friendly societies, for three reasons: this would oblige the societies to accept anybody who applied as a member, which would create problems in ideologically motivated organisations; it would promote the creation of a network of societies that were eligible for subsidies but not very efficient; and it would hamper the constitution of friendly societies in smaller towns, aggravating territorial imbalances. Nevertheless, during the 1920s and 1930s, the state did end up granting, upon request, small economic subsidies, funded from the General State Budget, to workers' mutuals offering medical and pharmaceutical care (Table 5.6). In fact, in the 1880s, the state had already published public tenders in order to subsidise the friendly societies with budget funds. During this preliminary stage, the subventions awarded amounted to 200,000 pesetas a year, a much higher figure than those awarded at the beginning of the twentieth century (Montero García 1988: 84). Taken together, all these subsidies implicitly reveal official recognition of the work carried out through popular solidarity in a field which concentrated the greatest failings of the state welfare system. However, the small number of societies subsidised and the limited quantity of official aid in the early twentieth century rule out the idea of a system of healthcare provision that was privately managed but subsidised by the state.

So what were the causes that led the state to abandon healthcare coverage? The historiography suggests that the main factors of the state's abandonment could be the complex infrastructure, the high cost of management demanded by the insurance in relation to the state's financial capacity and the obstacles interposed by the medical profession and the private insurance companies (Martínez Quinteiro 1984; Cuesta Bustillo 1988; Rodríguez Ocaña 1990; Porras Gallo 1999). However, the most serious of these obstacles was without doubt the lack of modernisation of the tax system which made it difficult for the state to increase its income through direct taxation and, thus, impeded the creation of all the healthcare infrastructure

Table 5.6 Official subsidies to workers' mutuals with medical-pharmaceutical care

State budget	No. of subsidised societies	Total subsidy (nominal pesetas)	Average subsidy per society (nominal pesetas)
1924	96	75,000	781.3
1925	76	35,000	460.5
1926[a]	76	17,500	230.3
1927	101	35,000	346.5
1929	96	35,000	364.6
1930	68	35,000	514.7
1931	101	50,000	495.1
1933	178	75,000	421.4
1935[b]	42	37,500	892.9

Source: Gaceta de Madrid of: 22/03/1925 (No. 163); 10/11/1926 (No. 314); 26/10/1927 (No. 299); 11/04/1928 (No. 102); 4/12/1929 (No. 338); 11/01/1931 (No. 11); 30/12/1931 (No. 364); 21/12/1933 (No. 355); 30/11/1934 (No. 334); 22/11/1935 (No. 326)

Notes: [a]Refers to the budget for the second half of 1926. [b]Refers to the first two quarters of 1935

necessary to apply sickness insurance to the entire population. In this respect, it should be remembered that, as from 1845, when the Mon-Santillán reform tried to transform the tax system typical of the Old Regime into another compatible with the liberal system, there were various attempts to direct the Spanish system of public finances towards a progressive model that would base the majority of its income on direct taxes. However, these attempts failed, in most cases due to the resistance of the wealthy classes, and the result was a low tax burden, low tax collection and a high public debt (Comín Comín 1994). On the other hand, the opposition of the majority of employers, medical associations, mutuals and insurance companies, who felt their private business interests to be at risk, continued. Even workers showed themselves to be unwilling to accept an insurance based on contributions, as they were hoping for greater state coverage without having to pay contributions, as was the case with old-age pensions. Nevertheless, in spite of the severe obstacles, we can point out two initiatives that were intended to promote state coverage of the risk of sickness.

First of all, an interesting political debate took place during the first decades of the twentieth century between representatives of the friendly societies and representatives of the state. The topic was, above all, the issue of healthcare (Vilar Rodríguez 2010). The National Conference on Sickness, Disability and Maternity Insurance, held in Barcelona in 1922, served as a forum for the non-profit-making entities where they could voice their legal and economic demands.[12] One of their main complaints was in relation to the lack of legislative protection that they had suffered throughout their long history. In contrast to other European countries, where friendly societies benefited from specific legislation, workers' mutuals in Spain continued functioning under the generic law of associations of 1887. In order to solve this problem, an ambitious preliminary draft law was presented. It contained 30 articles which pursued two fundamental objectives: to constitute a more solid legal framework for their operations and to guarantee their active participation in the incipient system of state welfare.

As had occurred in other countries, collaboration between the state and friendly societies could have served as a guide for the development of sickness insurance in Spain, but no agreement was reached. Both the presentation of the preliminary draft law by the friendly societies' representatives and its reception by the state were riddled with contradictions. On the one hand, the societies showed a desire to collaborate, which required a metamorphosis of the mutual system, but without concealing their rejection of having their activities controlled by the authorities. Although they were aware of the fact that they were risking a good part of their possibilities of survival in the process, they were at no time prepared to lose their own personality and autonomy.[13] In this sense, it is notable that the request for state

[12] INP (1922) and the interesting reflection on this document in Cuesta Bustillo (1994: 409–422). The representatives of the Federation of Friendly Societies of the Province of Barcelona assumed a prominent role at this forum.

[13] *Conferencia Nacional de Seguros de Enfermedad, Invalidez y Maternidad* (1922: 18). The representatives of the friendly societies maintained that the vigilance of their members obviated the

financial aid always occupied a secondary position in their demands. They were aware of the fact that accepting money from the state would require allowing the authorities a greater degree of control and intervention, something that was not desirable from their point of view. On the other hand, the state implicitly recognised the important work carried out by the workers' mutuals, but completely ignored their demands through a legislative silence and a lack of information.

The lack of understanding between the state project and the friendly societies, mainly related to the healthcare coverage of their members, resulted in a missed opportunity in the legislation of sickness risk in Spain. The Spanish government's late intervention in sickness coverage prolonged the survival of the friendly societies, which had been losing market share with the implementation of other state insurances, a factor that was already revealed as decisive in Rivera Blanco (1994: 142). Thus, for example, the approval of maternity insurance in 1929 led to the abandonment of the midwife service that the mutuals had been offering to women related to their members since the end of the second decade of the twentieth century.[14]

The second attempt to legislate sickness insurance before the Spanish Civil War was the work of the socialist Labour Minister, Largo Caballero, who tried to get a project of sickness insurance underway during the first 2 years of the Second Republic (1931–1936). The bureaucratic process became drawn out as the political make-up of the government changed during the second 2-year period of the Republic. Finally, the project was presented at the beginning of 1936, but now included in a wider scheme intended to bring about the unification of all different types of social insurance. Its main objective was to incorporate Spain into the European trend which advocated an integrated and universal insurance. However, the partial failure of the coup d'état of 18 July 1936 and the posterior outbreak of the Civil War prevented the passage of this legislation (Porras Gallo 1999).

While these attempts to approve a state sickness insurance were taking place, the friendly societies survived as a way to cover the risk of sickness among the common people. Accounting data indicate the increasingly significant weight of medical and pharmaceutical provisions compared with monetary pensions, verifying the concentration of objectives in healthcare coverage. However, during the Primo de Rivera dictatorship and the Second Republic, a series of factors were accumulating that explain the start of the crisis of this model. On the one hand, the previously mentioned increase in state intervention, as in the case of maternity insurance, eliminated some coverage needs. On the other hand, the creation of private insurance companies, created especially by the medical profession, and employers' relief funds, increased the private offer of coverage. The lack of interest of young workers in the friendly societies must also be taken into account. This led to an increase in

---

need for professional inspection.

[14]This was the case, for example, of the *Montepío de la Caridad*, a society founded in Palma de Mallorca in 1857 and which operated until 1951. In 1918 it had incorporated the service of two midwives, a service that was continued until 1930. As from 1931, this service disappeared from the society's list of expenses.

the average age of members, with the consequent increase in costs and medical fees. In some cases, the number of supporting members went down in view of the increase of class conflicts during the Second Republic (Rivera Blanco 1994). The *coup de grâce* for the friendly societies came from the Franco regime and the approval, finally, of a state-run compulsory sickness insurance.

The cost structure of *La Protección*, one of the oldest friendly societies founded in Majorca in 1856, allows us to see how most of the funds were devoted to sickness benefits and medical fees in the first decades of the twentieth century. However, the former lost weight in the total expenditure after the First World War, while the medical costs increased until they accounted for more than the half of the society's spending in the 1930s. At this juncture, protection of the income of the sick lost importance compared to the provision of medical and pharmaceutical care. Nor should it be overlooked that the cost of medical fees increased during the Second Republic (1931–1936), and especially in the first years after the Civil War, when medical associations approved substantial salary increases. In particular, Fullana and Marimón (1994) affirm that the society's most serious problem occurred in 1940, when the practitioners demanded substantial increases in their fees, approved by the medical association. This resulted in a 30% increase in the *montepío's* expenses. Meanwhile, some medical specialties were gradually incorporated into the insurance coverage during this period, including, among others, surgeons, ophthalmologists, dentists and the services of midwives.

On the other hand, despite the fact that it is not perceptible in the analysis of the expenditure of the mutual societies studied, there are qualitative sources that indicate that, during these years, medical advances and the application of new treatments and medicines (sulphonamides, etc.) increased pharmaceutical costs, upsetting the accounts of the mutual societies. The advances in bacteriology and immunology, thanks to the discoveries of Pasteur and Koch, galvanised pharmacological medicine. In 1928, Sir Alexander Fleming discovered the first antibiotic, penicillin, and the drugs started to come into circulation during the following decade, although they did not come into general use until the Second World War (Menéndez-Navarro and Rodríguez-Ocaña 2003: 207–16). Although in Spain in the 1930s most pharmacists continued to prepare their ointments from magistral formulas and using traditional methods, these professional practices had their days numbered. Industrially produced medicines would end up taking over the market (Rodríguez Nozal 2007: 137).

Industrial medication was legalised in Spain by the Stamp Act of 1892 and its corresponding implementing regulation. The Royal Health Council (*Real Consejo de Sanidad*) defined this product as "those medicines whose composition is wholly or partially unknown and which are dispensed in boxes, jars, bottles or packets with labels that state the name of the medicine, its uses and the dosage". After several failed attempts, the first Spanish regulation for the manufacture and sale of pharmaceutical specialities was published in 1919, but this legal measure was not actually implemented. Finally, the regulation of 1924 established the basic conditions. Medical and pharmaceutical advances undoubtedly affected the already precarious

Table 5.7 Expenditure of *Montepío La Protección* (1901–1950) (as percentage of total)

	Porter	Sickness benefit	Death benefit	Medical fees	Medical expenses	Other medicines	Total
1911	6.66	40.60	7.20	33.51	2.00	10.00	9381.01
1913	6.56	49.41	6.69	33.14	2.06	2.11	9713.44
1915	8.25	36.62	8.03	43.24	2.40	1.42	7465.63
1917	8.89	39.14	9.10	38.55	3.01	1.28	8235.42
1918	8.93	41.18	9.57	34.89	3.86	1.54	8879.69
1919	9.78	29.30	6.52	45.09	1.61	4.85	6893.85
1920	7.95	14.70	3.74	33.73	0.74	39.10	13,341.52
1930	11.95	24.31	6.61	54.46	2.08	0.56	9069.81
1931	11.72	28.56	5.97	50.91	2.10	0.71	9211.05
1932	12.27	28.08	5.68	50.69	1.33	1.92	8797.85
1933	13.92	20.37	4.51	57.74	1.81	1.62	7753.85
1934	13.63	23.90	4.41	55.95	0.90	1.18	7923.55
1935	14.74	13.90	8.19	57.69	1.28	4.16	7323.00

Source: *Archivo del Reino de Mallorca*, Gobierno Civil. Asociaciones 1583/55

budgets of the friendly societies (Table 5.7). In particular, the impact of the Spanish influenza of 1918–1920 can clearly be seen in society expense accounts.

From a territorial point of view, mutual insurance coverage in Spain continued to be very unequal, being concentrated above all in the most industrialised regions with a greater weight of urban population and wage-earners (Catalonia, the Basque Country, Madrid and Valencia). According to the figures available, the majority of friendly societies (not dependent on any company) were concentrated in Catalonia, which was home to 73.39% of these societies and 56.26% of their members in 1915 (INP 1927: 99). In particular, the province of Barcelona – the most industrial in Spain at this time – set itself up as the dynamic centre of Catalan associationism. In 1896 the Catalan Federation of Mutual Provident Societies was founded, the first of its kind in Spain, which then became the Federation of Friendly Societies of the Province of Barcelona in 1918. The intention was that the *Mancomunidad de Cataluña* (a federation of the four Catalan provincial councils) intervene directly in fomenting, regulating and organising social welfare in Catalonia. These demands were finally met in the Constitution of 1931 and the Catalan Autonomy Statute, which recognised the exclusive competence of the Catalan government over its mutual institutions. Later, the Catalan Act of 1934 established the legal bases for cooperatives, mutual societies and agricultural trade unions and dedicated a specific chapter to the Federation.[15] Catalan legislation was pioneering in Spain, where the outdated and imprecise law of associations of 1887 continued in force.

[15] For more on these aspects, see the official website (link: http://www.mutualitats.com), Moreta i Amat (1991) and Sola i Gussinyer (1994: 71–86). In 1935 the federation spread to the whole of Catalonia and became known as the Federation of Friendly Societies of Catalonia. These laws were repealed after Franco's victory in the Civil War.

Meanwhile, in the country's other main industrial zones, such as Asturias, Biscay, Guipúzcoa or Madrid, there was a greater number of societies linked to large companies typical of the Second Industrial Revolution (large-scale iron and steel industry, electricity, textiles, paper industry and transport), which had developed later and were of a more modern nature. This trend had already begun in the late nineteenth century in areas such as Biscay, where employers' *montepíos* were created in the iron and steel and transport industries in the 1880s (Pérez Castroviejo 2010: 137). In some cases, the management offered programmes of healthcare coverage with the aim of improving their workers' working and living conditions and thereby reducing strike action. In other cases, the management realised that in order to improve the conduct of their workers and maintain the loyalty of the employees most difficult to replace, it was necessary to combine discipline with a system of incentives geared towards supplementing wages and/or social coverage (Martínez Vara 2006: 105). Hence, these companies went from offering the services of staff doctors and nurses to attend to accidents that occurred in the workplace to creating associations with medical staff from outside the company who provided their members (workers of the company) free medical and pharmaceutical care. These associations were usually funded by employees' fees and by considerable contributions from the company itself. On occasions, the association entered into an agreement with an outside sanatorium for surgical operations and hospital convalescence, when this was required by the member, while the wage for the working days lost due to being off sick was the responsibility of the respective companies. This was the case with some electricity companies in Madrid, as Aubanell Jubany (2002) explains. Members' relatives could also voluntarily join the association on payment of the corresponding fees.

This phenomenon also spread to public companies such as tobacco factories or railway companies, sometimes located in less industrial zones. It seems clear that the high costs of the systematised system of protection limited the viability of the mutual societies founded by companies to firms of a certain size and number of workers, which had the capacity to organise and administrate complex programmes of welfare and healthcare coverage (Aubanell Jubany 1998). On the contrary, smaller companies could not meet these costs, so they opted for more paternalistic and interim practices.[16]

The functioning of these company mutuals had some special characteristics, as the majority were controlled by the firms and were funded by fees deducted from the workers' wages (around 2% of the wage) supplemented by contributions from the company itself, as can be seen in different case studies (Aubanell Jubany 2002; Martínez Vara 2006; Vilar Rodríguez 2010; Marín Casado 2015). Generally speaking, the company also reserved for itself the tutelage and patronage of the society; controlled the board of directors, where there was a minority workers' representation; and supervised the system of benefits. In most cases, the benefits and

---

[16] For more on the origin of the first company hospitals and the setting up of healthcare services within companies, see Menéndez Navarro (2010).

provisions were of better quality than in the workers' friendly societies, as they offered specialised medical attention for employees and their families, medicines in approved pharmacies, hospital admissions and surgical operations and also a cash benefit. In larger companies with a high risk of industrial accidents (such as in the mining operations of Rio Tinto Company in Huelva or La Unión in Cartagena), they installed their own hospitals and dispensaries to attend to workers who had suffered an accident and to carry out appropriate medical examinations (Menéndez Navarro and Rodríguez Ocaña 1992; Martínez Soto et al. 2012). Some of these facilities improved over time, setting up competent medical teams and incorporating some specialist hospital treatment. All in all, the workers who benefited from these systems were a minority as the average size of companies in Spain before the Civil War was fairly small (Soto Carmona 1989: 67).

5.4 Final Reflection

In conclusion it may be affirmed that the friendly societies in Spain, as in all the other countries that are industrialised today, fulfilled two key functions. On the one hand, they played an important economic role by providing aid to workers affected by the temporary or definitive inability to work (sickness, accident or old age); on the other hand, they reduced the uncertainty and helplessness that such situations created for workers' families. This solidary association spread in Spain from the late nineteenth century, despite the low purchasing power of the workers and the state's mistrust of workers' associationism. For these societies, sickness was the scheme with greatest coverage and the one which, in the long term, drove their dissemination and expansion.

In the first stages of development in the second half of the nineteenth century, cash aid to make up for lost wages while sick was the main help provided by these institutions. To this end, each society set up a bureaucratic and regulatory framework based on the figure of a supervisory doctor during the period of sickness and also auxiliaries who controlled fraud and infringements. Benefits were small, but nevertheless alleviated the lack of income for up to a few months while workers were unable to work, although they were not able to solve the problems of chronic illnesses. Over time, this initial pecuniary aid gradually lost weight in the expenditure of these entities, with the medical and pharmaceutical care of members being promoted as the twentieth century unfolded. The structure of these societies was modified with the creation of ever more complex medical teams and the introduction of coverage by specialists such as obstetrician-gynaecologists, midwives, dentists and eye specialists.

As with the process that Murray described for the United States, the decline of the friendly societies in Spain started in the 1940s. However, this was not so much due to the competence of private insurance companies, as in the former case, but rather owing to state intervention with the passage of compulsory sickness insurance and the exclusion of mutual associations from the system, as well as the rising cost of medical and pharmaceutical fees. Only a few friendly societies survived, by adopting the form, structure and management of health insurance companies. The rest languished, concentrating on recreational and social activities for their last years.

References

Alarcón CM (1975) El derecho de asociación obrera en España 1839–1900. Revista del Trabajo, Madrid

Aubanell Jubany AM (1998) La gestió laboral de l'empresa elèctrica madrilenya en el primer terç del segle XX. Recerques: Història, economia i cultura 37:137–164

Aubanell Jubany AM (2002) La elite de la clase trabajadora. Las condiciones laborales de los trabajadores de las eléctricas madrileñas en el periodo de entreguerras. Scripta Nova. Electronic Review, 119, 7. Link.: https://revistes.ub.edu/index.php/ScriptaNova/article/view/485

Beito DT (2000) From mutual aid to the welfare state: fraternal societies and social services, 1890–1967. University of North Carolina Press, Chapel Hill

Brückweh K, Schumann D, Wetzell RF, Ziemann B (eds) (2012) Engineering society. The role of the human and social sciences in modern societies, Palgrave-Macmillan, New York

Castillo S (ed) (1994) Solidaridad desde abajo. Trabajadores y Socorros Mutuos en la España Contemporánea. Unión General de Trabajadores y Confederación Nacional de Entidades de Previsión, Madrid

Castillo S, Ortiz de Orruño JM (coords) (1997). Estado, protesta y movimientos sociales. Universidad del País Vasco, Guipúzcoa

Castillo S, Ruzafa R (coords) (2009). La previsión social en la Historia. Siglo XXI, Madrid

Comín Comín F (1994) El Estado y la economía en la España del siglo XX. In: Velarde J, García Delgado JL, Pedreño A (eds) El Estado en la economía española. VIII Jornadas de Alicante sobre Economía Española. Civitas, Madrid, pp 39–65

Cuesta Bustillo J (1988) Los seguros sociales en la España del siglo XX. Hacia los seguros sociales obligatorios. La crisis de la Restauración. Ministerio de Trabajo y Seguridad Social, Madrid

Cuesta Bustillo J (1994) Las Sociedades de Socorros Mutuos en el primer tercio del siglo XX: Sociedad sin Estado: una relación fallida. In: Castillo S (ed) Solidaridad desde abajo. Trabajadores y Socorros Mutuos en la España Contemporánea. Unión General de Trabajadores y Confederación Nacional de Entidades de Previsión, Madrid, pp 409–422

Dreyfus M (1996) Mutual benefit societies in France: a complex endeavour. In: Van der Linden M (ed) Social security mutualism: the comparative history of mutual benefit societies. Peter Lang, Berna, pp 209–224

Dreyfus M (ed) (2009) Les assurances sociales en Europe. Presses Universitaires de Rennes, Paris

Duch Plana M (2019) El mutualismo en Cataluña: la incipiente construcción desde debajo de la ciudadanía social (1890-1936). Historia Contemporánea 61:797–833

Fullana P, Marimón A (1994) Història del 'montepío' de Previsió de l'Arraval de Santa Catalina. Centenari 1894–1994. Palma de Mallorca

Gorsky M (1998) The growth and distribution of English friendly societies in the early nineteenth century. Econ Hist Rev 51(3):489–511

Gorsky M, Sheard S (eds) (2006) Financing medicine: the British experience since 1750. Routledge, New York

Gereña JL (1994) El Espacio mutualista en la sociabilidad popular de la Restauración (1875-1900). El ejemplo asturiano. In: Castillo S (ed) Solidaridad desde abajo. Trabajadores y Socorros Mutuos en la España Contemporánea. Unión General de Trabajadores y Confederación Nacional de Entidades de Previsión, Madrid, pp 205–224

Guinnane TW, Jopp TA, Streb J (2012) The costs and benefits of size. In: Harris B (ed) Mutual insurance, sickness and old age in Europe and North America since 1850. Pickering & Chatto Publishers, London, pp 27–46

Harris B (2004) The origins of the British Welfare State. Social welfare in England and Wales. Palgrave Macmillan, New York, pp 1800–1945

Harris B (2009) The development of social policy in England and Wales, 1800-1945. In: Bochel H, Bochel C, Page R, Sykes R (eds) Social policy: themes, issues and debates. Palgrave, MacMillan, Basingstroke, pp 89–1909

Harris B (ed) (2012) Mutual insurance, sickness and old age in Europe and North America since 1850. Pickering & Chatto Publishers, London

Harris B, Bridgen P (eds) (2007) Charity and mutual aid in Europe and North America since 1800. Routledge, New York

Harris B, Gorsky M, Guntupalli A, Hinde A (2006) Age, sickness and longevity in the late nineteenth and early twentieth centuries: evidence from the Hampshire Friendly Society. Soc Sci Hist 30(4):571–600

INP (1922) Conferencia Nacional de Seguros de Enfermedad, Invalidez y Maternidad (1922). Sobrinos de Sucesora de M, Minuesa de los Ríos, Madrid

INP (1927) La cuestión del seguro de enfermedad ante la X reunión de la Conferencia Internacional del Trabajo, Ginebra, mayo 1927. Sobrinos de Sucesora de M. Minuesa de los Ríos, Madrid

Instituto de Reformas Sociales (1908) Estadística de las Instituciones de Ahorro, cooperación y Previsión el 1 de Noviembre de 1904. Imprenta de los Sucesores de M. Minuesa de los Ríos, Madrid

León-Sanz P (2012) Medical assistance provided by La Conciliación, a Pamplona Mutual Assistance Association (1902-84). In: Harris B (ed) Mutual insurance, sickness and old age in Europe and North America since 1850. Pickering & Chatto Publishers, London, pp 137–166

Marín Casado G (2015) Florecimiento y ocaso de una tipología asociativa. Socorros mutuos artesanos en Vitoria (1849–1949). Sancho el Sabio: revista de cultura e investigación vasca, 38. Link: https://revista.sanchoelsabio.eus/index.php/revista/article/view/39.

Martín Valverde A (1987) La formación del Derecho del Trabajo en España. Introducción. In: Valverde AM, Palomeque MC, Espinosa FP, Dal-Ré FV, Baamonde MEC, Murcia JG (eds) La legislación social en la Historia de España. De la Revolución Liberal a 1936. Congreso de los Diputados, Madrid, pp XV–CXIV

Martínez Quinteiro ME (1984) El nacimiento de los seguros sociales en el contexto del reformismo y la respuesta del movimiento obrero. Studia Histórica 4:61–83

Martínez Soto ÁP, Pérez de Perceval MA, Sánchez Picón A (2012) Entre miseria y dolor. Trabajo y salud en la minería del Sureste (segunda mitad del siglo XIX -primer tercio del XX). In: Cohen A (ed) El trabajo y sus riesgos en la época contemporánea: conocimiento, codificación, intervención y gestión. Icaria, Barcelona, pp 207–248

Martínez Vara T (2006) Salarios y Programas de Bienestar Industrial en la empresa ferroviaria MZA (1915–1935). Investigaciones de Historia Económica 4:101–138

Marucco D (1981) Mutualismo e sistema politico. Il caso italiano (1862–1904). Franco Angeli, Milán

Maza Zorrilla E (1991) El mutualismo y su polivalente papel en la España del siglo XIX (1839–1887). Investigaciones Históricas 11:173–198

Maza Zorrilla E (1995) Sociabilidad formal en Palencia: 1887–1923. In Valentina Calleja González M (coord.), Actas del III Congreso de Historia de Palencia: 30, 31 de marzo y 1 de abril de 1995 (p 425–444). Edad Moderna y Edad Contemporánea, Palencia

Maza Zorrilla E (coord) (2002) Sociabilidad en la España Contemporánea: historiografía y problemas metodológicos. Universidad de Valladolid, Instituto de Historia Simancas, Valladolid

Maza Zorrilla E (coord) (2003) Asociacionismo en la España contemporánea. Vertientes y análisis interdisciplinar. Universidad de Valladolid, Valladolid

Menéndez Navarro A (2010) Hospitales de empresa: los primeros pasos de la medicina del trabajo. In: VVAA (ed) Trabajo y salud: desde la protección a la prevención. Instituto Nacional de

Seguridad e Higiene en el Trabajo, Fundación Francisco Largo Caballero, Mutua Fraternidad-Muprespa, Madrid, pp 328–345

Menéndez Navarro A, Rodríguez Ocaña E (1992) Aproximación al estudio de los recursos asistenciales sanitarios en los establecimientos minero-metalúrgicos españoles a comienzos del siglo XX. In: Huertas R, Campos R (coord.), Medicina social y clase obrera en España (siglos XIX y XX) (pp. 263–293). Fundación de Investigaciones Marxistas, Madrid

Menéndez-Navarro A, Rodríguez-Ocaña E (2003) From "accident medicine" to "factory medicine": Spanish occupational medicine in the twentieth century. In: Grieco A, Fano D, Carter T, Iavicoli S (eds) Origins of occupational health associations in the world. Elsevier, Amsterdam, pp 207–216

Montero García F (1988) Los Seguros sociales en la España del siglo XX. Orígenes y antecedentes de la previsión social. Los seguros sociales en la España del siglo XX. Ministerio de Trabajo y Seguridad Social, Madrid

Moreta i Amat M (1991) Cataluña en el movimiento mutualista de previsión social en España. Unpublished manuscript

Murray JE (2007) Origins of American health insurance: a history of industrial sickness funds. Yale University Press, New Haven

Nieto Sánchez JA, Lopez Barahona V (2020) Guilds, confraternities and mutual support in medieval and early modern Spain. In: Hellwege O (ed) Professional guilds and the history of insurance. Duncjer & Humblot, Berlin, pp 193–216

Pérez Castroviejo P (2010) La asistencia sanitaria de los trabajadores: beneficencia, mutualismo y previsión en Vizcaya, 1876-1936. Revista de la Historia de la Economía y de la Empresa 4:127–152

Pons J, Vilar M (2011) Friendly societies, commercial insurance and the state in sickness risk coverage: the case of Spain (1880-1944). Int Rev Soc Hist 56(1):71–101

Pons J, Vilar M (2014) El seguro de salud privado y público en España: su análisis en perspectiva histórica (1880–2010). Prensas Universitarias de Zaragoza, Zaragoza

Porras Gallo MI (1999) Un foro de debate sobre el seguro de enfermedad: Las Conferencias del Ateneo de Madrid de 1934. Asclepio LI(1):159–183

Radelet M (1991) Mutualisme et syndicalisme. Presses Universitaires de la France, Paris, Ruptures et convergences de l'Ancien Régime à nos jours

Rivera Blanco A (1994) Desarrollo y crisis del modelo de sociedad de socorros (Vitoria, 1849–1938). In: Castillo S (ed) Solidaridad desde abajo. Trabajadores y Socorros Mutuos en la España Contemporánea. Unión General de Trabajadores y Confederación Nacional de Entidades de Previsión, Madrid, pp 142–143

Rodríguez Nozal R (2007) Sanidad, farmacia y medicamento industrial durante la II República (1931–1936). ILUIL 30:123–150

Rodríguez Ocaña E (1990) La asistencia médica colectiva en España hasta 1936. In: VVAA (ed) Historia de la Acción Social pública en España. Ministerio de Trabajo y Seguridad Social, Madrid, pp 321–360

Solà i Gussinyer P (1994) El mutualismo contemporáneo en una sociedad industrial. Anotaciones sobre el caso catalán. In: Castillo S (ed) Solidaridad desde abajo. Trabajadores y Socorros Mutuos en la España Contemporánea. Unión General de Trabajadores y Confederación Nacional de Entidades de Previsión, Madrid, pp 71–86

Solà i Gussinyer P (2003) El Mutualismo y su función social: sinopsis histórica. Ciriec – España. Revista de Economía Pública, Social y cooperativa 44:175–198

Soto Carmona Á (1989) El trabajo industrial en la España contemporánea, 1874–1936. Anthropos, Madrid

Van der Linden M (ed) (1996) Social security mutualism: the comparative history of mutual benefit societies. Peter Lang, Bern

Van Leeuwen MHD (2007) Historical welfare economics in the nineteenth century: mutual aid and private insurance for burial, sickness, old age, widowhood, and unemployment in the

Netherlands. In: Harris B, Bridgen P (eds) Charity and mutual aid in Europe and North America since 1800. Routledge, New York, pp 89–130
Vilar M, Pons J (2012) Economic growth and demand for health coverage in Spain: the role of friendly societies (1870-1942). In: Harris B (ed) Mutual insurance, sickness and old age in Europe and North America since 1850. Pickering & Chatto Publishers, London, pp 65–88
Vilar Rodríguez M (2010) La cobertura social a través de las sociedades de socorro mutuo, 1839–1935. ¿Una alternativa al Estado para afrontar los fallos de mercado? In: Pons Pons J, Silvestre Rodríguez J (eds) Los orígenes del Estado del Bienestar en España, 1900–1945: los seguros de accidentes, vejez, desempleo y enfermedad (p 85–122). Prensas Universitarias de Zaragoza, Zaragoza

Chapter 6
A Difficult Consensus: The Making of the Spanish Welfare State

Sergio Espuelas

Abstract Since the 1880s, the Spanish government tried to promote social insurance to achieve political stability. However, a proper welfare state did not develop until the late 1970s. Weak fiscal capacity plus persistent disagreement on who should assume the financial cost of new social programs explain this delay. Before the Spanish Civil War (1936–1939), social reform advanced very slowly. Given the lack of fiscal capacity, Spanish policy makers initially promoted contributory social insurance schemes, mostly financed by employers' and employees' compulsory contributions with little public subsidy. To reduce social conflict, rural laborers were included in these programs along with industrial workers. This, however, generated strong business opposition from both rural landowners and small-sized, labor-intensive businesses (which predominated in Spain). With the advent of democracy in 1931, new social programs were devised, but redistribution demands focused on land reform, an ambitious and controversial policy that eventually led to the outbreak of the Spanish Civil War. After the war, the Franco dictatorship consolidated a conservative social insurance model. Social benefits were kept very low and funding relied on employers' and employees' compulsory contributions. The repression of the labor movement alongside trade protectionism allowed companies to easily transfer the cost of social insurance to wages and final prices. The introduction of income tax, after the restoration of democracy in 1977, led to a new social protection model. Tax-funded, noncontributory programs increased and social protection was extended beyond those in stable employment. Unlike in 1931, in 1977, the political consensus necessary to develop social policy was reached. In addition to economic modernization and population aging, decreasing inequality and the example set by the social pacts that spread throughout Europe after World War II must have been crucial in this sense.

S. Espuelas (✉)
Universitat de Barcelona, Barcelona, Spain
e-mail: sergio.espuelas@ub.edu

P. Gray et al. (eds.), *Standard of Living*, Studies in Economic History,
https://doi.org/10.1007/978-3-031-06477-7_6

Keywords Social insurance · Labor movement · Social benefits · Income tax · Welfare state

6.1 Introduction

Political instability was a notorious feature of nineteenth- and twentieth-century Spain. It became particularly intense after World War I and peaked in the period 1936–1939 with the outbreak of the Spanish Civil War. Indeed, the country went through two dictatorships—that of Primo de Rivera (1923–1930) and that of Franco (1939–1977)—before the consolidation of democracy in 1977. From the inception of modern social policy, in the late nineteenth century, the explicit objective of the Spanish government was to promote social peace. However, unlike many of its European neighbors, Spain was unable to successfully establish most of the social programs that today we associate with the welfare state (such as old-age and disability pensions, public healthcare, or unemployment insurance). A proper welfare state did not develop until the late 1970s and early 1980s. Even today, when Spain is compared to other European countries, some deficiencies persist. What explains this late development? Why was Spain unable to develop a comprehensive welfare state earlier? Many studies have highlighted the importance of economic and demographic modernization plus the advent of democracy as key factors in the long-term development of the welfare state (Lindert 2004). A number of theories have also emphasized the role of specific actors. According to power resource theories, for example, the demands of the labor movement were crucial (Hicks 1999). However, employers (especially large-sized, capital-intensive companies) also supported social legislation in countries such as the UK or Germany (Mares 2003; Hellwig 2005). Similarly, in Scandinavia, the support of small- and medium-sized farmers was crucial for the development of universal social programs in the late nineteenth and early twentieth century (Baldwin 1990). This suggests that social policy outcomes are often the result of some sort of cross-class alliance and a mixture of social interests.

Several studies have indicated that it is easier to achieve political consensus for social policy expansion in relatively homogeneous and egalitarian societies, where social affinity (between different social groups) is usually higher and redistribution costs lower (Lindert 2004; Bénabou 2005). These factors seem to have played an important role in Spain. The Spanish government proved unable to raise funds to finance new social programs until the 1977 tax reform. Given this lack of fiscal capacity, Spanish policy makers placed an emphasis on contributory social insurance schemes (which were mostly financed by employers' and employees' contributions). However, this generated strong business opposition, especially from rural employers and small-sized businesses, which predominated in Spain. The different political regimes that existed in Spain throughout the twentieth century tried to promote various social protection models. However, the political consensus needed to create (and finance) a comprehensive social protection system was not reached until the late 1970s. The following sections explain the story of this difficult consensus.

6.2 Early Measures and Sources of Social Conflict

In 1883, the Spanish government created the Commission for Social Reform (in Spanish, the CRS: *Comisión de Reformas Sociales*), which was intended to study the living conditions of the working class and to propose measures to improve them. Two years earlier, in the German Reichstag, Bismarck had advocated for the promotion of social insurance to achieve political support from the working class. Shortly afterward, a comprehensive social insurance scheme was introduced that included sickness insurance (1883), workplace accident compensation (1884), and old-age pensions (1889). In Spain, the years 1881–1883 were marked by intense social unrest affecting both rural and urban centers. Some examples are the strikes in cities such as Barcelona, Valencia, and Madrid, or the events related to *La Mano Negra* ("The Black Hand") in Andalusia.[1] However, unlike the preceding decades, repression was not the government's only response. After decades of bitter political dispute (including three civil wars in 1833–1839, 1847–1849, and 1872–1876), the Conservative Party and the Liberal Party reached an agreement to alternate peacefully in office during the Bourbon Restoration (1874–1923). This allowed for some political stability, albeit at the price of widespread corruption. To guarantee this alternation in power, before each election, the incumbent party ceded power to an interim government led by the other party, which organized the election and was always able to guarantee its own victory by means of extensive political patronage, vote buying, mass fraud, and even direct coercion (Moreno Luzón 2007).

As part of these attempts to achieve more political stability, the government tried to integrate new emerging social movements (especially, the labor movement) and reduce social unrest in rural areas. Deployment of the police and even the army to deal with social unrest remained a commonplace during the Restoration period. However, in the period 1881–1883 (under the liberal rule of President Sagasta), labor protests became increasingly tolerated by the government. Shortly afterward, in 1887, the Associations Law was passed and union rights were recognized, allowing for the gradual growth of the labor movement (Pérez Ledesma 1990). The first mass demonstration of the Spanish labor movement took place in 1891, with the celebration of May Day. In 1890, the government complemented recognition of social rights with the extension of voting rights to all men. In parallel, publication of the encyclical *Rerum Novarum* in 1891 stimulated the rise of social Catholicism and Conservative Party factions more willing to support social policy. All this contributed to consolidate the reformist trends initiated in 1883.

In the preamble to the Royal Decree creating the CRS, Segismundo Moret (Minister of the Interior at that time) acknowledged that Spanish social policy was

---

[1] Allegedly, *La Mano Negra* was a secret anarchist organization to which the government attributed a number of violent actions, including the destruction of crops and even murders. According to Tuñón de Lara (1972), however, as a formal organization, *La Mano Negra* never existed. Rather, the Spanish government leveraged political violence in rural Andalusia as an excuse to initiate severe repression and quell peasant revolts.

underdeveloped compared to other European countries and that "it was not possible to maintain this situation without lessening public peace" (reproduced in Castillo 1985, p. CXLIII). The explicit objective of the CRS was to achieve "[social] peace (…) between the two large production factors: labor and capital" (p. CXLIV) and channel labor demands away from revolutionary measures. The government, however, focused not only on the *new* conflicts emerging in industrial cities but also on the *traditional* conflicts of rural areas. Nineteenth-century Spanish agriculture was characterized by high land inequality. In southern Spain, large estates (or *latifundios*) represented more than half of the total rural area, and peasant uprisings had been common since the early nineteenth century (Malefakis 1970). After the visit of Bakunin's envoy, Giuseppe Fanelli, to Spain in 1868, rural Andalusia became a breeding ground for anarchist militants. In fact, anarchist unions predominated among Spanish labor unions until at least the 1920s, and landless laborers always represented a large share of total union membership.[2] Since the government's objective was to deactivate revolutionary social movements, paying attention to rural areas was crucial. Spanish social reformers, however, never tried to implement any type of land reform to change the structure of land ownership. Rather, they hoped to find a way to "alleviate the evils affecting the rural working classes," so that "property can exist safely" (Castillo 1985, p. CXLV).

The CRS was initially charged with a number of social tasks: to promote the regulation of child and female labor, and of working conditions in general in industrial factories; to stimulate the creation of *Jurados Mixtos* (to resolve industrial disputes between employers and employees); and to encourage the creation of old-age and disability pension funds, as well as agricultural banks and reforms facilitating rural laborers' access to land (p. CXLIX). However, the only significant work undertaken by the Commission before 1890 was an ambitious study on the conditions of the working class that compiled a great deal of information but did not result in any specific policy measures. In fact, both socialist and anarchist unions viewed the CRS with skepticism and were convinced that it would not succeed in improving workers' living conditions (De la Calle 2004). In 1890, the CRS was reformed and became a sort of advisory body for the government; but again no specific measures were introduced until 1900, when the occupational accidents law was passed. This law obliged industrial employers to pay mandated benefits to their employees in case of work-related accidents. However, the initial impact of this measure was very limited. The benefits established by the government were low and employers often failed to fulfill their commitments due to lack of inspection

[2] In 1882, 20,915 of the 57,934 members of the Spanish Anarchist Federation were agricultural workers, mostly from Andalusia, and total Andalusian membership (38,349) still far exceeded that of industrial Catalonia (13,201) (Malefakis 1970, p. 159). In 1919, the anarchist union CNT (*Conferederación Nacional del Trabajo*) had 700,944 members, while the socialist union UGT (*Unión General de Trabajadores*) had 150,382 members (Silvestre 2003, appendix). The initial growth of the UGT was slower than that of the anarchist unions, and more restricted to industrial and urban areas such as Madrid and the Basque Country. When the UGT eventually surpassed the number of affiliates of the CNT in the 1930s, it was possible due to a large increase in its rural affiliates.

(Silvestre and Pons 2010). This anticipated two permanent features of social policy in Spain: employers' opposition to social reform and the inability (unwillingness perhaps) of the government to enforce social legislation.

6.3 From Voluntary, State-Subsidized Insurance to Compulsory Insurance

In 1903, the former CRS was replaced by the Institute of Social Reform (in Spanish, the IRS: *Instituto de Reformas Sociales*). Again, its objectives were to promote social legislation and oversee its enforcement. To achieve social legitimacy, the IRS was expected to include representatives from employees and employers alike in its decision-making bodies. Employer representation, however, was very limited, partly because employers showed little interest in participating, and partly because of a long-standing tradition of individualism among Spanish business groups. Labor representation was also very limited. The anarchist union, the CNT (*Confederación Nacional del Trabajo*), rejected any kind of collaboration with the government (as had already happened with the CRS), being convinced that the IRS was useless and a distraction from the (revolutionary) interests of the working class. In turn, the board of directors of the IRS did not consider the social Catholic unions to be genuine representatives of labor interests because they brought together within a single organization both employers and employees. As a result, labor representation relied almost exclusively on the socialist union, the UGT (*Unión General de Trabajadores*), which this time proved more willing to collaborate in the government's reformist agenda (Montero 1988).

The IRS was unable to promote the permanent social pacts between labor and capital sought by the government, but it played a very active role in promoting social legislation. One of the projects emerging from the IRS was the National Institute of Social Security (in Spanish, the INP: *Instituto Nacional de Previsión*), created in 1908 to manage what was known as the *Retiro Obrero*, or worker's retirement fund. This was a voluntary, State-subsidized old-age pension scheme. Potential beneficiaries were all wage earners (from industry and agriculture alike) with an annual income of less than 3000 pesetas, which was a high threshold at that time.[3] When designing the *Retiro Obrero*, the government followed the example of the voluntary insurance schemes, with little public subsidies, established in France, Belgium, and Italy, instead of the compulsory insurance model prevailing in Germany (Montero 1988; Murray 2003, 2007). This is in part explained for ideological reasons. Spanish social reformers believed that voluntary insurance had the advantage of ensuring that workers would be actively involved in obtaining a solution to their problems because in order to obtain the governmental subsidy, workers

[3] In 1910, the average daily wage in industry was 2.88 pesetas. Assuming 280 working days per year, this would indicate an annual wage of 806.40 pesetas (see Vilar (2004), p. 156).

had to voluntarily join an insurance fund (and pay the corresponding fees). In contrast, compulsory insurance, it was said, would not promote individual virtues, as "its automatic retentions on the pay-roll (…) do not compel the insured person to adopt a pro-saving attitude" (Eza 1914, p. 43).

However, voluntary insurance schemes were also preferred for practical reasons, since they entailed a much lower cost for the government. Compulsory insurance was considered an "overwhelming and monstrous bureaucratic mechanism," whereas voluntary State-subsidized insurance programs provided an effective means to "alleviate government burdens," as administration was left to private funds (González and Oyuelos 1914; pp. 230 and 267). Some social reformers even argued that social insurance would help reduce public spending on traditional poor relief: "The State budget cannot meet all social needs (…). The more the government promotes and channels social insurance, the less it will have to attend in the future to expenditure on poor relief, which is overwhelming for the public treasury" (Maluquer 1926, p. 220). As in Germany, more than fighting poverty, the Spanish government's objective was to integrate the labor movement politically. But unlike Germany, Spain tried to avoid compulsory insurance for as long as possible. The Spanish government was reluctant to assume any increasing cost to improve social protection, and refused to significantly alter the tax structure. As one might expect, the *Retiro Obrero* had a very limited impact in this context. In 1918, after 10 years in force, only around 1% of the active population was covered (Elu 2010).

Before World War I, the labor movement was too weak to influence government policies. There were some outbreaks of violence and mass demonstrations before 1913, such as the 1909 *Semana Trágica*, which plunged Barcelona into violent anticlerical riots, and the 1903–1904 wave of rural strikes. However, even in 1910, union membership only accounted for around 1% of the active population (Silvestre 2003). This changed quite suddenly during World War I. The economic disturbance caused by the war and the contagious effect of the Russian Revolution led to a huge increase in social unrest. Largo Caballero (a socialist representative in the Spanish parliament) attributed the "entire labor mobilization occurring from 1916 to the general strike in August [1917]" to "the high cost of living and the lack of work" (cited in Espuelas 2013a, p.87). Union density increased substantially in this context, reaching 12% of the active population in 1920. To regain political stability, the government tried to stimulate the development of social legislation. In 1917, in a *Conference for Social Insurance*, the government made a commitment to create a comprehensive social insurance system (covering workplace accidents, old age, illness, maternity leave, and unemployment). This time, the government recognized that, to be effective, social insurance had to be compulsory.

After the conference, the Socialist Party (which had won its first seat in parliament in 1910) demanded that the government honor its social promises. Several projects, including the creation of new unemployment and health insurance schemes and the extension of workplace accident insurance to agriculture, were discussed in parliament and within the INP. As shown by Domenech (2011), the greater executive powers of governments after 1917 in response to political crises allowed for a faster pace of reform. However, as for social insurance, the only program that came to fruition was the 1919 *Retiro Obrero Obligatorio* or Compulsory Worker's Retirement fund. As before World War I, the government remained reluctant to assume the financial cost of new social programs. Public deficits were constant during the early decades of the twentieth century, and the government proved unable to collect sufficient taxes to maintain a balanced public budget (Comín 1996). The creation of tax-funded programs, such as the 1891 Danish old-age pensions, was never contemplated in this context. And when the Compulsory Worker's Retirement scheme was established in 1919, workers were not required to make compulsory contributions. The government was trying to forestall labor opposition to its new social reforms, in a context of intense social unrest. However, this meant that employers would assume the bulk of the cost of social insurance.

In fact, business opposition to social insurance in Spain was fierce, especially among small-sized labor-intensive companies, as seems to have been the case in other European countries as well. Resistance to compulsory social insurance was often more severe among small-sized companies and rural landowners than among large-sized, capital-intensive companies, which in some cases even supported the introduction of social insurance as a means to enhance productivity growth, reduce labor unrest, or gain competitiveness over smaller rivals. Often, large firms had social insurance policies for their employees before mandated benefits were established (Murray 2007; Mares 2003; Hellwig 2005). In Spain, however, small-sized companies predominated (Comín and Martín Aceña 1996). Unlike Bismarck's Germany, Spain lacked a broad industrial base willing to support compulsory social insurance. Moreover, unlike many European countries, in which the rural population was often excluded from social insurance, the new Compulsory Worker's Retirement scheme covered both rural and urban workers. As mentioned before, revolutionary movements wielded great influence in rural Spain, especially in areas where large farms predominated. Since the government's objective was to reduce social unrest and channel labor demands through nonrevolutionary measures, extending social insurance to agriculture was crucial. However, this became an additional obstacle to social reform. When the Compulsory Worker's Retirement scheme came into effect, affiliation records in agriculture were very low (Elu 2010), and the combined opposition of rural landowners and small-sized companies frustrated plans to extend workplace accident insurance to agriculture and to create a new unemployment insurance scheme after World War I (Del Rey 1992; Espuelas 2013a).

The labor movement did not show full support for social reform either. Socialist sectors supported the government's social plans and indeed asked for more State intervention; however, revolutionary sectors, basically the anarchist movement, did not trust the government's intentions and viewed social insurance plans as a distraction from the true interests of the working class. The government's inability to fulfill its social promises and the slow pace of social policy development in Spain reinforced the revolutionary position and hindered political integration of the labor movement within the Restoration regime (Barrio 1997). Neither did the political changes of the early 1920s have a positive effect. Until then, the government had proved unable to make good many of its social promises. However, after the military coup of 1923 and the establishment of the Primo de Rivera dictatorship (1923–1930), post-World War I reform attempts were abandoned. The government only introduced some subsidies for large families in 1927, a policy consistent with the heightened influence acquired by the Catholic Church during the dictatorship (Velarde 1990). To regain momentum, social policy had to wait until the arrival of democracy in 1931.

6.4 The Second Republic: Momentum and Limitations

The advent of the Second Republic (1931–1936) marked the beginning of the first truly democratic period in Spanish history. This short period of time generated high hopes for reform among diverse social sectors that aspired to democratize Spanish political and social life. These expectations, however, soon turned into acute social tension, with the highest levels of political mobilization and social unrest in Spanish contemporary history (Pérez Ledesma 1990). During the Second Republic, the Socialist Party became the most voted party, although it never obtained sufficient votes to rule on its own: from 1931 to 1933, it was in office in coalition with other left and center-left parties, while in the second legislature, from 1933 to 1935, it was the main party in opposition, after right and center-right parties reached an agreement to form a government. The growth of the Socialist Party in this new democratic context was due not only to the broadening of its urban and industrial base but also to the rapid consolidation of a broad rural base. By 1932, the socialist union, the UGT, had 1,041,539 members, of whom 445,414 were rural laborers (Tuñón de Lara 1972, p. 857–858).

As in the preceding decades, rural interests conditioned the progress of social policy during the Second Republic. The implicit alliance between landless laborers and industrial workers gave the Socialist Party sufficient political power to launch its program of social reform, and several social rights were included in the 1931 Spanish Constitution. The right to social insurance, for example, was granted in Article 46: "The Republic guarantees to all workers the necessary conditions for a dignified existence. Its legislation will regulate the cases of sickness, accident, unemployment, old-age, disability, and survivor's insurance." Progress in social legislation was particularly striking from 1931 to 1932, when the Socialist Party was in office (Samaniego 1988). The government introduced maternity insurance (granting healthcare during childbirth and maternity leave for working women); created a voluntary, State-subsidized unemployment insurance scheme; and extended workplace accident compensation to agriculture. Moreover, a plan was devised to unify all existing social insurance programs plus new programs (providing healthcare, sickness leave, and disability and survivor's pensions) within a single social security system. However, discussion of the details of this plan dragged on for years, and the military coup of 1936 eventually prevented it from being passed (Samaniego 1988).

The obstacles faced by this unification plan were diverse. Mutual aid associations and commercial insurance companies providing sickness-related benefits opposed government plans because they feared being displaced by State insurance and instead advocated for voluntary programs. Doctors feared the loss of professional freedom that State insurance might entail. They believed that such a program would reduce "the medical classes to the role of simple civil servants, controlled by other administrative civil servants" (cited in Samaniego (1988), p. 368). The government also had to deal with the customary opposition from employers, and to a lesser extent with opposition from workers. In regions and provinces such as Catalonia, Zaragoza, Galicia, and Valencia, strikes were held, often promoted by the anarchist union, the CNT, in protest against the 1931 compulsory maternity insurance scheme. Working women rejected the corresponding mandatory contributions (Pons 2010). The government was aware of this potential opposition, but as the INP put it in a 1936 pamphlet, it hoped that workers' opposition to compulsory contributions would decrease "if the insured person receives instant benefits, such as those granted by health insurance" (INP 1936, p. 39).

A crucial characteristic of the new plan was that it "does not cast on the State any burden that has not already been recognized" (INP 1936, p. 74). This meant that the government would maintain public subsidies for preexisting old-age pension and maternity funds, but the new benefits devised in the unification plan (healthcare, sickness leave, and disability and survivor's pensions) would be entirely financed by employers' and employees' compulsory contributions. The government announced this as a virtue: taxpayers did not need to worry about any *unbearable* burden. But it was precisely this aspect that probably aggravated opposition from employers and employees. Above all, this reflects the Spanish government's persistent unwillingness to assume the cost of new social programs, which was in part the result of weak fiscal capacity. As mentioned before, public deficit was a constant feature of the early decades of the twentieth century, a situation that was exacerbated by World War I and the Great Depression. Left-wing governments in the Second Republic implemented several tax reforms to increase public revenues, raising tax rates on land ownership and industrial equity and introducing a new tax on gasoline. The most important measure was the creation of an income tax in 1932, but even this was a timid reform, unable to solve the government's financial problems.

Only people with annual incomes above 100,000 pesetas were subject to the new income tax, and tax rates ranged between a minimum of 1% and a maximum of 11% for incomes above 1,000,000 pesetas. The 1932 Spanish GDP was 1448 pesetas per person,[4] so the percentage of population subject to the new income tax was very low. Jaume Carner, Minister of Finance at the time, was convinced that this was the only feasible reform, believing that a more ambitious project would have met with insurmountable opposition. He hoped that in the future, the new tax could be gradually extended to a broader segment of the population by lowering the 100,000 peseta threshold (Costa 2000). After these reforms, State revenues increased, but the public deficit remained (Comín 1996).

[4] Prados de la Escosura (2003), p. 521

However, the most ambitious social reform undertaken during the Republican period was the agrarian reform, most actively promoted by the Socialist Party, which had a broad rural base. In launching this reform, the socialists were supported by Manuel Azaña and left-wing republicans, who believed that meeting the socialists' demands was the only way to guarantee that the working classes "would remain loyal to the Republic rather than succumb to Anarcho-syndicalist cries for total opposition" (Malefakis 1970, p. 192). The explicit objective of the agrarian reform was to achieve social peace in rural areas and contribute to economic and political democratization. However, the Spanish government was unable to overcome the predictable opposition from rural landowners and enlist the support of small- and medium-sized farmers. During the first legislature (under the republican-socialist coalition government), the reform advanced very slowly, while during the second (with a right-wing coalition in government), it was practically paralyzed. This first disappointed and then radicalized the Socialist Party's rural base. When the left returned to power in February 1936, the agrarian reform once again made headway, but was halted by the military coup of July 1936. A diversity of factors lay behind the outbreak of the Spanish Civil War, but tensions resulting from the agrarian reform played a crucial role (Simpson and Carmona 2020).

6.5 The Franco Dictatorship: A Conservative Social Insurance Model

The outcome of the Spanish Civil War (1931–1936) was the imposition of the Franco dictatorship (1939–1977). Unlike what had happened after previous civil conflicts, such as the Carlist Wars in the nineteenth century, this time there were no attempts at reconciliation. On the contrary, the goal was to inflict a definitive defeat on the enemy to avoid a re-emergence of the reformist ambitions of the Second Republic (Tusell 2005). The army led postwar repression and the country remained under military law until April 1948. Political parties were outlawed, with the exception of the Falange Española, the official party. In the domain of labor relations, employers and employees were forced to join the so-called vertical union. Independent labor unions were prohibited, as were strikes, which were considered sedition and therefore an offense punishable by death penalty (Pérez Ledesma 1990). Business associations, by contrast, remained legal and could even act as pressure groups (Molinero and Ysas 1998). Many businessmen and landowners became members of parliament, forming part of the dictatorship's political elite together with high-ranking civil servants, the military, the Catholic Church, and politicians from monarchic groups and the Falange (Jerez 1996).

The Spanish economy recovered very slowly after the Civil War. Pre-war income levels were not restored until 1952. Real wages performed even worse: industrial real wages did not recover pre-war levels until 1962–1963. In agriculture, real wages in 1959 represented only 77% of the real wage in 1936. This poor performance was mostly the result of curtailing workers' rights (Vilar 2004). As for social protection, most of the social insurance schemes created before the Civil War continued, the only exception being unemployment insurance, which was abolished and not reintroduced until 1961. The dictatorship's policy makers believed that unemployment benefits only contributed to laziness: Girón de Velasco, Ministry of Labor between 1941 and 1957, claimed that "unemployment insurance [in Europe] fatally engendered a tendency to indolence and indirectly contributed to vice and even degeneration" (1951, p.19). The Republican project for social insurance unification was also abandoned. The Franco dictatorship, however, did launch some new social programs. During the Civil War, the government created the *Auxilio de Invierno* (Winter Relief), an institution linked to the Falange, that shortly afterward was renamed the *Auxilio Social* (Social Relief). Its initial mission was to meet the social needs derived from the war on the side of pro-Franco rebels. Later on, as Franco's army advanced through Republican areas, the *Auxilio Social* became an instrument of propaganda, distributing bread to the population and organizing soup kitchens. Once the war was over, the *Auxilio Social* became a parallel welfare institution to traditional poor relief (Cenarro 2006).

Also during the war, a family allowance called the *Subsidio Familiar* was introduced, which provided bonus payments to all wage earners based on number of children. Pro-family (conservative) policies played a key role in the rhetoric of the dictatorship, and this allowance was largely an outcome of the regime's population ideology and the influence of the Catholic Church's social doctrine, which advocated for a *sufficient* family wage (Velarde 1990). The measure was also aimed at reducing female labor participation. Women's work was attributed with all kinds of social evils:

> mothers are forced to work outside the home because of a lack of resources (…) and the consequences are fatal. Increased maternal mortality during childbirth; increased infant mortality (…); a brutal drop in birth rates (…); no education for the children, [who are] abandoned to the evil teachings of the street; her housework skimped, making the home unpleasant and pushing her husband to the tavern and bar (…) Returning mothers to the home is the ideal and we need to move toward it. The Subsidio Familiar is the most effective way. (Aznar 1943, pp.16–17)

Lastly, a compulsory health insurance scheme (in Spanish, SOE: *Seguro Obligatorio de Enfermedad*) was also set up from 1942 to 1944. According to Girón de Velasco, the goal of this program was to improve health and increase workers' performance, in line with the virtues that nineteenth-century social reformers attributed to social insurance.[5] Girón de Velasco, moreover, attributed an explicitly political function to the new sickness insurance: "proselytism, [to] gain new adepts for the motherland and the revolution" (1943, p. 67). However, despite propaganda, social protection levels remained very low under the Franco dictatorship. In 1958, Spanish social spending was only 3.3% of the GDP, whereas in Italy or Greece, it was above 10% (Table 6.1). Coverage rates remained very low too. Rural workers were largely

[5] See, for example, INP (1936) and Maluquer (1926).

Table 6.1 Public social spending in selected European countries (% of GDP), 1950–2005

	European average	Germany	Belgium	Sweden	Greece	Italy	Spain
1950	8.55	14.67	10.26	7.72		7.37	3.73
1958	11.38	18.17	12.10	10.66	10.44*	12.33	3.33
1966	13.69	19.21	17.03	14.05	8.55	16.32	4.06
1975	19.65	27.15	26.74	21.16	8.64	20.94	11.66
1982	20.84	23.56	25.68	27.85	14.49	19.85	17.74
1990	21.77	22.28	24.89	30.20	16.47	19.95	20.61
1998	23.42	26.26	26.12	30.38	18.56	22.94	20.91
2005	24.38	26.75	26.40	29.43	20.55	24.98	21.06

Source: Espuelas (2013b). *1960

excluded from social protection before 1959,[6] but even in 1959, health insurance only covered 37% of the active population, and the total number of beneficiaries (including the insured person's family) only accounted for 38% of the total population. As for old-age pensions, coverage rates were even lower. In 1959, only 32% of the active population was included in the scheme.[7]

Pension benefits also remained very low in the 1940s and 1950s, as these were only partially indexed to inflation (in a context of high inflation rates). Table 6.2 shows the evolution of old-age pension benefits from 1940 to 1959. As is shown in column 1, average benefits in nominal terms increased gradually. However, when we analyze the evolution in real terms, the result is completely different (column 3). Average real pension benefits decreased constantly between 1940 and 1955. They recovered after 1956, but even in 1959, real benefits were similar to those of 1940. If replacement rates are analyzed, the results are similar. Taking as a reference the average unskilled industrial wage, average replacement rates oscillated between 20 and 30% over the entire time-period (column 5). This means that social protection remained limited to a minimum during the Franco dictatorship. Moreover, this meager social protection network was almost exclusively financed by employers' and employees' compulsory contributions. In 1959, government subsidies to social insurance funds (including old-age pensions, health insurance, and the *Subsidio Familiar*) accounted for 12% of total revenues (INP 1960). This allowed the Franco regime to finance (ungenerous) social insurance without increasing taxation.

Business groups showed little opposition to this social insurance model (at least until the 1960s). During the 1940s and 1950s, the Franco dictatorship adopted an aggressive import substitution policy, alongside very active State economic intervention. Wages and prices were subject to government regulation and labor unions were prohibited, which allowed employers to easily transfer the cost of social insurance to wages (as potential workers' opposition was silenced). In parallel, trade

[6] Rural laborers were excluded from old-age pensions before 1943. Permanent rural laborers were excluded from health insurance until 1953, and nonpermanent rural laborers until 1958.

[7] Data on insured persons and beneficiaries from INP (1960); data on active population and total population from Nicolau (2005)

Table 6.2 Old-age benefits (1940–1959)

Year	Old-age benefits (average) (current pesetas)	Consumer price index	Old-age benefits (average) (1959 pesetas)	Unskilled wage (average) nominal	Replacement rate (%)
1940	70	22.05	334		
1941	86	28.65	317		
1942	88	30.63	305		
1943	85	30.46	293	328	26
1944	81	31.81	268	326	25
1945	86	34.02	266	324	26
1946	96	44.64	227	393	24
1947	92	52.52	185	420	22
1948	93	56.08	174	450	21
1949	123	59.12	221	448	28
1950	148	65.53	239	523	28
1951	162	71.71	240	536	30
1952	150	70.29	226	535	28
1953	129	71.42	190	547	24
1954	134	72.30	197	581	23
1955	130	75.21	182	590	22
1956	248	79.62	329	1004	25
1957	316	88.20	379	1049	30
1958	303	100.00	321	1062	29
1959	309	105.72	309	1082	29

Sources: Average old-age pension benefits are total spending on old-age benefits divided by the number of beneficiaries. Data from the INP Bulletin of Statistical Information (*Boletín de Información Estadística*) (several years), and Jordana (1953); consumer price index from Maluquer (2009); unskilled industrial wage from Vilar (2004), p. 154

protectionism allowed employers to transfer part of the cost of social insurance to final prices and consumers (Espuelas 2012). This situation, however, changed gradually after 1959. To overcome the 1957–1959 crisis, the government devised the 1959 Stabilization Plan. The peseta was devalued to gain international competitiveness, and a strict monetary policy was implemented to defend the new exchange rate. In parallel, a number of liberalizing measures were gradually introduced, and the most aggressive forms of State intervention were abandoned. State control over private investment diminished, and the economy was increasingly opened up to international trade. After an initial recession in 1959–1960, the Spanish economy recovered very rapidly, growing at an average annual rate of 7% between 1960 and 1974.[8]

Economic growth stimulated social policy expansion. Urbanization and population aging generated new social demands, while rising incomes generated higher public revenues (Lindert 2004). Rural-urban migration helped to overcome rural

[8] GDP figures from Prados de la Escosura (2003)

landowners' traditional opposition to social insurance, as these became more willing to accept social insurance in order to retain the population in rural areas. In 1959, the government created the National Mutual Fund for Agrarian Social Security to "place the protection granted to agricultural workers on the same level as that for urban workers" (Decree 613/1959). The gradual growth of a clandestine labor movement also favored social policy expansion from the mid-1960s onward. Between 1956 and 1958, there were a number of strikes demanding higher wages, which started in Pamplona and extended to the Basque Country, Barcelona, and mining areas in Asturias. For the first time since the Civil War, the government's response consisted of a combination of repression and (some) social concessions (Pérez Ledesma 1990). In the context of the aforementioned economic liberalization, the 1958 Collective Agreement Act was passed, allowing employees to negotiate wages and working conditions with employers.

Strikes remained illegal, especially when involving political demands, but they were tolerated when held for economic reasons (i.e., when they were linked to the collective bargaining process legalized in 1958). The number of collective agreements increased rapidly thereafter. In 1962, the number of employees included in a collective agreement was above 2,300,000, while in 1969 it exceeded 3,700,000 (Maluquer and Llonch 2005). This allowed employees to obtain higher wages in exchange for increased productivity, which in turn stimulated economic growth. However, this measure also had unintended consequences for the government. It favored the rise of a new clandestine labor movement, which took advantage of the new organizational opportunities offered by the 1958 collective bargaining law to include political and social demands in labor mobilizations (Pérez Ledesma 1990; Molinero and Ysas 1998). In parallel, new opposition movements supporting workers' demands appeared in the mid-1960s and early 1970s, led by university students and social Catholic groups. In combination, these changes became the main source of political instability in the final years of the Franco dictatorship (Tusell 2005).

Once again, the government's response consisted of a combination of severe political repression and social policy expansion. A new Social Security Act came into effect in 1963/1967, bringing together preexisting social insurance programs under a single and more streamlined social security system. Coverage that had previously been limited to medium- and low-income workers was now extended to all wage earners. This represented some progress toward universal cover, albeit the population without stable ties to the labor market remained marginalized. Social spending grew very rapidly after the 1963/1967 reforms, rising from 4.06% of the GDP in 1966 to 11.7% in 1975 (see Table 6.1). However, the cost of social security remained borne almost exclusively by employers' and employees' compulsory contributions (with very little public subsidy during the entirety of the dictatorship). Growing labor demands and increasing exposure to international trade prevented employers from transferring the cost of social security to wages or final prices as easily as before. As a result, employers' complaints about the unbearable cost of social insurance became recurrent in the 1970s (Cabrera and Del Rey 2002). Moreover, even in 1975, Spanish social spending was only 59% of the European average (Table 6.1). For Spain to catch up with its European neighbors, it would be necessary to wait until the restoration of democracy in 1977.

6.6 Democracy and Convergence with Europe

After Franco's death in 1975, political change accelerated. The transition to democracy, however, coincided with a period of economic downturn and increasing unemployment. In this context, social policy proved crucial for political stability and democratic consolidation. The best example of the social consensus reached during the transition to democracy is the 1977 Moncloa Pacts. Workers' and employers' representatives plus the main political parties agreed to accept wage moderation and macroeconomic stabilization policies to curb inflation, in return for greater social protection, progressive taxation, and the consolidation of political freedoms. One very important outcome of the Moncloa Pacts was the 1977 tax reform and the introduction of income tax in 1978 (Torregrosa-Hetland 2018). This overcame one of the most important historical barriers to the development of Spanish social policy: the lack of fiscal capacity. Public subsidies to social security institutions increased, and the funding of social insurance no longer relied on employers' and employees' compulsory contributions as it had under the Franco dictatorship. In the 1980s, Spanish social spending reached similar levels to that of other southern European countries such as Italy or Greece, although it remained below that of the leading countries, such as Sweden or Germany (Table 6.1). Access to healthcare became universal in 1986, welfare benefits for disabled persons improved substantially after 1982, noncontributory old-age and disability pensions were introduced in 1990, and the regional governments gradually introduced minimum income programs for low-income families throughout the 1990s. All this represented a gradual improvement in social provision, and permitted the expansion of cover to sectors without stable ties to the labor market.

Unlike in 1931, with the arrival of democracy in 1977, the political consensus necessary to develop social policy was reached. There are at least two reasons that seem crucial in this respect. The first one has to do with the evolution of inequality. In 1977, overall inequality was significantly lower than in 1931 (Prados de la Escosura 2008). In egalitarian countries, social affinity between middle- and lower-income groups tends to be higher and the costs associated with redistribution smaller, resulting in more political support for social policy expansion (Lindert 2004; Bénabou 2005; Espuelas 2015). The *nature* of Spanish inequality in 1977 and in 1931 was also substantially different. Until the 1950s, inequality was mostly driven by the gap between property and labor incomes, and particularly by land inequality, which was the main asset of the economy. This helps explain both the insistence on agrarian reform by the progressive governments of the Second Republic and the subsequent political instability. Since land is an immobile asset (with no exit options), when there are threats of expropriation, landowners might be interested in supporting nondemocratic governments to avoid redistribution (Boix 2003). In 1977, instead, wage dispersion had become the main component of inequality. With industrialization, land rents gradually lost relevance in the economy, and inequality became much less dependent on land inequality. This would explain why tax-and-transfer redistribution replaced expropriation demands.

The international context must also have played a crucial role. In the Second Republic, redistributive struggles around land reform were mixed with the rise of fascism and left-wing revolutionary movements in interwar Europe. The outbreak of the Spanish Civil War was in part a precedent for the political violence that assailed the continent during World War II. By contrast, in 1977, Spain had as a reference the social pacts that spread throughout Europe after World War II and that served as a basis for the growth of the welfare state and for preserving political stability. The Moncloa Pacts were the Spanish equivalent of these social pacts. Actually, both the center-right UCD (the *Union de Centro Democrático*) and the Socialist Party stimulated social spending growth when they were in office in the late 1970s and early 1980s. However, the Keynesian consensus established after World War II gradually broke down in the 1980s, leading to social spending stagnation in many European countries. In Spain, social spending also stagnated in this time period, but at a lower level (Fig. 6.1).

From 1985 onward, and especially after the signing of the Maastricht Treaty in 1993, public deficit and inflation control became the main targets of economic policy. As a result, the Spanish government introduced a number of measures to limit social spending (under the rule of both the socialist and the center-right Popular Party). Just as with the 1977 Moncloa Pacts, when both center-right and center-left political parties accepted the Keynesian consensus, in the 1980s and 1990s, both the center-right and the center-left adopted what Offer and Söderberg (2016) call the *market turn*. Guillén and Álvarez (2004) qualify this and say that the Socialist Party *accepted* the European Union's prescriptions for limiting public spending, whereas the Popular Party actually *encouraged* these policies. In any event, it is in this context that the Toledo Pact was signed in 1995 with the support of almost all political representatives at the time. Its purpose was to guarantee the financial stability of the pension system by establishing a clear distinction in the funding sources for contributory and noncontributory pensions. Contributory pensions became linked to the availability of funds from employers' and employees' contributions, which allowed

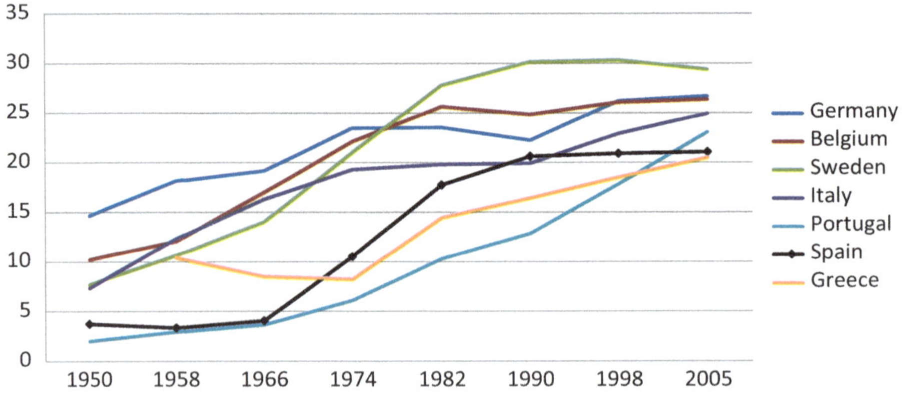

Fig. 6.1 Public social spending in Europe (% of GDP), 1950–2005. (Source: See Table 6.1)

Table 6.3 Public spending on family support (% of GDP), 1980–2010

	Germany	Belgium	Ireland	Sweden	Greece	Italy	Portugal	Spain
1980	2.0	2.9	1.1	3.5	0.3	1.0	0.6	0.5
1985	1.5	2.5	1.4	3.7	0.3	0.9	0.6	0.3
1990	1.8	2.2	1.9	4.0	0.7	0.9	0.7	0.3
1995	2.1	2.2	2.1	3.6	1.0	0.6	0.7	0.4
2000	2.0	2.5	2.0	2.8	1.0	1.2	1.0	0.9
2005	2.0	2.6	2.6	3.2	1.1	1.2	1.2	1.2
2010	2.2	2.8	3.7	3.4	1.4	1.3	1.4	1.5

Source: OECD.stat

for a reduction in government subsidies to social security funds. Noncontributory pensions, in turn, became exclusively financed by government subsidies.[9]

However, one of the main limitations of today's social protection in Spain is that the generosity of noncontributory benefits lags far behind that of contributory benefits. This has led to a kind of dualism in the sense that social protection is significantly better for labor market insiders (with long contribution records and access to contributory benefits). This in turn involves a gender bias, since women have historically had lower activity rates (especially under the Franco dictatorship) and therefore shorter contribution records (León 2002). On the other hand, Spanish public spending on family support remains below that of most European countries (Table 6.3). Parental leave provisions are shorter and family cash benefits and social services for child care are lower. This has limited female labor participation and widened the gender income gap (León and Salido 2016). To some extent, the precariousness of family policy in democratic Spain is a reaction to the central role assigned to (antifeminist) family policy in the propaganda of the dictatorship. The first democratic policy makers omitted references to family policy to avoid being identified with the authoritarian past (Valiente 1996). Later, the restrictions on social spending growth in the mid-1980s and early 1990s hampered the development of alternative (more pro-feminist) family policies. The current gap in aggregate social spending between Spain and Europe is to a large extent the result of this gap in public support to young families and new parents.

6.7 Conclusions

Since 1880s, the Spanish government tried to promote social insurance to achieve political stability, integrate the labor movement politically, and reduce social unrest in rural areas. However, unlike many of its European neighbors, Spain was unable

[9]To qualify for contributory pensions in the Spanish system, a previous contribution record is required, whereas for noncontributory pensions, it is not. Before the Toledo Pact, social insurance funds (receiving compulsory contributions plus government subsidies) could be used to finance either contributory or noncontributory benefits. For more details, see Comín (2010).

to successfully establish most of the social programs that today we associate with the welfare state. Weak fiscal capacity plus persistent disagreement on who should assume the financial cost of new social programs explain this delay. Before the Spanish Civil War, social reform advanced very slowly. Initially, Spanish social reformers promoted voluntary State-subsidized insurance schemes. The Spanish government was reluctant to assume any increasing cost to improve social protection, and (as one might expect) these measures had a very limited impact in this context. After World War I, in a context of intense social unrest, the government advocated for the creation of compulsory social insurance programs. Several projects were discussed. However, the only program that came to fruition was the 1919 compulsory old-age pension scheme. To forestall labor opposition, workers were not required to make compulsory contributions, and to deactivate revolutionary social movements in agriculture, coverage was extended to rural workers. However, this generated strong business opposition, especially from rural employers and small-sized businesses, which predominated in Spain.

With the advent of democracy in 1931, new social insurance programs were introduced, but traditional obstacles persisted. Weak fiscal capacity, plus the opposition from employers, some sectors of the labor movement, and specific interest groups (such as insurance companies or doctors), frustrated government plans to create a comprehensive social security system. However, redistribution demands during this period focused on land reform, an ambitious and controversial policy that eventually led to the outbreak of the Spanish Civil War. After the war, the Franco dictatorship consolidated a conservative social insurance model. Social benefits and coverage rates were kept very low. Even in 1958, Spanish social spending was only 3.3% of GDP, whereas in Italy or Greece, it was above 10%. Moreover, funding relied on employers' and employees' compulsory contributions, which allowed the government to finance (ungenerous) social insurance without increasing general taxation. Business groups showed little opposition to this model. The repression of the labor movement alongside trade protectionism allowed companies to easily transfer the cost of social insurance to wages and final prices.

This situation, however, changed gradually from the 1960s onward. The economy gradually opened up to international trade, economic growth accelerated, and a clandestine labor movement emerged. A new Social Security Act came into effect in 1963/1967, and social spending grew very rapidly thereafter, in part as a result of increasing political instability. Social security remained financed almost exclusively by employers' and employees' compulsory contributions. However, growing labor demands and increasing exposure to international trade prevented employers from transferring the cost of social security to wages or final prices as easily as before. The restoration of democracy in 1977 and the subsequent tax reform led to a new social protection model. Public subsidies to social security institutions increased, and the funding of social insurance no longer relied almost exclusively on employers' and employees' compulsory contributions as it had under the Franco dictatorship. In the 1980s, Spanish social spending reached similar levels to that of other southern European countries such as Italy or Greece, although it remained below that of the leading countries, such as Sweden or Germany.

Unlike in 1931, the arrival of democracy in 1977 did lead to the political consensus necessary to increase taxation and develop social policy. Rapid economic growth, urbanization, and population aging played a role in this sense, but two additional factors must also have been crucial. Firstly, in 1977, inequality was lower and much less dependent on land inequality than in 1931. This would explain why less controversial tax-and-transfer redistribution replaced 1930s' expropriation demands. Secondly, the international context was also very different. Instead of the political extremism that shook interwar Europe, 1977 Spain had as a reference the Keynesian consensus. Somehow, the 1977 Moncloa Pacts were the Spanish equivalent of the social pacts that spread throughout Europe after World War II.

Acknowledgments I thank Alfonso Herranz, Peter Lindert, Javier San Julián, Sara Torregrosa-Hetland, and the participants at the fifth Finland in Comparison Conference and the second Workshop on Public finance in the History of Economic Thought for their comments. Also acknowledged is Javier Silvestre's patience and help. The usual disclaimers apply.

Most of all, I would like to thank John E. Murray. I met John in 2008, when he visited the University of Barcelona as a visiting scholar. At that time, I was in the early stages of my PhD. I distinctly remember John being kind enough to discuss with me what, at the time, were just a few research ideas and bits of data. He made a number of suggestions and even gave me some ideas on how to start publishing my work. My later research departed a bit from the preliminary ideas that I presented to John. But for me (a young scholar who was just starting out) it was very important that a professor from the United States listened to me and gave me advice on how to continue. Of his work, I followed with particular attention his studies on social insurance. I always found his book on the Origins of American Health Insurance to be an excellent example of combining quantitative and qualitative methods. I admired his ability to illustrate through examples and testimonies of the time some of the most relevant findings of the book, as well as the attention that John paid to the incentive problems associated to the design of social insurance. Some of the ideas I had the opportunity to discuss with him are captured in this chapter.

References

Aznar S (1943) Fundamentos y motivos del seguro de subsidios familiares. Revista de la Facultad de Derecho de Madrid, enero-junio

Baldwin P (1990) The politics of Social Solidarity and the Bourgeois Basis of the European Welfare State, 1875–1975. Cambridge University Press, Cambridge

Barrio A (1997) El sueño de la democracia industrial en España. In: Suárez M (ed) La Restauración: entre el liberalismo y la democracia. Alianza, Madrid, pp 1917–1923

Bénabou R (2005) Inequality, technology and the social contract. In: Agion P, Durlauf SN (eds) Handbook of economic growth. Elsevier, Amsterdam, pp 1596–1638

Boix C (2003) Democracy and redistribution. Cambridge University Press, New York

Cabrera M, Del Rey F (2002) El poder de los empresarios: Política e intereses económicos en la España contemporánea, 1875–2000. Taurus, Madrid

Castillo S (ed) (1985) Reformas sociales, Información oral y escrita publicada de 1889 a, vol 1893. Ministerio de Trabajo y Seguridad Social, Madrid

Cenarro A (2006) La sonrisa de Falange: auxilio social en la guerra. Crítica, Barcelona

Comín F (1996) Historia de hacienda pública II. España 1808–1995. Crítica, Barcelona

Comín F (2010) Los seguros sociales y el Estado del Bienestar en el siglo XX. In: Pons J, Silvestre J (eds) Los orígenes del Estado del Bienestar en España, 1900–1945: los seguros de accidentes de trabajo, vejez, desempleo y enfermedad. Prensas de la Universidad de Zaragoza, Zaragoza

Comín F, Martín Aceña P (1996) Rasgos históricos de las empresas en España: un panorama. Revista de Economía Aplicada 12(5):75–123

Costa MT (2000) Biografía del ministro de hacienda Jaume Carner. In: Comín F (ed) La Hacienda desde sus ministros. Del 98 a la guerra civil. Prensas de la Universidad de Zaragoza, Zaragoza

De la Calle D (2004) La Comisión de Reformas Sociales: la primera consulta social al país. In: Palacio Morena JI (coord) La Reforma Social en España. En el centenario del Instituto de Reformas Sociales. Consejo Económico Social, Madrid

Del Rey F (1992) Propietarios y patronos. La política de las organizaciones económicas en la España de la Restauración (1914–1923). Ministerio de Trabajo y Seguridad Social, Madrid

Domenech J (2011) Legal origin, ideology, coalition formation, or crisis? The emergence of labor law in a civil law country, Spain 1880–1936. Labor Hist 52(1):71–93

Elu A (2010) Las pensiones públicas de vejez en España. In: Pons J, Silvestre J (eds) Los orígenes del Estado del Bienestar en España, 1900–1945: los seguros de accidentes de trabajo, vejez, desempleo y enfermedad. Prensas de la Universidad de Zaragoza, Zaragoza, pp 1908–1936

Espuelas S (2012) Are dictatorships less redistributive? A comparative analysis of social spending in Europe (1950-1980). Eur Rev of Econ Hist 16(2):211–232

Espuelas S (2013a) Los obstáculos al desarrollo de los seguros sociales en España antes de 1936: el caso del seguro de desempleo. Rev de Hist Indust 52:77–110

Espuelas S (2013b) La evolución del gasto social público en España. Estudios de Historia Económica. Banco de España, Madrid

Espuelas S (2015) The inequality trap. A comparative analysis of social spending between 1880 and 1930. Econ Hist Rev 68(2):683–706

Eza, Luis de Marichalar and Monreal, Vizconde de (1914) La previsión como remedio a la falta de trabajo. Conferencia dada en la Casa del Pueblo de Madrid el día 15 de febrero de 1913. Imprenta Bernardo Rodríguez, Madrid

Girón de Velasco JA (1943) Escritos y discursos. Ediciones de la Vicesecretaria de Educación Popular, Madrid

Girón de Velasco JA (1951) Quince años de política social dirigida por Franco. Ediciones OID, Madrid

González F, Oyuelos R (1914) Bolsas de Trabajo y Seguro contra el Paro Forzoso. Publicaciones IRS, Madrid

Guillén A, Álvarez S (2004) The EU's impact on the Spanish welfare state: the role of cognitive Europeanization. J Eur Soc Policy 14(3):185–299

Hellwig T (2005) The origins of unemployment insurance in Britain. A cross-class alliance approach. Soc Sci Hist 29(1):107–136

Hicks A (1999) Social democracy and welfare capitalism. A century of income security politics. Cornell University Press, London

INP (1936) La unificación de los seguros sociales, 3ª edición. Publicaciones INP, Madrid

INP (1952–57) Boletín de Información Estadística (3–21). INP, Dirección de servicios especiales, Asesoría actuarial, Madrid

INP (1960) Boletín de Información Estadística (30). INP, Dirección de servicios especiales, Asesoría actuarial, Madrid

Jerez A (1996) El régimen de Franco: elite política central y redes clientelares, 1938–1957. In: Robles A (coord) Política en penumbra. Patronazgo y clientelismo políticos en la España contemporánea. Siglo XXI, Madrid

Jordana L (1953) Los seguros sociales en España de 1936 a 1950. INP, Madrid

León M (2002) Towards the individualization of social rights: hidden familialistic practices in Spanish social policy. S Eur Soc Politics 7(3):53–80

León M, Salido O (2016) Políticas de familia en perspectiva comparada. In: León M (coord) Empleo y maternidad: obstáculos y desafíos a la conciliación de la vida laboral y familiar. FUNCAS, Madrid

Lindert PH (2004) Growing public: social spending and economic growth since the eighteenth century. Cambridge University Press, Cambridge

Malefakis EE (1970) Agrarian reform and peasant revolution in Spain: origins of the civil war. Yale UP, New Haven and London

Maluquer J (1926) Una campaña en pro del seguro y de la previsión popular. Publicaciones y Trabajos de Josep Maluquer i Salvador. Sucesora de M. Minuesa de los Ríos, Madrid

Maluquer J (2009) Del caos al cosmos: una nueva serie enlazada del producto interior bruto de España entre 1850 y 2000. Revista de Economía Aplicada 49(XVII):5–45

Maluquer J, Llonch M (2005) Trabajo y relaciones laborales. In: Carreras A, Tafunell X (coords) Estadísticas históricas de España. Fundación BBVA, Bilbao

Mares I (2003) The politics of social risk: business and welfare state development. Cambridge University Press, Cambridge

Molinero C, Ysas P (1998) Productores disciplinados y minorías subversivas. Clase obrera y conflictividad laboral en la España. Siglo XXI, Madrid

Montero F (1988) Los seguros sociales en la España del siglo XX. Orígenes y antecedentes de la previsión social. Ministerio de Trabajo y Seguridad Social, Madrid

Moreno Luzón J (2007) Political clientelism, elites and caciquismo in restoration Spain (1875-1923). Eur Hist Q 37(3):417–441

Murray JE (2003) Social insurance claims as morbidity estimates: sickness or absence. Soc Hist Med 16(2):225–245

Murray JE (2007) Origins of American health insurance: a history of industrial sickness funds. Yale University Press, New Haven

Nicolau R (2005) Población, salud, y actividad. In: Carreras A, Tafunell X (coords) Estadísticas históricas de España: siglos XIX y XX. Fundación BBVA, Bilbao

Offer A, Söderberg G (2016) The Nobel factor: the prize in economics, social democracy, and the market turn. Princeton University Press, Princeton

Pérez Ledesma M (1990) Estabilidad y conflicto social. España, de los íberos al 14-D. Nerea, Madrid

Pons J (2010) Los inicios del seguro de enfermedad en España. In: Pons J, Silvestre J (eds) Los orígenes del Estado del Bienestar en España, 1900–1945: los seguros de accidentes de trabajo, vejez, desempleo y enfermedad. PUZ, Zaragoza, pp 1923–1945

Prados de la Escosura L (2003) El progreso económico de España (1850–2000). Fundación BBVA, Bilbao

Prados de la Escosura L (2008) Inequality, poverty and the Kuznets curve in Spain, 1850–2000. Eur Rev Econ Hist 12:287–324

Samaniego M (1988) La Unificación de los Seguros Sociales a Debate. La Segunda república. Ministerio de Trabajo y Seguridad Social, Madrid

Silvestre J (2003) Los determinantes de la protesta obrera en España, 1905-1935: ciclo económico, marco político y organización sindical. Revista de Historia Industrial 24:51–80

Silvestre J, Pons J (2010) El seguro de accidentes del trabajo, 1900-1935. El alcance de las indemnizaciones, la asistencia sanitaria y la prevención. In: Pons J, Silvestre J (eds) Los orígenes del Estado del Bienestar en España, 1900–1945: los seguros de accidentes de trabajo, vejez, desempleo y enfermedad. Prensas de la Universidad de Zaragoza, Zaragoza

Simpson J, Carmona J (2020) Why democracy failed. The agrarian origins of the Spanish civil war. Cambridge University Press, Cambridge

Torregrosa-Hetland S (2018) Limits to redistribution in late democratic transitions: the case of Spain. In: Huerlimann G, Brownlee WE, Ide E (eds) Worlds of taxation: the political economy of taxing, spending, and redistribution since 1945. Palgrave, London

Tuñón de Lara M (1972) El movimiento obrero en la historia de España. Taurus, Madrid

Tusell J (2005) Dictadura franquista y democracia, 1939–2004. Crítica, Barcelona

Valiente C (1996) The rejection of authoritarian policy legacies: family policy in Spain (1975–1995). S Eur Soc Polit 1:95–114

Velarde J (1990) El tercer viraje de la seguridad social. IEE, Madrid

Vilar M (2004) Mercado de trabajo y crecimiento económico en España (1908–1963): una nueva interpretación del primer franquismo. Universitat de Barcelona, Dissertation

Chapter 7
The Effect of the 1918 Influenza Pandemic on US Life Insurance Holdings

Joanna Short

Abstract This paper examines the effect of a sharp rise in mortality, the 1918 influenza epidemic, on life insurance holdings in the USA. The BLS Cost of Living Surveys of 1918–1919 provide a unique opportunity to examine the effect of the pandemic—some households were surveyed before, and others during or shortly after the worst of the influenza outbreak. In addition, I use state-level insurance sales data to compare the increase in spending on insurance in states particularly hard hit by the epidemic, relative to those that were not. I find some evidence that, in the immediate aftermath of the epidemic, those in severely affected areas spent more on industrial insurance. They were less likely, though, to hold ordinary or fraternal policies and the effects appear to be short-lived. I consider a few explanations for the smaller-than-expected results.

Keywords Influenza · Mortality · Epidemic · Life Insurance · History · Insurance

7.1 Introduction

> Spanish Influenza! Can You Afford Sudden Death? If Not, Protect Your Family and Business By Life Insurance.
>
> Ad for Ives & Myrick Life Insurance Agency
> New York Times, October 1, 1918

The 1918 influenza pandemic caused immense suffering, fear, and economic disruption. In just a few months, influenza and pneumonia killed an estimated 550,000 Americans in excess of the expected mortality (Crosby 2003). This exceeds American combat deaths from World War I, World War II, and the Vietnam War combined. In areas most affected by the epidemic, real manufacturing wages rose sharply as markets adjusted to the decrease in labor supply (Garrett 2008). Survivors

J. Short (✉)
Augustana College, Rock Island, IL, USA
e-mail: JoannaShort@augustana.edu

P. Gray et al. (eds.), *Standard of Living*, Studies in Economic History,
https://doi.org/10.1007/978-3-031-06477-7_7

suffered persistent health effects, even decades after exposure to the disease (Almond 2006).

In contrast to most influenza outbreaks, young adults were much more vulnerable to the 1918 strain, recently identified as an H1N1 version of the virus (Taubenberger and Morens 2006). In the death registration area, deaths from influenza and pneumonia increased from 1.7 per thousand in 1917 to 6.0 per thousand in 1918. As a result, the mortality rate from all causes increased from 14.1 per thousand to 18.0 per thousand (Bureau of the Census 1922). Did a sudden and sharp rise in mortality, which particularly affected healthy young adults, convince many to seek out life insurance?

At this point, we know little about the effect of mortality risk on demand for life insurance. All else equal, it would seem that higher mortality risk, or perceived mortality risk, would make life insurance a better bet and lead to increased demand for it. Counter to this prediction, Kantor and Fishback (1996) have shown that industry accident risk did not affect the purchase of life and accident insurance in the 1917–1919 period. National-level studies on the effect of mortality risk on life insurance demand, for the late twentieth century, also offer mixed results.[1]

Despite its severity, the influenza epidemic was ultimately short-lived, even considering a flare-up in the spring of 1919. Thereafter, mortality continued its long-term decline. If households rationally considered life insurance before the epidemic, and anticipated that the mortality effects would be short-lived, there would be no need to reconsider insurance coverage during or after the epidemic. However, we might expect that households do not always consider life insurance rationally. Life insurance is somewhat unusual for a consumer good or service in that it is unpleasant to buy—one must consider one's own mortality or that of loved ones. For this reason, some may put it off, underinsure, or avoid buying insurance altogether, hence the industry's reliance on a sales force and advertising to help consumers overcome this reluctance. Zultowski (1979) reports on over a dozen studies dating from 1928 indicating that only 15–35% of insurance buyers report having initiated contact with an agent. Insurance agents typically report an even lower estimate of the proportion of sales that are client-initiated. To the extent that consumers put off or avoid life insurance, we might expect an epidemic could shock many consumers into action.

In addition, perhaps shocks to mortality, like the influenza epidemic, have a larger impact on life insurance demand than accident risk or overall mortality. There is some evidence that people respond to disasters by purchasing more insurance. Economic geographer Risa Palm (1995) surveyed California homeowners in 1989, 1990, and 1993 on their perceived risk of loss from earthquakes and purchase of earthquake insurance. She finds that *actual* risk, as measured by distance to an active fault, is unrelated to take-up of earthquake insurance. However, *perceived* risk of loss is consistently related to the purchase of earthquake insurance. Perceived risk and purchase of earthquake insurance increased dramatically among those who

[1] For example, Browne and Kim (1993) and Li et al. (2007).

experienced the Loma Prieta earthquake in 1989. In a similar vein, Stephen G. Fier and James M. Carson (2015) find that, from 1996 to 2008, the number of life insurance policies and amount in force was significantly higher in those states that suffered a catastrophic hurricane or tornado, in the year following the disaster. Perhaps earlier generations similarly responded to the 1918 influenza epidemic by buying more life insurance. In addition, even as actual mortality risk returned to normal, perceived risk may have increased if the epidemic caused a lack of faith in medical progress in general.

In looking for an empirical relationship between influenza mortality and life insurance holdings, we might expect the effect could vary with the type of life insurance. Several types of life insurance were available at the time, and they were generally used for different purposes. Ordinary and fraternal insurance typically provided a large amount of coverage for breadwinners, while industrial insurance provided less coverage for more members of the family. Essentially burial insurance, industrial insurance frequently covered women and children. We know much about the buyers of fraternal insurance, thanks to the work of Emery and Emery (1999) and Beito (2000). Recent work by Murray (2007) sheds much light on industrial sickness insurance, which usually also paid a small death benefit.

In this paper, I use the 1917–1919 Cost of Living Surveys to estimate a flu effect on holdings and spending on different types of life insurance. Both Whaples and Buffum (1991) and Kantor and Fishback (1996) have used Cost of Living Surveys to examine the probability of holding life insurance, in 1889 and 1917–1919, respectively. However, they do not break down the analysis by the different types of life insurance, nor do they look specifically for the effect of a mortality shock.[2] To supplement and extend the Cost of Living data, I also analyze state-level insurance sales data to see if sales increased more in those states particularly hard hit by the epidemic, relative to those that were not.

7.2 Early-Twentieth-Century Life Insurance

In the early twentieth century, life insurance provided a popular means to protect young families from the financial consequences of death. By 1918, 85% of middle-class households surveyed by the Bureau of Labor Statistics reported holding at least one life insurance policy (Kantor and Fishback 1996). In 1917, ordinary insurance was the most popular, representing nearly 60% of the life insurance in force in US companies (Stalson 1942, 822). Ordinary insurance was the earliest type commercially available, with premiums due annually, semiannually, or monthly.

[2] From the 1889 data on Michigan furniture workers, Whaples and Buffum cannot tell what type of insurance is held. Kantor and Fishback have access to data on different types of life insurance from the 1917 to 1919 survey, but largely examine the purchase of any type of life insurance policy. Also, given their interest in workers' compensation laws, Kantor and Fishback limit the sample to those with high-risk occupations.

Coverage was typically in the thousands, and these plans frequently paid dividends which could be paid in cash (effectively reducing the premium), used toward paid-up insurance, or used toward building a surrender value (Stalson 1942; Huebner 1923). The dividends provided a second potential purpose for purchasing life insurance beyond the death benefit—the policy could be used to build a nest egg through regular contributions. This savings function was apparently highly valued by consumers.[3] Although term insurance was available, and much cheaper than whole life or endowment plans, few bought it. In 1920, for example, 73% of the ordinary insurance in force was whole life, 20% was endowment, and the remainder other variations including term insurance (U.S. Department of Commerce 1925, 284). Coverage was typically subject to passing a medical exam.

Life insurance was also provided by some fraternal orders. Herb Emery (2001) classifies fraternal orders that provided benefits into two types: friendly societies, which typically offered sickness benefits and a small funeral benefit, and life insurance orders which offered stipulated life insurance, endowment, and annuity benefits. The amount of life insurance coverage varied, but life insurance orders could provide large amounts of coverage, generally at a lower cost than ordinary insurance companies. In part, this may be because fraternal organizations were less likely to offer participating policies. They may have realized some efficiencies from reducing adverse selection, and until 1912, faced little regulation in terms of reserve requirements (Emery and Emery 1999).

Industrial insurers sold smaller policies, generally for burial expenses, to the lower and middle classes. The premiums were collected by door-to-door salesmen weekly. These were very popular policies for women and children—by one estimate, these groups represented 70% of the policyholders (Pedoe and Jack 1978, 438). While these policies represented a small amount of the total life insurance in force (14%), in terms of the number of policies, industrial insurance represented the majority of policies in force. Instead of requiring a medical exam, industrial insurers generally paid only half of face value if death occurred within 6 months of taking out a policy (Huebner 1923, 291).

After 1911, a few large firms made insurance available to their employees. Group or establishment insurance represents insurance that covers a number of people, typically employees, under a single contract. Though growing rapidly, this insurance was still in its infancy in this period—representing only 0.1% of the total life insurance in force in 1917 (Stalson 1942, 804).

While troops were mobilized beginning in April of 1917, War Risk Insurance was briefly an important source of life insurance. The War Risk Insurance Act provided payments of $25 per month to qualifying war widows, and additional payments for additional dependents and disabled veterans. This coverage was automatic

[3] Ransom and Sutch (1987) show that tontine insurance policies were very popular until their sale was prohibited in 1906. After this prohibition, consumers continued to value participating policies that built a cash value or included an endowment feature. This may be due to the fact that the insurance company could invest in a diversified portfolio of real estate, bonds, and stocks in a way that few families could afford to do on their own.

upon enlistment. In addition, soldiers and sailors could elect to take out an additional $1000 to $10,000 in life insurance, offered at peacetime rates, with premiums deducted from pay (U.S. War Office 1918). As a result, the US government was for a short time the largest insurance company in the country. Although War Risk policies were convertible into ordinary life, most veterans dropped the coverage shortly after the war (Stalson 1942, 571; Buley 1967, 846).

7.3 The 1919 Increase in Demand for Life Insurance

Figure 7.1 shows the percentage change, over the previous year, in the face value sold of ordinary and industrial insurance, from 1908 to 1929 by US companies. There is a clear surge in life insurance sales in 1919 and 1920, particularly for ordinary insurance. Insurance executives and state insurance officials thought 1919 was a banner year for selling life insurance, and largely credit the epidemic for it. Thomas F. Tarbell, state actuary for Connecticut, reported that greatly increased business in the first half of 1919 was "a matter of common knowledge among

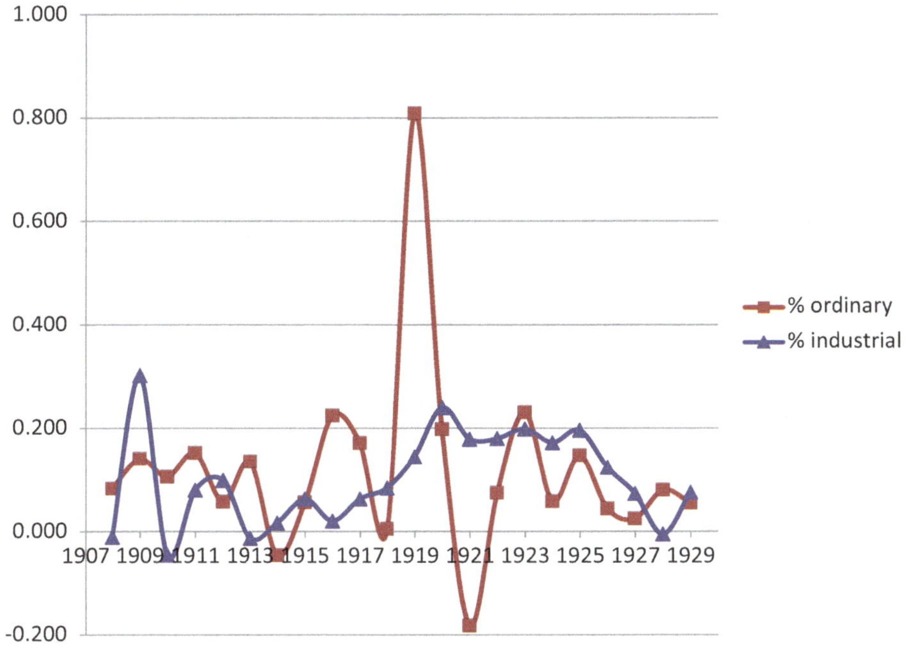

Fig. 7.1 Percentage change, over previous year, in face value of life insurance sold 1907–1929. (*Source*: Eugene N. White (2006), Table Cj723–726. Life insurance–sales, by type of insurance: 1854–1998. *Notes*: "Beginning in 1919, figures exclude revivals, increases, and dividend additions. Figures for industrial life insurance exclude revivals, increases and dividend additions starting in 1893")

insurance circles." By means of a survey of the 32 life insurance companies operating in the state of Connecticut, Tarbell estimates a 79% increase in life insurance written in the first 6 months of 1919, relative to the first 6 months of 1918. Similarly, the fraternal societies in the state reported an 84% increase in life insurance written (Tarbell 1919). The Eastern Underwriter (March 21, 1919) reported that "companies have been writing new insurance on an unprecedented scale, without making any drive to get it. The companies went through the epidemic in such fine shape that men and women who never thought much about insurance apparently have got the habit."

Despite the unusually high number of claims, few insurers failed in the wake of the epidemic. Prior to the epidemic, life insurers had been accused of using old mortality tables that predicted unrealistically high death rates. Many companies realized actual mortality rates less than 90% of expected rates. Even as mortality ratios increased (for Prudential from 86.4% in 1917 to 143.7% in 1918; for Kansas City Life from 44.9 to 101.7%), these companies were well positioned to weather the storm with minor rate increases (Bell 1997). A few insurance companies failed in late 1918 and 1919, and were absorbed by other insurers. The number of firms involved in these mergers (12 in 1918, 7 in 1919) was consistent with the number of failures in non-pandemic years, which averaged 12.75 for the years 1910–1917 (Best's Life Insurance Reports 1920).

The 1919 increase in life insurance sales appears to be driven more by demand than supply. If supply was the decisive factor, we would expect to see prices and insurance company profits declining in this period. Instead, most insurers held rates constant or increased them slightly in 1919 and 1920. For example, the largest insurer in the country, Metropolitan Life, held premiums on its most popular policies (20 payment life and 20 year endowment) constant from 1917 through 1919. By 1920, premiums for a 25-year-old increased by 7.66% and 6.45%, respectively. Meanwhile, dividends for existing policies were eliminated in 1919, effectively increasing the price of existing participating policies by 12–16%. At New York Life, premiums remained constant and dividends remained consistent throughout the period from 1917 to 1920.[4] Tarbell (1919) reports that three of 31 Connecticut insurers raised premiums in 1919, and an additional seven reduced dividends. Twelve of 32 fraternal societies raised rates or levied a special influenza assessment.

Premium income from life insurance for US companies increased by 21% in 1919 and another 16% in 1920 (White, 2006, Table Cj728). Underwriting profit for stock companies increased from $20 million in 1918 to $51 million in 1919 (White, 2006, Table Cj795). Increases in premiums, premium income, and underwriting profit all point to demand as the main source of the surge in life insurance sales in 1919. But can we attribute that increase in demand to the influenza epidemic?

Tarbell notes several possible reasons for the increase in new business in early 1919 including the epidemic, the advertising of life insurance provided by War Risk

[4] National Underwriter Company, Unique Manual-Digest of American Life Insurance, 1917, 1919, 1920.

Insurance, general prosperity, inflation, the rise of group insurance, and the corporation and inheritance tax. Of these factors, he surmises that "general prosperity is in the lead, with influenza and government insurance running a close second" (Tarbell 1919, 309).

Tarbell is likely correct in considering inflation, group insurance, and the estate tax as relatively minor influences on the surge in insurance sales in 1919. Despite the rapid inflation at the time, it is unlikely that policyholders frequently adjusted their coverage for inflation. White's series shows that the average size of ordinary policies in force increased only slightly, from $1840 to $1860 between 1918 and 1919. However, there was a more substantial increase to $1990 in 1920 (White, 2006 Cj720). Inflation might explain the 1920 increase in average policy size, as households eventually responded to inflation. Group insurance, while growing rapidly, still only represented about 3% of US life insurance in force in 1919 (White, 2006 Cj717). Thus, it is hard to imagine that increasing group coverage could have stimulated demand for other types of insurance that much. The Revenue Act of 1916 created an estate tax of 1–10% on estates exceeding $50,000 (Jacobson et al. 2007). Since life insurance proceeds are not taxable to the beneficiary, the estate tax encourages the wealthy to convert taxable estates into nontaxable insurance proceeds. However, at the time, the $50,000 threshold would have applied only to the very wealthy—taxable estates were involved in less than 1% of all adult deaths (Jacobson, 125). As Tarbell suggests, rising income, publicity from War Risk insurance, and the influenza epidemic remain as the most likely causes of the surge in life insurance demand in 1919.

7.4 The 1918–1919 Influenza Epidemic

The first wave of the influenza epidemic arrived in Kansas in the spring of 1918. Although illness rates were high, and some cases rapidly progressed to fatal pneumonia, death rates were not much higher than normal. The first wave went largely unnoticed by all but a few organizations, like army camps and prisons, which had complete control of their members and some responsibility for providing health care. A few pathologists noticed differences in the lung tissue of victims, but did not realize the significance until the second wave in the fall. As the first wave disappeared in the USA, it struck Europe, affecting military operations during the summer of 1918 (Crosby 2003).

The second, more deadly, wave of influenza first appeared in the USA at Commonwealth Pier, Boston, in late August of 1918. While it is not known whether the two waves were caused by the same virus, it is possible the virus mutated profoundly into a form against which few had immunity, and of course, there was no treatment (Taubenberger and Morens 2006). The disease spread within 3 weeks to Denver and cities along the Mississippi River. Within 4–7 weeks, interior and West Coast cities were affected (Eggo et al. 2011). In most cities, deaths from influenza and pneumonia peaked in September or October 1918, before quickly returning to near-normal. Some cities, like Philadelphia, struggled with the rapid increase in mortality, and briefly could not pick up and bury the victims in a timely manner. Many coastal cities attempted to quarantine new arrivals. Several cities closed schools, churches, and other places of entertainment for weeks. Some cities, like San Francisco, enforced mask laws for people in public. It is unlikely that these public health measures had much effect on mortality, as they were frequently enacted after influenza had appeared, or were unevenly enforced (Crosby 2003).

Mortality from the influenza epidemic was widespread, yet variable. Among 50 registration cities with population of 100,000 or more in 1920, the highest mortality rate from influenza and pneumonia was suffered by Pittsburgh, at 12.4 per 1000 (vs. 3.8 per 1000 in 1917). The lowest mortality rate occurred in Grand Rapids, Michigan, at 2.8 per 1000 (vs. 0.9 per 1000 in 1917). The most affected states (Pennsylvania, Montana, Maryland, and Colorado) had little in common geographically or economically. However, Clay et al. (2018) show that air pollution from coal-fired power plants contributed significantly to infant mortality during the epidemic. Briefly, in October 1918, those living in counties near military camps suffered higher mortality than those who lived further away (Hilt and Rahm 2020). Nonetheless, neighboring communities sometimes suffered at vastly different rates—the mortality rate in St. Paul was 70% higher than in neighboring Minneapolis. Brainerd and Siegler (2006) argue that differences in influenza and pneumonia mortality rates cannot be explained by state-level income, geography, or climate. Garrett (2008) finds that 1918 mortality was related to population density and race, but not as much as in 1915.

One of the few ways that people could respond to the epidemic was to adjust life insurance coverage. We can look deeper for an influenza effect on life insurance by more precisely examining consumer behavior at the household level, in the few months before and after the epidemic.

7.5 1918–1919 Cost of Living Surveys and Mortality Data

Household-level data on the purchase of life insurance may be derived from the Cost of Living Surveys conducted by the US Department of Labor in 1918–1919. This survey covered the families of wage and salary workers in 92 cities across the country. Most of the cities sampled were quite large—47 had a population greater than 100,000 in 1920, and another 31 had a population larger than 25,000. The purpose of the survey was to collect consumption and price data to use as the basis for wartime wage adjustments. Respondents were approached by door-to-door surveyors. Eligible respondents were households composed of at minimum husband, wife, and one child. Further restrictions include a salary limit of $2000 (but no limit on wage or other earnings), no "slum" or "charity" families, and no families living in the USA for less than 5 years (Bureau of Labor Statistics, 1918).

In comparing the Cost of Living Survey to an urban sample from the 1920 census, James J. Feigenbaum finds that the survey provides a representative, but slightly younger, sample of white urban middle-income families. While the age of the household head is slightly younger than in the census (around age 37 vs. 42), the average family size is similar (Fiegenbaum 2015). This survey provides a great deal of detail with regard to family income and expenses, including specific expenses on food, clothing for each member of the family, entertainment, and other expenses including life insurance premiums. Of course, since detailed questions were asked on income and purchases for an entire year, the responses are subject to recall bias. Survey respondents were asked the number of life insurance policies they owned, their amounts, and the premiums paid for four types of life insurance: ordinary or "old line," industrial, fraternal, and group.

Of the 12,818 families surveyed, 11,023 report paying premiums on one or more life insurance policies. Table 7.1 summarizes the coverage and cost reported by families for different types of insurance. Ordinary and fraternal insurance policies provided the most coverage, at a median of $1000, most likely just for the breadwinner of the household. While a decent sum, $1000 was not enough to maintain a family's standard of living very long, given that median husband's earnings was $1296. Fraternal plans provide a similar level of coverage at a lower cost than ordinary insurance companies, although this may in part reflect that ordinary plans are more likely to include an additional investment component. Industrial policies provided a smaller amount of coverage, for more members of the family. Similarly, group insurance policies provide a small amount of coverage at low cost; however, these plans are reported only by a small fraction of the respondents.

In looking for a surge in life insurance demand from the influenza epidemic, I divide the respondents according to the month surveyed. Each respondent was asked to provide details on income and spending for the previous year, ending with the last day of the month preceding the date of the survey. The earliest cities surveyed cover the year ending July 31, 1918. The latest surveys cover the year ending February 28, 1919. I consider the earliest surveys, covering the years ending July 31, August 31,

Table 7.1 Life insurance coverage by type of policy, 1917–1919

		Amount of insurance ($)		Cost of insurance ($)	
Type of policy(ies)	Median number of policies	Median	Average	Median	Average
Ordinary	1	1000	1354	32.68	41.88
($N = 4175$)					
Industrial	3	260	423	23.25	26.76
($N = 8336$)					
Fraternal	1	1000	1102	20.00	24.58
($N = 3487$)					
Group	1	300	559	12.00	15.29
($N = 494$)					
Other	1	250	621	12.00	18.33
($N = 221$)					

Source: BLS Cost of Living in the United States, 1917–1919. 1986
Note: Several respondents reported carrying more than one type of policy

and September 30, 1918 to be pre-flu, since they cover spending from just before to the beginning of the deadly second wave of the influenza epidemic, which first appeared in the USA in late August. Recall that mortality from the epidemic peaked in most cities in September or October. However, it is likely that many remained unaware of the scale of the epidemic until well into September. A review of *The New York Times* indicates that through September 15, the only articles on influenza involved issues on ships and at army bases. One could conclude, at this point, that the problem was contained to those areas. However, by September 17, there are mixed messages in the article "Close Camp Upton to Check Influenza." Despite "no deaths, not even any very serious cases," the army camp was closed, and in addition, 16 deaths in 6 hours were reported for the Greater Boston area. By September 21, it is clear that influenza is spreading in New York and elsewhere.[5] Small city and town newspapers also appear to have effectively reported on the epidemic. Roger Heinrich (2011) compares the flu coverage of *The New York Times* to that of the Knoxville *Journal Tribune*. The Knoxville paper ran its first story on the epidemic in Boston on September 12, 3 days before *The New York Times*. Both papers ran a similar number of stories on influenza, and both provided daily death tolls. Thus, it appears that information about the spread of the disease was widely available by mid-September. The later surveys, covering the periods up to October 1918 through February 1919, we consider post-flu.

7.5.1 Selection Concerns

It is important to note that those households that recently suffered the loss of husband, wife, or only child would not be included in the survey, given the requirements for participation. Given the relative randomness of influenza mortality, and the large sample sizes, it is unlikely that the pre-flu and post-flu samples differ significantly due to this sort of mortality selection. Of larger concern are possible selection effects from military buildup, moral hazard in the purchase of insurance, and differences in the timing of the surveys in different regions.

Sydenstricker and King (1920) note that at the height of the epidemic, the civilian population was about 400,000 lower than usual due to the military draft. This represents about 8% of the male population. These soldiers would not be included in the pre-flu sample, but could appear in the post-flu sample as soldiers returned home at the close of the war. While this is a concern, the effect is mitigated by the dominance of young single men in the military—who would be ineligible for the Cost of Living Survey anyway. We can also limit samples to just those households headed my men older than the military draft age.

[5] Sept. 21 p. 7, "31 New Influenza Cases in New York"; Sept. 25, p. 24 "Influenza Spreads, 150 New Cases Here"; Sept. 27, p. 6, "Bay State Asks Aid in Influenza Fight".

Another concern is that life insurance holdings may differ systematically between survivors who may be in our sample and non-survivors who are not. While flu mortality may have been fairly random, death from other causes was not, and we might expect that those who have health issues would be more likely to buy life insurance in general. In a limited sense, we can compare the mortality experience of policyholders and the general population. Dublin and Lotka (1937) note that the mortality risk of industrial policyholders at Metropolitan Life was about 15% higher than the general population in 1920. But industrial policyholders lived mainly in industrial centers, where the mortality rate was about 20% higher than in smaller cities and rural areas. Over long periods of time, the mortality rate of policyholders mirrored that of the general population. Thus, the mortality experience of industrial policyholders looks roughly comparable to that of the overall urban population.

A final concern is that the Bureau of Labor Statistics did not randomly survey throughout the country both before and after the flu—some regions were surveyed more heavily before, and others after. Table 7.2 shows differences in life insurance holdings for the households surveyed in the pre-flu and post-flu periods. At first glance, there does not seem to be a rush to buy life insurance once the worst of the epidemic hits. In fact, the proportion holding any life insurance policy falls slightly. It is important to note, though, that the pre-flu (earliest surveyed) cities were concentrated in the East, Midwest, and Pacific regions. In fact, the pre-flu observations are heavily influenced by results from New York City, Pittsburgh, and Baltimore which account for more than 35% of the pre-flu observations.

Table 7.3 shows the regional distribution of households surveyed, by the month the survey was conducted. Region matters in the purchase of life insurance. We know from the Kantor and Fishback (1996) study of the effects of state workman's compensation laws on insurance demand that families in the northern and eastern regions were much more likely than those in the West to buy life insurance. This may in part reflect differences in the concentration of life insurance companies and agencies, the cost of insurance, and the mortality rate. Hence, the regional makeup of the pre-flu and post-flu samples may explain why we see a decline in insurance coverage after the influenza epidemic. To limit this selection effect, in the analysis below for the most part, I consider only those regions that were widely surveyed both before and after the epidemic. This limits consideration to the New England,

Table 7.2 Proportion of families reporting holding one or more insurance policies, by survey month, 1918–1919

Proportion reporting one or more:	Pre-flu ($N = 3130$)	Post-flu ($N = 9687$)
Life insurance policies	87.3%	85.6%
Ordinary policies	33.5%	32.3%
Fraternal policies	20.0%	29.5%
Industrial policies	70.7%	63.2%

Source: BLS Cost of Living in the United States, 1917–1919. 1986

Note: Pre-flu includes all families surveyed for the years ending July 31, August 31, and September 30, 1918. Post-flu includes all families surveyed for the years ending October 31, 1918, through February 28, 1919

Table 7.3 Regional distribution of families surveyed, by survey month Cost of Living Surveys, 1918–1919

Region:	Jul	Aug	Sep	Oct	Nov	Dec	Jan	Feb	All months	Total pop'n
New England (%)	0.0	20.1	8.1	20.0	30.8	0.0	0.0	0.0	10.4	7.0
Mid Atlantic (%)	0.0	64.9	49.0	16.4	6.4	0.0	0.0	0.0	16.9	21.0
South Atlantic (%)	99.7	0.0	0.0	3.5	12.9	23.1	12.8	34.7	13.3	13.2
East North Central (%)	0.0	14.8	0.0	40.4	22.8	34.4	6.5	0.0	20.9	20.2
West North Central (%)	0.0	0.0	1.6	4.3	14.2	5.6	23.2	38.3	9.9	12.0
East South Central (%)	0.3	0.0	0.0	0.0	0.0	11.7	22.7	0.0	6.7	8.5
West South Central (%)	0.0	0.0	0.0	0.0	0.0	8.3	20.8	11.4	6.2	9.6
Mountain (%)	0.0	0.0	0.0	0.0	12.9	3.1	14.0	15.7	5.3	3.1
Pacific (%)	0.0	0.0	41.2	15.4	0.0	13.8	0.0	0.0	10.5	5.4
Sample size	302	1495	1334	2789	1195	2638	2401	658	12,812	

Sources: BLS Cost of Living in the United States, 1917–1919, 1986; U.S. Bureau of the Census 1996
Total population distribution is extrapolated for 1918 from 1910 and 1920 Census

Mid-Atlantic, South Atlantic, East North Central, and Pacific regions (see Table 7.3). This still encompasses 72% of the surveys, and limits the number of observations that are dropped due to lack of mortality rates.

Note also that the last few columns of Table 7.3 show the overall distribution for all months of the survey, compared to the overall population at the time. While the Bureau of Labor Statistics made some effort to include urban families throughout the country, it appears that some regions like New England and Pacific were oversampled in the Cost of Living Survey. Others, like the Mid-Atlantic region, were undersampled relative to the overall population.

7.5.2 *Variables and Predicted Effects*

In investigating how various factors, like the influenza epidemic, affected demand for life insurance, we could consider a few different dependent variables. From the Cost of Living Surveys, we can find how many insurance policies families held of each type (ordinary, fraternal, industrial, group, and other). So, we can use a binary variable for whether a family holds one or more policies of each type as the dependent variable.

Spending on each type of life insurance and the amount of insurance coverage could also be considered as dependent variables. Unfortunately, due to the substantial savings component of most policies, spending on insurance does not seem to be a good representation of insurance coverage. Hence, I only consider spending as a dependent variable when investigating industrial insurance. Although the amount of insurance coverage would be an ideal dependent variable, these data seem somewhat unreliable considering that about 20% of respondents who report holding policies and spending on insurance also report zero insurance coverage. This problem is most severe for industrial policyholders, probably because this insurance was typically "adjusted to the unit of premium" (Huebner 1923, 288). This means that the amount of insurance obtained for a given premium (generally a multiple of five cents per week) varied with age and frequently provided odd-figured insurance amounts. Many likely did not know the precise amount of coverage they had at any given time. Although ordinary and fraternal policies generally provided standard coverage amounts, in these cases, families may have simply misunderstood the question or mistaken it for the cash value of the insurance. In either case, we will consider insurance coverage, for those who appear to have reported it correctly, as a supplement to our analysis of the binary dependent variable.

Our main independent variables of interest are an indicator variable for post-flu, a measure of flu severity, and an interaction between post-flu and flu severity. Recall that we are considering surveys that measure spending through October 1918 or later to be post-flu observations. The coefficient on the post-flu variable will provide the overall time trend in the take-up of insurance or insurance spending.

Mortality rates are used to measure flu severity; however, they are only available in the death registration area. City-level death rates are available for large cities with populations of 100,000 or more in 1920. State-level death rates can also be obtained for smaller cities in one of the registration states. In 1917, 27 states were in the registration area, meaning they had consistent reporting of deaths and provided such data to the Census (Bureau of the Census 1922). The death registration area covered

Table 7.4 Number of cities and households in Cost of Living Survey, by region, in the death registration area in 1917

	Number of cities in Cost of Living Survey, by region and mortality rate availability			
	Have city mortality	Have state mortality	Have neither mortality	Total
Northeast	11	10	0	21
Midwest	12	12	8	32
South	9	5	14	28
West	6	10	2	18
Total	38	37	24	99
	Number of households in cost of living survey, by region and mortality rate availability			
	Have city mortality	Have state mortality	Have neither mortality	Total
Northeast	2638	858	0	3496
Midwest	2362	1042	547	3951
South	1577	380	1395	3352
West	957	906	155	2018
Total	7534	3186	2097	12,817

Source: BLS Cost of Living in the United States, 1917–1919, 1986; U.S. Bureau of the Census. *Mortality Statistics, 1920*. Twenty-first Annual Report. Washington, D.C.: GPO, 1922

most of the East and Midwest, but the South and West were not as well represented. Table 7.4 shows the number of cities and households in the Cost of Living Surveys where reliable city-level, state-level, or no mortality rate is available from census reports. Unfortunately, we will have to dismiss observations where we have no reliable death rates, and this will disproportionately exclude observations from the South. Many southern cities are excluded anyway, though, when we limit the analysis to just those regions surveyed both before and after the flu.

One measure of flu severity is an indicator variable for a large increase in the mortality rate from all causes from 1917 to 1918. For the cities in the survey with available mortality rates, the average increase in mortality was about 30%. Therefore, I use a 40% or greater increase in mortality as an indication that a city suffered particularly severe mortality from the epidemic. As an alternative measure of flu severity, I use the city's mortality rate from all causes in 1918. This is less specific to the epidemic, and an indication of the effect of overall mortality risk. The coefficients on these variables will provide the effect of living in a severe flu area (or high mortality area) on insurance take-up *prior* to the epidemic. Most important, for our question, is the effect of the interaction variable between post-flu and flu severity. This will indicate whether the increase in insurance take-up was significantly higher after the epidemic, in more severely hit regions, relative to the less severe regions.

In addition, we can control for several household-level variables that may affect the demand for insurance. These variables and their predicted effects are summarized in Table 7.5. For all types of policies, husband's age is predicted to have a quadratic effect, and number of young children is predicted to have a positive effect, on the probability of owning a policy. For the rest of the variables, the predictions are consistent with the general purpose of the type of life insurance. Ordinary and fraternal policies are generally purchased by the wealthy to protect the earnings of the household head, but the earnings of other members of the household could provide a substitute. In contrast, industrial insurance was generally purchased by poorer households to cover the funeral expenses of the wife and children, but earnings of

Table 7.5 Variables and predicted effects on probability of owning one or more policies, by type of insurance

	Predicted effect of variable on the Probability of owning one or more policies		
Variable	Ordinary	Fraternal	Industrial
Husband's age	+	+	+
Husband's age squared	–	–	–
Husband's earnings	+	+	–
Wife's earnings	–	–	+
Children's earnings	–	–	+
Savings	+	+	–
Home ownership	+	+	–
Number of young children	+	+	+
Number of older children	–	–	+

the household head could provide a substitute. Finally, regional dummies are included to account for differences in population density, supply, and other factors that may influence insurance demand.

7.5.3 Results

Table 7.6 shows the estimated coefficients and clustered standard errors for an ordinary least squares regression on industrial insurance spending. The first column includes only the difference-in-difference variables, while the second column includes household and regional controls. In Panel A, the interaction variable indicates that households surveyed after the flu in severe flu areas spent significantly more on industrial insurance—about $6 more, relative to median spending of $23, once controls are included. The coefficient on the post-flu variable indicates that the overall trend was to spend less on industrial insurance after the flu. The coefficient on the severe variable indicates that those living in severely affected areas tended to spend less on industrial insurance prior to the flu. The coefficients on the control variables are consistent with our expectations for industrial insurance. Panel B of

Table 7.6 Ordinary least squares coefficients and clustered standard errors on spending on industrial life insurance, 1918–1919

Panel A:	(1)	(2)	(3)
Variable	Mean	Difference-in differences	Add household and regional controls
Post-flu * severe	0.083	12.122**	6.180*
		(5.396)	(3.121)
Post-flu	0.633	−6.257**	−4.163**
		(2.452)	(2.003)
Severe	0.172	−10.087***	−4.080**
		(3.356)	(1.552)
R^2		0.022	0.162
N		8475	8475

Panel B:	(1)	(2)	(3)
Variable	Mean	Difference-in differences	Add household and regional controls
Post-flu * mort rate	12.079	0.691	0.722*
		(0.546)	(0.369)
Post-flu	0.649	−14.573†	−16.756**
		(11.007)	(7.352)
Mortality rate	19.378	1.053**	0.553††
		(0.521)	(0.373)
R^2		0.071	0.177
N		8868	8868

Source: BLS Cost of Living in the United States, 1917–1919. 1986
Note: *** 99% significance level, †† 85% significance level, ** 95% significance level, † 80% significance level, * 90% significance level

Table 7.6 shows similar results when the mortality rate for 1918 is used as our measure of flu severity. Each additional death per thousand added about $0.72 in spending on industrial insurance for those surveyed after the flu.

For ordinary and fraternal insurance, spending on insurance is not an appropriate measure of insurance coverage since much of the premiums typically went to a savings component of the policy. For these types of insurance, I use a dummy variable for one or more policies, and insurance coverage (excluding those who reported a policy and a zero coverage amount). In Table 7.7, I use indicator variables for holding one or more industrial, ordinary, or fraternal policy as the dependent variable. The coefficients are from ordinary least squares regressions, and the standard errors are clustered by city. Other than a significantly negative effect of young children on ordinary insurance, the coefficients on the control variables are broadly consistent with our expectations. In column 2, we see that those surveyed after the flu and living in severe flu areas were somewhat more likely to hold industrial insurance, though this is significant only at an 83% level of confidence. In contrast, these households were somewhat less likely to hold ordinary policies and significantly less likely to hold fraternal policies. These results are largely unchanged when we use the mortality rate as our measure of flu severity, and when we use probit specifications. Using insurance coverage as the dependent variable also leads to similar results.

Table 7.7 Ordinary least squares coefficients and clustered standard errors on holding one or more insurance policy, 1918–1919

	Industrial policies		Ordinary policies		Fraternal policies	
	(1)	(2)	(3)	(4)	(5)	(6)
Variable	Difference-in-differences	Add household and regional controls	Difference-in-differences	Add household and regional controls	Difference-in-differences	Add household and regional controls
Post-flu * severe	0.191††	0.079†	−0.102*	−0.112*	−0.163***	−0.161***
	(0.117)	(0.057)	(0.059)	(0.061)	(0.037)	(0.040)
Post-flu	−0.072††	−0.041†	0.011	0.029	0.095***	0.081***
	(0.044)	(0.030)	(0.035)	(0.030)	(0.029)	(0.025)
Severe	−0.196**	−0.071*	0.022	−0.030	0.093***	0.074**
	(0.080)	(0.038)	(0.040)	(0.038)	(0.026)	(0.028)
R^2	0.012	0.077	0.002	0.082	0.010	0.055
N	8475	8475	8475	8475	8475	8475

Source: BLS Cost of Living in the United States, 1917–1919. 1986
Note: *** 99% significance level
** 95% significance level
* 90% significance level
†† 85% significance level
† 80% significance level

There are a few reasons we might expect the flu epidemic would have a larger effect on industrial insurance than ordinary or fraternal insurance. First, as pure insurance with no savings component, it should be more affected by the disease environment. Second, it was easy to quickly obtain more from door-to-door salesmen. In contrast, ordinary and fraternal insurance was typically subject to a medical exam. Still, it is unexpected that households in severely affected areas would be *less* likely to hold ordinary and particularly fraternal insurance after the flu, particularly when we consider the large increase in ordinary and fraternal insurance sales that occurred in early 1919.

The overall trend for fraternal policies, given by the post-flu variable, is toward more policies. This effect was more than offset by the negative effect of living in severe flu areas. These areas may have suffered more disruptions that delayed households seeking more fraternal coverage. In addition, perhaps the surveys simply do not provide a long enough time period to see the surge that we were expecting.

7.5.3.1 Sensitivity Analysis

One concern with our analysis of pre-flu and post-flu surveys is the possible effect of the military draft. In the pre-flu period, many household heads were at war. Only households with husband, wife, and at least one child living at home were surveyed. Thus, the pre-flu sample may include many household heads ineligible for military service for medical or other reasons. If these household heads were less healthy, we might expect they were more likely to hold life insurance. This selection issue could cause an apparent decline in fraternal insurance holdings, for example, as samples of less healthy men are replaced by healthier men.

One way to limit the selection issue is to limit our sample to households headed by older men. The first two draft registrations, in June 1917 and June 1918, covered men aged 21–31. The third registration in September of 1918 was for men up to age 45 (National Archives, WWI Registration Cards). Thus, throughout the war, men older than 45 were not subject to military draft. If we limit our sample to households headed by men over 45, living in regions widely surveyed both before and after the flu, this limits the number of observations to 1375. Again, the results are fairly similar—although the interaction variable loses significance for the likelihood of holding ordinary policies, it remains significantly positive for spending on industrial insurance, and significantly negative for the likelihood of holding fraternal policies.

Another concern with our analysis is our assumption, throughout, that the effect of all the control variables remained consistent in the pre- and post-flu period. If these differ for some variables between the pre-flu and post-flu samples, it may indicate selection issues, or that the epidemic affected household responses to these variables. Table 7.8 shows means, coefficients, and standard errors for regressions on industrial insurance spending, estimated separately for the pre-flu and post-flu samples. Here the mortality rate for the pre-flu sample is the mortality rate in 1917, and for the post-flu sample, I use the mortality rate in 1918. Only for the mortality rate variable (along with the number of young children) do the means and

Table 7.8 Ordinary least squares coefficients and clustered standard errors on industrial insurance spending, 1918–1919

	Pre-flu		Post-flu	
	(1)	(2)	(3)	(4)
Variable	Mean	Coeff (St. err)	Mean	Coeff (St. err)
Mortality rate	15.41	−0.257	18.60	1.760***
		(0.445)		(0.188)
Husband's age	37.19	0.328*	37.01	0.335*
		(0.163)		(0.195)
Husband's age sq	1456.34	−0.003	1443.71	−0.002
		(0.002)		(0.001)
Husband's earnings	1307.92	0.002	1327.68	−0.000
		(0.002)		(0.001)
Wife's earnings	17.86	0.010*	16.33	0.010**
		(0.006)		(0.005)
Child earnings	105.87	0.007†	91.03	0.008***
		(0.005)		(0.002)
Own home	0.204	−3.335***	0.268	−3.082***
		(1.031)		(0.731)
Savings	64.48	−0.023**	77.43	−0.002†
		(0.009)		(0.001)
Children age 0–4	0.890	0.521	0.890	1.804***
		(0.524)		(0.325)
Children age 5–9	0.771	3.050***	0.786	2.153***
		(0.519)		(0.307)
Children age 10–14	0.543	2.308***	0.568	2.989***
		(0.681)		(0.452)
Children age 15+	0.327	4.084**	0.313	1.850**
		(1.516)		(0.719)
Regional dummies		Yes		Yes
R^2		0.217		0.182
N		3109		5759

Source: BLS Cost of Living in the United States, 1917–1919. 1986

coefficients change significantly between the pre-flu and post-flu samples, indicating that the post-flu households became more responsive to the mortality rate. This effect shows up again in Table 7.9, where the dependent variable is a dummy for holding one or more insurance policy. Here, in addition to the usual controls, we also include the holding of a fraternal policy, as a potential substitute for an ordinary policy, and vice versa. And we also see again that the mortality rate positively affected industrial insurance holdings after the epidemic, but had a negative effect on fraternal insurance holdings.

Table 7.9 Ordinary least squares coefficients and clustered standard errors on holding one or more insurance policy, 1918–1919

	Industrial policies		Ordinary policies		Fraternal policies	
	(1)	(2)	(3)	(4)	(5)	(6)
Variable	Pre-flu	Post-flu	Pre-flu	Post-flu	Pre-flu	Post-flu
Mortality rate	−0.004	0.028***	−0.005	−0.007	0.005	−0.008*
	(0.008)	(0.004)	(0.006)	(0.006)	(0.012)	(0.005)
Fraternal policy			−0.136***	−0.156***		
			(0.023)	(0.015)		
Ordinary policy					−0.103***	−0.143***
					(0.020)	(0.016)
Household controls	Yes	Yes	Yes	Yes	Yes	Yes
Regional dummies	Yes	Yes	Yes	Yes	Yes	Yes
R^2	0.122	0.075	0.096	0.080	0.041	0.061
N	3109	5366	3109	5759	3109	5759

Source: BLS Cost of Living in the United States, 1917–1919. 1986

7.6 1916–1923 Spectator Yearbook Life Insurance Sales Data

Analysis of the Cost of Living Surveys allows us to see the consumer response to the influenza epidemic only during a short time window. Given the timing of the surveys, we can only observe the response of the post-flu observations 1–5 months from the clear start of the pandemic. To extend the analysis, we can examine the annual insurance sales data published by the Spectator Company. Spectator provides annual data on insurance in force, ordinary insurance written, and industrial insurance written by each insurance company, in each state. This data is derived from the annual reports required by state insurance commissions, although Spectator notes, "a few States do not supply this information, and in such cases we have applied to the companies for particulars" (The Spectator Company 1919, 343).

From the Spectator Yearbooks, I have collected a panel of new life insurance written, by state, from 1916 to 1923. The amount of insurance written in each year is inflated to 1982–1984 dollars using the CPI (Williamson 2019). We might predict that real insurance written in a state in a particular year would vary with the state's population, urbanization, per capita income, enlistment rate, mortality rate, and fixed regional and year effects. Annual state population and urbanization rates are extrapolated from census data. State income estimates are infrequently available, so throughout I use Easterlin's estimates for 1919–21, again inflated to 1982–1984 dollars using the CPI (Easterlin 1957). The enlistment rate from April 1917 to October 1918 is included to look for a promotional effect from War Risk Insurance (U.S. War Office 1919). State mortality rates are available annually, but only for those states in the registration area.

Pooled cross-sectional estimates for these data are reported in Table 7.10. For both ordinary and industrial insurance, log real insurance written increases with population and urbanization. As we might expect, log real income per capita has a

Table 7.10 Ordinary least squares coefficients and clustered standard errors on log of real insurance written, by state, 1916–1923

Variable	Means	Ordinary written		Industrial written	
Mortality rate	13.41	−0.019	0.014	0.115***	0.100**
		(0.015)	(0.019)	(0.027)	(0.044)
Log population	14.43	1.024***	1.011***	1.091***	1.079***
		(0.029)	(0.038)	(0.069)	(0.131)
Urbanization rate	0.509	0.023	0.407*	3.907***	3.779**
		(0.243)	(0.241)	(1.001)	(1.431)
Log real inc/cap	8.29	0.716***	0.490**	−1.589**	−1.444
		(0.160)	(0.208)	(0.677)	(1.255)
Enlistment rate	0.040	4.736**	3.161	−22.800†	−20.768
		(2.144)	(2.470)	(17.401)	(18.651)
Fixed year effects		Yes	Yes	Yes	Yes
Regional dummies		No	Yes	No	Yes
R^2		0.968	0.976	0.891	0.892
N		257	257	256	256

Source: Spectator Insurance Yearbooks, 1916–1923. Life Insurance by States tables

positive effect on ordinary insurance, but not on industrial insurance. The enlistment rate does not affect insurance written, once we control for region. The mortality rate positively affects industrial insurance written, but does not affect ordinary insurance written. This seems consistent with our earlier results from the cost of living surveys. The magnitude suggests that each 1 per 1000 increase in the mortality rate is associated with about a 10% increase in real industrial insurance written.

One potential issue with our pooled cross-sectional analysis is the possibility of unobserved state effects that may be correlated with flu severity. These might include, for example, local attitudes toward life insurance and patriotism. In areas where life insurance is viewed more positively, we might expect such attitudes would attract more agents and advertising, which could also contribute to the spread of influenza. Similarly, more patriotic attitudes could lead to higher enlistment, which could in turn bring more flu home. Such effects would render our estimates biased and inconsistent (Wooldridge 2010).

To overcome this issue, we will assume that these effects are fixed over time, and difference them away by estimating the *change in* insurance written from 1 year to the next. Accordingly, we'll also difference the explanatory variables to see if states that suffered a large increase in mortality had a large increase in new insurance written, relative to similar states that did not. This differencing procedure will cause us to lose variables that do not change in our data, like real income per capita and the enlistment rate. In essence, we must assume that these and other differences between states are fixed over time.

Results from regressions of the change in log real insurance written on changes in the mortality rate, population, urbanization rate, and fixed year effects are reported in Table 7.11. The coefficients on all the change variables are relative to the change from 1916 to 1917. Here, we are most interested in the interaction between the year

Table 7.11 Ordinary least squares coefficients and clustered standard errors on change in log of real insurance written, by state, 1916–1923

Variable	ΔLog real ordinary written	ΔLog real industrial written
ΔMort rate	−0.025*	−0.000
	(0.014)	(0.018)
ΔMortRate × 1918	0.026***	−0.022†
	(0.009)	(0.013)
ΔMortRate × 1919	0.002	−0.025††
	(0.022)	(0.018)
ΔMortRate × 1920	0.000	−0.033†
	(0.031)	(0.020)
ΔMortRate × 1921	0.035	−0.035††
	(0.031)	(0.025)
ΔMortRate × 1922	0.031	−0.049**
	(0.027)	(0.023)
ΔMortRate × 1923	0.038†	−0.038††
	(0.025)	(0.027)
ΔLog population	0.858	−0.146
	(0.902)	(1.138)
ΔUrban rate	4.047†	−3.526
	(2.699)	(3.483)
1918	−0.526***	0.506***
	(0.130)	(0.185)
1919	0.671***	0.064
	(0.226)	(0.175)
1920	0.106	0.257†
	(0.317)	(0.168)
1921	−0.512**	0.422*
	(0.246)	(0.243)
1922	0.131	0.503***
	(0.207)	(0.135)
1923	0.110	0.083
	(0.092)	(0.224)
R sq	0.544	0.456
N	218	217

Source: Spectator Insurance Yearbooks, 1916–1923. Life Insurance by States tables
Note: *** 99% significance level
** 95% significance level
* 90% significance level
† 80% significance level
†† 85% significance level

and the change in the mortality rate from the previous year. We might expect particularly large effects from the change in mortality in 1918 and 1919, around the period of the flu epidemic. The fixed year effects are also of interest, since they provide the overall trend over time in insurance sales.

There are a few significant effects on the interaction variables, most notably in 1918 for ordinary insurance. The coefficient indicates a 2.6% increase in real ordinary insurance written from a one percentage point increase in the mortality rate from 1917 to 1918. This effect looks small, though, relative to the overall trend for 1918 which was large and negative for ordinary insurance. In 1919, the trend for ordinary insurance was large and positive, yet we cannot attribute this to the change in mortality. Similarly, for industrial insurance, there is a small negative effect on the interaction variable for 1918, but this appears small relative to the overall positive effect of 1918.

In most years, other than 1918 and 1919, the mortality rate steadily declined from the previous year. Perhaps using the change in mortality from 1 year to the next is not the best way to look for lingering effects of the flu epidemic on take-up of insurance. I have conducted a similar analysis using the change in an interaction between the year and whether a state suffered severe flu mortality (greater than 40% increase in mortality from 1917 to 1918). In this specification, none of the interaction variables have a significant effect on real insurance written. This indicates that the amount of insurance written was not significantly higher in severe flu states, relative to milder flu states, in the years immediately following the epidemic. It is important to note, though, that state mortality rates may not pick up the variations in flu mortality very well. In addition, even "mild" flu states suffered an unusual increase in mortality. We cannot rule out the possibility that the epidemic did stimulate insurance demand, but that reaction did not vary according to flu severity.

7.7 Conclusion

This paper investigates the cause of a surge in demand for life insurance in early 1919. Relative to 1918, sales of ordinary insurance increased by 80% and sales of industrial insurance increased by 15%. However, the apparent source of the surge varies by the type of insurance. I find some evidence that spending on industrial insurance increased more in areas more severely affected by the epidemic. Industrial insurance typically covered funeral costs for women and children, and had little investment value, so it seems reasonable that demand for these policies would be more sensitive to mortality risk. In addition, the door-to-door agents and lack of a medical exam made it easy to quickly pick up more industrial coverage. Also, the mortality rate consistently, or more strongly, affected industrial insurance only after the influenza pandemic. This lends support to the idea that shocks to mortality have a larger effect on insurance than overall mortality. Our results from the Cost of Living Surveys suggest that the four per thousand increase in the mortality rate could be responsible for increasing the probability of holding industrial insurance by about 7%. While not a monumental increase, this goes a long way toward explaining the 15% increase in industrial insurance sales.

In contrast, the holding of ordinary policies was not affected by the disease environment. While we expected a larger effect for industrial insurance, it seems a little strange that there is no effect for ordinary insurance, especially given the even stronger gain in sales. In the immediate aftermath of the epidemic, holdings of fraternal insurance were significantly lower in areas more affected by the disease. Recall that the Cost of Living Surveys only capture a small window of time immediately before and after the worst of the flu epidemic. The lack of positive effects on ordinary and fraternal insurance might be explained by the fact that such insurance was more difficult to obtain particularly considering the disruptions of the epidemic. Many were either convalescing or caring for convalescents for weeks or even months. Public health restrictions may have further made obtaining a medical exam difficult for a considerable period following the first appearance of the epidemic.

To look for lagged effects of the epidemic, we examine panel data on new life insurance written by state. Here, we find a positive effect from a large change in the state mortality rate on the change in new insurance written in 1918, but only for ordinary insurance, and none for any other year through the early 1920s. The effect on industrial insurance that we found in the immediate aftermath of the epidemic appears to dissipate very quickly, as mortality rates returned to more usual levels. We cannot rule out, though, that state-level data is not precise enough to pick up the effects of the mortality shock very well. Furthermore, we have assumed throughout that those living in areas with sharper increases in mortality would respond more. In the 1918 flu epidemic, though, severely affected areas suffered a 40% or more increase in mortality. Those "lightly" affected still saw a 20% increase in mortality. It is possible that the epidemic did cause many people to buy life insurance, but this response did not vary significantly between severe and lightly affected areas.

Recall that our leading candidates to explain the bump in life insurance sales in 1919 were the epidemic, publicity from War Risk Insurance, and the increase in income. Our results indicate that disease mortality was not a large factor in ordinary insurance sales. While not the focus of this paper, promotion from War Risk Insurance does not seem to be the likely cause. We found that state enlistment rates are not correlated with ordinary or industrial insurance holdings in this period, once region is controlled for. This leaves rising income as a leading candidate for explaining the surge in ordinary life sales. Some of this increase in income might be considered an indirect effect of the epidemic, though, as the disease reduced labor supply and contributed to an increase in wages.

Acknowledgments This chapter was much improved by the participants of the 2015 Cliometric Society Conference at the University of Michigan and the 2019 Social Science History Association Meetings in Chicago. Their contributions to this work are gratefully acknowledged.

Appendix: A Tribute to John

I did not know John E. Murray personally. I narrowly missed my best opportunity to meet him several years ago. Back in 2006, I presented my first effort to understand demand for life insurance at the SSHA meetings in Minneapolis. John was scheduled to be the discussant for the panel. By email, he seemed genuinely enthused to receive my paper. Unfortunately, he was ultimately unable to attend. I was somewhat disappointed given how much I admire John's work.

I am an avid fan of good work in economic history. I also introduce undergraduate students to the field. One of the main goals of my economic history course is for students to consider the qualities that make research strong and convincing. In the process, I hope that they also come away with an appreciation for economic history—but even if that does not occur, they should be able to recognize and emulate good research in any field. Outstanding work in economic history tends to have the following qualities: it is engagingly written. It sheds light on an important aspect in the lives of ordinary people. The insights we gain from the work may also help inform us on current or recurring issues. Great economic history brings data to the question in useful and convincing ways—while also providing qualitative evidence through old-fashioned archive work. It is carefully sourced and documented. Finally, the best work is evenhanded and respectful. Even when the research contradicts that of others, it does so without an apparent "axe to grind."

I have read (and reread) John Murray's books on industrial life insurance and the Charleston Orphan House several times. To me, they check all the boxes above, representing the best of what economic history can be. While reading, I frequently get the feeling that I am tagging along to explore the treasure of records that the author just found. Even among eminent economic historians, John's work seems particularly adept at achieving a balance between quantitative and qualitative evidence. When coupled with an unparalleled evenhandedness, his work is an absolute pleasure to read.

References

Almond D (2006) Is the 1918 influenza pandemic over? Long-term effects of in utero influenza exposure in the post-1940 U.S. population. J Pol Econ 114(4):672–712

Beito DT (2000) From mutual aid to welfare state: fraternal societies and social services, 1890–1967. University of North Carolina Press, Chapel Hill

Bell A (1997) 1918 flu pandemic hit insurers hard. National Underwriter, Life & Health (March 31, 1997), pp 46–47

Best AM Co Inc (1920) Best's life insurance reports—1920. Alfred M. Best Company, Inc, New York

Brainerd E, Siegler MV (2006) The economic effects of the 1918 influenza epidemic. CEPR discussion paper 3791

Browne MJ, Kim K (1993) An international analysis of life insurance demand. J Risk Insur 60(4):616–634

Buley RC (1967) The equitable life assurance society of the United States 1859–1964, vol 2. Meredith Publishing Company, New York

Clay K, Lewis J, Severnini E (2018) Pollution, infectious disease, and mortality: evidence from the 1918 Spanish influenza pandemic. J Econ Hist 78(4):1179–1209

Crosby AW (2003) America's forgotten pandemic: the influenza of 1918, 2nd edn. Cambridge University Press, New York

Dublin LI, Lotka AJ (1937) Twenty-five years of health progress: a study of the mortality experience among the industrial policyholders of the Metropolitan Life Insurance Company 1911–1935. Metropolitan Life Insurance Company, New York

Easterlin RA (1957) State Income Estimates. In: Lee ES, Miller AR, Brainerd CP, Easterlin RA (eds) Population redistribution and economic growth United States, 1870–1950, volume I: methodological considerations and reference tables. The American Philosophical Society, Philadelphia

Eggo RM, Cauchemez S, Ferguson N (2011) Spatial dynamics of the 1918 influenza epidemic in England, Wales, and the United States. J Roy Soc Interface 8(55):233–243

Emery H (2001) Fraternal sickness insurance. In: Whaples R (ed) EH.Net encyclopedia, http://eh.net/encyclopedia/article/emery.insurance.fraternal

Emery G, Emery JCH (1999) A young man's benefit: the independent order of odd fellows and sickness insurance in the United States and Canada, 1860–1929. McGill-Queen's University Press, Montreal

Fiegenbaum JJ (2015) Intergenerational mobility during the great depression. Working paper, December 1, 2015. https://scholar.harvard.edu/jfeigenbaum/publications/jmp

Fier SG, Carson JM (2015) Catastrophes and the demand for life insurance. J Insur Iss 38(2):125–156

Garrett TA (2008) Pandemic economics: the 1918 influenza and its modern-day implications. Fed Reserve Bank St Louis Rev 90(2):75–93

Heinrich R (2011) A small town newspaper and a metropolitan newspaper report on a deadly virus: a content analysis of the Spanish influenza pandemic of 1918. J Human Soc Sci 4(1):1–6

Hilt E, Rahm WH (2020) Financial asset ownership and political partisanship: liberty bonds and republican electoral success in the 1920s. J Econ Hist 80(3):746–781

Huebner SS (1923) Life insurance: a textbook. D. Appleton and Company, New York

Jacobson DB, Raub BG, Johnson BW (2007) The estate tax: ninety years and counting. SOI Bull Stat Income 27(1):118–128

Kantor SE, Fishback PV (1996) Precautionary saving, insurance, and the origins of workers' compensation. J Pol Econ 104(2):419–442

Li D et al (2007) The demand for life insurance in OECD countries. J Risk Insur 74(3):637–652

Murray JE (2007) Origins of American health insurance. Yale University Press, New Haven

National Underwriter Company (1917, 1919, 1920) Unique manual-digest of American life insurance. The National Underwriter Company, Cincinnati

Palm R (1995) The Roepke lecture in economic geography. Catastrophic earthquake insurance: patterns of adoption. Econ Geogr 71(2):119–131

Pedoe A, Jack CE (1978) Life insurance, annuities, and pensions: a Canadian text, 3rd edn. University of Toronto Press, Toronto

Ransom RL, Sutch R (1987) Tontine insurance and the Armstrong investigation: a case of stifled innovation, 1868–1905. J Econ Hist 47(2):379–390

Stalson JO (1942) Marketing life insurance: its history in America. Harvard University Press, Cambridge

Sydenstricker E, King ML (1920) Difficulties in computing civil death rates for 1918 with special reference to epidemic influenza. In: U.S. Public Health Service, Reprint No. 583 from the Public Health Reports

Tarbell, TF (1919) The effect of influenza on insurance. In: proceedings of the National Convention of Insurance Commissioners, 9–12 September 1919. Hartford, CT, pp 302–311

Taubenberger JK, Morens DM (2006) 1918 influenza: the mother of all pandemics. Emerg Infect Dis 12(1):15–22

The Spectator Company (1919) Life insurance by states—summary. In: The insurance year book 1918–1919: Life, casualty, and miscellaneous edition, p 343

U.S. Bureau of the Census (1922) Mortality statistics, 1920. Twenty-first annual report. GPO, Washington, DC, pp 12–13

U.S. Bureau of the Census (1996) Population of the states and counties of the United States: 1790–1990. GPO, Washington, DC
U.S. Department of Commerce (1925) Statistical abstract, 1924. GPO, Washington, DC
U.S. Department of Labor, Bureau of Labor Statistics (1918) Cost of living 1918 instructions, 1918. GPO, Washington, DC
U.S. War Office (1918) Allotments, family allowances, compensation, and insurance under War risk insurance act. GPO, Washington, DC
U.S. War Office (1919) Second report of the provost marshal general to the secretary of war on the operations of the selective service system to December 20, 1918. GPO, Washington, DC
Whaples R, Buffum D (1991) Fraternalism, paternalism, the family, and the market: insurance a century ago. Soc Sci Hist 15(1):97–122
White E (2006) Tables Cj713-732, and Cj766-786. In: Carter SB, Gartner SS, Haines MR, Olmstead AL, Sutch R, Wright G (eds) Historical statistics of the United States, earliest times to the present: millennial edition. Cambridge University Press, New York
Williamson, SH (2019) The annual consumer price index for the United States, 1774-present. Measuring Worth, URL: http://www.measuringworth.com/uscpi/
Wooldridge JM (2010) Econometric analysis of cross section and panel data, 2nd edn. The MIT Press, Cambridge
Zultowski WH (1979) The extent of buyer-initiated life insurance sales. J Risk Insur 46(4):707–714

Chapter 8
"Theft of Oneself": Runaway Servants in Early Maryland: Deterrence, Punishment, and Apprehension

Farley Grubb

Abstract Immigrant indentured and transported convict servants had an incentive to breech their labor contracts by running away. Masters and servants in colonial Maryland engaged in strategic behaviors to deal with this contract breech incentive. In the seventeenth century, masters altered the colony's statutory laws to deter and thwart servant escape, and servants chose the escape routes that offered the best chance of not being returned to Maryland. Strategic behaviors changed by the eighteenth century. Masters quickly advertised runaway servants in Maryland newspapers, and servants selected when to run that delayed the appearance of those ads as much as possible.

Keywords Indentures · Indentured servants · Theft of oneself · Contract breach · Apprehension

8.1 Introduction/Summary

Servants who voluntarily entered fixed labor contracts (indentures) comprised a majority of the immigrants arriving from Britain to seventeenth-century Maryland (Grubb 1985a; Smith 1947: 336). Before the late 1680s, and even as late as 1702, they also comprised a majority of the bound labor force in Maryland (Grubb and Stitt 1994). While African slaves became the majority bound labor force in Maryland after 1702, British voluntary indentured servants and transported convict servants continued to arrive in sizable numbers throughout the rest of the colonial period (Bailyn 1986; Grubb 1985a, 2000b).

Indentured immigrants and transported convict servants broke their contracts by running away. This act was called "theft of oneself." In the seventeenth century, both Virginia and Maryland passed laws to deter and punish such acts. However,

F. Grubb (✉)
University of Delaware, Newark, DE, USA
e-mail: grubbf@udel.edu

P. Gray et al. (eds.), *Standard of Living*, Studies in Economic History,
https://doi.org/10.1007/978-3-031-06477-7_8

Maryland made the legally prescribed punishment for running away harsher than the punishment enacted in the neighboring colony of Virginia. A simple economic model is used to account for this difference. In this model, society desires a "good" called "completed servant contracts." It produced this good using a cost-minimizing combination of inputs, namely, the apprehension mechanisms and punishments if caught in response to the gains from a successful escape, all of which varied by location within and between the colonies. The method of informing the public of runaway servants and so detaining them in seventeenth-century Maryland was only through "hue and cry"—information passed from one neighbor to the next. Maryland used harsher legal punishments than Virginia not because Maryland planters were crueler, but as a reaction to the greater probability of successful escape and gains from that escape that existed for Maryland servants compared with those faced by servants in Virginia.

By the mid-eighteenth century, Maryland's laws to deter and punish servants who ran away had become codified and fixed, no longer responsive to changing probabilities of successful escape and gains from that escape. Those probabilities, however, no longer varied substantially across colonies or by location within colonies. Maryland's method of informing the public of runaway servants and so detaining them had also changed from using just "hue and cry" to using the colony's weekly newspaper, the *Maryland Gazette*, to inform fellow colonists and county sheriffs of runaways.

The advertisements for runaway servants in the *Maryland Gazette* are used to assess the strategic behavior of runaway servants and their masters in mid-eighteenth-century Maryland. No matter the master's location within the colony, a runaway advertisement was typically placed in the *Maryland Gazette* within 2 weeks of the servant's act of running away, appearing in the next issue of the *Gazette* after the act of running away. Runaways were also more likely to select certain days of the week to run away, namely, the days that increased their chances of successfully escaping. The primary method of informing the public of runaway servants by the mid-eighteenth century led to predictable strategic behaviors on the part of servants and masters regarding contract compliance, enforcement, and apprehension of runaways.

8.2 The Puzzle in Runaway Law in Seventeenth-Century Maryland

The seventeenth-century colonies of Virginia and Maryland were similar. They resided next to each other with economies oriented toward Chesapeake Bay and the export of tobacco to England. Both relied on immigrant indentured servant labor as their principal bound labor force into the late seventeenth century when slaves thereafter became the principal bound labor force. Even so, thereafter immigrant indentured and convict servant labor continued to be imported and used throughout the rest of the colonial period, with most English indentured servants migrating to these two Chesapeake colonies. Trade and migration flourished between the two colonies with little restriction, even though each colony passed its own laws to govern its citizens (Grubb 1985a, 2000b; Grubb and Stitt 1994; McCusker and Menard 1985; Walsh 1977, 1987).

One glaring legal difference between the two colonies was over the treatment of indentured servants, in particular the legally prescribed punishment given the servant when the servant ran away from their master and was subsequently caught and prosecuted. This act of breaking the contract by running away was called "theft of oneself" and was deemed criminal in law in both England and the colonies. Abbot E. Smith (1947: 270, 276–7) summarized and explained the difference as follows:

> Why should the laws of Maryland in general have been so much more harsh than those of her neighbors? ... Why should a runaway serve ten [extra] days for one [absent] in Maryland, and only two for one in Virginia? Why should a person who harbored a runaway forfeit five hundred lbs. of tobacco for every night in Maryland, and only sixty pounds in Virginia? And most remarkable of all, why, when most colonies progressively made their penal codes milder, should Maryland after abandoning her original death penalty for runaways and substituting double service [two extra days of service for every one day absent], progressively make her code more severe? I know of no answer to these questions, except to assume that the planters of Maryland were a harsher breed than those of Virginia and Pennsylvania. This assumption appears foolish, but one certainly gains the impression from reading court records that not only the laws but also the magistrates of that colony were less merciful. ... Obviously the penalties of extra service were imposed principally for the enrichment of the master; there can be no possible reason for the Maryland law with a punishment five times as severe as that of Virginia except that the planters of that colony more openly pursued their own advantage.

Smith's assertion that differential punishments are due to differential values or tastes is a conclusion, not an explanation. This conclusion is the result of an absence of other explanations. Conclusions such as Maryland planters were harsher or greedier than Virginia planters have the disadvantage of suggesting an end to further investigation. Once an issue arrives at a difference in values, what more can be said? By contrast, the economic approach to explaining differences in servant punishment is to assume fixed values, tastes, and preferences, and look instead at differences in observed opportunities between the two colonies that affected the decision by servants to run away (Becker 1996: 24–49; Diamond 1982).

Published primary sources for the seventeenth century are scarce. The only published court records for Virginia are for Accomack County between 1640 and 1645. Published primary source evidence for Maryland is more plentiful. Secondary sources indicate that Virginia's penalty of double the time absent added to the contract was constant throughout the seventeenth century. Therefore, the issue to be explained is why Maryland laws differed from Virginia and why Maryland laws changed over time (see Table 8.1).[1]

Traditional sentences for violating criminal law in England involved some type of physical chastisement, such as whippings, brandings, or, in extreme cases,

[1] For Virginia see, Bruce (1896, vol. 2: 10–29). For Maryland see, *Archives of Maryland* (vols. 1, 2, 4, 10, 41, 49, 53, 54, 57, 60, 65, 66).

Table 8.1 Maryland laws regarding the punishment for runaway indentured servants

Year	Punishment
1638	Several lashes (a single case precedent, not an act)
1639	Hanging
1641	Death, unless the servant requests to exchange the penalty for extra service. Then the servant must serve double the time absent as extra service, but the total not to exceed 7 years
1650	Double the time absent as extra service, plus damages and costs occasioned by the absence
1666	For every day absent the servant must serve 10 days extra

Sources: Archives of Maryland (vols. 1, 2, 4, 10, 41, 49, 53, 54, 57, 60, 65, 66)

hangings (Beattie 1986). Once the punishment was meted out, the person found guilty of the crime (if still living) was returned to society. Incarceration was not used as a sentence or as punishment, but only to hold individuals awaiting trial. The point of punishment in criminal law was to deter similar criminal acts in the future.

In England, as in America, breaching a labor contract by the worker running off was considered a criminal act called "theft of oneself." Workers who ran off and were caught were returned to their employers to finish their contracts and could also be physically chastised—the physical chastisement being the deterrence part. In England, labor contracts were relatively short and absent workers could be more easily replaced than in colonial America. There was also little labor contract breaking in England due to how English labor contracts were structured (Grubb 2000a). In England, employers lost relatively less from workers running off compared with employers in colonial America.

The punishment of hanging implemented in early Maryland (1639) for the servant's act of running away from their master was a strong deterrent to servants breaching their contracts. But this punishment also left the master without the rest of the servant's contracted labor time. Given that servant labor contracts were several years long, the loss of labor value by the master could be substantial. Colonial masters desired compensation for the lost labor value for the time that servants had absented themselves from their masters.

Seeking compensation for damages from the person who breached their contract involves tort law. Immigrant servants had no resources to pay damages except their future post-contract labor time. The punishment in law—that is, requiring servants who ran off and were caught to not just finish their existing labor contracts but to serve extra time beyond the end of their contracts as compensation to masters for the lost labor value while the servants were absent—mixed criminal law (deterrence) with tort law (compensation to the wronged party for breaching a contract).[2]

[2] Slaves had no resources and no extra labor time with which to compensate slave owners for the lost labor time caused when slaves ran off. All the owner could get was the rest of the slave's labor life from the point when the slave was caught and returned. The lost labor time while absent was a total loss. Therefore, a slave owner's calculation of the resources to invest in recapturing a runaway slave was different than that for recapturing a runaway indentured servant. The loss of future labor

The extra time the servant had to serve as compensation for having run off had to be longer than the time the servant had absented himself because (1) it had to also serve to deter future acts of running away and (2) had to compensate the master for the lost time while absent. Because the extra days added to the contract were several years in the future, that future labor value had to be time-discounted back to the present. Everything else held constant, a day's labor value 4 years from now is worth less than a day's labor value today. Thus, the extra time served had to be more than the time the servant was absent to fully compensate the master for the lost labor value—to make the master "whole" as phrased in tort law. Colonial law after 1641 required that extra days be added to the end of the contract for the act of running away, more than the number of days the servant was absent (see Table 8.1).

Table 8.1 also shows a sudden shift in punishment in 1666 for the act of running away by the servant. From a level similar to that of Virginia, namely, 2 days extra servitude for every day absent, Maryland substantially increased its punishment in 1666 to 10 days extra servitude for every day absent. While this change generated increased compensation to the master, it also represented increased punishment deterrence to committing this crime. It is difficult to see this change as being driven by a correction in the required equitable compensation for damages. Thus, it looks like it may have been a response to the need for greater deterrence. To explore this, court cases involving runaway servants in Maryland are examined from 1653, the first court case of running away in the surviving records, to 1676, a full 10 years after the change in legal punishment, to explain the cause and effect of changes in Maryland's runaway laws.

8.3 The Structure of Indentured Servant Contracts and the Incentive to Run Away

Immigrant indentured servitude was a form of long-term labor contracting, basically a forward-labor contract, similar to English apprenticeship contracts and life-cycle-servitude in husbandry agreements (Galenson 1981; Grubb 1985b, 2000a; Kussmaul 1981; Laslett 1971). A key differentiating feature of immigrant indentured contracts was that a large portion of the contract's value was paid up front in the form of passage to the New World before any work was performed. Servants also received maintenance during the voyage and during the contract. To recoup this outlay, the labor contract had to extend over several years, typically 4 years for an

value if the slave successfully escaped was much greater than the loss of future contracted labor value if a servant successfully escaped—the rest of life for the slave versus a few years of labor for a servant. Thus, a slave owner's investment in recapturing a runaway slave would depend most on that future lost value. Masters of servants could get tort-damage compensation from the servant both for the lost labor time while absent and the cost of apprehension via being legally granted extra labor time added to the end of the servant initial contract. This was compensation a slave owner could not get.

adult (Grubb 1992a). In effect, the servant borrowed on his future labor a sum large enough to pay for passage across the Atlantic.

Prepayment of passage to the New World by masters may have been inescapable. Passage costs were sizable, equal to maybe a full year's income (Grubb 1985a). Servants did not have enough accumulated savings, and it would take many years to accumulate enough savings to pay such a high passage cost. Borrowing on their future labor by signing an alienable servant contract was likely their only option to secure passage to America.

This large up-front passage fare payment could not be effectively countered over the first half of the labor contract's length by requiring payment of a contract-completion bonus at the end of the contract. Such bonuses, required in colonial law, were called "freedom dues." The servant had to pay for any freedom dues contracted or legally due by working for it; thus, freedom dues simply extended the contract's length without altering the amount of labor time needed initially to repay the passage fare (Grubb 2000a).

When the lion's share of payment is made prior to the execution of the labor portion of the contract, when it is what is called a "frontloaded contract" from the worker's perspective, the result is an incentive by the workers to shirk or even breach the contract (Grubb 2000a). Why should the servant work hard or even stick around once the servant has received his passage to America? Having already been paid, i.e., having already been transported to America, the servant had an incentive to avoid the rest of the contract. The incentive was to run away and work for someone who would not have to deduct the cost of passage from the servant's remuneration.

The economic approach to crime and punishment takes the level of punishment and the probability of capture (conviction) as substitutes in controlling the crime rate (Becker 1976: 39–85; Bodenhorn 2015: 90–3; Ehrlich 1973). The crime here is the unilateral breaking of a labor contract by running away. Instead of thinking in terms of the supply and demand of crimes, it is more cogent to think in derived demand terms of a production function of completed indentured servant contracts. The society of colonial planters produced completed indentured servant contracts through a combination of inputs that influences the servants' behavior, namely, the likelihood of running away. Planters choose a set of inputs to minimize the cost of producing completed indentured servant contracts per an exogenously given payoff that the servant sees from a successful escape. Changes in the relative costs of these inputs, or changes in the payoff the servant expected from a successful escape, may explain changes in punishment levels inflicted on runaway servants who were caught.

Planters endeavor, through control of the legislature and to some extent the courts, to minimize the cost of producing completed indentured servant contracts. The production function of completed contracts contains a vector of inputs, including the probability of capture and conviction for running away, the degree of punishment for running away, and the expected alternative income if running away is successful. Planters will choose the combination of inputs to satisfy the first-order condition of cost minimization, namely input amounts will be adjusted until the ratio of cost-per-input-unit is equalized across all inputs.

Planters' control or influence over the inputs and their relative costs varied by location. Both the marginal payoff and the cost per unit of the various inputs can be location specific, thus altering the mix of inputs used to produce the optimal amount of completed contracts by location. The particular combination of inputs used by Maryland planters, via their control of the legislature and courts, was effective in that the number of runaway servants out of the total population of servants was not large (Grubb 2000b; Smith 1947: 270, 278).

8.4 Application to Seventeenth-Century Maryland

The impression in the historical literature is that the problem of runaway servants was large, taking up a substantial portion of court time in seventeenth-century Maryland. In fact, for the period 1653 through 1676, there are only 39 prosecutions of runaway servants. This is a minute fraction of the court's total time. Cases involving servants suing planters for nonpayment of freedom dues and other rights violations are more frequent (Grubb 2000a). Table 8.2 presents the runaway prosecution cases, their court locations, and the punishments handed down separated into the pre- versus post-1666 change in punishment laws.

The Maryland courts followed the letter of the law in meting out punishment except in Charles County after 1666. The number of prosecuted cases increases

Table 8.2 Prosecutions of runaway servants in Maryland, 1653–1676

Years	Court	Number	Punishment
1653–1666	Provincial	5	2 days extra for each day absent
	Kent County	1	25 lashes
	Charles County	4	7 to 27 lashes
1666–1676	Provincial	9	6 serve 10 days extra for each day absent
			3 have uncertain punishments
	Kent County	1	10 days extra for each day absent
	Talbot County	14	12 serve 10 days extra for each day absent
			2 have uncertain punishments
	Somerset County	2	1 serves 10 days extra for each day absent
			1 has uncertain punishments
	Charles County	3	1 received 10 lashes
			1 received 12 lashes
			1 was already whipped by his master, so no additional punishment was given

Sources: Archives of Maryland (vols. 1, 2, 4, 10, 41, 49, 53, 54, 57, 60, 65, 66)

after the punishment was increased in 1666. More information is needed on the number of servants present in the colony before this increase can be used to infer a rise in the incidence or percentage of servants running away. The number of unprosecuted runaway servants mentioned incidentally in the court records may more accurately reflect changes in the incidence of running away before versus after 1666. Table 8.3 reports these unprosecuted cases of running away in the court records. This evidence indicates that the increase in punishment did not by itself cause an increased incidence of running away.

Changes in punishment were part of a wider integrated shift in the use of inputs to produce completed indentured servant contracts. One of the other inputs to achieving completed indentured servant contracts was increasing the probability of capture, thus lowering the incentive to run away. Schemes to increase the probability of capture in the seventeenth century were more difficult to devise than ways to increase the punishment level. Nevertheless, a flurry of acts were passed by the Maryland assembly between 1666 and 1676 that attempted to increase the probability of capture. Table 8.4 lists the legislative acts passed to aid in the apprehension of runaway servants.

Changes in alternative income for successfully running away prior to 1666 was another event affecting the use of inputs to produce completed indentured servant contracts. In general, runaways would seek out other white settlements. The wilderness was not a serious option due to the threat from Native Americans and due to starvation. For the years prior to 1666, Virginia and Maryland were relatively isolated. Most runaways would stay within the two colonies or try to board ships leaving the Chesapeake. Many runaway servants were extradited from Maryland to Virginia. Prior to 1664, more runaways were extradited to Virginia from Maryland than were prosecuted as runaways from within the colony of Maryland. Prior to 1664, 14 runaway servants were extradited from Maryland to Virginia. From 1664 through 1676, none were. Also none were extradited to other colonies from Maryland prior to 1676 (*Archives of Maryland* vols. 1, 2, 4, 10, 41, 49, 53, 54, 57, 60, 65, 66). It may be safe to assume Virginia reciprocated and extradited Maryland runaway servants captured in Virginia back to Maryland.

After about 1660, a new destination for runaway servants appeared, namely, the Dutch-Swedish settlements on the lower Delaware River. Although there was some concourse between these settlements on the Delaware and the English colony of

Table 8.3 Unprosecuted runaway servants in the Maryland court records

Years	Court	Number
1653–1666	Provincial	27
	Kent County	4
	Charles County	3
1666–1676	Provincial	7
	Kent County	1
	Talbot County	10
	Charles County	3

Sources: Archives of Maryland (vols. 1, 2, 4, 10, 41, 49, 53, 54, 57, 60, 65, 66)

Table 8.4 Legislative acts to aid in runaway servant apprehension

Year	Legislation enacted
1638	Harboring or transporting another's servant out of the province shall be a felony
1641	Receiving a runaway servant shall be a felony
1662	No servant shall travel over two miles from his master's house without a pass written in the master's hand
1666	Fines for harboring runaway servants are 500 pounds of tobacco for the first night, 1000 pounds for the second night, and 1500 pounds for all other nights
1669	A prison is to be built on the northern escape route at Augustine Herman's bohemian manor; other governments are paid 400 pounds of tobacco for delivery of runaways, and Herman may work servants to pay for his cost; to redeem captured servants, a master must pay Herman 400 pounds of tobacco
1671	All former acts repealed; fine for harboring runaway servants is 500 pounds of tobacco a night; servants cannot travel over 10 miles from home without a pass from his master or out of the county without a sealed county stamped pass; reward for returning a runaway is 200 pounds of tobacco to be paid by the master; reward to Indians will be a match coat[a]
1674	Extend the fine for harboring runaway servants to cover ship captains
1676	Reward to Virginia, Delaware, and northern colonies will be 400 pounds of tobacco for the return of runaway servants to be paid by the master, except for Accomack County, Virginia, who will get only 200 pounds of tobacco

Sources: Archives of Maryland (vols. 1, 2, 4, 10, 41, 49, 53, 54, 57, 60, 65, 66)

[a]The significance of the difference in reward paid to Native Americans is hard to determine, in part because no examples of Native Americans collecting rewards for apprehending runaway servant were found in the data. Whether Native Americans were treated differently in colonial statutory laws that dealt with similar reward issues is currently unknown and so a topic for future research

Maryland, the atmosphere was hostile between the two governments, even after the English officially took over these Delaware settlements in 1665. Systematic English government on the Delaware does not appear until 1676. Even then, New Castle, formerly New Amstel (on the Delaware River), court records from 1676 to 1681 reveal no cases involving the extradition to Maryland from Delaware of runaway servants from Maryland. In fact, as late as 1678, the colonists of Delaware were petitioning their governor for the liberty to trade with Maryland for the purpose of acquiring slaves, servants, and utensils.

Delaware was a frequently mentioned destination by Maryland runaway servants. The Maryland court records reveal two specific escape routes to Delaware. One route was up the Elk River and the other route was up the Choptank River. The mouth of the Elk River was close to Augustine Herman's Bohemian Manor where a prison was established in 1669 to hold runaway servants apprehended nearby (see Table 8.4). The head of the Elk River was a short walk to the head of the Christina River which led directly to New Castle, Delaware. The head of the Choptank River was a short walk into the lower Delaware region. Apparently, escaped servants did not become servants in Delaware. Of the list of tithables for New Castle County in 1677, there were only 19 servants among the 307 inhabitants between the ages of 6 and 60.[3] Table 8.5 lists the destination mentioned in Maryland court records for runaway servants.

[3]New Castle Court Records (1904)

Table 8.5 Destinations of runaway servants in Maryland records

To Delaware and Farther North:		To Virginia and Further South:	
Assembly Records	1	Provincial Court	5
Kent County court	1		
Talbot County court	2		
Provincial court	14		
Total	18	Total	5

Sources: Archives of Maryland (vols. 1, 2, 4, 10, 41, 49, 53, 54, 57, 60, 65, 66)

Maryland formed a buffer between Virginia and the safe haven of Delaware. In a world where the standard form of apprehending runaway servants was through sending out a "hue and cry" through the population—neighbors passing information to the next neighbors—the probability of capture increases with the size of the friendly population between the master and the runaway's destination. Maryland in effect was performing part of Virginia's policing effort. Not only was there an increase in the alternative income available for successful runaways after 1660, namely, getting to the Delaware settlements, but the likelihood of successfully getting to Delaware was relatively greater for Maryland servants. Virginia servants faced a longer trek and a higher probability of apprehension because they had to traverse through Maryland to get to the safe haven of Delaware.

The increase in the alternative income occasioned a shift to other inputs such as punishment. The difference in the probability of capture between Virginia and Maryland runaway servants could explain the difference in punishment of their respective runaway servants. One implication of this view is that given some discretion in the county courts, the punishment would be tempered depending on the distance from Delaware, namely, on the probability of their runaway servants being apprehended. The interior counties would be expected to have less severe punishment than the counties on the Delaware frontier. Charles County, in the interior, never inflicted more than 27 lashes. Extra service was not added to the runaway's contract. Charles County became less severe in its punishment of its runaway servants over the period. By contrast, Talbot County, a county on the Delaware frontier, inflicted the maximum punishment allowed in law in all runaway cases.

The increase in punishment and the increase in the desired rate of apprehension can be seen as part of the same concerted effort to offset the change in some other input to the production of completed indentured servant contracts. That other input was an exogenous change in the probability and payoff from a successful escape occasioned by the presence of a new safe haven for runaway servants on the lower Delaware River.

8.5 Escape and Apprehension Strategies in Mid-Eighteenth-Century Maryland

By mid-eighteenth century, Maryland's laws to deter and punish runaway servants had become fixed, even ossified, no longer responsive to changing probabilities of escape and gains from escape. The Maryland Assembly saw fit to make no adjustments. However, those escape, and gains from escape, probabilities no longer varied substantially across colonies or by location within colonies. Maryland was now surrounded by other English colonies, i.e., Pennsylvania, Delaware, and Virginia, who advertised and returned servants who ran away from neighboring colonies' masters. For example, Johann Carl Buettner, a German immigrant indentured servant, ran away from his master in eastern New Jersey in 1775. He made it through Pennsylvania and Maryland and was finally picked up and jailed in Norfolk, Virginia. The Norfolk sheriff advertised his capture in the *Pennsylvania Gazette*, and Buettner's New Jersey master was able to recover Buettner from Virginia (Klepp et al. 2006: 186–9).

By mid-eighteenth century, Maryland's method of informing the public of runaway servants and so detaining them had also changed from just "hue and cry" to using the colony's weekly newspaper, the *Maryland Gazette*, to inform fellow colonists and county sheriffs of runaways. The *Maryland Gazette* was a weekly newspaper issued out of Annapolis. Issues exist from 1745 through 1789. The first page or two of each issue was devoted to news, much of it political, and the next two pages or so were devoted to advertisements. All sorts of things were advertised, including lots of runaways: runaway horses, runaway wives, runaway slaves, and runaway immigrant servants and transported convict servants.

A total of 1765 advertisements for runaway servants (netting out repeat ads) appear in the *Maryland Gazette* from 1745 through 1789. An advertisement for a runaway typically ran for several issues. Information was taken only from the first appearance of an ad. For an example of a first ad, see the following advertisement in the *Maryland Gazette*, Thursday, March 30, 1769:

> *March 29, 1769.*
>
> RAN away last Night from the subscribers, living on *Kent-Island*, Two Convict Servant Men, *viz.*
>
> EDWARD PONTING, born in *Bristol*, about 25 Years of Age, 5 feet 6 or 7 Inches high, has a pert impudent Look, thin Visage, with brown curled Hair, is by Trade a Shoemaker, has some blue Marks on the Upper Part of his Hands, near the Thumbs, which are unknown: Had on, when he went away, an old bloom coloured *Wilton* Coat, spotted Flannel Jacket, a Pair of half worn Leather Breeches, old blue ribb'd Stockings, old Shoes, with plated Buckles, half worn Castor Hat, and a Check Shirt.
>
> ... [description of second runaway belonging to Jonathan Roberts] ...
>
> Whoever takes up and secures said Convicts, so that their Masters may get them again, shall receive, for each, Thirty Shillings, besides what the Law allows, and reasonable Charges, if brought home, paid by SAMUEL BLUNT [Ponting's owner] ...

Male servants comprised 95% of these ads. Convict servants comprised 48%, immigrant indentured servants 48%, apprentices 1.5%, and re-indented servants

2.5% of these ads. Among the 1085 ads that identified the servant's ethnicity, 55% were English, 31% were Irish, 4% were Scots, 3% were Welsh, and 2% were German. Table 8.6 reports the counties of the masters of the runaways, from most to least runaways advertised. Three counties, Baltimore County, Annapolis, and Anne Arundel County accounted for over half the runaways.

Table 8.6 also reports the month the servant ran away based on the date advertised. Servants were more likely to run away in June through September, and less likely to run away in December through February. That servants chose the summer months and avoided the winter months to try and escape makes rational strategic sense on several levels. The opportunities to board a vessel to escape were higher in the summer than in the winter, and the ability to travel far and live off the land was greater in summer than in the winter. There was no nonrandom pattern in terms of what day in the month servants ran away.

Table 8.7 reports the day of the week servants chose to run away. Servants overwhelmingly chose to run away on Sunday. Given that most servants were given Sundays off as the Lord's day-of-rest and/or to attend Church, running on Sunday likely maximized the amount of time before the master would detect that the servant was missing. Choosing to run on Mondays and Tuesdays was also above random choices, whereas choosing to run on Wednesdays through Saturdays was below random choices. Given that the *Maryland Gazette* was issued on Thursdays, and given the time it took masters to get a letter to the newspaper to advertise the runaway, running away on Sunday through Tuesday likely meant that the master could not get an advertisement about the runaway into that week's newspaper. Thus, even if the master sent an ad in immediately after detecting that the servant had run away, the ad would not appear until the following week's Thursday issue. This time span

Table 8.6 Month when the servant ran and the county of owner

Month when ran	N = 1765	Top counties of owners of runaways	N = 1639
March	7.0%	Baltimore	22.9%
April	9.2	Anne Arundel	19.4
May	8.2	Annapolis	11.0
June	13.5	Prince George	7.7
July	13.2	Kent Island and	
August	13.4	Queen Anne	5.2
September	11.3	Charles	4.3
October	8.1	Kent/Chestertown	4.0
November	6.6	Frederick, Maryland	3.7
December	3.4	Calvert	3.1
January	3.2	Frederick, Virginia	3.1
February	2.9	Talbot	2.4
		Cecil	1.8
	100%		88.6%

Source: Maryland Gazette

Notes: Only 93% of the ads listed the county of the owner. If running away was random by month, then 8.3% would run away each month

Table 8.7 Day of the week the servant ran away

	N = 1336
Day	%
Sunday	32.0
Monday	17.6
Tuesday	16.0
Wednesday	10.5
Thursday	7.8
Friday	7.0
Saturday	9.1
	100%

Source: Maryland Gazette
Notes: Only 76% of the ads had information that allowed determination of the day of the week when the servant ran. If running away was random by day of the week, then 14.3% would runaway each day of the week

maximized the servant's time on the run, a full week and a half, before the public was alerted to the runaway through newspaper ads. This pattern is consistent with servants exercising considerable strategic behavior to maximize their chances of escape and avoiding quick apprehension.

Many masters dated the letter they sent to the *Maryland Gazette*; see the example above by the master Samuel Blunt. This evidence gives a sense of how long it took letters to get to Annapolis and then get the ad into the newspaper. Table 8.8 reports that evidence. Half of all the letters got to Annapolis in time to make that week's newspaper, with 3 days' time being the mode interval. Almost 80% of the letters got to the newspaper within 2 weeks, namely, by the next issuance of the weekly paper. This evidence indicates that masters did not wait long once detecting that the servant had run away, but more-or-less immediately sent a runaway ad to the *Maryland Gazette*. Given that masters could be compensated for the cost of placing an ad by having the servant's labor time extended beyond that required in law meant that masters saw little differential loss from advertising runaway servants regardless of the servant's contract type or labor value per unit time.

The incentive to advertise runaway slaves was different. Masters could not be compensated by the slave for the cost of advertising or apprehending the slave. Thus, slave owners had a different calculation, namely, they might consider the likelihood that a given runaway slave might return on his or her own, being just a brief absence for some reason, and so the master could avoid the advertising cost (loss). Only when it became clear the slave had permanently fled, and if the remainder of the slave's life if caught was of greater value, then the master would invest in more advertising and apprehension expenses (Bodenhorn 2015: 93–5).

Given that masters could be compensated for the cost of advertising runaway servants via extra labor time added to the end of the servant contract, beyond the extra time added as set out in law, and so had an incentive to quickly advertise all runaway servants, the strategic behavior of servants in choosing what day of the

Table 8.8 Days between when the owner's letter was posted and when the ad appeared and days between when the servant ran away and when the ad appeared

	Days between owner's letter and ad		Days between when the servant ran and ad	
	N = 859		N = 1339	
Days				
1	5.8%		2.3%	
2	8.1		4.7	
3	16.8		5.8	
4	3.1		14.5	
5	4.8		4.0	
6	4.8		3.2	
7	6.1		4.3	
First week total	49.5%		38.8%	
8	8.5%		4.2%	
9	5.6		6.3	
10	9.3		6.0	
11	2.4		8.3	
12	1.5		2.2	
13	1.4		1.5	
14	1.0		1.3	
	____	(cumulative)	____	(cumulative)
Second week total	29.7%	(79.2%)	29.8%	(68.6%)
Third week total	11.8%	(91.0%)	10.7%	(79.3%)
Fourth week total	3.7%	(94.7%)	7.2%	(86.5%)

Source: Maryland Gazette

Notes: Only 49% of the ads had a date listed for the letter sent by the owner to the newspaper. Only 76% of the ads had enough information to calculate the days between when the servant ran and the ad's date (the date the newspaper was issued)

week to run away makes sense. Servants wanted to maximize that Table 8.8 interval, and so try and push that interval into week 2, because they knew masters would advertise their escape as soon as it was detected. This pattern is internally consistent in a game-theoretic way between masters and servants and their incentives to react to each other's behaviors.

Table 8.8 also reports the number of days between when the servant ran away and when the ad appeared in the newspaper. Almost 40% of the ads appeared within the week of the act of running away, namely, by the next newspaper issue after running away. The mode interval was 4 days. Almost 70% of the ads appeared within 2 weeks, namely, by the second issue after running away. Again, this evidence indicates that masters did not wait long after detecting that the servant had run away, but more-or-less immediately sent a runaway ad to the *Maryland Gazette*. Comparing the two columns in Table 8.8 indicates that servants gained some time by strategically choosing what day to runway before the public was alerted to their act through a newspaper ad.

The behavior of masters and servants as revealed through the newspaper ads for runaways still has to be traced through the county courts to see how punishment was administered and whether it varied by location and type of servant contract. The runaway rate for servants in mid-eighteenth-century Maryland is difficult to assess given restrictive arrival sample sizes, though it looks like the runaway rate was about 16% for convict servants and 6% for indentured servants (Grubb 2000b: 108). How many runaways were actually apprehended, and how many of those apprehended were prosecuted and punished across the county courts in Maryland, is a project for future research.

8.6 Conclusions

Immigrant indentured servants and transported convict servants had an incentive to breach their labor contracts by running away. The contracts were frontloaded and so servants had a lot to gain by early departure. Masters and servants engaged in strategic behaviors to deal with this contract breach incentive. Servants maximized their chances of escape, and master maximized their ability to thwart successful escape, given their constraints. In the seventeenth century, that behavior involved masters altering the colony's statutory laws to mix together changing punishments and apprehension techniques to thwart servant escape. They adjusted these laws to changing locational opportunities of escape. Servants chose the best routes to escape that offered the best chance of not being returned to Maryland. Strategic behavior changed by the eighteenth century due to changing locational opportunities to escape and how runaways information could be delivered to the public. Masters quickly advertised runaway servants in newspapers, and servants selected when to run that delayed the appearance of those ads as much as possible.

Acknowledgments The author thanks Margarita Golod and Jianmin Zhang for research assistance done some time ago, and Howard Bodenhorn for helpful comments on an earlier draft.

Appendix: Grubb's Murray Tribute

John Murray's work on orphan apprenticeship in early America and my work on European immigrant indentured servitude in early America had much in common (for examples see Grubb (1992b, 2000a, 2006), Murray and Herndon (2002), and Murray (2013). Regarding these types of labor contracts, John and I often discussed contract structure, why particular contract designs were used, how contract compliance was enforced, and the behavioral incentives faced by masters, servants, and the government regarding contract performance. Typically, we discussed these issues in person at the annual meetings of the Economic History Association.

John was familiar with the work that is provided here through reading earlier working paper versions of it, but mostly through our in-person discussions of it over the years. He had encouraged me to publish it in some form. The initial working paper was written in 1980 as my first work on immigrant indentured servitude in colonial America when I was still a graduate student in economics at the University of Chicago. I sat it aside to work on other aspects of immigrant servitude. I returned to it often over the years, occasionally adding to it, but always setting it aside and not finishing it.

I aspired to use the paper as a vehicle for developing a complex mathematical model of crime and punishment, building on the work of my thesis advisor Gary Becker (1976: 39–85), and then use the colonial data to test the model. I hoped to place the piece in a general model-oriented economics journal. Alas, I have not been up to the task of mathematically modeling the issues as I envisioned them, nor do I think the data were strong enough to test the kind of model I had in mind. So while I frequently revisited the paper, I always sat it aside, waiting for better modeling inspiration that unfortunately (or fortunately) never came.

John liked the story and the data findings in the project and encouraged me to just publish the story and the evidence and not worry about trying to look modeling erudite for my economist peers. He felt that historians and economic historians would find the project interesting and a valuable addition to colonial labor history. As a tribute to his wise advice and, in a gentle way, his mentoring of an older scholar, I cleaned up the project, suppressed efforts to provide an explicit and original mathematical model of crime and punishment, and just presented the story and the evidence. Thanks John. I will miss our conversations.

References

Archives of Maryland, vols. 1–66 (1883–1972) Maryland historical society, Baltimore

Bailyn B (1986) Voyagers to the west: a passage in the peopling of America on the eve of the revolution. Knoft, New York

Beattie JM (1986) Crime and the courts in England, 1660–1800. Princeton University Press, Princeton

Becker GS (1976) The economic approach to human behavior. University of Chicago Press, Chicago

Becker GS (1996) Accounting for tastes. Harvard University Press, Cambridge

Bodenhorn H (2015) The color factor: the economics of African-American well-being in the nineteenth-century south. Oxford University Press, New York

Bruce PA (1896) Economic history of Virginia in the seventeenth century: an inquiry into the material condition of the people, based on original and contemporaneous records. Macmillan, New York

Diamond AM (1982) Stable values and variable constraints; the source of behavioral and cultural differences. J Bus Ethics 1:49–58

Ehrlich I (1973) Participation in illegitimate activities: a theoretical and empirical investigation. J Pol Econ 81:521–565

Galenson DW (1981) White servitude in colonial America: an economic analysis. Cambridge University Press, Cambridge

Grubb F (1985a) The incidence of servitude in trans-Atlantic migration, 1771–1804. Explor Econ Hist 22:316–339
Grubb F (1985b) The market for indentured immigrants: evidence on the efficiency of forward-labor contracting in Philadelphia, 1745–1773. J Econ Hist 45:855–868
Grubb F (1992a) The long-run trend in the value of European immigrant servants, 1654–1831: new measurements and interpretations. Res Econ Hist 14:167–240
Grubb F (1992b) Fatherless and friendless: factors influencing the flow of English emigrant servants. J Econ Hist 52:85–108
Grubb F (2000a) The statutory regulation of colonial servitude: an incomplete-contract approach. Explor Econ Hist 37:42–75
Grubb F (2000b) The trans-Atlantic market for British convict labor. J Econ Hist 60:94–122
Grubb F (2006) Babes in bondage? Debt shifting by German immigrants in early America. J Interdiscipl Hist 37:1–34
Grubb F, Stitt T (1994) The Liverpool emigrant servant trade and the transition to slave labor in the Chesapeake, 1697-1707: market adjustments to war. Explor Econ Hist 31:376–405
Klepp SE, Pfaelzer de Ortiz A, Grubb F (eds) (2006) Souls for sale: two German redemptioners come to revolutionary America: the life stories of John Frederick Whitehead and Johann Carl Büttner. Pennsylvania State University Press, University Park
Kussmaul A (1981) Servants in husbandry in early modern England. Cambridge University Press, New York
Laslett P (1971) The world we have lost. Scribner, New York
Maryland Gazette (1745–1789). Various issues
McCusker JJ, Menard RR (1985) The economy of British America, 1607–1789. University of North Carolina Press, Chapel Hill
Murray JE (2013) The Charleston orphan house: children's lives in the first public orphanage in America. University of Chicago Press, Chicago
Murray JE, Herndon RW (2002) Markets for children in early America: a political economy of pauper apprenticeship. J Econ Hist 62:356–382
New Castle Court Records, vol. 1, 1676–1681 (1904). The colonial society of Pennsylvania, Lancaster
Smith AE (1947) Colonists in bondage: white servitude and convict labor in America, 1607–1776. W. W. Norton, New York
Walsh LS (1977) Servitude opportunities in Charles County, Maryland, 1658–1705. In: Land AC, Carr LG, Papenfuse EC (eds) Law, society, and politics in early Maryland. Johns Hopkins Press, Baltimore, pp 111–133
Walsh LS (1987) Staying put or getting out: findings for Charles County, Maryland, 1650–1720. Will Mary Q 44:89–103

Chapter 9
Adult Guardianship and Local Politics in Rhode Island, 1750–1800

Ruth Wallis Herndon and Amílcar E. Challú

Abstract This essay asks two main questions. (1) How did Rhode Island town leaders use adult guardianship during the turmoil of the Revolutionary Era? (2) What factors explain each town's use of adult guardianships? Every town elected six councilmen each year to take care of local problems; these leaders had authority to enact discretionary guardianships to restrain and protect propertied adults whose behavior had caused complaint. Our analysis of data from 14 Rhode Island towns shows that town councilmen overall increased their use of adult guardianships significantly between 1750 and 1800. Guardianships declined during the height of warfare (1775–1781) but increased significantly after the war. Hopkinton showed the greatest use of this legal process and Providence the lowest. We found no significant correlation between a town's use of adult guardianship and that same town's population, wealth, or geographic region. The common factor appears to be the stress and disorder of the era. We investigated Hopkinton more closely and found that the town councilmen in this newest Rhode Island town put adults under guardianship in heavy-handed ways, especially in the 1780s and 1790s, often bypassing less intrusive and punitive solutions. The Hopkinton councilmen, we conclude, went to an extreme in using adult guardianship, but their actions were part of a widespread effort by Rhode Island town leaders to restore order in their communities after the Revolutionary War.

Keywords Adult guardianship · Probate · Town councils · Freeholders · Rhode Island

9.1 Introduction

This essay examines adult guardianship during the Revolutionary Era in Rhode Island. A guardianship is a legally appointed responsibility to manage the assets and decisions of another person. Minors who own financial or real estate assets, for instance, are often the subject of a guardianship. So are adults who are deemed to be

R. W. Herndon (✉) · A. E. Challú
Bowling Green State University, Bowling Green, OH, USA
e-mail: rwhernd@bgsu.edu; achallu@bgsu.edu

P. Gray et al. (eds.), *Standard of Living*, Studies in Economic History,
https://doi.org/10.1007/978-3-031-06477-7_9

incapable of making decisions on their own. The norms of guardianship are ingrained in the value system of a society and, expectedly, evolve and adapt according to the social context. Today, adult guardianship has become a widely discussed topic. As societies have aged demographically, social welfare professionals, legal scholars, and political activists have paid greater attention to the vulnerability of aged people and adults with disabilities (Quinn 2005; Wood 2016; Wood et al. 2017; Hardy 2008; Doron 2002). After almost a century of experience with centrally administered welfare institutions, proponents of reform believe that customary ways of protecting vulnerable adults are no longer effective (Wood 2019). Around the world, societies are shifting from "traditional" to "modern" systems of adult guardianship, often implying a bigger role for the state.[1] In the USA, this means legal reforms at the state level (Wood 2005, pp. 19–20, 31–32).[2] In the 1600s and early 1700s, American colonists inherited a system rooted in English common law, especially the concept of *parens patriae* ("parent of the country"); that is, the monarch served as "benevolent parent, taking care of those unable to care for themselves" (Wood 2005, p. 19).[3] In most American colonies, the monarch's authority was assumed by colonial governors, and after the American Revolution, state legislatures maintained the *parens patriae* concept. Thus, the American colonial system of adult guardianship "grew unexamined into state law" during the Revolutionary Era (Wood 2016, pp. 8–9).[4] Rhode Island had a unique system in that the responsibility of establishing and overseeing guardianships rested with the town council. Different towns showed different patterns of use of guardianships, particularly adult guardianships, providing an interesting window to explore the intersection of social norms and economic institutions during the critical and turbulent Revolutionary Era.

Adult guardianship was a powerful instrument in the hands of local authorities in eighteenth-century Rhode Island. It was a serious act to strip adults of the right to spend their money, sell their land, bequeath their property in wills, and conduct other important business of propertied persons. Before appointing a guardian, town leaders listened to complaints about someone's ill health or troublesome behavior. Family members, friends, and neighbors had to convince the town councilmen that the person in question was mentally incompetent, a spendthrift, a drunkard, or otherwise at risk of "wasting their estate" and becoming dependent on town welfare. As "fathers of the town," the councilmen were responsible for the good order of the whole community, and that included stewardship of the town treasury, which was

[1] In Japan and China, the legal responsibility for adult guardianship traditionally rested with the extended family, rather than with the state (Doron 2002, pp. 373–376; Yang 2019, pp. 12–15). In Germany and Sweden, guardianship stemmed from Roman law and traditionally rested on civil code (Doron, pp. 377–78, 383–84). In contrast, Israel took its system from English common law as it applied in Palestine by the British Mandate prior to 1948 (Doron, p. 380). Canada inherited a combination of English common law tradition and French civil law tradition (Yang, pp. 43–46). See also Sabatino and Wood (2012, pp. 35–55).

[2] For a study of changes in Maryland law over 300 years, see O'Sullivan and Hoffmann (1995/1996).

[3] See also O'Sullivan and Hoffman (1995/1996, pp. 13–17).

[4] See also Wood (2005, pp. 19–20) and O'Sullivan and Hoffman (1995/1996, pp. 13–17).

regularly replenished from taxes levied on the propertied inhabitants. Councilmen were ever alert to someone needing taxpayer support in the form of poor relief. Adult guardianship gave councilmen a way to bring order out of disorder both socially and economically – curb the worrisome behavior and simultaneously protect the town treasury.

The council minutes include striking details from the stories that townspeople poured out before the councilmen. Widow Abigail Pearce of Warwick was "an ancient woman" and "subject to fits" which made her "incapable of managing her estate."[5] Richard Barton of Warren had "for a considerable time gone to great excess in drinking and abusing his children."[6] The South Kingstown council appointed a guardian after hearing "sundry and repeated complaints" that brothers Job and Amos Smith were showing "want of discretion" in the form of "idleness, drunkenness, and making foolish bargains when intoxicated with strong drink."[7] The Cumberland council placed three men under guardianship in absentia because they had "absconded" from their wives and children, leaving them without support and necessitating the sale of the errant husband's real estate.[8] When John Lewis of Richmond died, the council appointed a guardian over his three adult daughters – "dumb girls" who were likely deaf as well as mute.[9] The Middletown council put Humility Coggeshall under guardianship when her niece (who also was her caretaker) reported that the older woman "was very troublesome, she being a person non compos mentis and utterly incapable of transacting her secular affairs."[10] Dramas of family distress thread through the council records of every town.

This essay analyzes the adult guardianships recorded in the council minutes of 14 Rhode Island towns between 1750 and 1800.[11] Altogether, the 14 study towns administered 1559 guardianships (See Table 9.1). 1181 of these (788 boys and 393

[5] Town council meeting of 26 September 1763, Warwick Town Council Records, 2:232. All Rhode Island guardianship information is taken from town council meeting minutes (hereafter TCM), written into the town council records (hereafter TCR) of each town. Additional information is taken from town meeting minutes (hereafter TM), written into the town meeting records (hereafter TMR) of each town. All town records are maintained in the town clerk's office at the town halls of the respective towns.

[6] TCM 24 August 1781, Warren TCR, 1:478.

[7] TCM 11 November 1782, South Kingstown TCR, 6:90.

[8] George Peck was placed under guardianship in 1783, Roger Brale in 1792, and Ibrook Whipple in 1796. See TCM 17 November 1783, Cumberland TCR, 5:503; TCM 28 January 1792, Cumberland TCR 3:280; and TCM 20 April 1796, Cumberland TCR 4:6.

[9] TCM 5 February 1753 and 5 March 1753, Richmond TCR 1:114-16. The Lewis daughters' guardian was directed to "take care of them and their estates" [emphasis mine]. The council records also refer to the cost of "nursing" the three women. TCM 3 May 1779, Richmond TCR 2:275–76.

[10] TCM 18 November 1782, Middletown TCR 2:107.

[11] The 14 towns are Cumberland, East Greenwich, Exeter, Glocester, Hopkinton, Jamestown, Middletown, New Shoreham, Providence, Richmond, South Kingstown, Tiverton, Warren, and Warwick. These towns constitute a stratified sample of Rhode Island's 37 towns in the Revolutionary Era, taking into consideration population, wealth, economic orientation, age, and geographic location. For a discussion of the selection of these towns, see Herndon (1992a, b, Appendix A, pp. 320–336).

girls) were protective guardianships for minors who would inherit property when they came of age. The remaining 378 (269 men and 109 women) were for adults who caused complaint because of their behavior or incapacity to manage their affairs. We compared each town's use of adult guardianship to its use of child guardianship; Hopkinton used adult guardianship the most (57% of its total guardianships were for adults), and Providence used it the least (8% of its total guardianships were for adults). (See Figs. 9.1 and 9.2.) We also compared the towns' per-capita rates of adult guardianship over the same period; again, Hopkinton had the highest per-capita rate (0.04155) and Providence had the lowest per-capita rate (0.00602). (See Tables 9.2 and 9.3 and Fig. 9.4.) We also graphed adult guardianships per capita over the entire study period. The use of adult guardianships declined significantly during the war itself and increased significantly after the war and in the 1790s. (See Fig. 9.3.) We also tested for correlations between the towns' use of guardianship and other factors. Neither geographic region, nor wealth, nor the size (or growth) of the population predicted the use of adult guardianship. Figure 9.1, for instance, indicates that the taxable wealth of the residents of a town did not predict a greater reliance on adult guardianship.[12] Figure 9.4 does not suggest a particular geographic pattern in the use of adult guardianships. These two visualizations serve as a sample

Table 9.1 Guardianships enacted in Rhode Island study towns, 1750–1800

Town	Adult guardianships	Minor guardianships	Total guardianships
Cumberland	38	96	134
East Greenwich	34	52	86
Exeter	20	132	152
Glocester	39	75	114
Hopkinton[a]	75	57	132
Jamestown	5	18	23
Middletown	8	46	54
New Shoreham	6	11	17
Providence	26	285	311
Richmond[b]	12	56	68
South Kingstown	45	94	139
Tiverton	23	77	100
Warren	17	113	130
Warwick	30	69	99
	378	1181	1559

Source: Guardianship statistics are drawn from the individual town council records
[a]Hopkinton records begin in 1757, when it separated from Westerly
[b]Richmond records end in 1783; town council records for 1783–1812 were lost in the nineteenth century

[12]While the graph shows the percentage of minor and adult guardianships, a panel regression of per-capita wealth and per-capita adult guardianships also supports this conclusion.

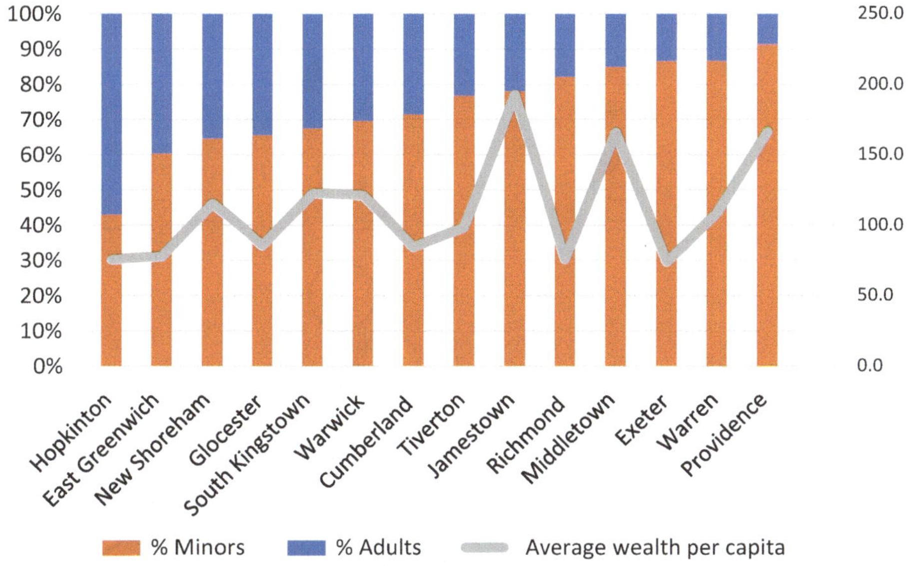

Fig. 9.1 Percent adult and minor guardianships in study towns and town per-capita wealth. (Sources: Guardianship statistics are drawn from the individual town council records. Per-capita wealth is the average of three valuations reported to the Rhode Island General Assembly. For the valuation of 1769, see Bartlett 1861, p. 576. For the valuation of 1782, see Bartlett 1856, p. 520. For the valuation of 1796, see manuscript copy included in the state estimate of 1800, at the Rhode Island State Archives.)

of our broader exploration of these relationships, without any statistically significant result.

Finally, we took a closer look at Hopkinton, which stood out because of its high overall use of adult guardianships. (See Figs. 9.4 and 9.6.) As we discuss below, Hopkinton councilmen administered adult guardianships in a heavy-handed way after the war, bypassing less intrusive and less punitive options. Every town had the same official options for dealing with disorder such as drunkenness, but other towns did not share Hopkinton's strong preference for the option of adult guardianship.

9.2 Rhode Island and Adult Guardianship

Rhode Island was the only colony/state that relegated the sensitive responsibility of adult guardianship to local leaders elected by town voters. Everywhere else, county-level probate court judges, appointed by the governor and his assistants, had this responsibility. In neighboring Massachusetts, for example, town selectmen's authority was limited on this point: they could identify "Common Drunkards, Tipplers, Gamesters"; they could "make inquisition respecting Ideots, Lunatics, or distracted persons"; and they could "complain of such persons to the Judge of Probate" – but

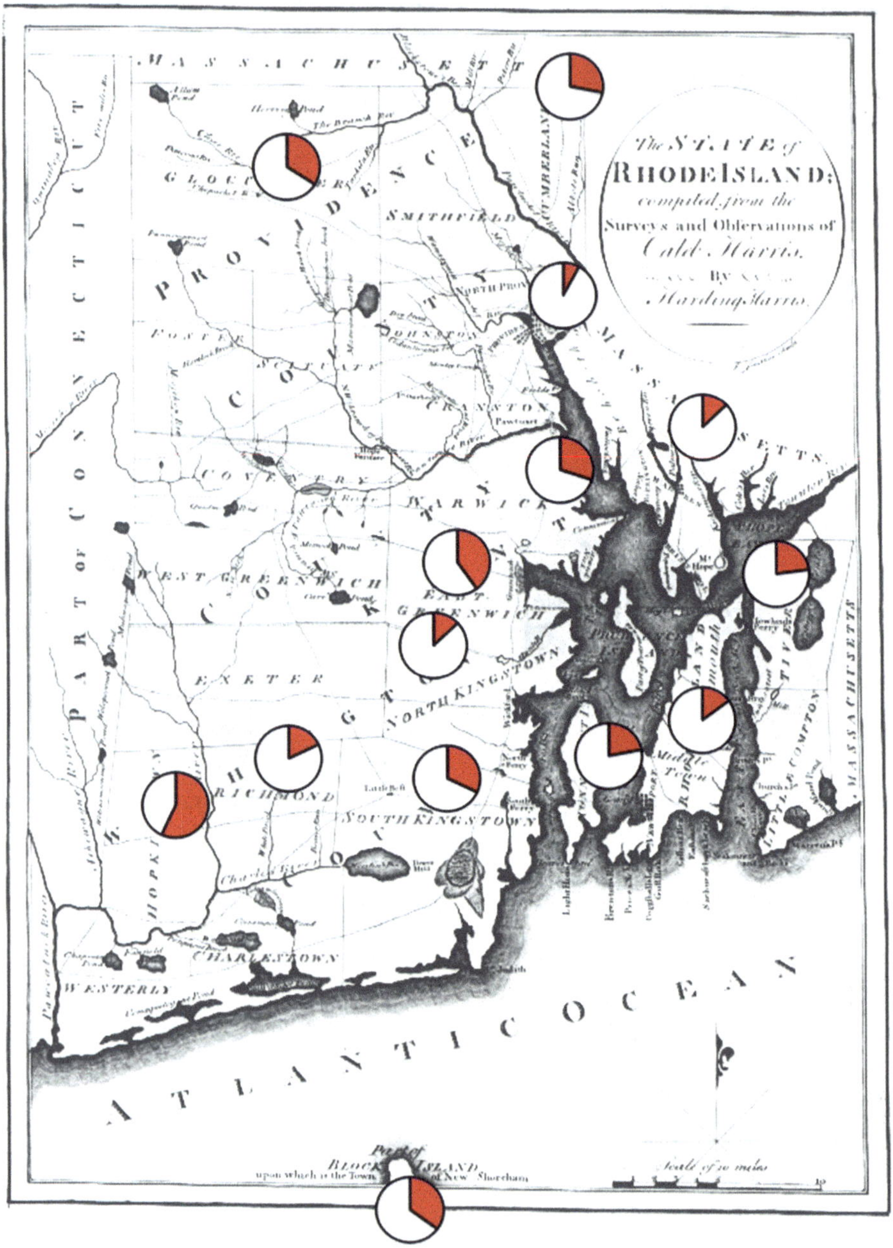

Fig. 9.2 Rhode Island's towns in 1795, showing percentage of adult and minor guardianships. The colored slice is the percentage of adult guardianships. Hopkinton has the largest colored slice and Providence the smallest colored slice. (Sources: Guardianships statistics are drawn from the individual town council records. Basemap from the David Rumsey Historical Map Collection, https://www.davidrumsey.com/luna/servlet/s/50v514 "The State of Rhode Island compiled from the Surveys and Observations of Caleb Harris, By Harding Harris. J. Smither sculp." Map, scale 1:285,000. Matthew Carey, 1795)

Table 9.2 Population of Rhode Island towns

Town	1755	1770	1782	1790	1800
Cumberland	1083	1756	1548	1964	2056
East Greenwich	1167	1663	1609	1824	1775
Exeter	1404	1864	2058	2495	2476
Glocester	1511	2945	2791	4025	4009
Hopkinton	--	1805	1735	2462	2276
Jamestown	517	563	344	507	501
Middletown	778	881	678	840	913
New Shoreham	378	575	478	682	714
Providence	3159	4321	4312	6380	7614
Richmond	829	1257	1094	1760	1368
South Kingstown	1913	2835	2675	4131	3438
Tiverton	1325	1957	1959	2453	2717
Warren	925	979	905	1122	1473
Warwick	1911	2438	2122	2493	2532

Sources: For 1755 and 1770 census counts, see Greene and Harrington (1966, pp. 67–69). For 1782 and 1790 census counts, see Holbrook (1979, p. viii). For 1800 census count, see Walsh (1987, pp. 722–23)

Table 9.3 Ratio of adult guardianships to population

Town	Total adult guardianships 1750–1800	1770 town population	Ratio of adult guardianships to 1770 population
Cumberland	38	1756	0.02164
East Greenwich	34	1663	0.02044
Exeter	20	1864	0.01073
Glocester	39	2945	0.01324
Hopkinton	75	1805	0.04155
Jamestown	5	563	0.00888
Middletown	8	881	0.00908
New Shoreham	6	575	0.01043
Providence	26	4321	0.00602
Richmond	12	1257	0.00955
South Kingstown	45	2835	0.01587
Tiverton	23	1957	0.01175
Warren	17	979	0.01736
Warwick	30	2438	0.01231

Sources: Guardianship statistics are drawn from the individual town council records. Population counts obtained from Greene and Harrington (1966), Holbrook (1979), and Walsh (1987)

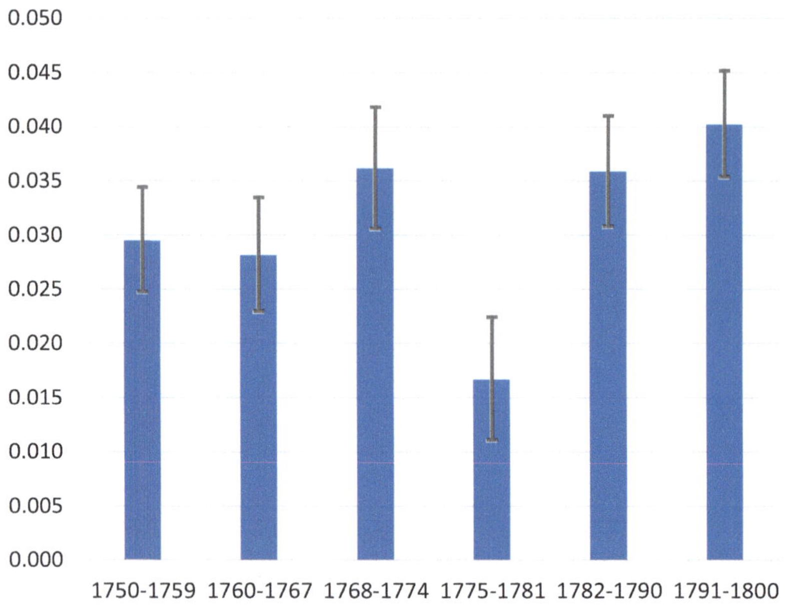

Fig. 9.3 Adult guardianships enacted in the 14 study towns, averaged by time period. (Source: Guardianship statistics are drawn from the individual town council records)
Notes: The thick bar represents the mean across all towns for each period, calculated as the fixed effects of the period binary variables; the thin bar represents one standard error. In total, the panel had 690 town-year observations

the county probate court judge actually appointed the guardians (Freeman 1791, p. 8).[13] Only in Rhode Island did locally elected town councilmen serve also as probate judges with all their associated powers.[14] In a unique development early in the colonial period, Rhode Island town councils had "inherited the function of probate courts, which clothed them in the garments of magistracy" (James 1975, p. 149). One historian has described Rhode Island town councils as "conclaves of village elders, to which had adhered the duties of a probate court" (James 2000, p. 165). Throughout the colonial era, Rhode Island "continued to elevate the

[13] See also Jimenez (1987, pp. 49–64). Jimenez (1987, p. 51) notes that Massachusetts towns "had little do with guardianship cases" except when someone disputed a court ruling; in those cases, "town selectmen made the determination of sanity." See also Montague (1895, pp. 5–11), who traced Massachusetts probate judges' county-level authority back to the early English county court system. For Montague's discussion of the Massachusetts probate courts' authority to appoint guardians over adults, see pp. 12–13, 23–24, 32-34.

[14] "An Act establishing Courts of Probate" and "An Act respecting Guardians," *The Public Laws of the State of Rhode Island and Providence Plantations* (Providence: Carter and Wilkinson, 1798), 1:276–79, 1:316–18. For the more complicated (and expensive) system of adult guardianship in Scotland, see Houston (2003, pp. 165–186). Houston notes that "guardianship procedures in eighteenth-century Massachusetts were similar to those in Scotland" (p. 179). For adult guardianship in England, see Neugebauer (1996, pp. 24–39) and Neugebauer (1989, pp. 1580–1584).

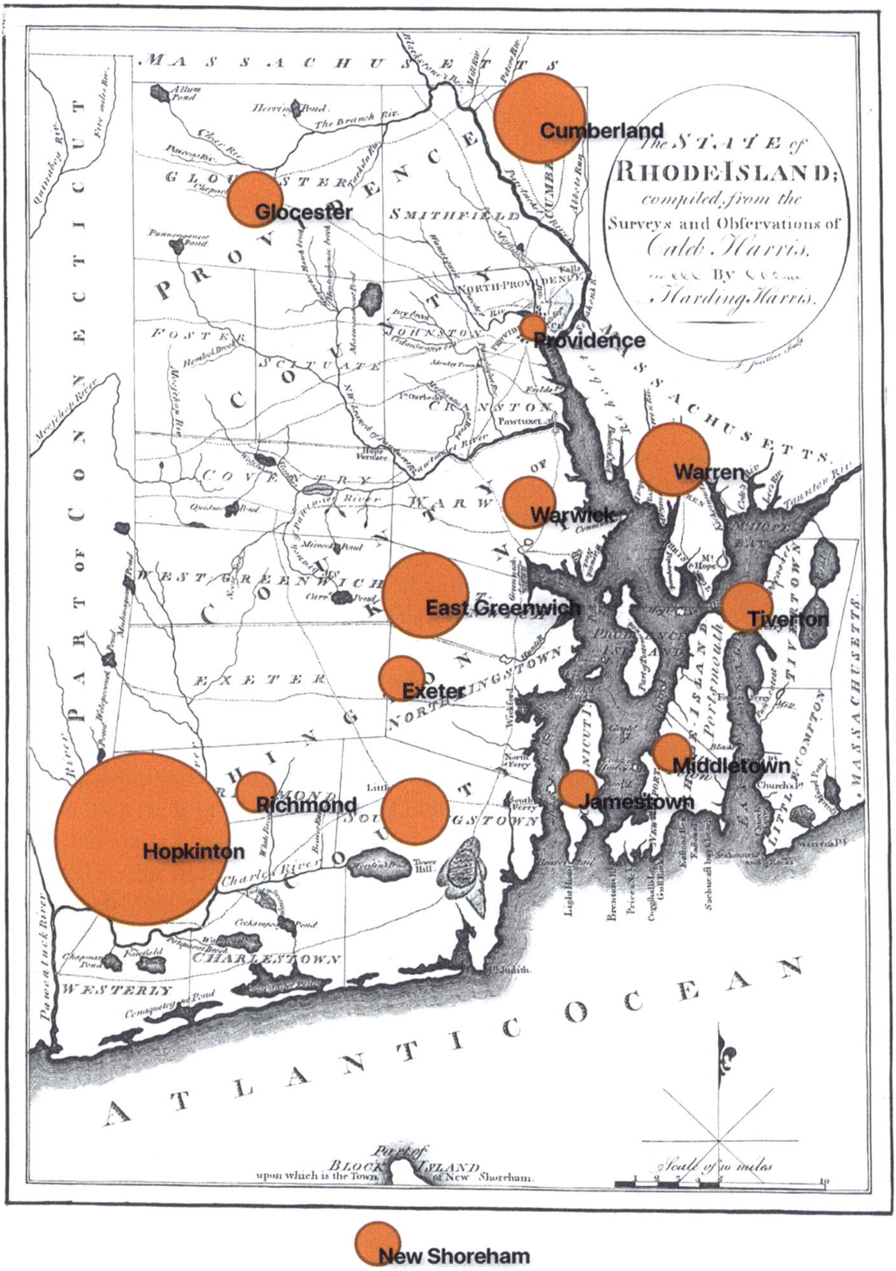

Fig. 9.4 Ratio of adult guardianships to 1770 population. (Sources: Guardianship statistics are drawn from the individual town council records. For 1770 town population, see Greene and Harrington (1966). Basemap from the David Rumsey Historical Map Collection, https://www.davidrumsey.com/luna/servlet/s/50v514 "The State of Rhode Island compiled from the Surveys and Observations of Caleb Harris, By Harding Harris. J. Smither sculp." Map, scale 1:285,000. Matthew Carey, 1795)

importance of the towns as opposed to the colonial government" (James 1975, p. 71). By 1750, town councils were well acquainted with the responsibilities of "judicial competence," including administering guardianships (James 2000, p. 121).[15]

Probate work, including appointing guardians to adults and minors, was only one part of the many responsibilities of Rhode Island town councils. Their nonprobate work included monitoring transient residents, granting departure certificates to legally settled inhabitants who wanted to move away, authorizing poor relief for the needy, authorizing the construction of roads, granting liquor licenses, and giving directions in emergencies such as an outbreak of smallpox or threat of enemy invasion during wartime (Herndon 1992a, pp. 186–187). Each year at the June town meeting, Rhode Island freeholders voted in a slate of local officials, starting with a town clerk and six town councilmen. These first-elected men were invariably social and economic elites who had earned the voters' confidence with their wealth, reputation, connections, and willingness to devote time to unpaid public service (Herndon 1992a, pp. 192–193; Cook 1976, chaps. 3 and 4; Daniels 1978, pp. 36–52). The Rhode Island General Assembly had fixed the council's number at "six good and sufficient freeholders" for each town, regardless of the town's population.[16] The councilmen's workload could become quite heavy in the more populous towns. In 1782, when town leaders were scrambling to respond to wartime upheaval, Providence's 6 councilmen (serving a population of 6380 inhabitants) convened 30 meetings; Hopkinton's 6 councilmen (serving a population of 1735 inhabitants) convened 14 meetings; and Warren's 6 councilmen (serving a population of 905 inhabitants) convened 8 meetings.[17]

Adult guardianship was the responsibility of town councilmen (acting as probate court) because it involved property that could be bequeathed and inherited, bought and sold. The probate court set the amount of the bond the guardian posted when taking up this responsibility; the court also had to "examine, allow and settle" the guardian's accounts periodically.[18] When Stephen Cottrell asked the South Kingstown council to put his son under guardianship for "leading a very irregular life" through "drinking to excess and idleness," the councilmen appointed Dr. Benjamin Wait as guardian and required that he post £100 bond, indicating that Stephen Jr. had a significant estate.[19] John Ladd conducted a full inventory when he

[15] During the period under study, some town clerks kept probate court business separate from nonprobate council business in the town books. In 1798, the Rhode Island General Assembly standardized record-keeping by requiring that clerks keep separate probate court minutes. See "An Act establishing Courts of Probate," *Public Laws of Rhode Island* (1798), 276–78.

[16] *Acts and Laws of The English Colony of Rhode-Island and Providence Plantations in New-England* (Newport: Samuel Hall, 1767), 261–62.

[17] Providence TCR vol. 5; Hopkinton TCR vol. 2; Warren TCR vol 1.

[18] "An Act respecting Guardians" (1798), Sec. 2, 316–17; "An Act establishing Courts of Probate" (1798), Sec. 1, 276.

[19] TCM 10 December 1781, South Kingstown TCR 10 December 1781.

became guardian to the Lewis daughters of Richmond, and he reported the value of their joint estate as £578.[20]

To place propertied adults under formal guardianship, councilmen needed good cause. They enacted a guardianship after "a due consideration" of a report, when they had concluded a complaint was "well founded."[21] The circumstances giving rise to a complaint were undoubtedly well-known to family, friends, and neighbors of the problem person. The doctor who attended the sick in the community, the pastor of the local church, the officer who headed the town militia, and the townsmen licensed to sell liquor at their inns – all these "worthies" had probably already been asked informally to bring their influence to bear. Assessing the process of adult guardianship in Scotland, R.A. Houston notes that the "simplest and least formal" alternative was "extra-legal protection of community opinion." That is, families could "rely on a consensus in the neighborhood about the impropriety of doing business with an individual who was plainly unable to manage his or her affairs" (Houston 2003, pp. 171–172).[22] Rhode Islanders likely relied on the same kind of informal procedure. It was up to the council to decide when and if a complaint should result in a formal guardianship. The absence of certain names in the minutes suggests that the council declined to act on complaints against elites. We reviewed the names of the top town leadership in each of the study towns – the head of the town council, the town clerk, the town treasurer, and deputies to the General Assembly.[23] Some of these men very likely became incapable of managing their

[20]The inventories were conducted 18 May 1752, and 1 January 1753, Richmond Wills 1:119–20. Ladd submitted two separate lists: the first (items held for them in a separate location) included cows, sheep, and household goods, totaling £370-13-9; the second (items already in their possession) included more household goods and cloth, totaling £207-15-6. When James Lewis died, his three disabled daughters Abigail, Hannah, and Ruth (by his first wife Abigail) were 35, 32, and 28 years old and still under their father's care. Lewis had bequeathed to them "one quarter part of my movables," stipulating that "beds, bedding, chests, boxes, wheels, chairs, clothing" and other goods "be equally divided between them" (Will of James Lewis, 5 April 1752 (probated 23 May 1752), Richmond Wills, 1:91–93). Lewis also stipulated that his unborn child by his second wife Susannah "whether it be son or daughter" should have "one fifth part of my lands before willed to my two sons." Daughter Patience was born to Lewis' widow 7 months after he wrote his last will (*Rhode Island: Vital Records, 1636-1850*, ed. James N. Arnold (Providence: Narragansett Historical Publishing Company, 1891); Richmond, 6–30).

[21]TCM 4 December 1797, 1 January 1798, and 12 February 1798, Tiverton TCR 5:59–60; TCM 15 December 1797, South Kingstown TCR 6:253. For example of "a due consideration" wording: The Tiverton council cancelled Abraham Burrington's guardianship after some family members protested the action; the council spent one meeting "hearing what was offered for and against the same." For example of "well founded" wording: The South Kingstown council concluded that Samuel Curtis should be put under guardianship, since Curtis had been "giving himself up to the practice of a daily inebriation, thereby disqualifying himself from taking a prudential care of his temporal interest."

[22]Houston (2003, p. 171) points out that the process of adult guardianship in Scotland was "potentially difficult, frequently expensive, and necessarily public," making informal alternatives much more appealing.

[23]Lower-level officials, such as town constables, were not treated with the same reserve as men who had been in the most prominent positions. In Jamestown, for example, the town council put

affairs in their old age, but only one suffered the indignity of formal guardianship: John Maxson of Hopkinton (discussed below). And when the Hopkinton council did put Maxson under guardianship, it caused such "uneasiness" that the council soon reversed their decision.[24]

Town councils enacted a guardianship when they deemed that the complaint described a person who was non compos mentis (literally "of unsound mind") and "likely to waste their estate." In the eighteenth century, the line between mental illness and physical illness was unclear (Rothman 1979, p. 4).[25] Today we might apply specific labels such as dementia, depression, or alcoholism to some of these cases.[26] In addition, we bear in mind that many soldiers returning from combat in this era exhibited a wide array of ailments and disabilities, both mental and physical, for decades afterward.[27] Other adults placed under guardianship – the Lewis daughters, for example – suffered from profound physical and mental disabilities their entire lives.[28] Still other adults, like Richard Barton of Warren, periodically "abused" family members.[29] And others, like George Peck, Roger Brale, and Ibrook Whipple, deserted their families. The Cumberland council was so outraged at Peck's abandonment of his wife and seven children that they publicly censured him for his "unnatural conduct," declaring that he was "greatly depraved and almost lost the natural feelings of common humanity."[30]

The councilmen heard details of unsettling and disorderly behavior and must have had no illusions about the intensity of distress in some households. Very likely, they were not surprised when people declined to take on a guardianship that would embroil them in family disputes or commit them to years of unpleasant service. Four men in quick succession declined to serve as guardian to John Lewis's "dumb" daughters, and the fifth resigned after 2 years. The records indicate that being guardian to these handicapped women involved finding appropriate nurses and caretakers

---

Benjamin Carr, a former town constable and tax collector, under guardianship when his son complained about this elderly man "squandering away his estate" (TCM 6 March 1784, Jamestown TCR 2:155).

[24] TCM 3 September 1793 and 2 December 1793, Hopkinton TCR 3:38, 41.

[25] For a good review of the scholarly literature on insanity in early America, see Jimenez (1987, pp. 1–11). See also Eldridge (1996, pp. 361–386), Neugebauer (1987, pp. 481–483), Grob (1994), Bell (1980), and Deutsch (1949).

[26] On attitudes toward and treatment of the elderly in early America, see Fischer (1977) and Achenbaum (1978, pp. 1–6); see also Field and Syrett (2020, pp. 370–384). On alcohol consumption in early America, see Rorabaugh (1979), Salinger (2002), and Lender and Martin (1982, Chap. 1).

[27] For a recent study of illness in early America that incorporates a discussion of Revolutionary War veterans, see Mutschler (2020, pp. 183–222). See also Resch (2002) and Blackie (2010).

[28] For a relevant study, see Dayton (2015, pp. 77–99).

[29] On domestic violence in early America, see Pleck (1987) and Daniels and Kennedy (1999).

[30] TCM 17 November 1783, Cumberland TCR 5:503.

as well as managing their financial affairs.[31] In other cases, the guardian perceived the task as intrusive or inappropriate. Moses Baker had been appointed guardian to his 21-year-old brother Pardon Baker when Pardon began drinking to excess after returning home from military service during the Revolutionary War. Seven years later, Moses told the Warwick council that "it was very disagreeable for him to act in that office any longer."[32] The council appointed a different guardian but had to revisit the case 3 years later, after they heard "great complaints" about the second guardian's neglect – so much so that Pardon's estate was "squandering away." The council appointed an assistant to the guardian to "procure an estate" where Pardon could "make a home for himself and family" and thereby avoid becoming a town charge.[33] The following year, the council "thought fit. . . to set Pardon Baker free from his guardianship, in hopes that he would refrain from his evil courses of life." But they soon learned that Pardon "persists in drinking too freely of spirituous liquors and spends much of his time at taverns and in idleness, whereby he is likely to bring himself and family to want and misery." Since they could persuade no reliable person to take on the guardianship, the council decided to serve collectively as guardian to Pardon, now 31 years old.[34] In this case, the council took quite seriously their responsibility as "fathers of the town," caring for a man who had apparently suffered a breakdown after his wartime service on behalf of the town.

Sometimes the adult placed under guardianship protested the council's action, embarrassed to have been publicly reduced in status. A year after the Warwick council placed George Wightman under guardianship because he showed "no discretion," his son Reuben told the council that his father "was got something uneasy at his being under guardian"; the councilmen "thought proper" to release the elder man from guardianship.[35] Two years later George Wightman's sons appeared before the council because "their father conducted in such a manner, that they apprehended unless there was a stop put to it, he would bring himself to want and misery," and the council once again appointed a guardian.[36] Before a year had passed, however, the sons were back to ask for their father's release once again because he "had of

[31] Edward Pierce of Charleston, George Lewis of Richmond, and the Samuel Kinyon of Charlestown all "refused to serve" when they were first appointed in February 1753. One month later, David Lewis, who had been appointed "in their stead," also refused. John Ladd of Charlestown agreed to serve, but he resigned in 1755, and the council recruited Jacob Lewis of West Greenwich. This appointment lasted. More than 20 years later, the Lewis daughters were still living in Jacob Lewis' household in West Greenwich, and the Richmond council was continuing to inspect the guardian's account, which included payment for "nursing and boarding" the three women. TCM 5 February 1753, 5 March 1753, 3 March 1755, 3 May 1779, and 2 December 1782, Richmond TCR 1:114, 1:115-16, 1:176, 2:275–76, 2:337.

[32] TCM 30 December 1777, Warwick TCR 3:40; TCM 15 December 1784, Warwick TCR 3:168.

[33] TCM 12 March 1787, Warwick TCR 3:200.

[34] TCM 28 April 1788, Warwick TCR 3:226.

[35] TCM 27 June 1767 and 13 June 1768, Warwick TCR 2:286 and 2:302. Reuben Wightman was one of the town constables at the time he made this complaint to the Warwick council; he was later elected as town sergeant, the chief law enforcement position.

[36] TCM 18 July 1772 and 21 March 1773, Warwick TCR 3:16 and 3:23–24.

late governed himself better" and (perhaps more to the point) he "hath an opportunity of disposing of his real estate at a good lay and to purchase another place whereby he would greatly advance his interest." The council "disannulled" the guardianship.[37]

The Warren council put shipwright Amos Bowen under guardianship in April 1756 because he was "discomposed and disordered" and "altogether unfit to manage his secular affairs."[38] Over the next 20 months, Bowen asked the council repeatedly that he "be restored to his former capacity," and in December 1757 the council finally agreed that he should be released from guardianship, settle accounts with his guardian, and take possession of his estate.[39] Three years later, though, "repeated complaints" from "credible persons" prompted the council to put Bowen back under guardianship because he was "so discomposed as well by excessive drinking as by other extravagant behavior."[40]

In another case, the father of a man under guardianship seemed to feel the public humiliation most keenly. The Warwick council put David Gorton under guardianship in 1796 because he "spends much of his time and money at public houses" and because of his "want of discretion in the management of his estate."[41] Eight months later, Gorton's father asked the council to discharge his son from this guardianship and allow him, the father, to "remove his son and family into some part of the state of New York, where he meant to settle them in such a manner, that [they] should not for the future be chargeable to this town." The council agreed and removed the guardianship "upon the condition that the said Joseph Gorton remove the said David and family out of this town, agreeable to promise."[42]

In yet another case, the Warwick council kept Benjamin Stone under guardianship for decades, suggesting that some underlying disability complicated the immediate problem of drinking too much. Stone was in his early 30s when the council put him under guardianship for "drunkenness" in 1750. There he remained for 39 years, living a surprisingly normal life under guardianship, even marrying.[43] In 1789, Stone (now in his 70s) wrote a petition (or had it written for him) "signed by a number of the inhabitants of the town of Warwick and [the neighboring town of]

[37] TCM 21 March 1773, Warwick TCR 3:23–24.

[38] TCM 5 April 1756, Warren TCR 1:126.

[39] TCM 5 December 1757, Warren TCR 1: 158.

[40] TCM 1 December 1760, Warren TCR 1:211.

[41] TCM 14 April 1796, Warwick TCR 4:393.

[42] TCM 10 January 1797, Warwick TCR 4:410.

[43] The original guardianship occurred at TCM 10 December 1750, Warwick TCR 2:88-89. He appeared in the Rhode Island 1774 Census (Cherry Fletcher Bamberg, "The 1774 Census of Rhode Island: Warwick," *Rhode Island Roots*, 30 (2004), p. 201). He appeared in the Rhode Island 1777 Military Census for Warwick, showing as "60+" years of age (*The Rhode Island 1777 Military Census*, transcribed by Mildred M. Chamberlain (Baltimore: Genealogical Publishing Company, 1985)). He appeared in the Rhode Island 1782 Census, with 1 adult male and 1 adult female in his household (Jay Mack Holbrook, ed., *Rhode Island 1782 Census* (Oxford, MA: Holbrook Research Institute, 1979), 119).

Cranston." The petition described "the embarrassment he labored under, by being deprived of the privileges of freemen." "Freemen," in eighteenth-century Rhode Island, referred to freeholders, men who owned sufficient property to qualify to vote in town meeting. Stone also pointed out that even while under guardianship he "made some improvements in his estate" and had behaved himself recently "in a prudent manner." The councilmen agreed and discharged him.[44] In the following 8 years, Stone could well have voted in town meeting and even prepared a will. In 1797, however, Stone (now in his 80s) was put back under guardianship because he was "infirm" and showed a "want of discretion." He died a year later, still under guardianship.[45]

The councilmen's wide discretion in imposing guardianship (and removing it) highlights the independence and autonomy of Rhode Island towns.[46] In the absence of an overriding authority at the county or colony/state level, councilmen were free to choose among a number of measures that might help secure peace and good order in the community during the Revolutionary Era. When they enacted adult guardianship, the town council in effect assumed the traditional *parens patriae* authority of the English monarch over adults deemed unable to care for themselves or their property.

Every Rhode Island town used adult guardianship to a greater or lesser extent, but overall towns increased their use of adult guardianship significantly between the 1750s and the 1790s (See Fig. 9.3.) This 50-year period was arguably the most tumultuous in Rhode Island's history.[47] The French and Indian War in the late 1750s and early 1760s required that towns raise troops and equip them for military campaigns. Revolutionary protest from the mid-1760s to the mid-1770s caused significant division among Rhode Island's townspeople. The Revolutionary War itself, from 1775 to 1783, directly and deeply affected Rhode Island: some port towns were occupied by British troops for several years, coastal towns came under fire from British ships, and all towns prepared for invasion. In the 1780s, people throughout the state felt the effects of severe postwar depression, as poor transients surged through towns in search of work and family and as settled inhabitants went bankrupt at alarming rates. In the early 1780s, Rhode Islanders argued over passage of a contentious law to begin the abolition of slavery; the law passed in the state legislature in 1784. In the late 1780s, the state experienced another political crisis over ratifying the new federal constitution; Rhode Island towns held meetings to vote on ratification in 1788 and resoundingly rejected ratification (238 for and 2714 against) (Herndon and Murray 2019). The state joined the union belatedly and reluctantly in

[44] TCM 14 September 1789, Warwick TCR 3:261.

[45] TCM 8 July 1797, Warwick TCR 4:420. See also Patricia Reed, "Henry Straight of Portsmouth and East Greenwich, R.I., and His Family," *Rhode Island Roots* 40 (2014): 192.

[46] Sydney James (1975, p. 56) found that each Rhode Island town "in its own way developed basic institutions" and "tried to bring into use daring ideas about the exercise of the body politic."

[47] On Rhode Island in this era, see McLoughlin (1986a), Polishook (1969), Lovejoy (1958), and Conley (1977). Rappleye (2006), Coughtry (1981), Sweet (2003), Withey (1984). See also Jones (1992), Coleman (1963), McLoughlin (1986b), and Lemons (1986).

1790. Rhode Island took its first step into the industrial revolution with the construction of a cotton spinning mill on the Blackstone River in Pawtucket, just north of Providence, in 1793. This not only began the state's turn toward textile production as its economic engine; it also signaled Providence's victory in the battle with Newport for economic dominance. A system of major roads to accommodate the increasing trade between Providence and the rest of New England began to snake through the Rhode Island countryside, ushering in the transportation revolution.

A Rhode Island resident born before 1750 witnessed a high level of political, economic, and social change in her town if she lived to 1800. Most towns experienced a dramatic population increase in the half-century, and some doubled in size. (See Table 9.2.) During the war itself, voters gathered more and more frequently in town meetings, scrambling to produce quotas of soldiers and raising taxes for bounties and supplies for the troops (Herndon 1992a, pp. 260–264). Town taxes increased 15-fold during the war (Herndon 1992a, pp. 271–274). The East Greenwich voters held a record 28 town meetings in 1779, while the Jamestown voters held no meetings at all that year, since the townspeople were all refugees scattered in nearby towns (Herndon, 1992a, pp. 270–271). In 1777, the Providence council called 51 meetings to deal with the most urgent problems of the war, while the Jamestown, Middletown, and New Shoreham councils did not convene at all because they were under British occupation.[48] After the war, towns were disrupted as Rhode Islanders found their way back home – or to a new home – and began to assess the cost of the war in blood and treasure. Not until the 1790s did Rhode Islanders begin to feel a respite from the chaos of the war (Herndon 1992a, pp. 310–311). Those who had endured the war years as adults must have welcomed the end of the century as a return to better times in many respects.

Figures 9.3 and 9.5 show that council activity putting minors under guardianship decreased overall, while council activity putting adults under guardianship increased overall.[49] These figures use the period 1750–1759 as a point of comparison and show the rise or fall in relation to that period. Enactments of adult guardianships stepped up significantly in the period 1767–1775, indicating an increased need to address disorder during the period of revolutionary protest. After the onset of war, council activity to put both minors and adults under guardianship decreased significantly, and this activity stayed low until 1781. This coincides with some towns being occupied by the British and all towns being preoccupied with wartime exigencies. Under these stressful circumstances, town councils did not prioritize

---

[48] Providence TCR 5:61–104; Herndon (1992a, pp. 292–95).

[49] Figure 9.3 shows changes in use of adult guardianships. A panel regression of the 690 counts of guardianships by year and town is behind these observations on the differences between periods. The 1775–1781 period is below all other coefficients with at least a 10% significance level; the 1791–1800 period is only significantly different relative to 1760–1767 and 1775–1781. Still, the trend suggests an increase in the towns' use of adult guardianships interrupted by the revolutionary war. Figure 9.5 shows changes in use of guardianships for minors. The dip during the revolutionary war and into 1790 is significant at the 5% level, according to a panel regression of the rate of minor guardianships with fixed effects by period. The decline of 1791–1800 relative to the 1750–1759 period is significant at the 10% level.

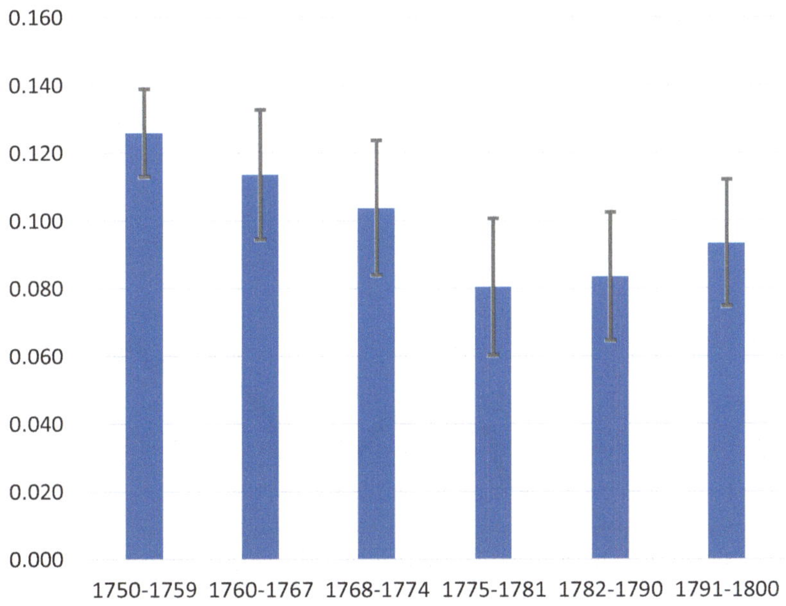

Fig. 9.5 Minor guardianships enacted in the 14 study towns, averaged by time period. (Source: Guardianship statistics are drawn from the individual town council records)
Notes: The thick bar represents the mean across all towns for each period, calculated as the fixed effects of the period binary variables; the thin bar represents one standard error. In total, the panel had 690 town-year observations

guardianship. At the end of the war, council activity to place minors under guardianship increased briefly, reflecting town councils catching up on the backlog of probate business. After that, however, enactment of minor guardianships trended downward until, by the 1790s, the rate of guardianships for children due to inherit property had fallen significantly below the per-capita levels of the 1750s. On the other hand, enactment of guardianships for adults deemed incompetent to manage their affairs returned to prewar levels and then increased significantly in the 1790s, well above per-capita levels of the 1750s.

9.3 Hopkinton

In April 1783, Elijah Burdick "personally appeared" before the Hopkinton town council and told them that "he suspected that sundry evil-minded persons was design[ing] to injure either his person or estate & that he believed he was not of a sufficient ability to defeat them."[50] He asked the council to appoint a guardian to

[50] TCM 21 April 1783, Hopkinton TCR 2:113.

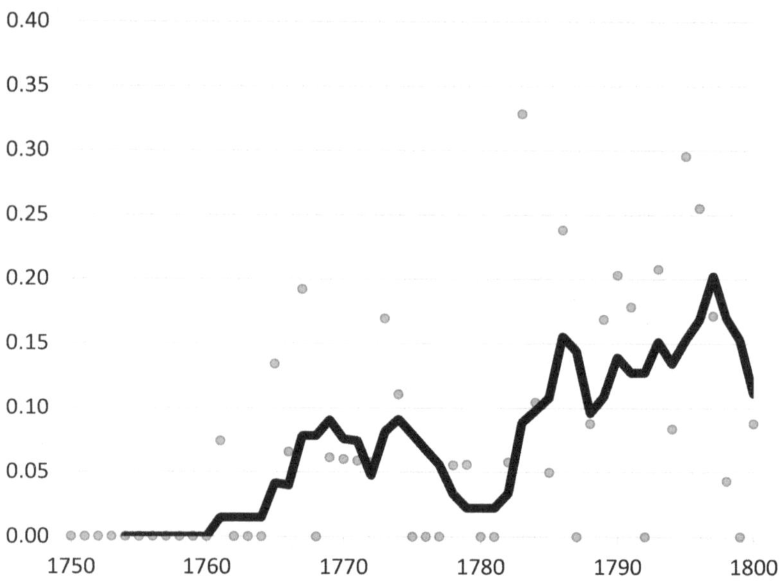

Fig. 9.6. Per-capita adult guardianships in Hopkinton, 1757–1800. (Sources: Guardianship statistics are drawn from Hopkinton Town Council Records, held at the Hopkinton Town Clerk's Office, Hopkinton Town Hall)
Notes: The gray dots represent the ratio of adult guardianships to Hopkinton population each year. The thick line represents 3-year moving average of each year

protect him, and the councilmen obliged. Burdick's anxiety suggests a kind of paranoia – was this one man's nightmare or was he pointing to an unusual pulse of fear and worry in Hopkinton?

Hopkinton stands out among the Rhode Island towns for its high rate of putting adults under guardianship in the 1780s and 1790s (See Figs. 9.4 and 9.6.) Hopkinton was not alone in suffering economically, socially, and politically during this period. All Rhode Island town councils worked hard to restore order after the war. But adult guardianship appears to have been Hopkinton councilmen's favorite solution for problems that affected every town. Further, Hopkinton's application of adult guardianship seems rather heavy-handed. The council put adults under guardianship when less formal measures might have served just as well. What prompted the Hopkinton councilmen to make such choices?

The answer may lie in Hopkinton's status as the newest Rhode Island town, having separated from Westerly in 1757.[51] For the town leaders, the pressures of making a new town must have been significant. Would Rhode Island's newest town be competently governed? Would their separation from Westerly be viewed in hindsight as

[51] "An Act dividing the Town of Westerly," *Acts and Laws of Rhode Island (1767).*

Fig. 9.7 Town council meetings in Hopkinton, 1757–1800. (Sources: Hopkinton Town Council Records, Town Clerk's Office, Hopkinton, RI, town hall)
Notes: The thick line represents the number of town council meetings in Hopkinton. The gray dots represent the number of council meetings in towns of similar size

a mistake, if they could not manage the disorder of the war as effectively as more established towns?

For Hopkinton, the Revolutionary Era was an unusually severe strain.[52] The inhabitants had to deal with turmoil almost from the moment they convened their first town meeting in the midst of the French and Indian War. Before the town meeting had opportunity to solidify itself as a group of voters, they were being pressured to officially protest various acts passed by the English parliament in the 1760s and 1770s. Before the town could firmly build its own alliances with neighboring towns, it was hearing calls for rebellion against the English monarch. Before the inhabitants had bonded as a community and put in place informal mechanisms to deal with disorder, they were engulfed in revolutionary turmoil that stirred up discord among neighbors. Before Hopkinton leaders could establish their own "best practices" for governing, they were faced with urgent wartime situations that demanded immediate responses. Adult guardianship might easily have seemed the most expedient solution for a council under such pressure.

The Hopkinton town council met more often than usual throughout the 1780s and 1790s, with a post-war peak of 27 times in 1796 (See Fig. 9.7.) Putting adults

[52] On Hopkinton in the late 1700s, see Herndon (1992a, pp. 18–49) and Herndon (1992b, pp. 103–115).

under guardianship was often on the agenda in these meetings. In 1 month alone – April 1783 – the council put four adults under guardianship. Between February 1782 and January 1785, Hopkinton put ten adults under guardianship; it would not experience another such "run" until 1795, when the councilmen appointed guardians over seven people in one 5-month period. The council gave reasons that varied from drunkenness to imprudence to selling land unwisely. This last concern deserves a closer look.

Every Rhode Island town clerk had charge of the land evidence books that documented the sale and purchase of privately owned real estate. Town councils had no authority over these private sales, yet Hopkinton's town councilmen cited a looming sale of real estate as cause for putting someone under guardianship. They implied that selling real estate would cause the seller to fall into poverty and then need town poor relief. Very likely, the town council was also trying to maintain some control over who had political power in the town. Owning real estate was key to becoming a freeholder and having the right to vote in town meeting (Herndon 1992a, pp. 89–91). Selling real estate signaled the potential loss of a freeholder; selling real estate to someone outside of Hopkinton potentially introduced a new freeholder, perhaps someone they did not approve.

In 1786, the Hopkinton council heard a "complaint" that Isaiah Button "is in a likely way to lose part of his estate by making sale of part of his lands if not speedily prevented." The council promptly put Button under guardianship explicitly to prevent the sale. Three years later, when Button wanted to "exchange some lands" with neighbor Ross Coon, an exchange that Button's guardian approved, the council lifted the guardianship so that Button could legally make this exchange.[53] In 1791, when the Hopkinton council learned that Elisabeth and Penelope Barber were "about to dispose of their land" – an action which the council considered "of bad consequence" – the councilmen appointed a guardian to prevent the sale.[54] In 1796, the Hopkinton council appointed Deacon Zaccheus Maxson to be guardian to Jonathan Dyer and his mother Rebekah, because Dyer "conducts imprudently and is about to convey his real estate" and his mother, Widow Rebekah Dyer, "is consenting to sign the deed and acquit her right of dower."[55] Adult guardianship seems an overbearing method of preventing a sale, when town leaders, friends, and neighbors might have exerted pressure more discreetly.

The Hopkinton council's heavy reliance on guardianship is especially evident in its dealings with the Button family. Isaiah Button's guardianship in 1786 was not the first encounter between the Buttons and the council. Twenty-one years earlier, in 1765, the Hopkinton council had put Rufus Button under guardianship because he had "through misconduct" gotten himself in debt "and likely to remain so." Given that Rufus Button had a wife and young child, the council thought it unlikely that he could get out of debt without the supervision of a guardian. By 1770, Rufus Button

[53] TCM 29 August 1786 and 7 June 1789, Hopkinton 2:257 and 2:305.

[54] TCM 13 December 1791, Hopkinton TCR 3:9.

[55] TCM 20 August 1796, Hopkinton TCR 3:84.

(with the assistance of his guardian) had cleared his debts and was released from guardianship.[56] In 1783, the Hopkinton council put Samuel Button, "an aged gentleman who is past labor," under guardianship because he was "about to sell his present inheritance which will likely render him in a suffering condition."[57] In 1786, another, younger Samuel Button (son of Amos) was put under guardianship "at the request of his parents," suggesting a serious problem in family relationships.[58] In 1794, the council put Rufus Button Jr. under guardianship because he "conducts himself very imprudently, in a very slothful, idle manner."[59]

Finally, in 1796, the council took comprehensive action against the latest generation of Buttons for being troublesome. The Hopkinton council heard "complaint" that Arnold Button and David Button Jr., two teenaged cousins, "conducts themselves in a very unbecoming manner, being idle, disobedient to parents & mischievous." The complaint also alleged that kinsman John Button "conducts imprudently." The council appointed guardians over the two teenagers, over their fathers (Rufus Button and David Button Sr.) and over John Button. The guardians? Renowned General George Thurston, veteran of the Revolutionary War, and William Tanner, Esqr., another of town's political and economic elite.[60] Perhaps the Hopkinton councilmen had decided that lesser measures did not work with members of the Button clan.

The Hopkinton council's biggest mistake over adult guardianship was John Maxson Sr. In September 1793, John Maxson Jr. reported to the Hopkinton town council that his father "conducts himself imprudently and very unbecomingly in several respects"; even worse, "some of his misconduct is well known by others."[61] John Maxson Sr. had been a prominent citizen of Westerly; his father and grandfather – both ministers – had established the Sabbatarian (Seventh Day Baptist) Church in the northern region of Westerly that would later hive off as Hopkinton (Denison 1878, pp. 60–61; Griswold 1877, pp. 70–71).[62] John Maxson Sr. was elected to Westerly's highest office, serving as one of their two representatives to the General Assembly in the 1740s (Denison 1878, pp. 156–157). Further, he was one of the "honored civil founders" of Hopkinton; in 1757, when the town separated from Westerly, he was the first man elected to the town council and served as its president for 3 years.[63] Starting in 1761, he was regularly elected to be one of

[56] TCM 18 November 1765, 21 March 1768, 6 March 1769, 1 January 1770, Hopkinton TCR 1:85, 1:119, 1:127, 1:139.

[57] TCM 7 April 1783, Hopkinton TCR 2:112.

[58] TCM 6 February 1786, Hopkinton TCR 2:245.

[59] TCM 24 March 1794, Hopkinton TCR 3:46.

[60] TCM 5 September and 3 October 1796, Hopkinton TCR 3:86–87.

[61] TCM 3 September 1793, Hopkinton TCR 3:38. John Maxson Sr. was born on April 21, 1701; his son John Maxson Jr. was born August 27, 1725. See *Rhode Island: Vital Records*, 1:117.

[62] At the time of Hopkinton's founding, the Sabbatarian Church was the only church in Hopkinton.

[63] TM 4 April 1757, Hopkinton TMR 1:1–5; Griswold (1877, pp. 17–18). John Maxson, Jr., who made the complaint against his father, was elected to the town council regularly from 1760 onward. He served as town clerk from 1768 to 1774. Hopkinton TMR vol 1 and 2.

Hopkinton's representatives to the General Assembly, and the clerk who recorded this election wrote "Esqr." behind his name, showing the widespread respect he had earned.[64]

Some 30 years later, the Hopkinton councilmen quickly realized they had made a mistake in not considering John Maxson Sr.'s long and distinguished service to the community and his still high status among the residents. They could have made an informal arrangement with kinfolk and neighbors to keep this venerable town father and the town council itself from the embarrassment of a formal guardianship. Three months after they put Maxson under guardianship, the councilmen reversed their decision because "there seems to have arisen some uneasiness" about it and "some think it best to discharge him therefrom."[65] Adult guardianship was indeed a powerful instrument; if townspeople believed the council had misused that instrument, they would talk about it. By lifting the guardianship of John Maxson Sr., the Hopkinton council acknowledged they had fallen short of the community's expectations.

9.4 Conclusion

Hopkinton's unusually high use of adult guardianships was likely due to its newness as a town. But Hopkinton was not alone; town councils throughout Rhode Island increased their use of adult guardianship throughout the era. There is no simple explanation, however, of this rise. The rise and fall in wealth or the pace of population growth did not predict a greater use of guardianships. Instead, we conclude that town councils responded to the disorder caused by war, in part, with increased use of adult guardianships. And some towns (Hopkinton being the paradigm) relied on this tool as a key way to restore order. The Revolution had introduced unprecedented turmoil at the local level and put town leaders under pressure to restore order. Towns clung to the traditional structure of government right through the chaos. In 1800, they still elected six town councilmen to solve their problems, and those councilmen relied more intensively on the familiar measures their counterparts had used in the 1750s. The increased use of adult guardianship was part of a larger effort to restore order in a time of crisis.

Appendix: Herndon on Murray

John Murray strongly influenced the direction of my scholarship. During the years that he and I were on faculty together at the University of Toledo (1996–2007), he helped me keep social history in conversation with economic history. He fed me

[64] TM 25 August 1761, Hopkinton TMR 1:41; Griswold (1877, 38–39).

[65] TCM 3 September 1793 and 2 December 1793, Hopkinton TCR 3:38, 41.

classic and recent books and articles that used economic data to tell a story about the past. One of the greatest benefits of being on the same campus with him was getting to hear his critiques of new scholarship; he had a new book in hand every time I walked into his office, and I always left with a recommended reading list. A conversation with John was even more productive than browsing through book reviews in a scholarly journal. Further, during those years at UT, John gave me a great gift of his time by reading every piece of scholarship I had produced, including my lengthy dissertation on Rhode Island towns during the Revolutionary Era. He had fruitful ideas for developing and publishing pieces of the dissertation. It has been a great sadness not to be able to consult him as I wrote this essay, which began with my dissertation and took on new life when John asked questions about adult guardianship that I couldn't answer. This essay answers some of John's questions.

References

Achenbaum WA (1978) Old age in the new land: the American experience since 1790. Johns Hopkins University Press, Baltimore

Acts and Laws of The English Colony of Rhode-Island and Providence Plantations in New–England (1767) Samuel Hall, Newport

Arnold JN (ed) (1891) Rhode Island: vital records, 1636-1850. Narragansett Historical Publishing Company, Providence

Bamberg CF (2004) The 1774 census of Rhode Island: Warwick. Rhode Island Roots 30:194–205

Bartlett JR (ed) (1856) Records of the State of Rhode Island, vol. 9 (1780-1783). AC Greene, Providence

Bartlett JR (ed) (1861) Records of colony of Rhode Island and providence plantations, vol. 6 (1757-1769). Knowles, Anthony, Providence

Bell LV (1980) Treating the mentally ill: from colonial times to the present. Praeger, New York

Blackie D (2010) Disabled Revolutionary War veterans and the construction of disability in the early United States, 1776-1860. Ph.D. dissertation, University of Helsinki

Coleman PJ (1963) The transformation of Rhode Island, 1790-1860. Brown University Press, Providence

Conley PT (1977) Democracy in decline: Rhode Island's constitutional development, 1776-1841. Rhode Island Historical History, Providence

Cook EM (1976) Fathers of the towns: leadership and community structure in eighteenth-century New England. Johns Hopkins University Press, Baltimore

Coughtry J (1981) The notorious triangle: Rhode Island and the African slave trade, 1700-1807. Temple University Press, Philadelphia

Daniels BC (1978) Diversity and democracy: officeholding patterns among selectmen in eighteenth-century Connecticut. In: Daniels BC (ed) Power and status: officeholding in colonial America. Wesleyan University Press, Middletown, pp 36–52

Daniels C, Kennedy MV (eds) (1999) Over the threshold: intimate violence in early America. Routledge, New York

Dayton CH (2015) 'The oddest man that I ever saw': assessing cognitive disability on eighteenth-century Cape Cod. J Soc Hist 49(1):77–99

Denison F (1878) Westerly and its witnesses, 1626-1876. JA & RA Reid, Providence

Deutsch A (1949) The mentally ill in America: a history of their care and treatment from colonial times, 2nd edn. Columbia University Press, New York

Doron I (2002) Elder guardianship kaleidoscope: a comparative perspective. Int J Law Policy Family 16(3):368–398
Eldridge LD (1996) 'Crazy brained': mental illness in colonial America. Bull Hist Med 70(3):361–386
Field CT, Syrett N (2020) Chronological age: a useful category of historical analysis. Am Hist Rev 125(2):370–384
Fischer DH (1977) Growing old in America. Oxford University Press, New York
Freeman S (1791) The town officer: the power and duty of selectmen, town clerks, town treasurers, overseers of the poor . . . and other town officers as contained in the laws of the Commonwealth of Massachusetts. Benjamin Tiscomb, Jr., Portland
Greene EB, Harrington VD (1966) American population before the federal census of 1790. Peter Smith, Gloucester
Griswold SS (1877) An historical sketch of the town of Hopkinton, from 1757 to 1876. Wood River Advertiser Press, Hope Valley
Grob GN (1994) The mad among us: a history of the care of America's mentally ill. Harvard University Press, Cambridge
Hardy DA (2008) Who is guarding the guardians? A localized call for improved guardianship systems and monitoring. M.J.S. thesis, University of Nevada-Reno
Herndon RW (1992a) Governing the affairs of the town: continuity and change in Rhode Island, 1750-1800. Ph.D. dissertation, American University
Herndon RW (1992b) 'On and off the record': town clerks as interpreters of Rhode Island history. Rhode Island Hist 50(4):103–115
Herndon RW, Murray JE (2019) An economic interpretation of Rhode Island's 1788 referendum on the Constitution. In: Hall JC, Witcher M (eds) Public choice analyses of American economic history, vol 3. Springer, New York, pp 117–135
Holbrook JM (ed) (1979) Rhode Island 1782 Census. Holbrook Research Institute, Oxford
Houston RA (2003) Legal protection of the mentally incapable in early modern Scotland. J Legal Hist 24(2):165–186
James SV (1975) Colonial Rhode Island: a history. Charles Scribner's, New York
James SV (2000) In: Skemp SL, Daniels BC (eds) The colonial metamorphoses in Rhode Island: a study of institutions in change. University Press of New England, Hanover
Jimenez MA (1987) Changing faces of madness: early American attitudes and treatment of the insane. University Press of New England, Hanover
Jones DP (1992) The economic and social transformation of rural Rhode Island, 1780-1850. Northeastern University Press, Boston
Lemons JS (1986) Rhode Island's ten turning points: a second appraisal. Rhode Island Hist 45:57–70
Lender ME, Martin JK (1982) Drinking in America: a history. Free Press, New York
Lovejoy DS (1958) Rhode Island politics and the American Revolution, 1760-1776. Brown University Press, Providence
McLoughlin WG (1986a) Rhode Island: a history. WW Norton, New York
McLoughlin WG (1986b) Ten turning points in Rhode Island history. Rhode Island Hist 45:41–55
Montague HB (1895) The origin, history and jurisdiction of probate courts in Massachusetts. Bachelor of Law Thesis, Cornell University
Mutschler B (2020) The providence of affliction: illness and the making of early New England. University of Chicago Press, Chicago
Neugebauer R (1987) Exploitation of the insane in the new world: Benoni Buck, the first reported case of mental retardation in the American colonies. Arch Gen Psych 44(5):481–483
Neugebauer R (1989) Diagnosis, guardianship, and residential care of the mentally ill in medieval and early modern England. Am J Psych 146(12):1580–1584
Neugebauer R (1996) Mental handicap in medieval and early modern England: criteria, measurement, and care. In: Wright D, Digby A (eds) From idiocy to mental deficiency: historical perspectives on people with learning disabilities. Routledge, London, pp 22–43

O'Sullivan JL, Hoffman DE (1995/1996) The guardianship puzzle: whatever happened to due process? Maryland J Contemp Legal Iss 7 (1995/96): 11–80
Pleck EH (1987) Domestic tyranny: the making of social policy against family violence from colonial times to the present. Oxford University Press, New York
Polishook IH (1969) Rhode Island the Union, 1774-1795. Northwestern University Press, Evanston
Public Laws of the State of Rhode Island and Providence Plantations (1798) Carter and Wilkinson, Providence
Quinn MJ (ed) (2005) Guardianships of adults: achieving justice, autonomy, and safety. Springer, New York
Rappleye C (2006) Sons of Providence: the Brown Brothers, the slave trade, and the American Revolution. Simon & Schuster, New York
Reed P (2014) Henry Straight of Portsmouth and East Greenwich, R.I., and his family. Rhode Island Roots 40:185–193
Resch J (2002) Suffering soldiers: Revolutionary war veterans, moral sentiment, and political culture in the early republic. University of Massachusetts Press, Amherst
Rhode Island 1777 Military Census (1985) Transcribed by Chamberlain MM. Genealogical Publishing, Baltimore
Rorabaugh WJ (1979) The alcoholic republic: an American tradition. Oxford University Press, New York
Rothman DJ (1979) Discovery of the asylum: social order and disorder in new republic. Little, Brown, Boston
Sabatino CP, Wood E (2012) The conceptualization of legal capacity of older people in western law. In: Doron I, Soden AM (eds) Beyond elder law: new directions in law and aging. Springer, New York, pp 35–55
Salinger SV (2002) Taverns and drinking in early America. Johns Hopkins University Press, Baltimore
Sweet JW (2003) Bodies politic: negotiating race in the American north: 1730-1830. University of Pennsylvania Press, Philadelphia
Town Council Records for Cumberland, East Greenwich, Exeter, Glocester, Hopkinton, Jamestown, Middletown, New Shoreham, Providence, Richmond, South Kingstown, Tiverton, Warren, and Warwick, Rhode Island. All council records are located in the Town Clerk's Office at the respective town halls
Withey L (1984) Urban growth in colonial Rhode Island: Newport and Providence in the eighteenth century. State University of New York Press, Albany
Wood E (2005) History of guardianship. In: Quinn MJ (ed) Guardianships of adults: achieving justice, autonomy, and safety. Springer, New York, pp 17–48
Wood E (2016) Recharging adult guardianship reform: six current paths forward. J Aging Longevity Law Policy 1(1):8–53
Wood E (2019) An interview with Erica Wood: a 40-year lookback on guardianship. Bifocal Je ABA Commission Law Aging 41(2):189–190
Wood E, Teaster P, Cassidy J (2017) Restoration of rights in adult guardianship: research & recommendations. American Bar Association, Washington DC
Walsh EF (1987) The state of Rhode Island and Providence Plantations, 1987-1998 manual. RI Secretary of State, Providence. Online version at: http://www.planning.ri.gov/documents/census/popcounts_est/pop_cities_towns_historic_1790-2010.pdf
Yang S (2019) The tradition and the modernization of adult guardianship system –from the comparative law perspective on adult guardianship systems in China and Canada. M.L. thesis, McGill University

Chapter 10
Later-Life Realizations of Maryland's Mid-Nineteenth-Century Pauper Apprentices

Howard Bodenhorn

Abstract *Children Bound to Labor* (2009) revealed the ubiquity and idiosyncratic nature of pauper apprenticeship across the eighteenth- and nineteenth-century United States. Despite local and regional differences, pauper apprenticeship served the three related purposes of poor relief, social control, and training for later-life economic independence. Most existing studies focus on whether and to what extent the system achieved the first two objectives. Less is known about later-life outcomes of pauper apprentices. This chapter offers insights into the system's contribution to the third objective by linking more than 2700 young males apprenticed by family members and by poor relief administrators in Maryland between 1820 and 1860 to the federal censuses of 1860 and 1870. Compared to boys apprenticed by family members, pauper apprentices were indentured at younger ages, but they were otherwise promised similar training, education, and freedom dues during their apprenticeships. In later life, however, pauper apprentices were less likely to be literate and conditional on marriage had fewer children. There were small differences in skilled employment, wealth, and mobility. A second well-documented feature of pauper apprenticeship was its racialized implementation. Maryland's poor blacks worked in less skilled occupations, were less literate, and amassed notably less wealth. If the system is to be judged by equitable treatment and sufficient training for later-life economic independence, it is not clear that the system succeeded. It took poor black children off the public dole but did not prepare them for more than scraping by in later life.

Keywords Apprenticeship · Poor relief · Social control · Racism · Census-linked

---

H. Bodenhorn (✉)
Clemson University, Clemson, SC, USA
e-mail: bodnhrn@clemson.edu

P. Gray et al. (eds.), *Standard of Living*, Studies in Economic History,
https://doi.org/10.1007/978-3-031-06477-7_10

10.1 Introduction

Eighteenth- and nineteenth-century Americans faced the issue of how best to deal with indigent members of their communities. The state's ability to provide relief was constrained by its limited bureaucracy, tax base, and state capacity. Other than private charity and parish relief, communities adopted various mechanisms to assist the poor and unfortunate, whether adults or children, including pauper auctions and pauper apprenticeship. Pauper auctions were conducted by local governments in which municipalities auctioned poor adults to householders willing to accept the lowest public subsidy in return for taking in an indigent person (Klebaner 1954; Smith 1988). Presumably, bidders expected to extract labor services from the poor during the contract period. That the system included a public subsidy points to the low expected labor productivity of the poor. Pauper apprentices were poor, orphaned, neglected, abused, or abandoned children who were taken in by local householders. The children were expected to work in return for their subsistence, a rudimentary education, and skill training during the remaining years of their minority. Most pauper apprentices labored in the householders' fields, tended their livestock, and received freedom dues at the expiration of the apprenticeship.

The existing literature on pauper apprenticeship documents the terms under which poor children were bound out and the conditions under which they lived during their apprenticeships. Masters signed contracts in which they promised to provide apprentices with food, drink, clothing, shelter, and medical care. Apprentices agreed to work, abide by the master's rules, and not drink, curse, gamble, and fornicate. We know that most apprenticed boys and girls were orphaned rather than simply indigent (Russo and Russo 2009; Whitman 2009). Most were bound out between the ages of 7 and 15, though some were apprenticed as early as a few months of age or as old as 20 years (Murray and Herndon 2002; Brewer 2009; Herndon 2009; Whitman 2009). Age at indenture increased over the eighteenth and nineteenth centuries (Brewer 2009). Apprenticed youth were promised to be taught the "art and mystery" of some trade. Most learned how to work a farm; others were provided with genuine craft training. Most were promised instruction in the three Rs; others were promised a cash payment at the end of their indentures in lieu of an education (Herndon 2009; Russo and Russo 2009; Whitman 2009; Bodenhorn 2003). Black apprentices received less generous indentures (Rohrs 2013). Apprentices were promised freedom dues; some received the traditional payment of two suits of new clothes, while others received cash (Whitman 2009).

Despite a now substantial literature on the subject, there is little agreement among historians about the purpose or the result of pauper apprenticeship. Seth Rockman (2009) interprets it as a coercive and exploitive mechanism designed to alleviate the chronic shortage of labor in early America. For Rockman, in its mobilizing the labor of the indigent and the unfortunate, pauper apprenticeship was a legal institution shaped to serve the interests of a wealthy landholding, often slaveholding, class and a nascent capitalist class. Karin Zipf (2005) also views pauper apprenticeship as a partial solution to labor shortages in the agricultural South, but because it marshaled a small fraction of the region's labor power, its true importance lay less in its economic contribution than in its social and political symbolism. For Zipf (2005, p.4), pauper apprenticeship was not so much an effort to mobilize labor as it was an effort to reinforce a "social order rooted in white male superiority." It was incumbent on a paternalist, patriarchal state to intercede in the raising of orphaned, indigent, and free black children.

Herndon and Murray (2009) offer a more benign interpretation, one that nods to a pragmatic solution to a social problem under conditions of limited state capacity. By their account, pauper apprenticeship provided the training and education that gave an indigent child a fighting chance at an independent adulthood. Apprenticeship "kept vulnerable children alive, it put them in a family setting, it put them to work at some useful occupation, and it familiarized them with the kind of manual labor that was the lot of most early Americans" (Herndon and Murray 2009, p. 2). Monique Bourque (2009), too, recognizes that the system was motivated by multiple factors and served multiple purposes. The binding out of children, according to Bourque (2009, p.72), was a labor transaction in which a child was turned over to a master who was expected to put the child to work, "but it was also an act of local governance, the administration of poor relief, the giving of charity, and a matter of neighborly observation and concern." The apprenticing of poor children was not a symbolic statement of patriarchy or a concerted effort by the wealthy to exploit a powerless underclass. Economists, more than most social scientists, tend to view statements of principle and public spiritedness skeptically, and not without reason, but that does not mean that local public officials and masters were not influenced by the era's much-discussed republican virtues and wanted to do right by parents, children, masters, and taxpayers, including themselves. Local officials can be, and sometimes are, motivated by a genuine spirit of public service (Besley 2005).

This chapter builds on one of Murray's research agendas in that it offers a longitudinal study of nineteenth-century American pauper apprentices. Besides Lockley's (2009) analysis of a small number of Savannah, Georgia's apprentices, there is more speculation about than understanding of apprentices' later-life realizations. It is fair to characterize the existing literature as doubtful. Despite a handful of well-known success stories – Benjamin Franklin, the printer's apprentice, being commonly invoked – historians believe that masters did little to alter the career or life trajectories of apprentices (Herndon 2009). Cycles of intergenerational poverty, it is believed, were not easily deflected.

To better understand the consequences of pauper apprenticeship, this chapter traces the life trajectories of Maryland boys who were apprenticed by their families into a craft or by the courts into crafts and husbandry between 1820 and 1860. The original sample of 2700 boys is linked to the 1860 and 1870 censuses to better understand their socioeconomic condition in adulthood. The 545 apprentices linked to the 1870 census provide a snapshot of the midlife realizations of former pauper and craft apprentices. Based on simple comparisons and without controlling for other factors, pauper apprentices were less likely than craft apprentices to work in a skilled occupation, were less upwardly mobile, held less wealth, were more likely to be illiterate, were less likely to be married, and headed households with fewer children. After controlling for differences in their baseline characteristics and indentures, the skilled employment and wealth differences between white pauper and craft apprentices disappear. The system was racialized, however, in that free blacks indentured in their youth experience much lower later-life realizations than their white counterparts.

10.2 Craft and Pauper Apprentices

Through much of the eighteenth and into the nineteenth century in North America, once a boy celebrated his 13th or 14th birthday, he began training in his chosen profession. The skills needed to practice that profession were passed on by his father, another male relative, or a master craftsman with whom the boy was apprenticed (Rorabaugh 1986). Among middling Americans, sons of farmers became farmers and sons of craftsmen trained in their fathers' crafts. But not every farmer's son wanted to farm; not every blacksmith's son was cut out for the rigors of hammer and forge. If a son was disinclined to pursue his father's trade, fathers and sons negotiated an apprenticeship agreement with a craftsman willing to train the boy in a chosen craft's practices.

The Old-World model of apprenticeship was one in which apprentices took up residence in the master's house, worked alongside their masters, and lived as part of the masters' families. Masters were expected by law and tradition to exercise the same paternalistic authority with their apprentices as they would with their own children (Steffen 1984). The usual age of apprenticeship was about 14 by which time boys had become large enough and strong enough that their labor would be useful to masters even though the boys did not yet have any specialized skills (Main 2009). When it worked as designed, apprenticeship provided boys with the knowledge and skills needed to earn a living at the end of the contract. In many trades, it is unlikely that an apprentice would have the capital or wherewithal to hang out a shingle upon completion of his indenture. He might have to work for a few years as a journeyman, during which time he acquired the tools and capital necessary to establish his own shop. Those jobs requiring the fewest and least expensive tools, like shoemaking and tailoring, were the easiest to enter, but they were among the earliest to be devalued with the emergence of factory-made, ready-to-wear apparel.

Apprenticeship was not just about skill training; the system served four functions: it provided for an education that facilitated the intergenerational transfer of skill training; it provided youth with a model of socially acceptable adult behavior; it advanced the moral development through the master's paternalistic reward and punishment system; and it was a means for controlling potentially disruptive male teenagers. Courts took the latter two functions as seriously as the first. Steffen' (1984) study documents recurring tensions between Baltimore's infamously rebellious and incorrigible youth and their allegedly despotic and tyrannical masters. Courts granted masters wide disciplinary latitude, though certain lines could not be crossed. In practical terms, it is not clear how well the European model of guild-supervised apprenticeship translated to a New-World economy characterized by labor shortages and cheap land. American apprentices had more outside options and more autonomy than their Old-World counterparts.

Despite challenges in its implementation, child pauper apprenticeship borrowed features from the craft apprenticeship tradition, and two lines of thought have emerged in the discussion of pauper apprenticeship. On the one hand, Neff (1996) contends that the normal rules of craft apprenticeship did not apply to pauper apprentices. She argues that few people cared about whether apprentices' situations were privately or socially beneficial so long as the children were fed, clothed, housed, and kept off public poor relief. All the system was designed to do was keep poor children busy and off the streets. Apprentices were rarely taught the skills needed to prepare them for employment, much less economic independence in later life.

Neff's contention is plausible in a one-period static framework, but it overlooks the reality that if pauper children represented a potential drain on the public purse, poor adults must have presented an even larger one. Unless local authorities expected most pauper children to move out of the jurisdiction when their apprenticeship expired or unless justices of the orphans' courts responsible for apprenticing them had high discount rates, making tomorrow's adult paupers unworthy of today's concern, orphans' court justices must have recognized the dynamic, multiperiod nature of the problem. In the absence of effective intervention, today's poor children would be tomorrow's poor adults. If poor adults are not particularly mobile, pauper children apprenticed with little concern for their education and training would in a few years' time become public charges. Poverty would become a lifelong condition and a recurring charge on the public purse.

Bourque (2009), on the other hand, contends that pauper apprenticeship advanced two potentially desirable objectives: it removed indigent, abused, and neglected children from households that were not providing them with appropriate moral and physical development; and it provided these children with an opportunity to learn skills that would help them be productive after they left the master's house. In the early republic, children needed to build character and develop habits of industry. Masters would, presumably, provide better guides in the process than would the apprentices' impoverished or inattentive parents. There were other options – almshouses, orphanages, and even outdoor relief – but apprenticeship was considered an effective way to transform disadvantaged children into productive adults.

It does not stretch credulity too far to believe that pauper apprenticeship was an exercise in craftsmen and farmers acquiring labor at, perhaps, below-market wages. Any number of plausible examples can be found in the Maryland records. Between 1823 and 1839, plasterer James Allison of Anne Arundel County, for instance, took in four teenage pauper apprentices. That he took on each new apprentice as the term of a previous apprentice expired suggests that he expected each to contribute to Allison's bottom line. It is a bit more difficult to reconcile a master's pure self-interest and the economic exploitation of pauper apprentices in the case of Anne Arundel farmer Henry Basford's taking in of three brothers ages 2 (George Calvert), 5 (John), and 9 (Charles) in 1846. The 9-year-old might immediately contribute to the household through light chores, but it would be years before George and John would be chopping wood or working the mule and plow. Fogel and Engerman (1974) show that slaves raised from infancy in the highly productive Cotton South circa 1850 did not earn enough to repay their maintenance costs until age 26. A 2-year-old taken in the less productive southern shore of Maryland would probably not pay his accumulated costs until later, almost certainly not by age 21, which is consistent with the fact that county courts sometimes paid masters modest sums for taking in very young children (Walsh 1988; Brewer 2009).

Basford's willingness to take in three young brothers seems more consistent with an institution concerned with public responsibility and the stewardship of community and family. Children were sometimes removed over their parents' protestations, to be sure and perhaps out of prejudice, but it seems unlikely that such was the norm. Overseers of the poor tried to find mutually beneficial matches between masters and apprentices, and "economic self-interest and class loyalty were not always more important than the welfare of individuals" (Bourque 2009, p. 79).

Children became involved in the pauper apprenticeship system because they had no living parents to see to their immediate welfare and long-term well-being. Others entered because their parents deserted, abused, or neglected their children. Relatives, guardians, family friends, and concerned neighbors asked magistrates to bind out these children to a responsible master. The watchword of pauper apprenticeship was "improvement" – improvement in the child's immediate situation, improvement in the child's long-term prospects. Masters were considered "agents who carried out the goals of the magistrates in preparing the youngest and poorest of the rising generation for a useful adulthood of service within the community" (Murray and Herndon 2002, p. 12).

If we take contemporaries at their word, pauper apprenticeship was designed to maintain children through their minority and train them to become productive adults. Because the records are silent on the issue, except for the cases brought by or on behalf of apprentices who believed that their masters were abusive or in breach of their contractual obligation to provide an apprentice with training or schooling, we must assume that masters abided by their agreement to provide food, clothing, shelter, medical care, and some sort of instruction and skill training. Extant records provide the materials needed to judge pauper apprenticeship on its second mission, namely, the training of disadvantaged youth for a productive adult life. The availability of online sources makes it possible to follow the life trajectories, if only in a limited way, of boys bound as apprentices through to their later appearance in the federal census records. Economic historians are now able to conduct large-scale longitudinal studies of citizens of the United States and elsewhere that were challenging, even daunting to all but the most indomitable, even two decades ago (Ferrie 1999; Baker et al. 2020; Leknes and Modalsli 2020).

Of 2751 male craft and pauper apprentices whose indentures were recorded in a sample of 4 Maryland counties, this study links 805 of them as adults to the 1860 federal census and 663 to the 1870 federal census, each of which provides information on the former apprentices' later-life occupations, wealth, and household structures. A study of the economic and familial conditions of these apprentices provides some much-needed perspective on the nature and consequences of pauper apprenticeship.

10.3 The Evolution of Pauper Apprenticeship in Maryland

Maryland enacted its first orphan law in 1654. The law required estate administrators who controlled orphan's property to submit regular reports to the county court (Carr 1977). The 1654 law and its seventeenth-century amendments provided for propertied orphans in that it required the protection of orphaned children, including a provision that they be maintained and educated consistent with their prior statuses. The law looked to preserve the orphans' heritable property. Propertyless orphans were to be bound out to learn a trade. Bound out orphans resembled indentured servants in certain regards (Grubb 1992, 2022). Their indentures could be transferred between masters, but, because bound orphans were not chattel, transfers required permission of the court (Daniels 2001). Transfers did not involve payments; the court sanctioned the transfer with a new indenture. When the court bound out infants, it often paid the child's master a small fee. Carr (1977) argues that masters requested such payments because young children were unproductive and often died before they could provide a return on the master's expenditures.

Post-Revolutionary Maryland revised its law requiring Orphans' Courts to bind out any orphan child whose estate was insufficient to provide for his or her support in 1793 (Kilty 1818). The revised act directed Orphans' Courts or its agents (county justices of the peace and trustees of the poor) to bind illegitimate and indigent children to masters who would provide them with food, drink, shelter, clothing and washing, training and education, and freedom dues. If one or more of the indigent child's parents were alive and could be brought before the court, their wishes as to whom the child should be bound were respected if their wishes were "just and reasonable" (Kilty 1818). It was not uncommon, in fact, for magistrates to record that an indigent child was bound with the consent of his or her mother.

In establishing its system of orphan care, Maryland drew on a legacy dating back to England's 1562 Statute of Artificers and Apprentices, which codified the apprenticeship system and supplemented the poor laws by directing justices to bind out unemployed and indigent children as apprentices in husbandry (Hicks 1989). Maryland's 1793 act consolidated several earlier colonial-era statutes in that all orphans without estate, bastards, and indigent children were to be bound out. Where pauper apprenticeship had once represented a mechanism to provide boys and girls with skill training, by the beginning of the nineteenth century, it had arguably reverted to its English roots. Historians contend that magistrates exchanged the maintenance of indigent youth for their unskilled labor on farms, in factories, or in the masters' homes; the system had, in large part, reverted to apprenticeship in husbandry or housewifery (Whitman 2009).

Carr (1977) shows that orphan and indigent children were a concern for Maryland lawmakers dating to the earliest days of the colony, but in the late eighteenth and early nineteenth centuries, a new social concern appeared – a growing population of free blacks. While some viewed manumission as the ultimate act of charity, others viewed it was a serious threat to the existing social order and sought ways to curtail, or at least, control it. Laws were passed throughout the colonial and early federal period to control various aspects of the lives of free blacks, and Orphans' Courts were enlisted in the effort (Wright 1971; Fields 1985; Whitman 2009). An 1808 amendment to Maryland's 1793 orphans act directed justices of the peace, trustees of the poor, county sheriffs, and Orphans' Court justices to bind out the "children of lazy, indolent and worthless free negroes" (Kilty 1818, Ch. 54). An 1818 amendment included mulattoes and eliminated the education requirement for the children of free people of color. In lieu of providing apprentices with an education, masters could pay apprentice $30 at the expiration of their indentures.

Rorabaugh (1986), Quimby (1985), Zipf (2005), and Brewer (2009) interpret such discriminatory laws in Maryland and elsewhere as a white patriarchy providing "for an alternative form of social control for young blacks that … reassured anxious white opinion by maintaining white supremacy" (Rorabaugh 1986, pp. 189–90). Hicks (1989) and Rockman (2009) argue that such laws, which disadvantaged free blacks, were a nod to politically powerful farmers who pressured magistrates to indiscriminately indent black children into hard work at subsistence wages. Daniels (2001) questions whether white property holders had the political power or the inclination to force free-born or manumitted children into something akin to involuntary servitude.

Regardless of the historian's perspectives on power and patriarchy, it is indisputable that magistrates did not treat all children equally; Herndon and Murray (2009) contend that the system was permeated with distinctions based on sex, race, age, and socioeconomic background. But this, too, was a nod to the pauper law's original intent, which was to provide for the orphaned and the indigent according to their station. Neither the legislators who wrote the law nor the officials who implemented it expected all pauper apprentices to be treated equally.

10.4 Data

10.4.1 A Sample of Maryland's Craft and Pauper Apprentices

Any assessment of the later-life realizations of Maryland's pauper apprentices requires not only information on the paupers themselves, but on a relevant and reasonable comparison group. One option, one not pursued here, would be to draw a random sample of similar-aged individuals from Maryland, the Middle-Atlantic region, or the entire United States. The availability of large online data sets through IPUMS or other sites makes this a viable option. The alternative, which is the approach adopted here, would be to narrow the comparison group based on one or more criteria. Given the ready availability of information on craft apprentices in the same sources that provides information on pauper apprentices, the comparison group used here is the group of male youth indentured by family members. There are several advantages to using this group, including that they were indented during the same years as pauper apprentices and that both groups were placed into an occupational training system that was on the wane by the second quarter of the nineteenth century. At the expiration of their indentures, Maryland's young men exiting an apprenticeship in a specific trade, whether pauper or craft, should have faced similar opportunities and constraints. This may not be true of a random draw of the population.

Information on Maryland's craft and pauper apprentices is taken from the Register of Wills from Anne Arundel, Baltimore, Frederick, Somerset, and Talbot counties. The earliest records date to 1822 in Anne Arundel County; the latest records are from 1860 in Baltimore, Frederick, and Somerset counties. Although the records differ in particulars across counties and through time, they all included the same basic information: introductory legal boilerplate; standard clauses in which the master agrees to provide adequate food, drink, clothing, shelter, and medical care and the apprentice agrees to behave and obey the master; the date of the indenture; the apprentices' full name; the date of the apprentice's birth; the date the indenture expires; the guardian representing the minor (father, mother, Orphans' Court, etc.); the name of the master or householder who agrees to take in the apprentice; the trade to which the apprentice will be trained; any agreed-on education, which might be a specified period of time or, more often, an agreement to provide the apprentice with the rudiments of reading, writing, and arithmetic (3Rs); and any freedom dues, either in kind or in cash, payable at the expiration of the indenture.

By way of example, Cornelius Howard of Anne Arundel County was apprenticed by the Orphans' Court on July 9, 1822. Cornelius had celebrated his 16th birthday 6 months earlier on January 21, 1822. Under the terms of the indenture, he was to serve an apprenticeship with William Taylor until his 21st birthday on January 21, 1827. During his 4-plus years of service, Cornelius was to be instructed in the wheelwright's trade and educated sufficiently to have a command of the three Rs. At the expiration of his indenture, Taylor was to provide Howard with "customary dues," or new shoes and two new suits of clothes (Anne Arundel 1822).

A close reading of Maryland's apprentices' contracts provides a lesson in the relative incidence of contemporary occupations. Apprenticed boys and youth were to be trained as barbers and blacksmiths, carpenters and cordwainers, plasterers and printers, saddlers and shoemakers, tailors and tinners, and waiters and watermen. A few were relegated to learning the trade of a common servant. Most pauper apprentices, not surprisingly, received a promise to be instructed in the ways of the farmer, given a rudimentary education, and sent into the world at the expiration of their indentures with some new clothes, or a few dollars in cash, or both.

Table 10.1 provides summary statistics on the number of craft and pauper apprentices by county, the years for which data was collected, and key variables. Boys and youth apprenticed by a family member, typically but not always a father, for craft training were about 2–3 years older than pauper apprentices. Pauper apprentices were more likely than craft apprentices to be black. Apprenticeship agreements that promised an education differed by county. In Anne Arundel, for example, about

Table 10.1 Summary statistics for craft and pauper apprentices

Variable	Craft		Pauper		Difference
	Mean	Std dev	Mean	Std dev	*p*-value
(**a**) *Anne Arundel (1822–1858)*					
Observations	92		716		
Age	13.16	(3.92)	11.12	(4.68)	0.00
Black	0.28	(0.45)	0.42	(0.49)	0.00
3Rs	0.29	(0.46)	0.24	(0.43)	0.25
Suits	0.66	(0.91)	0.80	(0.88)	0.15
Real NPV dues	23.59	(58.51)	20.47	(18.81)	0.29
(**b**) *Baltimore (1825–1860)*					
Observations	412		628		
Age	14.84	(3.23)	13.71	(3.59)	0.00
Black	0.12	(0.32)	0.25	(0.44)	0.00
3Rs	0.16	(0.36)	0.51	(0.50)	0.00
Suits	0.51	(0.56)	0.75	(0.61)	0.00
Real NPV dues	33.56	(84.68)	32.66	(46.11)	0.83
(**c**) *Frederick (1827–1860)*					
Observations	293		399		
Age	15.19	(3.15)	13.10	(4.02)	0.00
Black	0.12	(0.32)	0.28	(0.45)	0.00
3Rs	0.11	(0.31)	0.32	(0.47)	0.00
Suits	0.23	(0.57)	0.37	(0.73)	0.00
Real NPV dues	28.91	(28.45)	26.27	(13.51)	0.11
(**d**) *Somerset (1854–1859)*					
Observations	17		115		
Age	10.91	(3.93)	8.54	(4.45)	0.04
Black	0.35	(0.49)	0.63	(0.48)	0.03
3Rs	0.06	(0.24)	0.02	(0.13)	0.29
Suits	1.36	(0.86)	1.73	(0.58)	0.02
Real NPV dues	36.06	(55.08)	33.23	(24.85)	0.72
(**e**) *Talbot (1853–1860)*					
Observations	3		75		
Age	12.81	(8.49)	9.06	(4.05)	0.14
Black	0.67	(0.57)	0.56	(0.50)	0.72
3Rs	0	0	0.09	(0.29)	0.58
Suits	0.67	(1.15)	0.05	(0.32)	0.01
Real NPV dues	13.33	(11.54)	24.60	(28.33)	0.50

Sources: Author's calculations from sources discussed in text and listed in references
Notes: For definition of real net present value (NPV) of dues, see text. Years included in samples are years listed, except Baltimore. Indentures were gathered from Baltimore County records at approximately 5-year intervals between 1825 and 1860, except 1840. Records for 1840 were unavailable. Difference is the *p*-value of the critical value of a Student's t-test of the differences in sample means

one-fourth of both craft and pauper apprentices were promised instruction in reading, writing, and arithmetic (3Rs). In Baltimore, about one-half of pauper apprentices were to be provided with an education, compared to about one-sixth of craft apprentices. In rural Somerset and Talbot counties, less than 10% of all apprentices were to receive a basic education. The table also reveals that the tradition of apprentices receiving two suits of clothes (i.e., "customary dues") at the expiration of their apprenticeships was falling out of favor. In Anne Arundel, for instance, the average craft apprentice received two-thirds of a suit; the average pauper apprentice received 0.80 suits. In Somerset County, by contrast, the two-suit tradition persisted; into the late 1850s, county court officials continued to stipulate two suits for most pauper apprentices.

Rather than providing an education during the apprenticeship and two suits at expiration of the indenture, it became increasingly common for parents and officers of the court to contract for cash alternatives. Between 1825 and 1860, promises of cash dues instead of one or two suits of clothes payable at expiration quintupled from an average of about $7 in the mid-1820s to approximately $35 in the late 1850s. Additional cash payments in lieu of providing for schooling or instruction in the 3Rs increased from an average of about $0.50 in the early 1820s to $2 in the 1850s. Moreover, a few apprentices, mostly in Baltimore, contracted for small cash payments paid to themselves or their families during the terms of their indentures.

To account for the increasing diversity of non-subsistence payments, the final line in each panel of Table 10.1 reports the real net present value of the contractual dues whether payable in cash or in kind. I estimated the implicit contractual value of suits at the terminal date by estimating a regression of dues in lieu of suits on year. The estimated amounts were combined with all other payments to construct the net present value discounted back to the contract year using a 6% discount rate. These values were then adjusted for inflation using the Benzason Philadelphia wholesale price index (Carter et al. 2006). The resulting real net present value of dues calculations exhibits noteworthy features. First, between the mid-1820s and the mid-1850s, the average real discounted value of dues increased for pauper apprentices from about $20 to $40; they increased for craft apprentices from $30 to $50. Second, dues increased more in Baltimore than elsewhere and more so, relatively, for pauper apprentices. Third, dues increased more for black than white apprentices, surely a consequence of Maryland's 1818 law that specifically allowed masters to make cash payments in lieu of school to black apprentices. The law did not release masters from their educational obligations to white apprentices.

A histogram of craft and pauper apprentices' occupations listed in the court records is reported in Fig. 10.1. Approximately 10% of craft and pauper apprentices were indentured to train in one of a handful of unskilled positions – hod carriers, common laborers, servants, and waiters. Twenty percent of craft and 10% of pauper apprentices were to be trained in one of several semiskilled occupations, including brickmaking, broom making, carting, cigarmaking, draying, sawing, and ship caulking, among others. One-half of craft apprentices were, appropriately, indented to learn a skilled craft, compared to just less than one-third of pauper apprentices. Skilled trades ran the gamut from bricklaying, blacksmithing, and coopering to

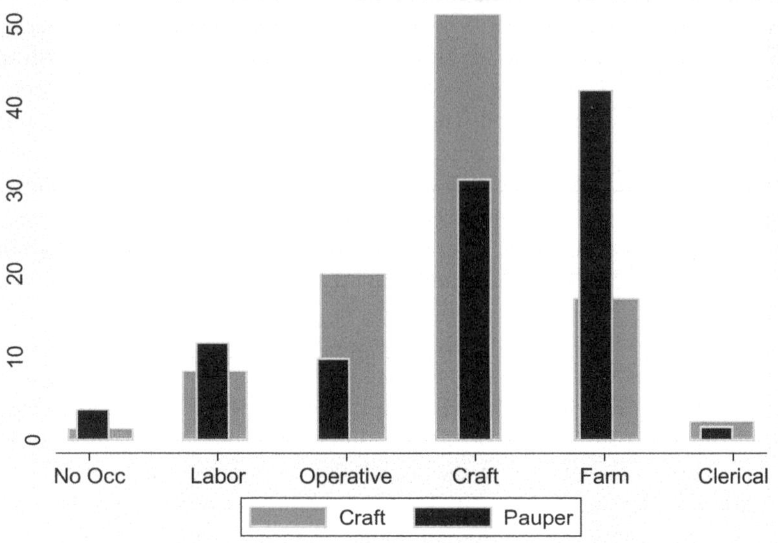

Fig. 10.1 Distribution of occupations in apprentice indentures, Maryland, 1822–1860. (*Sources*: author's calculations from information contained in Anne Arundel (1822--858), Baltimore (1825–1860), Frederick (1827–1860), Somerset (1854–1859), and Talbot (1853–1860))

printing, silversmithing, and watchmaking. The most common were shoemaking and tailoring. Very few teens were provided training as clerks. Farming was the most common trade in which pauper apprentices were trained; a smaller but non-negligible number of craft apprentices were indented to learn husbandry.

It is well known that pauper apprenticeship in the South was racialized in that black and white youth were not treated equally (Zipf 2005; Whitman 2009; Brewer 2009). The statistics reported in Table 10.2 are consistent with these previous studies. The table compares several contract features by race for craft and pauper apprentices. Black youth were apprenticed about 2 years earlier than whites, regardless of whether the contracts were negotiated by family members or county authorities. The occupational rank, based on a five-point categorization, for black and white craft apprentices was the same and consistent with the average apprentice being indentured into an operative or craft trade.[1] Only a small fraction of black youth was promised an education, though black youth received more dues in lieu of an education, both of which are consistent with Maryland's 1818 law that allowed masters to pay black apprentices rather than educate them.

In rural areas it was not uncommon for indentures to include a clause that released apprentices from their responsibilities to their masters to hire themselves out for a

[1]The scale is created such that 1 = laborer, 2 = operative, 3 = skilled artisan, 4 = farmer, and 5 = clerical. Boys indentured without a listed occupation were coded as no occupation = 0.

Table 10.2 Black and white pauper and craft apprentices

		Craft			Pauper	
	Black	White	Difference	Black	White	Difference
Observations	116	701	*p*-value	690	1243	p-value
Age	12.13	15.12	0.00	10.63	12.97	0.00
Birth year	1835.83	1823.49	0.00	1835.97	1829.55	0.00
Occupation rank	2.80	2.80	0.94	2.93	3.06	0.02
3Rs	0.02	0.17	0.00	0.05	0.48	0.00
Dues in lieu of school	0.93	0.24	0.05	3.48	0.32	0.00
Harvest release	0.00	0.93	0.00	0.03	0.39	0.00
Suits	0.66	0.41	0.00	0.84	0.65	0.00
Dues in lieu of suit	1.99	5.23	0.00	3.39	6.98	0.00
Real NPV dues	33.98	30.22	0.57	24.08	27.92	0.00

Sources: Author's calculations from data described in text

Notes: Age in years; occupation rank on a 5-point scale, 1 lowest skill; 3Rs = 0 if no, and 1 otherwise; dues in lieu of school in $; harvest release in days per year; suits in number; dues in lieu of school in $; real NPV dues in $

Difference is the *p*-value of the critical value of a Student's t-test of the differences in sample means

specific number of days during harvest. The average white craft apprentice received 1 day of release, though, when releases were negotiated, they tended to be for between 5 and 14 days. Guardians of pauper apprentices were less likely to negotiate harvest releases, which is consistent with the relatively large fraction of pauper apprentices assigned to farmers. It would have created an undue hardship on masters to release apprentices to hire their own time at the peak of the masters' labor demands. Blacks, whether craft or pauper, were more likely than whites to receive suits as freedom dues; whites received larger average payments in lieu of suits. Finally, the net present value of dues paid to black pauper apprentices was lower than those paid to whites.

10.4.2 Matching Maryland's Pauper Youth to Adults

Once the list of all boys and male youth indentured between 1822 and 1860 was compiled, the youth were linked to individuals who appeared in the eighth (1860) and ninth (1870) decennial federal censuses. If individuals were linked to both censuses, the information from each census was coded. I focus on the eighth and ninth censuses because these censuses recorded individual's name, age, sex, race, occupation, family situation, literacy, and the dollar value of real and personal property.

Individuals were hand linked using the Ancestry.com website based on first name, last name, birth year, race, and Maryland birth. The last restriction necessarily excludes Irish- and German-born youth who were indentured before reaching their 21st birthday, but the restriction was necessary to narrow the search results for individuals with common names. Initial searches restricted birth years to a relatively wide range of plus and minus 5 years, though the analysis reported below is restricted to a plus/minus 2-year window, which is consistent with machine matching procedures used elsewhere in the literature (Abramitzky et al. 2012; Baker et al. 2020; Ager et al. 2020). The results are not appreciably different when the sample window is extended to plus/minus 3 years. My aim throughout was to adopt a conservative match strategy to minimize the number of false-positive matches. Because the sample of 2700 apprentices is of relatively modest size and because Bailey et al. (2017) contend that, when feasible, hand matching or at least hand checking of questionable matches limits the acceptances of false-positive matches, I relied on hand matching.

The sample was not restricted to unique or uncommon names, but when multiple potential matches were identified some of which could not be eliminated based on age, race, or place of birth, the apprentice was not matched to an individual appearing in the census. This procedure surely generated false negatives, that is, apprentices who subsequently appeared in one of the censuses but were not matched, but the tradeoff in longitudinal matching studies is comparable to the Type I-Type II error tradeoff in statistics. Statistical theory concerns itself with the minimization of one or both errors, but neither can be eliminated. Given that my concern is with accurately accounting for later-life realizations, the conservative matching strategy is designed to reduce the occurrence of Type I error (false positives). An effort to avoid Type I error is unlikely to produce a representative sample but will not introduce the types of systematic and complicated biases that can be introduced using one of the less restrictive machine-linking algorithms (Bailey et al. 2017).

The matching strategy yielded 803 apprentices matched to the 1860 census (29.4% match rate) and 663 apprentices matched to the 1870 census (24.1% match rate) when all matches within +/− 5 years of age at indenture plus time. These match rates are consistent with match rates reported elsewhere. It might not be unreasonable to use the +/− 5-year sample given the extent of illiteracy (and, presumably, innumeracy) among apprentices, but the analysis below uses a sample based on +/− 2 years of age at indenture plus years since indenture, which should reduce the number of false-positive links.

Bailey et al. (2017) argue that matched samples with large proportions of false links tend to exhibit systematic correlations between match probabilities and baseline characteristics. As a first check for evidence of potential biases, Table 10.3 compares the mean values of key observable variables for matched and unmatched apprentices using the +/− 2-year linked sample.

Table 10.3 compares the mean values of key baseline characteristics for the two matched samples based on the +/− 2-year age window. Several baseline characteristics differ between the matched and unmatched 1860 sample. A smaller fraction of the matched sample were paupers and black. The matched sample consists of apprentices born earlier and observed at later ages, which is consistent with the smaller fraction of paupers who tended to be younger at indenture. Pauper

Table 10.3 Comparing matched and unmatched apprentices

	1860		Difference	1870		Difference
	Matched	Unmatched	*p*-value	Matched	Unmatched	*p*-value
Observations	456	1949		546	2090	
Pauper	0.59	0.71	0.00	0.72	0.69	0.24
Black	0.20	0.28	0.00	0.34	0.27	0.00
Age	14.56	12.87	0.00	13.44	12.94	0.01
Birth year	1822.85	1829.49	0.00	1828.52	1829.62	0.06
Occupation rank	2.87	2.97	0.06	2.94	2.95	0.96
3Rs	0.31	0.29	0.40	0.25	0.28	0.09
Dues in lieu of school	0.86	1.09	0.40	1.37	1.05	0.23
Suits	0.42	0.63	0.00	0.61	0.64	0.52
Dues in lieu of suit	7.40	5.54	0.00	6.10	5.37	0.14
Real NPV dues	26.57	27.18	0.79	27.21	28.06	0.70

Sources: Author's calculation from data discussed in text
Notes: See Table 10.2 for variable definitions and units of measurement

apprentices received fewer suits as freedom dues. There are no statistically significant differences in the other baseline characteristics. Baseline characteristics of the sample of apprentices matched to the 1870 census exhibit fewer statistically significant differences than the 1860 sample. The 1870 linked sample has a higher fraction of blacks and the average age is about one-half year greater.

To more rigorously investigate whether the later-life outcome reported below might exhibit unknown biases, probit models are estimated in which the dichotomous dependent variable (matched = 1, 0 otherwise) is regressed on the apprentices' observable characteristics at indenture. The baseline variables included in the probit estimation include the apprentice's age at indenture and its square, race, whether the indenture promised an education and release at harvest, the number of suits as freedom dues or cash freedom dues in lieu of school or suits, and controls for county of indenture and a linear time trend.

For ease of interpretation, Table 10.4 reports marginal effects of the influence of the baseline variables on the likelihood of matching an apprentice to the 1860 and 1870 census. Except for the linear time trend and the county of indenture, none of the baseline individual characteristics or indenture contract features influences the probability of matching apprentices to the 1860 census. A higher match rate for later-indented apprentices is not unexpected; later-indented individuals were released closer to 1860 and had not had time to move on, change names, or die. The 1870 census matches offer some small cause for concern about unknowable, but potentially attenuating, biases in the relationship between characteristics and observed outcome variables because race and release at harvest are correlated with the probability of matching apprentices (Bailey et al. 2017).

Table 10.4 Estimated marginal effects of likelihood of census match

Variable	Marginal effect (dy/dx)	Standard error	Marginal effect (dy/dx)	Standard error
	1860		1870	
Age	0.014	0.011	0.001	0.001
Age square	0.000	0.000	0.000	0.000
Black	0.015	0.023	0.078	0.021**
3Rs	−0.013	0.019	0.001	0.019
Harvest	0.000	0.003	0.011	0.003**
Suits	−0.017	0.013	0.014	0.013
Dues in lieu of school	0.000	0.002	0.001	0.001
Dues in lieu of suit	0.000	0.000	0.001	0.001
Linear time trend Anne Arundel	−0.005 Reference	0.001**	0.000	0.000
Baltimore	−0.056	0.021**	−0.067	0.022**
Frederick	−0.017	0.025	−0.031	0.025
Somerset	−0.181	0.035**	−0.108	0.038**
Talbot No occupation labor	−0.128 Reference	0.053*	−0.028	0.057
	−0.106	0.059	−0.104	0.054
Operative	−0.023	0.061	−0.026	0.057
Craft	−0.052	0.058	−0.067	0.054
Farm	−0.103	0.056	−0.061	0.051
Professional/clerical	−0.045	0.083	−0.049	0.084
Observations	2404		2635	
Wald chi-square stat	177.64		65.5	
Pseudo R-squared	0.07		0.02	

Sources: Author's calculations
Notes: * signifies p-value <0.05; ** signifies p-value <0.01

10.5 Comparing Later-Life Outcomes of Pauper and Craft Apprentices

10.5.1 Outcome Measures

The principal issue at hand is whether or how well pauper apprenticeship prepared indigent youth for an independent adulthood. There is no single measure that will fully capture the realizations of pauper apprentices in later life, but there are several economic and demographic factors associated with economic productivity, an ability to provide for oneself, overall well-being, and personal happiness. In general, economists believe that economic productivity increases with education, training, and experience and that income (and, perhaps, wealth) increases in productivity. They also recognize that well-being and happiness depend on other than material conditions, but they tend to assume that overall well-being and income move in the same direction (Easterlin 2003).

Given the weight nineteenth-century American placed on economic independence, economic and emotional well-being was likely influenced by self-directed employment, which depended in turn on the capacity to navigate the market in an increasingly literate and numerate society. Thus, two reasonable outcome measures are whether a former apprentice worked in a skilled occupation and whether he was illiterate.

In addition, Easterlin (2003) reports that, among individuals surveyed in the late twentieth century, the desire for and ownership of certain "big-ticket" items, including homes, cars, and other consumer durables, increases over the life cycle. Nineteenth-century data do not afford the opportunity to discern or directly document either the acquisition of big-ticket durables or their desirability, but the 1860 and 1870 censuses recorded dollar-value estimates of real and personal property held by each household. It is not unreasonable to assume that the nineteenth-century big-ticket items, such as farmland, livestock, as well as homes and their appointments, formed the basis for the census marshals' wealth estimates. Such were the big-ticket consumer durables of the mid-nineteenth century.

Well-being and happiness are influenced by how closely a household's ownership of consumer durables matches their self-reported desires for such things. In general life satisfaction increases in both the quantity of and the correspondence between durables owned and durables desired (Easterlin 2003). Mid-nineteenth-century Americans associated well-being with economic independence, which meant land ownership in rural areas and self-directed employment in urban areas. To understand the extent to which former apprentices might have experienced the well-being associated with economic independence, I consider the ownership of farmland in rural areas and employment in the skilled artisan trades in urban areas.

Well-being and happiness are also influenced by marriage and family formation. Easterlin (2003) reports evidence that married people report being happier on average than unmarried people and that happiness increases in the length of marriage. Children have mixed effects on happiness because the presence of children in a household can operate by way of two channels: children can increase satisfaction with family life; and children can represent a net financial burden, even if they work in their teen years (Zimmerman and Easterlin 2006).

Finally, westward expansion of the American population was one of the most significant economic and demographic transformations of the nineteenth century. Migration, whether internal or international, can be viewed as a type of investment – locational arbitrage — in one's productivity if labor productivity is higher in the destination than the county or state of origin (Vandenbroucke 2008; Gallman 1992). Nineteenth-century observers considered American's internal mobility as just one of several points of American exceptionalism (Tocqueville 2000, 361–65). Ferrie (2005) finds that more than one-half of American men over 30 years of age moved between counties; about 25% moved migrated across state lines. The median distance moved was 36 miles; the mean was 213 miles.

10.5.2 Realized Outcomes

These considerations and the types of information recorded in the censuses drove my choices about how best to draw meaningful comparative conclusions about the later-life well-being of pauper apprentices. Table 10.5 provides a first look at realizations of pauper and craft apprentices observed several years after the expiration of their indentures. Although craft apprentices observed in later life exhibit higher realizations than pauper apprentices, only a few differences are statistically significant. Former apprentices linked to the 1860 census were in their mid-30s, on average, and craft apprentices were about 2 years older. The average occupation rank on a five-point scale is consistent with a semiskilled operative.[2] The proportion of craft

Table 10.5 Comparisons of later-life outcome for pauper and craft apprentices

	1860			1870		
	Pauper	Craft	Difference *p*-value	Pauper	Craft	Difference *p*-value
Observations	271	185		392	154	
Age	36.01	38.22	0.00**	39.52	45.94	0.00**
Occupation rank	2.29	2.7	0.00**	2.16	2.54	0.00**
Skilled occupation	0.61	0.72	0.03*	0.44	0.59	0.00**
Real estate – variant 1	3277.96	2660	0.52	4025.13	5885.48	0.25
Personal estate – variant 1	1054.03	2112.22	0.19	1172.84	2277.89	0.06
Real estate – variant 2	931.38	992.11	0.86	1037.09	2407.69	0.02*
Personal estate – variant 2	598.97	1278.75	0.16	493.67	1301.65	0.00**
Landowning farmer	0.66	0.84	0.08	0.51	0.7	0.13
Illiterate	0.18	0.05	0.00**	0.38	0.19	0.00**
Married	0.73	0.89	0.18	0.74	0.91	0.00**
Children	2.33	2.66	0.18	2.06	2.7	0.00**
Miles moved	Na	Na		148.67	129.39	0.59

Sources: Author's calculations
Notes: Age in years; occupation rank on 0 to 5 scale; skilled occupation = 1 if occupation is skilled or professional; real and personal estate measured in current dollars; variant 2 of wealth replaces missing values with zero wealth; illiterate = 1 if census reported cannot read; married = 1 if wife appeared in census household; children = number of children; miles moved = distance in miles between county of apprenticeship and minor civil division of residence reported in 1870 census

[2] Instead of using the 100-point occupational rank (socioeconomic index) values, developed on relative occupational prestige circa 1950 and based on narrow occupational definitions, that are included in the IPUMS data sets, I categorized occupations on a five-point scale: 1 = common or unskilled laborers, 2 = semiskilled operatives, 3 = skilled artisans, 4 = farmers (not farm laborers = 1), and 5 = professionals and clerks. Those listed without occupation are coded as zero.

apprentices employed in skilled occupations exceeded that of pauper apprentices by 11 percentage points.

Lesser differences appear in other dimensions. Pauper apprentices were nearly four times more likely than craft apprentices to report being illiterate in 1860. Craft apprentices generally report greater wealth. Variant 1 values of wealth include only those households with non-missing data. Variant 2 values of wealth are calculated under the assumption common in the literature that missing values indicate zero reportable wealth. The landowning farmer category considers differences between craft and pauper apprentices who report farming as their occupation and any positive value of real estate. It seems reasonable to assume that these were owner-operator farmers, rather than tenants or renters. Boys apprenticed to farmers by a family member were about 18 percentage points more likely than boys apprenticed by the court to be owner-operators of their own farms in 1860. The difference is marginally statistically significant at usual levels.

Links to the 1870 census offer, perhaps, a more interesting comparison in that the former apprentices are linked as they were approaching midlife. Craft apprentices were nearly 46 years old on average; former pauper apprentices were approaching their 40th birthday. Former craft apprentices were more likely than pauper apprentices to be employed in skilled artisan or professional occupations. A histogram in Fig. 10.2 displays the fraction of former apprentices employed in each occupation category when observed in 1870. More than half of former pauper apprentices reported being employed as common laborers, including farm labor, or an unskilled

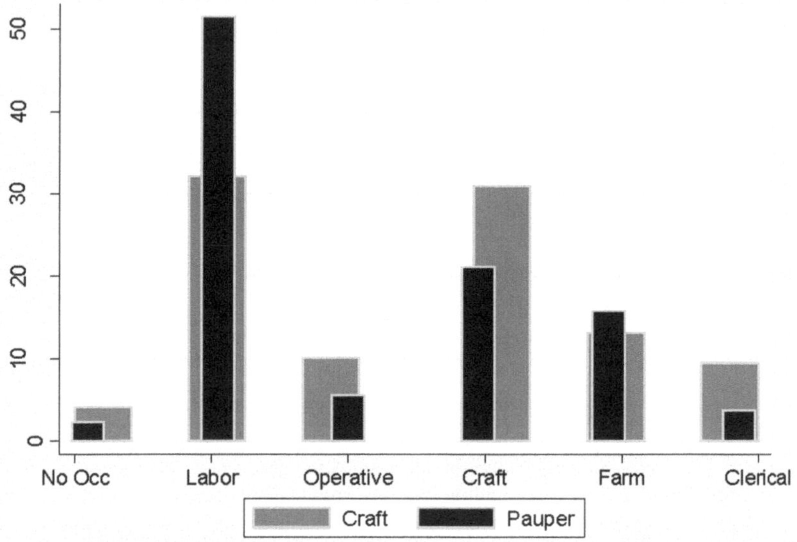

Fig. 10.2 Distribution of occupations among former apprentices in 1870. (*Sources*: author's calculations from information contained in Anne Arundel (1822–1858), Baltimore (1825–1860), Frederick (1827–1860), Somerset (1854–1859), and Talbot (1853–1860))

service occupation, such as waiter. Nearly one-third of former craft apprentices also reported being employed as laborers or in an unskilled job. Ten percent or less worked as semiskilled factory operatives. About one in three former craft apprentices reported employment in a skilled or artisan occupation in 1870 compared to just one in five former pauper apprentices.

One interesting result is that the fraction of boys apprenticed into husbandry by a family member and the fraction of men reporting farming in the 1870 census are nearly equal (see Fig. 10.1 for comparison) at about 15%. By comparison less than half as many men apprenticed into husbandry by the court (40%) reported farming in 1870 (15%). The clerical category includes managerial and professional occupations, and few boys were apprenticed as clerks. By 1870 10% of former craft apprentices worked as bank clerks, dry goods dealers, commission merchants, agents for steamboat companies, and so on. About half as many former pauper apprentices did so. Significant but not insurmountable hurdles stood in the way of upward occupational mobility for all apprentices. Downward slides were common, too, though more so for former pauper apprentices.

Table 10.6 provides occupational transition matrices for craft and pauper apprentices. Each cell, except the row and column totals, reports the percentage of apprentices apprenticed into one of five broad occupational categories that report being in one of those five categories in 1870 (i.e., the fraction appearing in each row).[3] The

Table 10.6 Occupational mobility from apprenticeship to 1870

1870						
Apprenticeship	Laborer	Operative	Skilled	Farm	Clerical	Row total
(**a**) Craft apprentices						
Laborer	87.5	0.0	0.0	0.0	0.0	8
Operative	15.8	29.0	21.1	13.2	10.5	38
Skilled	17.1	1.3	52.6	15.8	11.8	76
Farm	72.0	8.0	4.0	12.0	4.0	25
Clerical	0.0	0.0	0.0	50.0	50.0	2
Column total	45	14	49	21	16	151
(**b**) Pauper apprentices						
Laborer	73.7	10.5	2.6	5.3	5.3	38
Operative	26.3	21.1	18.4	26.3	2.6	38
Skilled	17.7	5.0	54.6	15.1	5.9	119
Farm	69.1	2.4	4.9	21.2	1.8	165
Clerical	0.0	16.7	33.3	33.3	0.0	6
Column total	188	23	85	71	13	387

Notes: Each cell, except row and column totals, reports the percentage of pauper or craft apprentices apprenticed into a certain occupation category (rows) and reported in a certain occupation category in 1870 (columns). Complete immobility implies entries only along the diagonal. Upward mobility implies higher percentages in lower, right diagonal; downward mobility implies lower percentages in the upper, left diagonal

[3] A transition matrix of the 1860 census yields similar results and is not reported.

table adds some interesting insights into the occupational mobility of apprentices. First, perfect occupational persistence would manifest as entries only along the diagonals of each transition matrix. Although the diagonals contain the largest percentage values – 87.5% of craft apprentices indentured into a laborer's trade report being employed in a laborer's trade in 1870 – which reveals strong persistence, there is considerable movement both up and down the occupational ladder.

Second, most youth apprenticed into husbandry transitioned to some other occupation; just 12% of craft apprentices established their own farm, and 21% of pauper apprentices farmed as adults. An apprenticeship in farming did not establish a foundation for advancement. Nearly three-quarters of craft and pauper apprentices who served their apprenticeship on a farm worked in unskilled occupations at midlife.

Craft apprentices were not only employed in more remunerative occupations, but they realized better outcomes in other aspects of their lives. In 1870 craft apprentices reported variant 2 real estate values 46% higher than pauper apprentices; craft apprentices reported variant 2 personal property values 2.32 times higher than former pauper apprentices. Craft apprentices were half as likely to be illiterate as former pauper apprentices; they were more likely to be married and to have more children.

Maryland's early nineteenth-century apprentices exhibited less mobility than did Americans generally. Of the apprentices linked to the 1870 census, 44% of adults in 1870 resided in the same county in which they were apprenticed; 83% remained in Maryland. Not surprisingly, about one-third of those apprenticed in rural counties who moved across county lines moved to Baltimore. Figure 10.3 presents the distributions of distance in miles between county of indenture and city of residence in 1870 among those who moved less than 500 miles.[4] There is no discernible difference in mobility between craft and pauper apprentices. The average distance moved for craft apprentices is 129 miles; the median is 42 miles. The average distance moved for pauper apprentices is 147 miles; the median is 41 miles. Maryland's apprentices were not a peripatetic lot.

A first pass through the linked data points to several preliminary conclusions. First, apprentices experienced more downward than upward occupational mobility, an asymmetry that was more pronounced among pauper apprentices. By 1870 only about half of former apprentices worked in a skilled occupation. Between one-half and three-quarters of apprentices in husbandry acquired their own farms by midlife, which is consistent with evidence on the nineteenth-century agricultural ladder (Atack 1989). Second, pauper apprentices were less likely to be literate, were less likely to be married, and had fewer surviving resident children at midlife. Former pauper apprentices were less likely to report wealth, but those who reported wealth reported holdings that were statistically equal to holdings of former craft apprentices.

[4]A handful of former apprentices moved to San Francisco, California, presumably in response to the gold rush, and a few moved as far west as St. Louis, Missouri, and one to Goliad County, Texas. These very long distances are dropped from the diagram, but not from the calculations of mean and median distances.

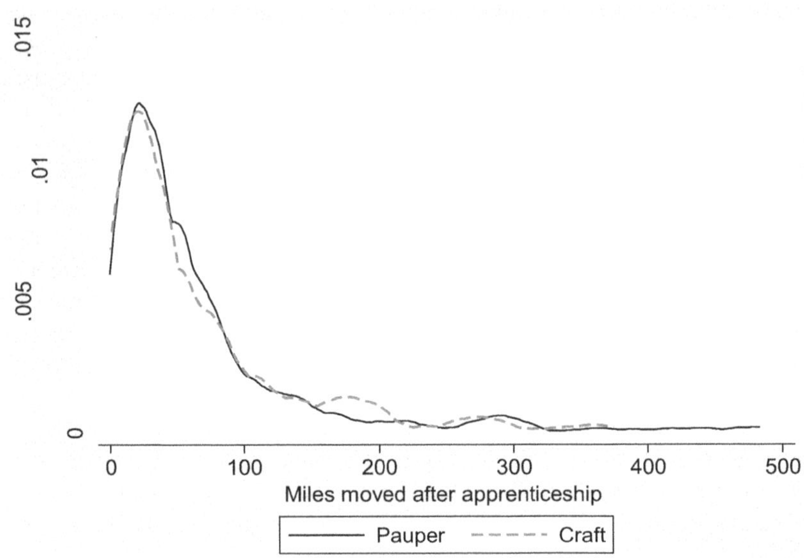

Fig. 10.3 Distributions of distance in miles between county of apprenticeship and residence in 1870. (*Source*: author's calculations from data discussed in text)

10.6 Regression Estimates the Relative Returns to Pauper Apprenticeship

A naïve approach to estimating the relative returns to pauper apprenticeship is to compare relevant outcomes of Maryland-born pauper apprentices observed after the expiration of their indentures to men who have been trained through craft apprenticeship according to the following equation:

$$
\begin{aligned}
y_{i,1870} = {} & \alpha_0 + \beta_1 \text{Pauper}_{i,\text{app}} + \beta_2 \text{Black}_{i,\text{app}} + \beta_3 \left(\text{Pauper}_{i,\text{app}} \times \text{Black}_{i,\text{app}}\right) \\
& + B_4 \text{Age}_{i,1870} + \beta_5 \text{Age}^2_{i,1870} + \beta_6 3Rs_{i,\text{app}} + \beta_7 \text{Real}\, NPV\, \text{dues}_{i,\text{app}} \\
& + \sum_{k=1}^{5} \text{Occupation Category}_{i,\text{app}} + \sum_{j=1}^{4} \text{Country}_{i,\text{app}} + \varepsilon_i
\end{aligned}
$$

where y represents one of the six outcomes of interest discussed above: occupation, literacy, marital status, wealth, and mobility. All the independent variables, except age, are measured when the youth was apprenticed. Age is reported age in 1870. The equations are estimated using probit, tobit, or OLS methods depending on the nature of the dependent variable, whether dichotomous outcomes (skilled employment, illiteracy, and marital status), continuous with excess zeroes (real and personal property), or continuous (miles moved between apprenticeship and adulthood). Because the literature emphasizes the racialized nature of the system and because blacks were overrepresented among pauper apprentices and underrepresented among craft apprentices, the equation includes an interaction term, which makes it possible to isolate the independent effects of race and indigency.[5]

One methodological concern, of course, is that of over-testing, as it is sometimes labeled, in which the investigator runs multiple regressions on a host of independent variables, which increases the likelihood that some dependent variable(s) will be statistically significant. Economic meaningfulness is then attached to the significant coefficient(s). Because the literature provides few clues concerning which outcomes reflect on later-life economic well-being or which features of apprenticeship might bear on those outcomes, it is reasonable to investigate the effect of baseline characteristics on several outcomes. The literature is, in the main, either agnostic or doubtful that any of the terms of the typical period of servitude, including training, education, and freedom dues, had powerful influences on later-life outcomes, so each is included as a regressor. Economic theory points to skill training, schooling, and early adulthood resources (freedom dues) as keys to adult achievement and well-being, so they are included as the principal explanatory variables (Becker 1992).

The estimated return to pauper apprenticeship relative to craft apprenticeship ($\beta_1 + \beta_3 *$ Black) will be the true return to apprenticeship if being indigent, abused, neglected, and selected into pauper apprenticeship was randomly assigned. An important form of endogeneity is self-selection, which occurs if choices made by the studied individual or some other individual (a father, e.g., or an Orphans' Court judge) connected to the individual influenced nonrandom entry into the sample. If selection into pauper apprenticeship was not random, estimates of $\beta 1$ will be inconsistent and biased because they will not converge to their true values (Clougherty et al. 2016).[6]

Heckman's (1979) canonical contribution to the empirical issue of self-selection recognizes that when individuals make choices that assign them into mutually exclusive treated and untreated groups based in part on unobservable characteristics (e.g., motivation, diligence, intelligence), those unobserved characteristics may be correlated with the outcome and predictor variables. If such correlations exist, the parameter estimating the effect of being in the treated group will be confounded with the selection process. The self-selection problem is a form of omitted-variable bias that results from nonrandom assignment into treatment and control groups, in that the choices we observe, such as the skills to be taught, the amount of education, and freedom dues paid at expiration of the indenture, are a function of courts altering contract features in response to preexisting differences and to influence

[5] Bodenhorn (2015) reports marked differences in outcomes for blacks and mixed-race individuals in the pre-Civil War South. Preliminary estimates of the equations included separate terms for black and mixed-race individuals indicate that mixed-race apprentices fared better than blacks in most outcomes, but the coefficients were not statistically different in any equation. For ease of reporting and interpretation, the reported regressions include all black and mixed in a single category.

[6] Bodenhorn et al. (2017, 2019a, b) discuss the theoretical and empirical issues that emerge due to self-selection in other historical contexts.

outcomes based on characteristics observable to the individuals making the choice to select into the treatment group that are not necessarily observable to the econometrician. Heckman's (1979) solution is to employ a type of instrumental variables approach. If the researcher can identify one or more instrumental variables that explain entry into a first-stage treatment equation that are uncorrelated with the error term in the equation of principal interest, variability in the second-stage error term is no longer affected by self-selection, and estimation yields a consistent estimate of the treatment effect (e.g., pauper apprenticeship). The challenge is to identify one or more first-stage instruments.

In the results reported below, I use apprentice race, age at indenture and its square, and the annual growth rate of real per capita gross national product (Carter et al. 2006). The existing literature suggests that blacks and the young children of indigent parents were at highest risk of being indented as pauper apprentices. It is also plausible that years in which real incomes (or unskilled wages) decline more low-income households descend further into poverty, which would expose children residing in such households to court-supervised apprenticeship. These instruments should satisfy the relevance and exogeneity criteria; age at indenture and economic downturns in youth should have small direct effects on outcomes 20 years hence, but they should influence whether local authorities considered a child eligible for pauper apprenticeship.[7] Weak instruments are a cause for concern in standard instrumental variables estimation. Using simulation techniques, Clougherty et al. (2016), however, show that a Heckman modeling approach even with small samples and weak instruments generates coefficient estimates closer to their true values than does OLS or two-stage least squares.

Table 10.7 reports summary statistics for the 1870 census-linked sample used for the regressions. Nearly three-quarters of those linked were pauper apprentices; one-third were black. The average age at indenture was 13 years and the average apprentice was promised \$27 in freedom dues. The average age in 1870 was 41 years, nearly one-half were employed in a skilled occupation, and former apprentices owned real and personal property combined worth about \$2100.

Given the nature of the data, which includes only apprenticed youth, the estimates and interpretations follow from the assumption that youths selected into pauper apprenticeship were at risk for placement into a craft apprenticeship and would have been so placed had the youth's parents been less indigent or negligent. It is a nontrivial, but not implausible, assumption. Prior to the emergence of the late-nineteenth-century, factory-based industrial economy, lower and middling households believed that economic independence and security were achieved through

[7] The models were also estimated using annual Baltimore alms house admissions per capita as an instrument to measure the incidence of poverty, which should place more children at risk of pauper apprenticeship (Baltimore City 1843–1854; Rockman 2009). The alms house data are available for fewer years, which reduces the 1870 regressions to 366 observations, so the results are not tabulated. The second-stage results are comparable to those reported in Table 10.8a, b. The alms house variable is marginally significant in every regression but one and the likelihood-ratio test statistics are significant at $p < 0.001$ in every case.

Table 10.7 Summary statistics

	(1)	(2)	(3)	(4)
Variables	Mean	Std dev	Minimum	Maximum
Characteristics at indenture				
Pauper	0.72	0.45	0.00	1.00
Black	0.34	0.48	0.00	1.00
Age at indenture	13.41	4.15	1.00	20.25
Age squared	197.07	98.19	1.00	410.06
3Rs	0.25	0.43	0.00	1.00
Real NPV dues	26.96	37.83	0.00	651.00
ln(Real NPV dues)	3.52	1.18	0.00	7.17
Characteristics in 1870				
Black	0.32	0.47	0.00	1.00
Mixed race	0.04	0.19	0.00	1.00
Age	41.33	11.54	22.00	65.00
Age squared	1841.32	948.92	484.00	4225.00
Skilled employment	0.49	0.50	0.00	1.00
Illiterate	0.32	0.47	0.00	1.00
Married	0.79	0.47	0.00	6.00
Real property	1440.82	5903.42	0.00	91,000.00
ln(Real property)	2.49	3.88	0.00	12.11
Personal property	709.00	3099.04	0.00	44,000.00
ln(Personal property)	3.12	3.51	0.00	11.39
Miles moved	142.93	379.19	0.00	3965.41
ln(Miles moved)	4.46	1.56	0.00	8.98
GNP growth rate	0.01	0.04	−0.06	0.17
$N = 547$				

land ownership and farming on one's own account in rural areas and the operation of artisan shops in urban areas. Middling- and laboring-class families sought apprenticeships for their children so that they might achieve independence and security. Indigent families surely shared that expectation.

To save space Table 10.8 reports the marginal effects of pauperism and race on the outcomes listed in the first column. The reported effects are those estimated using either standard or Heckman's selection-correction assumptions, depending on whether the likelihood-ratio test for independence of the error terms in the selection and outcome equation are highly correlated. Selection-corrected coefficients on the pauper variable can be interpreted as the average treatment effect (ATE) on pauper apprenticeship.[8] Testing for instrument validity in a Heckman-type model (e.g., an overidentification test) involves comparing the second-stage parameter estimates from the proposed specification to a specification that just

[8] Except for children, which is estimated using the -etpoisson command in Stata, the models are estimated using the -etregress command, so that the second-stage equations for dichotomous independent variables are linear probability models.

Table 10.8 Estimated marginal effects of pauper apprenticeship and race on later-life outcomes

Estimated marginal effects					
Dependent variable	Pauper	Black	Estimation procedure	LR independence *p*-value	Observations
Skilled employment	−0.105	−0.389***	Selection corrected	0.13	524
	(0.116)	(0.053)			
Illiterate	0.581***	0.374***	Selection corrected	0.00***	547
	(0.059)	(0.059)			
ln(Miles moved)	0.147	0.063	OLS	0.95	538
	(0.171)	(0.186)			
Married	−0.006	0.033	Probit	0.27	546
	(0.046)	(0.044)			
Children in household	−1.484*	−0.155	Selection corrected	0.04**	548
	(0.879)	(0.457)			
ln(Real property value)	1.812	−10.158***	Tobit	0.87	548
	(1.651)	(0.708)			
ln(Personal property value)	1.134	−5.754***	Tobit	0.34	548
	(0.926)	(0.565)			
Owner-operated farm	0.099	−0.198***	Probit	0.85	170
	(0.067)	(0.052)			

Notes: Robust standard errors in parentheses. LR independence test for correlated errors across equations. Likelihood-ratio test statistic for instrument relevance exceeds 50 ($p \leq 0.001$) in each case. *** $p \leq 0.001$, ** $p \leq 0.01$, *$p \leq 0.10$

identifies the second stage based on functional form using a likelihood-ratio test. If the likelihood-ratio test statistic is statistically significant, it implies that the instrumented model fits the data better than the non-instrumented alternative. In each specification, the test statistic is significant, though not all first-stage regressors are individually significant.

All regressions include additional controls for age in 1870 and its square, whether the individual was promised an education, the value of freedom dues, county of residence, and occupational category at indenture. To save space, these coefficient estimates are not reported. In general, the coefficients on age and its square, education, Baltimore residence at indenture, and skilled apprenticeship are statistically significant.

The dependent variables in the first three rows reflect on how pauperism and race affected later-life levels of human capital (skilled employment, illiteracy, and geographic mobility). The coefficient on pauper in the first row is small, negative, and insignificant; thus, there is no evidence that pauper apprenticeship per se reduced the likelihood of acquiring marketable skills relative to craft apprenticeship.[9] Black apprentices, about 85% of whom were pauper apprentices, were about 39% less likely than white apprentices to acquire skills marketable in later life.

How do we interpret this result? Was it that courts and skilled masters were prejudiced and discriminated against black youth in that courts were reluctant to place blacks in skilled positions? Were masters unwilling to take them on? Neither courts nor parents placed black youth in skilled apprenticeships. Of 411 apprentices placed by parents into skilled apprenticeships, just 4 were black, and of the 589 paupers so placed by the courts, just 41 were black. If it were true that there were few skilled apprenticeships available outside Baltimore, it is still the case that black youth did not receive skill training when placed in Baltimore. Of 208 youth placed by parents into a skilled training, just 1 was black; of 232 placed by the courts, only 8 were black.

It is apparent that skilled masters did not take in black apprentices. Their reluctance may have resulted from one of three sources of discrimination: employer, employee, or customer. It is likely that all three worked against black youth, but historians have documented the power of fellow-employee discrimination in keeping southern workplaces segregated. Berlin (1974, pp. 234–35) argues that southerners were quick to distinguish between white jobs and "Negro work," which included barbers, sawyers, brickmakers, stevedores, and carters. Not only did white workers avoid these jobs, but they raised legal and extralegal barriers designed to exclude black workers from other than these jobs. Segregation was rigidly enforced in Baltimore's shipyards, for example. Ship carpentering was overwhelmingly white and ship caulking was overwhelmingly black. Shipyard owners kept the peace in their workplaces only so long as they kept the races separated by task (Baltimore American 1858).[10] Master artisans almost surely faced similar demands to keep workplaces and occupations segregated. White youth probably refused to enter into apprenticeships that would have placed them shoulder to shoulder with black apprentices training for the same job.

In explaining labor-market outcomes, economists who study racially stratified economies delineate between premarket and market discrimination. Premarket discrimination occurs before the individual enters the labor market and may be the consequence of poor health or socialization associated with being raised in impoverished households or neighborhoods, unequal education or training, or disadvantages in other dimensions that limit their ability to navigate labor markets. The coefficients estimated in the illiterate model point to an additional reason former paupers and blacks rarely found skilled employment: they were much more likely to be illiterate and, presumably, innumerate. Illiteracy and innumeracy would have

---

[9] Although the likelihood-ratio test does not provide compelling evidence of a selection effect, the p-value on the test statistic is close to standard levels of significance, so the selection-corrected estimates are reported. The marginal effects generated by probit estimation were not qualitatively different.

[10] Donohue III and Heckman (1991) document comparable occupational segregation in southern textile mills in the early twentieth century.

been severe handicaps in an increasingly complex, impersonal marketplace in which success required formal contracting and good record keeping.

The extant information does not provide any clues whether it was masters or apprentices who did not take the promise to educate seriously. Educational agreements may have been treated as so much preprinted legal boilerplate rather than legitimate contractual agreements. Apprenticed youth may not have wanted to spend their free time studying. More needs to be done to understand why educational promises were not more effectual.

Estimates in the third row provide no evidence that pauper or black apprentices were less geographically mobile than craft apprentices. Craft apprentices, both black and white, moved an average of 130 miles between the date of indenture and 1870. Pauper apprentices, black and white, moved an average of 148 miles. Whatever the advantages that accrued to locational arbitrage, blacks and whites, paupers and not, took equal advantage of them.

Results reported in rows 4 (married) and 5 (children) provide some insight into Easterlin's (2003) and Zimmerman and Easterlin's (2006) findings that married people are happier and that children may or may not improve emotional well-being. There is no evidence that race or early-life indigency altered midlife marriage rates. After controlling for age (the analysis includes only those over 21 years), former paupers had markedly fewer surviving children still resident in the household. A count of children in a household is a crude measure of family formation in that it is not children ever born and does not control for age since marriage or years since first birth, but restricted samples, such as conditional on marriage and narrower age groups, reveal similar patterns. Former paupers had fewer children.

The final three rows reflect on former apprentices' acquisition of real and personal property. For purposes of estimation, property values were transformed using the inverse hyperbolic sine formulation, which mimics the natural log transformation except that zero wealth maps into zero in the transform. Whether the coefficients are estimated by tobit or corrected for selection, the coefficients imply that there were no statistically significant differences in wealth holdings between pauper and craft apprentices. Wealth holdings increase in age, which is consistent with the life-cycle hypothesis. The estimates coefficients imply that the value of real estate holdings was maximized around age 46; the value of personal property was maximized around age 48.

It is well known that free blacks found it difficult to acquire real estate in the pre-Civil War South (Bodenhorn 2015). In the real property model, the estimated marginal effect on the black coefficient is consistent with the absence of southern black property holders generally. Among former apprentices matched to the 1870 census, a single black man reported a modest $225 in real estate value. There are also notable differences in reported values of personal wealth by race. The estimated marginal effect implies that the average former black apprentice held just 0.3% of the personal wealth of former white apprentices. It is a challenge to interpret the meaning of personal wealth regressions based on census data. Census marshals were not given clear instructions concerning what types of property to include in the calculation, and most appear to have censored values at $100. Only 46% of individuals linked to 1870 report any personal property, and there are only three reported values less than $100. It is hard to imagine that 54% of households held no household durables, so it is not evident that blank cells in the census reports represent $0 wealth, but it seems reasonable to conclude that blank cells are indicators of household poverty. What is clear is that blacks held less of whatever was counted as personal property.

The final row considers the ability of apprentices bound to husbandry to farm on their own account in adulthood. The sample is restricted to apprentices indentured to farmers and linked to the 1870 census. Given the smaller sample, inferences are less certain, but the available evidence suggests no difference in the ability of former paupers to acquire their own farms. Blacks apprenticed to farmers were less likely to farm on their own account. A more complete understanding might be had with a study of the 1870 agricultural census, which would allow us to identify owners, tenants, and sharecroppers, but such is beyond the scope of this study.

10.7 Conclusions

Let us accept Gloria Main's (2009, p. 199) observation that in early America "children worked as a matter of course." Most households needed their children to contribute to household income, either directly by earning wages through outside employment or indirectly by taking on household chores that freed the parents for more hours of wage labor. Working poor families in early nineteenth-century American cities experienced recurrent bouts of unemployment and low wages in which they barely kept themselves fed, clothed, and housed (Rockman 2009). Children contributed when they could. When children and parents could not keep themselves off the poor rolls, local authorities intervened. In certain instances, raising a child above poverty meant removing the child from home.

It was not just families that wanted children to work. Social convention held that it was good to put children to work. Working served several purposes: it kept trouble-prone teenagers out of trouble; it continued to socialize youth into the place of deference, despite the leveling impulses and the challenge of balancing personal independence and the republican duty of citizenship that permeated the Jeffersonian and Jacksonian eras; it provided first-hand examples of the discipline, stick-to-itiveness, and dogged perseverance needed to succeed in a market-oriented economy; and, of course, it provided them with the skills needed to live useful, productive lives.

Based on the evidence discussed here, pauper apprenticeship receives both a passing and failing grade. Except for literacy and family size, former white pauper apprentices realized later-life outcomes comparable with craft apprentices. Pauper apprentices were no less likely than former craft apprentices to work at skilled occupations, be married, own real and personal property, or have climbed the agricultural ladder up to owner-operator. In terms of offering opportunities for a reasonably well-lived adult life, the system worked well for indigent white youth and receives a passing grade. The long-term consequences of racially disparate treatment in youth are apparent in nearly every economic outcome. Black apprentices exited apprenticeship with few skills and little education. They did not acquire property. They faced the prospect of lifelong poverty.

Coming full circle then, I return to Herndon and Murray's (2009) observation that the system was permeated with distinctions based on sex, race, age, and socioeconomic background. This chapter offers no insights into the consequences of pauper apprenticeship for girls caught up in the system, not because their stories are not interesting, but because of the challenges of following women once they marry and change their names. This chapter does speak to the other characteristics, however, and it shows that age at indenture and socioeconomic background, namely, childhood indigency, had smaller effects on later-life realizations than previously believed. Race, not surprisingly, loomed large. Blacks exited apprenticeships unskilled, uneducated, and unprepared for much more than a life of scraping by.

Acknowledgments I thank Pam Bodenhorn for exceptional research assistance and the late Lois Green Carr for her assistance in locating and interpreting some of the materials on pauper apprentices.

Appendix: Remembrance of John Murray

Though we met years earlier (at the 1994 EHA meetings in Cincinnati, if memory serves), I got to know John when he invited me to the *Children Bound to Labor* conference in Philadelphia in 2002. I joined John and Gillian Hamilton for dinner after the first day's sessions where we discussed their papers. Their enthusiasm for the larger pauper apprentice project that was to become the book was infectious. They convinced me to collect the data from the Maryland archives that underlies my contribution to this volume. John would occasionally inquire into the status of my pauper project, and he always seemed dismayed that I let it languish. We had a friendly, professional, casual acquaintance. As was John's wont, he sent kind notes of congratulation after he read one of my published papers, often with a prod to finish the pauper paper already.

John and I became friends when he submitted the manuscript that was to become *The Origins of American Health Insurance* to Yale University Press. He turned that early draft into a magnificent volume that deserved all the praise it received, and then some. But my lasting memory of John will be the kindness, generosity, and collegiality he showed me even while I worked on a series of papers that challenged one of his bedrock beliefs. He shared his data on the heights of Amherst College students knowing that I intended to use it in a line of study with which he fundamentally disagreed. Despite our disagreement on that issue, he invited me to Rhodes College. He offered insightful and useful comments on my paper, took me to dinner (Memphis barbeque, of course), and invited me to his home, which housed more books than some municipal libraries, where we shared a bottle of red wine sitting on his front porch on a warm spring Memphis evening. Once we agreed to disagree, we discussed the half-dozen books he was reading at the time. As I went back to my hotel, I knew that John and I were still friends. His deep respect for the academic enterprise and the value of friendship says a lot about the person – not the academic – John was.

I can finally say, "John, it's done." I regret that it is not in time to receive his kind note of congratulations on its publication.

References

Abramitzky R, Boustan LP, Eriksson K (2012) Europe's tired, poor, huddled masses: self-selection and economic outcomes in the age of mass migration. Am Econ Rev 102(5):1832–1856

Ager P, Eriksson K, Hansen CW, Lønstrup L (2020) How the 1906 San Francisco earthquake shaped economic activity in the American West. Explor Econ Hist 77(July):101342

Atack J (1989) The agricultural ladder revisited: a new look at an old question with some data from 1860. Agr Hist 63(1):1–25

Bailey M, Cole C, Henderson M, Massey C (2017) How well do automated linking methods perform? Lessons from U.S. historical data. J Econ Lit 58(4):997–1044

Baker RB, Blanchette J, Eriksson K (2020) Long-run impacts of agricultural shocks on educational attainment: evidence from the boll weevil. J Econ Hist 80(1):136–174

Baltimore American (1858) Issues 5–9 July 1858

Becker GS (1992) Human capital: a theoretical and empirical analysis, with special reference to education. University of Chicago Press, Chicago

Berlin I (1974) Slaves without masters: the free Negro in the Antebellum South. Pantheon Books, New York

Besley T (2005) Political selection. J Econ Perspect 19(3):43–60

Bodenhorn H (2003) Just and reasonable treatment: racial differences in the terms of pauper apprenticeship in antebellum Maryland. NBER working paper 9752

Bodenhorn H (2015) The color factor: the economics of African-American well-being in the nineteenth-century south. Oxford University Press, New York

Bodenhorn H, Guinnane TW, Mroz TA (2017) Sample-selection biases and the industrialization puzzle. J Econ Hist 77(1):171–207

Bodenhorn H, Guinnane TW, Mroz TA (2019a) Diagnosing sample-selection bias in historical heights: a reply to Komlos and A'Hearn. J Econ Hist 79(4):1154–1175

Bodenhorn H, Guinnane TW, Mroz TA (2019b) Theory and diagnostics for selection biases in historical heights samples. Res Econ Hist 35:59–89

Bourque M (2009) Community networks in Chester County, Pennsylvania, 1800–1860. In: Herndon RW, Murray JE (eds) Children bound to labor: the pauper apprentice system in early America. Cornell University Press, Ithaca, pp 71–83

Brewer H (2009) Apprenticeship policy in Virginia: from patriarchal to republican policies of social welfare. In: Herndon RW, Murray JE (eds) Children bound to labor: the pauper apprentice system in early America. Cornell University Press, Ithaca, pp 183–197

Carr LG (1977) The development of the Maryland Orphans' Court, 1654–1715. In: Land AC, Carr LG (eds) Law, society, and politics in early Maryland. Johns Hopkins University Press, Baltimore, pp 41–62

Carter SB, Gartner SS, Haines MR, Olmstead AL, Sutch R, Wright G (2006) Historical statistics of the United States: millennial edition. Cambridge University Press, New York

Clougherty JA, Duso T, Muck J (2016) Correcting for self-selection-based endogeneity in management research: review, recommendations and simulations. Org Res Methods 19(2):286–347

Daniels C (2001) 'Liberty to complaine': servant petitions in Maryland, 1652–1797. In: Tomlins CL, Mann BF (eds) The many legacies of early America. University of North Carolina Press, Chapel Hill, pp 219–249

Donohue JJ III, Heckman J (1991) Continuous versus episodic change: the impact of civil rights policy on the economic status of blacks. J Econ Lit 29(4):1603–1643

Easterlin RA (2003) Explaining happiness. P Natl Acad Sci USA 100(19):11176–11183

Ferrie JP (1999) Yankeys now: immigrants in the Antebellum U.S., 1840–1860. Oxford University Press, New York

Ferrie JP (2005) The end of American exceptionalism? Mobility in the United States since 1850. J Econ Perspect 19(3):199–215

Fields BJ (1985) Slavery and freedom on the middle ground: Maryland during the nineteenth century. Yale University Press, New Haven

Fogel RW, Engerman SL (1974) Philanthropy at bargain prices: notes on the economics of gradual emancipation. J Leg Stud 3(2):377–401

Gallman RE (1992) American economic growth before the Civil War: testimony of the capital stock estimates. In: Gallman RE, Wallis JJ (eds) American economic growth and standards of living before the Civil War. University of Chicago Press, Chicago, pp 79–115

Grubb F (1992) Fatherless and friendless: factors influencing the flow English emigrant servants. J Econ Hist 52(1):85–108

Grubb F (2022) Runaway servants in early Maryland: deterrence, punishment, and apprehension. In: Gray P, Hall JC, Herndon RW, Silvestre J (eds) Standard of living: essays on economics and history in honor of John E. Murray

Heckman JJ (1979) Selection bias as specification error. Econometrica 47(1):153–161

Herndon RW (2009) 'Proper' magistrates and masters: binding out poor children in southern New England, 1720–1820. In: Herndon RW, Murray J (eds) Children bound to labor: the pauper apprentice system in early America. Cornell University Press, Ithaca, pp 39–51

Herndon RW, Murray JE (2009) 'A proper and instructive education': raising children in pauper apprenticeship. In: Herndon RW, Murray J (eds) Children bound to labor: the pauper apprentice system in early America. Cornell University Press, Ithaca, pp 3–18

Hicks HS (1989) The black apprentice in Maryland court records from 1661 to 1865. Dissertation, University of Maryland at College Park

Kilty W (1818) Laws of Maryland, 1692–1818, 7 vols. Frederick Green, Annapolis

Klebaner BJ (1954) Some aspects of North Carolina public poor relief, 1700–1860. N C Hist Rev 31(4):479–492

Leknes S, Modalsli J (2020) Who benefited from industrialization? The local effects of hydropower technology adoption in Norway. J Econ Hist 80(1):207–245

Lockley TJ (2009) 'To train them to habits of industry and usefulness': molding the poor children of antebellum Savannah. In: Herndon RW, Murray J (eds) Children bound to labor: the pauper apprentice system in early America. Cornell University Press, Ithaca, pp 133–148

Murray JE, Herndon RW (2002) Markets for children in early America: a political economy of pauper apprenticeship. J Econ Hist 62(2):356–382

Neff C (1996) Pauper apprenticeship in early nineteenth century Ontario. J Fam Hist 21(2):144–171

Rockman S (2009) Scraping by: wage labor, slavery, and survival in early Baltimore. Johns Hopkins University Press, Baltimore

Rohrs RC (2013) Training in an 'art, mystery, and employment': opportunity or exploitation of free black apprentices in New Hanover, County, North Carolina, 1820-1859? N C Hist Rev 90(2):127–148

Rorabaugh WJ (1986) The craft apprentice: from Franklin to the machine age in America. Oxford University Press, New York

Russo JB, Russo JE (2009) Responsive justices: court treatment of orphans and illegitimate children in colonial Maryland. In: Herndon RW, Murray J (eds) Children bound to labor: the pauper apprentice system in early America. Cornell University Press, Ithaca, pp 151–165

Smith BG (1988) Poverty and economic marginality in eighteenth-century America. P Am Philos Soc 132(1):85–118

Steffen CG (1984) The mechanics of Baltimore: workers and politics in an age of revolution, 1763–1812. University of Illinois Press, Urbana
Tocqueville ADE (2000) Democracy in America, Mansfield HC, Winthrop D (trans). University of Chicago Press, Chicago
Vandenbroucke G (2008) The U.S. westward expansion. Int Econ Rev 49(1):81–110
Walsh LS (1988) Plantation management in the Chesapeake, 1620–1820. J Econ Hist 49(2):393–406
Whitman TS (2009) Orphans in city and countryside in nineteenth-century Maryland. In: Herndon RW, Murray J (eds) Children bound to labor: the pauper apprentice system in early America. Cornell University Press, Ithaca, pp 52–70
Wright JM (1971) The free Negro in Maryland, 1634–1860. Octagon Books, New York
Zimmerman AC, Easterlin RA (2006) Happily ever after? Cohabitation, marriage, divorce, and happiness in Germany. Popul Dev Rev 32(3):511–528
Zipf K (2005) Labor of innocents: forced apprenticeship in North Carolina, 1715–1919. Louisiana State University Press, Baton Rouge

Data Sources

Anne Arundel County (1822–1858) Register of wills (indentures). Maryland State Archives, Annapolis
Baltimore City Trustees for the Poor (1843–1854) Report of the Trustees for the Poor. In Ordinances of the Mayor and City Council of Baltimore... Printed by George W. Bowen & Co, Baltimore
Baltimore County (1825–1860) Register of wills (indentures). Maryland State Archives, Annapolis
Frederick County (1827–1860) Register of wills (indentures). Maryland State Archives, Annapolis
Main, GL (2009) Conclusion: reflections on the demand and supply of child labor inearly America. In: Herndon, RW, Murray JE (eds) Children bound to labor: the pauper apprenticeship system in early America. Cornell University Press, Ithaca
Somerset County (1854–1859) Register of wills (indentures). Maryland State Archives, Annapolis
Talbot County (1853–1860) Register of wills (indentures). Maryland State Archives, Annapolis
United States Census Office (1860) Eighth census, manuscript population censuses. Available at Ancestry.com
United States Census Office (1870) Ninth census, manuscript populations censuses. Available at Ancestry.com
Quimby, IMG (1985) Apprenticeship in colonial Philadelphia. Garland Publishing, New York

Chapter 11
Family Allocation Strategy in the Late Nineteenth Century

Trevon Logan

Abstract I analyze the intrahousehold allocation of resources among nineteenth-century industrial families. The narrative record and economic theory suggest that we should find allocation differences by gender. Using a large survey of industrial households in the late nineteenth century, I find no evidence of gender bias in household allocations to children, nor can I reject the hypothesis that allocations were efficient. These findings cannot be explained by parental egalitarianism. I find that parents were strategic out of necessity—the future cooperation of children was unknown and highly uncertain, tempering any desire for gender bias in household allocations. Narrative and quantitative evidence supports this conclusion.

Keywords Parental egalitarianism · Intrahousehold allocation · Gender bias · Earnings potential · Adult consumption

11.1 Introduction

Economists and historians have noted for some time that industrialization changed intergenerational relationships in fundamental ways (see, e.g., Gary Becker 1991). Our knowledge of family strategies in the industrial world of the nineteenth century gives us some clues about how families behaved in this period. We know, for example, that the earnings of children were important to family survival as households made the transition from agricultural to industrial work and that household resources, savings, and labor force participation were intimately related to the household's age structure and the earnings of children—the dominant secondary workers at the time (Angus and Mirel 1985; Hoover 1985; Rotella and Alter 1993; Haines 1979, 1981; Manacorda 2006).

T. Logan (✉)
The Ohio State University, Columbus, OH, USA
e-mail: logan.155@osu.edu

P. Gray et al. (eds.), *Standard of Living*, Studies in Economic History,
https://doi.org/10.1007/978-3-031-06477-7_11

We also know that cultural and social norms changed much more slowly than the economic environment. Even though children of both genders worked, young men had greater labor force attachment than young women and earned, on average, higher wages. Indeed, the independence that young women could experience with participation in the labor force could cause conflict within the family (Goldin 1980, 1981; Moehling 2005). In many ways the independence of young women was thwarted by cultural norms that dictated that young women should live in their families of origin until marriage, although the cultural variations on this theme were many (Glenn 1990, Goldin 1981, Woods and Kennedy 1913, Ewen 1979). At the same time, young women in the USA were among the most educated in the world in the late nineteenth century, although the majority of women would leave the labor force upon marriage (Goldin 1980, Carter and Savoca 1991).

Given the contradictory indirect evidence, we should ask if the allocation of resources in industrial households favored one gender over another. This gender differential in allocations could take place for several reasons. If parents desired to smooth consumption over the lifecycle, they could devote more resources to children who would earn more for the household in the future. Similarly, if young women contributed more in nonmarket work or old age support, this could play a factor in how parents chose to allocate resources in the household. Alternatively, altruistic parents could devote more resources to children with higher marginal utilities of consumption, and this would appear to favor children who had lower potential earnings in the labor market. Both lifecycle and altruistic arguments imply gender differences in household allocation strategies.

Beyond this question of the direction of any potential allocation bias, there is a more fundamental economic question: Was the allocation strategy efficient? Would it have been possible to make one group (parents, sons, daughters) better off without any change in the welfare of others? While we do know about how households made decisions, we know little about the welfare implications of those decisions. Furthermore, should we expect efficiency? In theoretical work, economists have concentrated on efficiency as the shared condition for a large range of household decision-making models, from those with a single dictator to those where household members bargain over resources. Households, then as now, have long-lived relationships with one another, one of the requirements for efficiency to hold (one-shot games need not be efficient). Narrative evidence suggests the same social and cultural forces that tied young women closer to the home than young men could be used to the parents' advantage, and it is easy to imagine such situations being suboptimal. As with the question of allocation differences by gender, conjectures point in both directions.

To answer these questions, I test whether the pattern of intrahousehold allocation differed by gender among late nineteenth-century industrial households in the USA and also test for the efficiency of the allocation strategy. In every test, I cannot reject the hypothesis that the allocation of resources was equal by gender. Furthermore, I cannot reject the hypothesis that the allocation of resources in these households was efficient. The failure to reject efficiency comes despite the fact that the earnings profiles of boys show that they earn roughly 40% more than their sisters during their teenage years.

Parents did not favor one gender over another and household allocations were efficient, yet we know that boys earned more than girls when they entered the labor market, and Rotella and Alter (1993) found that parents were forward-looking consumption smoothers. If parental allocations were efficient and parents were forward looking, then it must hold that parents perceived the expected income flows from sons and daughters to be equal or the marginal utilities of consumption for boys and girls to be equal. The perceived equal flows from sons and daughters could be due to either longer streams of wage income from daughters or greater nonwage contributions by daughters. Concentrating on labor market earnings only, I use the income profiles to estimate the probability that boys would not cooperate relative to girls. I find that boys age 12–24 in these industrial households were anywhere from 30% to 50% more likely than girls the same age to leave home. Narrative evidence is also consistent with this explanation—young men were allowed more freedoms, did fewer household chores, and retained more of their earnings than their sisters when they earned more in the labor market.

I conclude that parents were strategic out of necessity—because the future cooperation of children was unknown, parents allocated equally because the expected higher earnings of sons came with higher probability of noncooperation and/or greater bargaining concessions. This conclusion is supported by recent theoretical work that shows that intertemporal efficiency within households is unlikely because members cannot fully commit to future cooperation (Mazzocco 2007). Gender-neutral allocations were the best option for parents at this time.

11.2 Intrahousehold Allocation in the Historical Record

Before turning to the theory and empirical results, we should see what insights and hypotheses about gender differentials in household allocations can be found in the historical record. While there is a great deal of information in the historical narrative, those contemporaneous accounts of the phenomena are sometimes problematic. Many contemporary observers were known to be biased against the working class, industrial families, immigrants, and non-whites, and many of the sources were used as propaganda for policy agendas.

Therefore, we should look at the narrative record carefully and see what observations by contemporary observers are also supported by recent scholarship on the topic. Below, I analyze both contemporaneous and recent scholarship in an attempt to establish what is known about differentials in household well-being by gender in industrial households.

The changes brought about by industrialization changed traditional familial relationships. Not only did the wage economy change the location and tasks of household members, but also the types of contributions they could be expected to make to the household. Children of both genders worked outside of the household to supplement their father's income. Glenn (1990) points out:

> This pattern was a shift from the traditional way that… [Europeans] had defined the economic role of women…redistribution of economic responsibility was a behavioral shift more than a shift in values, but it represented the first in a series of changes that would redefine the nature of …womanhood. (p. 89)

In short, this change was momentous and changed the way the family functioned and was structured.

Poverty was common among these households, and Chapin (1909) notes that households with more than one wage earner were more likely to be impoverished. Streightoff (1911) summarizes many of the general findings of contemporaneous reports of living standards in the late nineteenth century. He further supports Chapin's claims about the poverty of multiple- earner households when he looked at the other surveys of industrial families from the late nineteenth century onward. Since children were the primary secondary workers at the time, Chapin and Streightoff's findings imply that families in which children worked were most in need of their incomes for survival.[1] Streightoff additionally noted that young working women seem to be particularly affected by fatigue brought about by undernourishment.[2] Such observations point to mistreatment in the household and perhaps unequal allocations at the dinner table.[3] Glenn (1990) notes that until 1903 New York law required only 4 years of schooling before a child could work, and "working papers" were easy to forge, further enabling children at very young ages to participate in the labor market. Additionally, families could exert greater social control over their daughters than sons.

Haines (1981) concludes that the highest-earning members of the household could be expected to receive better treatment than others, and this was usually the father or older son. Goldin (1981) claims that this could be the result of implicit investment choices by parents, where boys would receive a larger share of parental resources. In an analysis of Philadelphia households in the late nineteenth century, she concludes that "sons and daughters had differing relative productivities in the

[1] This is not a causal claim—there is an obvious endogeneity between the labor supply of household members and total household income.

[2] He reported that "The reason for this pitifully insufficient diet is well expressed by Mrs. Van Vorst in describing

her own experience as a working woman: 'I am beginning to understand why the meager lunches of preserves, sandwiches, and pickles more than satisfy the girls whom I was prepared to accuse of spending their money on gewgaws rather than on nourishment. It is a fatigue that steals the appetite. I can hardly taste what I put in my mouth; the food sticks in my throat. I do not want wholesome food…'" (Streightoff 1911, p. 91).

[3] There is further narrative evidence to support such claims. Glenn (1990) notes that "So important were a daughter's wages to the family that in some instances her marriage would be postponed until another child could earn enough to replace her…The economic needs and priorities of immigrant families frequently required daughters to drop out of school in order to become wage earners" (Glenn 1990, pp. 84–86).

household and in the market and required differing training for their future occupations inside or outside the home" (p. 293). To the extent that parents weighed market production more heavily than household production (or vice versa), we would expect differential allocations by gender.

Some social observers turned their attention to young women in the household. Unlike the investments that parents made in sons, observers claimed daughters were seen solely as a source of income. Some parents, it seems, were disinterested in the particulars of a daughter's work life:

> The family sense of responsibility for the girl who goes to work is universally admitted to be greatly underdeveloped ...The vital question is that of putting the girl at work; her safety is merely incidental. "I do not know where she works, but I know what she gets a week," fairly represents the attitude of the average parent. (Woods and Kennedy 1913, pp. 59–60)

This lack of concern could spill over to other areas as well. Young women could be made to do a large portion of the household chores in addition to working, and parents were often likely to deny young women free time for recreation or large amounts of spending money.[4] This created conflict in the household, and Goldin (1980) claims that this conflict drove some young women to leave home and live in boarding houses, which were controversial as young women living alone could be exposed to "moral corruption."

Young women also faced dangerous work environments. Metzker (1971) details several accounts of young women in precarious situations with morally questionable or abusive supervisors, consistent with Woods and Kennedy's (1913) claim that many young women routinely worked near "red light" districts and were sometimes solicited for prostitution. Even without these (literal) moral hazards, the working conditions of young women were nearly as demanding as those of young men.[5]

The treatment of young women in the household interacted strongly with social norms. Since there was a strong taboo against young women living on their own and against married women working, the only range of escape from the household would be through marriage. Furthermore, once the daughter married, she was no longer a "member" of the household, as she would now belong to the husband's family. This echoes Glenn's (1990) observations about parents placing the interest of the household before the daughter. This view is supported by contemporary scholarship that views this changing landscape as one that put new demands on mothers who had to navigate the transition and enforce codes of conduct on the family:

> While middle class women lost control over their family economy, immigrant women and working class women created the machinery of the family economy... The divorce between

---

[4] See Salmon (1906, 1911) for more on domestic service at this time. The subject of retained earnings will be discussed later.

[5] One woman described her working conditions as a weaver in the following way: "When I came in 1900, we worked from six in the morning till six at night. I worked solid...Even on the weekends I worked... It wasn't long till I did see where I was wrong. It was drudgery there; of course, it paid well, but it's regular drudgery" (Hareven and Langenbach 1978, pp. 44–48).

> production and consumption and the reliance upon wages as the sole means to survival made money and its control a dominate imperative. (Ewen 1979, pp. 119–122)

This review of the narrative literature establishes a number of facts that clarify the questions asked of the empirical analysis. The record indicates that parents exploited their children to a certain extent—taking advantage of their income to secure goods for the household and potentially more for themselves as well. Children of different genders had different economic values in the labor market (favoring boys) and different degrees of attachment to the home (favoring girls). Parents took advantage of existing taboos regarding gender and independent living. Parents also appeared to treat daughters differently than sons in a number of ways. This narrative review leads to the question: Is the empirical evidence consistent with the notion of differential treatment by gender?

11.3 Conceptualizing Intrahousehold Allocation

11.3.1 Theory

There are now several different models of household decision-making. The oldest class of models treat the household as a single individual who maximized utility subject to a budget constraint of total household resources (Becker 1991). Recent models treat the household as a collection of individuals who make group decisions and where the decision process takes into account the fact that household members may have different opportunity costs of household membership. This bargaining structure has different theoretical and empirical predictions about household behavior, and there is now a large literature that looks at the distinctions between these two classes of models (Thomas 1990, Udry 1996, Mazzocco 2007).

Recently, theorists have derived a methodology that is consistent with a large number of these models and that allows empirical test of their predictions (Browning, et al. 1994). The main contribution of this new development is that it allows us to sidestep, at first, the issue of how the allocation decision is made as long as we assume that the outcome of that decision-making process is efficient.[6] What this means is that, whatever each member of the household receives as a result of the allocation process, each member's individual utility function is maximized subject to their effective budget constraint. In other words, the maximization of an individual household member's utility function takes place *after* the household has decided how much to allocate to public goods and how much to allocate to each household member for their own private consumption. That is, each household member i maximizes a utility function

[6] The discussion that follows borrows from Deaton (1997).

$$\max v^i\left(q,\bar{\omega}\right)s.t.p^i q=\theta^i\left(p,p_{\bar{\omega}},y\right) \tag{11.1}$$

where q is the good, $\bar{\omega}$ is the optimal choice of public goods (goods that are shared by household members), p is the prices of all goods, $p_{\bar{\omega}}$ is the price of all goods, p^i is the price of goods consumed by household member i, y is total household resources, and $\theta^i\left(p,p_{\bar{\omega}},y\right)$ is the sharing rule, the function that determines how much person i will get for their own private consumption conditional on prices and total household resources. Maximization of the utility function will lead to a set of demand functions for each household member

$$q^i=g^i\left[\theta^i\left(p,p_{\varpi},y\right),p^i,\varpi\right] \tag{11.2}$$

That depends on the sharing rule, prices of the private goods, and the public goods allocation decided earlier. For ease of exposition, suppose that a household contained two members, i and j. The efficiency assumption allows us to write the household's budget constraint as

$$y=p_{\varpi}\varpi+\theta^i\left(p,p_{\varpi},y\right)+\theta^j\left(p,p_{\varpi},y\right) \tag{11.3}$$

because $p^i q^i = \theta^i(p,\ p_{\sigma},\ y)$. This is entirely intuitive; total household resources are devoted to either public goods, $\bar{\omega}$, or to the private consumption of each household member, q. We have limited information about who actually receives what in the household, and many items in the household are shared among household members. If there are goods that are only consumed privately (exclusively by one or only some members of the household), we could say that the demand for that good would be the sum of the *individual* demands as there would be no public component to it (a crude but vivid example would be undergarments). For such goods, the demand function would be

$$q_k=g_k^i\left[\theta^i\left(p,p_{\varpi},y\right),p^i,\varpi\right]+g_k^j\left[\left(y-\theta^i\left(p,p_{\mathrm{w}},y\right)-p_{\mathrm{w}}\varpi\right),p^j,\varpi\right] \tag{11.4}$$

If each household member (or, more generally, more than one household member) earned income, this could change the amount of resources available to each member under the sharing rule depending on how the household behaved. Different kinds of household behavior yield different kinds of sharing rules, and this is where the allocation process that was sidestepped earlier comes into play. If households pooled their income, individual earnings would not matter for individual demands, only total household income as given above, but if earnings reflected the opportunity costs of household membership or if household members bargained with one another over resources, then individual consumption (and the sharing rule) would depend on individual earnings. The earnings of each member of the household would affect the sharing rule because individual earnings act as an (outside) option of leaving the household if their demands are not met.

Leaving aside the prices and public goods to increase the exposition, this would give a demand function with

$$q_k = g_k^i\left[\theta^i\left(p,p_\pi,y,y^i,y^j\right)\right] + g_k^j\left[y - \theta^i\left(p,p_\varpi,y,y^i,y^j\right)\right] \tag{11.5}$$

(where $y = y^i + y^j$).[7] If we differentiate the function with respect to the individual earnings of each household member and derive one derivate by the other, we obtain

$$\frac{\partial q_k / \partial y^i}{\partial q_k / \partial y^j} = \frac{\partial \theta^i / \partial y^i}{\partial \theta^i / \partial y^j} \tag{11.6}$$

This expression tells us that the earnings of each member of the household (relative to the other member) make a difference with respect to demand in the same way that they matter for the sharing rule itself. Changes in individual earnings affect demand for private goods through the sharing rule, which in turn changes the budget constraint that each household member faces for their private consumption. Note that if the household pooled income, the left-hand side of (11.6) would equal 1 for all goods because the source of income would not matter for demand, and this is the basis for the tests of "pooled" income in the household.[8] Furthermore, we can test for efficiency by estimating the left-hand side of (11.6) and testing to see if these effects of income are equal to one another for the private goods.[9]

How can we incorporate children into this framework? The presence of children does yield some complications, particularly to the assumption of efficiency. McElroy (1985, 1990) notes that children may simultaneously determine household membership and labor force status. The future (expected) opportunity costs of family membership matter to the extent that opportunity costs increase the threat point (the maximum utility of not belonging to the household). The greater the opportunity costs, the more likely these household members can see their needs better reflected in the household's demand. This is analogous to asserting that these differences in the opportunity costs of membership in the household translate into different allocations within the household, so we would expect the characteristics of children to have some influence on the sharing rule. Becker (1991) has argued that household outcomes may be inefficient due to the inability of children to enter into contracts (bargain) with their parents and that children of different genders may receive different levels of investment from their parents because of the sexual division of labor.

[7] With prices and public goods, the demand function would be

$$q_k = g_k^i\left[\theta^i\left(p,p_\varpi,y,y^i,y^j\right),p^i,\varpi\right] + g_k^j\left[\left(y - \theta^i\left(p,p_\pi,y,y^i,y^j\right) - p_\pi\varpi\right),p^j,\varpi\right].$$

[8] See Thomas (1990) and Udry (1996) for classic examples.

[9] Equation 11.6 is a direct result of the efficiency assumption. See Browning et al. (1994) for the proof of the existence of the sharing rule. Some researchers have used public goods when performing the test, but Blundell et al. (2005) note that such tests fail to take account of the fact that the model only yields predictions for the allocations to private goods, whose allocation is decided conditional on the public goods allocation.

The theory on household decision-making usually argues that efficiency can be guaranteed because family members are involved in long-term relationships with one another, but Mazzocco (2007) has shown that long and enduring relationships are not sufficient to guarantee commitment to future allocations, even without the complications of adding children to the model.

Rather than having two members in the household, we can think of there being two groups in the household—parents and children. In the case of parents and children, the assumption about assignability of some goods in the household reduces to goods that are consumed by parents only. In the terminology of the theory, these goods would not only be assignable to adults, but they would also be exclusive—only consumed by adults.[10] Rather than subutility being separable for private goods as it was above, the model now requires utility to be separable for *adult* goods. Since all other (non-adult) goods are public, this is analogous to the assumption in the two-adult case. This aids in being able to identify the sharing rule itself because now the sharing rule would be the amount of expenditure on adult goods, which would be a function of household income, prices, and characteristics of parents and children. Put another way, we now assume that parents consume both the public goods and the adult goods.

The number (n) and characteristics (z) of children (C) will influence adult (A) consumption through the share of income devoted to children, which will be a function of the characteristics of children and adults. We can therefore modify the demand function in (11.5) to be

$$q_k = g_k\left[\theta^A\left(y,p,z^C,z^A\right),z^C,z^A,p,p_w\right] \tag{11.7}$$

where now the characteristics of children have the same effect as income from the other partner in the two-adult case. The sharing rule result now applies to the characteristics of children such that the result given in Eq. (11.6) is now

$$\frac{\partial q_k / \partial z^C}{\partial q_k / \partial y} = \frac{\partial \theta^A / \partial z^C}{\partial \theta^A / \partial y} \tag{11.8}$$

where once again the result is the same for all adult goods k. The test for efficiency is the same as in the two-adult case—namely, that the left-hand side of Eq. (11.8) is the same for all adult goods, which are the private goods in this setup.

We can further test, for two different demographic characteristics, C and C', whether

$$\partial q_k / \partial z^C = \partial q_k / \partial z^{C'} \tag{11.9}$$

[10] In practice, it is usually easier to argue that some goods are consumed only by parents than only by one adult in the household. Since the grouping here is between parents and children, I leave aside the issue of which of the parents consumes which adult items more than the other.

that is, whether children with different characteristics have different effects on demand for adult goods. If allocations were biased, there would be larger changes in demand for a child of type C than a child of type C'. This would reflect the (possibly) greater threat point for boys than girls and the fact that boys could secure greater resources based on their greater threat point. This is intuitive—if one child had different opportunity costs of household membership, this would affect the household's allocation decision in a distinguishable way. The theory, then, gives us two tests, one for the efficiency of household allocation and another for the same allocations across different child characteristics.

11.3.2 Empirical Strategy

To capture gender differentials, I use a variant of the Almost Ideal Demand System, which attributes changes in demand to the distribution of members in the household by age and gender. For each adult good in the data, w, I estimate

$$w_i = \alpha_i + \beta_i \ln\left(\frac{x}{n}\right) + \eta_i \ln(n) + \sum_{k=1}^{K-1} \gamma_{ik}\left(\frac{n_k}{n}\right) + \varepsilon_i \tag{11.10}$$

where w is the share of the total budget (expenditure) devoted to a particular good, n is the size of the family, x is total expenditure, and k is 5-year age sex categories (e.g., males 5–9, females 15–19, etc.).[11] I estimate the model above using ordinary least squares (OLS). If w is an "adult good" (e.g., a good consumed only by the mother and/or father), the size and sign of the γ coefficients gives the substitution away from (if negative) or toward (if positive) the consumption of that adult good if a given share of the household lies in that age-sex category.

If the γ coefficients are significantly different across genders for the same adult good and age grouping, then the adults can be said to sacrifice more of their consumption for one gender than for another. The basis of the type of gender differential is not child consumption, but parental *willingness to forgo consumption*. It can be thought of as a "top-down" measure of gender allocation, which follows directly from the theoretical discussion above since it relates to private (adult) goods. As such, it does have limitations—since this is a test based upon parental consumption, it will not capture different access by gender to services such as education and healthcare, for example. Even with these limitations, the allocation rules captured here are useful for thinking about and analyzing the allocation of goods within the

[11] As Deaton (1997) notes, the "transformation of expenditures to budget shares and of total outlay to its logarithm induces an approximate normality in the joint density of the transformed variables, so that the regression function is approximately normal" (p. 231). This joint normality justifies the use of OLS. Horrell and Oxley (1999) use a similar econometric strategy to test for gender discrimination among the British households in the 1888CEX. Since one potential control variable would be skill level, the results are disaggregated for metalworks and textile families.

household, particularly in light of the narrative evidence and the model described above.[12]

11.3.3 Data

The primary data analyzed in this paper comes from the "Cost of Living of Industrial Workers in the United States and Europe 1888-1890" (1888CEX) survey published by the US Department of Labor (2006).[13] The 1888CEX contains a sample of 6809 American families working in iron, steel, coal, textile, and glass industries in the USA. Homes from 24 states in the Northeast, Midwest, Mid-Atlantic, and South were surveyed. For the households surveyed, enumerators from the Department of Labor were sent to firms in the nine selected industries and collected information on the costs of production and the standard of living of the workers in the firms surveyed for costs of production. As Haines (1979) notes, how the household sample was chosen remains unclear, but the sample is broadly representative of industrial households in the USA at the time in the selected industries.

The data set contains detailed annual expenditure information for both food and nonfood items and annual income information for all members of the household (father, mother, and children). In addition, the data also contains demographic information on the household's age and sex composition, as well as a detailed enumeration of the husband's occupation. The occupations of children and wives are not included in this study, although their labor force status is recorded in the data.

There are several limitations to the data that may influence the empirical results. First, remittances from children not living at home are not recorded, although they could be listed under the "other income" category.[14] Second, the labor force and/or school enrollment for each child, individually, is not given. As such, we are unable to assign child income to particular children in the household, although we can

[12] Another important use of this approach is that it fits quite well with the historical era under consideration. In contemporary populations, it is unwise to think of household composition as exogenous. As Behrman (1997) has correctly noted, these types of regressions may fail to reject the hypothesis of gender equality even when there is substantial evidence that women are mistreated in the home. If parents are taking part in activity which eliminates young women from the household (e.g., sex-selective abortion, infanticide, etc.), the failure to find gender differentials in household allocation is not on a firm footing. Historically, there is no evidence of excess infant female mortality in the late nineteenth century—while household size was determined by the family, composition was not similarly constructed through sex-selective practice. Lifetables from the time suggest that the probabilities of dying in the first year of life were equal, and if anything were higher for boys than girls. For more see the Human Mortality Database (http://www.mortality.org)

[13] For more on the historical forces shaping the 1888CEX, see US Department of Labor *How American Buying Habits Change* (1959).

[14] The "other income" category provides very little income, on average less than 2.5% of household income.

assign income to children as a group and derive earnings profiles through a parametric method.

More importantly, these families come from a number of different industries that may have different patterns of household allocation. In many instances, children in textile families earned nearly as much as the household head, and the differences in earnings by gender were relatively small. In contrast, daughters whose fathers worked in iron or steel often had to secure employment in low-paying service jobs like domestic service. Although the focus in this paper is the general pattern of household allocation among these industrial households, I also present results for the families employed in metalworks (iron and steel) and textiles (wool and cotton) separately as a test of the robustness of the general pattern for households with highly unequal (metalworks) and equal (textiles) earnings for young workers. Since families in metalworks tended to concentrate in the Northeast and Midwest, while textile families were located in the Northeast and South, separation by industry also acts as a quasi-geographic control.[15] Table 11.1 lists the means and standard errors of the variables used in this analysis. As the table shows, the household shares were similar between textile and metalworks families overall. Expenditure shares on adult goods were largely similar as well, but families in metalworks had greater expenditure for alcohol and religious donations.

11.4 Intrahousehold Allocation in the Late Nineteenth Century

11.4.1 Gender and Intrahousehold Allocation

In the 1888CEX I identified six expenditure items that can be thought of as adult goods. Tobacco, alcohol, husband's clothing, wife's clothing, charity, and religious expenditures were most likely made by and for adults. I further aggregate these goods to create a seventh adult good to test for differential gender allocation. Of the six adult goods, tobacco, alcohol, husband's clothing, and wife's clothing expenditures were surely not made for children, particularly young children, and as such these four items were the most likely adult goods, and I aggregate these four "most likely" adult goods into an eighth adult good.[16] To test for differences in gender allocation, I test the null hypothesis that the age category coefficients are equal to one another across gender. The regression results are listed in Table 11.2.

---

[15] See Smith (1994) for more on the geographic differences by occupation.

[16] I also used savings, savings as a share of total income and expenditure, the share of protein in the diet, and the share of protein from animal sources as potential adult goods. As the results for these goods were the same as the most likely adult goods from the data, these results are not reported.

Table 11.1 Means and standard errors of variables, American sample of 1988 Cost of Living Survey

	Whole sample		Metalworks		Textiles	
Variable[a]	Mean	Std. error.	Mean	Std. error	Mean	Std. error
Log Per Cap. Exp.	9.491	0.461	9.517	0.454	9.453	0.419
Log Family Size	1.464	0.454	1.421	0.452	1.491	0.458
Tobacco	0.016	0.014	0.018	0.015	0.014	0.014
Liquor	0.019	0.121	0.025	0.244	0.008	0.020
Husb Cloth	0.054	0.031	0.064	0.031	0.041	0.024
Wife Cloth	0.040	0.026	0.044	0.028	0.033	0.024
Religion	0.013	0.264	0.024	0.550	0.012	0.014
Charity	0.004	0.007	0.005	0.005	0.002	0.005
Male 0–4	0.073	0.125	0.080	0.134	0.068	0.123
Male 5–9	0.065	0.107	0.065	0.107	0.059	0.102
Male 10–14	0.056	0.100	0.053	0.099	0.057	0.100
Male 15–19	0.037	0.087	0.027	0.077	0.045	0.095
Male 20–24	0.025	0.088	0.026	0.094	0.025	0.085
Male 25+	0.234	0.132	0.248	0.133	0.220	0.132
Female 0–4	0.073	0.125	0.077	0.128	0.065	0.120
Female 5–9	0.063	0.107	0.062	0.107	0.060	0.104
Female 10–14	0.051	0.096	0.047	0.093	0.056	0.099
Female 15–19	0.050	0.107	0.048	0.108	0.059	0.112
Female 20–24	0.057	0.126	0.057	0.130	0.058	0.124
Female 25+	0.211	0.147	0.208	0.147	0.218	0.152
N	6809		1568		3043	

Notes: [a]Unless otherwise noted, non-logged variables are the share of either total household expenditures (for consumption goods) or total number of persons in the household (for age-sex categories). Author's calculations using 1888CEX

Parents appeared to substitute away from the consumption of adult goods in the presence of young children, as can be seen by the negative regression coefficients. Similarly, it appears that the substitution lessened with age, although this certainly does not hold in a strict sense. We should expect such a result—as children aged, parents were less likely to decrease their consumption of adult goods, possibly because the earnings of children in the labor market could be devoted to securing more adult goods or because as children aged they provide services to the household which have an income effect, or a substitution effect away from public good consumption. When looking at the aggregate of the four most likely adult goods, it does appear that there was statistically significant variation with the age and sex composition of the household with respect to adult consumption.

The primary focus, however, is the comparison between genders in the same age category. Table 11.3 lists the Wald test statistics for the hypothesis of gender equality by age group for each of the regressions presented in Table 11.2 as well as the Wald test statistics for the test by industry for the metalworks and textile

Table 11.2 Gender allocation regression results for the American sample, 1988 Cost of Living Survey

	Tobacco	Liquor	Husb Cloth	Wife Cloth	Religion	Charity	All Adult	4 Adult
Intercept	0.117	−0.250	0.193	0.044	−0.049	−0.031	0.023	0.103
	(0.00602)	(0.04670)	(0.01165)	(0.00997)	(0.01609)	(0.00415)	(0.05444)	(0.05161)
ln (x/n)	−0.009	0.027	−0.006	0.004	0.004	0.004	0.026	0.018
	(0.00056)	(0.00411)	(0.00107)	(0.00094)	(0.00091)	(0.00039)	(0.00471)	(0.00459)
ln (n)	−0.010	0.017	−0.029	−0.027	−0.003	0.001	−0.052	−0.050
	(0.00076)	(0.01358)	(0.00161)	(0.00134)	(0.01034)	(0.00032)	(0.01729)	(0.01385)
Male 0–4	−0.009	−0.010	−0.024	0.006	0.003	0.001	−0.032	−0.037
	(0.00235)	(0.02184)	(0.00527)	(0.00412)	(0.01364)	(0.00108)	(0.02751)	(0.02368)
Male 5–9	−0.006	0.008	−0.031	0.010	0.032	0.000	0.013	−0.018
	(0.00247)	(0.00984)	(0.00563)	(0.00432)	(0.04452)	(0.00116)	(0.04686)	(0.01389)
Male 10–14	−0.006	−0.029	−0.042	−0.002	0.032	−0.001	−0.049	−0.079
	(0.00262)	(0.03338)	(0.00559)	(0.00448)	(0.04047)	(0.00106)	(0.05344)	(0.03469)
Male 15–19	−0.002	−0.043	−0.059	−0.020	0.016	0.000	−0.109	−0.124
	(0.00298)	(0.03019)	(0.00612)	(0.00468)	(0.02197)	(0.00117)	(0.03890)	(0.03192)
Male 20–24	0.001	0.014	−0.009	0.002	0.184	−0.003	0.189	0.007
	(0.00227)	(0.01942)	(0.00562)	(0.00477)	(0.18584)	(0.00094)	(0.18762)	(0.02168)
Female 0–4	−0.009	0.004	−0.025	0.006	0.000	0.001	−0.023	−0.024
	(0.00236)	(0.01032)	(0.00532)	(0.00409)	(0.01124)	(0.00111)	(0.01812)	(0.01378)
Female 5–9	−0.005	−0.009	−0.026	0.015	0.032	0.000	0.007	−0.024
	(0.00249)	(0.02574)	(0.00560)	(0.00434)	(0.13812)	(0.00097)	(0.05179)	(0.02754)
Female 10–14	−0.005	−0.035	−0.042	0.002	0.028	0.000	−0.054	−0.081
	(0.00259)	(0.03433)	(0.00568)	(0.00448)	(0.03706)	(0.00120)	(0.05156)	(0.03564)
Female 15–19	−0.006	−0.006	−0.064	−0.016	−0.002	−0.002	−0.096	−0.092
	(0.00251)	(0.01155)	(0.00556)	(0.00433)	(0.00572)	(0.00104)	(0.01622)	(0.01507)
Female 20–24	−0.010	−0.039	−0.073	−0.015	0.086	−0.003	−0.055	−0.137
	(0.00282)	(0.01853)	(0.00598)	(0.00489)	(0.08456)	(0.00110)	(0.08752)	(0.02138)
Female 25+	−0.010	−0.035	−0.100	−0.029	0.038	−0.002	−0.139	−0.175
	(0.00282)	(0.00981)	(0.00612)	(0.00512)	(0.03031)	(0.00105)	(0.03394)	(0.01471)
R Square	0.071	0.008	0.203	0.203	0.005	0.038	0.018	0.050

Notes: N = 6809 for all regressions. Robust standard errors listed in parentheses. The column in a regression in which the dependent variable is the share of the budget devoted to teach good in the column heading

households.[17] The most striking feature of Table 11.3 is that the hypothesis of gender equality is only rejected for children above the age of 20. When looking at Wald

[17] The Wald test statistics for metalworks and textile families are based on regressions on the form listed in Table 11.3. Since I use a robust variance-covariance matrix, the F-test for a set of linear restrictions for the regression is not appropriate. Fortunately, the Wald test (which must be used when employing the Eicker-White variance-covariance matrix) reduces to a standard F-test for my hypotheses. Under the null of gender equality, the Wald statistic has a chi-squared distribution with degrees of freedom equal to the number of linear restrictions imposed by the null hypothesis. Since I test each age category separately, each test has one degree of freedom.

Table 11.3 Wald statistics for the hypothesis of gender equality in household allocation, 1888 Cost of Living Survey

Age group	Tobacco	Liquor	Husb Cloth	Wife Cloth	Religion	Charity	4 Adult
American sample (N = 6809)							
0–4	0.035	0.305	0.027	0.004	0.029	0.008	0.204
5–9	0.053	0.388	0.409	0.738	0.000	0.002	0.038
10–14	0.069	0.020	0.000	0.397	0.005	0.104	0.002
15–19	1.455	1.317	0.246	0.424	0.608	1.647	0.845
20–24	8.365	3.927	60.215	5.941	0.234	0.184	22.366
Metalworks (N = 1568)							
0–4	0.0216	0.0879	0.0312	0.2309	0.0026	0.0382	0.0529
5–9	0.0001	0.2470	0.4695	0.5579	0.0010	0.0901	0.1112
10–14	0.2605	0.0055	0.2153	0.0322	0.0000	0.1775	0.0181
15–19	0.2716	1.2283	0.1647	0.2301	0.0350	0.0044	1.1235
20–24	0.4243	1.6485	3.8407	2.3557	0.6090	0.1893	2.7952
Textiles (N = 3043)							
0–4	0.045	0.812	0.665	0.001	0.987	0.403	0.000
5–9	0.040	0.438	0.033	0.119	0.009	0.002	0.412
10–14	0.029	0.488	0.270	0.080	0.464	0.048	0.000
15–19	1.013	3.921	0.921	0.184	0.003	0.029	3.810
20–24	4.659	0.919	52.033	1.210	0.879	0.006	27.374

Notes: The Wald test statistics are based on regression results presented in Table 11.2 (not reported for metalworks and textiles). The results test the hypothesis that the male and female coefficients in a given group are equal to one another for the specified adult good listed above. The critical value for the Wald test ($\alpha = 0.01$) is 6.64

test statistics for metalworks and textile families, the pattern is the same. The hypothesis of gender equality is never rejected for metalworks families, and for textile families only above the age of 20.

There are two problems with the results of Table 11.3. The first is that few of the demographic coefficients themselves are statistically significant, so the finding of gender equity could be a problem of a poorly specified regression. The second problem is that these results are not specified in a manner consistent with the theory outlined earlier. Demand for the adult goods should depend on the sharing rule, which is a function of household income and the characteristics of parents and children. In order to match the theory as closely as possible, I estimated the sharing rule and then test for gender equity. First, I estimated the sharing rule as

$$\theta_i = \alpha_i + \beta_i \ln\left(\frac{x}{n}\right) + \eta_i \ln(n) + \sum_{k=1}^{K-1} \gamma_{ik}\left(\frac{n_k}{n}\right) + \varepsilon_i \tag{11.11}$$

where θ is the total expenditure on all six adult goods, and as noted earlier is a function of household income, and the characteristics of parents and children. I then estimated the demand for each adult good as a function of the sharing rule and household income and demographics

$$w_i = \alpha_i + \lambda\hat{\theta}_i + \beta_i \ln\left(\frac{x}{n}\right) + \eta_i \ln(n) + \sum_{k=1}^{K-1} \gamma_{ik}\left(\frac{n_k}{n}\right) + \varepsilon_i \tag{11.12}$$

This is appropriate since the model assumes that the sharing rule is decided before the expenditure on individual adult goods. From this specification we can test for gender equity as before, where now we have accounted for the sharing rule itself.[18] Table 11.4 shows the results. Unlike the results of Table 11.2, the regressions in Table 11.4 show that the demographic characteristics have a statistically significant effect on the demand for the adult goods—and the sharing rule itself does have an effect on the demand for the adult goods. Even with this improved fit, the results for gender equity remain the same, and these are presented in Table 11.5. Also in Table 11.5 are the gender equity results when the sharing rule was estimated with child income and only for households where children earned income.[19] In no specification of the demand equation do I reject the hypothesis of gender equality in household allocations.

11.4.2 The Efficiency of Intrahousehold Allocation

Tests for efficiency in household allocation hinge on the hypothesis that changes in demand for adult goods due to household composition are the same as changes in the sharing rule due to changes in household composition, $\frac{\partial q_k / \partial z^C}{\partial q_k / \partial y} = \frac{\partial \theta / \partial z^C}{\partial \theta / \partial y}$ where z is the demographic category.[20] To test for efficiency I bootstrapped the sharing rule regression to obtain an estimate of the standard error for $\frac{\partial \theta / \partial z^c}{\partial \theta / \partial y}$ for each demographic category C that can then be compared to the estimate of $\frac{\partial q_j / \partial z^c}{\partial q_j / \partial y}$

[18] One would like to include nonlinear forms of the sharing rule such as those exploited by Browning et al. (1994). The issue for the paper is that there are several demographic categories, and one assumes that they have a linear effect on demand. While one would like to use nonlinear forms, I cannot because symmetry of the Slutsky matrix and the additive structure of the specification require a linear model (see Blundell et al. 2003 for a proof).

Chiappori and Browning, since they restrict their sample to two-adult households, do not have the number of demographic categories I use here, and this allows them to try several alternative specifications without regard to this consideration. I am not able to use nonlinear specifications of the sharing rule without the results being suspect and inconsistent with the theoretical model that they are supposed to correspond to.

[19] For child income the sharing rule is $\theta_i = \alpha_i + \phi \ln(y_{\text{child}})_i + \beta_i \ln\left(\frac{x}{n}\right) + \eta_i \ln(n) + \sum_{k=1}^{K-1} \gamma_{ik}\left(\frac{n_k}{n}\right) + \varepsilon_i$. Also, Wald test results for households where no children worked (N = 4826) are qualitatively similar to those where only children worked. See Appendix B.

[20] Since prices are fixed in the cross section, we can ignore them here.

Table 11.4 Gender allocation regressions with the sharing rule results for the American sample, 1888 Cost of Living Survey

	Sharing rule	Tobacco	Liquor	Husb Cloth	Wife Cloth	Religion	Charity	4 Adult
Intercept	0.023	0.113	−0.247	0.178	0.034	−0.048	−0.030	0.079
	(0.115)	(0.005)	(0.046)	(0.011)	(0.009)	(0.101)	(0.003)	(0.050)
Sharing rule		0.145	−0.103	0.624	0.404	−0.069	−0.001	1.070
		(0.011)	(0.097)	(0.022)	(0.019)	(0.212)	(0.006)	(0.105)
ln (x/n)	0.026	−0.012	0.028	−0.022	−0.005	0.007	0.004	−0.011
	(0.026)	(0.001)	(0.006)	(0.001)	(0.001)	(0.012)	(0.000)	(0.006)
ln (n)	−0.052							
	(0.016)							
Male 0–4	−0.032	−0.012	0.027	0.007	−0.002	−0.021	0.003	0.018
	(0.050)	(0.002)	(0.027)	(0.003)	(0.003)	(0.030)	(0.001)	(0.015)
Male 5–9	0.013	−0.016	0.051	−0.027	−0.019	0.009	0.002	−0.011
	(0.054)	(0.002)	(0.016)	(0.004)	(0.003)	(0.034)	(0.001)	(0.017)
Male 10–14	−0.049	−0.008	0.008	−0.001	−0.006	0.004	0.001	−0.006
	(0.056)	(0.002)	(0.017)	(0.004)	(0.003)	(0.038)	(0.001)	(0.019)
Male 15–19	−0.109	0.006	−0.011	0.020	0.000	−0.016	0.002	0.015
	(0.059)	(0.002)	(0.022)	(0.005)	(0.004)	(0.048)	(0.001)	(0.024)
Male 20–24	0.189	−0.029	0.046	−0.123	−0.082	0.190	−0.002	−0.188
	(0.045)	(0.003)	(0.028)	(0.006)	(0.005)	(0.061)	(0.002)	(0.030)
Female 0–4	−0.023	−0.013	0.041	−0.001	−0.007	−0.024	0.003	0.020
	(0.049)	(0.001)	(0.013)	(0.003)	(0.003)	(0.029)	(0.001)	(0.015)
Female 5–9	0.007	−0.014	0.033	−0.019	−0.011	0.009	0.002	−0.011
	(0.054)	(0.002)	(0.015)	(0.004)	(0.003)	(0.034)	(0.001)	(0.017)
Female 10–14	−0.054	−0.006	0.002	0.003	0.000	0.000	0.002	−0.001
	(0.058)	(0.002)	(0.018)	(0.042)	(0.004)	(0.040)	(0.001)	(0.020)
Female 15–19	−0.096	−0.001	0.025	0.008	0.000	−0.032	−0.001	0.033
	(0.053)	(0.002)	(0.017)	(0.004)	(0.003)	(0.037)	(0.001)	(0.018)
Female 20–24	−0.055	−0.010	−0.003	−0.027	−0.016	0.058	−0.001	−0.056
	(0.056)	(0.002)	(0.014)	(0.003)	(0.003)	(0.030)	(0.001)	(0.015)
R Square	0.018	0.068	0.007	0.202	0.197	0.005	0.038	0.050

Notes: N = 6809 for all regressions. Robust standard errors listed in parentheses. The column is a regression in which the dependent variable is the share of the budget devoted to each good in the column heading. The sharing rule is the share of total expenditure devoted to all six adult goods. The variable Sharing Rule is the unique predicted sharing rule for each household based upon the coefficients in the sharing rule regression and the household's income and composition

from the demand equation for each adult good.[21] Since I do not bootstrap the demand-equation estimates, the test here is conservative (e.g., if I fail to reject the

[21] Note that these demand equations include the sharing rule as a variable. Also, that identification of the sharing rule itself is actually not a requirement for the test—we could similarly test whether the demand-equation parameters were equal to one another (since they all must equal the ratio from the sharing rule, they therefore must be equal to some constant).

Table 11.5 Wald test statistics for the hypothesis of gender equality in household allocation, 1888 Cost of Living Survey

Age group	Tobacco	Liquor	Husb Cloth	Wife Cloth	Religion	Charity	4 Adult
Sharing rule included in demand equations							
0–4	0.145	0.235	2.650	1.299	0.003	0.021	0.012
5–9	0.451	0.652	2.983	3.074	0.000	0.003	0.000
10–14	0.297	0.061	0.007	1.233	0.007	0.146	0.024
15–19	4.143	1.741	3.968	0.000	0.068	1.684	0.358
20–24	30.906	2.432	183.258	114.677	3.788	0.077	15.363
Sharing rule that includes child income							
0–4	0.0081	0.5107	2.2143	0.9736	0.0069	0.0007	0.0286
5–9	0.2645	0.6186	2.7822	2.8070	0.0002	0.0016	0.0009
10–14	0.1865	0.0563	0.3060	1.1680	0.0061	0.2216	0.0178
15–19	1.1813	1.5922	2.3180	0.3733	0.1359	4.0447	0.7329
20–24	7.8760	1.6859	283.6953	103.3548	3.5678	5.3800	13.7260
Households with nonzero child earnings (N = 1982)							
0–4	0.189	2.037	0.937	0.148	0.477	0.011	2.219
5–9	0.003	0.560	0.381	0.416	0.009	0.219	0.411
10–14	0.020	0.000	0.132	0.197	0.022	0.008	0.004
15–19	1.937	0.345	8.403	5.006	0.461	4.081	0.007
20–24	4.099	1.255	1.448	0.622	2.557	0.001	1.920

Notes: The Wald test statistics are based on the regressions as described in the text. For all estimates the demand system included an estimate of the sharing rule. The bottom panel is based on regressions similar to those in Table 11.4 that only included households where children earned income. The critical value for the Wald test ($\alpha = 0.01$) is 6.64

hypothesis of equality here, I would surely fail to reject it in a test where the demand-equation estimate was allowed to vary).

Table 11.6 shows the results of the efficiency tests. For all of the adult goods, the hypothesis that household allocations are efficient cannot be rejected.[22] While there is some variation in the individual t-statistics for each test, the overall conclusion from Table 11.6 is that the allocations were efficient—it would certainly be difficult to support an argument that the allocations were inefficient. Even when expanding the number of potential adult goods to include savings and savings as a share of total income and expenditure, as well as the amount of protein in the diet, the hypothesis is not rejected. The robustness of the result to an expanded definition of adult goods, and even a different version of the sharing rule, adds further strength to the claim that household allocations were efficient.

[22] In only one instance is the hypothesis of efficiency rejected at the $\alpha = 0.001$ level. There are alternatives to estimating the variance of the quotient for the demand equation. If $\partial q_j/\partial z^C = \beta$ and $\partial q_j/\partial y = \lambda$, then by the delta method the variance of β/λ is $V(\beta/\lambda) = \frac{\sigma_\beta^2}{\lambda^2} - 2\left[\frac{\beta\sigma_{\beta\lambda}}{\lambda^3}\right] + \frac{\beta^2\sigma_\lambda^2}{\lambda^4}$. Hypothesis tests with estimates of the standard errors from the demand equations based on the delta method led to failure to reject the hypothesis in all instances.

Table 11.6 Efficiency test of household allocation, 1888 Cost of Living Survey

$\frac{\partial\theta / \partial z^C}{\partial\theta / \partial y}$		$\frac{\partial q_j^A / \partial z^C}{\partial q_j^A / \partial y}$						
		Tobacco	Liquor	Husb Cloth	Wife Cloth	Religion	Charity	4 Adult
Male 0–4	−1.251	1.046	0.941	−0.296	0.488	−2.996	0.875	−1.700
	(0.969)							
Male 5–9	0.504	1.341	1.810	1.238	3.706	1.259	0.474	0.995
	(1.797)							
Male 10–14	−1.893	0.656	0.295	0.023	1.140	0.613	0.362	0.529
	(1.872)							
Male 15–19	−4.252	−0.465	−0.396	−0.915	−0.050	−2.293	0.432	−1.380
	(2.264)							
Female 0–4	−0.879	1.114	1.452	0.026	1.344	−3.337	0.919	−1.911
	(0.869)							
Female 5–9	0.284	1.205	1.184	0.848	2.206	1.264	0.454	0.992
	(1.969)							
Female 10–14	−2.098	0.529	0.074	−0.133	0.041	−0.056	0.518	0.137
	(1.839)							
Female 15–19	−3.756	0.054	0.896	−0.346	−0.059	−4.499	−0.149	−3.044
	(1.773)							

Notes: Bootstrapped estimates of standard errors (B = 500) are listed in parentheses. The estimates from the demand equations come from a regression similar to those in Table 11.2, where an estimate of the sharing rule (a theta hat unique to each household) has been added as a covariate. N = 6809 for all regressions

There are some caveats to this result, however. Firstly, we have employed a linear form here, and although there are theoretical justifications for its use, more complex demand systems may give different results. Secondly, the choice of adult goods will influence the estimation of the sharing rule that forms the basis of the test. Even with these caveats, these results tell us that there were very little, if any, gender differentials in household allocations in the late nineteenth century, especially for young children. Additionally, the allocation of resources in these households appears to have been efficient. Lastly, both of these results are robust to a number of adult goods and alternative specifications of the sharing rule.

11.5 Explaining the Finding

Given the lack of gender bias in allocations and the efficiency of household allocations, we should seek to explain such a finding. If children of different genders had different earnings potential, why do efficient allocations coincide with gender equality in allocations to children? Differences in earnings would imply different allocations by gender if parents were allocating based in future contributions or if parents allocate more to children with higher marginal utility of consumption.

The first explanation for the efficiency of gender neutrality of allocations would be that parents desired to have gender equity in the household, and as such the substitution away from adult consumption is the same for both genders.[23] This explanation, however, is inconsistent with the theoretical model and the econometric test, and therefore parental egalitarianism cannot explain this finding. The method employed here looks at parental substitution away from adult consumption—not allocations to children directly. Since the test is indirect, parents could make themselves better off by increasing the consumption of adult goods when children who earn more are present or, similarly, consuming more when children with low marginal utilities of consumption were present.

To see the inconsistency of the parental egalitarianism explanation, consider the following example. Suppose that parents were egalitarian, but also that they valued their own consumption. Further assume that parents were forward looking and desire to smooth consumption over the lifecycle. If parents knew that children of one gender had greater earnings potential than another, parents could increase their own consumption while still ensuring gender equity in actual allocations to children, and if they were smoothing consumption over the lifecycle, this is what we would expect. But this would imply that parents could be made better off (through additional consumption) while leaving the utility of children unchanged, and this does not agree with the efficiency finding. While the finding of gender equality seems to be consistent with parental egalitarianism, the efficiency finding contradicts this explanation as increased parental consumption would be Pareto improving.

Since parental egalitarianism cannot explain this result, we must return to the theory outlined earlier to see what these results implied for parents and their decision-making process. If this result cannot be explained by egalitarianism, then it must be explained by another feature. If parents are forward looking and there was no differential allocation by gender, it must hold that parents viewed the stream of future benefits coming from sons and daughters as equal—the same would be true of the marginal utilities of consumption for both sons and daughters. If not, they could substitute more (less) away from their own consumption for the child who would earn less (more) in the future.[24]

---

[23] We must be mindful, however, to distinguish between altruism and egalitarianism in this context. In models of parental altruism, altruistic parents seek to ensure that children are equally well off, and this is achieved by allocating more resources to the child with the greater marginal utility of consumption. This supposes, then, that parents would allocate resources differentially to children by type insofar as that type signifies differing marginal utilities of consumption. The empirical test, however, does not look at allocations to children directly, only substitution away from adult consumption. While it could certainly be the case that substitution differentials would be highly correlated with allocation differentials, it need not be the case per se.

[24] It is important to note that discounting would matter, but the main point hinges on differences between young men and women. As it is unlikely that parents had different discount factor for the earnings of children of different genders, these are suppressed here.

Is the evidence consistent with this explanation? Below, I detail the ways in which this "strategic" explanation is consistent with both the quantitative evidence and the narrative record. First, I concentrate on the income from children and use wage profiles to calculate a "back of the envelope" relative probability of sons leaving home as opposed to their sisters. Second, we return to the narrative record to see what evidence exists about household chores and responsibilities for boys versus girls and how this nonwage activity could lead to equal streams of benefits from both genders.

11.5.1 Future Cooperation in the Household

If parents view equalized future income from children in a probabilistic setting, we can use wage profiles to uncover the underlying probabilities of leaving home, which we can take as relative probabilities of noncooperation. There are two things that parents must consider: (1) the possibility that a child of type k will leave in the home, r_k, and (2) the earnings of the child of type k, w_k. So parents must take into account $r_k\ w_k$ where $r_{boy} > r_{girl}$ and $w_{boy} > w_{girl}$. In fact, Moehling (2005), Woods and Kennedy (1913), Ewen (1979), and others tell us that parents would negotiate with children to keep them in the home once they began to work, so parents did not view the income of working children as an extra boon to the household coffers with absolute certainty. Parents negotiating with their children can be taken as evidence that parents were unsure about the future earnings stream coming from children. Similarly, social taboos against married women working and young women living alone outside of their parents' household insured that $r_{boy} > r_{girl}$. Combining these two facts with the absence of any gender differentials, it must hold that parents assumed that $r_{boy}\ w_{boy} = r_{girl}\ w_{girl}$. If not, parents could increase their current consumption more dependent on the gender of the child, and this would mean a differential in substitution away from (or toward) adult goods dependent on gender, which has been rejected.

Since the probability-weighted earnings are equal, we can use this conclusion to derive an estimate of $r_{boy}/r_{girl,}$ which would tell us the relative probability that a daughter would stay in the home (cooperate) relative to a son. We can estimate this over a number of ages since we have estimates of the wages of children by gender, but to be the most concrete, we should estimate it for younger ages when children are more likely to stay in the home and a time horizon that is short enough to represent the time horizon that parents can be said to be reasonable about.

If one had information on individual child earnings (and the age and sex of the child), a simple age profile based on each child's age and earnings could be constructed from an equation such as

$$y_i = \sum_{n=0}^{4} \left[\alpha_n age_i^n \right] + \varepsilon_i \tag{11.13}$$

where income would be a polynomial function of age. One could add a term that would designate the gender of the child in the household to capture potential gender differentials as well. Since the income from children is pooled and it is impossible to assign income from the data itself, I aggregate the right-hand side of Eq. (11.13) since child income is aggregated in the data. Further, I adopt a method that allows us to estimate earnings profiles for each gender in one procedure. I gauge the income of young men and women in the following specification:

$$\text{ChildIncome}_i = \sum_s \left[\sum_{n=0}^{4} \alpha_{n_s} age_{s_i}^{n} \right] + \varepsilon_i \tag{11.13}$$

where child income is regressed on a polynomial aggregated for the ages of all children in the household above the age of 12, with separate coefficients for each sex.[25] The estimated α's are then used to generate an income profile for young men and young women.

Table 11.7 lists the earnings of boys and girls at selected ages. From the table two facts are clear. Firstly, the earnings of young boys and young girls were similar, but the earnings of young men grew faster with age than the earnings of young women. For example, 15-year-old young women earned 80% of what 15-year-old young men earned, but by the age of 20, young women earned only 70% of what young men earned. In a broad sense, this result agrees with Goldin's (1980) observation that the earnings of young women peaked faster than the earnings of men. Secondly, the earnings of young men in the household were substantially lower than the earnings of men of the same age who are heads of their household. This implies that the earnings of men were also a function of the head of household status at the time.

By industry, the results show marked differences. As expected, families in textiles had very similar earnings, but in metalworks the earnings gap by gender was quite large, with boys earning several times what girls earned. This is entirely consistent with the notion that young women in iron and steel households could only secure employment in very low-paying jobs. Also note, however, that the earnings at very young ages were low for both boys and girls in metalworks but that by age 20 young men earned significantly more than the average 20-year-old man living at home, but less than the average 20-year-old man who was the head of his household.

We can turn to other sources to confirm a portion of these wage results. I used data from the "Report on Women and Child Wage Earners" report collected by Goldin (1980). The data comes from the *Report on Condition of Woman and Child Wage-Earners in the U.S. in 19 Volumes*, Vols. 86–104 (1910, 1911). Goldin's sample of women and child wage earners contains information on the individual wages,

[25] Note that both males and females have different intercepts and coefficients on the age terms, so that the two profiles are allowed to be as independent as possible in this specification. Specifications with age minimums of 9, 10, and 11 were also specified, and the income profiles were robust to the age cutoff. There is little narrative evidence that children below the age of 10 worked outside of the household in the USA at the time, and the vast majority who entered the workforce did so around the age of 12 or shortly thereafter.

Table 11.7 Estimated annual earning of children by gender, 1888 Cost of Living Survey

Age	Whole sample (N = 6809)		Metalworks (N = 1568)		Textiles (N = 3043)	
	Male	Female	Male	Female	Male	Female
13	36.17	30.95	8.33	1.09	54.91	54.38
14	80.09	59.04	29.73	9.30	100.35	89.88
15	117.43	82.82	70.29	16.54	136.38	119.23
16	148.68	102.67	120.34	22.82	164.27	143.03
17	174.35	118.99	171.71	28.13	185.24	161.87
18	194.89	132.13	217.76	32.49	200.39	176.30
19	210.77	142.45	253.40	35.92	210.75	186.83
20	222.45	150.27	275.06	38.45	217.25	193.97
21	230.36	155.91	280.67	40.12	220.73	198.20
22	234.94	159.66	269.74	40.98	221.94	199.95
23	236.60	161.82	243.25	41.08	221.56	199.64
Estimated annual earnings of male household head, 1888 Cost of Living Survey						
Age	Whole sample		Metalworks		Textiles	
18	409.24		481.18		349.71	
19	425.62		485.60		361.98	
20	441.35		491.27		373.64	
21	456.37		498.01		384.65	
22	470.65		505.64		395.01	
23	484.16		513.99		404.68	

Notes: Author's calculation based on 1888CEX. See the text for an explanation of the income estimation procedure for children

schooling, household structure (although not by age and sex), and retained earnings for over 3000 women and children employed in the cotton textile and clothing industries in New York, Massachusetts, Illinois, and North Carolina collected in 1907.[26] As the sample pertains to women generally but to males only for children, I restricted the sample to those below the age of 17 (the age of the oldest males in the sample; this resulted in a sample size of 1485) and estimated the log wages of the children as a function of age, sex, literacy, and household structure (the number and earnings of other household members). These wage regressions show that the coefficient on sex was statistically indistinguishable from zero, which would be consistent with the wage profiles generated here from the aggregate child earnings data for textile workers.[27]

Using the wage profiles of the 1888CEX, I calculate the wage ratio (boy/girl) for ages 13–14 and 13–17. Table 11.8 lists the results. The relative probabilities suggest that boys were around 30% more likely on average, according to their parents, to leave (not cooperate) as their daughters if parents viewed the probability-weighted

[26] For a full description of the data, see Goldin (1980).

[27] The regression coefficient on sex was −0.003 and the standard error was 0.004. This would imply a small (but statistically insignificant) penalty for females in textiles, which is consistent with the wage profiles from the 1888CEX.

Table 11.8 Relative male/female wages by age, 1888 Cost of Living Survey

Age	Whole sample (N = 6809)	Metalworks (N = 1568)	Textiles (N = 3043)
13	1.17	7.61	1.01
14	1.36	3.20	1.12
15	1.42	4.25	1.14
16	1.45	5.27	1.15
17	1.47	6.10	1.14
18	1.47	6.70	1.14
19	1.48	7.05	1.13
20	1.48	7.15	1.12
21	1.48	7.00	1.11
Average	1.42	6.04	1.12
13–14 Average	1.26	5.40	1.06
13–17 Average	1.37	5.29	1.11
Ratio of males to females by age group, 1888 Cost of Living Survey			
0–4	1.000	1.034	1.045
5–9	1.030	1.045	0.994
10–14	1.098	1.133	1.026
15–19	0.740	0.557	0.764
20–24	0.439	0.457	0.432

Notes: Estimates of relative male/female wages by age from top portion of the table are derived from the income estimates presented in Table 11.7. The ratio of males to females by age group is based on author's calculations based on 1888CEX

wages as equal.[28] In metalworks the probability is more than five times greater, while in textile families it is lower, only around 10%.

It is important to note that forward-looking hedging was a very real feature of industrial households at the time. In fact, it explains the degree to which the household political economy would change when children began to work outside of the home. Parents were willing to make concessions, in part, because they needed the income of the children, but also because they understood that the threat of their children leaving the home was very real. Even in the comments of the 1888CEX, there are notes that older sons had abandoned the family or no longer contributed to the home. Parents had to take this into account the distinct possibility of noncooperation when planning on the future income to the household that would be provided by children. Table 11.8 also shows the ratio of boys to girls in age groups. As the table shows, boys began disappearing from the household in the mid-teens. By these calculations, boys 15–19 were 25% more likely to leave the household than girls and more than 50% more likely to leave the household by the age of 24. Young men in metalworks families were much more likely to leave home than young

[28] An important caveat here is that once the wages were realized and the child chose to stay in the home, consumption could increase, and total household welfare could improve. Parents could not guarantee this, however, because of the inability to form contracts and agreements with children (Becker 1991).

women, entirely consistent with their higher earnings. Young men in textiles were less likely to leave home, consistent with their lower earnings.

How reliable are these estimates for leaving home? These estimates suggest that young men in industrial households left home at relatively early ages, certainly earlier than the ages produced by other scholars. In general the age at leaving home declined from the mid-20s in the mid-nineteenth century to the early 20s in the early twentieth century, but it is not clear how the age of leaving home varied by other factors.[29]

There are three confounding factors that should temper our desire to label this estimate an "age" of leaving home. The first is that the 1888CEX is not broadly representative of American households at the time. Indeed, we can only say that it is representative of households whose head was employed in the nine industries targeted in the original survey. Haines (1979) compared the age of household heads in the 1888CEX to the age of household head from the Census and found broad, general agreement. Modell (1978) also confirms the representativeness of the 1888CEX in this regard. It does appear, then, that the 1888CEX is representative of families employed in the selected sectors. The second factor is that this estimate is not one for an age at leaving home—it calculates the sex ratio as a function of age. Certainly some of the estimate could be due to mortality differentials by gender and sampling error, where working sons may be underrepresented. Third, absence from the home cannot (and should not) be taken, on its own, as noncooperation. For example, children who leave home earlier may have contributed more to the household's coffers while in residence. While this relative probability estimate is consistent with the arguments made here, it is not the only possible explanation. As a partial confirmation, however, the rates for leaving home reported here are also consistent with Horrell and Oxley's (1999) estimates for England in the late nineteenth century, which is based upon a British sample of the same industries. As such, as a relative probability, there is some independent support for these estimates.

11.5.2 Retained Earnings and Nonwage Benefits

Parents may treat children equally despite their unequal earnings, if the wages retained by parents were equal. If sons kept a larger portion of their income than their sisters, the additional income into the household's coffers could be equal (or nearly so). In fact, parents may be forced to let the higher-earning child retain more of their earnings if that would keep the child in the household. Parents may have been forced to provide incentives to work or make concessions in the way that Moehling (2005) and Tuttle (1999) describe to keep children contributing (cooperating) in some way. The percentages reported in Table 11.6 would also refer to the

[29] Steckel's (1996) estimates for the mid-nineteenth century (age 25 for males) are much higher than Gutmann and Pullman-Pinon's (2002) estimates (age 22 for males).

percentage of income that boys were able to retain.[30] There is narrative evidence that suggests that boys were allowed to keep a larger share of their earned income than girls. Ewen notes that:

> Boy children, in general, were allowed greater access to social life outside of the domain of family life than girl children...In a study of Italian working class life, the social workers observed that "it was assumed as a matter of course that the girl's pay envelope should be turned over to the mother intact," because "it wouldn't look nice to pay board to the mother who raised you...while the question as to whether the brothers also contributed everything to the home received the answer, 'Oh no, he's a boy.'" (Ewen 1979, p. 131)

Woods and Kennedy (1913) note the same phenomenon. This speaks to the fact that parents did treat their children differently once they began working, but perhaps out of necessity. Allowing the son more freedom may have been the only way to keep sons, and their earnings, in the household, while parents had the additional aid of social norms and taboos to coerce daughters to cooperate. More (1907) finds that treatment differentials by gender were quite common.[31] Chapin (1909) also documents how daughters were expected to contribute all of their earnings to the household coffers, while sons after adulthood would pay only board. In some households, the income of daughters was blindly turned over to the female head.[32]

There is historical data that allows us to look at this issue in finer detail. Returning to the Goldin data that was used to estimate the gender wage differential for children in textiles, we can see if children in textiles would retain different amounts of their earnings as we see that their wages were similar. In regressions for the log of retained earnings on age, sex, family size, and household earnings (once again restricting the sample to those below the age of 17), the coefficient on sex was not statistically distinguishable from zero, so young women in textiles did not retain less than their brothers, who were earning similar wages.[33] This would be entirely consistent with children retaining the same portion of their wages conditional on the wages themselves. The wage earnings received by parents were the same.

We can also address the issue of remittances, somewhat, from a different sample of the same Goldin data. The Goldin data also contains a sample of more than 1300

---

[30] That is, on average, boys could retain 30% more of their earnings than their sisters, assuming daughters gave all of their income to their parents.

[31] "It is the general custom for all boys and girls between 14 and 18 to bring pay envelopes to the mother unopened, and she has the entire disbursement of their wages, giving them from $0.25 to $1. a week spending-money, according to the prosperity of the family. After they are 18, the boys usually pay board of $4.–$8. a week, according to their wages...The girls are not usually boarders until they are over 21, and then they pay from $3. to $6 a week to their mothers. In some cases they continue to give all their wages to their mother, who supports them until they are married" (More 1907, p. 87).

[32] "Few Jewish daughters considered their wages their own; rather they understood them to be part of the family fund...And Nettie Licht, who began working as a milliner in 1910, faithfully gave her pay envelope to her parents without even bothering to open it...Many other Jewish daughters did the same: as one 1916 report noted, the majority of women in the New York shirtwaist factories gave their "untouched and unopened" pay envelopes to their parents" (Glenn 1990, p. 84).

[33] The coefficient on sex in the retained earning regression is −0.029, with a standard error of 0.114.

young women who were living at home in New York City and a sample of nearly 400 young women who lived apart from their families in New York City and Philadelphia.[34] In both instances the young women were employed in either stores or factories. Regressions of contributions to family members on the characteristics of these women show that, even controlling for rent and for transportation costs for young women who lived apart from their families, women apart their families contributed less than half of what women who lived with their families did.[35] This would be consistent with the narrative evidence that parents took pains to keep their daughters in the home because it resulted in more resources for them.

11.6 Conclusion

Rather than allocating more resources to the children who would earn more in the labor market or more resources to children who would earn less in the labor market, parents chose to allocate resources equally to both genders in the late nineteenth century. Theoretical models of the household allow us to discern the motivations behind this allocation strategy. Namely, the gender equity in resource allocation was not altruistic or egalitarian. Pure economic altruism would predict that parents would allocate more resources to the child who would earn less, and egalitarianism would predict that parents would allocate resources equally, but even when doing so they could increase their own consumption more when young boys were present in the household, and that has been rejected as well. The elimination of altruistic or egalitarian motives implies that parents were strategic. Parents treated children of different genders equally because, in the probabilistic setting, the future higher earnings of boys were offset by their higher probability of leaving the household. This explanation is also consistent with parents letting boys keep a larger share of their earnings and letting boys have more freedom and/or fewer responsibilities in the household. Each of these possibilities is supported by the narrative record. Parents were forced to treat children of different genders equally as young children because of an uncertain future. Parents knew boys would earn more than girls, but they also knew that boys could leave the household behind—the net result was gender equality in household allocations.

[34] These women are noted as being "adrift."

[35] This was estimated in two ways. First, I regressed the log of the wage on the contributions to family members, age, and experience. For women at home, the coefficient on contributions was 0.47 (0.03), while for women adrift it was 0.147 (0.03). I also regressed the log of contributions to family members on the log of earnings, age, and experience. These can be interpreted as elasticities, which would estimate for every percent increase in income what portion was contributed to the family. For women at home, the coefficient for the log of earnings was 0.924 (0.033), while for women adrift it was 0.492 (0.117). For women away from home, regressions also included education, board payments, and transportation costs—exclusion of these variables results in lower coefficient estimates for women away from home.

An important caveat is that the theory used here is static, yet many of the conclusions depend on dynamic parental decision-making. While it would appear to cause a problem, the results here agree with work by Mazzocco (2007) who finds that household members cannot commit to future allocation decisions, which is what parents and children could not do here.[36] These cooperation-related explanations agree not only with the gender equity result but also with the efficiency result. Ex ante, if parents and children were able to enter into an agreement before children entered the labor market, where parents agreed to give children a larger share of their income in exchange for children agreeing to stay in the household for a given time, both parties could have been better off. The reality is that parents had to make allocation decisions before the children made the cooperation decision, a decision made with uncertainty about future cooperation. Gender-neutral allocations were not efficient ex post, but were efficient ex ante.

Appendixes

Appendix A: Reflection on Murray

I first met John at meetings of the Economic History Association as an assistant professor. I had heard about him before then because my colleague Rick Steckel had referred to him often as the best student he had ever had. When I met John, I was struck by his intellect and his kindness, and I always looked forward to seeing him at the EHA or Social Science History Association meetings. When I was visiting at the University of Michigan, John invited me down to Toledo to give a seminar. It was at dinner where we discussed the paper in this volume, and John shared insights from his work that were quite important to how I came to think about this project. To this day, it is the longest dinner I have had after a seminar, and it was because of John's humor and the amazing conversation we had. John's recollection of data, conceptual frameworks, and models around the issues of household allocation, children as breadwinners, and the role of social norms and gender in parental decisions was powerful. When John moved to Rhodes, I remember filling him in on the great BBQ places that he could enjoy now that he was in the capital of the industry!

[36] Duflo and Udry (2004) and Ligon (2002) are recent attempts to analyze the intertemporal implications of the collective model. Formally testing the implications of the dynamic collective model (as in Mazzocco) requires the use of panel expenditure data that is unavailable in the historical record.

Appendix B: Expenditure Equivalent Ratios

The choice of adult goods and the test of efficiency are subject to numerous criticisms. For example, it is unclear if husband's and wife's clothing precludes the clothing expenditures of adult children, who could (presumably) fit and wear their parents' clothing. Similarly, the efficiency test was not particularly powerful, even in its conservative form, because of the large standard errors of the sharing rule derivative quotient. We would like additional information to strengthen the selection of adult goods and the efficiency results. Fortunately, such information exists. We can estimate expenditure equivalent ratios, which measure the percent change in per capita expenditure that would induce the same increase or decrease in expenditure on a particular adult good as an additional child of a certain age and gender. For example, an expenditure equivalent ratio for alcohol for a female aged 0–4 of −0.32 would tell us that per capita expenditure would have to decrease by 32% to induce the same change in alcohol demand as the presence of a girl aged 0–4 does. More precisely, the expenditure equivalent ratio for good *j* and demographic category *c* is[37]

$$\pi_{jc} = \frac{\partial q_j / \partial n_c}{\partial q_j / \partial x} / \frac{x}{n}. \tag{A1}$$

The expenditure equivalent ratio serves two purposes. If good *j* is an adult good consistent with the definition given earlier, then the expenditure equivalent ratio should be the same for all goods since it measures the derivative of the sharing rule (by Eq. 11.8). If gender equality holds, then the ratios will be equal by gender at particular ages. Variation of expenditure equivalent ratios between different goods would tell us if the variances of the sharing rule were spurious or reflected the true variances in the adult expenditure categories. As such, the ratios not only tell us which goods should be considered adult goods, but they serve as a robustness check on the gender neutrality and efficiency results.[38]

Table A1.1 shows the expenditure equivalent ratios for all households and households in metalworks and textiles separately. While the presence of children generally would result in lower per capita expenditures to achieve the same effect as the presence of a child, this is not always the case. Tobacco and alcohol consumption expenditure equivalent ratios suggest that children have the effect of increasing

[37] Calculation of the expenditure equivalent ratios is done by $\pi_{jc} = \frac{(\eta_j - \beta_j) + \gamma_{jc} - \sum_k \gamma_{jk}(n_k / n)}{\beta_j + w_j}$, where the means of the budget shares and demographic variables are used. See Deaton (1997) for calculation of the standard errors of expenditure equivalent ratios.

[38] One could argue that the efficiency result is due to the sharing rule being "unidentified." There is nothing in the theory, however, which allows us to distinguish "spurious" estimates of the sharing rule with "minimum variance" estimates. The use of the expenditure equivalent ratios here is a partial solution—if the variances of the sharing rule in Table 5 actually reflect variance in the underlying demand with respect to household composition, then the expenditure equivalent ratios will vary as well.

Table A1.1 Expenditure equivalent ratios, 1988 Cost of Living Survey

Whole sample (N = 6809)								
	Tobacco	Liquor	Husb Cloth	Wife Cloth	Religion	Charity	All Adult	4 Adult
Male 0–4	1.856	0.302	0.896	−0.730	−2.023	−0.442	−0.005	0.265
Female 0–4	1.771	0.015	0.921	−0.722	−1.855	−0.460	−0.061	0.180
Male 5–9	1.385	−0.086	1.028	−0.802	−3.608	−0.235	−0.268	0.140
Female 5–9	1.275	0.284	0.922	−0.922	−3.634	−0.227	−0.235	0.181
Male 10–14	1.481	0.711	1.269	−0.535	−3.604	−0.192	0.091	0.558
Female 10–14	1.348	0.858	1.272	−0.626	−3.393	−0.259	0.121	0.572
Male 15–19	0.838	1.016	1.627	−0.125	−2.706	−0.230	0.443	0.865
Female 15–19	1.481	0.217	1.712	−0.219	−1.715	0.029	0.369	0.643
Male 20–24	0.495	−0.200	0.578	−0.619	−12.153	0.060	−1.293	−0.034
Female 20–24	1.927	0.946	1.900	−0.240	−6.628	0.140	0.126	0.953
Metalworks (N = 1568)								
	Tobacco	Liquor	Husb Cloth	Wife Cloth	Religion	Charity	All Adult	4 Adult
Male 0–4	2.087	0.495	−0.457	−0.569	−1.233	0.373	−0.218	1.596
Female 0–4	1.917	0.423	−0.397	−0.419	−1.166	0.297	−0.310	1.389
Male 5–9	0.798	0.404	−0.524	−0.499	−1.621	0.610	−1.027	1.207
Female 5–9	0.789	0.534	−0.777	−0.752	−1.578	0.483	−0.705	1.533
Male 10–14	1.451	0.627	−0.180	−0.197	−1.603	0.706	−0.135	2.243
Female 10–14	2.118	0.647	−0.002	−0.260	−1.599	0.521	−0.024	2.380
Male 15–19	0.147	0.591	−0.178	−0.119	−1.395	0.800	−0.008	2.076
Female 15–19	0.855	0.277	−0.016	−0.295	−1.110	0.769	−0.580	0.958
Male 20–24	0.778	0.133	−0.667	−0.550	−3.577	0.639	−4.383	0.159
Female 20–24	1.545	0.448	0.012	−0.063	−2.545	0.811	−1.789	1.689
Textiles (N = 3043)								
	Tobacco	Liquor	Husb Cloth	Wife Cloth	Religion	Charity	All Adult	4 Adult
Male 0–4	1.406	−0.107	1.524	−0.661	0.715	0.489	0.643	0.634
Female 0–4	1.472	−0.467	1.665	−0.669	0.488	0.749	0.615	0.637
Male 5–9	1.336	0.080	1.935	−0.752	0.794	0.456	0.792	0.807
Female 5–9	1.267	−0.210	1.901	−0.835	0.817	0.435	0.709	0.698
Male 10–14	0.953	−0.075	2.119	−0.532	0.670	0.631	0.833	0.878
Female 10–14	1.012	0.234	2.019	−0.600	0.843	0.532	0.858	0.877
Male 15–19	0.758	−0.156	2.406	−0.062	0.581	0.140	0.996	1.127

(continued)

Table A1.1 (continued)

Whole sample (N = 6809)								
	Tobacco	Liquor	Husb Cloth	Wife Cloth	Religion	Charity	All Adult	4 Adult
Female 15–19	1.088	0.673	2.580	0.035	0.594	0.068	1.245	1.445
Male 20–24	0.504	0.233	1.388	−0.644	0.117	0.588	0.439	0.504
Female 20–24	1.182	0.618	2.639	−0.403	0.333	0.621	1.121	1.319

Notes: The calculation of expenditure equivalent ratios is given in the text of Appendix 2. Expenditure equivalent ratios for metalworks and textiles are based on separate regression for those samples

expenditure on these items, some by significant percentages.[39] As the table shows, there is marked variation of the expenditure equivalent ratios by goods and even for the same good by different samples. We should expect some variation between individual households and also between households employed in different industries, but it is not clear whether this is "too much" variation. This type of variation by adult good is consistent with other estimates of expenditure equivalent ratios, both contemporary and historical (Deaton 1997; Horrell and Oxley 1999).[40] Given such marked variation, we should expect the standard error to be large for the sharing rule derivative quotient, as it was in the bootstrapping procedure. Consistent with the gender neutrality finding, the expenditure equivalent ratios are very similar for males and females of the same age group.[41] Overall, the expenditure equivalent ratios confirm the gender neutrality of allocations and the underlying variability of the sharing rule for specific goods.

References

Angus DL, Mirel JE (1985) From spellers to spindles: work force entry by the children of textile workers, 1888-1890. Soc Sci Hist 9:123–142

Becker GS (1991) A treatise on the family, Enlarged edn. Harvard University Press, London

Behrman JR (1997) Intrahousehold distribution and the family. In: Rosenzweig MR, Stark O (eds) Handbook of population and family economics. Elsevier, Amsterdam, pp 125–187

Blundell R, Browning M, Crawford IA (2003) Nonparametric Engel curves and revealed preference. Econometrica 71(1):205–240

[39] Note that these adult good expenditures are (on average) a small percent of the budget—tripling expenditures on tobacco would still imply that tobacco was less than 5% of the household budget.

[40] Horrell and Oxley (1999) use age categories of 0–4, 5–14, 15–54, and 55+. Given the focus on the allocations to young children here, the 5-year categories to the age of 25 are used.

[41] It is important to note that the regressions used to estimate the expenditure equivalent ratios are done so with an estimate of $\hat{\theta}$, so the ratio acts as an additional robustness check of gender neutrality with the inclusion of the sharing rule in the demand equation.

Blundell R, Chiappori P, Meghir C (2005) Collective labor supply with children. J Pol Econ 113(6):1277–1306
Browning M, Bourguignon F, Chiappori P, Lechene V (1994) Income and outcomes: a structural model of intrahousehold allocation. J Pol Econ 102(6):1067–1096
Carter SB, Savoca E (1991) Gender differences in learning and earning in nineteenth-century America: the role of expected job and career attachment. Explor Econ Hist 28:323–343
Chapin RC (1909) The standard of living among workingmen's families in New York City. Charities Publication, New York
Deaton A (1997) The analysis of household surveys: a microeconometric approach to development policy. Johns Hopkins, Baltimore
Duflo E, Udry C (2004) Intrahousehold resource allocation in Côte D'Ivoire: social norms, separate accounts, and consumption choices. Unpublished manuscript, MIT
Ewen E (1979) Immigrant women in the land of dollars, 1890-1920. Ph.D. Dissertation, State University of New York at Stonybrook
Glenn SA (1990) Daughters of the shtetl: life and labor in the immigrant generation. Cornell University Press, Ithaca
Goldin C (1980) The work and wages of single women: 1870-1920. J Econ Hist 40:81–88
Goldin C (1981) Family strategies and the family economy in the late nineteenth century: the role of secondary workers. In: Hershberg T (ed) Philadelphia: work, space, family, and group experience in the nineteenth century. Oxford University Press, New York, pp 277–310
Gutmann M, Pullum-Pinon SM (2002) Three eras of young adult home leaving in twentieth-century America. J Soc Hist 35:533–576
Haines MR (1979) Industrial work and the family life cycle. Res Econ Hist 4:289–356
Haines MR (1981) Poverty, economic stress, and the family in a late nineteenth-century American city: whites in Philadelphia, 1880. In: Hershberg T (ed) Philadelphia: work, space, family, and group experience in the nineteenth century. Oxford University Press, New York, pp 240–276
Hareven TK, Langenbach R (1978) Amoskeag: life and work in an American factory-city. Patheon, New York
Hoover GA (1985) Supplemental family income sources: ethnic differences in nineteenth century industrial America. Soc Sci Hist 9(3):293–306
Horrell S, Oxley D (1999) Crust or crumb? Intrahousehold resource allocation and male breadwinning in late Victorian Britain. Econ Hist Rev 52:494–522
Ligon E (2002) Dynamic bargaining in households. Unpublished manuscript, University of California, Berkeley
Manacorda M (2006) Child labor and the labor supply of other household members: evidence from 1920 America. Am Econ Rev 96:1788–1800
Mazzocco M (2007) Household intertemporal behavior: a collective characterization and a test of commitment. Rev Econ Stud 74:857–895
McElroy MB (1985) The joint determination of household membership and market work: the case of young men. J Lab Econ 3:293–316
McElroy MB (1990) The empirical content of Nash-bargained household behavior. J Hum Res 25:559–583
Metzker I (ed) (1971) A bintel brief: sixty years of letters from the lower east side to the Jewish Daily Forward. Doubleday, Garden City
Modell J (1978) Patterns of consumption, acculturation, and family income strategies in late nineteenth-century America. In: Hareven T, Vinovskis M (eds) Family and population in nineteenth century America. Princeton University Press, Princeton
Moehling C (2005) 'She has suddenly become powerful': youth employment and household decision making in the early twentieth century. J Econ Hist 65:414–438
More LB (1907) Wage earners' budgets: a study of standards and cost of living in New York City. Henry Holt, New York
Rotella E, Alter G (1993) Working class debt in the late nineteenth century United States. J Fam Hist 18:111–134

Salmon LM (1906) Progress in the household. Houghton Mifflin, New York
Salmon LM (1911) Domestic service. Macmillan, New York
Smith DS (1994) A higher quality of life for whom? Mouths to feed and clothes to wear in the families of late nineteenth-century American workers. J Fam Hist 19:1–33
Steckel RH (1996) The age at leaving home in the United States, 1850-1860. Soc Sci Hist 20:507–532
Streightoff FH (1911) The standard of living among the industrial people of America. Houghton Mifflin, New York
Thomas D (1990) Intra-household resource allocation: an inferential approach. J Hum Res 25:635–664
Tuttle C (1999) Hard at work in factories and mines: the economics of child labor during the British industrial revolution. Westview Press, Boulder
U.S. Department of Labor (2006) Cost of living of industrial workers in the United States and Europe 1888-1890 [Computer File]. ICPSR Study No. 7711. Ann Arbor, MI: Inter- University Consortium for Political and Social Research [distributor]
Udry C (1996) Gender, agricultural production, and the theory of the household. J Pol Econ 104:1010–1046
Woods RA, Kennedy AJ (eds) (1913) Young working girls: a summary of evidence from two thousand social workers. Houghton Mifflin, New York

Chapter 12
Child Labor and Industrialization in Early Republican Turkey

Semih Gokatalay

Abstract The chapter provides a historical survey of child labor in early republican Turkey. Capitalist development and class differences were the two main factors that shaped child labor. Evaluating the Turkish experience of child labor within a broader, international context, the present study argues that capitalist development had an overall adverse effect on working-class children despite the official rhetoric that the nation owed to its children the best that it had to give. The emphasis on the problems of child labor in public speeches and several legal changes notwithstanding, political elites took no comprehensive step to ameliorate the socioeconomic conditions of child laborers.

Keywords Child labor · Industrialization · Urbanization · Capitalism · Labor laws · Income inequality

12.1 Introduction

This chapter considers the reasons for the persistence of child labor in early republican Turkey (1923–1945). Despite legal developments and public debates, child labor did not die out in post-Ottoman Turkey. First and foremost, child labor in early republican Turkey was part of a universal discourse of capitalist development.[1] The

[1] Several studies have claimed that there was no capitalist mode of production in Turkey prior to the 1980s. For a recent example, see Düzgün (2012). The findings in this chapter contradict these assertions. The historical development of child labor demonstrated that Turkey had been integrally part of the universal discussion about capitalism and child labor long before the 1980s.

S. Gokatalay (✉)
UC San Diego, La Jolla, CA, USA
e-mail: sgokatal@ucsd.edu

P. Gray et al. (eds.), *Standard of Living*, Studies in Economic History,
https://doi.org/10.1007/978-3-031-06477-7_12

employment of child labor in large-scale manufacturing facilities began to decrease in the developed world in the late nineteenth and the early twentieth centuries. The decline continued in the interwar period when international organizations, such as the International Save the Children Union, drew attention to child rights on the international scene (Bolzman 2008). The effects of the disappearance of child labor from the workforce, however, were uneven and created a marginalized market for child labor (Cunningham 2000, p. 409; Eichengreen and Hatton 1988, p. 43). In the undeveloped world, too, both politicians and nongovernmental organizations tried to raise public awareness about child labor after World War I (Littell-Lamb 2011). As in the developed countries, the success of such campaigns varied across underdeveloped ones. In the colonies where children were forced to work in plantations and other workplaces, child labor did not cease (Byfield 1997, p. 96; Walters 2016). At the same time, states in the politically independent and economically undeveloped countries attempted to combat child labor. But there were gaps between the visions of governing elites and the expectations of lower-class families. Although governments, for economic and ideological reasons, discouraged families from putting their school-age children to work, many poor families did not send their children to schools so that they could contribute to the family income (Blum 2011, p. 68; Papathanassiou 2004, p. 337; Purs 2004; p. 99; Vergara 2018).

Turkish elites countered the same dilemma as their counterparts in countries that had already integrated into the capitalist world economy as periphery and semiperiphery countries. The Kemalists, ruling elites of early republican Turkey, viewed child labor as a major social problem in need of reform. But the effectiveness of reforms depended on the realities of the Turkish economy and society. Not only was it culturally accepted for Anatolian children to support their families and resist official policies of compulsory education, but a lack of decent work for parents, overweening financial pressures, and disparities between the rich and the poor also helped to sustain the use of child labor in Turkey. As elsewhere, child labor in early republican Turkey was intrinsically associated with poverty and closely related to the power of the working classes. During the period under consideration, workers' organizations were weak, and their influence on political decisions remained limited (Koç 2013, p. 21). The weakness of organized labor contributed to the persistence of child labor in Turkey.

To explore the ways in which class differences and capitalist development affected child labor in Turkey, this chapter consults a wide range of primary and secondary sources. Its empirical backbone is legal decisions, reports sent by provincial authorities to the political center, parliamentary speeches, and local and national newspapers with different political leanings. It argues that an analysis of childhood in early republican Turkey should take the economic and social backgrounds of children into account. It is true that the Kemalist reforms brought many advantages, including compulsory education and the control and prevention of infectious diseases, to Turkish children (Halman 1999, pp. 17–24).[2] Nonetheless, the effects of the reforms were unevenly distributed along social class lines. Many children were in no position to take advantage of the industrialization, subsequent economic growth, and Kemalist reforms. On the contrary, child labor was often necessary to achieve this industrialization. By contextualizing child labor within the discourse of capitalist development, this chapter intends to contribute to the burgeoning field of the history of childhood in modern Turkey.

The remainder of the chapter is chronologically organized and divided into four sections. Section 12.2 deals with child labor in Turkey in the 1920s, with an emphasis on the legacy of the Ottoman Empire, World War I, and the Turkish War of Independence. The mid-to-late 1920s saw the initial efforts by policymakers to control child labor. Section 12.3 explores child labor in the early-to-mid-1930s when both the Great Depression and state-led industrialization encouraged child labor. The same period also witnessed the most serious steps to regulate child labor and workers' rights, exemplified by the enactment of the new labor law in 1936. Section 12.4 deals with the immediate aftermath of the law and the early 1940s when child laborers felt the disastrous effect of World War II in their lives. It discusses the limited implementation of the Labor Law of 1936 and the persistence of child labor. Section 12.5 presents the conclusion that the story of child labor was intimately linked to capitalist development in post-Ottoman Turkey.

12.2 Child Labor in the 1920s

Before a historical analysis of child labor, a definition of child labor should be given. A child laborer in early republican Turkey, as specified in the law, was an individual above the age of 10 (12 after 1930) and under the age of 18. Once a laborer reached age 18, he was considered an adult under the laws. As will be elaborated on in the next sections, despite legal restrictions, many children under the age of 12 were employed. Building on the insights of Georges Kristoffel Lieten, this study makes a distinction between child labor and child work. While the latter "would refer to any type of physical (or mental) engagement done for any purpose," the former "could better be restricted to the production of goods and services, including work in the household, that interferes with the normative development of children" (Lieten 2009, p. 30). Furthermore, this chapter attaches a central place to child laborers in urban centers, ranging from children who worked in factories to shoeshine boys and girls. Children who performed agricultural labor on a seasonal or permanent basis were of secondary importance because of the urban bias of available sources although a large number of children worked in agricultural jobs in a period when mechanization was low (Talas 1961, pp. 85–87). Children who looked

[2] Other studies in the same volume also meticulously demonstrate the multiple ways in which Kemalist reforms benefited Turkish children.

after sheep in the countryside and those who worked for any business owned by their parents were excluded from the analysis due to data availability.[3]

There were three major factors that affected child labor in Turkey in the 1920s: the socioeconomic legacy of the Ottoman Empire, the effects of wars, and the influence of external migration. The integration of the Ottoman economy into the world system drove the capitalist mode of production into more corners of the empire throughout the nineteenth century. The social and economic transformation did not only increase the number of child laborers in factories but also gave rise to the wage labor market for children who involved in domestic work in the closing decades of the century (Araz and Kokdaş 2020, pp. 81–82; Erişçi 1951, p. 7). The series of wars that began with the Italo-Ottoman War of 1911–1912 and the Balkan Wars of 1912–1913 had repercussions for social life, including child labor. World War I worsened the livelihood of child laborers (Fişek 1969; Okay 2007). During the war, government intervention in the business sphere increased, and the government pursued economically nationalist policies. Accordingly, child laborers, predominantly orphans, played an important role in factory and workshop production (Maksudyan 2014, p. 81). State authorities tried to enact new laws to improve the health conditions and ensure the dignity of child laborers (Toprak 1982, p. 306). Nonetheless, the official attempts to find a permanent alternative to child labor met with no success (Velipaşaoğlu 2018, p. 107). On the contrary, the long-standing issue of child labor exacerbated toward the end of the war. More children began to be employed, even outside the empire. For example, the Ottoman government sent hundreds of Ottoman children to its war-time ally Germany to work in German factories (Maksudyan 2016; pp. 141–172). Although the end of the war reduced the severity of child labor, the problem of child labor existed in the remaining Ottoman provinces under the Allied occupation (The Christian Science Monitor, 20 November 1922, p. 7). During the transition from the empire to the nation-state, different forms of child labor, such as domestic workers, persisted.[4]

Even though the use of child laborers can be traced back to the late Ottoman Empire, the prevalence of child labor in the republican period was not merely an expansion of an already long-established practice. The formation of the republic considerably altered the nature of the child labor debate and the importance of child labor for the national economy. Turkish ruling elites propagated children as "the future of the nation" (Libal 2002). The reason behind this emphasis was the depopulation caused by pandemics, scarcity, and wars (Yılmaz 2013). After the wars ended, the male population returned to the land, which decreased the demand for child labor in the countryside. Nonetheless, the poverty of the village life pushed many peasants to seek work in the urban centers in the first years of the republic. In the mid-to-late 1920s, Turkey was integrating into the capitalist world economy as an exporter of raw materials and importer of industrial consumer goods (Boratav 2008,

[3]On the absence of data, see Fişek (1969), p. 63.

[4]Such children "were neither slave nor adopted children" but they "were treated as both slaves and adopted children" in the late Ottoman Empire and early republican Turkey (Özbay 1999), p. 28.

pp. 50–51). Since many peasants sought to complement their agricultural income, instead of finding permanent jobs in urban centers, they worked at factories temporarily, which adversely affected the stability of the labor supply (Akkaya 2008, p. 55; Başbakanlık Cumhuriyet Arşivi [The Turkish Republican Archive] (hereafter BCA), 30.18.1.1.12.61.2, 7 December 1924). The serious shortage of industrial workers encouraged the employment of a higher number of children in factories.

Another major development that increased child labor was international population movements between Turkey and countries around it. As the Ottoman Empire lost most of its provinces in Europe, hundreds of thousands of refugees and immigrants came to the empire in the late nineteenth and early twentieth centuries. After they settled in modern-day Turkey, children had to work in a variety of jobs. While girls mostly worked as domestic workers (BCA, 272.0.0.14.75.24.10, 23 December 1920), boys were encouraged by officials to work as apprentices (BCA, 272.0.0.14.76.25.7, 26 June 1921). Likewise, among the White Russian émigrés in Turkey who had escaped from the Russian Civil War, there were thousands of children and women who had to work (New York Herald Tribune, 15 January 1928, 2). The most influential population movement was the population exchange between Greece and Turkey in 1923. The exchange and the subsequent influx of 350,000–400,000 refugees into Turkey caused a dramatic rise in child labor in the rest of the decade. The immigrants could not set up their stalls and take a job in the immediate aftermath of their arrival in Turkey (Arı 2000, p. 129). The ill effects of the population exchange were evident in child labor as well. Refugee children whose parents could not work and who lost their parents had to work as a survival strategy (BCA, 272.0.0.12.54.133.2, 21 September 1927, 1).[5] As such, internal and international movements of the population played a decisive role in the persistence of child labor in Turkey in the mid-to-late 1920s.

Within this volatile atmosphere, political authorities were seeking remedies for the long-standing issue of child labor. Although a single political party (the Republican People's Party) formed and ran the government in Turkey at that time, the governing elites did not constitute a monolithic block. They can be divided into smaller groups in regard to their worldview and ideological outlook, including their approaches toward the elimination of child labor. As Benjamin Fortna has observed, there were "competing agendas in the political, social, economic and cultural spheres" regarding the child question in post-Ottoman Turkey (Fortna 2016, p. 173). Fuad Umay represented the most expansive program among the progressive members of the party. As MP for the province of Kırklareli from 1923 to 1950, he proposed scores of laws addressing child education, health, labor, and protection (Akın 2000, pp. 55–77). Umay was truly concerned about child laborers, especially those who were forced to work in the informal economy. His speeches in the Grand National Assembly of Turkey tried to focus national attention on the abysmal conditions of children in factories, which he found inexcusable under any circumstances.

[5]The population exchange led to the mass entrance of children into the workforce in Greece as well. For details, see Adamopoúlou (2016).

He urged other MPs to get children out of the workforce (Türkiye Büyük Millet Meclisi Tutanakları [Minutes of the Grand National Assembly of Turkey] (hereafter TBMM), 4 November 1925; TBMM, 9 November 1925).[6] The existence of politicians like Umay illustrates that there was no lack of awareness among political circles regarding children's workplace issues.[7]

The Kemalist ambition to transform Turkey into an industrialized country, however, conflicted with efforts to decrease the number of child laborers.[8] The Law for the Encouragement of Industry in 1927 was a clear illustration of these competing Kemalist objectives. It was an outcome of the Kemalist intention to strengthen the power of local capitalist classes through incentives (Ahmad 2002, p. 96). The desire to encourage capitalist development overshadowed the effort to eradicate child labor even before the state-led industrialization of the 1930s. Some public figures and newspapers favored training of a new generation of workers by bolstering the employment of children and teaching them important life skills by master craftsmen, which would prepare them to facilitate economic growth as adults (İkdam, 23 April 1929, 2).

Beyond question, child labor was not limited to manufacturing sectors. In a petition written to the government in 1929, Abdüllatif Naci [Eldeniz] (MP for the province of Cebel-i Bereket) stated that there were many unaccompanied young boys and girls who had migrated from rural areas to bigger provinces. While some boys and girls were jobless, others worked as carriers, shoeshiners, and street hawkers. He wanted the government to monitor and report on the issue of street children. His main purpose, however, was not the well-being of street children but the rupture that they could cause in the social order (BCA, 30.10.0.0.8.48.6, 20 May 1929). Abdüllatif Naci's emphasis on social order can be placed into the broader context of interwar Kemalism. Kemalist elites evaluated the issue of abandoned children in terms of their nationalist and modernist agenda (Libal 2000, p. 58). As discussed in the next two sections, however, they would not solve the issue of unprotected children. The growing population of neglected children in working-class neighborhoods, even in the heart of the country's capital, can be also connected to the broader development of capitalism in Turkey. Although Ankara, as the political center of Kemalist Turkey, symbolized the modernist aspect of the republic, capitalist development led to the emergence of shantytowns in the city that functioned as a critical supply of labor (Dölek 2019). The uneven capitalist development across Turkey played a key role in the persistence of child labor.

Raising concern among policymakers who were calling for new laws to control child labor in the late 1920s contributed to the enactment of the Public Health Law

---

[6] Umay also played a decisive role in the enactment of laws concerning child labor in the decades that followed.

[7] Another important figure was Emin Sazak (MP for the province of Eskişehir) though he was a political conservative. Sazak complained about child laborers who were quarrying with their bare hands for hours but not compensated for their labors (TBMM, 17 April 1930, 67).

[8] There were 22,684 children under the age of 14 who worked in industrial production in 1927. For details, see Devlet (1969).

in 1930 (T.C. Resmî Gazete, 6 May 1930, Law No: 1593). Articles regarding child labor were a part of the law. Employment of all children under the age of 12 as laborers and apprentices in all kinds of industrial enterprises, such as factories and manufacturing plants, and mining works was prohibited.[9] Girls and boys between the ages of 12 and 16 could not be employed for more than 8 hours a day (T.C. Resmî Gazete, Article 173, 8903). Children between the ages of 12 and 16 could not work after 8:00 PM (T.C. Resmî Gazete, Article 174, 8903). More importantly, the employment of children under the age of 18 in the entertainment industry, including bars, cabarets, dance halls, coffee houses, casinos, and public baths, was prohibited (T.C. Resmî Gazete, Article 176, 8903). At the same time, what types of jobs were unhealthy for children from 12 to 16 years, along with women, was left for a future labor law to define (T.C. Resmî Gazete, 8904). The Public Health Law demonstrated the widespread recognition of the problem of child labor by political elites. Although it was a step in the right direction, there was a divergence between intent and implementation, as discussed in the next section.

12.3 The Labor Law of 1936

Child labor had a central place on the political agenda in Turkey in the early-to-mid-1930s. The Great Depression was the main factor behind its centrality. The international economic downturn had a crippling effect on the Turkish economy chiefly because Turkish exports were hit by the global slowdown in demand, and Turkish agriculture went into steep decline (Pamuk 2014, p. 186). As a result, unemployment rates quickly rose. Confronted by such challenges, the government tried to formulate a new economic policy. As in many states in the undeveloped world, the Global Depression resulted in economically nationalist and protectionist policies in Turkey. The years from 1933 to World War II represented etatism, which brought about the establishment of state-owned enterprises all around the country. Etatism became a crucial stage of capitalist development in Turkey (Boratav 2008, pp. 62–69). As John Rapley (2013, p. 36) put it, "it was in Turkey that one of the boldest early moves into state-led development took place." Nonetheless, state-led industrialization did not generate enough jobs. The political establishment tried to address poverty and the continuing increase in unemployment via a set of populist policies, such as agricultural subsidies. The economic dependence of the government on the capitalist classes, however, limited the scope of populism (Özbek 2003). In a period when male breadwinners were unable to find work and the government struggled to ameliorate social tensions, economic concerns gave a new impetus to political debates on child labor.[10]

---

[9] Enterprises that employed fewer than five laborers, however, were excluded (TBMM, 19 April 1930, 97).

[10] One more time, the Turkish experience was inseparable from wider global trends. To give but one example, rising unemployment among men brought new restrictions on the use of child labor in

In addition to unemployed adults, the education of children heightened the concern over child labor, another point in which one can compare the Turkish experience with the rest of the world. Both in the developed and undeveloped countries, governmental authorities devoted considerable effort to democratize schooling in the interwar period (Benson 2007, pp. 58–59; Goldberg 2004, p 5; Lassonde 2005, p. 161). As elsewhere, the employment of children retarded the growth of literacy in Turkey, which contradicted the developmental and modernist agenda of the Kemalist elite. The Turkish press claimed in the early 1930s that the government was working on a new labor law, which would regulate the education of child laborers. According to reports, the law would prevent children who had not completed their elementary education from being employed in factories (Son Posta, 10 October 1931, 1). Yet, it took until 1936 for a new law to be finalized by the government. Meanwhile, child labor did not tend to decline. On the contrary, in the face of economic crisis, hundreds of children were applying for jobs in factories because households resorted to child labor to cope with job losses by adults. Due to the oversupply of child labor, employers did not struggle to find low-wage child laborers who were willing to work 12 hours a day, even during weekends (Cumhuriyet, 19 January 1932, 5). Regarding such children as a "social problem," Turkish newspapers wanted the government to ensure children enough time to take advantage of their educational opportunities (Yeni Mersin, 21 February 1935, 3).

Although the government aimed to protect children from more strenuous types of work, it often failed to combat illicit forms of child labor. Children were working not only in state-owned facilities, which were relatively safer places, but also in privately owned businesses in which the laws against child laborers under the age of 12 were widely ignored. As child laborers were forced to work long hours in crowded and unhealthy conditions, work-related accidents frequently took place, leading to physical injuries to the bodies of children and causing lifelong psychological disorders. Employers had total control over child laborers whose working days stretched to 12 long hours with no rest. Many child laborers received no more than TL0.10 per day in child-dominated workplaces. Certain newspapers attempted to change attitudes toward child labor and raise public consciousness regarding the treatment of working children. They warned employers about the potential problems of employing children, which led to health-related problems. Girls were uniquely vulnerable as they received little protection from physical and sexual abuse at work. Journalists hoped that the forthcoming labor law would safeguard children from unscrupulous practices and ameliorate workplace abuses (Haber, 21 March 1936, 2).

Both internal and external factors contributed to the birth of the Labor Law. Domestically, the ruling elites tried to avoid potential class conflicts by enhancing the overall status and power of workers and had tried to formulate a new labor law since the mid-1920s (Akkaya 2010, p. 74). The government worked in collaboration

factories and workshops in Greece, one of Turkey's neighbors, as well (Bada and Hantzaroula 2017, p. 19).

with laborers. Official experts consulted with laborers and shaped several articles based on workers' feedback (Belenli 2016, p. 23). Technical advisors and other officials traveled through the country during the preparations for the law, visiting all the factories in the provinces. Their focus was centered around large industrial facilities where they checked on the working conditions of children and women (Yeni Asır, 9 November 1935, 2; Yeni Asır, 20 November 1935, 2). Furthermore, business organizations influenced the government during the preparation of the law (İstanbul Ticaret Odası Mecmuası 7 (1928), pp. 253–255; Ertürk 1934, 12). External developments went hand in hand with internal factors. The International Labour Organization (ILO) had fought against the employment of child labor in industrial sectors since its formation in 1919 and adopted four conventions regarding child labor in other sectors as well in the 1930s (Cullen 2007, p. 2). Turkey joined the ILO in 1932. Turkey's affiliation with the organization accelerated the legislative process for the new labor law.

Inspired by national and international developments, the National Assembly finally enacted the new labor law on June 8, 1936, which specified the rights of all employees in Turkey (T.C. Resmî Gazete [The Official Gazette of the Republic of Turkey], Law No: 3008, 15 June 1936). The law also covered laborers of all ages, dividing them into four major categories: children between the ages of 12 and 16, children over 16 and under 18, female workers aged 18 and over, and male workers aged 18 and over. Every employer was obliged to keep a record of his workers by drawing up separate charts of the categories (T.C. Resmî Gazete, Article 51, 6627). The Labor Law of 1936 further restricted the maximum hours that children could work. Children under the age of 16 were prohibited from working more than 8 hours a day, regardless of work. The goal behind the restriction was to make sure that children could attend schools. The working hours of those who attended the primary school were regulated in a way that would not interfere with the school hours. The course hours were counted within the 8-hour working period (T.C. Resmî Gazete). Violators would be fined from TL10 to TL100 (T.C. Resmî Gazete, Article 110/13, 6635).

The Labor Law also dealt with economic sectors in which children could work. It prohibited child labor in hazardous work environments and criminalized the employment of children in certain forms of labor. The law forbade the employment of boys under the age of 18 and girls and women of all ages, without exception, in underground or underwater jobs, such as mining works, cable laying, sewer, and tunnel construction (T.C. Resmî Gazete, Article 49, 6627). Employers who did not comply with the sectoral restrictions would be fined at least TL25 (T.C. Resmî Gazete, Article 110/14, 6635). Furthermore, children above the age of 12 would be inspected by facility doctors to ensure their physical endurance according to the work to be done. If workplaces had no doctor, governmental and municipal doctors would conduct the inspection (T.C. Resmî Gazete, Article 60, 6629). The Labor Law became effective on June 15, 1937 (İktisat Vekâleti, iii), but it is not easy to detect the immediate effects of the Labor Law across the country. Cunningham and Viazzo (1996, pp. 11–39) have observed that even if laws were sporadically implemented, they still improved the conditions of child laborers. As discussed in the next

Table 12.1 Workers in Aydın, Denizli, and Muğla (1938)

Sector	Number	Female laborers	Male laborers	Child laborers	Total	Child laborers (%)
Textile factory	1	288	1130	448	1866	24
Others	97	360	1201	423	1984	21.32
Cotton factory	47	800	1100	116	2016	5.75
Licorice factory	4	100	241	15	356	4.21
Olive oil factory	45	–	691	–	691	–
Construction	39	–	2311	–	2311	–
Mining	19	6	2665	–	2671	–
Flour factory	13	–	192	–	192	–
Soap factory	4	–	148	–	148	–
Raki factory	4	12	51	–	63	–
Leather factory	2	–	50	–	50	–
Total	275	1566	9780	1002	12,348	8.11

Sources: Aydın, 29 October 1938, 7. The last column was calculated by the author

section, however, the articles about child labor were radical decisions that mostly remained on paper.[11]

12.4 The Aftermath of the Labor Law

Several obstacles stood in the way of enforcing the Labor Law (Avni 1937, 4; Algün 1938, 3–4). The first was the limited power of the government. Governmental authorities faced challenges in enforcing industrial discipline even in public enterprises.[12] Second, the Labor Law did not incentivize employers to hire adults instead of children. As can be observed from newspaper classified ads, employers wanted to hire boys and girls for factories even after the law came into effect (Son Telgraf, 21 September 1937, 8). Third, the distribution of child labor across sectors was uneven. For example, Table 12.1 shows factories in Aydın, Denizli, and Muğla, which were three of the economically most developed provinces in Turkey, in 1938. Most of those working in factories were adult males, but children were working alongside men and women. Child labor was particularly abundant in the textile and other labor-intensive industries.

The implementation of restrictions on working hours was an even more serious problem. Not all employers took maximum hour requirements seriously, and

[11] Turkey was hardly alone in this. For example, as another politically independent country in the interwar Middle East, Egypt did not consistently enforce laws that regulated child labor (*Tribune*, 26 February 1937, 6). For details on Egypt, see Goldberg (2004).

[12] For details, see Arnold (2012).

children had to work long, arduous hours at their jobs in many enterprises (Alkan 1938, p. 79). Aside from employers, the decisions of state officials led to non-compliance with hour restrictions. According to the Labor Law, night work should start by 8:00 PM, not extend past 6:00 AM, and not exceed 11 hours (T.C. Resmî Gazete, Law No: 3008, 15 June 1936, Article 43, 6626). It was forbidden to employ boys under the age of 18 and girls and women of all ages in industrial works at night (T.C. Resmî Gazete, Article 50/I, 6627). If a violation was discovered, employers would pay fines, ranging from TL10 to TL100 (T.C. Resmî Gazete, Article 110/15, 6635). Nonetheless, the articles were not strictly implemented in the following years. The main reason for the loose implementation was actually another article of the Labor Law, which stated that "based on the social and economic necessities," the Ministry of Economy had the right to permit the employment of children at nights for the 4 years that would follow (T.C. Resmî Gazete, Article 50/II, 6627).

The ministry was tasked with enforcing laws and monitoring their violations (Tan, 16 June 1936, 1), but politicians were aware that such far-reaching decisions could not be carried out easily. As a consequence, the ministry used the right and postponed the implementation of the abovementioned article multiple times (Haber, 23 June 1937, 6, Son Posta, 13 June 1940, 3). Although the right was granted for 4 years, the ministry lifted the restriction on night works even after the deadline. In 1941, for example, children above the age of 12, as well as women, were permitted to be employed in the textile industry both during the day and at night (BCA, 30.18.1.2.94.13.1, 18 January 1941).

The persistence of night work and the repeated extensions could be understood within the global context of labor markets in the 1930s. In their study of the textile industry in the southern United States in the interwar period, Martha Shiells and Gavin Wright (1983, p. 332) find a relationship between the common practice of night work and excess labor supplies. One can observe a similar case in Turkey. Unlike the United States, an enormous mass of reserve workers was absent in Turkey, but textile industries were still driving forces of Turkey's industrial strategy in the 1930s. They were dependent on child labor and became one of the main ways that children entered the labor market. As such, although the government restricted the hours during which children were allowed to work, it was the same government that did not enforce overtime regulations and delayed full implementation of the Labor Law.

The poor enforcement of the Labor Law in the late 1930s can be also understood by considering the education of children, more specifically that of orphans. At its Fourth General Congress in 1935, the ruling party had declared its intention to protect orphans (C.H.P. 1935, p. 84). The governing elite, however, confronted several interrelated problems regarding the schooling of orphans and other children from modest backgrounds (Libal 2016, p. 51). Although there were certain individuals who opened orphanages for abandoned children, the state bore the main responsibility of ensuring the educational opportunities of orphaned children. Both local and central authorities offered up various reform plans to employ orphans as child laborers, because, according to the authorities, the presence of jobless orphans inhibited economic development (BCA, 30.10.0.0.178.234.1, 22 March 1937, 22; BCA,

30.10.0.0.178.234.1, 25 March 1938, 28). In official correspondence to the Prime Ministry, Minister of Health and Social Assistance Ahmet Hulusi Alataş requested that the government provide apprenticeship opportunities to orphans over the age of 6 not only to nurture the next generation of Turkish artisans and to help children acquire hands-on experience but also to prevent juvenile delinquency. Alataş wanted municipalities to take care of orphans until the age of 12. Thereafter, the government should employ orphans in state-owned enterprises. Since the Public Health Law in 1930 prohibited the employment of children under the age of 12, however, he desired to change the law to permit the employment of orphans younger than 12 (BCA, 30.10.0.0.178.234.1, 24 June 1939, 1–2). Other top-level politicians, such as the minister of economy and the minister of national education, also wanted both orphans and children of poor families to work to gain experience and develop a work ethic (BCA, 30.10.0.0.174.201.6, 28 May 1940, 6; BCA, 30.10.0.0.174.201.6, 22 October 1940, 1–2). Consequently, along with the profit motivation of private actors, public authorities accounted for the persistence of child labor.

The enforcement of the laws regarding child labor became more troublesome during World War II. The war changed the family structure and drove many couples to divorce, which further increased the number of abandoned children (Metinsoy 2007, pp. 391–422). Although Turkey was able to stay out of the war until its final phase, the advent of the war had an adverse influence on Turkey's society and economy. The war and the subsequent mobilization withdrew hundreds of thousands of men from the labor force in Turkey, especially in the countryside, and accelerated the flow of children into the labor market by opening a growing number of jobs held by adults to children in the city centers (Kazgan 2006, p. 69). The availability of these positions led many poverty-stricken families to pull children from school. Table 12.2 shows that 2,650,000 children aged between 7 and 16 were out of school across the country in 1940. Education was not a viable option for most Turkish children.

Figure 12.1 shows the extent to which children dropping out of school became a nationwide problem in war-time Turkey. But school absenteeism was far more prevalent for children in economically less developed eastern provinces where child marriage was also common. Children rarely completed primary school in these provinces. Moreover, school absenteeism at the primary level was especially common in the rural areas where children rarely had access to education and parents

Table 12.2 The distribution of school-age children in Turkey (1940)

Category	Boys	Girls
The number of children (aged 7–16)	2,040,000	1,710,000
Children who completed elementary schools	148,000	69,000
Children who were currently going to elementary schools	599,000	285,000
The number of students who were school-age but did not continue their education	1,356,000 [66.4%]	1,294,000 [75.7%]

Source: BCA, 30.10.0.0.25.141.1, 22 January 1941, 1–2

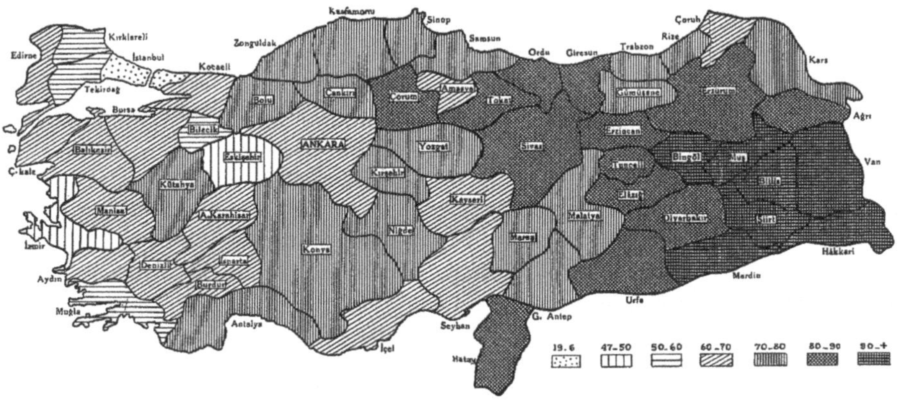

Fig. 12.1 Percent of children who were not enrolled in school in 1940 (%). (Source: BCA, 30.10.0.0.25.141.1, 22 January 1941, 3)

were unwilling to force children to go to school.[13] Even Istanbul, the most developed province of Turkey, suffered from inadequate access to education. One-fifth of children were not in the education system in the province. As war conditions deprived more children of education, central and provincial authorities attempted to take measures to ensure education for "abandoned and vagrant children" in the remainder of the war. Western countries offered a template for Turkey to deal with eradicating child labor through education and professional training (BCA, 30.10.0.0.185.274.10, 16 June 1943, 1–2; BCA, 30.10.0.0.179.236.5, 2 July 1943, 1). Nevertheless, school absenteeism did not cease. Widespread poverty continued to force many children into the workplace, while housework and caring for siblings kept others at home (Cumhuriyet, 9 October 1944, 1).

The war did not only affect child labor quantitatively. The conditions of employment deteriorated for both child and adult laborers as well.[14] As the general trend was toward loosening the restrictions in laws dealing with child labor, the war years left laborers – especially children – with less protection. The diets of child laborers became monotonous and less healthy throughout the war. Even though the government gave cards to state employees and those with flexible incomes to purchase bread, children received significantly less bread than adults even taking body differences between adults and children into account (En Son Dakika, 21 October 1942, 1). While real average earnings decreased for most workers, the government financially supported civil servants via subsidies in order to keep their real income unchanged during the war (Koç 1998, p. 38). Child laborers in particular were not paid the wages they deserved. Although children did the same work as adults in most cases, they earned less than both men and women. For example, a match

[13] Even in the places where schools existed, children could help their families in the field to make ends meet in the rural parts (Balkır 1998, pp. 127–128).

[14] For details, see Nacar (2009).

factory in Istanbul paid men and women an average hourly wage of from TL1 to 1.70 and from TL 0.75 to TL1.10, respectively. Child laborers, however, received an average hourly wage of TL0.65 (En Son Dakika, 1 August 1942, 2). In other words, the government's continued tolerance of child laborers gave employers a golden opportunity to hire two laborers for the price of one on average.

As the state failed to ameliorate the social consequences of the war for child laborers, some concerned officials tried to find ways to eliminate child labor. For example, according to a report written by Lütfi Kırdar, who was both the mayor and governor of Istanbul, desolate and deserted children came mostly from working-class families who fled from Anatolia. In his opinion, a prime factor that fostered migration was the harsh poverty of farm life. Kırdar thought that extramarital affairs, divorce, and mobilization of urban men were the main factors that gave rise to street children and child laborers. There were 2516 street boys and 332 street girls in Istanbul alone in 1943. Kırdar's proposition was not to decrease child labor. By contrast, he presented the employment of such children as a solution to prevent juvenile crime (BCA, 30.10.0.0.179.236.5, 12 April 1943, 2–3). War conditions increased rather than reduced the number of child laborers in formal and informal sectors. According to official statistics, the number of child laborers rose from 23,347 to 51,871 from 1937 to 1943 (Makal 2007, pp. 335–346). Both local and central authorities were desperate to address the root causes of child labor.

12.5 Conclusion

Child labor remained on the agenda of Turkish governments throughout the period under consideration. Legal developments, parliamentary speeches, and press coverage demonstrated a deep awareness of child labor and an aspiration among the elite to remove children from the workforce. Although many public and private figures did not turn a blind eye to the problems of child labor, the political commitment and will of central and local governments to get rid of child labor were insufficient. Regulations to protect child laborers, such as the Labor Law of 1936, were difficult to enforce. The advent of World War II was another major impediment to the intention to eradicate child labor. The war touched the lives of nearly every Turkish child. Aside from those at the top of the social hierarchy, who were relatively sheltered from the destructive effects of the war, a growing number of children from lower-income groups were forced to leave school and work. In effect, even before the war, the government had often rolled back child labor protections and showed no progress in eliminating child labor.

This chapter has made two interconnected arguments. First, an analysis of the drivers of child labor in early republican Turkey reveals that child labor was rooted in income inequality. The harmful effects of the global economic crisis and the war were not distributed equally. The harsh economic and social conditions hit lower-class children particularly hard. The outbreak of World War II and the conscription of thousands of men placed further unique burdens on these children. Child labor perpetuated disadvantages and social exclusion and made class divisions even deeper before and during the war. Second, the scourge and persistence of child labor during this period were related to the development of capitalism. The Turkish experience was similar to other cases in both developed and undeveloped parts of the world. Like their counterparts all around the globe, the Turkish ruling elite saw industrialization as necessary to counter the crippling effects of the Great Depression and promote the general welfare of the people. Although industrialization was incomplete and Turkey did not become a fully developed country, industrial progress decreased Turkey's dependence on Western economies and made Turkey a regional power in the Balkans and the Middle East. Yet, the economic and social conditions of child laborers, especially those who worked in the informal economy and on the night shift, deteriorated in the same period.

Acknowledgments I would like to thank Reuben Silverman for his careful reading and constructive feedback on an earlier version of this chapter. I also thank Gözde Emen for her invaluable comments on different versions of this chapter.

Appendix: Remembrance of John Murray

Unfortunately, I did not meet John E. Murray in person. I began to read his studies when I was an undergraduate student in Turkey. Since then, his scholarly interests in and studies on the history of ordinary people, particularly poor children, have inspired me as a student of economic history. That's why I wanted to contribute to the edited volume by an essay on child labor in early republican Turkey in honor of him and in memory of my grandfathers, both of whom were child laborers in Turkey during the period under consideration.

Bibliography

Primary Sources

Archival Sources
Başbakanlık Cumhuriyet Arşivi (BCA) [The Turkish Republican Archive]
Periodicals
Aydın
Cumhuriyet
En Son Dakika
Haber
İkdam
İstanbul Ticaret Odası Mecmuası
New York Herald Tribune
Son Posta

Son Telgraf
T.C. Resmî Gazete
Tan
The Christian Science Monitor
Tribune
Yeni Asır
Yeni Mersin

Published Primary Sources

Alkan İ (1938) Endüstri İşletme Ekonomisi ve Esas Meseleleri. İstanbul Üniversitesi İktisat Fakültesi, Istanbul
C.H.P. (1935) Dördüncü Büyük Kurultayı Görüşmeleri Tutulgası, 9–16 Mayıs 1935. Ulus Basımevi, Ankara
İktisat Vekâleti (1936) İş Kanunu. Başvekâlet Matbaası, Ankara
Türkiye Büyük Millet Meclisi Tutanakları (TBMM) [Minutes of the Grand National Assembly of Turkey]

Secondary Sources

Adamopoúlou M (2016) To Víoma tis Paidikís Ergasías stous Mikrasiátes Prósfyges tis Thessaloníkis (1922–1930). University of the Aegean, Mytilene
Ahmad F (2002) The making of modern Turkey. Routledge, London
Akın V (2000) Bir Devrin Cemiyet Adamı - Doktor Fuad Umay (1885-1963) Atatürk Araştırma Merkezi, Ankara
Akkaya Y (2008) Kapitalizmin Hapishanelerinde Ödünç Hayatlar - Sınıf Mücadeleleri, Avrupa Birliği, "Küreselleşme". Eksen Yayıncılık, Istanbul
Akkaya Y (2010) Cumhuriyet'in Hamalları İşçiler. Yordam, Istanbul
Algün N (1938) İş Kanunu Birinci Tatbik Yılını Tamamlarken. Türk Akdeniz II(9):3–4
Araz Y, Kokdaş İ (2020) In between market and charity: child domestic work and changing labor relations in nineteenth-century ottoman Istanbul. International Labor and Working-Class History 97:81–108
Arı K (2000) Büyük Mübadele - Türkiye'ye Zorunlu Göç (1923–1925). Tarih Vakfı Yurt Yayınları, Istanbul
Arnold CE (2012) In the Service of Industrialization: Etatism, social services and the construction of industrial labour forces in Turkey (1930-50). Middle East Stud 48(3):363–385
Avni H (1937) İş Kanunu Nasıl Tatbik Ediliyor. Yeni Adam 4(201):4
Bada K, Hantzaroula P (2017) Family strategies, work, and welfare policies toward waged domestic labor in twentieth-century Greece. J Mod Greek Stud 35(1):17–41
Balkır SE (1998) Eski Bir Öğretmenin Anıları. Cumhuriyet, Istanbul
Belenli T (2016) İş Kanunu Layihası (1927) Hakkında İkdam Gazetesi Tarafından Düzenlenen Bir Anket. Cumhuriyet Tarihi Araştırmaları Dergisi 12(23):1–30
Benson SP (2007) Household accounts: working-class family economies in the interwar United States. Cornell University Press, Ithaca
Blum AS (2011) Speaking of work and family: reciprocity, child labor, and social reproduction, Mexico City, 1920-1940. Hisp Am Hist Rev 91(1):63–95
Bolzman L (2008) The advent of child rights on the international scene and the role of the save the children international union 1920-45. Refug Surv Q 27(4):26–36
Boratav K (2008) Türkiye İktisat Tarihi, 1908–2007. İmge Kitabevi, Ankara

Byfield J (1997) Innovation and conflict: cloth dyers and the interwar depression in Abeokuta. Nigeria Journal of African History 38(1):77–99
Cullen H (2007) The role of international law in the elimination of child labor. Brill, Leiden
Cunningham H, Viazzo PP (1996) Some issues in the historical study of child labour. In: Cunningham H, Viazzo PP (eds) Child labour in historical perspective 1800–1985. Case studies from Europe, Japan and Colombia. Istituto degli Innocent, Florence, pp 11–39
Cunningham H (2000) The decline of child labour: labour markets and family economies in Europe and North America since 1830. Econ Hist Rev 53(3):409–428
Devlet İstatistik Enstitüsü (1969) Sanayi Sayımı, 1927. Devlet İstatistik Enstitüsü, Ankara
Dölek Ç (2019) Erken Cumhuriyet Ankarası'nda Emeği Zapt Etmek: Altındağ'da Polisin Toplumsal Tarihi. Mülkiye Dergisi 43(1):63–110
Düzgün E (2012) Class, state and property: modernity and capitalism in Turkey. European Journal of Sociology/Archives Européennes de Sociologie 53(2):119–148
Eichengreen B, Hatton TJ (1988) Interwar unemployment in international perspective: an overview. In: Eichengreen B, Hatton TJ (eds) Interwar unemployment in international perspective. Kluwer, Dordrecht, pp 1–59
Erişçi L (1951) Türkiye İşçi Sınıfının Tarihi (Özet Olarak). Kutulmuş Basımevi, Istanbul
Ertürk S (1934) İş Kanunu Hakkında Manifaturacılar Cemiyetinin Teşebbüsleri Esnaf Meslek Mecmuası 4:12
Fişek K (1969) Türkiyede Kapitalizmin Gelişmesi ve İşçi Sınıfı. Doğan Yayınevi, Ankara
Fortna BC (2016) Bonbons and bayonets: mixed messages of childhood in the late ottoman empire and the early Turkish republic. In: Fortna BC (ed) Childhood in the late ottoman empire and after. Brill, Leiden, pp 173–188
Goldberg E (2004) Trade, reputation and child labor in twentieth-century Egypt. Palgrave Macmillan, New York
Halman T (1999) Çocuk Cumhuriyeti. In: Onur B (ed) Cumhuriyet ve Çocuk: 2, Ulusal Çocuk Kültürü Kongresi: 4–6 Kasım, vol 1998. Ankara Üniversitesi, Ankara, pp 17–24
Kazgan G (2006) Tanzimat'tan 21. Birinci Küreselleşmeden İkinci Küreselleşmeye Yüzyıla Türkiye Ekonomisi. Istanbul Bilgi Üniversitesi, Istanbul
Koç Y (1998) 100 Soruda Türkiye'de İşçi Sınıfı ve Sendikacılık Hareketi. Gerçek Yayınevi, Istanbul
Koç Y (2013) Kemalizm Devrim CHP ve İşçi Sınıfı (1919–1946). Kaynak Yayınları, Istanbul
Lassonde S (2005) Learning to forget: schooling and family life in New Haven's working class, 1870–1940. Yale UP, New Haven
Libal K (2000) The Children's protection society: nationalizing child welfare in early republican Turkey. New Perspect Turk 23:53–78
Libal K (2002) Realizing modernity through the robust Turkish child, 1923-1938. In: Cook DT (ed) Symbolic childhood. Peter Lang Publishing, New York, pp 109–130
Libal K (2016) Child poverty and emerging Children's rights discourse in early republican Turkey. In: Fortna BC (ed) Childhood in the late ottoman empire and after. Brill, Leiden, pp 48–72
Lieten GK (2009) Toward an integrative theory of child labor. In: Hindman HD (ed) The world of child labor - a historical and regional survey. M.E. Sharpe, London, pp 26–32
Littell-Lamb E (2011) Caught in the crossfire: Women's internationalism and the YWCA child labor campaign in Shanghai, 1921-1925. Frontiers 32(3):134–166
Makal A (2007) Ameleden İşçiye. İletişim, Istanbul
Maksudyan N (2014) Orphans and destitute children in the late ottoman empire. Syracuse University Press, New York
Maksudyan N (2016) A triangle of regrets: training ottoman children in Germany during the first world war. In: Fortna BC (ed) Childhood in the late ottoman empire and after. Brill, Leiden, pp 141–172
Metinsoy M (2007) İkinci Dünya Savaşı'nda Türkiye - Savaş ve Gündelik Yaşam. Homer Kitabevi, Istanbul

Nacar C (2009) 'Our lives were not as valuable as an animal:' Workers in State-run Industries in world-war-II Turkey. Int Rev Soc Hist 54(S17):143–166

Okay C (2007) War and child in the second constitutional period. In: Georgeon F, Kreiser K (eds) Enfance et Jeunesse dans le monde Musulman / childhood and youth in the Muslim world. Maisonneuve & Larose, Paris, pp 219–232

Özbay F (1999) Turkish female child labor in domestic work: past and present. ILO/IPEC, Istanbul

Özbek N (2003) Kemalist Rejim ve Popülizmin Sınırları: Büyük Buhran ve Buğday Alım Politikaları, 1932-1937. Toplum ve Bilim 96:219–238

Pamuk Ş (2014) Türkiye'nin 200 Yıllık İktisadi Tarihi: Büyüme. Kurumlar ve Bölüşüm, Türkiye İş Bankası Kültür Yayınları, Istanbul

Papathanassiou M (2004) Aspects of childhood in rural Greece: Children in a Mountain Village (ca. 1900-1940). Hist Fam 9(3):325–345

Purs A (2004) Unsatisfactory National Identity: school inspectors, education and National Identity in interwar Latvia. Journal of Baltic Studies 35(2):97–125

Rapley J (2013) Understanding development: theory and practice in the third world. Routledge, London

Shiells M, Wright G (1983) Night work as a labor market phenomenon: southern textiles in the interwar period. Explor Econ Hist 20(4):331–350

Talas C (1961) İçtimai İktisat. Ajans-Türk, Ankara

Toprak Z (1982) Türkiye'de "Millî İktisat" 1908–1918. Yurt Yayınları, Ankara

Velipaşaoğlu DY (2018) Weaving for war & peace: education of the children in the Hereke factory campus (1912-1918). Cihannüma Tarih ve Coğrafya Araştırmaları Dergisi 4(1):93–129

Vergara Á (2018) Identifying the unemployed: social categories and relief in depression-era Chile (1930–1934). Labor 15(3):9–30

Walters S (2016) 'Child! Now you are': identity registration, labor, and the definition of childhood in colonial Tanganyika, 1910-1950. The Journal of the History of Childhood and Youth 9(1):66–86

Yılmaz H (2013) Becoming Turkish - nationalist reforms and cultural negotiations in early republican Turkey, 1923–1945. Syracuse University Press, New York

Chapter 13
Orphans, Widows, and the Economics of the Early Church

Patrick Gray

Abstract The New Testament describes "religion that is pure and undefiled" as consisting of "care for orphans and widows in their distress." This essay surveys the demography of orphans and widows in the Greco-Roman world and considers how the economic ramifications of these realities in early Christian communities can help interpreters make sense of otherwise opaque biblical texts.

Keywords Orphans in early Christianity · Widows in early Christianity · New Testament, economic interpretations of · First Letter to Timothy (New Testament)

13.1 Introduction

The historical study of economics and religion, as John Murray (2013b) notes, is typically approached from one of two directions. One approach employs economic ways of thinking to understand religious beliefs and behaviors. A second approach examines religious beliefs and behaviors in terms of the influence they have exerted on various economic aspects of the societies in which they are embraced.

This essay falls in the former category and intersects with Murray's own research on the dynamics of life in religious communities and the welfare of women and children (1992, 1995, 2013a; Murray and Cosgel 1998). It takes as a point of departure the New Testament description of "religion that is pure and undefiled" as consisting of "care for orphans and widows in their distress" (James 1:27). I will briefly survey the demography of orphans and widows in the Greco-Roman world before considering how the social and economic ramifications of these realities in early

P. Gray (✉)
Rhodes College, Memphis, TN, USA
e-mail: grayp@rhodes.edu

P. Gray et al. (eds.), *Standard of Living*, Studies in Economic History,
https://doi.org/10.1007/978-3-031-06477-7_13

Christian communities can shed light on otherwise opaque biblical texts, in particular Acts 6:1–6 and 1 Timothy 5:3–16.

13.2 Orphans in the Greco-Roman World

Most present-day languages apply the term "orphan" to children who have lost their parents. In ancient Greece and Rome, by contrast, the term (Gk. *orphanos*; Lat. *orphanus*, *pupillos*, *orbus*) typically denoted a child who had lost either parent. This definition of "orphan" lasted well into the early modern period. More commonly in antiquity, status as an orphan implied the loss of one's father, even if the mother was still living. Shorter life expectancies for males and females alike, due to such factors as malnutrition and poor sanitation, created the conditions in which high numbers of children would lose a parent. Insofar as men married for the first time at an older age than women—perhaps a difference of 7 or 8 years on average (Saller 1987)—fathers would therefore be more likely to die before mothers, all else being equal. Mortality rates for women related to complications from pregnancy and labor were high, while frequent warfare led to higher mortality rates for men. Athens and some other Greek city-states had public programs for the care of war orphans, such as provision for a girl's dowry, but this was the exception rather than the rule (Fitzgerald 2016, p. 37–39). Fewer legal arrangements are found on the books in Rome of the late republic and early principate, where attention was focused on regulation of guardians, many of whom were more interested in expropriating the inheritance of their charges than in seeing to their welfare (Saller 1994, p. 182–189; Miller 2003, p. 30–31).

By their teenage years, it is estimated that over one-third of children in the first-century Roman Empire were fatherless and therefore counted as orphans (Krause 1994, p. 9; Scheidel 2009). Census records suggest that 7 percent of children were "complete" orphans, though Hübner (2009, p. 523-524) suggests the figure was likely much higher. Only 20 percent of children would have reached adulthood with both parents still alive (Saller 2007, p. 91). Orphanhood might be a temporary status in the event that a widow was able to remarry.

Given their ubiquity in the ancient Mediterranean world, it is surprising to see how rarely orphans appear in the New Testament writings. Unambiguous references to orphans are found in only a few passages. Jesus (John 14:18) and Paul (1 Thess. 2:17) use orphan language figuratively to describe the sense of loneliness and abandonment that often arises when the disciple is separated from the master. Only in James 1:27 is there an explicit, if fleeting, mention of the *orphanos*, alongside the widows for whom believers are exhorted to provide care. Yet there are a few other texts in which an ancient reader would naturally assume the presence of orphans. The son of the widow of Nain, whose death is recorded in Luke 7:12, would count as an orphan by the ancient definition, as would the children of the widows in 1 Timothy 5:3–16 (see below). Orphans would also likely have accompanied the widows receiving assistance from the early Christian community as described in Acts 6:1–2. The analogy used by Paul in Galatians 4:1–2 likewise presupposes orphan status for the child under the care of a guardian (Dunn 1993, p. 210–11). Finally, the enigmatic priest-king Melchizedek described in Hebrews 7:3 as "without father, without mother" might also technically qualify, though it appears he never had parents to lose in the first place, since he is also "without genealogy."

13.3 Widows in the Greco-Roman World

Among the consequences of high mortality rates for males was not only a large population of orphans but of widows as well. This partly explains why they are so frequently mentioned together in biblical texts (Exod. 22:22–24; Deut. 10:18; 24:17; 27:19; Isa. 1:17; Ezek. 22:7). Most women in the Roman world would acquire the status of widow (Gk. *chēra*; Lat. *vidua*) at some point in their lives, at least once if not multiple times. At any given time, it has been estimated that 25–30% of all women were widows (Kraus 1994, p. 67–73). Widowhood might be a brief state for some women, but many would have remained without a husband for a considerable length of time before remarriage or death. Because women would often become widows in their early 30s, the image of an elderly woman conjured by the term "widow" for English speakers is somewhat inaccurate. (According to Kraus 1994, p. 68, the age of the average widow was 52.6.) On account of lower life expectancies, elderly women—if "elderly" is reserved for those above, say, 60 years of age—would have been relatively rare.

Women of childbearing age were generally encouraged and expected to remarry. The pressure to remarry could take legal forms, as in the Augustan legislation of the first century that imposed testamentary disabilities on women up to age 50 who remained single (*Lex iulia de maritandis ordinibus*; cf. Saller 2007, p. 91). By age 50, however, the likelihood of remarriage for a widow would have already declined significantly. Remarriage carried no social stigma in the Roman world, yet the ideal in many circles was for a widow to remain single, out of devotion to their deceased husbands. Thus, while widows could suffer from a reputation for being headstrong, busybodies, sexually profligate, and given to drink (Walcot 1991; Kartzow 2005), they could also be idealized as longsuffering exemplars of fidelity, praised in literature and in epitaphs as a *monandros* (Gk.) or *univira* (Lat.) (Rawson 1986, p. 33–34; McGinn 1999, p. 621).

Whereas many widows appear to have enjoyed the freedom from male authority afforded by their circumstances (too much so, in the eyes of many pagan and, later, Christian observers), the burdens imposed would have outweighed this benefit for widows without the means to support themselves. Constant reminders by Greco-Roman moralists to respect and care for the elderly is an indication that the duty was often neglected. There existed very little in the way of a publicly funded "safety net" for the needy. Without property or an inheritance, widows had only their relatives for support. Under Jewish law, the institution of levirate marriage (Deut. 25:5–10) dictated that a widow would come under the protection of the dead husband's relative, who would be expected to father a child to carry on the name of the deceased and inherit his property, in addition to supporting the widow. No such laws were on the books among Gentiles until the second century AD (Parkin 1997). Care for widows remained a feature of Jewish synagogues in the Roman period.

Widows might receive an inheritance from their husbands but were typically dependent on their grown children, who were more commonly favored in their father's will. Having many children was thus considered a blessing. It comes as no surprise, however, to encounter literary and legal discussions of children who refused to meet their responsibility to their mothers or carried out their duties only begrudgingly (Malherbe 2008). Mothers could make use of their minor children's inherited assets (usufruct) in coordination with a legally appointed guardian, when the terms of the will permitted (Grubbs 2002, p. 219–262). Remarriage, however, remained the best solution to the problem of support for a woman left alone by the death of her husband. Widows often needed a dowry to remarry, and some children naturally resented the way in which this would have adverse financial consequences for their own inheritance.

In comparison with orphans, widows appear in the pages of the New Testament with great frequency. The scribes and Pharisees are castigated for "devouring widows' houses" out of greed (Matt. 23:14). In a memorable parable, Jesus tells of a widow who wears down a corrupt judge who finally agrees to take her case, if only to stop her constant complaining (Luke 18:2–5). A number of individual widows past and present are also singled out for their special faith (Luke 2:36–37; 4:25–26). Jesus effusively praises a particular poor widow who, in contributing her last two coins, is more generous than the wealthy (Mark 12:42–43; Luke 21:2–3). Another is comforted by Jesus when he raises her only son from death (Luke 7:12–15). A group of widows likewise accompanies Peter when he raises Dorcas from the dead (Acts 9:36–42). In response to the Corinthians' question about matters pertaining to marriage, Paul counsels "the unmarried and widows" to remain single for the time being, so long as they can control their passions (1 Cor. 7:8–9). Many of these passages presuppose the same precarious status that is reflected in discussions of widowhood in the wider Greco-Roman world (Bremmer 1995).

13.4 Two Case Studies

Orphans and especially widows feature prominently in two New Testament texts that come into clearer focus when viewed through an economic lens: Acts 6:1–6 and 1 Timothy 5:3–16.

13.4.1 Acts 6:1–6

Widows appear in the *Acts of the Apostles*, the first "sequel" to the Gospels chronicling the early days of the Christian movement after the death of Jesus. In Acts 6:1–6, "the Hellenists" (Greek-speaking Jews) complain against "the Hebrews" (Aramaic-speaking Jews) because their widows are being neglected in the daily distribution of food. The numbers of widows in both groups are high enough to merit the immediate attention of the community's leaders. The solution to this inequitable treatment is the appointment of special "deacons" who can oversee these daily affairs, thereby leaving the apostles free to teach and preach the good news about Jesus. Pressures exerted by Augustan legislation on widows to remarry resulted in a situation where the relatively large number of widows in early Christian communities would have been conspicuous. Indeed, the large number of widows and orphans in the church was noted late in the second century by Lucian of Samosata, a satirist, in his account of the charlatan Peregrinus and his conversion to Christianity (*Peregr.* 12). As outsiders sought to understand the nature of this new movement, its attention to widows and orphans led many to think of it as similar to other mutual aid societies found around the Mediterranean (Clark 2004, p. 21). Care for widows had also been a feature of the Jewish synagogue in the first century. Inasmuch as the Christian church in many ways modeled itself on the synagogue as an institution, members and nonmembers alike perhaps assumed that it would perform many of the same functions the synagogue was expected to perform, especially as the earliest members of the movement were almost exclusively Jewish (Winter 2003, p. 27).

The author notes in Acts 6:1 that the internal tensions over the provision of food for widows arose "when the disciples were increasing in number." Sadly, no membership figures are available, hindering any attempt at a precise statistical analysis of the problem. According to Acts 2:41, 3000 people joined the fledgling movement in response to Peter's Pentecost sermon. Most were pilgrims visiting for the Jewish Festival of Weeks (Shavuot) and would have returned to their homes elsewhere. The community of believers at Jerusalem, then, was probably much smaller.

Scarcity of resources surely exacerbated the preexisting tensions between the Greek-speaking and Aramaic-speaking members. Problems of scale also provide the context for understanding the situation in Jerusalem. After Pentecost, the faithful were "of one heart and soul, and no one said that any of the things which he possessed was his own" (Acts 4:32–34). Many landowners sold their property, and with the proceeds "distribution was made to each as any had need" (2:44–45). In addition to shared meals, study, and prayer, this idyllic gathering "held all things in common" (2:43). How long this practice continued is unclear, and historians are divided on the accuracy of this snapshot of the church's early period (see, e.g., Ascough 2000; Capper 2002). From Mikhail Gorbachev, who called Jesus "the first socialist," all the way back to Karl Kautsky and Friedrich Engels, Marxists have long pointed to these texts in support of the claim that early Christianity was a utopia guided by collectivist principles from which it quickly deviated. According to

Acts, however, this experiment in communal living operated on a voluntary basis. There is no demand for the abolition of private property, and when Jesus' disciples are exhorted to give up their possessions, they are to be delivered directly to the poor or to the church for redistribution.

By the time the widows make their appearance—with orphans in tow, if their circumstances were typical—the community has expanded numerically. Whatever system was in place before this growth and however efficiently it may have met the group's needs, it does not appear to have scaled very well. It is a problem that does not get any better with time. Two decades later, the Apostle Paul is still traveling around the Mediterranean, from Turkey in the east through Greece and Italy, with plans to visit Spain in the west, collecting funds to support the community in Jerusalem by collecting charitable gifts from Gentile Christians in the diaspora (Rom. 15:14–32; 1 Cor. 16:1–4; 2 Cor. 8:1–9:15). It is in this context that Paul tells the Corinthians that "God loves a cheerful giver" (2 Cor. 9:7). This relief effort occupies a great deal of Paul's energies over a long period of time, and it stands as a reminder that the church in Jerusalem was destitute. Part of the arrangement with Peter, James, and John in devising a missionary strategy was that Paul would "remember the poor" in Jerusalem (Gal. 2:10). This was a symbolic gesture of solidarity across ethnic and cultural lines intended to strengthen ties between groups naturally inclined to distrust one another, but it also addressed a very concrete need. They appreciated the thoughts and prayers contained in Paul's letters, but they also sorely needed the financial assistance. Judged in purely economic terms, then, this putative experiment in socialism proved incapable of attaining financial self-sufficiency.

13.4.2 1 Timothy 5:3–16

The document known as 1 Timothy is a letter sent by the Apostle Paul to one of his trusted co-workers, Timothy, with instructions on how to oversee a Christian community in first-century Ephesus, one of the largest cities in the Roman Empire. Along with 2 Timothy and Titus, it is one of three documents usually called the Pastoral Epistles because, unlike the bulk of his correspondence which addresses whole groups in the form of an "open" letter, it is addressed to an individual and dispenses advice on stereotypically "pastoral" concerns.

This traditional understanding of the letter has been called into question over the last two centuries. A majority of scholars now consider it to be a pseudonymous composition written perhaps as late as 170 CE, a century after Paul's death. Linguistic, theological, and sociocultural factors play a large role in this consensus. In this reading, a Christian writing in Paul's name seeks to perpetuate the apostle's legacy and bring his authority to bear on circumstances facing the church a few generations after his death. Interpreters who endorse this reading believe the pseudonymous author wants to "rehabilitate" and "domesticate" Paul after his writings have become popular among "radical" Christian sects in the second century. The widows discussed in 1 Timothy 5:3–16 are of particular interest to the author, according to this view, because they represent a dangerously egalitarian cadre of itinerant female missionaries or an ascetic "order" or "office" that threatens the patriarchal structures of the early Christian community by opening up previously closed avenues to power and agency outside traditional gender roles (Davies 1980; Bassler 1984, 2003; Thurston 1989, p. 36–55; Maier 2021).

When one takes proper account of the demographic realities and economic considerations of the implied situation, however, the heuristic value of speculative theories about the motivations of unnamed disputants in a second-century ideological struggle declines. This is not to say that traditional views of authorship, audience, and the like are therefore vindicated in every detail; only that a simpler explanation for the group dynamics and Paul's advice becomes much more viable.

In 1 Tim. 5:3–16, Paul tells Timothy to "honor widows who are really widows." From the following verse describing the religious duty of children and grandchildren as "repayment," it is clear that "honor" (*tima*) here refers to financial support (Winter 1988; later applications of the biblical commandment in Exod. 20:12 to "honor thy father and mother" further illustrate that "honoring" them included caring for them in their old age). In v. 8, family members who do not provide for relatives, especially those of one's own household (*oikos*), are considered "worse than an unbeliever." Widows over the age of 60 and who have been married only once are to be put on a list. Women on this list merit community assistance so long as they have been actively involved in church ministries (e.g., "shown hospitality, washed the saints' feet, helped the afflicted"). Younger widows are to be left off the list, as they are more prone to sensual desires and more likely to remarry, as well as engaging in "idle" pursuits such as gossip. Leaving aside questions about the accuracy of this generalization, it is noteworthy that Paul does not condemn remarriage in the case of younger widows. To the contrary, he encourages widows who have the opportunity to remarry, bear children, and manage their household. Paul concludes his instructions by urging believers to assist those of their relatives who are "really widows" (*hai ontōs chērai*). "Let the church not be burdened," he says, "so that it can assist those who are real widows" (5:16).

The situation provides a fascinating glimpse into the social dynamics of the early Christian movement. Many scholars see here an attempt to regulate a formal "order" of widows exercising an unusual degree of autonomy and thereby to reclaim them for the patriarchal institution of marriage. To be sure, there is some evidence for such a contest over ecclesiastical power early in the second century in the letters of Ignatius of Antioch (*Polycarp* 4.1–3; *Smyrnaeans* 13.1) and at the turn of the third century in the writings of Tertullian (*De virginibus velandis* 9; *De pudicitia* 13). Yet it is certainly not self-evident that this is the only or even the most likely explanation for the specific scenario described in 1 Timothy. A number of economic concepts help in imagining the original context without the distraction of speculative theories.

First, scarcity of resources is a basic fact of life, whether it is the first or the twenty-first century. In an era where government-funded welfare programs and nonprofit organizations attempt to meet a wide range of social and economic needs, it is sometimes easy to forget that the vast extent of these undertakings is exceptional and that scarcity was experienced in a much more immediate way in antiquity than it is in the developed world today. To the modern ear, it may sound cold and heartless to say that a class of needy individuals might have no claim to material assistance. In a hypothetical world of unlimited resources, it would indeed be cruel to deny widows access to the goods and services they need to survive. Many churches today possess considerable wealth yet still lack the resources to accomplish all the good they would like. It does not appear that the church in Ephesus enjoyed the same position as modern churches, nor that its resources would have been sufficient to meet the needs of the widows seeking assistance. This reality is so fundamental that economics has been defined as the study of how to allocate scarce resources to satisfy unlimited needs and desires in the most efficient manner possible. It is also imperative to remember that a "church" (*ekklēsia*) in the first century was a gathering of people and that the term did not denote a building. Separate buildings dedicated to Christian worship do not appear until the third century or later; thus "the church" would not have possessed the property most modern Christian communities have that they might liquidate to meet the needs of the poor in their midst.

Second, due to scarcity, the community's need to confront difficult trade-offs cannot be ignored. As uncomfortable as it may have been, it was essential for the church at Ephesus—a newly founded group without the longevity, stability, or institutional inertia conjured up by the English word "church"—to make an intentional and self-conscious determination about the scope of its financial obligations and, by extension, about the very nature of its core mission. In a very literal sense, here this means recognizing the truth of the adage that "there's no such thing as a free lunch." Daily food distribution to the needy was a feature of the Jewish synagogue in the first century and throughout the rabbinic period (*Bava Batra* 8b). The arrangement reflected in the situation in Acts 6 was modeled on this practice and also demonstrates that limited resources necessitated a hard look at opportunity costs; to wit, if we provide assistance to one individual or group, we will be unable to provide it to another individual or group. Hence the need to formulate a list of criteria for who qualifies for aid from the community chest.

Distinguishing "real" widows from those who, in the author's reckoning, do not qualify as "genuine" widows is critical to this process. This distinction is attended by a paradox, namely, not all women with dead husbands were "real widows," and some women with living husbands, furthermore, could be considered "widows" insofar as *chēra* could often denote any "manless" woman (Barclay 2020, p. 271), as in cases where newly converted women were divorced by their pagan husbands. Setting the age limit at 60 would automatically reduce the number of eligible women considerably, not to mention reducing the number of years for which the church would be responsible for giving aid, though Paul is not likely consulting actuarial tables in arriving at this figure. Once-married women would also, on average, have fewer children or grandchildren on which she might depend for support. Caring for children and nursing the sick are forms of "good works" that demonstrate commitment to the community that has pledged to support them. (It is conceivable but uncertain that such service might have included care for orphans.) When the needy in a city as large as Ephesus are so numerous, it is reasonable that the church would expect reciprocity in this manner. Such a policy would also mitigate what economists call "free riding," when outsiders join simply in order to take advantage of the benefits of membership without making a commensurate contribution to the community (Iannaccone 1992). Those widows who are "idle, gadding about from house to house" (v. 13), are not plugged into the household networks where "the routine benefactions that tie the community together" occur (Barclay 2020, p. 281). Their ability to conduct themselves in this way, not working but not suffering economic privation, may also indicate their relative affluence (Johnson 2001, p. 267).

True financial need is the most important element of the means test spelled out in this passage. Criticism of widows who "live for pleasure" (v. 6 NRSV) accentuates this requirement, though it is obscured in many translations. "Living self-indulgently" (RSV) is a more accurate rendering of the participle *spatalōsa*, which avoids the connotation of sexual immorality and fits better with the immediate literary context highlighting the defining quality of the "real widow, left alone, [who] has set her hope on God" (v. 5). Self-indulgence is not an option for those who are mired in abject poverty. Younger widows have a greater likelihood of rescue from this fate through remarriage. Paul's encouragement of remarriage comports with Augustan social legislation (probably the least of his priorities) while recognizing natural human desires and at the same time acknowledging a legitimate solution to the fiscal constraints experienced by the church. Late in the second century, in *Ad uxorem* Tertullian will argue against remarriage for widows on the grounds that, if wealthy widows remarry, any dowries or legacies in their possession will no longer be available to fund church ministries. This goes against the grain of Paul's instructions in 1 Timothy, but the bottom line is the same in that both Paul and Tertullian are concerned that the church not be unnecessarily "burdened" and thus hindered from assisting real widows. The key difference is that whereas remarriage in 1 Timothy eases the financial stresses on the church, remarriage of wealthy widows in Tertullian's north African context a century later results in lost resources with which to aid the needy (Wilhite 2009).

Third, implicit in Paul's instructions in 1 Timothy is the concept of moral hazard, the tendency of parties insulated from risk to behave differently than if they were not protected from that risk. Incentives matter, and when a group or individual perceives that there is little danger or downside to taking a certain course of action, it is not uncommon to witness riskier or less responsible behavior. Here the parties engaged in moral hazard are the relatives of the widows. They bear much of the brunt of Paul's criticism. In 1 Tim. 5:4, children and grandchildren are to "learn their religious duty to their own family and make some repayment to their parents." Jesus had earlier criticized a spurious loophole in the Ten Commandments by which children could dedicate a portion of their agricultural produce as a sacrifice to the Temple and thereby avoid caring for their parents (Mark 7:9–13). Paul's characterization of this neglect in 1 Tim. 5:8 emphasizes lack of careful planning or calculation in his use of the verb *proneō*, "to think of or take into consideration beforehand" (Marshall 1999, p. 590). Whether out of carelessness or willful avoidance, it is unacceptable. It is another linguistic paradox found in this passage that many of Paul's targets here would technically be orphans, in the sense that anyone—even an adult—whose father had died was an orphan even if the mother still lived. But they are not let off the hook by virtue of their "orphan" status. Failing to provide financial support of parents and placing them on the church's "list" is to neglect a basic religious duty. This framing of the issue distinguishes between the church as the "house of God" (*oikos theou*) and the mundane household (*oikos*) as the basic unity of society, whatever the similarities as expressed in kinship language (e.g., fellow believers as "brothers and sisters"). The two institutions do not serve the same precise functions, even if there is overlap in their missions (Johnson 2001, p. 274).

13.5 Conclusion

The author of 1 Timothy (1:4) states that one of his purposes in writing to his co-worker is to urge him to cultivate the *oikonomia theou* among his followers. To reason, on the basis of a wooden rendering of this Greek phrase, that this text is about "God's economy" would be to commit a version of the etymological fallacy, assuming that the present meaning of a word reveals the meaning of the word from which it is derived. ("Divine training" [NRSV] is a more common translation.) Economic considerations are not a skeleton key unlocking the many exegetical mysteries of this text. For example, the impropriety of a communal welfare program administered by males for the benefit of young, unmarried females lacking any other form of social support or protection should be readily apparent, and economic analysis adds relatively little to our appreciation of the potential for abuse in such an arrangement. As John Murray (2013b, p. 150) has noted, the "a posteriori nature of examining given religious texts through social scientific lenses is inherently *ad hoc*" and in many cases would be more convincing with greater empirical support, if only such quantitative data were available.

Nevertheless, by approaching the scenario in 1 Timothy 5:3–16 with an eye turned toward a few basic economic factors at play, it may be possible to avoid violating the principle of Ockham's razor in elucidating the social and cultural contexts of the situation behind the text. Put differently, when a simpler explanation accounts for the facts of the case, all else being equal, it is to be preferred to a more complicated explanation. Opportunity cost, scarcity, incentives, and moral hazard are hardly the most sophisticated concepts guiding the work of economists, but in the cases considered here, they keep the interpreter from making matters even more complicated than they already are.

References

Ascough RS (2000) Benefaction gone wrong: the "sin" of Ananias and Sapphira in context. In: Wilson SG, Desjardins M (eds) Text and artifact in the religions of Mediterranean antiquity. Wilfrid Laurier University, Waterloo, pp 91–110

Barclay JMG (2020) Household networks and early Christian economics: a fresh study of 1 Timothy 5.3-16. New Testament Studies 66:268–287
Bassler J (1984) The widows' tale: a fresh look at 1 Tim 5:3-16. J Biblic Lit 103:23–41
Bassler J (2003) Limits and differentiation: the calculus of widows in 1 Timothy 5.3-16. In: Levine AJ, Bickerstaff M (eds) A feminist companion to Paul: deutero-pauline writings. T&T Clark, London, pp 122–146
Bremmer J (1995) Pauper or patroness: the widow in the early Christian church. In: Bremmer J, van den Bosch L (eds) Between poverty and the pyre: moments in the history of widowhood. Routledge, London, pp 31–58
Capper BJ (2002) The church as the new covenant of effective economics: the social origins of mutually supportive Christian community. International Journal for the Study of the Christian Church 2:83–102
Clark G (2004) Christianity and Roman society. Cambridge University, Cambridge
Davies SL (1980) The revolt of the widows: the social world of the apocryphal acts. Southern Illinois University, Carbondale
Dunn JDG (1993) The epistle to the Galatians. A&C Black, London
Fitzgerald JT (2016) Orphans in Mediterranean antiquity and early Christianity. Acta Theologica Supplementum 23:29–48
Grubbs JE (2002) Women and the law in the Roman empire: a sourcebook on marriage, divorce, and widowhood. Taylor & Francis, London
Hübner SR (2009) Adoption and fosterage in the ancient eastern Mediterranean. In: Grubbs JE, Parkin T, Bell R (eds) The Oxford handbook of childhood and education in the classical world. Oxford University, Oxford, pp 510–531
Iannaccone LR (1992) Sacrifice and stigma: reducing free-riding in cults, communes, and collectives. J Polit Econ 100:271–291
Johnson LT (2001) The first and second letters to Timothy. Doubleday, New York
Kartzow MB (2005) Female gossipers and their reputation in the pastoral epistles. Neotestamentica 39:255–272
Krause J-U (1994) Witwen und Waisen im Romischen Reich, vol 1. Steiner, Stuttgart
Maier HL (2021) The entrepreneurial widows of 1 Timothy. In: Taylor JE, Ramelli ILE (eds) Patterns of women's leadership in early Christianity. Oxford University, Oxford, pp 59–73
Malherbe AJ (2008) How to treat old women and old men: the use of philosophical traditions and scripture in 1 Timothy 5. In: Gray P, O'Day GR (eds) Scripture and traditions. Leiden, Brill, pp 263–290
Marshall IH (1999) A critical and exegetical commentary on the pastoral epistles. T&T Clark, London
McGinn T (1999) Widows, orphans, and social history. Journal of Roman Archaeology 12:617–632
Miller TS (2003) The orphans of Byzantium: child welfare in the Christian empire. Catholic University Press of America, Washington DC
Murray JE (1992) Communal living standards and membership incentives: the Shakers, 1780–1880. Ohio State University, Dissertation
Murray JE (1995) Determinants of membership levels and duration in a Shaker commune, 1780-1880. J Sci Study Relig 3:35–48
Murray JE (2013a) The Charleston orphan house: children's lives in the first public orphanage in America. University of Chicago, Chicago
Murray JE (2013b) Economic history and religion. In: Whaples R, Parker RE (eds) Routledge handbook of modern economic history. Routledge, London, pp 147–155
Murray JE, Coşgel MM (1998) Market, religion, and culture in Shaker swine production, 1788-1880. Agric Hist 72:552–573
Parkin T (1997) Out of sight, out of mind: elderly members of the Roman family. In: Rawson B, Weaver P (eds) The Roman family in Italy: status, sentiment, space. Oxford University, Oxford, pp 123–148

Rawson B (1986) The Roman family. In: Rawson B (ed) The family in ancient Rome: new perspectives. Cornell University, New York, pp 1–57

Saller RP (1987) Men's age at marriage and its consequences in the Roman family. Class Philol 82:21–34

Saller RP (1994) Patriarchy, property, and death in the Roman family. Cambridge University, Cambridge

Saller RP (2007) Household and gender. In: Scheidel W, Morris I, Saller RP (eds) The Cambridge economic history of the Greco-Roman world. Cambridge University, New York, pp 87–112

Scheidel W (2009) The demographic background. In: Hübner SR, Ratzan DM (eds) Growing up fatherless in antiquity. Cambridge University, New York, pp 31–40

Thurston BB (1989) The widows: a women's ministry in the early church. Minneapolis, Fortress

Wilhite DE (2009) Tertullian on widows: a north African appropriation of Pauline household economics. In: Longenecker BW, Liebengood KD (eds) Engaging economics: new testament scenarios and early Christian reception. Grand Rapids, Eerdmans, pp 222–242

Winter BW (1988) Providentia for the widows of 1 Timothy 5:3-16. Tyndale Bulletin 39:83–99

Winter BW (2003) Roman wives, Roman widows: the appearance of new women and the Pauline communities. Grand Rapids, Eerdmans

Walcot P (1991) On widows and their reputation in antiquity. Symbolae Osloenses 66:5–26

Chapter 14
An Economic Approach to Religious Communes: The Shakers

Metin Coşgel

Abstract The Shakers were a religious society well known for their commitments to celibacy, pacifism, joint ownership of property, and communal lifestyle. John E. Murray wrote the first economic analysis of the Shakers in his Ph.D. dissertation in 1992. Proposing that Shaker membership and prospective entrants responded to the incentives created by the difference between Shaker and worldly living standards, he developed a model of community formation and faith requirements, quality of life, and entry and exit behavior. He tested the implications of the model by using demographic, epidemiologic, anthropometric, and economic data recovered from Shaker manuscripts. He went on to write a series of articles, some coauthored by Metin Coşgel, which examined various aspects of the Shaker lifestyle and business organization. These articles showed that membership decisions within Shaker communal societies were influenced by both religious belief and economic incentives; despite communalism, Shaker farms and shops generally performed just as productively as their neighbors; the organization of Shaker communes under the Family system was a compromise that balanced communal ideals with the costs of motivation and coordination; eastern and western Shakers farmed in ways that were more similar to their neighbors than to each other; and Shakers' dairy operations were just as productive as nearby family farms or larger commercial operations. This essay examines these topics in a coherent manner with the dual objective of discussing Murray's contributions to the literature and uncovering the basic elements of an economic approach to understanding the behavior, organization, and relative performance of the Shakers.

Keywords Shakers · Religious commune · Living standards · Incentives · Membership · Productivity

---

M. Coşgel (✉)
University of Connecticut, Storrs, CT, USA
e-mail: metin.cosgel@uconn.edu

P. Gray et al. (eds.), *Standard of Living*, Studies in Economic History,
https://doi.org/10.1007/978-3-031-06477-7_14

14.1 Introduction

The Shakers were a religious society well known for their commitments to celibacy, joint ownership of property, and communal lifestyle. John E. Murray wrote the first economic analysis of the Shakers in his Ph.D. dissertation in 1992. Proposing that Shaker membership and prospective entrants responded to the incentives created by the difference between Shaker and worldly living standards, he developed a model of community formation, living standards, and entry and exit behavior. He tested the implications of the model by using demographic, epidemiologic, anthropometric, and economic data recovered from Shaker manuscripts.

Murray went on to write a series of articles on the Shakers, some coauthored by Metin Coşgel, which examined various aspects of the Shaker lifestyle and economy. These articles showed that membership decisions within Shaker communal societies were influenced by both religious belief and economic incentives; despite communalism, Shaker farms and shops generally performed just as productively as their neighbors; the organization of Shaker communes under the Family system was a compromise that balanced communal ideals with the costs of motivation and coordination; Shakers' dairy operations were just as productive as nearby family farms or larger commercial operations; and eastern and western Shakers farmed in ways that were more similar to their neighbors than to each other. This essay will examine the living standards and membership selection in Shaker societies and the organization and market integration of their businesses, with the dual objective of outlining the basic elements of an economic approach to the Shakers and discussing Murray's contributions to the literature.

14.2 The Shakers

The Shakers, whose official name was the United Society of Believers in Christ's Second Appearing, were (and are, but since John Murray's research was focused on the Shakers of the past, the past tense will be used here) a Christian communal society. Their distinctive religious beliefs included celibacy, pacifism, sexual equality, communal lifestyle, and joint ownership of the Society's assets. They were inspired by their foundress, an unlettered Englishwoman named Ann Lee, to live celibate lives, confess sins to elders, and pray in such a way as to experience direct contact with the divine. They believed in the existence of a male and female Godhead, from which followed sexual equality. Early in the Society's history, they adopted a form of communalism, in which all assets were owned jointly and Believers (a Shaker term for members of the sect) worked for the community without wages. Each community was further divided into Families which were essentially autonomous and consisted of 50 to 100 Shakers. Economically, the Shakers aimed at balancing the isolation that promoted their unusual brand of spiritualism and the interaction with worldly markets that provided goods they needed to maintain their community, but were unable to make themselves.

The Shakers were originally founded in England in the 1740s and then established in the United States in the 1780s. They were among the most successful of the hundreds of American communal societies that survived long enough to leave some historical record. By the year 1800, the Believers numbered 1373 and maintained 11 communities in New York and New England. In 1850 the US census recorded the greatest number of Shakers, when 3842 members lived in 21 communities located between Maine and Kentucky. Since then, their numerical decline has continued as members left or died without replacements by new converts. Only 12 Shaker communities were left in 1920. Many communities were abandoned to become museums, schools, and state prisons. The only active Shaker community today is in Sabbathday Lake, Maine, with a few remaining members.

Shaker history presents numerous interesting puzzles and important questions to an economist. Shaker communalism, for example, meant that Believers and prospective Believers responded to a different set of incentives than other people. Celibacy likewise put a significant barrier to their ability to grow through procreation. Their distinct beliefs had direct implications for their membership makeup and economic performance. As Murray (1992: 3-4) asked in his Ph.D. dissertation, "[w]ho were the Shakers? What were they like in non-spiritual terms? Had they different levels of human capital from other contemporary Americans? How did they change between 1790 and the end of the nineteenth century? Why did they become Shakers? Why did some choose apostasy and others remain? How well did they live, and how did that affect recruiting and retention?" Starting with these questions, Murray set out to develop an economic approach to the Shakers and wrote a series of articles, some coauthored by Metin Coşgel, which examined the living standards and skill composition of the Society's membership and the organization and market integration of its businesses.

14.3 Living Standards

Certain distinctive features of the Shaker lifestyle had direct implications for the health and living standards of Believers. Communal life and religious practices meant that hundreds of Believers constantly lived and worshipped in close proximity to each other, making Shaker villages more susceptible than other communities to the spread of infectious diseases. Epidemic disease could enter the community through Shaker interactions with neighbors and travels to nearby towns and far cities. Although their villages were typically set off in rural areas, the Shakers were never completely isolated from the outside. The celibacy condition required their leaders to venture out to recruit new members to ensure the continuity of their membership. Believers frequently traveled outside to conduct legal affairs and business transactions. They bought equipment, grains, and raw materials from outside businesses and sold in outside markets their seeds, brooms, furniture, medicinal herbs, and other products that were in high demand.

We have much to learn from studying the health and disease environment of the Shakers. In nineteenth-century America, diseases like pulmonary tuberculosis (the "white plague") could have a devastating impact on communal societies like the Shakers. Despite recent medical improvements, such diseases continue to assert their importance today, as the recent COVID-19 outbreak has shown. Crowded situations in contemporary schools, workplaces, social gatherings, and care facilities have much in common with the Shaker communities in spreading infectious diseases. By studying Shaker attitudes and actions toward such diseases, we would gain important insights into the effectiveness of various public health measures for prevention and treatment.

Murray (1994) used surviving records of three representative communities (in terms of size and geography) to study tuberculosis in Shaker communities in the nineteenth century. He focused on nutrition, sanitation, and isolation as the three factors that have been proposed in the literature to explain differences in tuberculosis mortality. His results showed that Believers of the mid-nineteenth century died at elevated rates from tuberculosis. The differential was probably unrelated to diet because the Shaker diet was adequate. Likewise, the sanitary environment was unlikely to be a factor, or even a factor in favor of the Shakers, because of their attitudes toward cleanliness and availability of clean water. The likely source of the problem, according to Murray, was isolation, because the Shakers did not (or could not) isolate infected members. He found that the rise and fall of tuberculosis mortality in Shaker communities was closely related to the rise and fall of population in their villages. This finding suggests that the decline of the disease in the nineteenth century was a function of the decline of crowded living spaces.

If certain Shaker practices or the realities of communal life led to disease problems, did Believers have shorter lives than non-Shakers? Contrary to this implication, the Shakers themselves claimed to have longer lives due to their distinct lifestyle, as recorded in their pamphlets and interviews with outsiders. Using techniques of demography and epidemiology, Murray (1993a) compared health conditions and mortality in some nineteenth-century Shaker communes with other contemporary populations. As primary sources, he used available membership, population, and death records of representative Shaker communities and the journals kept by their physicians.

The results showed that Shakers did indeed live unusually long lives, as seen in three different measures: age at death, expected years of life at age 20, and age-adjusted mortality rate. Comparing age at death for samples of Shakers and various rural New Englanders (for which comparable data are available from cemetery gravestones and town vital records) showed that New England Shakers died at later ages than a small sample of contemporary Massachusetts residents during the period between 1784 and 1830. Because mean age at death can be a misleading mortality statistic (especially since Shakers' celibacy excludes infant mortality), Murray looked at another statistic for confirmation, namely, expected years of life at age 20. Comparing life expectancy of this age group of Shakers with known statistics regarding other cohorts around the world showed that young Shakers could expect to live at least a decade longer than others, a surprisingly large differential. Finally,

Murray looked at differences in death rates for another comparison of mortality. Although Shaker communities had higher crude death rates than Massachusetts, this was the result of unusual Shaker demographic structure skewed toward older adults. Comparisons of age-adjusted mortality rates indicated higher longevity among the Shakers.

Notwithstanding the distinctive features of the Shaker lifestyle, can we utilize their archival records to learn about the living standards of the general population? Since direct quantitative information on the well-being of the general population is not available for historical studies, scholars have used stature as a proxy measure. This information, however, may be biased because they are typically derived from the records available for samples of students, soldiers, or slaves. To determine whether these samples are representative of the general population, we need to compare them with other samples. Moreover, since some of these samples are exclusively for males or children, an ideal comparison would be with a sample that includes adult females.

Findings regarding the stature of a sample of Believers might provide a useful comparison with the sample of students, soldiers, and slaves. Since the Shakers practiced celibacy, most individual members joined as adults who grew up outside the commune. Their stature thus likely represented more the living standards of their childhood conditions than the unique features of the Shaker lifestyle. In addition, a sample of Shakers would include adult females.

Murray (1993b) studied stature of men, women, and children who lived in a Shaker commune near Albany, New York, between 1840 and 1865. He examined how heights changed over time within this Shaker community, varied among age and gender groups, and compared with other non-Shaker samples. He found that Shaker men were about the same height as male slaves but shorter than Union Army soldiers. Over time, men's heights followed a similar trend to that observed in the Union Army, specifically a U-shaped trend between the late eighteenth century and the 1830s, followed by a decline. Interestingly, the trend for adult women was instead a long decline throughout the first half of the century, as successive birth cohorts became generally shorter over time, associated with the influx of shorter urban women. Shaker women were much shorter than Shaker men, likely a reflection of broader sexual differences in net nutrition. Shaker children were shorter than children in samples for later American populations.

14.4 Membership

The distinctive Shaker practices of celibacy and communalism had direct implications for the levels and duration of membership and their demand for nonmember labor. Given the restrictions imposed by celibacy and the incentive problems created by equal compensation of members under communalism, we would expect membership levels and duration in Shaker communes to decline, proportion of illiterate members to rise, and employment of nonmembers to increase, over time.

Decisions of individual Shakers were influenced by both religious beliefs and economic incentives. Although this clearly presented free-rider problems for Shaker communalism, the Society did not screen out prospective members who might have been attracted purely for pecuniary reasons or those who had little to contribute to productive activities. Preferring open membership, the Shakers rarely rejected potential entrants or expelled existing members. Entry and exit decisions typically belonged to individual members.

To test the implications of free entry and exit for the levels and duration of Shaker membership, Murray (1995a) used population data from the Church Family at the New Lebanon Shaker Community, near Albany, New York, for the period between 1785 and 1882. These data provide entrance and exit dates on individual members, from which changes in levels of overall population over time can be calculated. Using this information, Murray investigated whether the skill levels of entrants to Shaker communities declined over time and whether they were successful in keeping young members in the sect.

The results showed that the New Lebanon Church Family suffered from three types of membership problems. First, over time new recruits increasingly came from the largest urban areas of the United States and Britain. Less well suited for life on a rural commune, these members were significantly less likely to persist as Shakers than those who came from rural areas and small towns. Second, the Society was unable to deal with the "second-generation problem." Although adults chose to join the Shakers as converts, children either entered with their parents or were picked up from the outside as orphans or apprentices. The likelihood of staying longer in the community was greater for adults than children, confirming the greater importance of choice over socialization for membership continuity. Finally, membership in the community was influenced by economic fluctuations in the greater American society. When the economy took a downturn, the community's population increased. Men (but not women) who joined during economic downturns were less likely to persist as members.

Another important implication of Shaker communalism concerned the levels of skills and productivity among Believers. Although religious beliefs were important in affecting people's decision to join the Shakers, the incentive structure created by equal compensation of members could also be a factor. In general, if everyone received the same return in team production, we would expect those with low marginal productivity to join the team and those with high productivity to leave for better opportunities, consequently causing the average productivity of the team to fall over time. Regarding the Shakers, we would expect average levels of skills and productivity to fall among Believers over time, a problem of adverse selection caused by their commitment to communalism.

To test for the presence of adverse selection in Shaker communities, Murray (1995b) studied levels of literacy among Believers as an indicator of human capital. Based on the association between human capital and marginal productivity, he examined how Shaker literacy rates changed over time and differed from those of people in nearby areas. To determine literacy among the Shakers, he looked at whether Believers signed their names on certain documents, specifically covenants and entrance agreements, of the North Union, Ohio, and South Union, Kentucky, communities for which manuscripts are available to determine signature literacy.

The results showed that economic incentives adversely affected membership decisions for the Shakers. Although early Shakers were literate and highly skilled individuals, average literacy rates declined over time. New members were less literate than established Believers as well as people in nearby areas. These findings indicate that the changing quality of members over time may have been the main cause of the numerical decline of the Society in the nineteenth century.

Yet another consequence of the Shaker lifestyle concerned the relationship between Believers and nonmember labor. The Shakers often hired outside workers to perform a variety of tasks in their farms and businesses, as did many other religious and secular communal societies. Hiring nonmember workers, however, may pose problems for a collective organization, especially one formed for ideological reasons, because nonmembers may respond to different incentives than do members. This may cause a dilution of the group's values and a decline in membership over time, eventually causing the group's demise.

Murray (2000) examined the Shaker practice of hiring nonmember workers to determine whether the numbers of hired hands increased over time and whether employing nonmembers raised the risk of communal dissolution. He used data on Shaker hiring of outsiders in the nineteenth century from two different types of sources, namely, the manuscripts and account books of the Shakers themselves and a survey published by Charles Nordhoff that recorded the numbers of Shakers and hired hands employed by all Shaker communities in 1874.

Shaker employment records from early in the nineteenth century and the 1874 survey suggest that the Society indeed employed greater numbers of outsiders over time. Regarding the impact of this employment on Shaker membership, however, Murray's (2000) analysis of anecdotal and survey evidence did not find an association between outside labor and communal decline. The findings showed that the Society hired nonmembers from early in Shaker history and that such employment was complementary to Shaker labor, with no adverse effects on communal values and membership persistence. Indeed, surprisingly, the results showed that greater employment of hired hands led to decreased probabilities of community dissolution.

14.5 Productivity, Organization, and Land Accumulation

The Shakers met numerous economic and political constraints in implementing their religious ideals in the real world. Coşgel and Murray examined three specific examples of the way such constraints affected the Shaker economy. First, communal sharing presented a classic example of an incentive problem in production. Since Believers shared the fruits of each other's productive activities, they could face inadequate incentives to work hard. Second, the Society similarly had to carefully balance religious ideals with economic concerns in determining the scope of communal sharing. Although all members would ideally live, work, and consume together in each community, this would be less feasible as the size of membership grew, raising the question of how best to maintain communal sharing in larger communes. Third, as Shaker communities grew, they had to deal with challenges caused by large amounts of accumulated land over time. For example, they had to take controversial positions regarding policy proposals for land reform and faced questions regarding land use as membership declined. Focusing on the interaction of religious and economic concerns in Shaker communities, Coşgel and Murray wrote a series of essays to examine implications regarding the productivity of their business operations, the organization of communes, and the accumulation of land, as detailed below.

A comparison of Shaker farms and businesses with their neighbors would provide broad insights regarding the relative productivities of communes and conventional producers. Unlike a conventional firm, a commune distributes output to its members according to rules, such as equal sharing, that do not depend on members' effort. Because this independence between income and effort creates a potential for an incentive problem, those who emphasize the role of incentives on productivity would argue that a conventional firm should be more productive than a commune, all else being equal. Those who consider the presumptions of the standard theory as being inapplicable to communes, on the other hand, might argue that work incentives in a commune, shaped by such things as a communal work ethic and interdependence, are adequate to prove a commune to be just as productive, if not more, as a conventional firm.

To compare the productivity of Shaker farms and enterprises with other producers, Coşgel and Murray (1998) used information recorded in the enumeration schedules of the US agriculture and manufacturing censuses. Available for the period between 1850 and 1880, this information makes it possible to identify the Shaker entries in the schedules and to construct a random sample of other farms and shops for a comparison based on consistent data. Because the comparison sample is drawn from the schedules of the same townships as the Shakers, these neighboring farms and shops faced similar local constraints. Coşgel and Murray (1998) estimated the average productivities of the two groups of producers, identified and controlled for consistent nonorganizational differences between them that might have affected their relative productivities, and assessed the role of organizational differences.

The results provide support to the contention that communes need not always suffer from reduced productivity. Shaker farms and shops generally performed just as productively as their neighbors; when differences did exist between their productivities, there are good reasons to attribute them to factors other than the organizational form.

An important dilemma faced by growing communes is whether to maintain sharing in a single commune or break into a network of smaller independent units. Although the latter option might be more efficient from an organizational perspective, economic independence might have adverse consequences for the fundamental communal principles within the whole network since some communes may own more wealth or generate more income per member than do the others. Given the potential for such a conflict with communal principles, questions arise as to whether and why a commune might choose an organizational structure of a network consisting of economically independent units and what the consequences would be for inequality among units.

During the nineteenth century, the Shakers established several communities in seven states. A distinct feature of the Shaker organization of communes was to further divide each community into economically independent subdivisions called "Families." The Shakers faced a trade-off of sorts. One large commune for all Shakers, at least for each community, would have better matched communal ideals. Costs of motivation and coordination associated with the carrying out of economic activities, however, would have risen with group size. The compromise of several smaller Families within the larger community balanced these costs. Moreover, incentive effects and distribution costs prevented the Shakers from establishing a formal distribution mechanism that could have transferred resources across Families toward greater equality.

Using data from the 1850, 1860, and 1870 US census enumeration schedules, Coşgel et al. (1997) estimated the wealth and income per capita of Shaker Families in order to examine the consequences of the Shaker organizational structure of a network of independent Families. The results showed that both wealth and income per capita differed substantially across Shaker communities and even among Families within the same community. That is not to say that the Shakers failed entirely to meet their communal principles; in fact there is every reason to believe that distribution was very equitable within each Family and that the distribution of Shaker wealth and income was much more equal than the distribution in the fallen "World." But strict application of communal principles and complete distributional equality among all Shakers could have been achieved only at very high costs in the face of growing membership.

Another important dilemma faced by growing communes is whether to live by their communal principles within the larger economy, especially in land ownership. True, the Shakers held their land and its products in common, with no private property among the members. But their position within the larger economy presented an anomaly by the late nineteenth century, because they had become local monopolists with ownership of thousands of acres of land on which ever fewer Shakers were available to work. Whereas Shaker land policies attracted the attention of fearful neighbors and state legislators early in the nineteenth century, the large size of their land holdings became an increasingly urgent issue within the Society in the later nineteenth century as membership declined.

Murray (1996) studied the Shaker dilemma regarding land ownership in the late nineteenth century. To discern the evolution of the Society's attitudes, he focused on the writings of prominent Shaker elder Frederick W. Evans regarding the single tax proposal of Henry George. Evans wrote numerous pamphlets and letters to newspapers urging both the Society and the outside world to adopt George's ideas. He believed that the single tax proposed by George offered the possibility of more equitable land distribution. As another motivation, he believed that these proposals would help with the Society's own dilemma. Whereas the Shakers had successfully resisted proposals for quantitative restrictions on land ownership while they were growing early in the century, they were now in an uncomfortable position suffering from the result of their collective selfishness. Recognizing the increasing burden of Shaker land holdings and the inability of the Society to find a solution on their own, Evans ardently supported the land reform proposals of Henry George to curb their land hunger.

14.6 Market Integration and Specialization

With respect to external markets, the Shakers had originally sought separation from the outside world and economic self-sufficiency, as has been common among religious communes. To remain truly untouched by the "World," however, they would have needed an economic self-sufficiency that would spare them from having to trade with outsiders for various necessities. This ideal was never quite realized. Like any other economic agent, the Society produced goods that others would accept in trade, in addition to producing goods that were for their own consumption, to obtain what they wanted but could not (or chose not to) make themselves. The Society's integration with the markets raises important questions regarding how Shaker religious beliefs influenced production decisions, whether Shaker communities differed in regional specialization, and how their market behavior changed over time.

Murray and Coşgel (1998) examined the influence of Shaker religious beliefs on production decisions, specifically in swine raising. The Shakers raised hogs because they were enthusiastic pork eaters. Up to the 1840s, the Shakers made pork production decisions based on market information. Despite limited involvement in pork factor and product markets, they processed available price information efficiently and acted as economic theory would predict. They also made systematic efforts to increase meat yields through breeding and creative slaughtering.

Then in 1841 a ban was placed on pork as "cursed and unclean," a foodstuff that was "positively unfit for the children of Zion." Despite the evident pleasure that consumed pork provided to the Shakers and the care with which they made pork production decisions, the society as a whole grappled with the issue of banning pork consumption throughout the 1840s. While some communities obeyed the ban immediately, others continued to raise swine and produce pork throughout the nineteenth century. The Shakers were unable to end pork production altogether, in large part because of the demands of hired hands for pork. Western Shakers, for example, seem to have obeyed the prohibition on eating pork themselves, even while continuing to produce it for consumption by others.

Murray and Coşgel associated the uneven acceptance of the ban not with strictly economic motivations but with more general cultural issues. Overall, the results showed a complex of motivations that influenced the decision of whether and how much pork to produce. The fact that prices were one influence among several is not a sign of their unimportance but rather evidence that, even in relatively isolated communes dedicated to things otherworldly, the influence of the worldly economy was considerable.

Another business in which Shaker religious beliefs could influence production decisions and performance was dairy farming. Shaker dairies produced milk, butter, and cheese for the Shakers' own consumption and milk and cheese for sale, and the Shakers lavished considerable effort to expand dairy production through careful breeding of livestock and ingenious design of barns. Market integration of the Shakers in dairying raises interesting questions about how their religious beliefs affected production decisions and performance.

To analyze Shaker dairy operations and compare their productivity with other farmers, Murray and Coşgel (1999a) used data from the Shaker manuscript record and the enumeration schedules of the federal agricultural censuses. The results showed that the Shakers made production decisions consistent with positive supply elasticities, based on prices formed in nearby markets from the beginning of data series in the 1830s. Regarding comparative productivity, the authors found that at the middle of the nineteenth century, Shaker dairies produced more milk per cow than ordinary family-run dairies, even in the most important dairying states. Further, regression analysis showed that the greater Shaker productivity remained at midcentury.

After midcentury, the Shakers adopted religiously inspired production restrictions (i.e., the ban on lard, with implications for increased demand for butter) and, as a result, stopped basing their decisions on price signals. The decline in dairy productivity that followed this move mirrored the Shakers' numerical decline. Faithfulness to commands of the spirit was not without costs. Although the Shakers responded to price signals, they clearly were not a profit-maximizing firm in the usual sense of that phrase. Their religious beliefs, and the practices that flowed from them, constrained them in their consumption and hence in their production.

In specialization and crop choices, did the Shaker communities in different regions resemble each other or the non-Shaker farms and businesses around them? When the Shakers expanded westward and established communal farms in the Ohio Valley, they encountered a new agricultural environment that was substantially different from the familiar soils, climates, and markets of New England and the Hudson Valley. Despite the regional diversity among Shaker settlements, Murray and Coşgel (1999b) noticed that some of the literature on the Shakers often treated these communes as being almost identical. Regional differences in the ways new communities responded to local conditions had not been well documented.

To examine patterns of specialization among the Shakers, Murray and Coşgel (1999b) used information from the manuscript schedules of the federal agricultural censuses from 1850 through 1880. For each Shaker community, they also recorded a random sample of five farms in the same township for comparison. For a quantitative analysis of regional differences, the authors estimated measures of specialization and crop choice for the sample of Shaker communities and the random sample of neighboring comparison farms, in each census year from 1850 to 1880.

The results showed systematic and consistent differences between eastern and western Shaker communities. The eastern Shakers were more specialized than the western Shakers. In particular, their output consisted of a higher percentage of perishables, a lower percentage of grains, and a higher percentage of livestock-related items, relative to western Shaker production. Considering that these differences parallel the systematic differences between other farmers (neighbors, county, state) in the east and the west, they showed the regional diversity of Shaker farming strategies through their adaptation to local conditions. Western Shakers thus resembled more their neighbors in the west than other Shakers in the east.

14.7 Conclusion

As this brief survey illustrates, John Murray made outstanding contributions to the literatures on the economics of religion and American economic history by laying the foundations of an economic approach to religious communes and applying it to the history of the Shakers. He introduced the first economic model of communal membership in his Ph.D. dissertation. A topnotch economic historian, he analyzed the model's implications by using information from the enumeration schedules of the US censuses and economic data uncovered from various Shaker manuscripts, including letters, membership lists, legal and business documents, and diaries and journals.

In a series of publications that followed, Murray examined various important questions regarding the duration of membership and standards of living in Shaker communities and the organization and market integration of their businesses. I am fortunate and honored to be a part of his quest to understand the economic history of the Shakers.

Appendix: Coşgel on Murray

I got to know John in 1992, when he contacted me to ask for a copy of my paper on the bequest motive of the Amish, which I was scheduled to present at the upcoming annual meeting of the Economic History Association. When we met in person, we quickly realized we had a lot of research interests in common in the newly emerging field of the economics of religion. He was working on his Ph.D. dissertation on the Shakers, and learning about his approach to the Shakers was instrumental in shaping my own views on American religious communes and the relationship between religion and culture. Although we were originally asking different questions, our interests eventually converged as we met several times a year at the annual meetings of the Economic History Association, Social Science History Association, and Allied Social Science Association. Numerous lunch and dinner conversations during these meetings were memorable opportunities for learning, friendship, and discussing preliminary ideas that turned into several coauthored papers on the Shakers.

References

Coşgel MM, Murray JE (1998) Productivity of a commune: the Shakers, 1850-1880. The Journal of Economic History 58:494–510
Coşgel MM, Miceli TJ, Murray JE (1997) Organization and distributional equality in a network of communes: the Shakers. American Journal of Economics and Sociology 56:129–144
Murray JE (1992) Communal living standards as membership incentives: the Shakers 1780–1880. Ohio State University, Dissertation
Murray JE (1993a) A demographic analysis of Shaker mortality trends. Communal Societies 13:22–44
Murray JE (1993b) Stature among members of a nineteenth century American Shaker commune. Annals of Human Biology 20:121–129
Murray JE (1994) The white plague in utopia: tuberculosis in nineteenth-century Shaker communes. Bulletin of the History of Medicine 68:278–306
Murray JE (1995a) Determinants of membership levels and duration in a Shaker commune, 1780-1880. Journal for the Scientific Study of Religion 34:35–48
Murray JE (1995b) Human capital in religious communes: literacy and selection of nineteenth century Shakers. Explorations in Economic History 32:217–235
Murray JE (1996) Henry George and the Shakers: evolution of communal attitudes towards land ownership. American Journal of Economics and Sociology 55:245–256
Murray JE (2000) Communal viability and employment of non-member labor: testing hypotheses with historical data. Review of Social Economy 58:1–16
Murray JE, Coşgel MM (1998) Market, religion, and culture in Shaker swine production, 1788-1880. Agricultural History 72:552–573
Murray JE, Coşgel MM (1999a) Between god and market: influences of economy and spirit on Shaker communal dairying, 1830-1875. Social Science History 23:41–65
Murray JE, Coşgel MM (1999b) Regional specialization in communal agriculture: the Shakers, 1850-1880. Communal Societies 19:73–84

Chapter 15
Religion, Human Capital, and Economic Diversity in Nineteenth-Century Hesse-Cassel

Kristin Mammen and Simone A. Wegge

Abstract We document the religious diversity of the German principality of Hesse-Cassel in the mid-nineteenth century. Over 63% of the villages and towns were majority Protestant, and 13% were majority Catholic. Only 23% of Hessian villages and towns, however, were home to Jews, who typically made up less than 10% of the inhabitants in these places. Still, we find that Jews made up 2.6% of the principality, a larger percentage than has been estimated for Germany as a whole at this time. Our maps show the principality's extraordinary variety in the different principal Christian denominations, the Jewish population, and minority Christian enclaves. Protestant-majority communities were spread across most districts, as were communities with any Jews. Catholic-majority communities were clustered in two districts, while Christian minorities could only be found in Protestant-majority localities. Meaningful differences in the socioeconomic characteristics of communities existed, with majority-Protestant places a bit more urban than majority-Catholic ones and places with Jews the most urban. We document the occupations of the Jewish population, finding many traders, consistent with the literature, but a surprisingly large number of farmers and fewer moneylenders than might be expected. Hessians were segregated to a large degree by religion, and this was related to various economic, social, and demographic outcomes.

Keywords Christians · Hesse-Cassel · Jews · Occupations · Protestants · Religious diversity · Religious minorities · Religious segregation

K. Mammen (✉)
College of Staten Island, City University of New York, Staten Island, NY, USA
e-mail: kristin.mammen@csi.cuny.edu

S. A. Wegge
College of Staten Island and the Graduate Center, City University of New York, New York, NY, USA

P. Gray et al. (eds.), *Standard of Living*, Studies in Economic History, https://doi.org/10.1007/978-3-031-06477-7_15

15.1 Introduction

In several papers, John Murray and co-authors examined how Shakers balanced the use of market principles versus religious principles in making their organizational, production, and allocation decisions, and the consequences of that balance (Coşgel et al. 1997; Coşgel and Murray 1998, Murray 1995, 2000; Murray and Coşgel 1998, 1999). His work was an important contribution to the line of inquiry that asks, to what extent do religious principle and practice influence economic outcomes?

We contribute to this literature by studying the German principality of Hesse-Cassel, which was mostly Protestant in the eighteenth and nineteenth centuries but was also home to a substantial mix of Jewish and Catholic citizens. Economically Hesse-Cassel was known for its backwardness, poverty, and slow path to industrialization: outdated guild laws remained in place until 1866, and the main sector was agriculture (Bovensiepen 1909, p. 17; Frank 1994, p. 93; Kukowski 1995, p. 6; Pedlow 1988, p. 11). Using a rich dataset on over 1000 Hessian towns and villages, for about 75% of the Hessian principality (comprising almost 550,000 citizens), collected in the mid-1850s from an *Ortsbeschreibung* (Community survey), we analyze the religious diversity along with the socioeconomic makeup for each community.[1] These data provide us an opportunity to assess religious diversity for one area of Central Europe 200 years after the Thirty Years' War and examine whether there were links between religious practice and economic outcomes.

Our study generates a number of interesting results. First, we find that while most villages and towns were predominantly Protestant, there were both entirely Catholic and majority-Catholic communities as well. Further, most of the Hessian communities had no Jews. Those with Jews typically had a population that was less than 10% Jewish, while only one community was majority-Jewish.[2] We show that majority-Catholic villages and towns were clustered together geographically, while communities with Jewish populations were widely scattered across Hesse-Cassel.

We also document the prevalence of the different Protestant denominations. The communities that were majority Reformed Evangelical and thus followed Calvinist teachings dominated more than half of the 19 districts of the contiguous territory of Hesse-Cassel. In contrast, other Protestant groups had a smaller presence.

The economic characteristics and the occupational structures of the villages and towns differed by religion in some stark ways. Comparing such outcomes for these three religions is an active area of research in the current economics of religion. For example, Botticini and Eckstein (2012) show that religiously motivated increases in Jewish learning in the eighth and ninth centuries influenced entry into highly skilled occupations and contributed to Jewish economic success centuries later. Becker and

---

[1] Noted historian of Germany Mack Walker considered towns to have at least a population of 750 people (Walker 1971, pp. 27, 30). We will do the same and use the term "towns" when we refer to places with 750 or more in population and the term "villages" for places with less than 750 people. The average population for a Hessian community was 600 people (Bestand H3).

[2] This was the village of Rhina in the district of Hünfeld.

Woessmann (2009) examine the effects on Protestant outcomes of Martin Luther's support of universal schooling to enable all Christians to read the Bible. They find positive effects for Protestants in nineteenth-century Prussia, and argue that the mechanism is the greater literacy of Protestants relative to Catholics, rather than the "Protestant work ethic."

The last section of our paper examines Jewish human capital in our data. The survey provides rich information for the Jews in each community and lists how they earned their living: common occupations included traders, butchers, artisans, and farmers. Some of these findings, e.g., the presence of farmers, are perhaps surprising given the occupational barriers Jews faced through the centuries in much of Europe including German-speaking areas, but Jews gained emancipation in Hesse-Cassel in 1833, and our findings may reflect an increased portfolio of opportunities available to Jews. Below we begin with some historical background and follow it with the analysis of our results.

15.2 The Principality of Hesse-Cassel: Religion and Politics

The Landgraviate of Hesse and with it the House of Hesse were established in 1264 with Henry I.[3] It was part of the Holy Roman Empire. Upon the death of Philip I in 1567, Hesse was divided among four sons, and the Landgraviate of Hesse-Cassel came into existence. Over 200 years later, in 1803, it gained the honorific of being made an electorate of the Holy Roman Empire. Napoleon Bonaparte dissolved the Empire in 1806 and made Hesse-Cassel a part of the new Kingdom of Westphalia and its capital city of Kassel the capital of this kingdom, installing his brother Jérôme Bonaparte as the ruler. This lasted until 1814, when the Vienna Congress reestablished the principality of Hesse-Cassel and made its ruler an Elector. In 1866 Prussia annexed Hesse-Cassel along with a number of other German states, a prelude to the nation-state of Germany established in 1871 under Otto von Bismarck. Over its 300-year history, the Electorate of Hesse-Cassel went through many territorial and border changes and covered a much larger geographic area in 1866 than in 1567.[4] In 1850 Hesse-Cassel bordered Thuringia and Saxony to the east, Hannover, Waldeck, and Westphalia to the north, Hesse-Darmstadt (Grand Duchy of Hesse) to the west and south, and Bavaria to the south. In addition, the Free City of Frankfurt, on the navigable Main River, bordered the Hessian district of Hanau.

Our research draws on the community surveys of Hesse-Cassel from the 1850s, carried out by the Historical Commission for Hesse.[5] A representative from every

[3] The term Landgraviate is comparable to the term count, and signifies a noble with jurisdiction and sovereign rights over a large territory; it is a title used in the Holy Roman Empire.

[4] Maps presented in this paper show the boundaries in the 1850s. While Hesse-Cassel was technically an electorate between 1806 and 1866, we also use the term principality.

[5] This survey can be found at the Hessisches Staatsarchiv Marburg (HStAM), the Hessian State Archive in Marburg Germany. We refer to this survey as Bestand H3. Munter (1983), especially

village and town in the principality filled out this survey of 186 questions (some questions with several parts), divided across 17 themes. The questionnaire addressed the social, religious, geographic, and economic characteristics of each community. Typically a local mayor or teacher filled out this survey. We have gathered information about the religious makeup of the population of each community as well as their occupations.

Historically, local European rulers had great influence on which religious confessions could be practiced within their respective territories.[6] Thus religious history is intimately tied with political history. Before the Reformation of the sixteenth century, the dominant religion in German-speaking regions was Catholicism; those who practiced Judaism made up a small minority.[7] The start of the Reformation was marked by Martin Luther's 95 theses in 1517 and the Edict of Worms in 1521, both events that predated the establishment of Hesse-Cassel. During this time, in the 1520s, the Landgraviate of Hesse was ruled by Philip I (the "Magnanimous"), who was an early supporter of Protestant movements and sought to unite the different Protestant reformers: in 1529, in his own castle, he hosted the Colloquy of Marburg, which was attended by Martin Luther and the Swiss reformer Huldrych Zwingli. In 1527, he founded one of the first European Protestant universities, Philipps Universität Marburg (now public). Upon his death, the division of the Landgraviate of Hesse among the four sons led to the establishment of Hesse-Marburg, Hesse-Rheinfels, Hesse-Darmstadt, and Hesse-Cassel under William IV.

In subsequent decades, two of the four sons died leaving no heirs, and the lands of Hesse-Marburg and Hesse-Rheinfels were split between Hesse-Cassel and Hesse-Darmstadt. In the meantime, after 1567, each of the four sons wrestled with religious ideas, with most of them choosing Lutheranism; their own decisions on confession settled the religious question for their respective subjects. Throughout the 1500s, it is unclear how much the prospect of economic and political independence as opposed to religious ideas motivated these rulers. William IV at first supported uniting Protestant reformers, like his father Philip I, but ultimately decided on Lutheranism as the main religion for Hesse-Cassel. His son, Moritz (Maurice), the Landgrave of Hesse-Cassel from 1592 to 1627, however, converted from Lutheranism to Calvinism in 1605. Doing so meant that his subjects were also now followers of Calvinism. With this conversion he faced opposition from his Lutheran subjects, especially those in the areas that were not part of the original Hesse-Cassel territory. Moritz was not to be deterred and produced a set of *Verbesserungspunkte* ("points of improvement"), which instructed Hessians in how to abide by Calvinist principles; in addition, and where he could, he replaced Lutheran pastors with Calvinist ones (Theibault 1995, p. 36-7).[8] He hired Calvinists into his court and

---

Appendix B, provides documentation.

[6]Confession is used here with the meaning of a religious denomination.

[7]Evidence exists that Jews had lived in villages along the Rhine River from at least the fourth century. See *German Virtual History Tour (2021)*.

[8]It was not easy. Some pastors had to tread a path between the Calvinist Moritz and local Lutheran nobles.

established a college in his court as a way of influencing future diplomats (Collegium Mauritianum). Even though the main early centers of Calvinist thought were to the south in Zurich and Basel, Moritz succeeded in "making Kassel into a node of the international Calvinist network" (Gräf 1997, p. 1169).

On the eve of the Thirty Years' War (1618–1648), a war over religious differences, the largest Protestant group in Hesse-Cassel were the Calvinists. Some of these Calvinists were probably reluctant ones, and the principality was also home to some Lutherans who blended in or were tolerated.[9] After the initial conversion from Catholicism to Calvinism, many communities switched a second time to Lutheranism: for example, Schönstadt in the district of Marburg switched to Calvinism in 1526 and then to Lutheranism in 1624; similarly, Dörnholzhausen in the district of Frankenberg became Calvinist in 1530 and Lutheran in 1624.[10] Hesse-Cassel was also home to Jews in areas designated by principality officials (Theibault 1995, p. 64). In Hessian communities, access to full village rights depended on whether one followed the local religion (Theibault 1995, p. 63). This was how outsiders, like Jews, could be excluded from certain village rights.

Very sadly, the Thirty Years' War, which was supposed to settle religious differences across the various German states and entities, turned out to be a disaster for the people of Hesse-Cassel, with about 40–50% of the populace dying during the conflict (Fox 1976, p. 19). In some parts of the principality, it appears the war was even more devastating, with some villages in the Eschwege district losing 65% to 75% of their populations (Theibault 1995, pp. 171–173). It did not help that the principality was at the geographic crossroads of Germany, in the middle of religious debates, and that the elector of Hesse-Cassel was in conflict with his counterpart of Hesse-Darmstadt.

Over the next two centuries, a few important changes occurred. Before 1833, Jews were required to pay protection money; in October 1833, Jews were fully emancipated (Pedlow 1988, p. 242; Deutsch et al. 1906). The principality acquired various territories: in 1736, Hanau became part of Hesse-Cassel, and at the 1815 Vienna Congress the former Bishopric of Fulda (secularized in 1803), and the territories of the former Archbishopric of Mainz in the Kirchhain district, were all made part of Hesse-Cassel (Pedlow 1988, p. 7).

[9] Some Catholics may have lived in Hesse-Cassel in 1618, but probably they were a very minor group. Theibault comments on the northeastern part of the principality, "Catholicism had more or less disappeared from the region..." (Theibault 1995, p. 65). At this time, Hessians who wanted to worship as Catholics could move (in some cases) to the Catholic enclaves under the Archbishopric of Mainz (Fritzlar, Amöneburg, Neustadt) or to the Bishopric of Fulda. Both were states of the Holy Roman Empire until 1803 and thus not a part of Hesse-Cassel in 1618. Lutherans are discussed in archival records of the district of Eschwege from the early 1600s, but there is no census data on their numbers from this time. The district bordered on Saxony, a Lutheran state, so Hessians near the border could cross over to practice in a Saxon church (Theibault 1995, pp. 65–66).

[10] We found one village that switched three times. Bischhausen in the district of Eschwege, became Calvinist in 1535, converted to Lutheranism in the late 1620s and again converted back to Calvinism after that. These conversions are documented in the Landgeschichtliches Informationssytem Hessen (LAGIS) (2021).

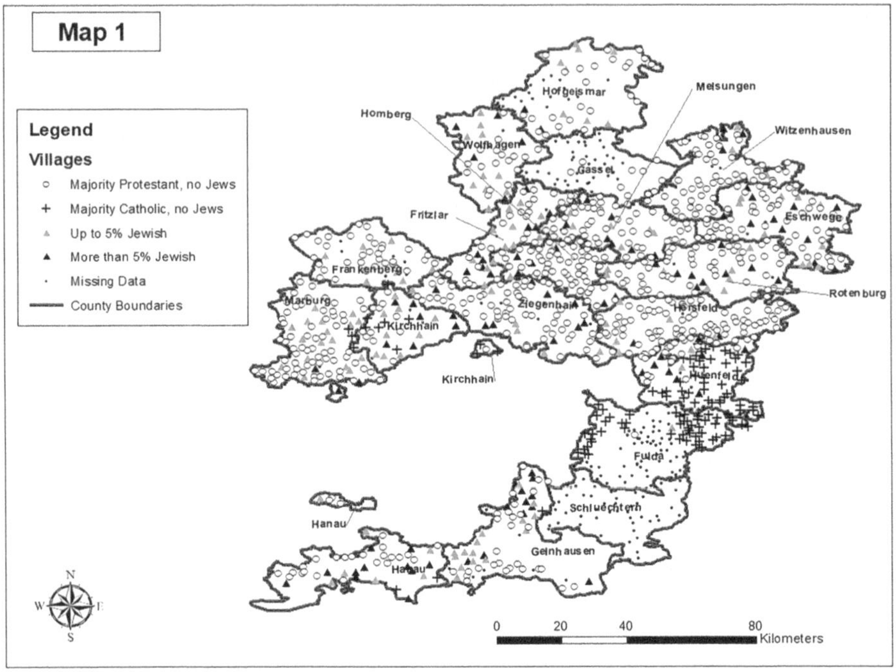

Fig. 15.1 Distribution of Protestants, Catholics and Jews by community. (*Source*: Community survey data: Germany, HStAM, Bestand H3)

By the 1850s, the principality of Hesse-Cassel consisted of 21 districts (*Kreise*), with 19 of them in the contiguous area shown in Fig. 15.1. From the community survey we know that Hessians practiced various faiths, including a number of Protestant confessions, Catholicism and Judaism.

15.3 The Geography of Religious Faith

15.3.1 Where Did the Protestants, Catholics, and Jews Live?

At this time in the 1850s a host of different Christians lived alongside Jews in the principality of Hesse-Cassel. Our data show that Protestantism predominated throughout Hesse-Cassel, with 82.4% Protestants, 15% Catholics, and 2.6% Jews overall (tabulations not shown). Estimates of the size of the Jewish population in 1850s Germany as a whole come from Botticini et al. (2019), who estimated the number of Jews in Germany at 1.04% in 1852 and 1.05% in 1861. They cite other scholars who assess the German-Jewish population at 1% as well.[11] In contrast, our

[11] For discussion of their methodology, see the online appendix of Botticini et al. (2019).

data show that the percentage of Hessians who were Jewish in the 1850s was 2.6%, two and half times more. Our number is significantly higher. Several factors may have contributed to this higher percentage. First, the principality of Hesse-Cassel lay next door to the Free City of Frankfurt, a city with a sizable and thriving Jewish population; in this respect, the growing Jewish population in Frankfurt as well as the space limits placed on them by the Frankfurt City Council may have served as a source of Jews for nearby Hessian communities, with Jews drawn to the Hessian communities in the countryside near Frankfurt (Soliday 1974, pp. 196–97).[12] In this way it could be possible that the Hessian states had higher number of Jews relative to other German states. Secondly, our estimates are based on micro data, specifically individual community surveys and our specific knowledge of the Jewish population for 1016 of the 1376 communities in Hesse-Cassel. The figures Botticini et al. (2019) derive seem to be conservative guesstimates based on macro data from other scholars. Is it possible that Jews have been undercounted in nineteenth-century Germany overall? We do not know and can only comment on Hesse-Cassel. It is worthy of further investigation.

Despite the predominance of Protestants, the data show great diversity in the mix of Protestants, Catholics, and Jews in the various towns and villages, and in the variety of confessions found among the Protestants. Table 15.1 demonstrates that religious distributions within communities vary in interesting ways. We find, as might be expected, that 85% of communities are largely Protestant – 49.3% entirely so and another 35.9% where Protestants lived alongside Catholics or Jews or both, but outnumbered them. However, predominantly Catholic places were a non-negligible 14.6% of the total, with 7.8% entirely Catholic, and 6.9% with Catholic proportions larger than the Protestant and Jewish proportions. Correspondingly, only 8% of localities had no Protestants, while 60% had no Catholics and 77% had no Jews. There are also meaningful proportions of the other possible configurations: communities with a mix of all three religions (13%); with Protestants and Catholics only (19.5%); and with Protestants and Jews only (10.3%). Only two (0.2%) villages had only Catholics and Jews.[13]

Table 15.2 conveys further information about the religious distributions within communities, showing the extent to which Catholics and Jews mixed with the majority Protestant population and each other. The rows show the count of communities in each percentage-Catholic category; the columns show the count of communities in each percentage-Jewish category; so the percentage-Protestant in the communities in each cell can be approximately inferred. For example, in row 1, column 1, the 524 places with zero percent Catholics and zero percent Jews obviously have 100% Protestants. Moving to the southeast, the cells along the diagonal

[12] To restrain the growth of its Jewish community, the Frankfurt City Council imposed marriage and immigration restrictions. These laws were certainly active in the seventeenth and eighteenth centuries (Soliday 1974, pp. 178–79, 196–97).

[13] From Table 15.1: percentage of communities with inhabitants of all three religions: 1.9% + 9.4 % + 1.1% + 0.6% = 13.0%; Protestants and Catholics only: 14.5% + 5% = 19.5%; Protestants and Jews only 10.2% + 0.1% = 10.3%; Catholics and Jews only = 0.2%.

Table 15.1 Distribution of communities by predominantly Protestant, Catholic, or Jewish

	$n = 1063$	(1)	(2)
(1)	**Predominantly Protestant (906 communities)**	0.852	**0% Protestant**
(2)	**100% Protestant (524)**	0.493	0.080
(3)	**<100% Protestant (382)**	0.359	(85)
(4)	*% Protestant > % Catholic > % Jewish (174)*	0.164	
(5)	% Protestant > % Catholic, 0 Jews (154)	0.145	
(6)	% Protestant > % Catholic > % Jewish (nonzero) (20)	0.019	
(7)	*% Protestant > % Jewish > % Catholic[a] (208)*	0.196	
(8)	% Protestant > % Jewish, 0 Catholics (108)	0.102	
(9)	% Protestant > % Jewish > % Catholic (nonzero)[a] (100)	0.094	
(10)	**Predominantly Catholic (156 communities)**	0.147	**0% Catholic**
(11)	**100% Catholic (83)**	0.078	0.595
(12)	**<100% Catholic (73)**	0.069	(633)
(13)	*% Catholic > % Jewish > % Protestant (14)*	0.013	
(14)	% Catholic > % Jewish, 0 Protestants (2)	0.002	
(15)	% Catholic > % Jewish > % Protestant (nonzero) (12)	0.011	
(16)	*% Catholic > % Protestant > % Jewish[b] (59)*	0.056	
(17)	% Catholic > % Protestant, 0 Jews (53)	0.050	
(18)	% Catholic > % Protestant > % Jewish (nonzero)[b] (6)	0.006	
(19)	**Predominantly Jewish (1 community)**	0.001	**0% Jewish**
(20)	**<100% Jewish (1)**	0.001	0.766
(21)	% Jewish> % Protestant, 0 Catholics (1)	0.001	

Source: Community survey data: Germany, HStAM, Bestand H3
Subsample sizes in parentheses
[a] Includes two communities with % Jewish = % Catholic
[b] Includes one community with % Protestant = % Jewish

Table 15.2 Distribution of communities by percent Catholic, Jewish, and Protestant

			(1)	(2)	(3)	(4)	(5)	(6)	(7)	(8)
			Jewish							
			0%	<1%	1–<5%	5–<10%	10–<20%	20–<100%	100%	Total
(1)	Catholic	0%	**524**	10	51	31	11	6	0	633
(2)		<1%	90	**6**	36	19	11	1	–	163
(3)		1–<5%	47	2	**18**	13	3	1	–	84
(4)		5–<10%	11	0	1	**2**	1	0	–	15
(5)		10–<20%	4	0	1	1	**0**	0	–	6
(6)		20–<100%	55	1	13	7	2	**1**	–	79
(7)		100%	83	–	–	–	–	–	–	83
(8)		Total	814	19	120	73	28	9	0	1063

Source: Community survey data: Germany, HStAM, Bestand H3

show the communities with roughly equal proportions (in the same percentage category) of Jews and Catholics, with Protestants comprising the remainder (so decreasing as we go down the diagonal). Cells to the southwest of the diagonal display communities with more Catholics than Jews – a sizeable number – 318 or 30%. Cells to the northeast show communities with more Jews than Catholics – a smaller but not inconsequential proportion – 194 or 18%. Most places had no Jewish population, but a quite a few had appreciable Jewish communities of up to 10% of the population; the modal category for Jewish population was 1–5% Jewish (120 communities). A few towns had between 10% and 20% Jews; very few towns had more than 20% Jews.

In Table 15.3, means are presented for communities stratified simply into three groups: majority Protestant (no Jews), majority Catholic (no Jews), and communities with any Jewish population. Means are statistically different at the 5% level (and often 1%) unless otherwise noted. Table 15.3 displays proportions Protestant, Catholic, and Jewish, giving us a more summary view relative to the detailed religious distributions in Tables 15.1 and 15.2. We see that the "typical" all-Christian communities were heavily dominated by either Protestants or Catholics: the average majority-Protestant community was 99% Protestant and 1% Catholic, while the average majority-Catholic community was the reverse, 99% Catholic and only 1% Protestant. The average community with any Jewish population was heavily Protestant (85%), but housed Catholics (9%) as well as Jews (6%).

Figure 15.1 shows the geographic distribution of communities with a slightly more complex stratification: majority Protestant, no Jews, denoted by empty circles; majority Catholic, no Jews, denoted by plus signs; communities with a Jewish population of up to 5%, denoted by grey-shaded triangles; and those with a Jewish population of greater than 5%, denoted by black triangles.[14] Communities for which we have no data are denoted by black dots.[15] We see that many of the majority Catholic communities were clustered in the districts of Fulda and Hünfeld, parts of which (mostly Fulda) had constituted the Bishopric of Fulda, a principality belonging to the Holy Roman Empire from the eleventh century until 1803. The Vienna Congress treaty transferred the Fulda Bishopric territory over to Hesse-Cassel in 1815. The district of Fulda was especially Catholic: most Fulda communities had no Jews as well as no Protestants living in them, which may reflect something about its Catholic past and the way the Bishopric had operated in terms of outsiders. The city of Fulda, one of the three largest towns in all of Hesse-Cassel, was the main exception: with 9547 residents, 80.4% were Catholics, 16.2% Protestants, and 3.4% Jews (tabulation not shown).

[14] It can be seen in Table 15.2 that of the 110 communities with more than 5% Jews, (73/110)*100 = 66% were 5–10% Jewish, (28/110)*100 = 25% were 10–20% Jewish, and only (9/110)*100 = 8% were more than 20% Jewish. We disaggregate the geographic distribution of Protestant denominations below in Fig. 15.2.

[15] Some data are missing because the manuscripts went missing over the decades, which is the case for the districts of Kassel and Fulda. For the same reason 16 out of the 51 villages and towns in the district of Hofgeismar are missing as well. In the case of the district of Schlüchtern, we have not finished cleaning the data for its 52 communities. In terms of how this affects the results, we believe Catholics may be undercounted, given the sizable amount of missing data in Fulda.

Table 15.3 Community mean characteristics by religious category

Variable	Majority protestant communities (no Jews)	Majority Catholic communities (no Jews)	Communities with any Jews
# Communities[a]	678	136	249
Religion			
Proportion Protestant	0.99	0.01	0.85
Proportion Catholic	0.01	0.99	0.09
Proportion Jewish[b]	0.00	0.00	0.06
Elevation, landholding, living arrangements			
Elevation in Rhine feet	839	1062	735
Average landholding in acker	15.6	22.5	10.7
Family Size, 1858	5.3	6.2	5.1
Number Persons per House, 1858[c]	6.6	7.2	7.0
Families per House, 1858	1.26	1.17	1.38
Urban and rural characteristics			
Population, 1858[b]	347	339	1037
Density (persons per acker), 1858	0.24	0.18	0.39
#/% of these communities which have city designation[b]	3/0.4%	0/ 0%	43/17%
# Markets[b]	0.09	0.07	1.35
# Types of specialized artisans	0.6	0.4	3.6
Average land price	68.7	47.4	81.3
# Supported per capita[b]	0.019	0.018	0.024

Source: Community survey data: Germany, HStAM, Bestand H3; Population data: Hessen-Kassel (1843, 1860). *Kurfürstlich Hessisches Hof- und Staatshandbuch*

Means significantly different at the 5% level (usually 1%) unless otherwise noted

[a] Number of communities differs for some variables because of missing values

[b] Majority-Protestant communities not significantly different than Majority Catholic communities

[c] Majority-Catholic communities not significantly different than communities with any Jews

Other majority Catholic communities could be found here and there scattered around the principality, but mostly in the districts of Kirchhain, Gelnhausen, and Hanau. Most of the Catholic communities in these districts were originally part of the Archbishopric of Mainz, one of the three most important political entities of the Holy Roman Empire. That Martin Luther addressed his famous 95 Theses to the Archbishop of Mainz emphasizes this point. With the dissolution of the Empire in 1803, a few years later in 1815 the Vienna Congress assigned these districts (or parts thereof) to the principality of Hesse-Cassel.

In contrast to the clustering of majority-Catholic communities, those with any Jewish population are widely scattered across the principality. Localities typically placed stringent residency restrictions on all kinds of "outsiders," including Jews

(Knodel 1967; Lowenstein 2005, p. 99); this likely contributed to the patchwork of communities with any Jewish population across Hesse-Cassel. Lowenstein (2005, p. 95) remarks on the uneven distribution of Jews across the regions of Germany as well as within the neighborhoods of specific communities.[16]

15.3.2 A Diversity of Protestants

Figure 15.2 shows where the different Protestant groups lived, specifically which communities were Reformed Evangelical (Calvinist) majority, Lutheran majority, United Evangelical majority, or Catholic majority. The symbols for communities with Protestant minorities like Anabaptists, Mennonites, Pietists, Baptists, and Irvingians have a dot in the middle.[17] Smaller dots not sitting inside a shape signify communities for which we have no data. Clearly there are distinct geographic patterns. The Reformed Evangelicals, who followed Calvinist teachings, were the dominant group at this time (squares) and could be found in nine districts in the north and northeast of the principality.[18] Of our sample of over 1000 communities (out of a total of 1376 communities), those who followed Reformed Evangelism were 60% of the population. In contrast, Lutherans had strong holdings in only three districts and United Evangelicals in only two and perhaps three districts.[19] Lutherans were 12.2% of our sample population, and majority Lutheran communities could be found in the west in the districts of Marburg, Kirchhain, and Frankenberg. One of the largest towns in the principality was Marburg, with almost 8000 residents; it is here where Philip the Magnanimous established the first European Protestant university in 1527 with the goal of supporting Lutheranism, in terms of its faculties in law, medicine, philosophy, and theology. The United Evangelical church was the majority religion in most of the communities in the southern districts of Hanau and Gelnhausen and made up 12.0% of the population.[20]

Sometimes Hessians were living in a community that diverged from their own faith for what seem like mostly specialized occupational reasons, indicating that some Hessians had no issue with hiring other Hessians of different denominations:

[16] Lowenstein (2005, p. 98) notes: Some "large village communities showed little segregation; five of 17 families in Schenklengsfeld, Hesse-Kassel, lived on the marketplace, and fewer than half of the Jews had immediate Jewish neighbors. . . . In towns with sparse Jewish population, Jews usually lived scattered among Christian neighbors."

[17] Anabaptists began with the teachings of the Swiss Ulrich Zwingli in Switzerland in the 1520s. Today's Mennonites, Amish, and Hutterites trace their founding back to Zwingli. The Irvingian Church, named after Edward Irving, but also called the Catholic Apostolic Church, was started in Scotland in 1831.

[18] The district of Kassel, for which data are missing, was most likely Evangelical Reformed as well, which would bring the number to ten districts.

[19] The district of Schlüchtern may have been mostly United Evangelical, making it three, but we are not sure. We will know this when we have finished cleaning data for this district.

[20] A uniting or united church was the result of a merger of two Protestant Christian faiths.

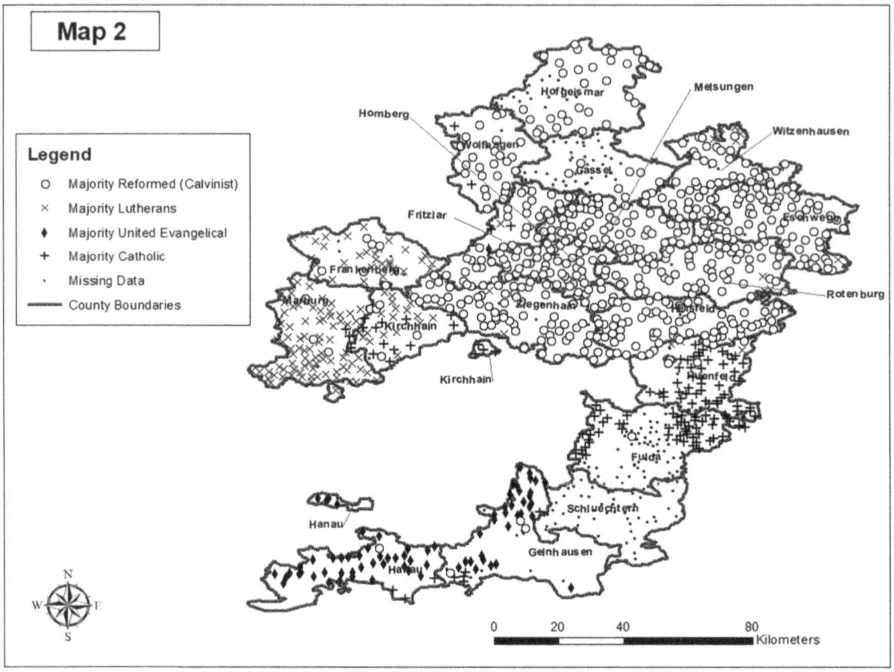

Fig. 15.2 Distribution of Christian confessions by community. (*Source*: Community survey data: Germany, HStAM, Bestand H3)

for example, everyone in the village of Ginseldorf (district Marburg) was Catholic except for the family of the forester; the Catholics in the Lutheran community of Treis an der Lumbde (district Marburg) were described as civil servants; the sole Catholic in the town of Rosenthal (district Frankenberg) was a lawyer; all in the village of Merzhausen (district Ziegenhain) were Reformed Evangelical except for a few servants who were Lutheran.

It is further interesting to note that we found not a single instance of a person following one of the Protestant minority confessions (Anabaptism, Mennonite, etc.) living in a majority Catholic community.[21] Any such followers were in majority Protestant communities. Perhaps this is not surprising, as such individuals had mostly splintered off from Protestant denominations and may have had a difficult enough time living among those who followed the mainline Protestant faiths. We found the use of the term "dissident" a few times in the records, as one referring to those not following the main (single) Protestant religion practiced in the community.

[21] Fulda is the one large Catholic town with many different Protestants. It is possible that there were Christian minorities living in the town of Fulda, given the large number of Protestants living there, but it is not mentioned in the survey.

15.4 Hessian Communities and Their Diverse Socioeconomic Structures

We now turn to describing the main differences in communities by the simplest stratification into the three religious categories, majority-Protestant communities, majority-Catholic communities, and communities with some Jews. The means in Table 15.3 show that majority-Catholic communities were found at the highest average elevation, majority-Protestant communities at lower elevations, and communities with some Jews at the lowest. As seen in Fig. 15.1, most of the Catholic communities were in the mountainous *Kreise* of Hünfeld and Fulda, explaining their high elevation, while we suspect that the presence of Jews at lower elevations was because they likely clustered in communities that were more accessible to trade and migration routes.[22] Osmond (2003, p. 80) notes that Jewish presence was greater in market towns. Lowenstein (2005, p. 132) notes that Jewish traders traveled by foot, or by wagon if more prosperous, to sell their wares, in both rural and city areas. Traders divided up territories (*medinas* or *Gäue*) so as not to compete, which may have divided them geographically.

Table 15.3 also shows that majority-Catholic communities had the highest average landholding at 22.5 Acker per household (an Acker was 0.59 of an acre, U.S.), followed by majority-Protestant communities at 15.6, while communities with some Jews had the smallest average landholding of 10.7 Acker. In this pre-industrialized economy land was the major asset (Mendels 1972, p. 242), so this distribution indicates that Catholic communities were the wealthiest on average. Figure 15.3 adds further detail on the allocation of land across households in each type of community. Large farmers are those who own at least 20 Acker; small farmers up to 20. Homeowners are those who own just a house and garden with no other landholding, while renters rent their home and own no land. The proportion of citizens in each category tells us something about the social structure in the community as well as the wealth distribution, since landowners had the most status, while landless laborers and artisans were of a lower rank in society (Vits 1993). Majority-Catholic communities have the greatest proportion of large farmers and of farmers overall, with smaller proportions of homeowners and renters, compared to both the majority-Protestant communities and those with some Jews. These large farmers would have been well-to-do, and these majority-Catholic communities would have been the most agricultural in nature. Correspondingly, the communities with some Jews had fewer farmers and more homeowners and renters than the majority-Protestant communities, lending to their more urban character, discussed further below.

The survey respondents were asked to give the number of persons, houses, and families in the community, allowing us to glean a bit of detail about living arrangements. It is not surprising to find that majority-Catholic communities had the largest average family size (computed as number of residents divided by the number of

[22] In addition, the former Bishopric of Fulda, the main source of Hessian Catholics in the nineteenth century, just happened to be at a higher elevation.

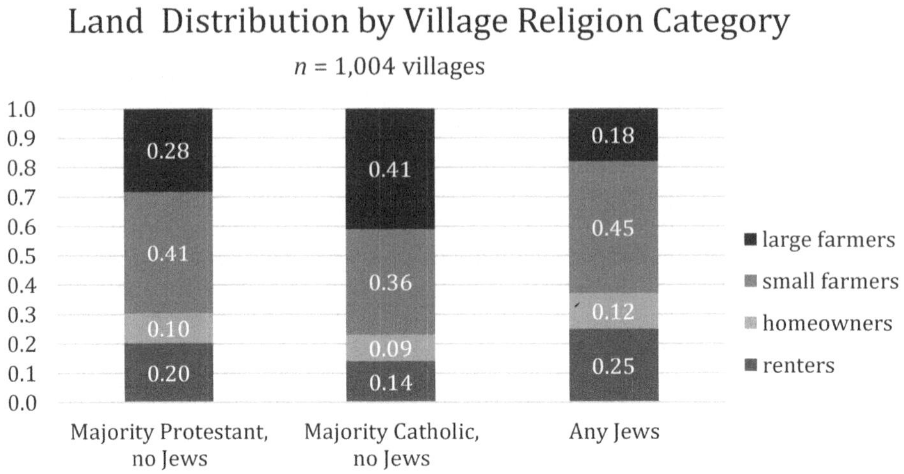

Fig. 15.3 Land distribution by majority-Protestant, majority-Catholic, and any Jewish population. (*Source*: Community survey data: Germany, HStAM, Bestand H3)

families) of 6.2 persons, with family size in majority-Protestant communities and communities with some Jews essentially equal at 5.3 and 5.1.[23] However, both the majority-Catholic communities and communities with some Jews had more people living in each house, 7.2 and 7.0 (number of residents divided by number of houses) than did the majority-Protestant communities. It appears there were more, smaller families per home in the communities with some Jews at 1.38 (computed as number of families divided by number of houses), followed by 1.26 in majority-Protestant communities and 1.17 in majority-Catholic communities. Lowenstein (2005, p. 105), evaluating differences in living standards between German Jews and non-Jews in this period, notes, "What was probably specifically Jewish was the crowding into multiple dwellings caused by legal limitations on Jewish homeownership."[24] Communities with any Jews were also more urban in character, which could have contributed to a higher number of person per home even outside of Jewish households.

This urban character is illustrated in Table 15.3, where we see that communities with some Jews have a strikingly larger population average and higher density relative to majority-Protestant and majority-Catholic communities, where population averages are very close but density is a bit higher in the majority-Catholic communities, perhaps related to the larger family sizes. Breuilly (2003, p. 197) remarks more broadly on the presence of Jewish settlements in larger German towns. But while a certain population may have accompanied the presence of Jews in a town,

[23] Hajnal notes that the average household size in pre-industrial Europe was five persons (Hajnal 1983, p. 65).

[24] Soliday comments on the growing Jewish population and the need for more space in the Free City of Frankfurt in the seventeenth and eighteenth centuries (Soliday 1974, pp. 175–197).

they were not found in abundance in the largest German cities because of residence restrictions.[25] Lowenstein (2005, p. 97) notes, "Only a small minority of German Jews lived in large cities.... Some important Jewish communities were located in villages or smaller cities just outside large cities that excluded Jews." Forty-six of the Hessian communities in our data had the official designation of *Stadt*, which translates into English as "city" or "town." This term conferred rights to hold more types of markets and allow more types of high-skilled artisans to operate and thus designated more metropolitan communities with more complex economies (Bovensiepen 1909). The vast majority of these "cities," 43, housed some Jews, again indicating that Jews clustered in more urban places. We can see that the number of markets and the number of types of high-skilled artisans allowed in the communities with some Jews were accordingly higher than in the majority-Protestant and majority-Catholic localities.

The average land price was also higher in communities with some Jews, likely related to the higher density and a greater turnover in land, relative to the more staid Catholic-majority communities where families likely held on to land over the generations, with the majority-Protestant land price somewhere in the middle.[26] The number of poor supported by the town was higher in communities with some Jews, possibly reflecting the fewer landowners and a more unsettled population.

15.5 Occupation and Religious Identity

In the 1850s, the principality of Hesse-Cassel was known for its relative poverty (Kukowski 1995; 6). The three main occupations were farmer, artisan, and laborer, with large farmers occupying the highest status in most places (Vits 1993). Still at this time, in place were old-fashioned guild laws which permitted most localities only a narrow set of artisan professions, including ones like baker, smith, butcher, shoemaker, carpenter, and a few others (Bovensiepen 1909).

Our information on the occupations of Jews is uniquely detailed, because for localities with Jewish residents, the community survey asked an additional question about the kind of occupation or business Jews were involved in. We thus have occupational information for the Jews in the 255 Hessian communities where they resided. Table 15.4 lists the different occupations mentioned in the records.[27] All we know is whether an occupation was practiced by Jews. The figure of 25% listed in Table 15.4 for artisans does not mean that 25% of Jews were artisans. What it means

[25] The three majority Protestant cities in Hesse-Cassel were Homberg in the district of Homberg and Lichtenau and Grossalmerode, both in the district of Witzenhausen. Remarkably, no Jews resided in any of these three officially designated cities.

[26] See Bestand H3, Community Survey.

[27] In addition, these occupations and/or life circumstances were mentioned once and for a single community: teacher, veterinarian, brewer, lawyer, miller, restaurant/bar owner, lives from own money, lives from support of relatives, and lives from support of sons in America.

Table 15.4 List of occupations for Jews

Occupation	#Communities found in	% of Communities with Jews
Trade (*Handel*)	192	75.3%
Trade, small trader (e.g., grocer)	38	14.9
Trade, distressed, petty trade (*Nothhandel*)	85	33.3
Rag picker	6	2.4
Artisans	65	25.5
Butchers	29	11.4
Seller of delicatessen/spices (*Speierei*)	17	6.7
Farming	66	25.9
Day labor	7	2.7
Factory workers	1	0.4
Brokers (*Mäkler*)	4 or 5	1.6 or 2.0
Lives from charity	3	1.2

Source: Community survey data: Germany, HStAM, Bestand H3

is that the occupation of artisan was mentioned as an occupation in which Jews were engaged in 65 of these 255 communities, specifically 25% of them.

The most common occupation was some involvement in trade. Surveys for a total of 192 communities, over 75% of the communities with Jews in our data, mentioned "trade" (*Handel* in German). In some cases this was a vague and incomplete statement and could mean a merchant, a businessman running a small store or a less prestigious form of trade, such as petty trade. In many other cases, it was better specified: at least 50 of these 192 communities mentioned trade in livestock, which could mean a bigger operation than peddling. As Stephen Lowenstein has noted, many Jews well-to-do enough purchased small amounts of land but although registered as farmers." spent the bulk of their time in the cattle trade" (Lowenstein 2005, p. 139). This seems to have been the case for Hesse-Cassel.

A number of communities were more explicit about the size of a trading operation and listed the presence of small stores (38 communities or 14.9%), butchers (11%), and the activity of petty trade or distressed trade, known as *Nothhandel* in German (85 communities, 33%). Trade is a common theme in the literature on Jewish history, and petty trade was a specialty of Jews.

Until the emancipations of the nineteenth century, European Jews had been blocked from engaging in many occupations. Various types of trade, though, had been accessible. Distressed trade involved peddling goods within communities or from village to village or selling goods at market stands; often traders employed credit. In the rural areas, peddlers traveled long distances by foot, or if better off, by wagon. Peddlers could be found in more urban areas as well. The emancipation of Jews made it possible for a transition from peddling or ambulatory trade to shopkeeping.[28]

[28] Lowenstein (2005, pp. 132–135) provides an in-depth discussion.

Our comparison groups come from stylized facts other scholars have found about the occupations of Jews. Botticini and Eckstein (2012, p. 188) state the following, albeit for a much earlier period:

> In the Hebrew record from the second half of the tenth century onward, shopkeeping, local trade, long-distance commerce, toll-collection, minting, and money changing were the main occupations of German Jews. They also could and did own land, gardens, orchards, and vineyards, in which they employed Christian tenants and agricultural laborers. Soon thereafter, many German Jews became heavily engaged in lending money at interest.

Stephan Lowenstein's discussion is much closer in time to our analysis. He elaborates on the various changes for Jews in the nineteenth century, partly due to the many emancipation laws passed as well as the pressures stemming from the industrial revolution. He concludes the following (Lowenstein 2005, p. 143):

> Until about 1840, most Jews of Germany had to struggle to make a bare living, usually as ambulatory petty traders in the countryside. Some attempted to improve their lot by switching into crafts. A growing minority opened retail businesses selling a variety of goods. In the period from 1840 to 1870, as the Industrial Revolution took hold in Germany, the economic position of Jews changed more rapidly. Despite the continued existence of pockets of poverty, most German Jews moved in the middle class.

Both sets of authors mention trade as a common occupation, which is what we find as well. Lowenstein mentions the move into crafts, which aligns with our finding that *artisan* was mentioned as an occupation for Jews in a fourth of the Hessian communities they lived in.

A surprise in our data is the extent, at 25%, that farming shows up so frequently as an occupation for Jews. Other scholars have not found this. While Botticini and Eckstein mention Jewish ownership of land for the period from 1000 AD to 1492, they argue elsewhere, and in contrast, that a miniscule number of German Jews were working in agriculture in 1933, less than 1% of all Jewish workers in Germany (Botticini and Eckstein 2012; 65). Similarly, Kaplan (2005, p. 217) finds that in both 1895 and 1907, 1% of German Jewish workers were working in the agricultural sector; the comparable figures for non-Jewish German workers are 36% in 1895 and 29% in 1907.[29]

Another surprise, perhaps, is the lack of a large number of Jews involved in moneylending. We find only four or five communities where the term *Mäkler* is mentioned; most of these were found in villages in the district of Gelnhausen, near Frankfurt, and all with populations of 500 to 700 people. One money lender lived in the town of Langenselbold, a town with a population over 2600 people, in the eastern part of the district of Hanau, but a bit closer to Frankfurt than the other villages with moneylenders. We reason that the close proximity to the bustling city of Frankfurt helped moneylenders to run their businesses. We wonder if, with the rise in savings institutions and other banking enterprises in the first half of the nineteenth century, whether the demand for moneylending services had declined.

---

[29] It is not clear from her work whether this counted both agricultural laborers and farmers (owners of land).

Lowenstein argues that moneylenders were a small percentage of all Jewish occupations. In addition, he explains that Jewish retailers, grocers, and cattle traders extended credit as well (Lowenstein 2005; pp. 132, 136).

15.6 Conclusion

During the sixteenth century, the principality of Hesse-Cassel was at the center of debates involving the Reformation. Geographically, it occupied a central location within the area that became Germany and thus lay to some degree at important political crossroads of Europe. Prince-Electors' personal decisions on which religion to adopt as well the aftermath of the Thirty Years' War determined the religious faiths for the majority of their Hessian subjects.

Skipping forward two centuries, to a time when Hessians had gained many civil liberties and could not really be considered subjects any longer, we document the variety of religions practiced in Hesse-Cassel by using micro data from an 1850s Hessian community survey. These data have established the religious makeup of over 1000 villages and towns across the contiguous area of the principality (see Figs. 15.1 and 15.2). We found that in the middle of the nineteenth century most mainline Christian groups were clustered, with the Evangelical Protestants dominating the northern and eastern districts, the Lutherans in three western districts surrounding the university town of Marburg, the United Evangelicals in two districts in the south close to Frankfurt, and the Catholics in former bishoprics, mostly in the east. In contrast, Jews lived in communities scattered across the region but only in about 23% of the communities in our sample. Protestant minorities were also scattered but in an even smaller number of places. In this analysis, a particularly noteworthy finding concerns the Hessian Jews. Based on our sample, Jews made up a much larger percentage of the Hessian population than other scholars have found for Germany overall.[30]

We examined the main differences between majority Protestant, majority Catholic, and communities with some Jews. This analysis produced several interesting and statistically significant results. Majority Catholic places were typically starkly different from those with some Jews living in them, while Protestant majority communities were in between the two. Catholics lived at higher elevations, while Jews lived at lower ones. The communities with the highest number of large farms were in Catholic places, while the opposite was true where there were Jews. The latter signifies more importantly that Jews lived in places that were more urban in character, essentially communities with larger populations, a greater variety of economic activity, more types of artisans, and more markets. Majority Catholic communities were on average the opposite. The differences were not just economic or geographical but also demographic: for example, majority Catholic towns had the

[30] See Botticini et al. (2019).

largest average family size, whereas majority Protestant places and places with Jews both had much lower average family sizes.

Lastly, the community survey provided the most detailed occupational information for Jews, allowing us to document the variety of occupations that they engaged in. About one quarter of villages and towns with Jews listed them as engaged in farming and/or with some artisan craft, and the overwhelming majority mentioned trade as a main occupation.

We believe we have documented a relationship between religious beliefs and socioeconomic outcomes. While we do not make any causal claims, we provide evidence for mid-nineteenth century Hesse-Cassel that meaningful economic and social variation existed between communities that differed in terms of the dominant religion practiced. We plan to expand on our findings by exploring in future work what may have driven these differences.

Appendix: Wegge on Murray

Generous of heart and giving of his time and ideas, John E. Murray was truly a special person in the world of academia. For those of us in the field of economic history, he was a great listener, a careful thinker, and a fantastic role model. Scholars young and old flocked to him for professional advice and guidance on their research projects. Journal editors and other intellectual leaders sought him out for editorial board positions, referee reports, and book reviews. When I managed the economics panel for the internal grant competition at the City University of New York in 2009, John assisted me with several referee reports. Others have remarked that he was a superb colleague within his own home institutions and more widely within the economic history profession. His C.V. is a testament to the immense amount of academic service he was involved in, both at lofty and less glamourous levels.

It was a joy to work with John and to speak with him at conferences, partly because he was not only smart and gifted but also humble and approachable. He was a devout Christian, a person devoted to his family, and a person confident in his own gifts and talents. At least this is what I saw outwardly, and I like to think he had no need for more external rewards since well-researched and consummately written scholarship was the ultimate prize. Another reason I and so many other academics enjoyed being around John is that he loved learning, teaching, and writing, and always wanted to do more, whether it was in economics, religion, history, or languages, but especially in all of them at the same time. Over the very long run he found a way to improve his knowledge of math, philosophy, theology, history, and languages. He was always working on his tool kit. John was an academic's academic, and many of us wanted to be in his orbit and absorb something from the way he looked at the world and operated in it.

In his 26 years as a professor, post-Ph.D., and according to my own counting, John published three books, at least 37 refereed journal articles, numerous other articles in other outlets, and 28 book reviews. It is an admirable record! He had a keen interest in special historical and often marginalized population groups, including the Shakers in Ohio, paupers in Early America, and orphans in Charleston. His research on the Shakers is noteworthy for several reasons. In a series of papers, many with co-authors (especially Metin Coşgel), John analyzed how a religious society that operated as a commune tackled production issues: he and his co-authors studied their production in dairying and swine and examined how they balanced their economic, religious, and cultural priorities, all in a commune. John was ahead of his time in studying the economics of religion and communes.

At the risk of being repetitive, John cared very much about great research, and his *Weltanschauung* was clearly interdisciplinary. Had he lived longer, I can imagine him being elected as president of the Social Science History Association (SSHA). He would be pleased at the way the Religion network at the SSHA has strengthened over the years and is now sponsoring many more sessions at the annual conference than 10 years ago.

I miss John, his friendship, his spirit, his ideas, and his contributions to academia. I hope that this volume would make him proud. I also hope that this book will bring some collective and communal solace to his colleagues, friends, and family, near and far, who miss him so dearly.

References

Becker SO, Woessmann L (2009) Was Weber wrong? A human capital theory of Protestant economic history. Q J Econ 124:531–596

Botticini M, Eckstein Z (2012) The chosen few: how education shaped Jewish history, 70–1492. Princeton University Press, Princeton

Botticini M, Eckstein Z, Vaturi A (2019) Child care and human development: insights from Jewish history in Central and Eastern Europe, 1500–1930. Econ J 129:2637–2690

Bovensiepen R (1909) Die kurhessische Gewerbepolitik und die wirtschaftliche Lage des zünftigen Handwerks in Kurhessen von 1816–1867. Elwert, Marburg

Breuilly J (2003) Urbanization and social transformation, 1800-1914. In: Ogilvie S, Overy R (eds) Germany: a new social and economic history, since 1800, vol III. Arnold, New York, pp 192–226

Coşgel MM, Murray JE (1998) Productivity of a commune: the Shakers, 1850-1880. J Econ Hist 58:494–510

Coşgel MM, Miceli TJ, Murray JE (1997) Organization and distributional equality in a network of communes: the Shakers. Amer J Econ Sociol 56:129–144

Deutsch G, Salfeld S, Kottek H (1906) Hesse. Jewish Encyclopedia, https://www.jewishencyclopedia.com/articles/7651-hesse. Accessed 27 Mar 27 2021

Fox GT (1976) Studies in the rural history of Upper Hesse, 1650–1830. PhD dissertation, Vanderbilt University

Frank H (1994) Regionale Entwicklungsdisparitäten im deutschen Industrialisierungsprozeß 1849–1939. Lit, Münster

German Virtual Jewish History Tour (2021) Jewish Virtual Library. https://www.jewishvirtuallibrary.org/germany-virtual-jewish-history-tour. Accessed 26 Mar 26 2021

Germany, State of Hesse. Hessisches Staatsarchiv Marburg (HStAM). Marburg, Germany. Bestand H3 (Community survey), 1850s.

Gräf HT (1997) The Collegium Mauritianum in Hesse-Kassel and the making of Calvinist diplomacy. Sixteenth Cent J 28:1167–1180

Hajnal J (1983) Two kinds of preindustrial household formation system. In: Wall R, Robin J, Laslett P (eds) Family forms in historic Europe. Cambridge University Press, Cambridge, pp 65–104

Hessen-Kassel (1843) Kurfürstlich hessisches Hof- und Staatshandbuch. Waisenhaus, Cassel. http://opacplus.bsbmuenchen.de/title/514509-0

Hessen-Kassel (1860) Daily life in Germany 1618–1945. Oxford University Press, New York, pp 173–205

Kaplan MA (2005) As Germans and as Jews in Imperial Germany. In: Kaplan MA (ed) Jewish daily life in Germany 1618–1945. Oxford University Press, New York, pp 173–205

Knodel J (1967) Law, marriage and illegitimacy in nineteenth-century Germany. Pop Stud 20:279–294

Kukowski M (1995) Pauperismus in Kurhessen: ein Beitrag zur Entstehung und Entwicklung der Massenarmut in Deutschland 1815–1855. Hessische Historische Kommission Darmstadt & Historische Kommission für Hessen, Marburg

Landgeschichtliches Informationssytem Hessen (LAGIS) (2021) Historical gazetteer. https://www.lagis-hessen.de/en/. Accessed 29 March 2021

Lowenstein SM (2005) The beginning of integration, 1780-1870. In: Kaplan M (ed) Jewish daily life in Germany 1618–1945. Oxford University Press, New York, pp 93–171

Mendels F (1972) Proto-industrialization: the first phase of the industrialization process. J Econ Hist 32:241–261

Munter C (1983) "Das Land der Armen Leute": poverty in the Marburg region of Hesse in the nineteenth century. PhD dissertation, Johns Hopkins University

Murray JE (1995) Human capital in religious communes: literacy and selection of nineteenth century Shakers. Explor Econ Hist 32:217–235

Murray JE (2000) Communal viability and employment of non-member labor: testing hypotheses with historical data. Rev Soc Econ 58:1–16

Murray JE, Coşgel MM (1998) Market, religion, and culture in Shaker swine production, 1788–1880. Ag Hist 72:552–573

Murray JE, Coşgel MM (1999) Between God and market: influences of economy and spirit on Shaker communal dairying, 1830–1875. Soc Sci Hist 23:41–65

Osmond J (2003) Land, peasant, and Lord in German agriculture since 1800. In: Ogilvie S, Overy R (eds) Germany: a new social and economic history, since 1800, vol III. Arnold, New York, pp 71–105

Pedlow GW (1988) The survival of the Hessian nobility 1770–1780. Princeton University Press, Princeton

Soliday GL (1974) A community in conflict. Frankfurt Society in the 17th and early 18th centuries. The University Press of New England, Hanover

Theibault J (1995) German villages in crisis: rural life in Hesse-Kassel and the Thirty Years' War, 1580–1720. Humanities Press New Jersey, Atlantic Highlands

Vits B (1993) Die Wirtshafts-und Sozialstruktur ländlicher Siedlungen in Nordhessen vom 16. bis zum 19. Jahrhundert. Im Selbstverlag der Marburger Geographischen Gesellschaft, Marburg/Lahn

Walker M (1971) German home towns: community, state and general estate, 1648–1817. Cornell University Press, New York

Chapter 16
Productivity, Mortality, and Technology in European and US Coal Mining, 1800–1913

Javier Silvestre

Abstract European coal production underwent a period of dramatic increase from the early nineteenth century to 1913. A consensus exists, however, for a depiction of the coal industry as, to a high degree, technologically stagnant throughout the long nineteenth century. Macro-inventions, or general-purpose technologies, in fact, appeared at either end of the period. Steam power to drive water pumps and shaft elevators was introduced in the eighteenth century, while the application of mechanical power to different tasks and the electrification of mines were advances that became pervasive in the twentieth century. In the interregnum, therefore, the increase in European coal production would have mainly been the result of adding more labor rather than developing new technology. This paper aims to revise this interpretation. First, long-term series of labor productivity and fatality rates data are presented for the four main coal-producing European nations, Great Britain, Belgium, France, and Germany. Second, a link between improvements in Europe both in productivity and safety in conjunction with a series of "small-scale" technological innovations is proposed. These technologies, which emerged and diffused to affect different aspects of mining production, did not involve huge investments in labor-replacing capital. They were, for the most part, complementary to labor and closely related to questions of safety. A comparison of both estimates, labor productivity and safety, for the European countries is also established with those of the United States, a latecomer to the exploitation of coal resources.

Keywords Long nineteenth-century coal mining · Productivity · Mortality · Technology · Europe · United States

J. Silvestre (✉)
Universidad de Zaragoza, Zaragoza, Spain
e-mail: javisil@unizar.es

P. Gray et al. (eds.), *Standard of Living*, Studies in Economic History,
https://doi.org/10.1007/978-3-031-06477-7_16

16.1 Introduction

The fuel of the European Industrial Revolution was coal. Data for eight European countries compiled by Kander et al. (2013, pp. 131–132) show that coal consumption per capita grew sevenfold between 1820 and 1910. More than four-fifths of Western Europe's energy supply came from coal on the eve of World War I (Kander et al. 2013, p. 132). Britain was the leader in coal exploitation, in large measure due to its development of coking and pumping technologies (Allen 2009).[1] However, although in the second half of the nineteenth century Britain still produced more coal than the rest of Continental Europe combined, a few countries became large-scale producers. Between the early 1830s (a point when statistical sources on coal improved for some of the major producing nations) and 1913, coal production in Britain and Belgium grew by a factor of 9, and a factor of 20 in France. While in Germany (Prussia), between 1850 and 1913, coal production grew by a factor of 41 (See Table 16.1). In 1913, these four countries accounted for 86.6 percent of the European output, according to data collected by Mitchell (1992) (See Table 16.2).

The different parts of Europe from which coal was won tended to be highly localized. In a broad geological sense, much of Europe's coal formed a discontinuous belt from coalfields in the North and the Midlands of Britain to Silesia, via the Nord and Pas-de-Calais coalfields in France, central Belgium, and the Ruhr. Other important coalfields included those in South Wales, the Loire Valley, and the Saar-Lorraine (e.g. Pounds and Parker 1957; Wrigley 1961; Leboutte 1997). It is true that, for example, France had many scattered coal basins throughout the country, but most of them were of little importance. The actual availability of coal has been one of the main topics in the discussion about the causes of the European Industrial Revolution.[2] It has been argued that coal could have been transported, as indeed it was to non-producing regions and countries. In spite of the uneven advance of coal across Europe over the nineteenth century (Kander et al. 2013, p. 137; Henriques and Sharp 2021), national and international coal markets became more integrated, especially up to the turn of the century, reflecting a decline in transaction costs (Murray and Silvestre 2020).

Table 16.1 Output of coal, in thousands of metric tons

	Britain	Belgium	France	Prussia	United States
c. 1830	30,500	2531	2047		799
1850	62,500	5803	4252	4419	7580
1913	287,500	22,842	40,051	180,058	517,059

Sources: See Figs. 16.1, 16.2, 16.3, 16.4, and 16.5
Notes: Britain: 1830; Belgium: 1833; France: 1834; United States: 1830

[1] See also Otojanov et al. (2020).

[2] As recently reviewed by Fernihough and O'Rourke (2014), Murray and Silvestre (2020), Henriques and Sharp (2021) and Ranestad and Sharp (2021). See also, for example, Foreman-Peck (2006).

Table 16.2 Share (%) of European coal production

	Britain	Belgium	France	Germany	Rest of Europe	Total
1830	83.1	6.3	5.2	4.9	0.5	100
1850	77.7	7.2	5.5	8.5	1.2	100
1913	39.9	3.3	5.6	37.8	13.4	100

Source: Own elaboration from Mitchell (1992, pp. 416–425)
Notes: Rest of Europe includes Russia. Hard coal (here, anthracite and bituminous) and lignite combined

A stronger consensus, however, exists for another of the main topics involving coal: the coal industry has been depicted as, to a large extent, technologically stagnant, and unable to make significant gains in productivity throughout the long nineteenth century. Far-reaching macro-inventions, or general-purpose technologies, in fact, appeared at either end of the period. On the one hand, steam power to drive water pumps and shaft elevators was introduced in the eighteenth century. The Newcomen engine, mainly but not exclusively, was first adopted in Britain and then in the main Continental European coalfields (e.g. Pounds and Parker 1957, pp. 81–82; Wrigley 1961, pp. 14, 27; Leboutte et al. 1998, p. 46; Allen 2009, pp. 161–163; Mokyr 2009, pp. 269–270; Kander et al. 2013, p. 165).[3]

On the other hand, the application of mechanical power to different tasks pertaining to coal extraction and (horizontal and vertical) transportation of coal, miners, and equipment, as well as the electrification of mines, although in some cases introduced during the period being studied (or earlier), were advances that, with some exceptions, did not become pervasive until the twentieth century. For example, coal-cutting machines, at first usually powered by compressed air and later by electricity, diffused slowly because of problems of motive power, maintenance, and reliability, not to mention the geological conditions of mines, safety issues, and the reorganization of labor. On the eve of World War I, 8 percent of coal was mechanically cut in Britain (although 20 percent in Scotland), 10 percent in Belgium, and below 3 percent in the Ruhr (Bézy 1951, p. 39; Milward and Saul 1973, p. 187; Greasley 1990, p. 883; Scott 2006, p. 27; Jopp 2016, p. 1117).[4] As a consequence of the adoption of more productive coal-cutting machines, another sweeping innovation, the conveyor (as a replacement for wagons and rails), was first used in Britain in 1902. By 1928, only 11.8 percent of British coal was face conveyed (Scott 2006, p. 27). In Continental Europe, the expansion of conveyors first began in Germany (Rice and Hartmann 1939, p. 167).

Drilling may have required less energy than coal cutting and, consequently, may have been more diffused. But, again, compressed air technology, even if well established by the 1880s, had its limitations (e.g. Lamb 1976, p. 165; Hickey 1985, p. 112; Church 1986, p. 344; McIvor and Johnston 2007, p. 34). The use of steam

[3] See also, for example, Otojanov et al. (2020).

[4] See also, for example, Abel (1889, pp. 16–17), Rice and Hartmann (1939, pp. 46, 151–158), Lamb (1976, pp. 161–164), Gillet (1984, p. 110), and Burghardt (1995, p. 139).

Fig. 16.1 Labor productivity and the fatality rate in coal mining, Great Britain, 1800–1913. (*Notes*: Production includes coal extracted from open quarries. The records do not generally distinguish between bituminous and anthracite, but only small amounts of the latter were produced. The fatality rate for 1813 and 1842 refers to the North-East coalfield only. *Sources*: Productivity, 1800, 1816 and 1820: Mitchell (1984, p. 317); 1831 and 1841: Church (1986, p. 472). Production, 1851–1913: Church (1986, p. 86). Workers, 1851–1913: Wright (1905, p. 416) and Church (1986, pp. 304–305). Fatality rate, 1813 and 1942: Hair (1968, pp. 553, 559–560). Fatalities, 1851–1903: Wright (1905, p. 444); 1904–1913: data compiled by Arthur McIvor, originally taken from Board of Trade, Abstract of Labour Statistics (various years). See also Murray and Silvestre (2015) for the sources used for cross reference purposes)

and compressed air for transportation purposes, although it gradually became more prevalent, also suffered from limitations in power transmission and safety (e.g. Hay 1924; Poole 1924). Electric locomotives appeared or began to consolidate only at the end of the period. Similarly, some portable electric lights appeared in the final years of the century, but (perhaps) the most successful early electric lamp did not materialize until 1912, in Germany (Maurice 1937, p. 367). While (safer) electric detonators were beginning to appear by the end of the nineteenth century (Guttmann 1895a, p. 333).

In the interregnum, therefore, the dramatic increase in European coal production would have mainly been the result of adding more labor rather than developing new technology. References, usually brief, to the illumination and ventilation of mines, the use of explosives, or better transport systems are actually not uncommon in the economic and social history literature. However, as epitomized by Milward and Saul (1973, p. 187), in the nineteenth-century coal industry, "Like house building, the industrial revolution to a major degree passed it by." And, as more recently argued by Stewart (2003, p. 518) with regard to mining in general, "real productivity gains would have to await the substitution of capital for labor in the drilling, boring, and movement of ore underground." For the particular case of Britain, Wrigley (2016, p. 42) concludes, "It is an interesting irony of the period during

Fig. 16.2 Labor productivity and the fatality rate in coal mining, Belgium, 1833–1913. (*Sources*: Production, 1833–1903: Wright (1905, pp. 113–114); 1904–1913: Ministère de l'Intérieu (1904–1913). Workers, 1833–1903: Wright (1905, p. 118); 1904–1913: Ministère de l'Intérieu (1904–1913). Fatalities, 1833–1903: Wright (1905, p. 141); 1904–1913: Ministère de l'Intérieu (1904–1913). See also Murray and Silvestre (2015) for the sources used for cross reference purposes, as well as Feldman and Tenfelde (1990, pp. 396–400))

which the English economy was transformed by the energy derived from coal that manpower productivity in the coalmining industry barely changed…." Similar arguments can be found in Benson (1989, p. 7), MacRaid and Martin (2000, p. 29), Ó Gráda (2016, p. 230), and the works cited therein. Thus the question is posed by Clark and Jacks (2007, p. 47): "Might the absence of an 'unceasing flow of technical advances'—safety lamps, gunpowder in shaft excavating, improved winding gearing, ventilation systems, and so on—have driven up costs in the nineteenth by hundreds of percent?"[5]

Studies of coal mining productivity at national or regional levels tend to share two characteristics. First, they usually focus on the late-nineteenth and early-twentieth centuries, a period of stagnant or even decreasing productivity (an issue to which I will return below), thus overlooking the dynamics of a longer-term evolution (e.g. Lamb 1976, esp. p. 155; Greasley 1990; Burghardt 1995, p. 382; Scott 2006; Broadberry and Burhop 2007; Burhop 2008; Burhop and Lübbers 2009). However, Clark and Jacks' (2007) estimates focus attention on the early English Industrial Revolution, between 1700 and 1869, showing a very modest productivity growth.[6] Longer-term analyses include Mitchell (1984, esp. p. 317), Church (1986,

[5] Quotation marks in "unceasing flow of technical advances" are used by the authors, referring to Flinn (1984).

[6] The authors also review previous literature, including the cliometric account of coal in the British Industrial Revolution.

Fig. 16.3 Labor productivity and the fatality rate in coal mining, France, 1834–1913. (*Notes*: Small amounts of anthracite and lignite were produced, and usually reported separately. Production of bituminous, anthracite, and lignite combined are included here. *Sources*: Production, 1833–1903: Wright (1905, pp. 184–185); 1904–1913: Ministère des Travaux Publics (1904–1913). Workers, 1833–1903: Wright (1905, p. 197); 1904–1913: Ministère des Travaux Publics (1904–1913). Fatalities, 1833–1903: Wright (1905, pp. 209–210) and, for 1859, Conus and Escudier (1997a); 1904–1913: Ministère des Travaux Publics (1904–1913). See also Murray and Silvestre (2015) for the sources used for cross reference purposes, as well as Feldman and Tenfelde (1990, pp. 396–400))

esp. pp. 470–496), and Jopp (2017).[7] Second, these studies predominantly refer to Britain and Germany, specifically the Ruhr area.[8] While granting less coverage to other major producing countries such as Belgium and France. Exceptions would include Wibail (1914), de Bivort de La Saudée (1939), Bézy (1951), and Wauthelet (1997).

This essay aims to revise the interpretation of the European coal industry as, in essence, technologically stagnant. In the next section, long-term series of labor productivity and fatality rates data are presented for the four main coal-producing European nations, Britain, Belgium, France, and Germany. The measurement of productivity used, although elementary, suggests a less bleak picture, with marked increases, notably in Continental Europe, up to approximately the late 1880s, or a little earlier in the case of Britain. The consideration of safety responds to the key fact that the capital introduced into mines was, for the most part, complementary to labor and closely related to questions of safety. Fatality rates show a considerable decline up to the turn of the century. A comparison of both estimates, labor productivity and the fatality rate, is established between the European countries and the United States, a latecomer to the exploitation of coal resources. Between 1850 and

[7] Jopp (2016, p. 1117) reviews previous studies for the Ruhr coalfield. See also related research reviewed by Broadberry and Burhop (2007).

[8] The Ruhr accounted for about 48 percent of German coal in 1880 and about 58 percent in 1913 (Burhop and Lübbers 2009, p. 503).

Fig. 16.4 Labor productivity and the fatality rate in coal mining, Prussia, 1852–1913. (*Notes*: Steinkohle (hard coal). *Sources*: Production and workers: Fischer (2011). Fatalities, 1852–1903: Wright (1905, p. 326); 1904–1911: Horton (1913, p. 66); 1912: US Bureau of Labor Statistics (1916, p. 65); 1913: Rice and Hartmann (1939, p. 257). See also Wright (1905) and Murray and Silvestre (2015))

1913, however, production in the United States grew by a factor of 68 (see Table 16.1). While its share of world production raised fourfold, to reach almost 40 percent of the world total (see Table 16.3).

Section 16.3 proposes a link between "small-scale" technological advances and improvements both in productivity and safety, as previously argued by Murray and Silvestre (2015) for the case of safety. Although no new large-scale technology appeared, or entered mainstream use, over the period, a series of relatively small-scale technologies emerged and diffused, within and between countries, to affect different aspects of mining production. Unlike the later mechanization of coal extraction and transportation, technologies in mine construction, working methods, transport, lighting, ventilation, and explosives did not tend to involve large scale investments in labor-replacing capital (e.g. Lamb 1976, p. 219; Mokyr 2010, p. 45; Murray and Silvestre 2015).[9] These methods permitted much more work without interruptions due to serious accidents, as well as an increase in job-specific human capital. The consequences of the aforementioned small-scale innovations have largely been overlooked, especially in the economic history literature.[10]

[9]The causes and effects of mechanization were actually varied. For Britain, see, for example, Jevons ([1915] 1969, pp. 212–213), who summarizes the general report of the Royal Commission of Coal Supplies, 1905. See also Melling (1996), McIvor and Johnston (2007, pp. 36–38), and the works cited therein. For Germany, see, for example, Spencer (1984, p. 94) and Jopp (2017, pp. 944–945). For the United States, see, for example, Rice and Hartmann (1939, p. 152) and Boal (2017).

[10]Although exceptions include Mitchell (1984) and Church (1986). Recent work by Singleton (2020, 2022) deals with rescue systems.

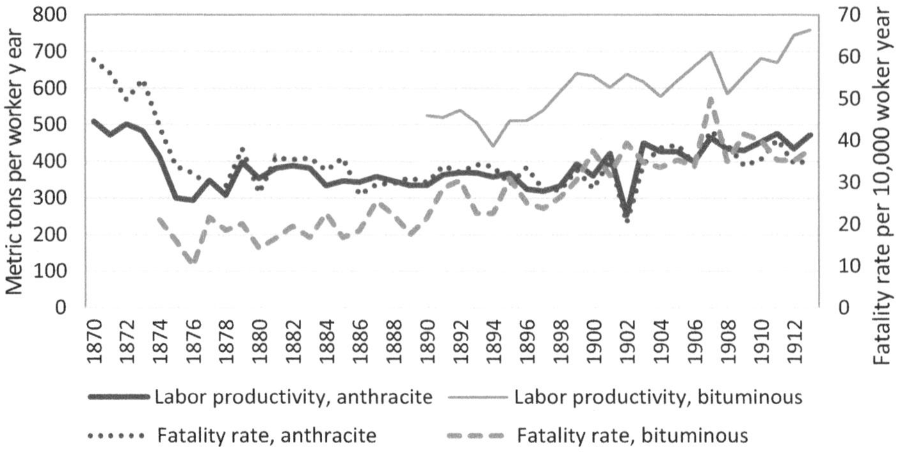

Fig. 16.5 Labor productivity and the fatality rate in coal mining, the US, 1870–1913. (*Sources*: Production and workers: Wright (2006, pp. 4–300-307). Fatality rates: Aldrich (1997a, pp. 300–301))

Table 16.3 Share (%) of world coal production

	Britain	Belgium	France	Germany	United States	Rest of the world	Total
1830	81.3	6.1	5.1	4.8	2.1	0.5	100
1850	71.0	6.6	5.0	7.7	8.6	1.1	100
1913	21.8	1.8	3.0	20.7	38.6	14.1	100

Sources: Own elaboration from Mitchell (1992, pp. 416–425), Mitchell (1993, pp. 306–311), and Mitchell (2003, pp. 352–359)
Notes: Rest of the world refers to up to 27 countries. Hard coal (here, anthracite and bituminous) and lignite combined

16.2 Labor Productivity and Fatality Rates in the Long-Term

Figures 16.1, 16.2, 16.3, 16.4, and 16.5 report (mostly) annual estimates of labor productivity and fatality rates for the four major European producing countries and the United States. Data for Prussia rather than Germany are used, since official statistics of accidents for the whole country seem not to have been published (Wright 1905, p. 326; Horton 1913, p. 66). Most German production occurred within the boundaries of Prussia, however. The collection of European data by labor statistician Carroll Wright (1905) was the starting point.[11] Wright (1905) was also used as a guide in order to check values and extend some series forward, as he included an exhaustive list of primary sources, i.e. government publications. The database was completed using secondary literature, particularly in the cases of Britain and

[11] On Carroll Wright's work, see Leiby (1960).

Germany. The main US data (in Fig. 16.5) are taken entirely from (Gavin) Wright (2006) and Aldrich (1997a). The list of sources used for each period is included in the Notes to Figs. 16.1, 16.2, 16.3, 16.4, and 16.5. Supporting data reported in Tables 16.4, 16.5, and 16.6 are mainly taken from US official publications.

Productivity is simply defined in terms of output per worker. As for the numerator, Figs. 16.1, 16.2, 16.3, 16.4, and 16.5 refer to the types of coal considered.[12] Both under and above ground work were considered when forming the denominator. Under ground work normally comprised three broad actions: hewing, transportation (of coal and miners), and development and maintenance (for example, roofing). Above ground work included the preparation and transport of coal, working the engines (such as those of pumps and fans), and a wide range of jobs that were necessary for mining operations (e.g. Church 1986, pp. 311–385; McIvor and Johnston 2007, pp. 28–32). The relative number of above ground workers may vary between countries (Aldrich 1997a, p. 65).

More precise measures of productivity, such as output per shift, output per hour, and total factor productivity, have been estimated for some countries, regions, or firms before World War I (e.g. Mitchell 1984; Church 1986; Greasley 1990; Scott 2006; Clark and Jacks 2007; Burhop and Lübbers 2009; Jopp 2016, 2017; Montant 2020). However, given the scarcity of data, these estimates usually refer to relatively short periods or specific dates. Trends, in any case, tend to coincide with simpler measures. Discrepancies may nevertheless emerge, for example, that between Church (1986, pp. 474–480) and Greasley (1990) concerning output per hour at the turn of the century. Table 16.4 reports an international comparison of daily productivity for the 1901–1913 period.

Table 16.4 Daily coal production per underground worker, in tons of 2000 pounds

	Britain	Belgium	France	Prussia	United States
1901	1.50	0.84	1.05	1.22	3.37
1902	1.49	0.87	1.05	1.22	3.55
1903	1.52	0.85	1.08	1.23	3.46
1904	1.53	0.83	1.07	1.24	3.52
1905	1.55	0.85	1.10	1.28	3.56
1906	1.53	0.85	1.09	1.31	3.70
1907	1.45	0.83	1.07	1.28	3.69
1908	1.43	0.82	1.04	1.24	3.72
1909	1.42	0.83	1.04	1.24	n.a.
1910	1.35	0.84	1.04	1.26	3.78
1911	1.36	0.82	1.06	1.29	3.72
1912	1.22	0.82	1.08	1.30	3.95
1913	1.28	0.80	1.08	1.32	3.85

Source: Adams (1920, p. 126)

[12] See also Murray and Silvestre (2020, pp. 673–674).

Table 16.5 Deaths per worker and deaths per metric ton

	Britain	Belgium	France	Prussia	United States
Panel A. Deaths per 10,000 worker year					
c.1850	43.8	32.5	40.2	17.9	
1860	35.7	24.6	33.2	23.8	
1871	27.5	25.9	27.8	29.8	55.0
1880	22.3	29.3	16.7	31.2	28.1
1890	18.3	14.4	24.2	27.2	26.5
1900	13.4	10.6	13.3	23.1	32.8
1912	13.3	10.6	12.2	22.9	35.7
Panel B. Deaths per 1000,000 metric tons mined per year					
c.1850	14.3	24.9	28.1	12.1	
1860	11.4	20.3	23.9	14.1	
1871	8.6	17.1	17.1	14.3	12.3
1880	7.5	18.1	9.4	11.7	6.6
1890	6.1	8.3	11.4	9.8	6.0
1900	4.6	6.2	6.4	8.7	6.0
1912	5.3	6.7	6.1	8.4	5.4

Sources: For Europe, see Figs. 16.1, 16.2, 16.3, and 16.4; for the United States, Fay (1916, pp. 10–11)
Notes: Three-year averages, except for Prussia, 1911–1912. c.1850 refers to 1851–1853, for Britain; 1851–1853, for Belgium; 1853–1855, for France; and 1852–1854, for Prussia. US data prior to 1889 represent only certain portions of the country, as inspections began in different states at different times. The number of workers represented 91 percent of the country total in 1889 (the first year for which this figure is reported in the source), 96 percent in 1900, and 100 percent from 1909 onwards. Production represented 47.4 percent of the country total in 1870, 74.3 percent in 1880, 92.7 percent in 1890, 96.5 percent in 1900, and 100 percent from 1909 onwards

Table 16.6 Deaths per 1000 workers calculated on the basis of a 300 working-day year

	Belgium	France	US
1901	1.2	1.3	4.5
1902	1.1	1.2	5.6
1903	1.1	1.0	4.4
1904	0.9	1.1	5.2
1905	0.9	1.1	5.1
1906	0.9	7.8	4.8
1907	1.0	1.1	6.3
1908	1.1	1.0	5.6
1909	0.9	1.2	5.3
1910	0.9	1.1	5.3

Source: Horton (1913, p. 90)
Notes: Workers employed under ground

The lack of reliable statistics in Britain before 1872, and especially before 1854, has led to a lively debate (e.g. Mitchell 1984; Church 1986; Minchinton 1990; and the works cited therein). In Fig. 16.1, I took the liberty of, essentially, splicing in

Church's (1986) annual (from the middle of the century) and decennial (1831 and 1841) estimates with Mitchell's (1984) roughly decennial (1800, 1816, and 1820) estimates. The big jump over the 1820s is remarkable and, to a large extent, possibly determined by, first, the fact that 1800, 1816, and 1820 were depression years (Mitchell 1984, p. 313); and, second, Church's (1986, pp. 85–88) upward re-estimation of output from 1831 onwards. Furthermore, sparse information on output and the number of workers for the early decades of the nineteenth century points to considerable regional variation (Flinn 1984, pp. 361–366).

The alternative approach by Clark and Jacks (2007) shows modest productivity growth between 1700 and 1860. Nevertheless, the authors' estimates may have underplayed, to some extent, the role played by the steam engine in mine drainage. Thus, it would not only have been a matter of costs, but also the existence of technological constraints in the use of horses in the deepest mines (Kander et al. 2013, p. 165).[13] This point was made previously by the mining engineer and colliery manager Robert L. Galloway ([1882] 1969, p. 82). It has also been argued that Clark and Jacks (2007) may have understated improvements such as those in ventilation, which became essential as depth increased (Mokyr 2009, p. 102). (I will return to mine depth below).

The fatality rate, i.e. deaths per 10,000 workers, is used as the measure of safety. Non-fatal accidents may also have been considered, but data are less widespread and much more ambiguous (e.g. Murray and Silvestre 2015, p. 901).[14] Both below and above ground workers again form the denominator. An alternative measure of safety, deaths per 1000,000 metric tons mined, is reported in Table 16.5, and will be particularly helpful in the Europe-US comparison. Table 16.6 accounts for differences in the number of working days.

As the British expansion of coal started earlier than the systematic record of fatalities, Fig. 16.1 includes estimates of risk for 1813 and 1842 provided by Hair (1968). It must be noted that these fatality rates refer only to the North-East coalfield, for which the available information is more abundant and reliable. The North-East was the most important coalfield, accounting for 30 percent of total output and 23 percent of total employment around 1800, and 22 percent of total output and 20 percent of total employment between 1830 and 1850 (Flinn 1984, pp. 26, 363–365; Church 1986, pp. 10, 189). However, it was also the most dangerous coalfield in terms of explosions, and that in which safety improved the most over the first half of the century thanks to the control of mine gases. In the other British coalfields, the decline in death rates from explosions was probably lower, and the decline in death rates from other causes may have been slight at best. Therefore, "it is probable that all the gassier coalfields showed some improvement, and it is possible that the remaining coalfields showed little or no improvement" (Hair 1968, p. 560).

---

[13] See also Fouquet (2008, p. 78) and Allen (2009, p. 162).

[14] Chronic occupation-related diseases are studied in works such as that of McIvor and Johnston (2007).

International, long-term comparisons of productivity and safety are not straightforward. Productivity and risks were, first and foremost, determined by natural conditions, such as geological folding and faulting, thickness and depth of coal seams, the strength of roofs and the presence of gasses, and the resultant mining methods. In broad terms, the US and the Upper Silesian coalfield (the second German coalfield in importance, after the Ruhr) had less difficult conditions than Britain, which in turn had better than or similar conditions to the Ruhr coalfield; while the northern (Nord and Pas-de-Calais) French coalfields and Belgium, in particular, tended to display the most difficult mining conditions (Horton 1913, pp. 88–89; Rice and Hartmann 1939, esp. pp. 55, 88, 94, 255, 312; Pounds and Parker 1957, esp. p. 131; Aldrich 1997a, ch. 2; Scott 2006, p. 23; see also Wrigley 1961, p. 55). Other, sometimes interrelated, factors, such as the number and the length of working days, labor relations, and differences between the US and Europe in the extent of mechanization and government intervention in safety will be (briefly) addressed below. In any case, all of these are limitations to be borne in mind when interpreting the evidence.

In Figs. 16.1, 16.2, 16.3, and 16.4, the series of productivity and accident risk for the main European producing countries reveal largely similar trends. Productivity in Continental Europe increased up to approximately the late 1880s, when it stagnated or even declined slightly. In Prussia, from mid-century, productivity jumped by two-thirds to about 250 tons. From the early 1830s, French and Belgian miner productivity doubled. British increase, up to the early 1880s, was lower. From that point onwards, productivity tended to fall. Therefore, a convergence process occurred among the less productive countries, which came to approach the relatively static British levels of productivity. Prussia caught up with Britain by the early 1890s, while the smaller producers, Belgium and France, increased productivity more gradually. Differences in productivity levels tend to reflect differences in natural disadvantages (see also Table 16.4).

In Britain, several causes acting simultaneously have been proposed so as to understand the generally poor performance from the 1880s to 1913.[15] It seems that the evolution of geological conditions could be the most determining factor, in the form of higher average depths, exhaustion of thicker seams, and aging of mines, the latter resulting in higher transportation and maintenance costs. Labor-related factors, such as absenteeism and reduction in work effort or hours worked, the latter mainly as a result of legislation, in general, seem to play a minor role in the long-term explanation (Mitchell 1984, 321–326; Church 1986, 470–496; Greasley 1990).

In reality, Figs. 16.1, 16.2, 16.3, and 16.4 may suggest that forces common to all major producing nations contributed to flattened out productivities from the end of the century onwards. As the nineteenth century progressed, worsening mining conditions resulting from the increasing scale of production and the length of time the mines were in operation have also been emphasized for Continental European countries (Wibail 1914, pp. 11–12; de Bivort de La Saudée 1939, p. 23; Gillet 1984,

[15] Short-term factors help to explain the sharp decline and rise in productivity in the 1870s and 1890s (Mitchell 1984, pp. 318–320, 325; Church 1986, pp. 471–472, 487–488, 491).

p. 17; Leboutte et al. 1998, 49). Thus, for example, in Belgium the average depth was 210 meters in 1838, 361 meters in 1856 (in the west of Mons), and 437 meters in 1866 (in the same area) (Pounds and Parker 1957, p. 131). In the Ruhr coalfield, the average depth was 134 meters in 1850, 172 meters in 1861, and 523 meters in 1913 (Jopp 2011, p. 82). A similar process occurred in France (Lamb 1976, p. 182). To the best of my knowledge, the effect of labor-related factors in Continental Europe is also not clear-cut. Regardless of which, in all the major coal-producing nations, including Britain, the labor movement strengthened and the incidence of strikes tended to rise from approximately the late 1880s onwards (Feldman and Tenfelde 1990, esp. pp. 25–27, 133, 226, 275–278; see also Hickey 1985, pp. 170–171; Parnell 1994 pp. 22–23; Wauthelet 1997).

Safety improved markedly throughout the period being studied. In Britain, Belgium, and France (Figs. 16.1, 16.2, and 16.3; Table 16.5) the risk of a fatal accident declined at least from when there are systematic records, from midway through the century, whereas in Prussia such a decline began later but was still evident from the mid-1880s (Fig. 16.4; Table 16.5). Belgian and French data compiled by Leboutte (1991) and Conus and Escudier (1997b), respectively, show that, as also probably happened in Britain, the decline could have started in earlier decades. Turning to the Figures presented here, in British and French mines the risk of mortality dropped by about 75 percent, from roughly around 40 per 10,000 in the middle of the century to just over 10 per 10,000 by the early 1910s.[16] In Belgium, the risk of death fell by two-thirds, from about 30 to 10 deaths per 10,000 workers. This is remarkable given the dangerous geological conditions of Belgian mines. Death rates in Prussia at the end of the period, although uneven, were uniquely high in Europe (see also Leboutte 1989; Martin 2009). Overall, declining trends in European countries applied to death rates from different causes, such as explosions and cave-ins, which were usually the most destructive (e.g. Hall and Snelling 1907; Murray and Silvestre 2015).

While the fundamental argument of this essay is that new technologies were hugely important in explaining trends in productivity and safety, the emphasis on technology alone as the causal agent in improvements cannot be entirely accurate. It has been proposed that, in general, regulation and technological change are interrelated; to put it simply, newer and better technologies may be adopted as a response to regulatory incentives (Pouliakas and Theodossiou 2013, p. 195), a point that has actually been made regarding the adoption of more productive and safer technologies and methods in European coal mining in the nineteenth century (e.g. Lamb 1976, p. 252; Leboutte 1989, p. 88; Singleton 2016, p. 111). Over this period government action included mine inspection laws that aimed to prompt mine owners into making collieries safer under threat of legal sanctions. In Britain, for example, mining was one of the first industries to be regulated (Singleton 2016, p. 109).

[16] In Britain, the spike in 1866 is associated with the explosion at the Oaks Colliery, which killed 334 men. A second explosion killed 27 members of a rescue team (e.g. Harvey 2016). In France, the spike in 1906 is associated with the explosion at the Courrières works in the Nord and Pas-de-Calais coalfields, which killed around 1100 miners (e.g. Neville 1978).

However, the British case indicates little direct effect of legislation on actual safety conditions (e.g. Bartrip and Burman 1983; McIvor and Johnston 2007, esp. p. 47; Mills 2010). Public intervention in the nineteenth-century coal industry was complex to design and implement, with the interests of several groups at stake (e.g. Mills 2010). The evidence for other European countries seems to be mixed (e.g. Lamb 1976, esp. pp. 244–252; Reid 1981; Leboutte 1989, 1991; Conus and Escudier 1997b; Murray and Silvestre 2015), though the Belgian record above all has received considerable attention, as mentioned above. In the words of Jevons ([1915] 1969, p. 375): "[It] reflects credit upon the mine engineers and the legal regulation for the protection of the workers".

In any case, it appears from the secondary literature that detailed and rigorous government regulation in Europe tended to occur after the onset of the decreasing trend in the risk of fatal accident. As an example, mainly from the 1880s onwards, government-appointed commissions collected evidence that helped to delineate revisions of already existing safety regulations regarding explosion risks, acknowledging coal dust as a factor; and the Courrières disaster in 1906 reinvigorated research on the prevention of explosions (Murray and Silvestre 2021). Two further determinants that may have contributed to an improvement in safety were accident insurance systems, which, when well-designed, provided incentives to reduce workplace dangers[17]; and stronger unions, which took up the cause of mine safety.[18] But, again, these were factors that tended to appear toward the end of the period being studied.

It is worth comparing Europe with the United States. The abundance of wood delayed the latter's transition to coal (Wright 2015). The anthracite coalfields of Pennsylvania were fully opened in the 1830s (Chandler 1972; Aldrich 1997b). But anthracite was overtaken by bituminous coal, the extraction of which expanded rapidly after the Civil War. Output and employment, even if they fluctuated, grew considerably until the early 1920s (e.g. Dix 1977, p. xiii; Fishback 1992, pp. 19–21; Matheis 2020; see also Table 16.1).

Figure 16.5 shows that productivity levels in the United States were higher than in Europe (as shown in the previous figures). At the end of the period (three-year average around 1912) productivity in anthracite US mining was approximately 2–3 times higher than in Europe.[19] Productivity in US bituminous mining, by comparison, was approximately 2.5–4.5 times higher.[20] Daily productivity per underground worker reported in Table 16.4 provides largely similar estimates (with respect to

[17] Although see Guinnane and Streb (2015) on the limited success of the first compulsory German industrial accident insurance.

[18] The relationship between unions and safety has generated an intense debate on its own. For Britain, see Mills (2010), and the works cited therein. For the United States, see, for example, Fishback (1992, esp. pp. 111–112) and Boal (2009, 2018).

[19] The fall in productivity and the fatality rate in 1902 is associated with the so-called anthracite coal strike (Aldrich 1997b; Healey 2007).

[20] The number of days worked was lower in the United States than in European countries (e.g. Adams 1920; Fishback 1992, p. 20).

bituminous coal in the United States). As explained above, natural conditions tended to be more advantageous in the United States than in Europe. Mark Aldrich (1997a, pp. 42–43) demonstrates that in the United States, less difficult, and therefore cheaper, access to coal, and more expensive labor and capital, together with the abundance of timber (for roof control), led to room-and-pillar working methods being preferred to longwall mining. Room-and-pillar methods yielded quicker returns and higher labor productivity than longwall techniques, which however spread from the 1830s onwards first in Britain and then in Continental Europe (Aldrich 1997a, pp. 44, 63; see also Church 1986, p. 336). (I will return to this issue in the next section). The mechanization of coal extraction and transportation also spread faster in the United States, notably in bituminous mines. The use of coal cutting machines, first introduced in the 1870s, accelerated in the early decades of the twentieth century. In 1915, 55.3 percent of the total national coal was mechanically cut; the percentages were higher in the four main producing states (in 1900): Illinois, Ohio, Pennsylvania, and West Virginia (Dix 1977, p. 20). The application of mechanical power to the transportation of coal, including locomotives, also accelerated in the same period (Rice and Hartmann 1939, p. 161; Dix 1977, p. 28).

The inverse in US mining was that, for a number of reasons, the predominant room-and-pillar methods tended to not only be more productive but also more dangerous (Aldrich 1977a, pp. 63–65). Safety was also costly to miners (Boal 2018). In addition to this, the mechanization of different tasks, although often leading to increasingly less hazardous working environments, may also have brought their own risks at first (Rice and Hartmann 1939, pp. 50–51, 268; Aldrich 1997a, pp. 58–60). Furthermore, in many respects, state intervention in the United States may not have been as relevant to the reduction of risks as interventions in European countries toward the end of century probably were (Fishback 1986, 1987, 1992, ch. 7; Aldrich 1995, 1997a, esp. pp. 67–75; compare with Boal 2018, p. 135). As an example, an expedition of three well-respected European experts made recommendations on the backward state of safety in the United States (Watteyne et al. 1908).[21] In short, safety deteriorated as production increasingly intensified. Figure 16.5 shows that the fatality rate (per 10,000 workers) in bituminous mining worsened from the 1880s onwards, while it did so in anthracite mining from the 1880s or 1890s onwards.[22] Table 16.5 provides a combined rate, including both bituminous and anthracite mining. Whereas Table 16.6, for selected countries, reports a contemporary estimate that accounts for both differences in the number of days worked and the actual number of miners working underground. Table 16.5 consists of the safety rate on the basis of employees (Panel A) and also of production (Panel B). This

[21] See Aldrich (1995, p. 491), for the contextualization of this, and other, reports. See also, for example, Hall and Snelling (1907, p. 6).

[22] The spike in the bituminous fatality rate in 1907 is associated with the explosion at the Monongah mine, which officially killed 362 miners (McAteer 2014).

complementary rate, however, is much more favorable to the United States as a result of its greater capacity for production.[23]

16.3 Small-Scale Technologies in Europe: A Brief Review

In the virtual absence of large-scale technologies, I focus on small-scale innovations that may have contributed to the improvement of both productivity and safety throughout the long nineteenth century.[24] Mokyr's (1990, p. 13) definition of "micro-inventions" as "small, incremental steps that improve, adapt, and streamline existing techniques already in use," and Engerman and Rosenberg (2016, p. 442) references to the incremental, rather than discontinuous, nature of certain innovations and the "learning by using" process, are helpful here.[25]

It may be added that, although technologies appeared to manage discrete problems of coal mining, the effectiveness of each sometimes depended on others, as in the case of the interaction between lighting, ventilation, and explosives. Improvements in these three particular areas were, in large part, the response to explosions provoked by methane gas (firedamp) and, sometimes, its interaction with coal dust. As stated above, together with landslides and cave-ins, explosions tended to be the most important determinant in the high numbers of death and injuries to coal miners. Moreover, although statistically infrequent, explosions often caused further costs derived from the interruption of the mining activity and the destruction of the capital stock, as well as, from a certain time onwards, workers' compensation schemes. Explosions were certainly feared, as reflected in the press and folklore around mining communities.

An essential part of the success of innovations was their smooth national and international diffusion. The results of research appeared in government publications, privately-issued memoirs, and the mining press continent-wide.[26]

The works of boring for prospecting purposes, shaft sinking, and road construction were the first steps in the mining process. Prospecting actually started with geological research. In Britain, from the late eighteenth century onwards, the reliance on geology grew along with its practical, local-based approach, which was close to the mining industry (Veneer 2006; Mokyr 2009, p. 140). Geological and related knowledge expanded and systematized across Europe as the century progressed (Ranestad and Sharp 2021). A key advance was the identification of

[23] The coefficient of correlation between the two rates is 0.985 for Britain (1851–1913), 0.967 for Belgium (1851–1913), 0.966 for France (1853–1913), 0.523 for Prussia (1852–1912), and 0.707 for the United States (1870–1913).

[24] Specific incentives to innovate are not considered here. Ongoing work includes the extent of patenting in technologies such as mechanical ventilators. On early safety lamps, see, for example, James (2005, p. 212) and Holmes (2008, pp. 371–375).

[25] See also, for example, Allen (2009, p. 136) and Kander et al. (2013, p. 26).

[26] As argued by Murray and Silvestre (2015, esp. pp. 891–892; 2020, p. 678; and 2021).

flooding risks (e.g. Conus and Escudier 1997b, p. 53). Boring technology, albeit slowly, improved throughout the entire period. Several innovations, such as the application of steam power, the use of water to lubricate the chisel, the possibility of using ropes (instead of rods), and diamond core drilling, were introduced or consolidated in the middle decades of the nineteenth century (Lupton 1893, pp. 51–79; Brown 1924a, pp. 27–28; Church 1986, p. 313). Given the depth of European mines, sinking vertical shafts was, by far, the most common way of accessing coal.[27] Sinking technology evolved considerably in order to overcome difficulties such as the presence of water and firedamp (Jevons ([1915] 1969, pp. 181–201; Church 1986, pp. 315–318). For example, the use of just one compartmentalized shaft was often replaced with the construction of two separate shafts, an improvement that reduced the number of fires and explosions. The downcast shaft carried fresh air into the mine from above, and the upcast shaft carried warmer stale air and firedamp to the surface. Underground, main, and secondary, roads (and pillars) permitted access to the seams, and sustained transportation, ventilation, and water drainage. Different techniques across countries were developed over time to avoid landslides and cave-ins (e.g. Leboutte 1991, pp. 727–730).

As explained above, in Europe room-and-pillar mining tended to be replaced with longwall mining as the nineteenth century advanced (see also Jevons ([1915] 1969, pp. 202–209; Lamb 1976, pp. 176–177; Mitchell 1984, pp. 71–75; Church 1986, pp. 328–340; Weisbrod 1990, p. 140; Burghardt 1995, pp. 80–86; Mills 2010, pp. 117–118). In room-and-pillar methods the miners worked in the midst of the vein (the room), removing some coal and leaving great blocks of it to hold up the roof (the pillars). In longwall methods many miners worked on a long face. The removed stone, slate, or other scrap materials were packed in their wake, forming the gob or goaf that held up the roof. In terms of safety, longwall methods were frequently necessary at great depths, and more suitable to larger spaces. For example, longwall mining required less ventilation and was less subject to roof and wall collapses (e.g. Murray and Silvestre 2015).

Transport in the mining process involved the movement of coal from the face to haulage roads and shaft bottom, and then to the surface, and the movement of miners and equipment between surface and work site (Church 1986). At the beginning of the nineteenth century, women and children were typically employed to drag baskets of coal or push wheeled tubs. As women and children began leaving mines, they tended to be replaced with ponies, as well as mules or horses. Moreover, a number of procedures were created to enable the tubs to be moved with a minimum of effort, such as slopes and supplementary rails carrying counterweights. Later, different devices such as endless ropes powered by steam engines pulled the tubs toward shafts (e.g. Poole 1924, pp. 89–100; Mitchell 1984, pp. 77–79; Church 1986, pp. 367–369). From the 1830s and 1840s onwards, usually steam-operated, winding apparatus that substituted early systems based on baskets, or ladders, included, first in Prussia, stronger wire ropes that replaced hemp ropes; guided shaft cages and

[27] Sometimes, outcrops permitted access to coal horizontally or by means of slopes.

protected shafts to avoid impacts from oscillation; and, more commonly in Continental Europe, ratchets on which the cage would be caught in the guiding rail should the central rope break (Galloway [1882] 1969, pp. 211–219, 259; Brown 1924b; Lamb 1976, pp. 170–172; Leboutte 1991, p. 727; Conus and Escudier 1997b, p. 58). In Britain, in the case of overwinding, safety hooks which disengaged the cage tended to be preferred (Abel 1889, p. 112).

The fundamental challenge of lighting in coal mines was to keep the source of the light away from the ambient methane that formed naturally with coal. Certain concentrations of gas would explode in the presence of an open flame, such as that of a candle. The problem with other kinds of illumination, such as reflecting the sun's rays from a mirror or generating sparks from striking a flint, was that they yielded very little light (e.g. Smyth 1890, pp. 190–192). The earliest safety lamps, including the best known by Sir Humphry Davy (1815), appeared in Britain early on in the nineteenth century. All worked on roughly the same principle: metal screens shielded the flame from the methane, producing relatively little light but more safely than open flames. Safety lamps were also used to detect the presence of firedamp. In its presence, flames became blue and elongated. The earliest safety lamps, designed to work in still air, however, became obsolete when mechanical ventilators created a continuous current along the galleries that extinguished the flames.[28] The first generation of safety lamps was a great step forward, although they remained problematic (e.g. Galloway ([1882] 1969, p. 268; Church 1986, pp. 325–326; James 2005; Mills 2010, p. 16).

Thus, although these lamps became widely used until the century was well advanced, newer lamps, or modified versions of old ones, provided by many inventors appeared elsewhere (e.g. Hardwick and O'Shea 1915, p. 620; Trotter 1982, ch. 1). For example, the Mueseler lamp was invented in 1831. Endorsement by a Belgian government commission followed by a government mandate requiring those lamps in 1851 led to its widespread adoption in that country's mines (e.g. Leboutte 1991, pp. 722–723). The Mueseler lamp was also used in coalfields in other countries, at least until their limitations were demonstrated (Dickinson 1884; Abel 1889, pp. 88–89). This pattern was very common. Testing was continuous, because balancing all desired attributes in a safety lamp was difficult. A key issue was their capacity to detect firedamp at low concentrations, as the interaction of firedamp with coal dust could reduce the minimum level of concentration needed for ignition (Murray and Silvestre 2021). Another area of interest for research before electrification concerned lamp fuels. But perhaps the most remarkable characteristic of research on safety lamps was scope: the sheer numbers of lamps that were tested and the number of laboratories, governmental and private, built to test them throughout Europe (e.g. Heinzerling 1891; Hardwick and O'Shea 1915; Paul et al. 1924). As an example, among many others, a Royal Commission on accidents in mines appointed by the British government examined more than 250 safety lamps from

[28] Moreover, miners, rather than returning to central lighting stations, could try relighting the lamp on the spot and risk an explosion of undetected firedamp.

Britain, Belgium, France, and Germany (Great Britain. Parliament. House of Commons Papers 1886, esp. p. 69).

The (to some extent) inaccuracy of lamps in detecting firedamp gave rise to the need for new ventilation systems to clear the air and new explosives to be used in the presence of small amounts of gas. In the mid-nineteenth century, apart from natural ventilation, the baseline method placed a furnace near the bottom of an upcast shaft. The hot air rose, drawing stale air out of the galleries toward the shaft and sending it upwards (e.g. Hinsley 1969). Many variations and improvements were developed, such as compound ventilation by Mr. Buddle (Moss 1924).[29] An alternative method was to produce steam (e.g. Atkinson 1892, pp. 55–65). A boiler could be built on the surface, to force steam downwards through a pipe that heated air in the shaft; or a boiler at the bottom of the shaft might either release steam or force it upwards. Furnaces and boilers, even in their most advanced forms, were relatively inexpensive, though at the same time often inefficient and unsafe. Efforts in Britain and Belgium to increase efficiency of steam jets proved futile, at least until the steam injector was developed in Germany in the early 1870s.

The ultimate successor of these (and other) technologies was the mechanical ventilator. These machines became more efficient over time. They were typically powered by steam engines, although attempts to provide underground ventilation through water-powered ventilators date as far back as the early seventeenth century. A mid-nineteenth century technology used steam to operate an air pump. A plunger worked like a piston and a so-called bell like a cylinder in a conventional steam engine. Horizontal ventilators enjoyed some popularity. The Archimedes' screw principle may also have been applied. (e.g. Galloway [1882] 1969, pp. 253–254; Lupton 1893, pp. 214–217). By the early 1850s, inventors had produced ventilation machines that worked on different principles, which were subject to continual testing (e.g. Jicinsky 1905; Cory 2005, ch. 1).

Over the second half of the century the coal-producing nations engaged in further, related, research, often, as in the case of lamps and explosives, promoted by governmental commissions. Ventilation was also an active research area of mine safety. The desire to solve problems was decidedly strong in Belgium due to the widespread prevalence of firedamp (e.g. Decamps 1888–1889, pp. 92–93). Eventually the most effective technologies involved centrifugal fans, first developed there in 1841 (e.g. Hinsley 1969, p. 32). Rather than a set of rotary blades as in a common window fan, the typical arrangement for a centrifugal fan fixed blades onto a cylinder, which spun so as to direct the air flow across the axis of the cylinder rather than parallel to it. Centrifugal fans reversed the action of a waterwheel: rather than the fluid rotating the wheel to generate power, the power source rotated the wheel to push the fluid along. This simple description belies a host of technical problems, however, that needed to be resolved.

Some ventilation technologies gained popularity only within a certain region, while others were, albeit temporarily, adopted internationally. An excellent example

[29] Swinging doors and road partitions or air pipes permitted fresh air to be directed where needed.

of the international diffusion of a superior design was the machine patented in 1858 by the French-born engineer Théophile Guibal, who settled in Belgium (e.g. Arnould 1877, p. 121; Atkinson 1892, pp. 67–72, 94–95; Church 1986, p. 323). The shares of mines ventilated by mechanical fans had reached high numbers in European coalfields at the end of the period being studied.[30]

Explosive materials were another technology that needed careful introduction into mines. Properly employed they could be a partial substitute for labor, in the digging of shafts and roads, and the releasing of coal from rock strata, but learning to use them took time and a willingness to experiment (Guttmann 1895a, b; Marshall 1915; see also Church 1986, pp. 340–341). By the early nineteenth century, gunpowder was used in some places. Methods of applying gunpowder in the actual winning of coal (as distinct from constructing a mine), in reality, changed little into the nineteenth century (e.g. Lupton 1893). The miner used a tool with a threaded head to drill a long and narrow hole into the coal, near the floor of the gallery so that the coal would be less likely to fall and shatter. He poured gunpowder into the hole and led a train of powder back to an acceptably safe waiting place. After lighting his end of the trail, he waited for the blast.

However, sources of potential improvement encompassed two types of explosive technologies: first, new kinds of explosives, and second, new ways to transmit the charge to the explosive material. In a parallel with safety lamps, it was critical to prevent energy that was intended for the explosive charge from contacting ambient explosive materials. The nature of those ambient materials, especially firedamp and coal dust, engaged the minds of some of Europe's best-known scientists and engineers (Murray and Silvestre 2021).

Safety fuses, for example, to keep sparks from the firedamp and coal dust developed in Europe from the 1830s onwards. Innovations included the use of potassium chlorate ($KClO_3$), the wrapping with a cable of jute and string, (then) metal or gutta-percha cases, as well as fuses that reached the charge more quickly (which enabled several shots to be fired at once); a sparkless fuse was patented in 1886 (e.g. Marshall 1915, p. 28; Crankshaw 1924). Developments in the explosive materials themselves also occurred over broad swathes of Europe (e.g. Leboutte, p. 724). At first, questions of stability limited the diffusion of new explosives (Guttmann 1895b, pp. 225–226). Not until the 1860s, when Alfred Nobel combined the extremely unstable compound nitroglycerin with diatomaceous earth to create dynamite, was a nitroglycerin-based compound stable enough to be widely used (Marshall 1915, pp. 31–32). Further developments included carbonite (a mixture of nitroglycerin, saltpeter, and flour), and ammonium nitrate (NH_4NO_3)-based explosives. At the end of the century, for example, improved management of the instability of potassium chlorate led to the British development of cheddite, which became widely used in French and German mines as well as those in Britain (Marshall 1915, pp. 31–36). Before widespread adoption, new explosives and detonating materials were extensively tested, usually by governmental commissions which appointed permitted lists

[30] Own unpublished data.

in some countries or required specifications in others (e.g. Rice 1914, p. 555; Murray and Silvestre 2021).

16.4 Conclusions

The production of coal in Europe throughout the long nineteenth century grew dramatically. Economies of scale and increasing populations and incomes per capita have been proposed as the main contributing factors to this expansion, whereas there would have been few signs of a technological revolution (Clark and Jacks 2007, esp. pp. 39, 68–69). However, in the major European producing countries, increased demand seems to have been compatible with a series of small-scale technological innovations, beyond any new large-scale or general-purpose technologies, which may have contributed to the gain in labor productivity and safety. These innovations did not involve huge investments in labor-replacing capital (with the partial exception of explosives). Instead, the technologies were complementary to labor, as well as reducing accident-related interruptions and increasing job-specific human capital.

In terms of productivity, the Continental European nations exhibited a tendency toward convergence with Britain, the stagnating leader. In terms of safety, in three of the four major European producing nations the fatality rate fell to reach a plateau around 10 per 10,000 workers at the end of the period. The exception was Prussia, which along with other newer producing nations, such as the United States, tended to display worse safety records (Leboutte 1989, p. 85). However, a key difference between the Prussian and US safety trends was the opposing direction of their respective evolutions. In fact, in Europe, with the exception of the early Prussian case, increasing productivity and decreasing risk of fatal accident seem to have gone hand-in-hand. Intuitively, it might seem if workers were intent on extracting ever greater amounts of coal from ever more inaccessible deposits, the two variables would be positively rather than negatively related.

In any case, flattened out productivities and safety rates at the end of the period suggest that pre-World War I technological improvements presented decreasing returns as a result of mines becoming older and natural conditions worsening (Lamb 1976, p. 151; Mitchell 1984, p. 323; Church 1986, p. 482; Leboutte et al. 1998, p. 49: Jopp 2011, p. 82). New, and large, increases in, for example, productivity had to wait until the—it may be said—delayed mechanization and rationalization of the European coal industry that, with some national or regional variations, would take place in the Interwar period (Rice and Hartmann 1939, pp. 311–312; Greasley 1990; Scott 2006; Jopp 2016, 2017; Montant 2020, p. 98).

Acknowledgement Although only my name is listed as author, this paper is a revision of a book project proposal John E. Murray (Rhodes College) and I wrote as part of a submission process, from which I decided to withdraw after John passed away in 2018. I hope my simplification and many alterations have not spoiled the main idea of John's account. This essay would not have been possible without the contribution of Patrick Gray, who generously sent me John's books, electronic documents, and computer programs on coal. I am grateful to Joel Mokyr, who helped us to refine early and incomplete drafts of the book proposal, Roger Fouquet, for sharing with me his unpublished co-authored manuscript, and Ruth Herndon and Timothy Guinnane for their support. I also benefited from comments by Jim Bessen, Ewout Frankema, Tamás Vonyó, and the rest of the participants in the Economic History Seminar at the Universidad de Zaragoza, the "Pre-industrial and modern trade" session at the XI European Social Science History Conference (Valencia), and the "The New Economic History of Patents and Innovation" session at the XVIII World Economic History Conference (Boston), where sections of earlier versions of this work were presented, as well as from bibliographical suggestions on the US by Mark Aldrich and William Boal. Arthur McIvor, Catherine Mills, and John Singleton kindly helped me to complete the British series on fatalities with information or inaccessible data during the pandemic Spring of 2020. The Government of Spain (research projects PGC2018-095529-B-I00 and PGC2018-096640-B-I00) and the Government of Aragon-European Fund for Economic and Regional Development (2020-2022) (research project S55-20R) have provided financial assistance.

References

Abel FA (1889) Mining accidents and their prevention. Scientific Publishing Company, New York

Adams WW (1920) A miner's yearly and daily output of coal. Mon Labor Rev 11:522–530

Aldrich M (1995) "The needless peril of the coal mine": the Bureau of Mines and the campaign against coal mine explosions, 1910–1940. Technol Cult 36:463–518

Aldrich M (1997a) Safety first: technology, labor, and business in the building of American work safety, 1870–1939. Johns Hopkins University Press, Baltimore and London

Aldrich M (1997b) The perils of mining anthracite: regulation, technology and safety, 1870–1945. Penn Hist: J Mid-Atlantic Stud 64:361–383

Allen RC (2009) The British industrial revolution in global perspective. Cambridge University Press, Cambridge

Arnould G (1877) Mémoire historique et descriptif: bassin houiller du Couchant de Mons. Hector Manceaux, Mons

Atkinson AA (1892) A key to mine ventilation. Colliery Engineer Co, Scranton

Bartrip PWJ, Burman SB (1983) The wounded soldiers of industry: industrial compensation policy, 1833–1897. Clarendon Press, Oxford

Benson J (1989) British coalminers in the nineteenth century: a social history. Longman, London and New York

Bézy F (1951) Les phases de la conjoncture au sein de la firme: Les agencements cycliques des coûts de production dans un charbonnage belge, 1836–1939. Bulletin de l'Institut de Recherches Économiques et Sociales 17:29–74

Boal WM (2009) The effect of unionism on accidents in US coal mining, 1897–1929. Ind Relat 48:97–120

Boal WM (2017) The effect of unionization on productivity: evidence from a long panel of coal mines. Ind Lab Relat Rev 70:1254–1282

Boal WM (2018) Work intensity and worker safety in early twentieth-century coal mining. Explor Econ Hist 70:132–149

Broadberry S, Burhop C (2007) Comparative productivity in British and German manufacturing before World War II: reconciling direct benchmark estimates and time series projections. J Econ Hist 67:315–349

Brown EOF (1924a) The history of boring and sinking. In: The Mining Association of Great Britain (ed) Historical review of coal mining. Fleetway Press, London, pp 26–41

Brown EOF (1924b) The history of winding. In: The Mining Association of Great Britain (ed) Historical review of coal mining. Fleetway Press, London, pp 170–182
Burghardt U (1995) Die Mechanisierung des Ruhrbergbaus, 1890–1930. CH Beck, Munich
Burhop C (2008) The level of labour productivity in German mining, crafts, and industry in 1913: evidence from output data. Eur Rev Econ Hist 12:201–219
Burhop C, Lübbers T (2009) Cartels, managerial incentives, and productive efficiency in German coal mining, 1881-1913. J Econ Hist 69:500–527
Chandler AD (1972) Anthracite coal and the beginning of the industrial revolution in the United States. Bus Hist 46:141–181
Church R (1986) The history of the British coal industry, vol 3. 1830–1913, Victorian pre-eminence. Clarendon Press, Oxford
Clark G, Jacks D (2007) Coal and the industrial revolution, 1700–1869. Eur Rev Econ Hist 11:39–72
Conus MF, Escudier JL (1997a) Les transformations d'une mesure: la statistique des accidents dans les mines de charbon en France, 1833–1988. Histoire et Mesure 12:37–68
Conus MF, Escudier JL (1997b) Sécurité et transformations du système productif: application a l'industrie française du charbon (1817–1988). Enterprises et Historie 17:49–71
Cory WTW (2005) Fans & ventilation. Elsevier, Amsterdam
Crankshaw HM (1924) History of explosives used in coal mining. In: The Mining Association of Great Britain (ed) Historical review of coal mining. Fleetway Press, London, pp 82–88
De Bivort de La Saudée E (1939) Des rythmes séculaires d'expansion des industries houillères européennes dans leurs rapports avec les prix et les coûts de production. Bulletin de l'Institut de Recherches Économiques 11:3–38
Decamps G (1888–1889) Mémoire historique sur l'origine et les développements de l'industrie houillère dans le basin du Couchant de Mons. Mémoires et Publications de la Société des Sciences, des Arts, et des Lettres du Hainaut Series 5, 1, pp 7–274
Dickinson J (1884) On the Marsaut safety lamp. T Manchester Geol Soc 17:185–195
Dix K (1977) Work relations in the coal industry: the hand-loading era, 1880–1930. West Virginia University, Morgantown
Engerman SL, Rosenberg N (2016) Innovation in historical perspective. In: Diebolt C, Haupert M (eds) Handbook of cliometrics. Springer, Heidelberg, pp 433–445
Fay AH (1916) Coal-mine fatalities in the United States, 1870–1914. Statistics of coal production, labor, and mining methods, by states and calendar years. US Bureau of mines bulletin no 115. GPO, Washington, DC
Feldman GD, Tenfelde K (eds) (1990) Workers, owners and politics in coal mining: an international comparison of industrial relations. Berg, New York, Oxford and Munich
Fernihough A, O'Rourke KH (2014) Coal and the European industrial revolution. University of Oxford Discussion Papers in Economic and Social History no 124
Fischer W (2011) Steinkohle Königreich Preußen (1850–1914). In: Germany's mining production statistics from 1850 to 1914. GESIS data archive https://dbk.gesis.org/dbksearch/sdesc2.asp?no=8448&db=e&doi=10.4232/1.10308. Accessed 15 June 2020
Fishback PV (1986) Workplace safety during the progressive era: fatal accidents in bituminous coal mining, 1912–1923. Explor Econ Hist 23:269–298
Fishback PV (1987) Liability rules and accident prevention in the workplace: empirical evidence for the early XXth century. J Leg Stud 16:305–328
Fishback PV (1992) Soft coal, hard choices: the economic welfare of bituminous coal miners, 1890–1930. Oxford University Press, New York and Oxford
Flinn MW (1984) The history of the British coal industry, vol 2. 1700–1830, The industrial revolution. Clarendon Press, Oxford
Foreman-Peck J (2006) A model of later-nineteenth century European economic development. In: Dormois JP, Lains P (eds) Classical trade protectionism 1850–1914. Routledge, London and New York, pp 318–341

Fouquet R (2008) Heat, power and light: revolutions in energy services. Edward Elgar, Cheltenham and Northampton
Galloway RL ([1882] 1969) A history of coal mining in Great Britain. David & Charles Reprints, Newton Abbot
Gillet M (1984) Histoire sociale du Nord et de l'Europe du Nord-Ouest. Recherches sur les XIXe et XXe siècles. Université de Lille, Lille
Greasley D (1990) Fifty years of coal-mining productivity: the record of the British coal industry before 1939. J Econ Hist 50:877–902
Great Britain Parliament. House of Commons Papers (1886) Final report of her Majesty's commission appointed to inquire into accidents in mines. Eyre and Spottiswoode, London
Guinnane T, Streb J (2015) Incentives that (could have) saved lives: government regulation of accident insurance associations in Germany, 1884–1914. J Econ Hist 75:1196–1227
Guttmann O (1895a) The manufacture of explosives, vol 1. Whittaker & Co, London
Guttmann O (1895b) The manufacture of explosives, vol 2. Whittaker & Co, London
Hair PEH (1968) Mortality from violence in British coal-mines, 1800–50. Econ Hist Rev, 2nd ser 21:545–561
Hall C, Snelling WO (1907) Coal mine accidents: their causes and prevention. A preliminary statistical report. US Geological Survey Bulletin no 333. GPO, Washington, DC
Hardwick FW, O'Shea LT (1915) Notes on the history of the safety-lamp. T Instit Mining Eng 51:548–724
Harvey B (2016) The Oaks colliery disaster of 1866: a case study in responsibility. Bus Hist 58:501–531
Hay D (1924) The development of mechanical and electrical power in collieries since 1850. In: The Mining Association of Great Britain (ed) Historical review of coal mining. Fleetway Press, London, pp 195–203
Healey RG (2007) The Pennsylvania anthracite coal industry, 1860–1902: economic cycles, business decision-making and regional dynamics. University of Scranton Press, Scranton and London
Heinzerling C (1891) Schlagwetter und Sicherheitslampen: Entstehung und Erkennung der Schlagenden Wetter und Konstruktion der Wichtigeren Typen der Sicherheitslampen. Verlag der J.G. Cotta'schen Buchhandlung, Stuttgart
Henriques ST, Sharp PR (2021) Without coal in the age of steam and dams in the age of electricity: an explanation for the failure of Portugal to industrialize before the Second World War. Eur Rev Econ Hist 25:85–105
Hickey SHF (1985) Workers in Imperial Germany: the miners of the Ruhr. Oxford University Press, Oxford
Hinsley FB (1969) The development of coal mine ventilation in Great Britain up to the end of the nineteenth century. T Newcomen Soc 42:25–39
Holmes R (2008) The age of wonder: how the romantic generation discovered the beauty and terror of science. Pantheon Books, New York
Horton FW (1913) Coal-mine accidents in the United States and foreign countries. Department of the Interior. US Bureau of Mines, GPO, Washington, DC
James FAJL (2005) How big is a hole?: the problems of the practical application of science in the invention of the miners' safety lamp by Humphry Davy and George Stephenson in late Regency England. T Newcomen Soc 75:175–227
Jevons HS ([1915] 1969) The British coal trade. Augustus M Kelley, Publishers, New York
Jicinsky J (1905) Manuel de la ventilation des mines. Librairie Polytechnique, Paris
Jopp TA (2011) The hazard of merger by absorption: why some Knappschaften merged and others did not, 1861 to 1920. J Bus Hist 56:75–101
Jopp TA (2016) How technologically progressive was Germany in the interwar period? Evidence on total factor productivity in coal mining. J Econ Hist 76:1113–1151
Jopp TA (2017) Did closures do any good? Labour productivity, mine dynamics, and rationalization in interwar Ruhr coal mining. Econ Hist Rev 70:944–976

Kander A, Malamina P, Warde P (2013) Power to the people: energy in Europe over the last five centuries. Princeton University Press, Princeton

Lamb GJ (1976) Coal mining in France, 1873 to 1895. Dissertation, University of Illinois

Leboutte R (1989) Pour une histoire des catastrophes charbonnières aux XIXe-XXe siècles. Bulletin du Département d'historie économique et sociale, Université de Genève 19:73–101

Leboutte R (1991) Mortalité par accident dans les mines de charbon en Belgique aux XIXe-XXe siècles. Revue du Nord 73:703–736

Leboutte R (1997) Vie et mort des bassins industriels en Europe, 1750–2000. Éditions L'Harmattan, Paris

Leboutte R, Puissant J, Scuto D (1998) Un siècle d'historie industrielle: Belgique, Luxembourg, Pays Bas. Industrialisation et sociétés, 1873–1973. Sedes, Paris

Leiby J (1960) Carroll Wright and labor reform: the origin of labor statistics. Harvard University Press, Harvard

Lupton A (1893) Mining: an elementary treatise on the getting of minerals. Longmans, Green & Co, London and New York

MacRaid DM, Martin D (2000) Labour in British society, 1830–1914. McMilland, London

Marshall A (1915) Explosives: their manufacture, properties, tests and history. J. & A. Churchill, London

Martin M (2009) Allgegenwärtiger Tod. Arbeitsbedingungen und Mortalität im Ruhr-Bergbau bis zum Ersten Weltkrieg. Hist Soc Res 34:154–173

Matheis M (2020) Production, prices, and technology: a historical analysis of the United States coal industry. Essays Econ Bus Hist 38:70–104

Maurice W (1937) The evolution of the miners' electric hand lamp. J Instit Elect Eng 81:367–380

McAteer D (2014) Monongah. The tragic story of the 1907 Monongah mine disaster: the worst industrial accident in US history. West Virginia University Press, Morgantown

McIvor A, Johnston R (2007) Miners' lung: a history of dust disease in British coal mining. Ashgate, Aldershot

Melling J (1996) Safety, supervision and the politics of productivity in the British coalmining industry, 1900–1960. In: Melling J, McKinlay A (eds) Management, labour and industrial politics in Modern Europe: the quest for productivity growth during the twentieth century. Edward Elgar, Cheltenham and Brookfield, pp 145–173

Mills C (2010) Regulating health and safety in the British mining industries, 1800–1914. Ashgate, Farnham

Milward AS, Saul S (1973) The economic development of continental Europe, 1780–1870. Routledge, Abingdon

Minchinton W (1990) The rise and fall of the British coal industry: a review article. Vierteljahrschrift für Sozial- und Wirtschaftsgeschichte 77:212–226

Ministère de l'Intérieu (1904–1913) Annuaire statistique de la Belgique et du Congo Belge. Imprimerie A Lesigne, Brussels

Ministère des Travaux Publics (1904–1913) Statistique de l'industrie minérale et des appareils à vapeur en France et en Algérie. Imprimerie nationale, Paris

Mitchell BR (1984) Economic development of the British coal industry 1800–1914. Cambridge University Press, Cambridge

Mitchell BR (1992) International historical statistics: Europe, 1750–1988, 3rd edn. Stockton Press, New York

Mitchell B (1993) International historical statistics: the Americas, 1750–1988, 2nd edn. Stockton Press, New York

Mitchell BR (2003) International historical statistics: Africa, Asia & Oceania, 1750–2000, 4th edn. Palgrave McMillan, Basingstoke, Hampshire, and New York

Mokyr J (1990) The lever of riches: technological creativity and economic progress. Oxford University Press, New York and Oxford

Mokyr J (2009) The enlightened economy: an economic history of Britain, 1700–1850. Yale University Press, New Haven and London

Mokyr J (2010) The contribution of economic history to the study of innovation and technical change: 1750–1914. In: Hall BH, Rosenberg N (eds) Handbook of the economics of innovation, vol 1. North-Holland, Amsterdam, pp 11–50
Montant G (2020) Expansion, depression and collusion: the Belgian coal industry, 1901–1945. J Eur Econ Hist 49:55–108
Moss KN (1924) Ventilation of coal mines. In: The Mining Association of Great Britain (ed) Historical review of coal mining. Fleetway Press, London, pp 126–149
Murray JE, Silvestre J (2015) Small scale technologies and European coal mine safety, 1850–1900. Econ Hist Rev 68:887–910
Murray JE, Silvestre J (2020) Integration in European coal markets, 1833–1913. Econ Hist Rev 73:668–702
Murray JE, Silvestre J (2021) How do mines explode? Understanding risk in European mining doctrine, 1803–1906. Technol Cult 62:780–811
Neville RG (1978) The Courrières colliery disaster, 1906. J Contem Hist 13:33–52
Ó Gráda C (2016) Did science cause the industrial revolution? J Econ Lit 54:224–239
Otojanov R, Fouquet J, Granville B (2020) Factor prices and induced technical change in the industrial revolution (manuscript)
Parnell MF (1994) The German tradition of organized capitalism: self-government in the coal industry. Clarendon Press, Oxford
Paul JW, Ilsley LC, Gleim EJ (1924) Flame safety lamps. US Bureau of mines bulletin no 227. GPO, Washington, DC
Poole G (1924) The history and development of underground haulage. In: The Mining Association of Great Britain (ed) Historical review of coal mining. Fleetway Press, London, pp 89–104
Pouliakas K, Theodossiou I (2013) The economics of health and safety at work: an interdisciplinary review of the theory and policy. J Econ Surv 27:167–208
Pounds NJG, Parker WN (1957) Coal and steel in Western Europe. Indiana University Press, Bloomington
Ranestad K, Sharp PR (2021) Success through failure? Four centuries of searching for Danish coal. Bus Hist (forthcoming)
Reid D (1981) The role of mine safety in the development of working-class consciousness and organization: the case of the Aubin coal basin, 1867–1914. French Hist Stud 12:98–119
Rice GS (1914) Investigations of coal-dust explosions. T Amer Instit Mining Eng 50:552–585
Rice GS, Hartmann I (1939) Coal mining in Europe: a study of practices in different coal formations and under various economic and regulatory conditions compared with those in the United Sates. US Bureau of mines bulletin no 414. GPO, Washington, DC
Scott P (2006) Path dependence, fragmented property rights and the slow diffusion of high throughput technologies in inter-war British coal mining. Bus Hist 48:20–42
Singleton J (2016) Economic and natural disasters since 1900: a comparative history. Edward Elgar, Cheltenham
Singleton J (2020) Origins of disaster management: the British mine rescue system, c. 1900 to c.1930. Bus Hist (forthcoming)
Singleton J (2022) Breathing apparatus for mine rescue in the UK, 1890s–1920s. In: Gray P, Hall J, Herndon RW, Silvestre J (eds) Standard of living: essays in economics, history, and religion in honor of John E. Murray. Springer Nature, Cham
Smyth WW (1890) A rudimentary treatise on coal and coal mining. Crosby Lockwood and Son, London
Spencer EG (1984) Management and labor in Imperial Germany: Ruhr industrialists as employers, 1896–1914. Rutgers University Press, New Brunswick
Stewart JI (2003) Mining. In: Mokyr J (ed) The Oxford encyclopedia of economic history, vol 3. Oxford University Press, Oxford, pp 512–527
Trotter DA (1982) The lighting of underground mines. Trans Tech Publications, Montreal
US Bureau of Labor Statistics (1916) Coal-mine fatalities in the United States, 1915, and during the period 1870 to 1914. Monthly Rev US Bureau Labor Stat 3:61–72

Veneer L (2006) Provincial geology and the industrial revolution. Endeavour 30:76–80
Watteyne V, Meissner C, Desborough A (1908) The prevention of mine explosions: report and recommendations. US Geological Survey Bulletin no 369. GPO, Washington, DC
Wauthelet JM (1997) Accumulation and return on capital in the Belgian coal industry, 1850–1914. In: Van der Wee H, Blomme J (eds) The economic development of Belgium since 1870. Edward Elgar, Cheltenham, pp 205–219
Weisbrod B (1990) Entrepreneurial politics and industrial relations in mining in the Ruhr region: from managerial absolutism to co-determination. In: Feldman GD, Tenfelde K (eds) Workers, owners and politics in coal mining: an international comparison of industrial relations. Berg, New York, Oxford and Munich, pp 118–202
Wibail A (1914) L'évolution économique de l'industrie charbonniére Belge depuis 1831. Bulletin del'Institut des Sciences Eonomiques 6:3–30
Wright CD (1905) Coal mine labor in Europe. Twelfth special report of the Commissioner of Labor. GPO, Washington, DC
Wright G (2006) Natural resource industries. In: such R, Carter SB (eds) Historical statistics of the United Sates: earliest times to the present. Millennial edition, vol 4, part D: economic sectors. Cambridge University Press, Cambridge, MA, pp 4-275-394
Wright G (2015) The USA as a case study in resource-based development. In: Badia-Miró M, Pinilla V, Henry W (eds) Natural resources and economic growth: learning from history. Routledge, London and New York, pp 119–139
Wrigley EA (1961) Industrial growth and population change: a regional study of the coalfield areas of North-West Europe in the later nineteenth century. Cambridge University Press, Cambridge
Wrigley EA (2016) The path to sustained growth: England's transition from an organic economy to an industrial revolution. Cambridge University Press, Cambridge

Chapter 17
Breathing Apparatus for Mine Rescue in the UK, 1890s–1920s

John Singleton

Abstract Breathing apparatus for use in irrespirable atmospheres in coal mines was developed in Britain and other countries in the late nineteenth and early twentieth centuries. Inspired in some respects by diving gear, the apparatus was used in mine rescue work and operations to recover mines after an explosion. The chapter focuses on the network of mining engineers, academics and businesses involved in the design and improvement of mine rescue apparatus. Although the profit motive was by no means absent, many of those working on breathing apparatus were inclined to share their ideas, particularly through the framework provided by the Institution of Mining Engineers, its regional affiliates and the journal *Transactions of the Institution of Mining Engineers*. Such collaboration was far from unique in the early stages of a technology, as economists and economic historians have shown in work on collective invention, open-source invention and user innovation.

Keywords Mining · Mine rescue · Breathing apparatus · Explosions · Collective invention

17.1 Introduction

Some of John Murray's later work, written in collaboration with Javier Silvestre, focuses on aspects of mine safety in the nineteenth and early twentieth centuries. Their 2015 article on small-scale technologies and declining fatality rates in

J. Singleton (✉)
Sheffield Hallam University, Sheffield, UK
e-mail: j.singleton@shu.ac.uk

P. Gray et al. (eds.), *Standard of Living*, Studies in Economic History,
https://doi.org/10.1007/978-3-031-06477-7_17

European coal mining between 1850 and 1900 will be of enduring value to researchers (Murray and Silvestre 2015). The objective of the current chapter is to examine the progress of a new safety and rescue technology – breathing apparatus for use in an irrespirable atmosphere underground – with the help of insights from the literature on collective invention and user innovation.

Breathing apparatus was used in mine rescue and related activities in the UK and other European countries from the late nineteenth century onwards. This chapter is a historical case study, grounded in a qualitative analysis of surviving records of mine rescue stations in the local government archives at Rotherham and contemporary articles and discussions in the *Transactions of the Institution of Mining Engineers* (hereafter *Transactions*). Collective invention and user innovation offer valuable lenses through which to observe the process of innovation and adaptation in the field of breathing apparatus.

Whilst not a direct component of the standard of living, mine safety impinged on living standards in several ways. The earning power of injured miners, and those suffering from industrial disease, was affected either temporarily or permanently. Despite the availability of compensation and other forms of relief, the dependants of miners killed at the pit were placed in difficult financial circumstances.[1]

The next section sets out the chapter's conceptual framework, reviewing relevant literature on collective invention and user innovation. Some historical context, especially on fires and explosions in coal mines, is given in the third section. The origins and design of breathing apparatus are discussed in Sect. 17.4. Section 17.5 examines the network working to improve breathing technology. Section 17.6 focuses more narrowly on debate within this community, as facilitated by the Institution of Mining Engineers (IME) and *Transactions*. Section 17.7, which examines the Rotherham and District Rescue Station, shows how breathing apparatus was chosen and adapted at the local level.

17.2 Collective Invention, Open-Source Invention and User Innovation

Collective invention, open-source invention and user innovation are the economic concepts employed in this chapter to make sense of the activities contributing to the improvement of breathing apparatus during the late nineteenth and early twentieth centuries.

According to Allen (1983), inventive activity may be performed by commercial enterprises, individual inventors, non-profit entities such as universities and governments, or networks of practitioners who swap ideas and technical information in a process of collective invention; in practice, several types of entity may be involved. Collective invention requires a mechanism to promote the exchange of technical

[1] For the social impact of the Hulton Colliery disaster in 1910 see Griffiths (2001).

information, perhaps not in full but in enough detail to spur other network members to take the technology further. Collective invention is more likely to occur when technical change is hard to patent or keep secret. Allen investigated the ironworks of Cleveland in England in the nineteenth century, where firms competed to improve performance by increasing the height and temperature of blast furnaces. Little was then known of the science pertaining to blast furnace design, and incremental improvements were the result of trial and error and could not be patented. Blast furnaces, moreover, were too big to hide. Ironmasters boasted of their achievements in the technical press, especially the *Journal of the Iron and Steel Institute*, a practice that encouraged efforts to surpass their achievements. Reverse engineering was relatively easy. Nuvolari (2004) offers support for the collective invention thesis in an article on steam pumping engines in Cornwall. Having been tormented by Watt's patent until 1800, Cornish engineers were disposed thereafter to share technical information. Collective invention was facilitated by a monthly publication, *Lean's Engine Reporter*, founded by mine managers in 1811. This journal recorded the technical specifications, method of operation and fuel efficiency of each new engine. Exchange of engineering information accelerated the development of pumping technology. Research on the Clyde shipbuilding industry in the nineteenth century demonstrates that family and friendship ties, and professional relationships strengthened by membership of the Institution of Engineers and Shipbuilders in Scotland, resulted in the exchange of technical information between apparent competitor firms (Schwerin 2004; Ingram and Lifschitz 2006).

Open-source technology is a term frequently given to technology that is not patented. Meyer (2007, 2013) argues that profits are elusive in the early days of a technology. Personal computing, for example, began as a hobby for tinkerers, and only later became immensely profitable. Meyer is interested in the motivation of inventors when technical success is uncertain and commercial viability a distant prospect. Research and experimentation will continue if inventors have some non-financial goals. Intrinsic motivations include a delight in tinkering and overcoming a challenge, or a desire for fame and honours; extrinsic motivations include a wish to help others by making the world a better or safer place. Where patents are used, this may be less to deter competitors than to advertise a promising technical development. Information brokers, including the authors and publishers of textbooks and bibliographies, perform an important role. Meyer illustrates open-source invention by examining collaboration between inventors working on powered flight before the emergence of a viable technology after 1900.

Unlike Allen's ironmasters, firms in the pottery industry during the Industrial Revolution showed no inclination to share technical information, yet they did not resort to patenting to safeguard their intellectual property. The key technical developments occurred in the mixing and processing of materials. Reverse engineering was virtually impossible, and recipes could be hidden from rivals, so patents were of little value (Lane 2019). Work on the English brewing industry finds that inventors deployed a range of appropriation strategies in relation to intellectual property, including secrecy, openness, patenting and a hybrid approach of selective openness. Information was more likely to be shared if it could neither be hidden nor patented, or if an inventor calculated that being open would enhance their career and reputation (Nuvolari and Sumner 2013). Clearly, much depended on the circumstances, including the industry and the characteristics of its main technologies.

Users are the experts in how equipment performs in practice. The users of a technology often modify and improve it, sometimes in cooperation with the manufacturers, and sometimes sharing their results freely with other users (von Hippel 2006). User innovation was common in the UK textile machinery industry in the mid-nineteenth century, and was also instrumental in the development of equipment for mountain climbing and related activities (Cookson 2018; Parsons and Rose 2009). The tea-shop company, J. Lyons, adapted the scientific computer to make the world's first business computer in 1949 – surely one of the most surprising examples of user innovation (Land 2000). Although user innovation need not involve information sharing and collaboration, it often does, and for the same reasons as those applying to collective invention (Harhoff and Lakhani 2016). Collaboration may involve other users, manufacturers or both. The contribution of users to the development of a technology varies, with some lead-users pushing the technology forward, whereas others confine themselves to adapting it to local conditions (Bogers et al. 2010).

Many of the practices discussed above can be seen in the following account of innovation in breathing apparatus. A network of engineering companies, mining companies, academic consultants and engineering societies worked to develop better breathing apparatus. This network extended beyond the UK to continental Europe, and to Germany in particular. Some inventions were patented, but others were shared freely, and there was a wide exchange of information and opinion through the auspices of the regional constituents of the IME and *Transactions*. Some network members were interested in profit, others in making the mines safer for workers and/or their businesses. Users adapted technologies to resolve defects, and sometimes came up with notable improvements. The development of mine safety breathing apparatus illustrates important aspects of collective invention and user innovation.

17.3 Underground Perils

Murray and Silvestre (2015) show that fatality rates in coal mining in the UK and other European countries were falling in the late nineteenth century. They argue that small-scale technical changes, including the adoption of reliable safety lamps and better ventilation techniques, played an important role in this trend. Tighter regulation may also have contributed to lower fatality rates, although enforcement was patchy, not least because of the underfunding of inspection (Mills 2010). Despite such improvements, however, around 1000 miners died each year in UK coal mines in the early twentieth century.[2] As the Welsh miners' leader and MP, William Brace, explained in the House of Commons in 1913: "Every year, broadly, the number of lives that are destroyed [in the coal mines] are equal to the number of lives which went down with the 'Titanic' when she was wrecked in the Atlantic".[3] Many more were injured, some seriously.

Most deaths at the pit were due to small-scale accidents involving individuals or a handful of men buried by collapsing roofs or roadways or crushed by waggons. The media barely noticed minor accidents, but explosions that took hundreds of lives in a matter of minutes or hours generated widespread public and political concern. Table 17.1 provides a list of the worst mining disasters in the UK in the early decades of the twentieth century.[4]

As well as destructive of life, explosions and fires were costly for the coalowners.[5] Little is known of the magnitude of such costs, but it could take months to restore a devastated colliery to full production and profitability.[6] Compensation had also to be paid to the injured and bereaved under legislation introduced in the 1890s. On the other hand, both coalowners and workmen, many of whom were pieceworkers, were tempted to trade off safety for higher production. Only a few mines exploded, and the probability that disaster would strike on any one shift was negligible. Several innovations designed to increase productivity, such as mechanical coal cutters and electrical power, actually made explosions more likely. Mechanical coal cutters generated more coal dust than hand tools, whilst primitive electrical apparatus often gave off sparks (Jones 2006; Rockley 1938, p. 23).

The best solution to the problem of explosions and fires was prevention. Improved ventilation, safer explosives and greater care during blasting could all lower the risk of disaster. Until after the outbreak of the First World War, however, there was no consensus as to the most effective means of preventing explosions involving coal

Table 17.1 Coal mine disasters with over 100 fatalities in the UK, 1900–1939

Date	Colliery	County	Fatalities
11 July 1905	National	Glamorgan	119
16 February 1909	West Stanley	Durham	168
11 May 1910	Wellington	Cumberland	137
21 December 1910	Hulton	Lancashire	344
14 October 1913	Senghenydd	Glamorgan	439
12 January 1918	Podmore Hall	Staffordshire	155
22 September 1934	Gresford	Denbighshire	265

Source: Durham Mining Museum, "In Memoriam", http://www.dmm.org.uk/names/index_19.htm. Accessed 6 July 2021

[2] This chapter excludes consideration of deaths from industrial diseases contracted in mining.

[3] House of Commons Debates, 2 July 1913, vol. 54, col. 1972.

[4] On Senghenydd see Singleton (2016, pp. 108–123), and on Gresford see Williamson (1999).

[5] The term given to directors and large shareholders of mining companies.

[6] For a description of the recovery of a damaged colliery see Garforth (1909, pp. 52–72).

dust. The ignition of firedamp (methane gas) and/or coal dust could be devastating. Firedamp, which seeped naturally out of coal deposits, was liable to explode upon meeting a naked flame or spark when comprising between 5 and 15 per cent of the air. Thick and highly inflammable coal dust coated most underground surfaces. A firedamp explosion often ignited the coal dust as well, spreading destruction along the roadways for a considerable distance. Most fatalities in explosions were caused not by the initial blast, but rather by the inhalation of afterdamp (carbon monoxide) produced by burning coal dust and wood (Boyns 1986).

Coal dust was implicated in many disasters, and it could be ignited even in the absence of a prior firedamp explosion. Three solutions were proposed: extracting coal dust from the mine, spraying it with water on a regular basis, or spreading inert stone dust in the areas clogged with coal dust to prevent the temperature reaching ignition point. Experimental work on the coal dust problem was conducted in the UK, the USA and other countries. Only after the outbreak of the First World War, however, did a consensus in favour of stone dusting emerge. From 1920 it was compulsory to apply stone dust in most UK coal mines.[7]

Slow progress with prevention stimulated research into the second-best solution of improved rescue facilities and technology. A Royal Commission on Accidents in Mines (1886, p. 8) expressed support for the employment of breathing apparatus in rescue work. The first report of the later Royal Commission on Mines (1907, p. 10) reviewed each type of breathing apparatus then available. Collieries in Austria and Saxony were already required by law to keep breathing apparatus. Some Westphalian mines opted to invest in breathing apparatus despite the absence of compulsion. Although sympathetic in principle to the employment of breathing apparatus, the Royal Commission did not recommend compulsory adoption in the UK in 1907, on the reasonable grounds that the technology was as yet imperfect.

In the opening years of the twentieth century, employers' groups in several districts, with Yorkshire in the forefront, opened or planned to open joint rescue stations to hold breathing apparatus and train miners in its use (Habershon 1900–1901, 1904–1905; Singleton 2020). Pressure for change was accumulating, and in its second report the Royal Commission on Mines (1909, p. 170) warned that legislation to force coalowners to fund a national network of rescue stations equipped with breathing apparatus would be forthcoming unless the industry acted on its own initiative. An explosion that took 137 lives at Wellington Pit in 1910 proved to be the final straw. Located on the isolated Cumberland coast, the stricken pit lacked access to breathing apparatus, and had to send to distant Newcastle and Sheffield for help. Whether or not a faster response would have saved those trapped underground is debatable (Redmayne and Samuel Pope 1911). But the conclusion drawn by the unions, the public and the Mines Inspectorate was that breathing apparatus must now be provided, if not at every mine, then within each district. Embarrassed by the strength of feeling, the government responded with the Mines Accidents (Rescue

[7] Stone dust cooled the coal dust and held it in place (Rockley 1938, pp. 353–355). For an American perspective on explosions and stone dusting see Aldrich (1995).

and Aid) Act, 1910, which was soon reinforced by the Coal Mines Act 1911. Under this legislation the government issued statutory orders to compel coalowners to establish a network of rescue stations equipped with breathing apparatus.

The pace of change now accelerated, and by 1921 there were 49 rescue stations and 1758 sets of breathing apparatus in place on UK coalfields (Mines Department 1922, pp. 132–133). In the event, the cost of constructing, equipping and operating rescue stations was by no means onerous, not least because it was shared by groups of firms in each locality (Singleton 2020).

17.4 Varieties of Breathing Apparatus

Mine rescue breathing apparatus had a long gestation period. John Roberts, a miner from Wigan in Lancashire, demonstrated his protective hood in 1825, spending 20 minutes in a "cast-iron drying stove" filled with noxious fumes at a Manchester foundry before emerging unharmed.[8] In evidence to the Select Committee on Accidents in Mines in 1849, John Hutchinson, a London doctor, suggested that breathing apparatus employed in the Paris sewers, comprising a mask with valves connected to a bag of air kept in a basket on the wearer's back, could be adapted for use in mines (Rescue Regulations Committee 1926, pp. 6–7; House of Lords 1849, pp. 140, 160–162).

The first practical breathing apparatus for rescue and salvage work in mines was invented by Henry Fleuss. Coming from a maritime background, Fleuss devised a primitive self-contained underwater breathing apparatus (scuba) in 1879. This apparatus dispensed with the vulnerable air hose connecting the diver to the surface. Divers now carried a self-contained compressed oxygen supply, and a contrivance to regenerate oxygen from exhaled carbon dioxide. Fleuss obtained patents and began to collaborate with Siebe, Gorman & Co. of London, the premier makers of diving equipment in the UK. Surviving in a poisonous atmosphere underground presented a similar challenge to surviving underwater. A society of mining engineers invited Fleuss to exhibit an apparatus modified for use underground at an event in Chesterfield in 1881 to mark the centenary of George Stephenson's birth. Shortly afterwards, the apparatus was used in work to reopen Seaham Colliery after an explosion, and in rescue work at Killingworth Colliery where some miners were trapped by a falling roof. Siebe, Gorman manufactured and distributed the Fleuss apparatus, but it was expensive and not adopted widely. Nevertheless, the design, including the mechanism for regenerating oxygen with caustic soda, was highly influential. Fleuss and Siebe, Gorman continued to work together to perfect

[8] "Local Intelligence", Manchester Courier and Lancashire General Advertiser, 19 February 1825, p. 3.

improved models of mine rescue apparatus (Foregger 1974; H.M. Inspectors of Mines 1883, pp. 318–319; Jackson 2002).[9]

Two basic types of breathing apparatus were developed: the compressed oxygen system and the liquid air system.[10] Austria and Germany led the way in the 1890s and early 1900s. Walcher (Austrian) and Shamrock, Giersberg and Draeger (all German) breathing apparatus or "pneumatophores" used compressed oxygen cylinders, and a chemical process to "regenerate" exhaled air in a breathing bag strapped to the body. The rescuer wore an airtight helmet or mask. A mouthpiece was connected by tubes to the breathing bag and oxygen cylinder(s). The pneumatophore was similar in principle to the Fleuss machine.[11] The liquid air apparatus or Aerolith, designed in Austria by O. Suess, was a radical departure from the Fleuss design. Liquid air was poured into a pack on the wearer's back as he was about to start work. A tube connected the backpack to the wearer's mouth. Although simpler to operate than compressed oxygen apparatus, the liquid air apparatus had drawbacks. Unlike compressed oxygen, liquid air could not be stored for long. Rescue stations adopting this technology had to invest in an expensive liquid air producing plant and fragile vacuum storage flasks to convey liquid air to the colliery (Cremer et al. 1906–1907).[12]

New British models appeared in the early 1900s. The Proto compressed oxygen apparatus, introduced in 1906, and manufactured by Siebe, Gorman, was the fruit of cooperation with Fleuss. The Meco (1906), made by the Mining Engineering Company, Sheffield, was almost identical to the Shamrock. Both the Proto and the Meco introduced compressed oxygen into the circuit at a constant rate (Department of Scientific and Industrial Research Advisory Council 1918, pp. 7–10). William Garforth's Weg (1906) apparatus was more advanced, with the supply of compressed oxygen adjusting automatically to meet the wearer's requirements (Garforth 1905–1906). Henry Simonis & Co. of London, a firm best known for fire-fighting equipment, introduced the Aerolith system to Britain (Simonis 1906–1907). The original Aerolith suffered from the defect of not supplying the wearer with enough air. An improved and safer liquid air apparatus, known as the Aerophor (1910), was developed by mining engineers associated with the Elswick mine rescue station at Newcastle upon Tyne. The Aerophor, which also incorporated a purifier to

[9] Fleuss was influenced by earlier inventors, including the Belgian physiologist, Théodore Schwann, who had constructed a prototype breathing apparatus in 1854. On Schwann's contribution see Meyer (1905–1906, pp. 574–581).

[10] For the best overview of these technologies see McAdam and Davidson (1955).

[11] Another device, the pneumatogen (also Austrian), dispensed with the heavy compressed oxygen cylinders, and relied totally on the regeneration of exhaled air through a chemical process involving peroxides. A small pneumatogen was designed as a "self-rescuer" for use by trapped miners. A larger pneumatogen intended for rescue work was not popular in Britain (Cremer 1897–1898, 1906–1907; Meyer 1905–1906, pp. 581–601).

[12] An alarming feature of the liquid air system was its use of asbestos. The liquid air container carried on the wearer's back was "filled with asbestos fibre which absorbs the liquid air as it is poured in and prevents it from running into the [breathing] tubes in liquid form" (Elliston 1922, p. 329).

regenerate exhaled air, was manufactured by Simonis. Here, we have an important example of user innovation in mine rescue (Bulman and Mills 1921, pp. 54–59, 90–101).

If properly maintained, and worn by healthy and well-trained personnel, breathing apparatus could sustain life in irrespirable conditions for between 90 minutes and 2 hours. The dangers included defects or damage to the headgear, tubes and breathing bags, resulting in leakage of oxygen or inflow of poisonous gas, not to mention the wearer's exhaustion, perhaps hastened by overheating caused by chemical reactions, and sometimes panic.[13]

The Society of Arts invited designers and makers to enter their breathing apparatus for evaluation in a competition in 1911. Gold medals were awarded to Siebe, Gorman and Garforth and silver medals to Draeger and Meco.[14] By 1916, there were 913 Proto sets in use in the British coal industry, 455 Meco, 220 Draeger, 132 Weg and 96 Aerophor sets (Department of Scientific and Industrial Research Advisory Council 1918, p. 7). The Proto extended its leadership after 1918, with a reputation enhanced by its deployment by the army in rescue work in tunnels under the Western Front (Logan 1918–1919).[15] But updated versions of the Aerophor continued to have advocates, and remained in service at nationalisation in 1947 (McAdam and Davidson 1955, pp. 35–47).

17.5 The Inventive Community

Having surveyed the technology in the previous section, the time has come to introduce the main participants in the network that designed, produced, tested, adapted and used mine rescue breathing apparatus in the UK.

To begin with, there were the commercial suppliers. Siebe, Gorman was strong in both design and manufacturing. It enjoyed economies of scope arising from the similarities between scuba equipment for diving and mine rescue. Siebe, Gorman was a London firm selling a high-technology product to firms in the UK's industrial heartlands (Foregger 1974; Compton-Hall 2004). Marketing was another strong point of the company, and circa 1915 it distributed a glossy brochure of testimonials from satisfied Proto users from as far afield as Illinois and New Zealand (Rice 1927–1928, p. 426).[16] Henry Simonis & Co., a London-based maker of fire engines,

[13] Good teeth were required to grip the mouthpieces used in most models, a factor that excluded many miners from rescue work.

[14] "Life-saving apparatus for use in noxious atmospheres", The Engineer, Vol. 111, 23 June 1911, pp. 651–52.

[15] As late as the 1950s, the Proto was "undoubtedly the most popular breathing apparatus used in British mines, and … in common use in Africa, Australia, New Zealand, Canada, and India" (McAdam and Davidson 1955, p. 6).

[16] Mining Institute Archives, Newcastle, Siebe, Gorman, Rescue and recovery: bulletin of a few cases where the "Proto" (patent) breathing apparatus has been used, undated (possibly 1915).

and Meco, a producer of mining equipment in Sheffield, were dabblers in mine rescue breathing apparatus, and lacked the staying-power of Siebe, Gorman.[17] The Lubeck firm of Draeger specialised in technologies that used compressed oxygen and other gases, including advanced medical equipment. Draeger was a strong competitor in the UK market for breathing apparatus until the First World War.[18]

Regional associations or "institutions" (sometimes institutes) of mining engineers, and their national federation the IME, occupied a strategic position in relation to innovation. There were 1.2 mining engineers per British coal mine in 1914 (Church 1986, p. 429). By no means every director, agent (the owners' representative) or manager was a mining engineer, but the profession was forging ahead. Some mining engineers, particularly those who chose to engage in the activities of the institutions, had interests that stretched beyond short term commercial success. They were fascinated by technology, and they were committed by the founding documents of their profession to the quest for safer methods. The North of England Institute of Mining Engineers, established in 1852, undertook to meet regularly to "discuss the means for ventilation of coal mines for the prevention of accidents and for general purposes connected with the winning and working of collieries" (Strong 1988, p. 108).

Members kept abreast of developments by attending meetings of their regional mining institution and by reading *Transactions.* This journal contained scientific papers read at institution meetings by practitioners and sometimes by academics. In addition, *Transactions* reported on the discussions that followed the papers. *Transactions* showed great interest in the causes of explosions, the prevention of accidents, the design and testing of breathing apparatus, the organisation of rescue stations, and the conduct of rescue operations. Readers would soon have become familiar with the advantages and disadvantages of the Proto, the Draeger, the Meco, the Aerophor and the Weg. Occasionally, mining engineers were accused of showing too much enthusiasm for the latest kit. At the annual general meeting of the South Midland Coal Owners' Rescue Station in 1913, one member "objected to so many engineers being on the Committee" and felt it was "necessary to take some commercial men on". He added that he was worried about the cost to member firms.[19]

A key individual member of the breathing apparatus network was William Edward Garforth, inventor of the Weg. The son of a Manchester ironworks and colliery owner, Garforth trained as a mining engineer, and was appointed agent of Pope

---

[17] A summary of Meco's catalogue in 1910 mentioned rescue apparatus last, after an "automatic rope greaser, a guide greaser, an electric rotary drill, a percussive coal cutting machine, automatic feed apparatus for drills, [and] a hand drilling machine". The Engineer, vol. 109, 13 May 1910, p. 502.

[18] Dräger, The History of Dräger. www.draeger.com/corporate/content/the_history_of_draeger_2.pdf. Accessed 8 July 2021. Richard Jacobson of London represented the German company in Britain, The Engineer, vol. 109, 13 May 1910, p. 502. The Draeger was the first type of breathing apparatus to be used in the USA in 1907 (Rice 1927–1928, p. 426). Both Draeger and Fleuss (Proto) sets were used at the North Butte copper mining disaster in 1917 (Punke 2016, p. 49).

[19] Leicestershire Record Office, DE1177/15, Minute Book of the Leicestershire and South Derbyshire Mine Rescue and Fire Station, 11 March 1913.

and Pearson's collieries in Yorkshire in 1879. He would become managing director and chairman of the company, president of the national employers' group, the Mining Association of Great Britain (MAGB) in 1907 and 1908, and president of the IME between 1911 and 1914 (Lloyd 1921–1922). Deeply affected by an explosion at Pope and Pearson's Altofts colliery, which extinguished 22 lives in 1886, Garforth began to investigate the scientific and organisational aspects of mine safety. He published a set of guidelines for use by managers after an explosion, established the UK's first rescue station at Altofts, and built experimental facilities for studying explosions. In collaboration with the MAGB and the government, Garforth and his team played an important role in confirming the stone dusting theory (Garforth 1909, 1912–1913). Garforth invented a coal cutting machine and owned the Diamond Coal Cutter works at Wakefield. He took out patents in relation to parts of the Weg apparatus and sold over 100 units. Whereas Garforth the inventor of coal-cutting machines sought profits, Garforth the inventor of breathing apparatus was guided seemingly by more altruistic motives. Although he declined to give away the key "lung-governing valve" at the heart of the Weg, he encouraged colleagues in the IME to make their own use of any other elements of the apparatus, for "everything associated with the saving of life should be as free to use as the air that we breathe" (Garforth 1905–1906, p. 653).

Garforth could have made more of the Weg, but seems to have been distracted by other commitments; nevertheless, his design inspired later generations of breathing apparatus, especially in the USA and Germany (McAdam and Davidson 1955, p. 21).[20] At the close of the First World War, Garforth called for a competition to develop a standard "British" model of breathing apparatus. He contended that progress would be rapid when "it becomes known that there is nothing to be patented, but that everything is to be done for the benefit of the miners" (Walker et al. 1918–1919, p. 246). But no standard "British" apparatus emerged to supersede the Proto.

Significant refinements to breathing apparatus were made by the users, the rescue stations and their staff and board members. The work of the Rotherham rescue station is considered in a later section, and the focus here is on the Durham and Northumberland Collieries Fire and Rescue Brigade (DNCFRB) and its leading lights William Cuthbert Blackett and Frederick P. Mills. The DNCFRB's first rescue station at Elswick worked closely with the fire brigade of the neighbouring Armstrong Whitworth shipbuilding and armaments complex (Blackett 1910–1911). Blackett, the chairman of the DNCFRB's management committee, was managing director of Charlaw and Sacriston collieries, and president of the IME in 1919 and 1920 (Tate 1934–1935). Patents for the Aerophor, the improved liquid air apparatus

[20] US mine safety experts and the embryonic Bureau of Mines were interested in the Weg, but disappointed when Garforth failed to develop his device commercially for the overseas market. This prompted the Americans to develop substitutes including the Gibbs apparatus (Rice 1927–1928, p. 427).

that Simonis would manufacture, were published in Blackett's name in 1911.[21] Frederick P. Mills, a mining engineer and manager, was appointed chief officer of the DNCFRB in 1913. Together with G.L. Brown of the North Midland Coal Owners' Rescue Stations (NMCORS), Mills worked on further refinements to the liquid air apparatus. Patents relating to the Brown Mills Aerophor were published in 1922, the applicants this time being Brown, Mills, the DNCFRB and the NMCORS (McAdam and Davidson 1955, p. 37).[22] In short, there was a community of mining engineers dedicated to improving existing rescue apparatus.

Foremost amongst the academics interested in explosions and rescue apparatus was John Scott Haldane. The UK's leading expert on physiology and respiration, and a Fellow of New College, Oxford, Haldane began investigating the effects of poisonous gases on coal miners in the late nineteenth century. He was active in the IME, holding the presidency between 1924 and 1927, a mark of acceptance by practical men. Although not an inventor of mine rescue apparatus, he commented extensively on the merits and demerits of each model on behalf of the government, the IME and coalowners. In 1912, whilst still on the staff at Oxford, he also became director of the Doncaster Coal Owners' Research Laboratory, where he oversaw research into a range of problems including spontaneous combustion, coal dust inhalation, and the defects of breathing apparatus.[23] Haldane exercised an important influence over the inventive community.

Henry Briggs, a lecturer at Heriot Watt College, and later professor at the University of Edinburgh, also made a mark. An academic entrepreneur, Briggs sought government support for research into rescue apparatus, and proposed a system of official inspection and authorisation. Heriot Watt trained colliery managers and cooperated with local collieries and the Carnegie Trustees to establish the Heriot Watt mine rescue station during the First World War.[24] The college principal contacted the Privy Council Commission on Scientific and Industrial Research in 1916 to propose working with the government on improvements to rescue apparatus.[25] Briggs hoped to develop an "apparatus which would combine …the more useful features of [the five or six] existing types, with the final object of evolving a design which could be officially recommended".[26] The Commission viewed this

[21] Espacenet patent database: GB191017589 (A) 1911-02-09 and GB191122507 (A) 1911-12-14. Patents may be accessed through the website of the European Patent Office, www.epo.org

[22] Espacenet patent database: GB179094 (A) 1922-05-04; GB179126 (A) 1922-04-12; GB188612 (A) 1922-11-16; GB188677 (A) 1922-11-23.

[23] For a popular biography see Goodman (2007). For Haldane's contribution to the IME see Graham (1935–1936).

[24] Part of a training session at the Heriot Watt rescue station in 1938 may be viewed at http://movingimage.nls.uk/film/1862 starting at 19 minutes 45 seconds [accessed 6 July 2021]. The University of Birmingham also operated a mine rescue station.

[25] The National Archives, Kew [hereafter TNA], DSIR3/234, A. P. Laurie to the Secretary, Privy Council Commission for Scientific & Industrial Research, 12 July 1916.

[26] TNA, DSIR3/234, Henry Briggs to the Secretary, Privy Council Commission for Scientific & Industrial Research, 18 July 1916.

approach sceptically, but Garforth, hearing of Briggs's plans, made a small donation.[27] A tragedy in South Wales turned the tide in Briggs's favour. In 1917 three rescuers were asphyxiated in a training session at Duchy colliery, deaths that were attributed to faults in their Draeger apparatus (Department of Scientific and Industrial Research Advisory Council 1918, pp. 22–23). The Home Office now approved work along the lines suggested by Briggs.[28] Funded by the Department of Scientific and Industrial Research (DSIR), the research project was based at Heriot Watt and assisted by Haldane's Doncaster laboratory. An official Mine Rescue Apparatus Research Committee (MRARC), comprising William Walker (acting Chief Inspector of Mines), Haldane and Briggs, oversaw the research.[29] Briggs's team developed a new design of compressed oxygen breathing apparatus, incorporating several improvements including an improved purifier.[30] This apparatus would later be manufactured by Meco, but although serviceable the Briggs-Meco failed to break the stranglehold of the Proto.

Until 1917, the government had at first chivvied and then compelled coalowners to invest in mine rescue facilities, but it had not funded research into breathing apparatus. The formation of the MRARC foreshadowed greater intervention. Several reports were published by the committee. Existing models of breathing apparatus were evaluated in the first report and certain improvements were suggested. The second report concluded that enforced standardisation would constrain future research, but urged the government to test each type of apparatus before approving it for use (Department of Scientific and Industrial Research Advisory Council 1920, p. 5). A new regulation was issued in 1920 to the effect that: "No Breathing Apparatus shall be used except such as is approved by the Secretary of State [for Mines] (Bulman and Mills 1921, pp. 51-52)". Several types of apparatus were approved, albeit after modification, providing rescue stations with almost as much choice as before the war.

17.6 The Institution of Mining Engineers and *Transactions*

The IME and *Transactions* offered a platform for the exchange of information and opinion about types of breathing apparatus. They linked together the network described in the previous section.[31] Although this forum was largely British, some

[27] TNA, DSIR3/234, Notes on Heriot Watt proposal, 8 December 1916.

[28] TNA, DSIR3/234, Memorandum on a proposal from the Home Office to establish a research committee to investigate the best form of mine rescue apparatus, 23 May 1917; minutes of Advisory Committee of the Department of Scientific and Industrial Research, 23 May 1917.

[29] TNA, DSIR3/234, Communication to be made to the press, 11 July 1917.

[30] In one test of the Briggs apparatus the wearer was required to climb Arthur's Seat in Edinburgh (Department of Scientific and Industrial Research Advisory Council 1920, pp. 41–53).

[31] The contribution of the IME and *Transactions* to the circulation and testing of new methods and technologies is mentioned briefly in Scott (2006, pp. 25–26).

foreign equipment was examined, and several overseas experts were invited to speak at meetings and to contribute articles. Some examples of the contributions made through the IME are given below.

The years 1905–1907 saw the publication in *Transactions* of several detailed accounts and evaluations of breathing apparatus. G.A. Meyer of Shamrock colliery in Germany read a paper on the history of breathing apparatus, also describing the work of Westphalian rescue teams at the Courriéres colliery disaster in 1906 in which 1100 French miners died. Some of the German explorers at Courriéres had worn the Shamrock apparatus, designed by Meyer himself (Meyer 1905–1906).[32] Meyer was billed as Germany's premier expert on rescue apparatus, and his paper provoked a lively debate. Haldane noted that Meyer's latest model incorporated new safety features, but another mining engineer claimed that the Shamrock was too complicated for the average user. Doubts were expressed over the claims that the Shamrock could be worn safely for 2 hours. H.E. Gregory of Cortonwood colliery mentioned problems with an earlier version of the Shamrock. He criticised other models, including the Draeger, which incorporated a helmet rather than a mouthpiece on the grounds that the helmet caused discomfort and possibly danger (Gerrard et al. 1905–1906). The discussion brought together practitioners (mining engineers and managers), a leading British scientist (Haldane), a representative of the Mines Inspectorate, and a respected foreign designer. Anyone with access to *Transactions* could have studied the article and debate.

Shortly afterwards, the characteristics of the Weg and the Aerolith were explained in articles by Garforth (1905–1906) and Simonis (1906–1907) respectively. R. Cremer, a Leeds mining engineer, published a paper comparing five different types of breathing apparatus made on the European continent. He produced a table evaluating them according to 12 criteria, from the length of time they could be worn safely to the purchase and running costs (Cremer 1906–1907, pp. 68–69). Garforth's new apparatus also sparked controversy. Members of the IME were invited to attend a demonstration of the Weg at Altofts. Some were impressed, but W.C. Blackett questioned the value of "so-called rescue-appliances" and said he could not remember a single occasion when he would have felt safer wearing one. He wondered whether rescuers could be sufficiently well-trained to wear and operate complicated apparatus without putting their own lives at risk (Blackett et al. 1906–1907, p. 180).[33] Blackett, developer of the Aerophor, would soon change his tune, which suggests open-mindedness.

The most searching evaluation of existing types of breathing apparatus was supplied by Haldane in two articles in 1914. Haldane was tasked to recommend a type of breathing apparatus for the new Doncaster rescue station. The number of rescue stations was growing rapidly, Haldane's verdict was worth taking seriously, and the Doncaster coalowners were content for him to reprint his findings in *Transactions*.

[32] On Courriéres see Neville (1978).

[33] A later paper was even more brutal, describing breathing apparatus as "absurd walking 'fitters' shops'" that would never be of any value to rescuers (Harger 1911–1912, p. 139).

Haldane and his staff subjected each model of apparatus to extensive testing. Serious and potentially dangerous defects were found in each of them. For example, the Proto was prone to overheating which made breathing painful; the Weg leaked both inwards and outwards and needed an expert operator; the helmets of the Draeger and the Meco also leaked; carbon dioxide was liable to accumulate in the Draeger and the Aerophor; finally, the Aerophor was judged experimental and unsuitable for adoption (Haldane 1913–1914). Haldane could recommend no apparatus to the Doncaster coalowners. A second article recorded improvements hurriedly made to several types of apparatus including the Aerophor. Haldane now concluded that the Proto, despite some remaining deficiencies, was the best available, and it was adopted at Doncaster (Haldane 1914–1915).

Haldane's articles caused testy debate in the institutions. Dismissing Haldane as a mere academic, Jonathan Piggford accused him of unfair bias against the Aerophor. Piggford mounted a detailed defence of the liquid air apparatus, an early version of which was in service at his local rescue station, Mansfield (Piggford et al. 1914–1915, p. 585). Garforth deplored Piggford's outburst, and said that Haldane's first report "had done more good than anything else" in recent years, and that his criticism of existing models "had been taken advantage of by the makers" to improve their equipment. Although the Weg had cost over £1000 to develop, Garforth offered to share it with anyone in the interests of saving lives (Piggford et al. 1914–1915, p. 590).

An active community of experts keen to debate the merits of different types of breathing apparatus was sustained by the IME, not least in the pages of *Transactions*. Opposing viewpoints on technical matters were aired in detail, sometimes heatedly. The mining engineering profession was certainly highly argumentative. Informed debate fed back into the work of the designers of breathing apparatus, both professional and amateur. Collective invention and user innovation flourished, albeit within certain constraints for the commercial makers at least were interested in making a profit.

17.7 The Rotherham Apparatus

User innovation and tinkering were prominent in the affairs of the Rotherham mine rescue station which opened in 1914. Rotherham was an important mining, steel and engineering centre near Sheffield. Rotherham coalowners who sat on the management committee of the rescue station took their duties very seriously. Before choosing breathing apparatus for the new rescue station, they visited other stations to evaluate their equipment and methods, and found a variety of models in use at

Elswick (Aerophor), Howe Bridge (Proto), Mansfield (Meco), Altofts (Weg) and Wath (Draeger).[34]

Consideration was given to developing a hybrid breathing apparatus, taking the best features of several types, but this option was not pursued.[35] In 1913, the suppliers of the Draeger, Proto, Meco and Aerophor were invited to Rotherham, and their apparatus put through a series of tests and practices in a special gallery designed to replicate underground conditions. Although the Aerophor liquid air apparatus was worn by the most inexperienced rescue man attending the tests, he experienced the least discomfort and distress. It was resolved to adopt the Aerophor as the principal model of breathing apparatus for the Rotherham rescue station, supplemented by some Meco compressed oxygen sets, a decision which may have indicated some lingering doubts about the Aerophor. The liquid air system had a higher capital cost but lower running costs than the compressed oxygen system. The internal report on the trials said that cost not been a consideration in the choice of apparatus but expressed the hope that the best system would prove the cheapest in the long run.[36]

An order for Aerophor sets and liquid air plant was placed with the Simonis company. After the release of Haldane's damning report on the Aerophor, the Rotherham coalowners, desperate for reassurance, approached the famous scientist for advice. He recommended several modifications, which Simonis agreed to make.[37] When the Aerophors started to arrive at Rotherham in 1914, they were discovered to have faults which the rescue station decided to have fixed by local firms.[38] Relations with Simonis were becoming soured by disputes over cost, delays and poor quality work. Significant improvements to the design of the Aerophor were made locally in 1915. Simonis undertook to produce the remaining sets to the modified "Rotherham" design, but further defects were found upon delivery in 1916. At this point Simonis was dropped, and the Rotherham coalowners resolved to proceed with their own refinements to the liquid air sets.[39] Sergeant Major Elliston, the chief instructor at the rescue station, was instrumental in the development of what became known as the Rotherham apparatus. This was a classic case of tinkering. When appointed, Elliston had no prior experience of mine rescue work, having been a

---

[34] Rotherham Archives and Local Studies (hereafter RALS), 185/B/9/1/1, Rotherham and District Rescue Station, Minutes of meeting, 4 November 1912; Notes on a visit to the Northumberland and Durham Rescue Station at Elswick, Newcastle upon Tyne, 29 May 1912; Visit to Howe Bridge Station, Lancashire, 12 June 1912; Visit to Mansfield Station, 19 June 1912; Notes of a Visit to Wath Rescue Station, 2 October 2 1912; Visit to the Altofts station to inspect the "W.E.G." Apparatus, 26 June 1912.

[35] RLAS, 185/B/9/1/1, Minutes of Breathing Apparatus Committee, 14 August 1913.

[36] RLAS, 185/B/9/1/1, Record of demonstrations with various apparatus at the new rescue station, 3 September 1913.

[37] RLAS, RLAS, 185/B/9/1/2, Minutes of General Meeting, 31 March 1914.

[38] RLAS, RLAS, 185/B/9/1/2, Minutes of General Meeting, 14 October 1914.

[39] RLAS, RLAS, 185/B/9/1/2, Minutes of General Meeting, 11 June 1915; Aerophor, 1 October 1915; Minutes of Breathing Apparatus Committee, 29 September 1915; Minutes of General Meeting, 14 October 1915; Secretary's Report for year ending 30 June 1916.

drill, musketry and engineering instructor in the Royal Engineers.[40] The improvements to the Aerophor were sufficiently extensive for the Rotherham device to be regarded as a distinct model, and it became the first type of liquid air apparatus endorsed by the Mines Department after 1920 (Elliston 1922).

In the early 1920s, the government Mines Department required further modifications to all types of breathing apparatus, including the Rotherham model which now acquired a better purifier and a protector for the breathing bag. Irritation was expressed that other rescue stations were copying these improvements without acknowledgement, and it was decided to seek patent protection.[41] In order to defray the cost of modifications and patents, other liquid air stations (including Mansfield, Elswick and Brierley) were invited to re-equip with the Rotherham apparatus, but they declined to do so.[42] The Rotherham apparatus was battle tested at the Maltby Main disaster in 1923. Although no lives could be saved on this occasion, the apparatus performed creditably in subsequent salvage and restoration operations.[43]

Rotherham coalowners worked closely with Simonis (and Haldane) on modifications to the liquid air breathing apparatus, but eventually went their own way when the performance of the London firm proved unsatisfactory. They sought help from other rescue stations when evaluating breathing apparatus, but later found some of them to be untrustworthy. Not surprisingly, the historical record offers a rather untidy illustration of collective invention and user innovation in this and other instances.

17.8 Conclusion

Strong elements of collective invention and user innovation were present in the network that developed rescue apparatus for use in coal mines in the UK in the late nineteenth and early twentieth centuries. Participants included commercial enterprises (Siebe, Gorman, Simonis and Meco), public spirited employers and engineers (Garforth and Blackett), academic scientists (Haldane and Briggs), the staff of mine rescue stations (Mills and Elliston) and government officials. The Institution of Mining Engineers and its journal *Transactions* provided a crucial platform for the exchange of information and ideas. Collective invention and user innovation were not to be found in their pure forms, but rather in somewhat untidy versions. Some, but not all, technical advances were shared freely. Cooperation was qualified by rivalry and tempers sometimes flared. Users and manufacturers worked together

[40] RLAS, 185/B/9/1/1, Minutes of General Meeting of the Board, 2 December 1913; 185/B/9/1/2, Note on miscellaneous matters, 17 September 1918.

[41] RLAS, 185/B/9/1/2, Minutes of General Meeting, 23 March 1922.

[42] RLAS, 185/B/9/1/2, Minutes of General Meeting, 14 June 1922 and 24 August 1922.

[43] Two miners trained as rescuers at the Rotherham station died at Maltby, but they were not involved in the rescue operation. RLAS, 185/B/9/1/2, Minutes of AGM, 11 October 1923; Minutes of General Meeting, 6 March 1924 and 28 May 1924. See also Mottram (1924).

some of the time, but they could also fall out. Nevertheless, the story that emerges is one of a dynamic innovative network, which collaborated to develop a new technology for use in mine rescue and recovery. Breathing apparatus may not have saved many lives in British coal mines in the period examined – its finest hour was not until 1950 – but it did provide a measure of insurance.[44] This study of mine rescue apparatus offers important insights into how advanced technologies were developed in Britain in the early twentieth century. The inventive network in question was able to span the worlds of practical mine engineering, commercial research and development, and the universities, and at its centre sat the Institution of Mining Engineers.

Acknowledgements I wish to thank Chris Corker, Sarah Holland, and Alan Malpass for research assistance; the staff at Rotherham Archives and Local Studies and Jennifer Hillyard of the North of England Institute of Mining and Mechanical Engineers, Newcastle upon Tyne for their help; and Javier Silvestre for illuminating email discussions of mine safety and rescue.

Appendix: Singleton on Murray

After moving from Wellington, New Zealand to Sheffield, Yorkshire at the end of 2010, I wanted to find a research topic with a local dimension and hit upon coal mine safety. Yorkshire was an important coal mining region until comparatively recently – the last Yorkshire (and UK) deep coal mine shut down in 2015. The publication in 2015 of an excellent article by John Murray and Javier Silvestre on the impact of better safety technology in European coal mines in the late nineteenth century gave a boost to what until then was a relatively neglected area of research. I was hoping to meet John at the Economic History Society Conference at the University of Keele in April 2018 where we were both scheduled to present papers on mine safety. John did not appear and a couple of days later I heard from Javier that he had died suddenly. The chapter presented here is based on my own paper from the conference at Keele.

References

Aldrich M (1995) 'The needless peril of the coal mine'. The Bureau of Mines and the campaign against coal mine explosions, 1910–1940. Technol Cult 36:483–518

Allen RC (1983) Collective invention. J Econ Behav Organ 4:1–24

Blackett WC (1910–1911) The fire- and rescue-station of the Durham and Northumberland collieries fire- and rescue-brigade. T I Mining Eng 41:253–271

Blackett WC et al (1906–1907) Discussion of Mr WE Garforth's paper on a new apparatus for rescue-work in mines. T I Mining Eng 33:180–182

---

[44] 116 trapped men were saved by rescuers equipped with Proto apparatus at Knockshinnoch Castle Colliery in 1950 (Bryan 1951).

Bogers M, Afuah A, Bastian B (2010) Users as innovators: a review, critique and future research directions. J Manage 34:857–875
Boyns T (1986) Technical change and colliery explosions in the South Wales coalfield, c. 1870–1914. Welsh Hist Rev 13:155–177
Bryan A (1951) Accident at Knockshinnoch Castle Colliery, Ayrshire: report, Cmd. 8180. HMSO, London
Bulman HF, Mills FP (1921) Mine rescue work and organization. Crosby, Lockwood & Son, London
Church R (1986) The history of the British coal industry, vol 3. Clarendon Press, Oxford
Compton-Hall R (2004) Davis, Sir Robert Henry (1870–1965). In Oxford Dictionary of National Biography. Oxford University Press, Oxford. http://www.oxforddnb.com/view/article/56874. Accessed 10 Oct 2017
Cookson G (2018) The age of machinery: engineering the industrial revolution, 1770–1850. Boydell, Woodbridge
Cremer R (1897–1898) The Walcher pneumatophore, and the employment of oxygen for life-saving purposes. T I Mining Eng 14:575–585
Cremer R (1906–1907) The pneumatogen: the self-generating rescue-apparatus, compared with other types. T I Mining Eng 32:51–71
Cremer R et al (1906–1907) Discussion of Mr Otto Simonis's paper on liquid air and its use in rescue apparatus. T I Mining Eng 32:539–550
Department of Scientific and Industrial Research Advisory Council (1918) First report of the mine rescue apparatus research committee. DSIR, London
Department of Scientific and Industrial Research Advisory Council (1920) Second report of the mine rescue apparatus research committee. DSIR, London
Elliston EC (1922) The "Rotherham" rescue apparatus. Colliery Guardian 11 August:329–330
Foregger R (1974) Development of mine rescue and underwater breathing apparatus: appliances of Henry Fleuss. J Hist Med 29:317–330
Garforth WE (1905–1906) A new apparatus for rescue-work in mines. T I Mining Eng 31:625–654
Garforth WE (1909) Suggested rules for recovering coal mines after explosions and fires, Revised edn. Colliery Guardian, London
Garforth WE (1912–1913) A record of the origin of the principle of stone-dusting for the prevention of explosions. T I Mining Eng 45:562–575
Gerrard J et al (1905–1906) Discussion of Mr GA Meyer's paper on rescue-apparatus and the experiences gained therewith at the Courriéres collieries. T I Mining Eng 31:614–624
Goodman M (2007) Suffer and survive: gas attacks, miners' canaries, spacesuits and the bends: the extreme life of J.S. Haldane. Pocket, London
Graham JI (1935–1936) Memoir of the late John Scott Haldane. T I Mining Eng 91:417–420
Griffiths T (2001) The Lancashire working classes, c. 1880–1930. Oxford University Press, Oxford
Habershon MH (1900–1901) A joint colliery rescue station. T I Mining Eng 21:100–110
Habershon MH (1904–1905) The work of a joint colliery rescue-station. T I Mining Eng 28:254–263
Haldane JS (1913–1914) Self-contained rescue-apparatus for use in irrespirable atmospheres: report to the Doncaster Coal-Owners' (Gob-Fire Research) Committee. T I Mining Eng 47:725–776
Haldane JS (1914–1915) Self-contained rescue-apparatus and smoke-helmets: second report to the Doncaster Coal-Owners' (Gob-Fire Research) Committee. T I Mining Eng 48:550–585
Harger J (1911–1912) The prevention of explosions in mines. T I Mining Eng 43:132–152
Harhoff D, Lakhani KR (eds) (2016) Revolutionizing innovation: users, communities and open innovation. MIT Press, Cambridge, MA
HM Inspectors of Mines (1883) Reports of the inspectors of mines to Her Majesty's Secretary of State for 1882, C. 3621. Eyre and Spottiswoode, London
House of Lords (1849) Report from the select committee of the House of Lords appointed to inquire into the best means of preventing the occurrence of dangerous accidents in coal mines, C. 613. HMSO, London

Ingram P, Lifschitz A (2006) Kinship in the shadow of the corporation: the interbuilder network in Clyde River shipbuilding, 1711–1990. Am Sociol Rev 71:334–352
Jackson P (2002) O_2 under H_2O: the Fleuss apparatus: a short history of the re-breather. Hist Diver 10:26–31
Jones AV (2006) Towards safer working: the hazards and the risks of introducing electrical equipment in British coal mines up to about 1930. T Newcomen Soc 76:115–126
Land F (2000) The first business computer: a case study in user-driven innovation. IEEE Ann Hist Comput 22:16–26
Lane J (2019) Secrets for sale? Innovation and the nature of knowledge in the early industrial district: the Potteries, 1750–1851. Enterp Soc 20:861–906
Lloyd WD (1921–1922) Memoir of the late Sir William Garforth. T I Mining Eng 62:202–205
Logan DD (1918–1919) The difficulties and dangers of mine-rescue work on the Western Front; and mining operations carried out by men wearing rescue-pparatus. T I Mining Eng 57:197–222
McAdam R, Davidson D (1955) Mine rescue work. Oliver & Boyd, Edinburgh
Meyer GA (1905–1906) Rescue-apparatus and the experiences gained therewith at the Courriéres collieries by the German rescue-party. T I Mining Eng 31:574–613
Meyer PB (2007) Networks of tinkerers: a model of open-source technology innovation Bureau of Labor Statistics Working Papers, No. 413
Meyer PB (2013) The airplane as an open-source invention. Revue économique 64:115–132
Mills C (2010) Regulating health and safety in the British mining industries, 1800–1914. Ashgate, Abingdon
Mines Department (1922) First annual report of the Secretary of State for Mines for the year ending 32st December 1921 and the annual report of HM Chief Inspector of Mines, HMSO, London
Mottram T (1924) Explosion at the Maltby Main Colliery, Yorkshire: report, Cmd 2047. HMSO, London
Murray JE, Silvestre J (2015) Small-scale technologies and European coal mine safety, 1850–1900. Econ Hist Rev 68:887–910
Neville RG (1978) The Courrières colliery disaster, 1906. J Contemp Hist 13:33–52
Nuvolari A (2004) Collective invention during the British Industrial Revolution: the case of the Cornish pumping engine. Camb J Econ 28:347–363
Nuvolari A, Sumner J (2013) Inventors, patents, and inventive activities in the English brewing industry, 1634–1850. Bus Hist Rev 87:95–120
Parsons M, Rose MB (2009) Lead-user innovation and the UK outdoor trade since 1850. Bus Econ Hist Online 7: 1–30 Lead User Innovation and the UK Outdoor Trade since 1850 (thebhc.org). https://thebhc.org/sites/default/files/parsonsandrose.pdf. Accessed 7 July 2021
Piggford J et al (1914–1915) Discussion of Mr JS Haldane's paper on self-contained rescue-apparatus and smoke-helmets. T I Mining Eng 48:585–595
Punke M (2016) Fire and brimstone: the North Butte mining disaster of 1917. Borough, London
Redmayne RAS, Samuel Pope S (1911) Explosion and underground fire at the Wellington Pit, Whitehaven Colliery. Report on the causes of and circumstances attending an explosion and underground fire which occurred at the Wellington Pit, Whitehaven Colliery on the 11th May 1910, Cd. 5524. HMSO, London
Rescue Regulations Committee (1926) Report of the Departmental Committee appointed by the Secretary of State for Mines to investigate the existing arrangements for the provision and maintenance of rescue appliances and for the formation and training of rescue corps and brigades. HMSO, London
Rice GS (1927–1928) Mine-rescue work in the United States. T I Mining Eng 75:426–444
Rockley E (1938) Royal Commission on safety in coal mines: report, Cmd. 5890. HMSO, London
Royal Commission on Accidents in Mines (1886) Final report, c. 4699. Eyre and Spottiswoode, London
Royal Commission on Mines (1907) First report of the Royal Commission on Mines, Cd. 3548. HMSO, London

Royal Commission on Mines (1909) Second report of the Royal Commission on Mines, Cd. 4820. HMSO, London

Schwerin J (2004) The evolution of the Clyde region's shipbuilding innovation system in the second half of the nineteenth century. J Econ Geog 4:83–101

Scott P (2006) Path dependence, fragmented property rights and the slow diffusion of high throughput technologies in inter-war British coal mining. Bus Hist 48:20–42

Simonis O (1906–1907) Liquid air and its use in rescue apparatus. T I Mining Eng 32:534–538

Singleton J (2016) Economic and natural disasters since 1900. Edward Elgar, Cheltenham

Singleton J (2020) Origins of disaster management: the British mine rescue system, c. 1990 – c. 1930. Bus Hist 2020:1–23

Strong GR (1988) A history of the institution of mining engineers 1889–1989. Institution of Mining Engineers, Doncaster

Tate RS (1934–1935) Memoir of the late Colonel William Cuthbert Blackett. T I Mining Eng 89:339–341

von Hippel E (2006) Democratizing innovation. MIT Press, Cambridge, MA

Walker GB et al (1918–1919) Discussion of Lt Col. Logan's paper on accidents due to structural defects of apparatus or injury to apparatus; and the future of the Proto apparatus. T I Mining Eng 57:238–259

Williamson S (1999) Gresford: the anatomy of a disaster. Liverpool University Press, Liverpool

Chapter 18
Grain Market Integration in Late Colonial Mexico

Amílcar E. Challú

Abstract This paper assesses the degree of integration of grain markets in late-Bourbon New Spain using standard econometric tools applied in other international cases. I find that grain market integration in Bourbon Mexico attained a degree comparable to other regions in the world, despite its poor transportation technology. Bourbon Mexico was not a market economy, but markets were effective tools in funneling resources from the countryside to the cities. An increase in prices in a leading market increased prices throughout the viceroyalty. For example, maize prices in Antequera, in the southern region of Oaxaca, within a year absorbed changes in prices in markets as distant as Guadalajara or San Luis Potosí (800 km). Likewise, wheat prices in Mexico City reacted to changes in the flour markets of the Gulf, such as Campeche (900 km away). These findings place grain markets in New Spain at a level of performance that is comparable to that found in the United States and some European regions. Spatial arbitrage (the buying in high-price regions and selling in low-price regions) was a driving force that broke local monopolies, opened the participation to other actors and created more diversified and integrated grain markets.

Keywords Market Integration · Maize · Wheat · Mexico

18.1 Introduction

In his biannual report of harvest and market conditions for the second semester of 1794, the local magistrate of the jurisdiction of Tepatitlán, located 40 miles east of Guadalajara, reported the maize harvest "was abundant, but because it is scarce in the neighboring jurisdictions of Guanajuato, to an extreme degree, it sells today at eight reales [per fanega] when it usually sells at four." Underneath this brief statement lies a story of price adjustments that we can reconstruct with the use of

A. E. Challú (✉)
Bowling Green State University, Bowling Green, OH, USA
e-mail: achallu@bgsu.edu

P. Gray et al. (eds.), *Standard of Living*, Studies in Economic History,
https://doi.org/10.1007/978-3-031-06477-7_18

evidence of prices from other similar reports.[1] The shortage affected the mining city of Guanajuato, located 50 leagues to the east, which experienced an increase in prices from 9 reales in the first semester of 1793 to 15 reales in the first semester of 1794. The price difference with Tepatitlán's typical price (4 reales) was close to the cost of transportation (12 reales per fanega). In the coming months the price surged to 23 reales. By now the difference in prices widely exceeded the costs, making it convenient to buy in Tepatitlán and sell in Guanajuato. The increase in demand translated into higher prices in Tepatitlán, but (as more places engaged in trade) it also increased maize supply in Guanajuato and drove its price down to 19 reales in early 1795, even as the new harvest would only be available by the end of the year. The evolution of prices in the two areas is not explained by a similar climatic trend: as the local magistrate of Tepatitlán made clear, and other reports from Guadalajara confirm, the harvest failure was contained to Guanajuato. It is the mutual dependence of markets that explains the trajectory: Guanajuato's high price made it irresistible to buy from places such as Tepatitlán, increasing the prices in the producer areas and mitigating prices in the consumer center.

In this essay, I inquire the degree of market integration in late colonial Mexico. By market integration I understand the scenario in which trade connects two localities when the price difference between them exceeds the cost of transportation. The interdependence of markets across the space is the defining characteristic of market integration. Supply and demand forces in one market are not isolated but are propagated through other integrated markets via price adjustments. A major driver of integration is *spatial arbitrage*: if two markets are integrated, whenever the price difference between them exceeds costs, actors will buy low in one market and sell high in the other one (Ravallion 1986, p. 103; Roehner 2000, p. 179). As actors engage in buying and selling, the extraordinary profits dissipate and the price differential decreases to match transportation and transaction costs. Prices in one market, then, adjust to the other market (and vice versa) to finally restore the price ratio that reflects transportation and transaction costs between the two markets.[2]

Integration does not mean that actors were directly trading from one market to the other. As John H. Coatsworth put it, "markets are not defined by the geographic space in which transactions actually occur, but by the space in which they may potentially occur given appropriate price signals" (1989, p. 539). Moreover, we can generalize the idea of integration to a system of markets in which the exchange between some of its components has effects throughout the system. Two distant consumer markets may not trade with each other but may still adjust to each other because of the existence of chain effects that affect conditions of supply and demand, and hence prices, in their suppliers (Ejrnæs and Persson 2000).

[1] Archivo General de Indias [Seville, Spain], Indiferente General, 1560, report from Guadalajara, February 1795.

[2] Federico (2018) distinguishes price convergence as the outcome of integrated markets, and the speed of adjustment as an indicator of market efficiency. Both measures, convergence and speed of adjustment, are the key metrics to compare and assess the integration of markets.

Grain market integration is a central theme, even a subfield, with a long tradition in economic history. The study of grain markets has progressed significantly in the last quarter century. Methodologically, the adoption of error- or equilibrium-correction models, dynamic factor analysis, and other statistical techniques have brought new awareness on the twin processes of adjustment and price convergence. A second revolution is the broadening of the scope to regions outside of Europe (Federico 2018). Against a Euro-centric and lineal interpretation that saw grain markets as progress toward modern economic growth, economic historians have shown that regions that did not share Western institutions, such as China, had a degree of market integration comparable to continental Europe in the eighteenth century (Li 1992; Marks 1998; Shiue and Keller 2007; Wong and Perdue 1992). Dobado-González et al. (2012) similarly showed that it was the entire Atlantic region, including Hispanic America, that evidenced traits of greater market integration in the eighteenth century. Scholars now see grain market integration as contingent on local characteristics, political priorities, and structural factors, rather than a lineal process of ever-increasing penetration of markets (Federico 2018, p. 18). In the case of Mexico, Dobado and Marrero (2005) found that corn market integration was increasing fast by the turn of the twentieth century and was comparable to more advanced economies.

The degree of the integration of grain markets in Mexico's colonial period has deserved some attention although it has not been studied in detail. Two ideas are clearly discernable. One view proposes that market fragmentation prevailed and this was manifest in the pronounced variability of prices (Garner 1993, pp. 55–57; Hamnett 1986, p. 115; Morin 1979, p. 195; Salvucci and Salvucci 1987). The high variability and volatility in prices is a reminder that transportation costs still loomed large in the connectedness of markets and that these costs were unlikely to have changed over time. High transportation costs limited the frequency of transactions, but they do not necessarily indicate lack of integration. On the other hand, prices in different markets showed a high level of co-movement (Espinosa Morales 1995; Lindo-Fuentes 1980). I showed elsewhere that maize prices in four regional capitals and Mexico City shared a break in the trend in the early 1780s and that they tended to follow a common pattern (Challú 2007, pp. 206–207). The correlation between these series, in absolute values or in their rate of change, is very high and significant. While co-movement is a feature that we come to expect in integrated markets, at the same time it might indicate common climatic changes, changes in the money supply and, more broadly, common shocks that lift or depress prices simultaneously (Klein and Engerman 1990, pp. 14–17; Lindo-Fuentes 1980). These two views are limited in that they do not focus on the dynamic adjustment of prices to changes in price differentials (Ravallion 1986, p. 102).

This essay seeks to bridge the gap in our knowledge about market integration in late colonial Mexico by focusing on a limited set of consistent maize and wheat price series and analyzing them with a standardized set of techniques to measure market integration. Four questions, in particular, guide this inquiry: Were grain markets less integrated in Mexico than in other areas of the world? Given the typical distinction between commercial and subsistence agriculture, were the markets of wheat (the cereal produced for trade) more integrated than the markets of maize (the cereal produced primarily for subsistence)? Was market integration changing over the period? Did grain markets cease working in times of famine, drought, or climatic stress? I deal with these questions by presenting different measures of market integration. I particularly focus on the use of equilibrium- or error-correction models (ECM) since they provide a superior framework to describe the process of dynamic adjustment of prices.

18.2 Maize and Wheat Prices

Prices provide critical information to assess the degree of integration of markets. Maize, wheat, and flour prices from different locations of New Spain are used to assess the degree of market integration. The series include maize, wheat, and wheat flour prices in Antequera (present-day Oaxaca, maize prices only), Campeche (flour only), Guadalajara (only maize), Mexico City, Puebla, San Luís Potosí, Valladolid (present-day Morelia), Veracruz and Zacatecas (only short-run monthly maize series). The locations are mapped in Fig. 18.1. Maize and wheat represented the bulk of agricultural production and of the food supply, and both were widely traded. The prices are primarily based on purchase and sale transactions from different sources that were averaged by year; ancillary information from related products and nearby locations and interpolation filled remaining gaps. The markets were important trading centers on major roads and distant 200 to 900 km from each other. In

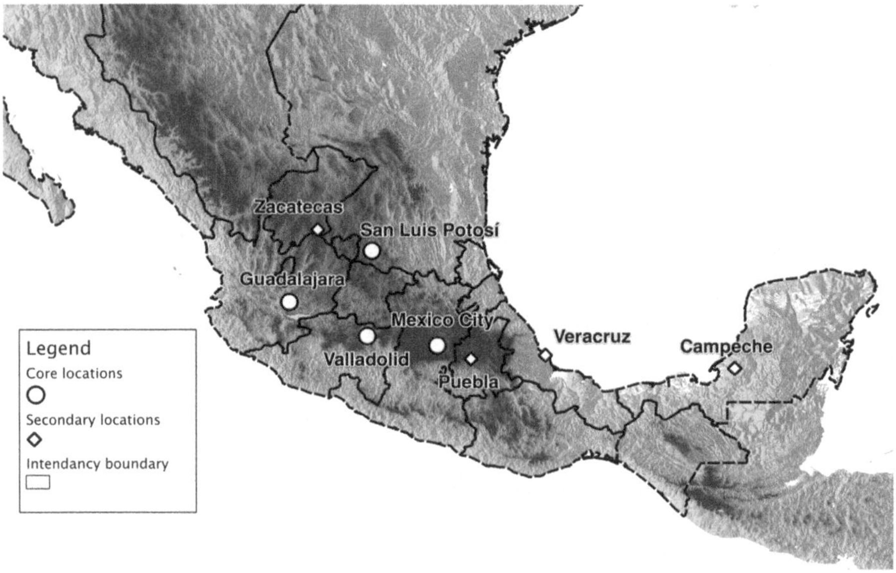

Fig. 18.1 Locations of price series

terms of their population the smallest was San Luis Potosí, which had almost 8600 inhabitants by 1790. Veracruz, Valladolid, Campeche, and Antequera had 16 to 18,000 inhabitants; Guadalajara was near, with 20,000 but was growing very fast and nearing Puebla's population in the early postindependence. Puebla was near 60,000 inhabitants and Mexico exceeded 100,000.[3]

The multiple transactions and large volumes of trade diffuse the effect of outliers. The use of annual averages further helps reduce the error in measurement, and it does not hinder detecting patterns in price movements given our knowledge of the speed of adjustment of prices in other international cases (MacKinnon 1996, pp. 614–615; Froot et al. 2019). Higher frequency data would have certainly been preferable to do a more fine-grained estimation of changes over time and to avoid the smoothing effect of price aggregation (Taylor 2001), but the monthly or quarterly series ran for short periods of 1–5 years (with the exception of Mexico City) that are unsuitable to obtain reliable estimates of price adjustment. Still, in the case of the estimation of volatility I used higher-frequency data to calculate more precise estimates that are comparable to other international cases.

The population experienced increasing difficulties in obtaining their food supply in this period, most especially since the 1780s. The trajectories of cereal prices attest to these difficulties. The spikes circa 1749–1750, 1785–1786, and 1808–1809 coincide with the three main famines of this time period. Of them, the one in 1785–86 became known as "the year of the famine" for its high mortality. Even in more regular times the changes from year to year were dramatic, more noticeably in the maize series. Yet, underneath the variability there is also a clear increase in the price level in the 1780s. Even after prices receded in the years following the year of the famine, they remained high in comparison with previous decades. The highest consistent level for a prolonged period of time is in the 1810s, when the insurrection, epidemics, and bad harvests disrupted the harvests and commercialization. It is in this context of famine, inflation, and high variability of prices that the question of market integration becomes more pressing to gauge market integration as a way to assess, more generally, the role of markets in the unequal access to food.

Maize was the staple in Mexican diet and it was primarily a subsistence crop. As peasant communities grew in number and were constrained to production in their existing lands we can expect that the pressures to retain it locally increased (Van Young 1981, pp. 80–87). In general its price was low relative to the high transportation costs, implying that maize traveled short distances. The closest distance between two of the locations was 220 km, long enough that it would be unprofitable to conduct trade except in extraordinary circumstances. On top of high transportation costs, maize harvests were highly variable, since maize was not irrigated and long-term storage was problematic. From a regulatory point of view, local authorities could impose restrictions on trade potentially limiting the degree of market integration (Challú 2013).

[3]All population figures from Instituto Nacional de Estadísticas Geografía e Informática (2014, Table 1.4), with the exception of Campeche, which is from Farris (1982, p. 448).

Wheat was a more expensive crop, which meant that transportation costs weighed less on its price and made it possible to travel over longer distances. The population of the cities was the primary destination of wheat and for that reason wheat production was more oriented to the market than maize. The locations used in the analysis include San Luis Potosí in the west and northern region, Mexico City in the center, and Puebla, Valladolid, and Veracruz in the south. Some of these locations traded with each other: Valladolid supplied Mexico City, Puebla supplied Mexico City and Veracruz, and the latter supplied Campeche. Wheat was traded primarily in wholesale operations in flour mills. There were few regulations at the wholesale level and, by contrast to maize, use of prohibitions to trade was extremely exceptional. Compared to maize, wheat is the most favorable crop for market integration: it was produced for the market, it had a higher price-to-volume ratio and was less encumbered by the interference of local authorities. Our work will shed light on whether these advantages translated into a higher degree of market integration.

Such differences between maize and wheat are important to address Regina Grafe's criticism that grain products were targeted in public policies as a response to moral economic expectations and not market expectations (2012, pp. 41–45). There are two responses to this potential criticism. First, by studying maize and wheat market integration I do not intend to make broader inferences about the degree of penetration of markets throughout the Mexican economy. I am primarily concerned with how the market mediated the access to food and facilitated transfers from producing to consuming areas. Although corn was not just food but also the fuel on which the mining economy and transportation ran, a broader set of products would be better suited to evaluate the integration of the economy as a whole. Second, the differences in types of regulation and market structure of corn and wheat provide us with two contrasting cases of substitute cereal products, helping to balance the bias introduced by relying in only one product.

18.3 Volatility

One important characteristic of maize and wheat prices that can be discerned in Appendixes 1 and 2 is the high degree of variation from one year to another. The expectation is that well-integrated markets feature less volatility than isolated markets because traders move grain from lower-price regions to profit with high prices, and in doing so reduce the peak prices (as we showed in the story of Guanajuato in 1794 that opened this essay). Volatility helps assess changes in market integration over time and draw comparisons with other international cases, although comparisons across products and countries also need to take into account the differences in cultivation and storage (Reher 2001; Salvucci and Salvucci 1987, pp. 77–78).

In Table 18.1, I use two different approaches to calculate price volatility within each series. Panel A shows the coefficient of variation of maize and wheat prices for series with more than 10 years of continuous information. The coefficient of variation is the standard deviation as the percentage of the series average. It is a rough

Table 18.1 Volatility of grain prices in Mexico

Panel A: Coefficient of variation of maize and wheat (annual frequency)		
	Maize	Wheat or flour
1. Guadalajara	(1748–1817) 51%	
2. Mexico City	(1725–1816) 41%	(1742–1812) 27%
3. S.L.Potosí	(1726–1817) 55%	(1726–1775) 42%
4. Valladolid	(1725–1814) 42%	(1725–1785) 26%
5. Puebla	(1804–1815) 26%	(1754–1776) 17%
6. Veracruz		(1777–1803) 16%
7. Campeche		(1781–1809) 18%
1–4, average	41%	
1–4, Average, 1780–1817	41%	

Panel B: Standard deviation of first log differences in monthly maize prices			
Place	1725–1779	1780–1817	Total
1. Guadalajara	0.150	0.120	0.136
2. Mexico City	0.072	0.091	0.082
3. S. L. Potosí	0.173	0.237	0.199
4. Zacatecas	0.293	0.317	0.309
5. Puebla		0.081	
6. Valladolid	0.115		
1–4, average	0.172	0.191	0.154

Challú 2007; Martín Ornelas 2008

Notes: With the exception of Mexico City, monthly prices typically span over 1–5 years and are scattered over the entire period. The data for San Luis Potosí in the 1780s was reported by quarters. I calculated the ratio between monthly and quarterly results in other places, and then applied that ratio to the data in the 1780s

measure of volatility that facilitates the comparison with other international cases. Panel B summarizes the typical monthly variation in maize prices in a slightly different set of locations; in most cases, we only have continuous runs of monthly data from one to five continuous years. Nevertheless, Panel B's indication of monthly volatility has the advantage of providing a more relevant measure of how the swings in prices affected consumers, and it follows the same methodology used in studies from China and Europe (Persson 1999; Shiue and Keller 2007, pp. 106–113).

The first noticeable pattern is that the price of maize was considerably more volatile than wheat or flour. In Table 18.2, Panel A, maize had a coefficient of variation in the 26–55% range, while the range of wheat and flour was 16–42%. At first glance this difference seems to confirm the notion that wheat and flour were products channeled through markets, while maize was primarily a subsistence crop marginally traded. Yet, other factors beyond market integration have an effect. First and foremost, wheat harvest was more stable and predictable output because it was often cultivated in irrigated lands. A second factor that explains the difference in price volatility is that wheat could be stored for longer periods and had immense storage facilities in the mills of major cities, particularly those in Mexico City and Puebla. Such facilities could not be easily switched from one crop to another. By contrast,

Table 18.2 International comparisons of volatility

Panel A: Coefficient of variation (CV) on annual data			
	Number of Series	Period	CV
Mexico, maize	5	1725–1817	43%
Mexico, wheat, and flour	6	1725–1817	24%
Castile, wheat	3	1691–1788	27%
Western Europe, wheat	5	1764–1794	17%
India, wheat	3	1764–1794	62%
India, rice	2	1764–1794	34%
Yangtze Delta, rice	1	1764–1794	19%

Panel B: Standard deviation (SD) of first monthly log differences		
	Number of series	SD
Mexico, maize	6	0.16
Western Europe, wheat, 18th c.	15	0.14
Provincial capitals in Southern China, 18th c., rice	10	0.09

Sources: (Llopis Agelán 2001; Persson 1999, p. 412; Shiue and Keller 2007, p. 1197; Studer 2008, p. 417)
Notes: The standard deviation of monthly differences is controlled by seasonal effects following Shiue and Keller's methodology

maize was less suitable for storing because its higher moisture content made it more vulnerable to spoiling.

From a geographic point of view, Mexico City, Valladolid, and Puebla had the lowest degree of volatility, while the western and northern locations of Guadalajara, San Luis Potosí, and Zacatecas had the highest. The pattern is consistent in the two cereals and in the two frequencies (annual or monthly). The major explanation for the difference is that the markets in the north and western regions were tightly connected to the demand in the mines, which were in arid areas and relied on shipments from long distances. The three locations (one of which was a major mining center itself) had to compete with demand from other mining centers as well, such as Guanajuato, Real de Catorce, and Sombrerete, among others. If the rains failed, not only was the grain supply scarcer but transportation was even more difficult as the pastures were nonexistent, increasing the consumers' dependence on maize and freight costs (Suárez Argüello 1997, p. 183). The case of Guadalajara surrounded by fertile areas but also close to the supply areas of the mining districts illustrates the limitations of volatility as a benchmark of market integration: the high variations in prices were likely produced by it being integrated to markets, than by its lack of integration.[4]

There were no significant changes in the long run in maize price volatility before and after 1780, a pivotal moment in economic and political trends (Challú 2010).

[4] In smaller markets this is even more true, as it is illustrated in the semester reports of harvests and prices in the case of Tepatitlán, with which we opened the chapter. On market size and volatility, see Salvucci and Salvucci (1987, p. 78).

The coefficient of variation of annual prices was roughly the same before and after 1780: 41% in the four maize series that span the entire period. The standard deviation of monthly differences had a very moderate increase (from 17% to 19%). While the lack of improvements in volatility can be taken as a sign of no major changes in market integration, this finding has to be countered by the greater level of climatic volatility that affected harvests and, hence, prices. The frequency of El Niño events, tree-ring reconstructions of drought conditions, and documentary evidence point to more variability and more climatic stress after 1780, which should have made supply more variable. Two generalized famines also took place after 1780 (in 1785 and 1809), compared to one before 1780 (1750), and conditions were critical in the 1810s. If anything, we should expect that these conditions should have produced a higher degree of volatility in the price series if markets were dysfunctional.

Compared with other contemporary cases in other regions of the world, grain prices in Mexico were more volatile than in Western Europe, but they were comparable to Spain and lower than in India (Table 18.2). The volatility of annual maize prices was particularly very high and only inferior to that of Indian wheat. Wheat and maize monthly variations, however, show Mexico much more in line with the European cases. We can see the same factors operating here that I pointed out in the differing volatility of maize and wheat in Mexico. The highest measurements of variation correspond to rain-dependent crops: wheat in India and maize in Mexico. At the other end of the spectrum, the Yangtze Delta and Southern China in the Qing period both enjoyed an outstanding system of grain storage and extensive use of waterways for grain transportation as well as irrigation; to a lesser degree similar conditions apply to Western Europe in this period (Shiue and Keller 2007; Studer 2008). The high variation in annual and monthly grain prices was not necessarily related to market failures or the absence of spatial arbitrage. The use of irrigation, the climatic cycle, and the availability of storage made maize prices intrinsically volatile.

18.4 Dispersion of Prices Across Different Markets

The spread of prices across central Mexico remained at similar levels over the period. Spread and volatility may arise some confusion, since both deal with variations in prices. While in the previous section I measured volatility through different measures of variation of prices within each series, here I measure the geographical dispersion of prices by calculating, in any given year, the coefficient of variation of prices in all different locations (Fig. 18.2). The locations examined here are Guadalajara, Mexico, San Luis Potosí, and Valladolid, which have a reasonably long overlap in their price series.[5] The average for the entire period was close to

[5] Use of alternative subsets using isolated observations (e.g. from Antequera, Puebla or Zacatecas) from other locations does not change these conclusions.

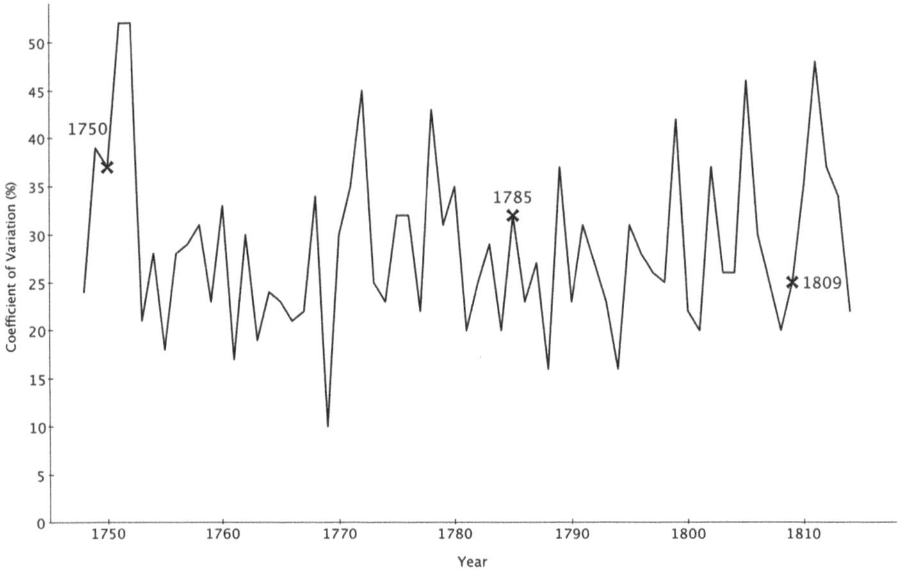

Fig. 18.2 Coefficient of variation in maize prices. Notes: The coefficient of variation is constructed as the standard deviation of the prices of Guadalajara, Mexico City, San Luis Potosí, and Valladolid, divided by their average. The marked years correspond to famines

29%, and 28% for the period after 1780. The prices of wheat in Mexico City, Puebla, San Luis Potosí, and Valladolid from 1757 to 1775 (the only period in which they overlap) had a slightly lower dispersion of prices: 23%. The difference between the geographic dispersion of maize and wheat prices is primarily attributable to transportation costs. Wheat has a lower coefficient of variation because transportation costs weigh less relative to the price. This logic also implies that the flat trend indicates the absence of major improvements in transportation costs.

The coefficient of variation in times of famine provides a good indication of whether markets were working more or less efficiently under such circumstances. If failing markets were behind a given famine, we would expect the coefficient of variation to be higher than average as speculation or barriers to trade placed limited the exchange of grain. Figure 18.2 shows that the famine of 1750 had a larger than average dispersion of prices and was followed in the next 2 years by the historical maximum of the series as conditions improved in the Bajío but remained bleak in Mexico City. This high point is indicative of limitations in the way markets corrected distortions. Yet, in the next two famine events, the coefficient of variation was not remarkably different than the average. In the 1785–1786 crisis, as prices shot up the variations from the high average were close to the average. The low coefficient of variation is even more remarkable because the authorities explicitly authorized restrictions to trade, but did not intervene prices. Similarly, the famine of 1808–1809 had below-average dispersion, although it increased in 1810 in part due to the disruptions of the insurrection to grain trade. These last two famine crises show that markets seemed better able to adjust to shocks in supply and this coincides with observations that volatility improved in the last two famines of the period. This increased ability to adjust does not mean that famines were less devastating, but rather that markets performed as expected in these events.

The spread of prices in Mexican maize and wheat markets was comparable to other grain markets in the world, even despite the highly localized tendency of its trade and the poor, mule-based transportation network. The average coefficient of variation across central Mexican markets was 29 percent for maize and 23 percent for wheat. In India, from 1760 to 1820, the coefficient of variation in rice prices was 60 percent, although it was a geographically larger area with many locations. In early eighteenth-century France, it was 30 percent in normal years and hit 45 percent during three famine episodes. In four states of the northeastern United States, from 1780 to 1820, the coefficient of variation was lower but not by much: 26 percent for maize and 20 percent for wheat. Only in the rice markets in northern China was the coefficient of variation remarkably lower: about 12 percent from 1738 to 1818 (Li 2000, p. 675; O'Gráda 2000, p. 721; Studer 2008).[6] In most of these areas there was no trend, like in the case of Mexico. It was not until the mid-nineteenth century when price convergence took place in Europe, India, China, and the United States (Jacks 2005; Studer 2008). This process was delayed in Mexico until the relatively late construction of railroads in the last quarter of the nineteenth century. At that point prices converged and the coefficient of variation became, once again, comparable to other international cases (Dobado and Marrero 2005, pp. 110–111).[7]

18.5 Adjustment to Shocks in Price Ratios

The problem of the measures of volatility and price spread used so far is that they do not distinguish between effects of spatial arbitrage, long-run price differentials, and storage. As we have seen, wheat prices were more stable than maize prices, but this tells us little to nothing about whether traders and producers from a given region were willing to send maize to a region experiencing a shortage and having high, attractive prices. Similarly, we cannot surmise from this data the extent to which the higher coefficient of variation of maize prices related to inefficiencies in maize markets or to the larger weight of transportation costs in a low-cost crop.

Equilibrium- or error-correction models (ECM) allow us to overcome these deficiencies and test if a long-run equilibrium price between two markets existed, and how fast prices adjusted to restore the equilibrium. In different variants they have been widely used in contemporary and historical studies of grain markets (Bateman

[6]The calculation for the United States is based on the series of Maryland, Massachusetts, Pennsylvania and Vermont, via "Global Price and Income History," http://gpih.ucdavis.edu

[7]Using data kindly facilitated by Rafael Dobado, the average coefficient of variation in maize prices for a similar subset of locations was 19%, that is, an improvement in ten points from our figures.

2011; Llopis Agelán and Sotoca 2005; O'Grada 2003; O'Gráda and Chevet 2002; Persson 1999; Shiue and Keller 2007; Studer 2008). Here I adopt, with minor modifications, Studer's equilibrium-correction model used in his analysis of annual grain price series of India (Persson 1999, pp. 114–130; Studer 2008, pp. 408–409):

$$\Delta p_{i,t} = -\alpha_1 \times \left(p_{i,t-1} - p_{j,t-1} + \tau \right) + \varepsilon_{1,t} \tag{18.1}$$

$$\Delta p_{j,t} = \alpha_2 \times \left(p_{i,t-1} - p_{j,t-1} + \tau \right) + \varepsilon_{2,t} \tag{18.2}$$

The subindices *i* and *j* designate the two markets in the pair, *t* is the time unit (the year), *p* is the log price, Δp is the annual change in the price, and ε is the error term, the variation from the expected long-run equilibrium value in a given year and location. This type of model is known as equilibrium or error-correction because the present value of the variable corrects the errors caused in the equilibrium level ($p[i,t-1] - p[j,t-1] + \tau$). The speed of the adjustment in each market is determined by the coefficients α, which have a range of 0 (no adjustment) to 1 (full adjustment in one time unit). We refer to the sum of both α coefficients as the γ, which represents the speed at which both markets restore the long-run equilibrium level. We calculate γ as a differentiated derivation of the previous equations:

$$\Delta \left(p_{i,t} - p_{j,t} \right) = -\gamma \left(p_{i,t-1} - p_{j,t-1} + \tau \right) + \varepsilon_t \tag{18.3}$$

where γ is the sum of α_1 and α_2. The coefficients are obtained with ordinary regressions for each possible market pair, and are calculated for the entire period, and also for the pre- and post-1780 subperiods.[8]

What results are expected if markets are integrated? First, in a condition of market Integration, we expect that γ is significantly different than zero and rejects the Augmented Dickey-Fuller unit root test. If γ is not significantly different from zero, we cannot conclude that there is a long-run equilibrium price that causes one or both markets to adjust, as is expected in a scenario of market integration (Froot et al. 2019; Studer 2008). Time aggregation and perhaps the time span of the series likely introduce downward biases in these calculations that run against the hypothesis of market efficiency (Taylor 2001). Second, we also expect that the coefficients for γ and α_1 are bound by 0 and -1, and that α_2 is bound by 0 and 1. The closer γ is to -1, the faster the equilibrium price is restored in one time unit. The speed of adjustment is an indicator of market integration, in that it reflects how fast actors respond (through spatial arbitration) to the profit incentives generated by a relative rise in prices. The ratio between the maximum and minimum absolute α indicates how

[8] In a standard regression, Eq. (18.3) becomes $\Delta(p_{1,t} - p_{2,t}) = a + b * (p_{1,t-1} - p_{2,t-1}) + \varepsilon_t$, where $b = \gamma$, $a = \gamma\tau$; b is expected to be negative.

symmetrically the two markets adjust to changes in the equilibrium price. If only one market has a significant α, the system is said to be "weakly exogenous" in that only one market is correcting to the equilibrium level. While mutual adjustment is an indicator of greater market integration, we can expect that larger markets are less influenced by small-size markets. Third, in a process of reductions of transportation costs and reduction of other trade costs, we expect the constant τ to decline. However, we do not expect this long-run differential to fall in this time period given that there were no major changes in transportation technologies (Bateman 2011; O'Rourke and Williamson 1999). Fourth and final, as Studer (2008) aptly indicates, the correlation between the regression residuals of Eqs. (18.1 and 18.2) measures the degree of co-movement between the two markets. Both prices may move together in response to common shocks (such as climatic conditions, economic conditions), but it is also a sign that traders are acting upon common information that is shifting prices in expectation of future changes (Roehner 2000, p. 179).

My results of the ECM models for the twenty market pairs, shown in Table 18.3, indicate that prices in each pair were adjusting to a long-term equilibrium level, that is, that a change in prices in the price ratio initiated a mechanism of price correction. Let us first focus on the total adjustment to shocks in the equilibrium (γ) and co-movement (ρ). All γ coefficients in all pairs reject the unit-root test, which indicates the existence of a long-term equilibrium level. Almost all α and γ coefficients are in the expected range, from 0 to 1 (and the exceptions are not significantly different from those boundaries). Looking at the total adjustment speed (γ), on average maize prices absorbed 87% of a shock in one year, and wheat prices 74%. That means that, according to our calculations, it took 14 and 16 months, respectively, to correct the prices to the equilibrium level, although in almost all pairs the γ coefficient is not significantly different than the unity, which indicates a full correction in one year. Only three cases have a speed of adjustment below 0.7 and they all involve the northern town of San Luis Potosí. These coefficients are likely to be biased toward a slower estimate because the annual data likely aggregate too much of the change that can be better gauged with a higher-frequency series. The true estimate of speed adjustment is 20–30 percent faster according to Taylor's analysis (2001, p. 7).

The results of the ECM models for the 20 market pairs indicate that prices in each pair were adjusting to a long-term equilibrium level, that is, that a change in prices in the price ratio initiated a mechanism of price correction. Let us first focus on the total adjustment to shocks in the equilibrium (γ) and co-movement (ρ). All γ coefficients in all pairs reject the unit-root test, which indicates the existence of a long-term equilibrium level. Almost all α and γ coefficients are in the expected range, from 0 to 1 (and the exceptions are not significantly different from those boundaries). Looking at the total adjustment speed (γ), on average maize prices absorbed 87% of a shock in one year, and wheat prices 74%. That means that it took 14 and 16 months, respectively, to correct the prices to the equilibrium level, although in almost all pairs the γ coefficient is not significantly different than the unity, which indicates a full correction in one year. Only three cases have a speed of adjustment below 0.7 and they all involve the northern town of San Luis Potosí.

Table 18.3 ECMs of market pairs in Mexico, 1725–1817

Panel A: Maize

Pair	Dist. (Miles)	$\alpha 1$	$\alpha 2$	γ	ρ	Max α /Min α	τ
Mexico–Valladolid (1725–1814)	184	[−0.13]	0.75	−0.88	0.71	5.77	−0.53
Guadalajara–Valladolid (1748–1814)	179	−0.58	0.36	−0.94	0.74	1.62	0.00
Valladolid–S. L. Potosí (1725–1814)	249	[−0.16]	0.47	−0.64	0.69	2.93	0.41
Guadalajara–S. L. Potosí (1748–1817)	214	[−0.21]	0.45	−0.65	0.67	2.14	0.35
Mexico–S. L. Potosí (1725–1816)	262	[−0.11]	0.65	−0.76	0.63	5.85	−0.13
Mexico–Antequera (1788–1815)	305	[−0.13]	0.84	−0.97	0.62	6.60	−0.23
Mexico–Guadalajara (1748–1816)	337	−0.25	0.73	−0.97	0.61	2.96	−0.50
Valladolid–Antequera (1788–1814)	486	[−0.21]	0.77	−0.97	0.30	3.66	0.39
Antequera–S. L. Potosí (1788–1815)	554	−0.68	0.27	−0.95	0.53	2.50	−0.04
Guadalajara–Antequera (1788–1815)	641	[−0.20]	0.81	−1.01	0.55	4.03	0.32
Average				−0.87	0.60	3.80	0.29

Panel B: Wheat and flour

Pair	Dist. (miles)	$\alpha 1$	$\alpha 2$	γ	ρ	Max α/Min α	τ
Mexico–Valladolid (1747–1799)	184	−0.35	0.42	−0.77	0.64	1.2	−0.38
Mexico–Puebla (1757–1776)	83	[−0.30]	0.41	−0.71	0.55	1.3	−0.09
Valladolid–S.L. Potosí (1756–1775)	249	−0.67	[0.21]	−0.89	0.19	3.2	0.41
Mexico–S.L. Potosí (1742–1775)	262	−0.22	0.51	−0.73	0.10	2.3	−0.01
Puebla–Valladolid (1757–1776)	267	−0.20	0.68	−0.88	0.13	3.4	0.48
Puebla– S.L. Potosí (1757–1775)	344	[−0.10]	0.53	−0.62	0.12	5.4	0.10
Valladolid–Veracruz* (1778–1799)	433	−0.43	0.29	−0.72	0.39	1.5	1.49
Mexico-Veracruz* (1777–1803)	248	−0.58	[0.12]	−0.70	0.63	4.9	1.09
Mexico–Campeche* (1782–1809)	616	−0.50	[0.21]	−0.71	0.37	2.4	1.22
Veracruz*–Campeche* (1782–1803)	368	[0.26]	1.10	−0.84	0.82	4.2	0.12
Average				−0.74	0.55	3.25	0.98

Notes: The star indicates a flour price series. All gammas reject the unit-root hypothesis at the 1% level using an Augmented Dickey-Fuller test. α coefficients in squared brackets indicate that the coefficient is not significant at the 10% level, which is taken as weak exogeneity. Pairs with less than 20 observations were excluded from the analysis

Most pairs involve markets of unequal importance, and such importance typically reflects on an unequal correction to price shocks. One market in the pair typically had an adjustment that was three to four times larger than the other market. This unbalance is shown in the ratio of maximum-to-minimum alpha. Even more, in 13 of the 20 pairs, the lowest alpha is not significantly different than zero, meaning that one market is "weakly exogenous" to the equilibrium-correction mechanism. The weakly exogenous market is said to be a "leader" and the other the "follower." There are two patterns that stand out in the leader-follower structure of market pairs in Bourbon Mexico. First, is that, with some exceptions, the smallest market in the pair is the follower and the most important is the leader. This is particularly obvious in the maize market pairs: Mexico City is always the leader and, on the other end, San Luis Potosí is always a follower. Second, the market size pattern breaks in the case of Veracruz, which is always a leader in price adjustment. Even Mexico City is a follower of Veracruz. The Veracruz market not only supplied its own population (of a size comparable to San Luis Potosí), but its importance lay in the fact that it supplied the fleets, other towns in the Gulf of Mexico (such as Campeche) and Havana. This trade is typically considered of importance for the Puebla region, but the fast adjustment in Mexico City and Valladolid suggests that the flour export trade was also consequential to grain markets elsewhere in the viceroyalty (Sennhauser 1996, pp. 107–109; Stein and Stein 2003, pp. 245–246; Suárez Argüello 1985, pp. 112–117).

The τ coefficients show that the long-run price differential between markets reflects trade costs only in markets that directly traded with each other (Jacks 2005, p. 384; Roehner 2000). In maize markets direct trade between even the closest of these markets was extraordinary. Only in 2 years the price differential exceeded the transportation cost between Mexico City and Valladolid. Instead, the price differential (τ) between markets with no direct trade primarily responds to the gap between high-price consumer markets, and low-price producer markets. By contrast, transportation costs weigh heavily in the case of wheat and flour, where many of the pairs had direct trade. The τ coefficients are, in general, reflective of transportation costs. Consider, for instance, how the τ of Valladolid and Puebla is equivalent to the sum of the τ's of Mexico–Valladolid and Mexico–Puebla. Such proportionality in trade costs is a good indicator of consistency in the series.

The distance and transportation cost between markets is also an important factor behind the co-movement of prices. We measure co-movement in ρ, which is the Pearson correlation between the residuals of the two ECM equations. A high ρ indicates that common trends were important drivers of local prices. Common climatic and economic cycles as well as short-term price adjustments are behind this co-movement (Studer 2008). We discussed before the similarities in the evolution of the price series and the ρ confirms this perception. The average correlation between the residuals of the ECM equations is 0.60 and 0.55 for maize and wheat, respectively, meaning that over 30% of the annual variations are explained by the common movement of prices from one year to another. We expect that common trends are stronger the closer the markets are, and our results confirm this expectation. In maize market pairs there is a clear distance-co-movement gradient. Markets within

200 miles had a co-movement coefficient above 0.7, while those farther than 450 miles had a co-movement of less than 0.55. The shorter periods and the use of boat shipments to supply Campeche complicate the picture in the wheat market pairs. If we compare the series by those with coverage before and after 1780, the degree of co-movement does trace distance closely. Before 1780 (rows 1–6), the pairs under 200 miles (Mexico–Puebla and Mexico–Valladolid) have a ρ over 0.55, while the other pairs have a very low ρ, in the 0.10–0.19 range. In the series covering the post-1780 period (rows 1 and 7–10), transportation cost (the lowest in the case of Veracruz–Campeche, and proportional to distance in the other cases) is well related to co-movement.

The results contrast with the characterization that grain market was fragmented in colonial Mexico. The comparison between maize and wheat markets, and between the southern market of Antequera with those in the western and northern highlands illustrate this point. First, there is no substantial or significant difference between market integration in maize or wheat markets. Maize was the crop primarily destined to subsistence and the major production in peasant households. Wheat, by contrast, was the crop oriented to the market and primarily taking place in haciendas. There is no substantial or significant difference between the two products: both were similarly responsive to shocks in equilibrium prices.[9] The case of Antequera similarly defies expectations of market fragmentation. Antequera was a provincial capital surrounded by a predominant indigenous, peasant agriculture. Supply typically involved the neighboring valleys and had a shorter reach than most of the other markets considered in the analysis. Despite its distance and stronger reliance on peasant agriculture for its supply, maize prices in Antequera showed similar if not better signs of market integration to other markets than Guadalajara and Valladolid. Antequera suggests the interdependence of local grain markets even in the absence of direct trade.

Instead of market fragmentation, my findings in Table 18.3 support the idea that there was a certain degree of market integration. This is certainly not the equivalent of a market economy and does not also mean that changes were instantaneous, as they will become later in the nineteenth century, but it points to a certain level of integration in which, within 1–2 years, changes in major markets and common trends affected all corners of the viceroyalty (or at least its central region). A 10% rise in the price of maize in Mexico City increased, within one year, 6.5–8.5% the prices in all other locations. A similar 10% increase in the price of flour in the Gulf markets produced an adjustment of 4.3% in Valladolid and 5% in Mexico City and of a likely similar dimension in San Luis Potosí. Antequera's maize prices reacted to prices from as far as Guadalajara. Market integration and common economic trends (reflected in the high degree of co-movement of prices) made local prices dependent on changes from other corners of the viceroyalty.

[9] The greater reliance of storage in wheat trade may explain its slightly slower speed of adjustment (Shiue and Keller 2007, p. 1204).

To further corroborate the assertion of a high level of market integration, we compare the findings for Mexico with four international cases in Table 18.4. The speed of adjustment was similar or higher than other contemporary cases. We rely for the comparison on comparable studies (India, Spain, and Western Europe), and our own analysis based on published series (Northeast United States and Mexico at the turn of the twentieth century). The case of Spanish wheat markets is the most revealing in that Mexico and Spain shared similar institutions and a fragmented geography (Coatsworth and Tortella Casares 2002). Market integration was incipient in Spain in the eighteenth century. The price ratios between Spanish wheat markets were stationary, like in Mexico, but the speed of adjustment was much slower: 0.45, implying that the price correction took more than 2 years to close the gap opened by a shock. The speed of adjustment was faster in India wheat and rice markets. The large majority of price ratios were stationary and the adjustment was faster: 0.64 (19 months to correct). Perhaps the halting effect of the Monsoon season on trade, or the fragmentation of authority in this period (the sample includes cities under native and British control) put India in disadvantage in this time period. It was only by the late nineteenth century, when India was unified under one authority and railroads provided fast connections, that the average speed of adjustment became comparable to Mexico's.

Table 18.4 International comparisons of speed of adjustment to equilibrium level

	γ	Months to restore equilibrium [a]
Spain, wheat, 1725–1806	−0.45 [b]	27
India, wheat and rice, 1750–1830	−0.64 [c]	19
India, wheat and rice, 1870–1910	−0.88 [c]	14
Western Europe, wheat, eighteenth century [d]	N/A	12
Western Europe, wheat, mid nineteenth century [d]	N/A	5
Northeast U.S., maize, 1755–1822 [e]	−0.81	15
Mexico, maize, 1885–1908	−0.80	15
Mexico, maize, 1725–1817	−0.87	14
Mexico, wheat, 1725–1809	−0.74	16

Notes: All data are annual. [a] Calculated as $12/\gamma$, with the exception of the pairs from Western Europe. [b] Based on Llopis Agelán and Sotoca (2005); pairs with a second lag component were not included in this summary. [c] Based on Studer (2008); this is the average of pairs within a range of 150 and 600 km of proximity. [d] based on Persson (1999, Ch. 5); the adjustment speed for Western Europe (England, France, Italy) is based on monthly data, hence the γ is not reported; only pairs in a range of 150–600 km were selected. [e] Includes Maryland, Massachusetts, Pennsylvania, and Vermont, extracted from the Global Price and Income History Dataset. [f] Data extracted from Instituto Nacional de Estadísticas Geografía e Informática (2014) includes Jalisco, Mexico City, Michoacán and San Luis Potosí

Table 18.5 Changes in average speed of adjustment and co-movement

Subperiod	γ	ρ
A. Comparison of all available pairs, before and after 1780		
1725–1779	−0.84	0.48
1780–1817	−0.83	0.65
B. Comparison of four markets in two 30-year windows		
1750–1779	−0.80	0.47
1780–1809 (Antequera excluded)	−0.94	0.72

Notes: The γs of the market pairs are statistically significant at the 5% level

The performance of grain markets in Bourbon Mexico resembles much more that of emerging market economies such as western Europe (Persson 1999) and the northeast United States (Rothenberg 1992), as well as India in the late nineteenth century (Studer 2008). In four maize markets in the United States, price corrections took 15 months. Grain markets in central Mexico, in fact, were comparable with those of the turn of the twentieth century in Mexico (and India) when railroads resolved most of the problems of communication, information flowed much more efficiently and there were no domestic barriers to trade (Dobado and Marrero 2005). Only when we compare Mexico's annual estimates with monthly estimates from Western Europe, particularly those of the mid and late nineteenth century, do we find that Mexico lagged. The comparison is not straightforward in that the higher frequency of European data provide a more fine-grained analysis and eliminates the bias of the low-frequency data that is present in the other studies that rely on annual series (Studer 2008, p. 412–413; Taylor 2001). The difference between Mexico's 14-month and Europe's 12-month adjustments point is remarkably close, even more if we consider the likely time aggregation bias that makes the Mexican estimates higher. All points to the fact that Mexican grain markets did not respond less efficiently than the most integrated grain markets of the time.[10] It was later in the nineteenth century when it is apparent that Mexican grain markets lagged behind Europe, although only higher frequency data would allow a better comparison.

Where there changes over time? The longer maize prices allow a break-down by subperiods in order to assess how market integration changed over time. A summary of changes in the average speed of adjustment (γ), co-movement (ρ) and the balance in the adjustment of each market is reported in Table 18.5. The periodization pivots in 1780. In the first panel, all available series are used in constructing the average, that is, the second period includes Antequera. In the second panel, only the four markets with long series are used, and the periods have the same dimension. The

[10] China also had a high degree of market integration in this time period, but the metric is not comparable (Shiue and Keller 2007). Another comparative point is Froot et al. (2019), which studied deviations from the law of one price in annual differentials of commodity prices between England and Holland from the fourteenth to the twentieth century. Their approach is similar to our Eq. (18.3) but without a constant (that is, plain deviations from the law of one price). The γ for their entire period (from the fourteenth to the twentieth century) is 0.21; our average γ using the same methodology (averaged across all our maize and wheat market pairs) is 0.39.

1810s were excluded because civil war and the fragmentation of monetary authority very likely had a negative effect on market integration. Given that the frequency is annual, the number of observations is limited and it should therefore be noted that this affects the reliability of the results.

From these data we glean some changes in market integration over time. Panel A shows that the speed of adjustment (γ) and co-movement (ρ) were very similar. When we constraint the comparison to comparable sets and we eliminate the 1810s (Panel B), a picture of improvements in market integration more clearly emerges. The speed of adjustment increased 11 points, from 0.81 to 0.92, and common movements climbed from 0.57 to 0.80. The results are consistent with moderate improvements in market integration from 1780 to 1809. More cases and higher-frequency data would be needed to sort out these hints of tighter integration, but at this point the most important feature that stands out in the equilibrium-correction analysis is the consistently high degree of adjustment throughout the period, and a seeming deterioration in market integration after the outbreak of insurgency in 1810.

18.6 Mutual Adjustment of Maize and Wheat Prices

If markets were efficient in responding to changes in supply and demand, we should not only expect spatial market integration but also an adjustment between prices of substitute products. If maize becomes more expensive, then wheat would become a more attractive substitute; as its demand increases its price would increase as well. We can approach this issue in an equilibrium correction framework as we approached the issue of spatial market integration. Did an equilibrium relationship exist between the price of maize and wheat? If so, how fast did prices adjust to correct a shock?

Table 18.6 displays the results of the equilibrium-correction models for maize and wheat in three markets. The better availability of data for Mexico City makes it possible to use quarterly data to provide a more accurate measurement of the adjustment speed. The coefficients are very consistent across the cases. They all confirm that a long-run equilibrium relationship existed between the prices of the two products. The differential in prices was also significant—wheat was more expensive than maize (about twice, on average, when using the same unit of measurement). Maize adjusted 57–61% of the shock in the equilibrium within one year (using annual data), and the response of the price of wheat is much slower and insignificant outside of Mexico City. The more detailed use of quarterly data enables to identify a faster adjustment than the annual data: within three quarters (9 months) the prices have corrected the shock and restored equilibrium. Overall, the conclusion of this analysis is that the two major cereals in New Spain were not independent of each other. Instead, maize and wheat were part of an integrated grain market in which shocks in the price in one product, or in one region, initiated changes in price levels in other regions and products. The mutual adjustment of maize and wheat markets extended the micro-effects that connected distant markets with each other even in the absence of direct trade.

Table 18.6 ECM of maize and wheat in select markets

Pair	α_1	α_2	γ	Cons.
Mexico City, annual, 1742–1812	−0.57	0.14	−0.71	0.62
Mexico City, quarterly, 1764:1–1792:4	−0.24	0.08	−0.32	0.66
San Luis Potosí, annual, 1727–1775	−0.57	(0.09)	−0.66	0.73
Valladolid, annual, 1757–1785	−0.61	(0.04)	−0.65	0.78

Notes: $\alpha 1$ and $\alpha 2$ indicate the speed of adjustment of maize and wheat, respectively. All γs significant at 5% using the ADF test. The parentheses indicate not significant at the 10% (i.e., weak exogeneity). The model using quarterly data uses four lags

18.7 Shortages and Market Integration

The issue of market integration is of particular interest when considering the severe droughts, other strong climatic shocks, and recurrent famines that debilitated the Mexican highlands in the late colonial period. In this section I examine the relationship between food shortages and market integration, and I compare the effects of food shortages on the maize and wheat markets. Previously, I showed that famine times were not remarkably different from the point of view of the spread of prices. Here I extend the equilibrium-correction models to gauge the extent to which shortages affected the integration of markets.

The approach I follow here is a cross-panel regression of the price differentials, in which the coefficient for the total speed of adjustment (γ) is interacted with a variable of climatic conditions in order to evaluate their effect on the speed of adjustment.[11] I proceed by extending Eq. (18.3) (the simplified version of the ECM):

$$\Delta q_{ij,t} = -\gamma \times q_{ij,t-1} + \varphi \times C_{i-1} + \nu \times C_{t-1} \times q_{ij,t-1} + \mu_{i,j} + \varepsilon_{ij} \tag{18.4}$$

where each market pair combination (i, j) forms a panel, q is $p_i - p_j$, C is a binary ("dummy") variable of climatic conditions that offsets the long-term price differential, ϑ is the interaction term, and $\mu_{i,j}$ is the pair's fixed effect. The coefficients γ, φ, and ϑ remain constant for all the pairs because I intend to gauge the common effect of climatic conditions on adjustment speeds and price differentials in all market pairs. Given that the adjustment speeds of the six market-pair regressions were in a similar range, having a fixed γ effect is not a problematic assumption. The sum of γ and ϑ is the adjustment speed under the conditions of climatic adversity.

I use droughts as indicators of climatic conditions. There were 23 years with known droughts in central Mexico, which are marked in a dummy variable. Droughts may have a double effect on grain trade: on the one hand, the increase in prices stimulates long-distance trade, but lack of pasture and more expensive fodder raise transportation costs. I also create another variable to identify the 8 years with famines: 1748–1750, 1785–1786, and 1808–1810. These famines had the lethal climatic combination of summer drought and fall frost that cannot be accurately

[11] This approach is inspired in O'Gráda and Chevet (2002), while the idea to use a cross-panel setting comes from Dobado and Marrero (2005).

Table 18.7 Adjustment speed and shortages, 1725–1817

	Drought		Famine	
	Maize	Wheat	Maize	Wheat
γ (adjustment speed in normal years)	−0.81	−0.66	−0.77	−0.79
$\gamma + \vartheta$ (adjustment speed in adverse years)	−0.63	−1.07	(−0.71)	(−0.70)

Sources: Droughts in central Mexico were identified from Florescano (1995). The famines in this period were 1749–1750, 1785–1786, and 1807–1809

Notes: Using a cross-panel regression with fixed effects, where each market pair (e.g., Guadalajara-Mexico) is a panel. Pairs involving Campeche were eliminated from the analysis as the climate in Yucatán follows different patterns. The parentheses indicate that ϑ is not statistically significant at the 5% level

captured in the drought variable. These generalized famines prompted strong reactions of central and local authorities, mostly to limit trade to guarantee the supply of local producer communities. If famines had a climatic origin, the effect should be similar to a drought; but if they stemmed from increased barriers to trade, then the mutual adjustment of prices should be slower.

The interactions of crisis years and the speed of adjustment, reported in Table 18.7, provide a key insight on how the maize and wheat markets operated. The adjustment during famine years was somewhat slower than in normal years but the difference is not statistically significant. This finding casts doubt on the idea that sharp increases in prices were caused by market failures or that interventionism was a powerful factor in either deterring or stimulating markets. Instead, the results suggest that the market continued to function properly during times of famine conditions. By contrast, the effects of drought conditions on the adjustment speed were significant and the change in adjustment speed was much more pronounced. However, the changes in adjustment speeds for maize and wheat occurred in opposite directions: a drought year slowed down the adjustment in maize prices from 15 to 19 months and accelerated the adjustment of wheat prices from 18 to 12 months.[12] These differences provide a key insight on the two markets. On the one hand, maize, as a subsistence crop grown in nonirrigated lands was more susceptible to droughts and climatic anomalies. Being so critical to the livelihood of peasants and workers, local communities and even the hacendados were more likely to retain the grain (maize) in times of crisis, which would translate in a slower speed of adjustment. This slower speed of adjustment explains the establishment of grain purchasing commissions in the cities to secure the provisioning of the population (Challú 2013). On the other hand, wheat was less susceptible to climatic risk as it was grown in irrigated lands, and it was predominantly produced in haciendas for the market. The faster adjustment for wheat prices was likely a response to the slower adjustment of maize as cities relied more heavily on wheat under conditions of food shortages caused by drought. While, on average, we found that maize and wheat had similar speeds of adjustments they had a different type of response in drought and normal years.

[12] El Niño events had similar effects but lacked statistical significance.

18.8 Conclusion

I initiated my inquiry into grain market integration with the expectation that Mexican grain markets were segmented relative to other international experiences. I also anticipated a "two gear" grain market, in which the "commercial" crop, wheat, had more price convergence and adjusted faster to shocks than the "subsistence" crop, maize. The prevailing narrative about Mexican grain markets emphasizes prohibitive transportation costs for bulk products such as maize under normal climatic circumstances. This prevailing narrative postulates that wheat, sold at a premium price, was the only viable commercial crop preferred by profit-driven farmers. Similarly, in some accounts maize and wheat are considered separate markets, in which wheat catered to the Spanish population, and maize to the lower classes and natives (Crossgrove et al. 1990). In other related views, markets are presented as broad (encompassing multiple actors), but stunted in that geography and elite collusion created insurmountable barriers (Salvucci 1999). This analysis of prices further challenges these characterizations of grain markets.

The alternative thesis that I present is that Bourbon Mexico had a high degree of grain market integration considering the limitations of its geography, technology, and communications. In the majority of market pairs analyzed here the estimated adjustment speed to shocks to the equilibrium level was close to the theoretical maximum, one. Moreover, the high degree of co-movement of the series (the ρ parameter) suggests that shocks were corrected within a year and that this analysis would benefit from monthly series. From a comparative perspective, the only measure in which Mexico was behind markets usually considered as integrated was the volatility of maize prices, which may well be related to the strong dependence of maize on variable summer rainfall. In all other comparisons price spreads and adjustment speeds compared favorably with other scenarios involving similar distances and geography. Grain markets in Mexico corrected a price disequilibrium faster, for instance, than in Spain and as fast as in other regions of the world. These general conclusions are corroborated by contemporaries who compared Mexico with Europe and did not cast Mexico in a negative light in regard to market integration. For example, Yermo in his report on the state of agriculture after the 1785–86 famine indicated that the grain trade in Mexico was less regulated than in Spain, and that it was such lack of regulation propagated climatic made prices more variable than in Europe (Florescano 1981, p. 620). Likewise, Humboldt criticized the extent of poverty and inequality in Mexico, but he praised the supply of grain to the cities (Humboldt 1811, p. 444–483).

Despite the prevailing view of fragmented markets, my findings on Mexican grain markets as integrated and efficient for their time is consistent with a historical scholarship that has revealed a high degree of versatility in the Mexican economy in this period. Commercial organization was more sophisticated and had more complex trade networks than previously thought, featuring a growing degree of specialization (Gálvez and Ibarra 1997; Miño Grijalva 2001; Moreno Toscano 1998; Van Young 1981); financial instruments facilitated long-distance and inter-temporal transactions (Pérez Herrero 1988); a well-organized and efficient transportation industry, the arriería, connected local markets despite tremendous geographic obstacles (Suárez Argüello 1997). The efficiency of grain markets challenges the notion that Mexican underdevelopment can be traced to backward institutions or an immutable colonial legacy (Sokoloff and Engerman 2000). Instead, our findings highlight the deep roots of markets in Mexico (Coatsworth 1978, 2008; Tutino 2011).

While it is true that the tyranny of distance limited the scope of most grain transactions to short distances, I have shown that the connections between grain markets extended over long distances throughout central Mexico. All corners of central Mexico were interconnected, making a large regional focus such as this one is an appropriate and necessary scale to examine food supply. The precise nature of these interconnections escapes the possibility of a quantitative analysis, but the major mechanisms that connected distant markets likely involved the integration of maize and wheat markets and chain connections between intermediate markets. Wheat markets operated at longer distances and likely sped up the price adjustments in the substitute product (maize). In another place, I showed a dense mesh of social and geographic relationships that substantiates the hypothesis that chained connections at the local sphere created indirect links between distant markets (Challú 2013).

The indicators of market integration did not change in major ways in the period under analysis. The higher degree of co-movement of prices, as well as the more balanced adjustment from 1780 to 1809 indicate small improvements in market integration, but volatility and dispersion of prices remained similar over time. In this, late colonial Mexico is no different than other areas in the world, since it is in the nineteenth, not the eighteenth century, when the revolution in grain markets took place as improvements in transportation first integrated national markets, and then international markets (Bateman 2011; Federico et al. 2021; O'Rourke and Williamson 1999). But this is not to say that nothing changed before the transportation revolution. Federico et al. (2021) convincingly argue that there were integrating forces operating in the early modern period and the eighteenth century in Europe, while Dobado-González et al.'s (2012) analysis of Atlantic wheat markets find substantial progress in market integration over the eighteenth century. All maize price series show a simultaneous and significant increase in prices in the 1780s and the 1800s, suggesting that actors adjusted their expectations of the equilibrium price upwards. Because all markets were well integrated and prices adjusted to each other, the inflationary trend affected the entire territory and did not spare even those rural areas with abundant supply. The 1810s were also a time in which markets lost the high degree of integration of previous years, a finding that coincides with existing knowledge about the disruption of markets and the fragmentation of monetary authority (Irigoin 2010). Economic policies and political arrangements that favored trade to supply cities and mining centers seem to be particularly relevant in creating the conditions for market efficiency that we see in this study (Federico 2018, p. 23).

At the time when markets were still successfully integrated prior to 1810, there were both positive and negative results for average Mexicans trying to meet their nutritional demands. Due to the ability to trade across significant distances a good harvest in a given area likely lowered prices in other areas. And yet the opposite was also true. A rising urban population and an increase in inequality that favored those with higher purchasing power created a demand for marketable food; in the countryside, the increasing power of landowners and the loss of autonomy in peasant agriculture similarly skewed the access to food. As prices raised in the last quarter of the eighteenth century due to increased demand and limitations in supply, the urban dwellers found an advantage in attaining grain because rural producers would be more motivated to sell scarce crops to the higher bidder in urban areas, as opposed to those in other rural districts with less purchasing power. Integrated markets helped the urban population and underlie the relative declines in wellbeing for rural dwellers as well as the immigration to the cities.

18.9 Appendix: Challú on Murray

John Murray and I met regularly in the late 2000s. He was a Professor of Economics at the University of Toledo, and I was an Assistant Professor of History at Bowling Green State University. We first met at the annual conference of the Economic History Association, and we then started meeting more regularly, eventually in the context of a formalized mentoring grant that let us carve out time for meetings and discussion of work in progress. John was not only encouraging but also an inspiration and a springboard for ideas about how I was approaching the study of grain markets in late colonial Mexico. I particularly recall with joy our discussion of panels on market integration at the World Economic History Congress in Utrecht in 2009. Later, John and I discussed the findings and arguments that I eventually put into this chapter. His influence is reflected in two ways. First, John was interested in studies of market integration that exceeds the traditional use of price convergence and that emphasizes the importance of policies and political arrangements, as demonstrated in the joint study of John and Javier Silvestre on European coal markets. Second, John also encouraged me to connect economic arguments, social history, and narrative. I hope that this contribution honors his legacy.

References

Bateman VN (2011) The evolution of markets in early modern Europe, 1350–1800: a study of wheat prices. Econ Hist Rev 64:447–471

Challú AE (2007) Grain markets, food supply policies and living standards in late colonial Mexico. Harvard University, Cambridge

Challú AE (2010) The great decline: biological well-being and living standards in Mexico, 1730–1840. In: Salvatore RD, Coatsworth JH, Challú AE (eds) Living standards in Latin American history: height, welfare, and development, 1750–2000. Harvard University David Rockefeller Center for Latin American Studies, Cambridge, pp 23–67

Challú AE (2013) Grain markets, free trade and the Bourbon reforms: the real Pragmática of 1765 in new Spain. Colon Lat Am Rev 22:400–421

Coatsworth JH (1978) Obstacles to economic growth in nineteenth-century Mexico. Am Hist Rev 83:80–100

Coatsworth JH (1989) Comments on "The economic cycle in bourbon central Mexico: a critique of the Recaudación del diezmo líquido en pesos," by Ouweneel and Bijleveld. II. Hispanic Am Hist Rev 69:538–545
Coatsworth JH (2008) Inequality, institutions and economic growth in Latin America. J Lat Am Stud 40:545–569
Coatsworth JH, Tortellas Casares G (2002) Institutions and long-run economic performance in Mexico and Spain, 1800–2000. Paper prepared for presentation at the XIIIth Congress of the International Economic History Association, Buenos Aires, Argentina, July 2002
Crossgrove W, Egilman D, Heywood P, Kasperson J, Messer E, Wessen A (1990) Colonialism, international trade, and the nation-state. In: Newman LF, Crossgrove W, Kates RW, Matthews R, Millman S (eds) Hunger in history: food shortage, poverty and deprivation. Wiley-Blackwell, New York, pp 215–240
Dobado R, Marrero GA (2005) Corn market integration in Porfirian Mexico. J Econ Hist 65:103–128
Dobado-González R, García-Hiernaux A, Guerrero DE (2012) The integration of grain markets in the eighteenth century: early rise of globalization in the west. J Econ Hist 72:671–707
Ejrnæs M, Persson KG (2000) Market integration and transport costs in France 1825–1903: a threshold error correction approach to the law of one price. Explor Econ Hist 37:149–173
Espinosa Morales S (1995) Análisis de precios de los productos diezmados. El Bajío oriental. 1665-1786. In: García Acosta V (ed) Los Precios de Alimentos y Manufacturas Novohispanos. Mexico City, Centro de Investigaciones y Estudios Superiores en Antropología Social and Instituto Mora, pp 122–172
Farris N (1982) Maya society under Spanish rule. Princeton University Press, Princeton
Federico G (2018) Market integration. In: Diebolt C, Haupert M (eds) Handbook of cliometrics. Springer, Berlin, pp 1–26
Federico G, Schulze MS, Volckart O (2021) European goods market integration in the very long run: from the black death to the first World War. J Econ Hist 81:276–308
Florescano E (1981) Fuentes para la historia de la crisis agrícola de 1785–1786. Archivo General de la Nación, Mexico City
Florescano E (1995) Breve historia de la sequía en México. Universidad Veracruzana, Xalapa
Froot KA, Kim M, Rogoff K (2019) The law of one price over 700 years. Ann Econ Financ 20:1–35
Gálvez MA, Ibarra A (1997) Comercio local y circulación regional de importaciones. La feria de San Juan de Lagos en la Nueva España. Hist Mex 46:581–616
Garner R (1993) Economic growth and change in bourbon Mexico. University Press of Florida, Gainesville
Grafe R (2012) Distant tyranny: markets, power, and backwardness in Spain, 1650–1800. Princeton University Press, Princeton
Hamnett BR (1986) Roots of insurgency: Mexican regions, 1750–1824. Cambridge University Press, Cambridge
Humboldt A (1811) Political essay on the Kingdom of New Spain. Longman, Hurst, Rees, Orme, and Brown, London
INEGI (2014) Estadísticas Históricas de México. INEGI, Mexico City
Irigoin A (2010) Las raíces monetarias de la fragmentación política de la América española en el siglo XIX. Hist Mex 59:919–979
Jacks DS (2005) Intra- and international commodity market integration in the Atlantic Economy, 1800–1913. Explor Econ Hist 42:381–413
Klein H, Engerman SL (1990) Methods and meanings in price history. In: Johnson L, Tandeter E (eds) Essays on the price history of eighteenth-century Latin America. University of New Mexico Press, Albuquerque, pp 9–21
Li LM (1992) Grain prices in Zhili province, 1736–1911: preliminary study. In: Rawski TG, Li LM (eds) Chinese history in economic perspective. University of California Press, Berkeley, pp 69–99
Li LM (2000) Integration and disintegration in North China's grain markets, 1738–1911. J Econ Hist 60:665–699
Lindo-Fuentes H (1980) La utilidad de los diezmos como fuente para la historia económica. Hist Mex 30:273–289

Llopis Agelán M (2001) El mercado de trigo en Castilla y León, 1691–1788: arbitraje espacial e intervención. Historia Agraria 25:13–68
Llopis Agelán E, Sotoca S (2005) Antes, bastante antes: La integración del mercado español del trigo, 1725–1808. Historia Agraria 36:225–262
MacKinnon JG (1996) Numerical distribution functions for unit root and cointegration tests. J Appl Econ 11:601–618
Marks RB (1998) Tigers, rice, silk, and silt: environment and economy in late imperial South China. Cambridge University Press, Cambridge
Martín Ornelas JM (2008) La organización económica regional y el abasto urbano: el trigo y el maíz en Zacatecas, 1749–1821. Universidad Autónoma de Zacatecas, Zacatecas
Miño Grijalva M (2001) El mundo novohispano: Población, ciudades y economía, siglos XVII y XVIII, Fideicomiso Historia de las Américas. El Colegio de México, Fondo de Cultura Económica, Mexico City
Moreno Toscano A (1998) Economía regional y urbanización: ciudades y regiones en Nueva España. In: Silva Riquer J, López Martínez J (eds) Mercado Interno En México. Siglos XVIII–XIX. Instituto Mora, Mexico City, pp 64–93
Morin C (1979) Michoacán en la Nueva España del siglo XVIII: Crecimiento y desigualdad en una economía colonial. Fondo de Cultura Económica, Mexico City
O'Gráda C (2000) Black '47 and beyond: the great Irish famine in history, economy, and memory. Princeton University Press, Dublin
O'Grada C (2003) Adam Smith and Amartya Sen: markets and famines in pre-industrial Europe. Working Paper
O'Gráda C, Chevet JM (2002) Market segmentation and famine in ancien régime France. J Econ Hist 62:706–733
O'Rourke KH, Williamson JG (1999) Globalization and history: the evolution of a nineteenth-century Atlantic economy. MIT Press, Cambridge
Pérez Herrero P (1988) Plata y libranzas: la articulación comercial del México borbónico. Centro de Estudios Históricos and Colegio de México, Mexico City
Persson KG (1999) Grain markets in Europe 1500–1900: integration and deregulation. Cambridge University Press, Cambridge
Ravallion M (1986) Testing market integration. Am J Agr Econ 68:102–109
Reher DS (2001) Producción, precios e integración de los mercados regionales de grano en España. Revista de Historia Económica 19:539–572
Roehner BM (2000) The correlation length of commodity markets 1. Empirical evidence. Eur Phys J B 13:175–187
Rothenberg WB (1992) From market-places to a market economy: the transformation of rural Massachusetts, 1750–1850. University of Chicago Press, Chicago
Salvucci R (1999) Agriculture and colonial heritage. In: Adelman J (ed) Colonial legacies: the problem of persistence in Latin American History. Routledge, New York
Salvucci R, Salvucci L (1987) Crecimiento económico y cambio de la productividad en México, 1750-1895. HISLA. Revista Latinoamericana de Historia Económica y Social 10:67–89
Sennhauser RW (1996) Veracruz y el comercio de harinas en el Caribe español, 1760–1830. Estudios de historia social y económica 13:107–122
Shiue CH, Keller W (2007) Markets in China and Europe on the eve of the industrial revolution. Am Econ Rev 97:1189–1216
Sokoloff KL, Engerman SL (2000) History lessons: institutions, factor endowments, and paths of development in the new world. J Econ Perspect 14:217–232
Stein SJ, Stein BH (2003) Apogee of empire: Spain and New Spain in the age of Charles III, 1759–1789. Johns Hopkins University Press, Baltimore
Studer R (2008) India and the great divergence: assessing the efficiency of grain markets in eighteenth-and nineteenth-century India. J Econ Hist 68:393–437
Suárez Argüello CE (1985) La politica cerealera en la economía novohispana: el caso del trigo. Centro de Investigaciones y Estudios Superiores en Antropología Social, Mexico City

Suárez Argüello CE (1997) Camino real y carrera larga: la arriería en la Nueva España durante el siglo XVIII. Centro de Investigaciones y Estudios Superiores en Antropología Social, Mexico City

Taylor AM (2001) Potential pitfalls for the purchasing-power-parity puzzle? Sampling and specification biases in mean-reversion tests of the law of one price. Econometrica 69:473–498

Tutino J (2011) Making a new world: founding capitalism in the Bajío and Spanish North America. Duke University Press, Durham

Van Young E (1981) Hacienda and market in eighteenth-century Mexico: the rural economy of the Guadalajara Region, 1675–1820. University of California Press, Berkeley

Wong RB, Perdue PC (1992) Grain markets and food supplies in eighteenth-century Hunan. In: Rawski TG, Li LM (eds) Chinese history in economic perspective. University of California Press, Berkeley, pp 126–144

Chapter 19
William McKinley, Optimal Reneging, and the Spanish-American War

Joshua R. Hendrickson

Abstract President William McKinley's decision to go to war with Spain in 1898 is not well understood. Since McKinley kept very few written records, little is known about his actual thought process. As a result, historians have struggled with the apparent inconsistency between McKinley's initial commitment to peace and subsequent decision to go to war and tend to focus on identifying outside forces that can explain the reversal. In this paper, I develop a model of optimal reneging. Contrary to conventional narratives among historians that McKinley's decision to go to war was inconsistent with his earlier position, my model suggests that McKinley's decision can be understood as an optimal timing problem. I start with the premise that a country would prefer to enter conflict only when its military capability is sufficient to make a victory likely. Thus, a country will commit to peace until its military capability reaches some threshold. Once military capability reaches this threshold, it is optimal to renege on a commitment to peace. I conduct simulations of the model to determine the likelihood that McKinley would renege during his first term. I find that if the ex ante estimate of the benefits of war was 2–2.6 times the ex ante estimate of cost, then the probability of reneging after one year is approximately 1–18%. If the perceived benefits were 2.7 times the ex ante estimate of cost (or greater), entry during McKinley's first term is certain.

Keywords War · Political economy · William McKinley · Spanish-American war

JEL Classifications H56 · N41

J. R. Hendrickson (✉)
University of Mississippi, Department of Economics, University, MS, USA
e-mail: jrhendr1@olemiss.edu

P. Gray et al. (eds.), *Standard of Living*, Studies in Economic History,
https://doi.org/10.1007/978-3-031-06477-7_19

19.1 Introduction

Among historians, there are three predominant explanations of President William McKinley's decision to go to war with Spain in 1898. One popular explanation is that McKinley gave in to the pressure by yellow journalists to go to war with Spain (Beard and Beard 1934; Wisan 1934). A second popular explanation is that McKinley was pushed into the conflict by business interests who sought expansion into foreign markets (Williams 1972). Finally, the third narrative is that McKinley was a political pragmatist who ultimately gave in to pressure from Congress (Gould 1982; Offner 1992, 2004). In each case, McKinley is depicted as an advocate of peace who was unable to withstand the public pressure to go to war with Spain. However, as Kapur (2011, p. 23) points out, these narratives fail to take into account "the fact that Congress moved so rapidly to make war on Spain, but only *after* it had secured McKinley's stamp of approval, and *after* acceding to all of his stated wishes." As Kapur argues, it is hard to reconcile how much power McKinley seemed to wield with Congress with the idea that McKinley was weak and prone to succumb to public pressure.

In this paper, I propose an alternative explanation of McKinley's decision to go to war. The Cuban rebellion against Spain that began in 1895 significantly reduced trade between the United States and Cuba. In addition, the strategies employed by both the Cubans and the Spanish threatened to destroy a significant number of investments made by US firms in Cuba. As a result, there were potential benefits to an intervention that restored trade and limited the destruction of wealth. However, war comes with significant costs. In determining whether or not to use military intervention, a leader must consider the expected net benefits of conflict, realizing that the benefits of intervention only occur with victory, but the costs are paid regardless of the outcome. Against this backdrop, it might be optimal to maintain a commitment to peace until some cost-benefit threshold is reached.

When President McKinley took office, he expressed a commitment to peace. However, he also threatened to use military action if necessary. A credible commitment to peace with the threat of military action creates an optimal timing problem. In other words, given a credible commitment to peace, McKinley's decision is to choose the optimal point in time (if any) to renege on his commitment to peace. The basic idea is that McKinley would ideally like to avoid war until the likelihood of victory is sufficiently high. I present a theory in which the decision about when to renege is equivalent to choosing an optimal threshold for the expected net benefit of military conflict. I assume that the probability of victory, and therefore the expected net benefit from war, is a function of the relative military capabilities of the United States and Spain. If there is uncertainty about relative military capabilities, then this timing problem cannot determine a precise point in time at which military action will occur; instead, there will be a distribution of optimal reneging times.

I conduct a Monte Carlo simulation of the model, which is calibrated using data on relative military expenditures of the United States in comparison to Spain. I show that the probability of reneging within McKinley's first term is dependent on (1) the ex ante estimates of the benefits of a successful war, (2) the ex ante estimates of the cost of war, and (3) the expected future time path of the relative military capability of the United States. If the perceived benefits of a successful war are double the cost, then the probability of McKinley reneging after only a year in office is 1%. If the perceived benefits are 2.6 times the cost, this probability is 17%. If the perceived benefit is 2.7 times the cost, McKinley is certain to enter in 1898. This suggests that, given the time path of the relative military capabilities of the United States, the probability of reneging depends critically on the magnitude of ex ante beliefs about the benefits of a successful military engagement.

Overall, the model suggests that when judging McKinley's decision to go to war, one must take into account the perceived benefits and costs of the conflict. Some back-of-the-envelope calculations suggest that the perceived benefit-cost ratio might have been 2.5 or higher. This implies that McKinley's decision to go to war should not be considered a sign of weakness or ineptitude, but rather a response to incentives associated with the benefits and costs of war.

The contribution of this paper is two-fold. First, historians see McKinley's commitment to peace and his subsequent reversal as an inconsistency. In their attempt to identify some triggering factor that led to this inconsistency, they are forced to appeal to outside influences. In contrast, I present an argument and a corresponding model that is able to show that McKinley's decision to renege on his commitment to peace need not imply inconsistency in his decision-making. Second, my model allows me to consider the role of uncertainty and the relevant counterfactuals ex ante. By using a Monte Carlo experiment, I am able to predict how likely McKinley is to renege on his commitment, given the perceived benefits and costs, the relative military capability of the United States when McKinley took office, and the expected future time path of relative military capability.

19.2 McKinley and the Decision to Go to War

19.2.1 Background

The Cuban rebellion against Spain began in 1895. The Cubans had previously attempted to oust the Spanish in 1868. After a war that lasted until 1878, the conflict ended when the Spanish government offered reforms. These reforms never materialized.

The rebellion that began in 1895 was better organized. The Cubans had learned their lesson from the previous war. Knowing that they were unlikely to defeat the Spanish militarily, the Cubans resorted to the outright destruction of wealth. The idea was that by destroying capital and other forms of wealth, this would convince Spain that nothing was to be gained from the island and they would decide to leave. Rather than leave, the Spanish committed to a policy of "reconcentration." This entailed taking Cubans from the countryside and relocating them to towns controlled by the Spanish. Once the Cubans were removed from the countryside, their villages and crops were burned. The conditions that Cubans faced after this relocation were harsh. Approximately 15 percent of the Cuban population died as a result of disease and starvation (Offner 2004, p. 51). The idea behind the reconcentration policy was to cut off resources and the food supply of those participating in the rebellion as well as fragment the Cuban population. The result was that "both the Cubans and the Spanish engaged in economic warfare that devastated the island. Agricultural production and foreign trade plummeted" (Offner 2004, p. 51). Nonetheless, this did not stop the rebellion.

When McKinley took office in 1897, he sent his friend and former Illinois state representative William Calhoun to Cuba to get an idea of the state of the conflict. When Calhoun returned, he brought back stories of human suffering due to the reconcentration policy of the Spanish. McKinley followed by calling for the Spanish to put down the rebellion "within humane limits" (Gould 1982, p. 28). He sent a representative, Stewart Woodford, to Spain calling for this change in Spanish tactics within three months. If the Spanish did not comply, he threatened that the United States would take action. However, while his representative was traveling to Spain, the Spanish prime minister was assassinated. The new government initially seemed willing to acquiesce to McKinley's demands:

> On October 23, 1897, Woodford was told that the decrees granting autonomy to Cuba would soon be issued. During the next month the Spanish suspended the reconcentration policy, declared an amnesty for political prisoners, and released Americans who were in Cuban jails. (Gould 1982, p. 30)

Nonetheless, McKinley prepared the United States for the possibility of conflict. He sent the USS Maine to dock in Florida and "the Navy discussed contingency plans for sending a ship to Havana" (Gould 1982, p. 31).

The Spanish promise of autonomy meant that the Cubans would have more power over domestic decision-making, but the Spanish would still control foreign affairs. The policy was officially put in place at the beginning of 1898. However, just two weeks later, Spanish military officers led riots in Havana. In the United States, this created "fear that Spain was losing its grip on the island and that future riots might harm U.S. citizens" (Offner 2004, p. 56). As a result of these fears,

> McKinley sent the USS Maine to Havana harbor, and the Navy Department repositioned a portion of the North Atlantic fleet from Hampton Roads to Key West and the Gulf of Mexico. Some U.S. naval ships also dropped anchor in Lisbon and others gathered in Hong Kong near the Philippines. (Offner 2004, p. 56)

Shortly afterward, a private letter from the Spanish minister appeared in the US press that presented a dim view of McKinley and suggested that the Spanish government was merely buying time by offering token appeasements to the United States in the hopes of putting down the rebellion in the meantime. Less than a week after the letter surfaced, the USS Maine exploded off the coast of Cuba. McKinley called for an investigation into the explosion, but also asked Congress for a $50 million appropriation to prepare the military. While the investigation was underway, McKinley sought a diplomatic solution with Spain. However, his requests of Spain were at least partially rejected. On April 11, 1898, McKinley asked Congress for a declaration of war.

19.2.2 Explanations for McKinley's Decision to Go to War

The two earliest narratives constructed to explain McKinley's decision to go to war focused on outside influences. Historian Lewis Gould presents a summary and critique of these early views:

> At the center of the controversy stands William McKinley. His actions and policies toward Spain and Cuba from March 1897 to April 1898 have received close attention and since the First World War, almost uniform censure. That McKinley gave in to jingoist pressure from a hysterical press and an overheated public and therefore accepted war with a nation that had capitulated to American demands has become a staple of textbook accounts of his presidency.
>
> During the 1960s an alternative hypothesis evolved. Departing from the usual picture of a feckless leader, some scholars have depicted a Machiavellian and cunning executive, bent on expansion and heedless of the interest of Cubans and Filipinos, whom Americans believed they were assisting. Sensitive to every wish of the business community, McKinley went to war when conditions were right for economic imperialism that relied on overseas markets.
>
> Neither of these portrayals does justice to the complexity of diplomatic problems that Spain and the United States encountered over Cuba between 1895 and 1898, and neither captures how McKinley sought, in the end unsuccessfully, to discover a way out of the impasse in which both nations found themselves. What is significant is not that war came. The divergent perceptions of Spanish and American national interests made conflict likely, once revolution began in Cuba in 1895. McKinley's ability to postpone war for as long as he did and to control the terms on which the United States commenced hostilities indicates that his presidential leadership during the coming of war was more courageous and principled than his critics have realized. (Gould 1982, p. 19–20)

Gould's dismissive attitude with respect to early criticisms is not unfounded. These earlier views tend to take a normative view of the Spanish-American War and then try to explain McKinley's decision to enter the war through backward induction from that initial premise. In other words, the basic premise of the early criticism of McKinley is that the war was unnecessary, either because the Spanish had made concessions to the United States or because the war was seen an attempt at US imperialism. Given the premise that the war was unnecessary, one must then determine how and why President McKinley would end up in an unnecessary war. The conclusion reached by early historians is that McKinley caved either to public pressure spurred on by yellow journalism or pressure from US business interests.

One problem with this line of thinking is that it fails to construct a proper counterfactual. For example, if yellow journalism was the cause of McKinley reneging on his commitment to peace, then in the absence of journalistic pressure, McKinley would not have gone to war. There is little evidence in favor of this counterfactual. Gould argues that it is hard to ascertain the direction of causation between the public support of the Cubans and yellow journalism. In fact, Gould (1982, p. 24) argues that prominent publishers of yellow journalism, such as William Randolph Hearst and Joseph Pulitzer, represented "only a small part of the journalistic community, and they reflected what the public wanted, rather than shaping it." The idea that public opinion might have been driving the coverage of the Cuban rebellion and not the reverse has some merit based on pre-existing opinions of Americans about

Spain. Offner (2004, p. 52) argues that "Americans had long disparaged Spain" and that many in the United States saw the Cuban rebellion as part of a "historical trend of the New World throwing off the tyrannical restraints of Old World political, economic, and religious domination."

Scholars like Williams (1972) argued that business interests wanted to expand into foreign markets to deal with problems of overproduction. Economists tend to take a dim view of overproduction theories. If firms produce more than individuals want to purchase at a given price, then the price will have to decline to clear the market. This certainly occurs. For such theories to be valid, however, would require that firms systematically and consistently overproduce, despite experience. Furthermore, an advocate of the view put forth by Williams would have to believe that not only do firms systematically make the same error, but that the only way to correct this error is to sell this excess production into foreign markets. Of course, the logical flaws in this argument do not preclude political adherence to such a theory. However, Williams "offered little, if any, supporting evidence for his assertions" (Kapur 2011, p. 21).[1] Furthermore, Offner (2004, p. 52) argues that firms with business interests in Cuba were divided on the war. Some wanted the United States to intervene to protect their interests. Others wanted cooperation with Spain to put down the Cuban rebellion. In addition, Gould (1982, p. 24) argues that business leaders without a direct stake in Cuba wanted to avoid war and the uncertainty that went along with it.

Subsequent scholars moved on from journalists and business interests to argue that it was Congressional pressure that ultimately caused McKinley to go to war. Historians such as Gould (1982) and Offner (1992, 2004) argue that McKinley was indeed committed to peace and tried to exhaust every opportunity for peace before going to war – even after the explosion of the USS Maine. Offner (2004) points out that as many as 100 Republicans had sought to align themselves with Congressional Democrats to declare war on Spain without the consent of the president. In fact, Offner depicts McKinley as trying to pursue peace until April 10, just one day before he asked Congress for a declaration of war.

The problem with explanations based on Congressional pressure is that they ignore key facts. The most important of these facts is that Congress failed to take any action before being explicitly asked by President McKinley. Also, it was McKinley who had requested $50 million in funding for the US Navy in the aftermath of the explosion of the USS Maine. And perhaps most importantly, McKinley

[1] Historians, such as Williams and even Gould, seem to suggest that McKinley gave some credence to this overproduction view. However, the support for this argument seems to be from one speech that McKinley gave in 1895. The speech, however, was clearly a call for reciprocity in trade, a view McKinley adopted in 1891 (Gould 1982, p. 10). The only indication that this relates to overproduction is McKinley's use of the word "surplus." However, his use of surplus hardly indicated he accepted this overproduction view. His use of the term "surplus" seems to imply that production in both countries would be higher than it would be with only domestic customers. When one considers that McKinley had long been a protectionist before he pivoted to the idea of reciprocity, the speech can just as easily be seen as an inarticulate attempt to explain the mutual benefits from reciprocity in trade.

"never showed any sign of regret for any 'failure' to secure peace" (Kapur 2011, p. 36).[2]

In short, each of the popular narratives denies McKinley agency. Perhaps McKinley wanted to avoid war, but circumstances beyond his control pushed him into war. One critical flaw in this analysis, as Kapur (2011, p. 23) argues, is that these historians traditionally focused on "what his actions were, and why they failed, rather than *why* his actions were, and whether he thought of them as failures." In this paper, I present a complementary idea. What I argue is that rather than starting with a premise that is based on information available ex post and then reasoning through backward induction, one should consider the incentives faced by McKinley ex ante.

19.2.3 An Alternative View

The view that I put forth is this paper is similar to that of Gould in the sense that I assume that conflict between the two countries is likely. However, I depart from Gould's argument that McKinley's decision to go to war represented a submission to Congressional pressure. The basic idea that I put forward begins with the assumption that conflict is likely. Given that conflict is likely, McKinley would prefer to wait to enter into such conflict until the United States is in a position of power and likely to emerge victorious from the conflict.

I present a model in which McKinley's decision is to choose a threshold for reneging on his commitment to peace. I assume that there are particular benefits from going to war. These benefits might include preventing the destruction of capital in Cuba that belonged to individuals and firms in the United States, a recovery of trade with Cuba that had declined significantly during the Cuban rebellion, greater US hegemony over the Western Hemisphere, and McKinley's own reelection prospects. There are also costs in terms of the direct cost of the government and the loss of human lives. The benefits of going to war are only realized in the event of victory, whereas the costs are paid regardless of the outcome. Furthermore, I assume that the probability of victory is a function of the relative military capability of the United States. As a result, McKinley's decision is to choose a threshold for relative military capability (or equivalently, a threshold for the expected net benefit) such that he would be willing to renege on his commitment to peace once the threshold is reached.

---

[2] McKinley probably produced fewer written records than most modern presidents. However, there is some indication that McKinley was savvy enough to use the written records for political purposes. He once sent a letter to his political ally and financier, Mark Hanna, indicating that it was improper to give public contracts for political reasons. Hanna was angry that McKinley had submitted this letter to the public White House file, thereby making it part of the public record (Kapur 2011, p. 31–32).

My model provides a way to think about the decision to renege on a commitment to peace that relies on only three factors: (1) the prospective benefits from conflict, (2) the prospective cost, and (3) the expected future path of the military capacity of the United States relative to that of Spain. Back-of-the-envelope calculations suggest that the prospective loss of wealth is sufficient to make war somewhat likely. Thus, one does not need to argue that journalists, Congressmen, or calls for economic expansionism pushed the United States into war. Furthermore, the focus is exclusively on the decision to go to war. Whether the war was necessary, worthwhile, or justified is beside the point.

19.3 The Model

Suppose that the United States has credibly committed to peace with the Spanish, such that Spain believes that the United States has no desire to enter a military conflict. However, the commander-in-chief of the US military, in this case William McKinley, has threatened to use military force, if necessary. Given the credible commitment, McKinley's decision to enter the conflict is a timing decision. He wants to choose the optimal point in time to renege on the US commitment to peace.

Let B and C denote the benefit of successful military aggression and the cost of conflict, respectively. The benefits from military aggression are the direct benefits that accrue to the state, government, and political leaders in the event of success. This could include the accumulation of land, prestige, and/or international power as well as any political benefits associated with success. The costs include political costs, the destruction of military infrastructure, as well as the human cost. I assume that the benefits of conflict are only received if the military action is successful. The costs are paid regardless of whether the action is successful.Suppose that the probability of victory, $p(M)$, is given as

$$p(M) = \frac{M}{1+M} \tag{19.1}$$

where M is the relative military capability of the United States in comparison to Spain. This implies that the probability of victory is a sigmoid function of relative military capability such that $\lim_{M \to 0} p(M) = 0$, $\lim_{M \to \infty} p(M) = 1$. Furthermore, suppose that M is random. In particular, assume that the relative military capability of the United States follows a jump diffusion:

$$\frac{dM}{M} = \mu dt + \sigma dz + \phi_1 dq_1 - \phi_2 dq_2 \tag{19.2}$$

where μ is the expected rate of change, σ is the conditional standard deviation, dz is an increment of a Wiener process, and dq_1 and dq_2 are each increments of two independent Poisson processes with arrival rates λ_1 and λ_2, respectively.[3] What this implies is that the relative military capability of the United States ordinarily follows a geometric Brownian motion. However, there are rare instances in which M experiences a "jump." In particular, given the assumptions above, $q_1 = 1$ and $dq_2 = 1$ with probabilities $\lambda_1 dt$ and $\lambda_2 dt$, respectively. When $dq_1 = 1$ or $dq_2 = 1$, these are referred to as "jumps." The magnitudes of the jumps in M are determined by ϕ_1 and ϕ_2. With probability $(1 - \lambda_i)dt$, $dq_i = 0$, $i = 1, 2$ (no jump occurs). Later, I show that jump processes are necessary to match the data.

Given these assumptions, for President McKinley, the decision about when to go to war is an optimal timing problem. The outcome of war is uncertain. Ideally, the president would like to wait until a point in time at which victory appears very likely. In the meantime, the president would like to communicate a commitment to peace. Since fluctuations in the relative strength of the US military are stochastic, it is not possible for any decision-maker to pinpoint an actual point in time in which to initiate conflict. For example, if the president sets a particular timetable, he might find that the US military doesn't have a sufficient advantage at that time. Or, the United States might have an advantage earlier than anticipated. In other words, this suggests that the timing problem is best understood in terms of a threshold for relative military capability. This description suggests that there is some threshold, M^*, at which the expected value of initiating conflict is sufficiently high to renege on a commitment to peace.

When presented in this context, the opportunity to renege on the United States's commitment to peace can be thought of in terms of its option value.[4] The objective of the president in determining when to renege is to choose a threshold, M^*, that maximizes the value of the option to initiate conflict. If $M \geq M^*$ when this threshold is determined, then the president should initiate conflict immediately. However, if $M < M^*$, then the president should continue to communicate a commitment to peace until $M \geq M^*$ and then renege on this commitment and initiate conflict.

Let $V(M)$ denote the value of the option for the United States to be the aggressor in conflict with Spain. Consider an interval of time of the size Δt. Let M be the relative military capability of the United States at the beginning of this interval and M' be the relative military capability at the end of this interval. It follows that the value of the option to initiate conflict at time t is the expected present discounted value of the option at the end of the time interval:

$$V(M,t) = \frac{1}{1 + r\Delta t} EV(M', t + \Delta t)$$

[3] I assume that $E(dq_1 dz) = E(dq_2 dz) = E(dq_1 dq_2) = 0$.

[4] The logic of treating the decision to enter the conflict as similar to the decision of whether to exercise an option is that McKinley had the option, but not the obligation to go to war. This option has value. This is therefore similar to Hendrickson and Salter (2016), who treat the decision to participate in a revolution as akin to exercising an option, albeit strategically.

where r is the real interest rate used to discount the future and E is the expectations operator. Multiplying both sides of this expression by $(1 + r\Delta t)$ and re-arranging yields:

$$rV(M,t)\Delta t = EV(M',t+\Delta t) - V(M,t)$$

Dividing both sides of this expression by Δt and taking the limit as $\Delta t \rightarrow 0$, yields a continuous time representation of Bellman's equation:

$$rV(M) = \frac{1}{dt}EdV \tag{19.3}$$

where $dV = \lim_{\Delta t \rightarrow 0}\left[V(M',t+\Delta t) - V(M,t)\right]$. Using Eq. (19.2) in conjunction with Ito's Lemma, Eq. (19.3) can be written as

$$rV(M) = \mu MV'(M) + \frac{1}{2}\sigma^2 M^2 V''(M) + \lambda_1\left\{V\left[(1+\phi_1)M\right] - V(M)\right\}$$
$$+\lambda_2\left\{V\left[(1-\phi_2)M\right] - V(M)\right\}$$

Or, by re-arranging,

$$(r+\lambda_1+\lambda_2)V(M) = \mu MV'(M) + \frac{1}{2}\sigma^2 M^2 V''(M)$$
$$+\lambda_1 V\left[(1+\phi_1)M\right] + \lambda_2 V\left[(1-\phi_2)M\right] \tag{19.4}$$

Note here that $V(M)$ is some unknown function. In order to solve for the optimal threshold, M^*, I need a solution to $V(M)$. Guess that

$$V(M) = \alpha M^{\beta} \tag{19.5}$$

Note that this implies that

$$V'(M) = \alpha\beta M^{\beta-1}$$

$$V''(M) = \alpha\beta(\beta-1)M^{\beta-2}$$

Thus, Eq. (19.5) is a solution to Eq. (19.4), if β satisfies:

$$\frac{1}{2}\sigma^2\beta(\beta-1) + \mu\beta + \lambda_1(1+\phi)^{\beta} + \lambda_2(1-\phi_2)^{\beta} - (r+\lambda_1+\lambda_2) = 0 \tag{19.6}$$

The solution for β can be obtained using numerical methods. However, note that there is more than one solution for β in the equation above. In order to solve for the threshold, M^*, I need to impose boundary conditions on $V(M)$. I impose two boundary conditions using economic reasoning.

The threshold, M^*, chosen by the government should meet two criteria. First, since the option value can be understood as the value of the option to wait, as long as the option value of initiating conflict is greater than the expected value of conflict, the government should not exercise the option. It is only when the option value is less than or equal to the expected value of the conflict that the option should be exercised. It follows that the president should choose to initiate conflict at the precise point at which the option value is equal to the expected value of conflict. Formally, this implies that

$$V\left(M^*\right) = p\left(M^*\right)B - C \tag{19.7}$$

Second, note that the value of the option to initiate conflict should be strictly increasing in M. In fact, as M gets arbitrarily small, the option to initiate conflict becomes worthless. Formally, this implies that

$$\lim_{M \to 0} V\left(M\right) = 0 \tag{19.8}$$

This latter condition implies that the solution to Eq. (19.6) must be positive. Further, from Eqs. (19.5) and (19.7),

$$V\left(M^*\right) = \alpha\left(M^*\right)^{\beta} = p\left(M^*\right)B - C$$

Solving this expression for α and substituting it into Eq. (19.5) yields

$$V\left(M\right) = \underbrace{\left(\frac{M}{M^*}\right)^{\beta}}_{\text{DiscountFactor}} \times \underbrace{\left[p\left(M^*\right)B - C\right]}_{\text{ExpectedNetBenefit}} \tag{19.9}$$

This equation illustrates the option value of reneging. The option value is the product of a stochastic discount factor and the expected net benefit of aggression. Note that M^* has been defined, but not determined. From Eq. (19.9), it is clear that there is a trade-off that the president faces when choosing the threshold for initiating conflict. If the president chooses a high threshold for relative strength, this increases the likelihood of victory. However, this also implies that the president will have to wait longer than if he chooses a lower threshold. As a result, the present discounted value of that future action is lower. The president's problem is to choose the threshold that optimally balances this trade-off. In short, the president wants to choose M^* to maximize the option value. The value of M^* that maximizes Eq. (19.9) satisfies:

$$(\beta B - C)(M^*)^2 + [(\beta - 1)B - 2C]M^* - C = 0 \tag{19.10}$$

Note that, as long as $(B/C) > (1/\beta)$, this equation has a positive and negative solution.[5] However, since M cannot be less than zero, then M^* cannot be less than zero. Thus, it follows that

$$M^* = \frac{-[(\beta - 1)B - 2C] + \sqrt{[(\beta - 1)B - 2C]^2 + 4(\beta B - C)C}}{2(\beta B - C)} \tag{19.11}$$

The threshold for reneging on the commitment to peace is a function of the benefits of successful conflict,

B, the costs of the conflict, C, and, from Eq. (19.6), the parameters that determine β.

An important conclusion from this model is that the threshold is expressed in terms of the relative military capability of the United States and not an explicit period of time. In fact, let T^* denote the time at which the president will renege on his commitment to peace. The time at which it is optimal to renege is the earliest point in time at which relative military capability crosses the optimal threshold. Formally, this can be written as

$$T^* = \inf\{t > 0 \mid M \geq M^*\} \tag{19.12}$$

Since M is stochastic, this point in time cannot be known with certainty. Rather, given some initial value of $M(0) = M_0$, there is a probability distribution for T^*. In the next section, I use a Monte Carlo experiment to simulate a distribution for T^*.

19.4 Implications and Discussion

In the model I presented above, the decision about when to renege on the commitment to peace is determined by a threshold for the relative military capabilities of the United States in comparison to Spain. The underlying idea is one that is prevalent in international relations research. For example, Most and Starr (1989) point out that military capability affects both a country's ability and its willingness to enter conflict. Using data for the United States, Fordham (2004) finds that greater military capability leads to a more frequent use of force.

In the model, I made the assumption that the relative military capability of the United States generally follows a geometric Brownian motion, but that there are also

[5] Notice that this implies that there is no meaningful threshold for reneging on a commitment to peace unless the benefit is at least some mark-up above the cost. In other words, this implies that in some scenarios, one should not even consider reneging.

rare, discrete "jumps" in relative military capabilities between the two countries. As such, the purpose of this section is two-fold. First, I present three different measures of relative military capabilities and I examine the time series properties and the distributions of each of these measures to determine whether the characteristics of the data are consistent with the assumptions in my model. Second, given the characteristics of the data that I identify, I conduct a Monte Carlo experiment of the model to determine the probability of reneging for specific, perceived benefit-cost ratios.

19.4.1 Relative Military Capability: Measurement, Time Series Properties, and Fat Tails

Consider Eq. (19.2) without the possibility of jumps and define $m := \ln(M)$. Using Ito's Lemma, it follows that without jumps, the evolution of m can be expressed using the following stochastic differential equation:

$$dm = \left(\mu - \frac{1}{2}\sigma^2\right)dt + \sigma dz$$

This equation can be written in discrete time using a random walk approximation:

$$m_t = \left(\mu - \frac{1}{2}\sigma^2\right) + m_{t-1} + \sigma\varepsilon_t \tag{19.13}$$

where E_t is drawn from a standard normal distribution. It is useful to use this random walk approximation because it highlights two important empirical properties. First, it implies that the logarithm of the relative military capability of the United States follows a random walk (with drift if $\mu - (1/2)\sigma^2 \neq 0$). Second, it follows that the expected change in the logarithm of the relative military capability of the United States has a normal distribution. Thus, to determine whether the data on the relative military capability of the United States is consistent with the assumptions of the model, I conduct unit root tests on the logarithm of each measure. I then use quantile-quantile plots of the log difference of these measures to examine whether the measures are drawn from a normal distribution.

I measure military capability using three distinct variables: (1) real military expenditures, (2) the stock of military capability, and (3) military personnel.

The use of real military expenditures is straightforward in the sense that military expenditures will tend to be positively correlated with military capability. As such, it might be a useful proxy. Nonetheless, the use of military expenditures is not without flaws. For example, military expenditures are a flow. In contrast, military capability is perhaps best thought of as a stock. Kugler et al. (1980) suggest the following method to measure the stock of military capabilities. Let M denote the stock of military capability and assume that military capability depreciates at a constant rate, (1

$-\ \delta$). It follows that the law of motion of the stock of military capability can be written as

$$M_t = E_t + \delta M_{t-1}$$

where E_t is military expenditures. Since the stock of military capabilities cannot be directly measured, this equation has the following equivalent representation:

$$M_t = E_t + \delta E_{t-1} + \delta^2 E_{t-2} + \ldots$$

I use this weighted lag approach to calculate the stock of military capabilities for both the United States and Spain. Finally, I measure military capability using military personnel. Again, this might not be a perfect indicator of military capability because changes in technology can affect military capability without having any effect on military personnel. However, these concerns should be lessened (somewhat) given the time period of the nineteenth century.

Figure 19.1 plots the natural logarithm of the ratio of US military expenditures to Spanish military expenditures over the course of the nineteenth century. The data are obtained from the Correlates of War Project.[6] As shown, there is a slight upward trend over the sample with a sizable temporary increase during the US Civil War. I test for a unit root using the augmented Dickey-Fuller test. The first row of Table 19.1 shows the test statistic and the corresponding 5% critical value. As shown, the null hypothesis of a unit root cannot be rejected.

In the model, I assumed that military capabilities follow a jump diffusion. In the absence of jumps, it follows from Eq. (19.13) that the log-difference of relative military capability follows a normal distribution with a mean of $\mu - (1/2)\sigma^2$ and a variance of σ^2. If, however, there are discrete jumps in M, then the distribution of M will have "fat tails" in the sense that extreme values are more likely than the normal distribution would predict. To examine this property, I present a quantile-quantile plot in Fig. 19.2. This figure plots the quantile of the log-difference of relative military expenditures against the corresponding quantile of a normal distribution. If the variable of interest follows a normal distribution, then each of the plotted points will lie on the 45-degree line. When points lie below the 45-degree line in the bottom left corner of the figure, this is evidence of a fat left tail. When points lie above the 45-degree line in the upper right corner of the figure, this is evidence of a fat right tail. As shown in Fig. 19.2, there is some evidence of fat tails since there is a point that lies significantly above the 45-degree line in the upper-right corner of the figure

[6] The data are from the Correlates of War project: http://www.correlatesofwar.org/data-sets. In particular, I use data from the project used to construct the material capabilities of the state. The project itself constructs an index of material capability, which includes data on military expenditures and military personnel, among other factors. I do not use the index because the way that the index is constructed implies that each component of the index as a perfect substitute for all other components. For more on this material capabilities project and corresponding data, see Singer et al. (1972) and Singer (1987).

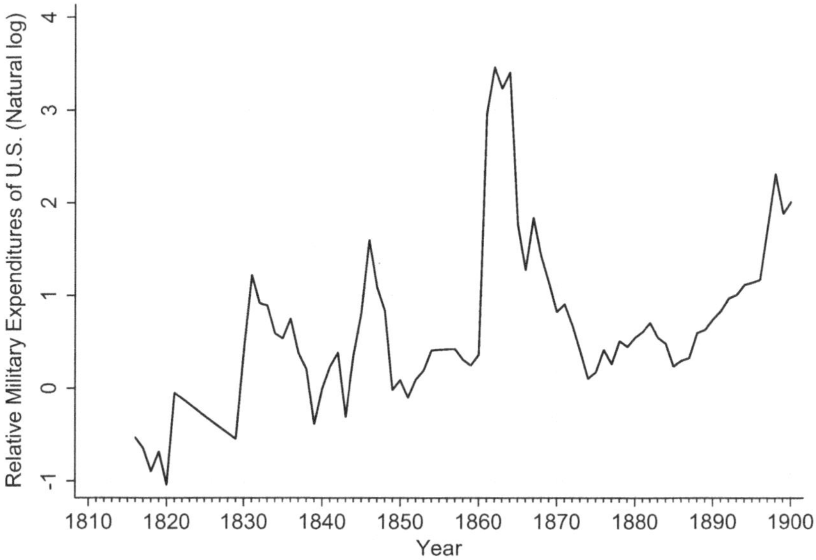

Fig. 19.1 Relative Military Expenditures, U.S. (Natural Logarithm). This figure plots the ratio of US military expenditures to Spanish military expenditures. (*Source*: Correlates of War Project)

Table 19.1 Unit root tests

Variable	Test statistic	5% Critical value
Military expenditures	−3.22	−3.48
Stock of military capability	−2.27	−2.93
Military personnel	−2.91	−3.47

and a point that lies significantly below the 45-degree line in the lower-left corner of the figure.

It is possible to argue that the two extreme values in the far ends of the tail of the distribution are due to the Civil War and that the large increase (and subsequently large decrease) in relative military expenditures do not reflect changes in military capability, but rather reflect the temporary cost of war. To examine this, I remove the years 1860-1866 from the sample and present a quantile-quantile plot of the modified sample in Fig. 19.3. As shown, the existence of fat tails is evident in this plot as well. In fact, the evidence of a fat right tail is more pronounced in the subsample than it was in the entire sample.

In order to calculate the stock of military capabilities as outlined above, I set $\delta = 0.75$, as in Kugler et al. (1980). This implies a depreciation rate of 25%. I then construct the stock measure using the data on military expenditures for each country. The natural logarithm of the relative stock of military capability of the United States is plotted in Fig. 19.4. I first test for a unit root using an augmented Dickey-Fuller

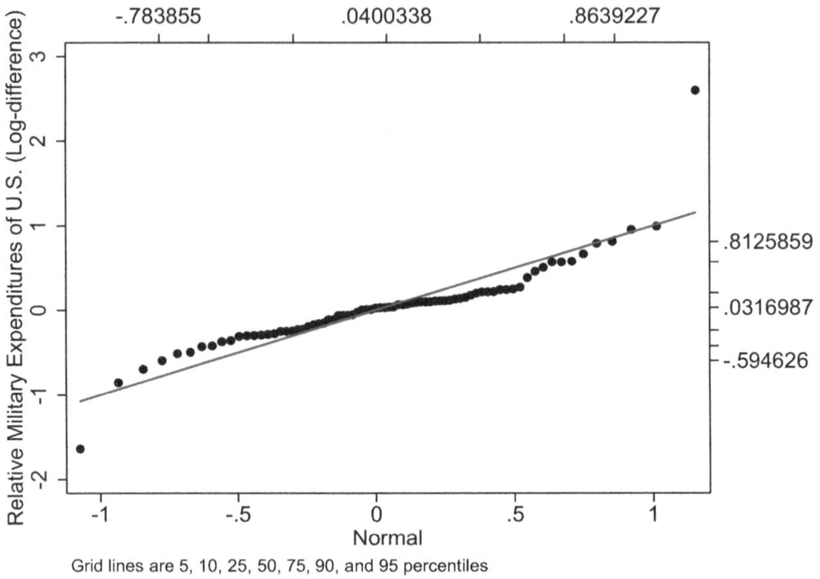

Fig. 19.2 Q-Q plot: relative military expenditures

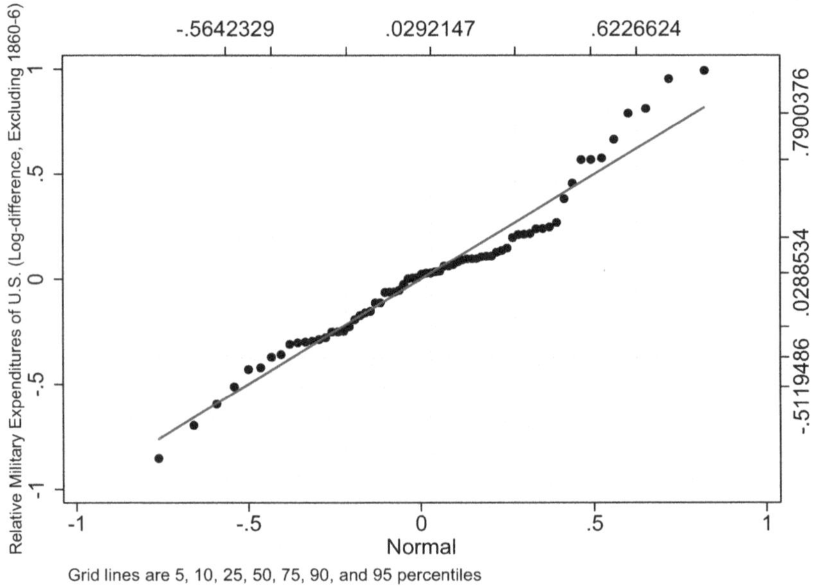

Fig. 19.3 Q-Q Plot: relative military expenditures (excluding 1860–1866)

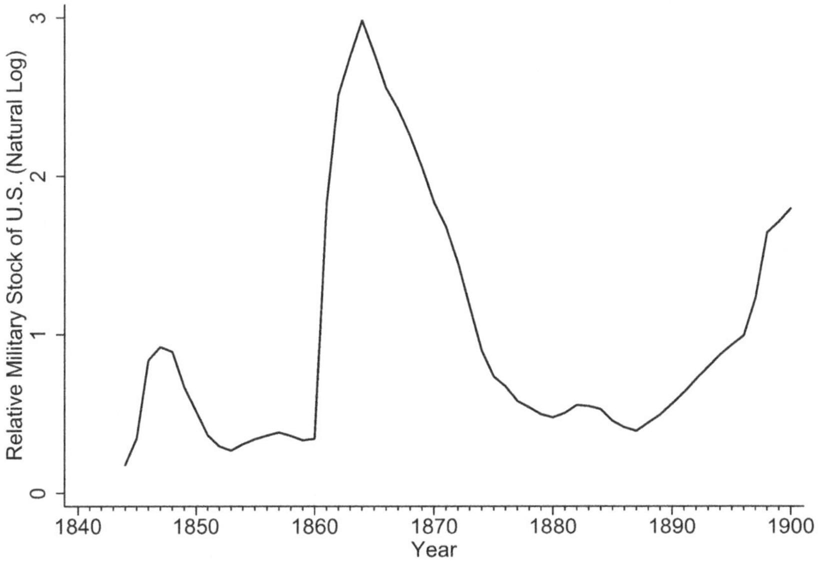

Fig. 19.4 Relative Stock of Military Capability, U.S. (Natural Logarithm). The figure plots the ratio of the stock of US military capability to the stock of Spanish military capability. (*Source*: Correlates of War Project, author's calculations)

test. The results are shown in the second row of Table 19.1. As shown, one cannot reject the null hypothesis of a unit root.

In Fig. 19.5, I present a quantile-quantile plot of the log-difference of the stock of military capacity. As shown, there is no evidence of a fat left tail, but there is some evidence of fat right tail. However, this series does not appear to be consistent with a normal distribution, even in the absence of fat tails.

Finally, Fig. 19.6 plots the natural logarithm of relative military personnel of the United States. The data are again from the Correlates of War project. The measure shows a slight upward trend with a large increase during the US Civil War. The results of an augmented Dickey-Fuller test are shown in the third row of Table 19.1. As shown, one cannot reject the null hypothesis of a unit root.

In Fig. 19.7, I present a quantile-quantile plot using the log-difference of the relative military personnel of the United States. As shown, there is again evidence of fat tails in the distribution.The implications of the model presented in this paper are predicated on the assumption that Eq. (19.2) is an accurate representation of the time path of relative military capability. For each measure of military capability used in this paper, there is evidence of a unit root and evidence of jumps that are larger than would be predicted by a normal distribution. It therefore seems reasonable to argue that a president weighing the expected net benefit of war and also aware of the historical evolution of relative military capability, would behave in a manner that is consistent with the model I have outlined above. In the next section, I conduct Monte Carlo experiments to determine the probability of reneging for various perceived benefit-cost ratios.

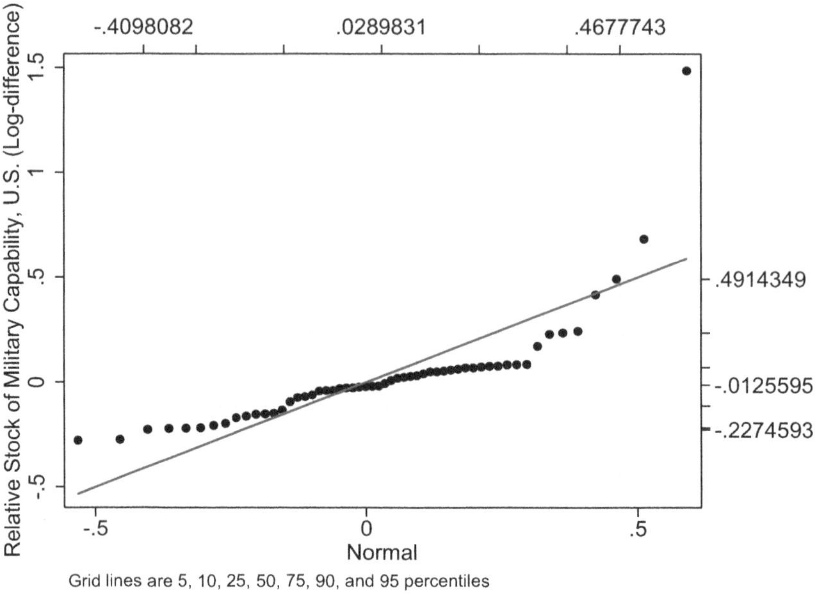

Fig. 19.5 Q-Q plot: relative stock of military capability

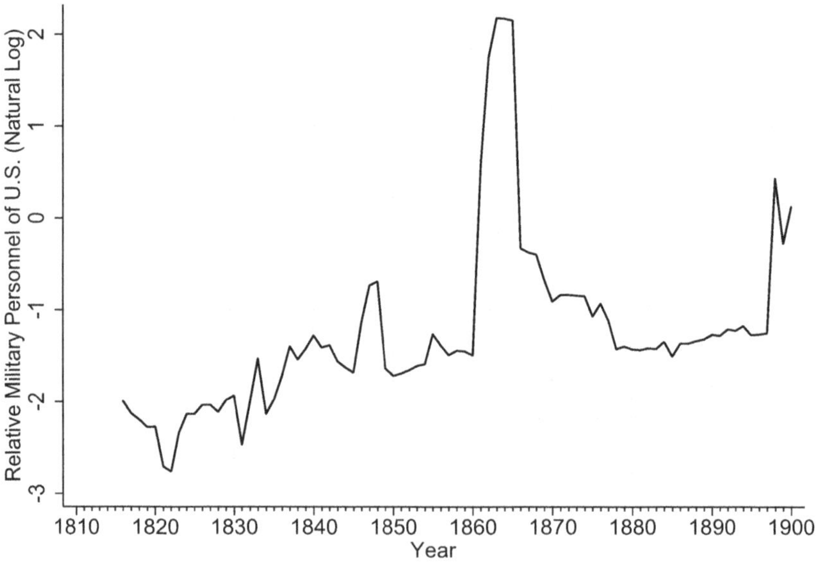

Fig. 19.6 Relative military personnel, U.S. (natural logarithm). This figure plots the ratio of US military personnel to Spanish military personnel. (*Source*: Correlates of War Project)

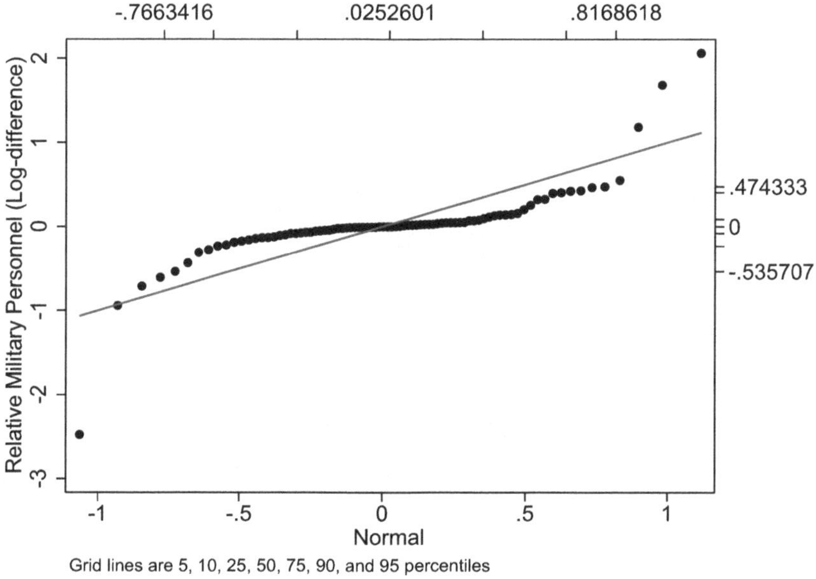

Fig. 19.7 Q-Q plot: relative military personnel

19.4.2 A Monte Carlo Experiment

In this section, I conduct Monte Carlo experiments to determine the probability of reneging on a commitment to peace, given that relative military capability behaves according to eq. (2). The idea behind the Monte Carlo experiment is to construct relevant counterfactuals. Using data on military capabilities and Eq. (19.2), I can simulate hypothetical paths for relative military capabilities during McKinley's first term in office. I can then estimate the probability that relative military capabilities hit the threshold for reneging and initiating conflict. What this does is allow me to get a sense of the probability that McKinley would have reneged on his commitment to peace based solely on my model and the historical data. The experiment thus gives a sense in which reneging is likely. To do this, I simulate 100,000 different paths for M, given this initial value and given the assumption that it behaves according to Eq. (19.2). For a given perceived benefit, B, and cost, C, I calculate a cumulative distribution function for the probability that $t \leq T^*$, for $t = 1, 2, \ldots, T$. I then plot the CDF for the first term of the McKinley administration.

To perform the Monte Carlo experiments, I need to calibrate the parameters of Eq. (19.2). In the Monte Carlo experiment, and consistent with the assumption of the model, I assume constant jump sizes, ϕ_1 and ϕ_2. In reality, the magnitude of the jump should also likely be considered a random variable. However, by treating the jump size as exogenous, this allows me to calibrate the jump sizes to be consistent with the data that I presented in the previous section.

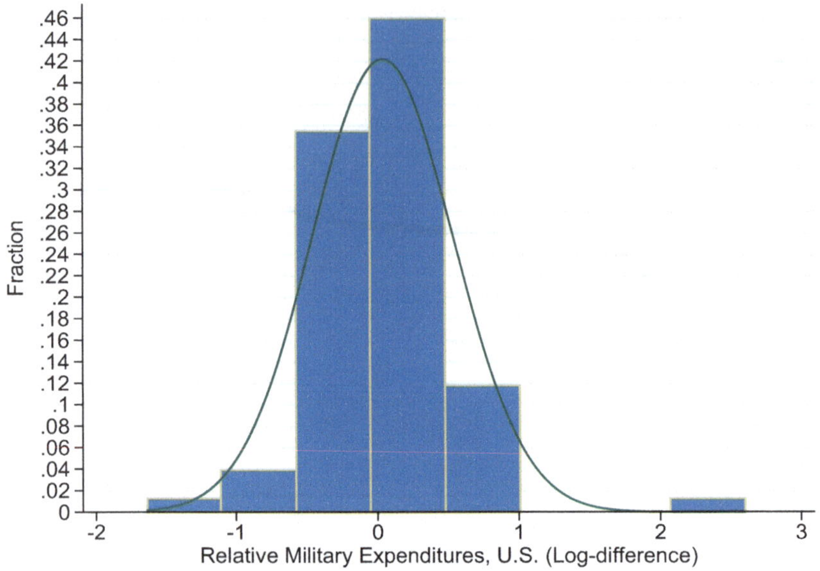

Fig. 19.8 Histogram of log-difference of relative US military expenditures

Figure 19.8 presents a histogram of the log-difference of relative military expenditures. A normal distribution overlays the histogram. Based on this histogram, I set $\lambda_1 = \lambda_2 = 0.01$, $\phi_1 = 8.49$, and $\phi_2 = 0.78$.[7] To calibrate μ and σ, I estimate the mean and variance of the log-difference of military expenditures. The average change in the logarithm of the ratio of US military expenditures to Spanish military expenditures is 0.04 with a standard deviation of 0.5. Thus, I set $\sigma = 0.5$. To calibrate μ, recall that $dm = [\mu - (1/2)\sigma^2]dt + \sigma dz + \phi_1 dq_1 - \phi_2 dq_2$. Thus, the expected value of the log-difference of M satisfies

$$\mu - (1/2)\sigma^2 + \lambda_1\phi_1 - \lambda_2\phi_2 = 0.04$$

It follows that $\mu = 0.0879$. Finally, I set the initial value of relative military expenditures to $M_0 = 4.4$, which is the average ratio of military expenditures between 1896 and 1897.

I consider three perceived benefit-cost ratios. I assume that the perceived benefits are 2, 2.5, or 2.6 times the cost of the conflict.[8] It is important to note that, in terms of the model, these are ex ante estimates of the benefits and costs associated with

[7] All else equal, the jumps imply that $M_t = (1 + \phi_1)M_{t-1}$ and $M_t = (1 - \phi_2)M_{t-1}$. It follows that the log-difference is $\ln(M_t/M_{t-1}) = \ln(1 + \phi_1)$ and $\ln(M_t/M_{t-1}) = \ln(1 - \phi_2)$. The value in the left-tail of the distribution is approximately −1.5. The value in the right tail is approximately 2.25. Using these formulas, this implies that $1.5 = \ln(1 - \phi_2)$, or $\phi_2 = 0.78$, and $2.25 = \ln(1 + \phi_1)$, or $\phi_1 = 8.49$.

[8] Here, I am defining the benefit-cost ratio in terms of the model as B/C. In the Monte Carlo experiments, I normalize $C = 1$ and then set B equal to the corresponding values.

war. Unfortunately, it is hard to know (or quantify) these ex ante estimates. Ex post, the budgetary cost of the Spanish-American War was approximately $270 million (Rockoff 2012; Edwards 2014).[9] Thus, assuming that the true cost of war was known, these ratios assume that the perceived benefit of going to war was between $540 million and $702 million.

To get an idea of how accurate these perceived benefits are, consider that prior to the Spanish- American War, firms had invested approximately $50 million in Cuba (Gould 1982, p. 24). Assuming this was all invested in tangible capital, a real interest rate of 5% and a depreciation rate of 10% would imply the present discounted value of that capital is approximately $333 million. Thus, the destruction or confiscation of wealth alone would amount to a benefit-cost ratio of 1.3. Prior to Cuba's war with Spain, trade between the United States and Cuba amounted to approximately $100 million annually. However, during the Cuban rebellion, this declined by two-thirds (Offner 2004). If the United States expected this decline in trade to continue indefinitely, this would imply a present discounted value of $1.32 billion of lost trade. Even if one imagines that the United States could only recover one-quarter of the trade that had been lost, it would still seem reasonable to assume a perceived benefit-cost ratio between 2 and 2.6 based on economic factors alone. Furthermore, it is important to note that this justification for benefit-cost ratios is basely solely on the direct economic benefits associated with war. There are additional benefits to politicians, such as McKinley and others, that they would accrue if victorious. In addition, the United States would stand to benefit in terms of military prestige and greater power in the Western Hemisphere. These benefits are hard to quantify, but certainly bolster the case for the assumption I've made about the benefit-cost ratios used in the Monte Carlo experiments.

In Figs. 19.9, 19.10, and 19.11, I plot the cumulative distribution functions for the Monte Carlo experiments associated with the benefit-cost ratios of 2, 2.5, and 2.6, respectively, for McKinley's first term as president. Each figure plots the probability that the United States will have hit the optimal threshold and entered the war at or before the corresponding time period. By presenting the probabilities in terms of time, it is possible to examine the timing of entry within McKinley's first term. For the case in which $B/C = 2$, the threshold is $M^* = 9.97$. According to the model, this corresponds to a probability of victory of 91%. As shown in Fig. 19.9, the probability of reneging on the commitment to peace and entering the war by the end of McKinley's first term is 4%. The probability of entering by some point in 1898 is approximately 1%.

If the perceived benefit-cost ratio is 2.5, the threshold is $M^* = 5.12$. According to the model, this corresponds to a probability of victory of 84%. As shown in Fig. 19.10, the probability of McKinley reneging on the commitment to peace by the end of his term is approximately 17%. In addition, the probability of reneging after only one year of McKinley's presidency is approximately 4.6%.

[9] As both Rockoff and Edwards note, the cost of the war turned out to be larger than its budgetary outlay due to things like pensions for veterans. Edwards also considers the uncompensated costs associated with war-related injuries. Nonetheless, I use the budgetary cost as a baseline estimate.

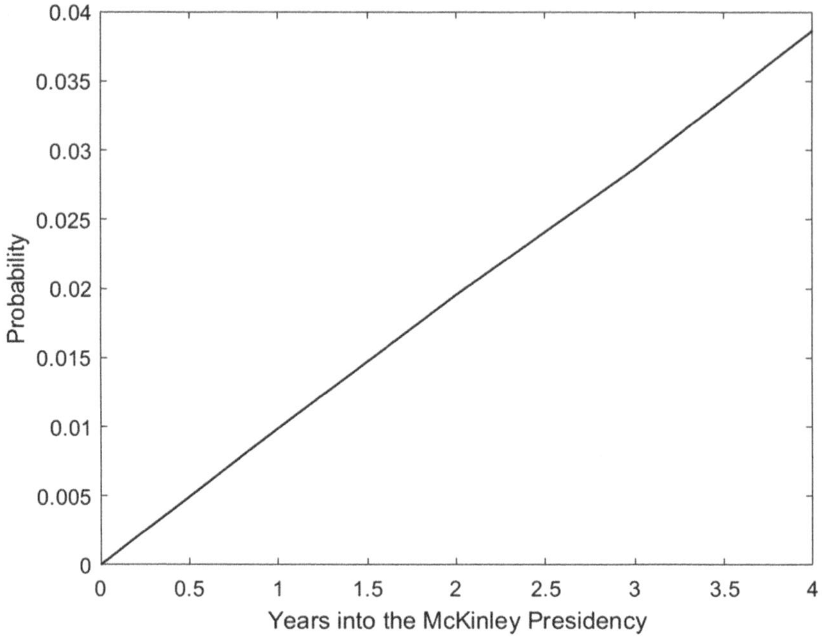

Fig. 19.9 Cumulative distribution function of reneging. This figure plots the probability that the United States would renege on its commitment to peace at or before time *t*, assuming a benefit-cost ratio of 2

If the perceived benefits were 2.6 times the cost, then the threshold is $M^* = 4.71$. According to the model, this corresponds to a probability of victory of 82%. As shown in Fig. 19.11, the probability of reneging on the commitment to peace by the end of McKinley's first term is nearly 35%. In addition, the probability of reneging in 1898 is 17.5%. It is important to note that once the perceived benefit gets to 2.7 times the cost, the probability of reneging at any point during the first term of McKinley's presidency is 100%, given the initial relative military capabilities of the United States.

The results of these simulations capture the basic idea of the model. The decision to go to war should ideally be made from a position of power. If a country does not have the military capabilities to make a victory sufficiently likely, then it is optimal to commit to peace and try to avoid conflict. However, there is some threshold of relative military capability at which it becomes optimal to renege on the commitment to peace and to enter into conflict.

The simulations illustrate that as the perceived benefits of war increase relative to the costs, a country lowers its threshold of relative military capability. This has two implications. First, it suggests that as the perceived benefits of war increase, a country is willing to enter conflict with a lower probability of victory. Second, the results suggest that as the perceived benefits increase, a country is likely to renege on its commitment to peace *sooner* than it would for a lower benefit.

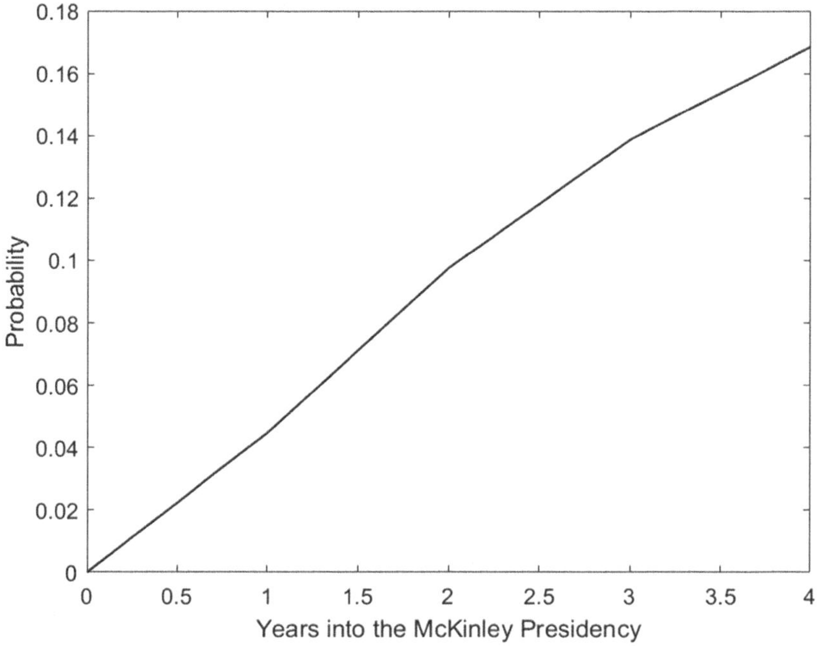

Fig. 19.10 Cumulative distribution function of reneging. This figure plots the probability that the United States would renege on its commitment to peace at or before time *t*, assuming a benefit-cost ratio of 2.5

The takeaway with regard to the Spanish-American War is particularly important. While the popular narratives among historians suggest that McKinley's decision to go to war was due to his weakness in the face of pressure, this paper provides an alternative explanation. In particular, my model suggests that the decision about whether or not (and when) to renege on McKinley's commitment to peace depends on the perceived benefits and costs associated with conflict and expectations about the relative military capacity of the United States. The model shows that if the perceived benefits of war were 2.6 times the perceived costs, then the probability of reneging within McKinley's first term is quite high. Whether or not this is an accurate estimate of the perceived costs and benefits depends on the counterfactual. In other words, what did McKinley, and others, believe would happen if the United States maintained the commitment to peace indefinitely? Suppose, for example, that McKinley and others believed that abstaining from the conflict would result in a destruction of the capital investment of US interests in Cuba or a continuation of the collapse of trade with Cuba. In this context, and given the investment and trade figures presented above, it is likely that the perceived benefits of preventing the destruction of capital and a loss of trade with Cuba would be sufficiently large on their own to generate a benefit-cost ratio of 2.6 or greater. This is not to mention the benefits to decision-makers, such as McKinley, who might stand to gain from better

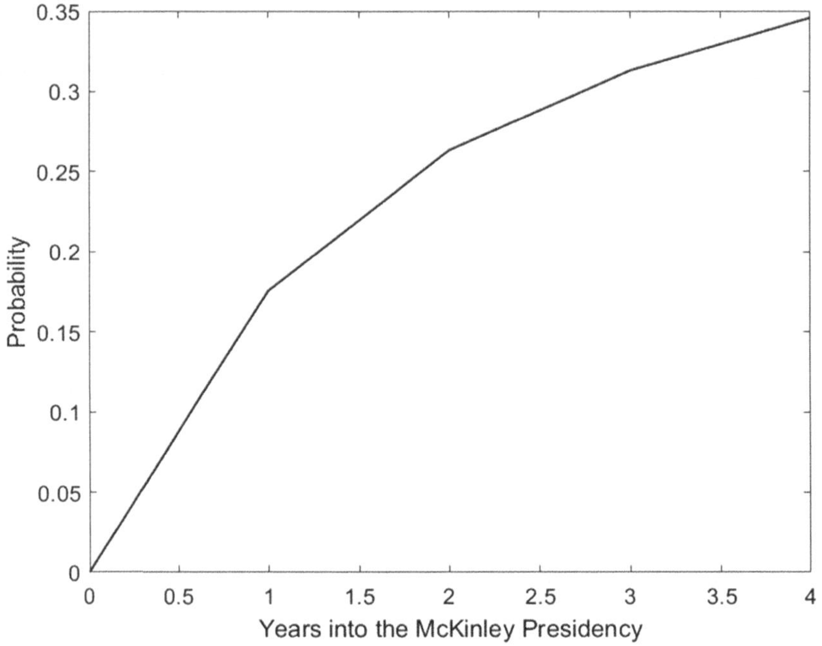

Fig. 19.11 Cumulative distribution function of reneging. This figure plots the probability that the United States would renege on its commitment to peace at or before time *t*, assuming a benefit-cost ratio of 2.6

re-election prospects and a greater standing in the world of the United States and its military.

It is also particularly important to note that the probability of entering conflict in this model should be seen as a *lower bound* estimate. The reason is that the model assumes that the only things that the president cares about are the perceived benefits, the perceived costs, and the expected future path of relative military capabilities. In reality, other events can influence decision-making. My model, for example, does not account for the explosion of the USS Maine off the coast of Havana in February 1898. Nonetheless, the model does present an important starting point to considering the possibility of conflict without attempting to ascertain the true nature and/or inner thoughts of William McKinley.

Finally, the model does not draw any normative conclusions. My simulations and subsequent discussion should not be seen as my attempt to say that the Spanish-American War was a good idea or a bad idea. Similarly, the purpose of my paper is not to draw any conclusions about whether William McKinley was a good or a bad president. Rather, the point of my paper and of my model is to say that if we take seriously the notion that countries are more likely to use force when they are in a position of power, then we can better understand the decision-making process of leaders by modeling their decision-making with this characteristic in mind.

19.5 Conclusion

When President William McKinley took office, he claimed to be committed to peace with Spain. However, by 1898 the United States was at war with the Spanish. A common narrative among historians is that McKinley's inability to maintain peace is due to his weakness in the face of mounting pressure for war. These narratives seem to stem from a normative premise. For example, if one begins with the premise that the Spanish-American War was unnecessary, then one must explain why William McKinley reneged on his commitment to peace in such a short period of time. Historians seem to have accepted this premise and therefore have traditionally looked for factors that might explain why McKinley had a change of heart. If one accepts the premise that the war was unnecessary, then the abundance of evidence regarding the presence of outside pressures makes it easy to accept the conclusion that McKinley simply caved to external pressure.

However, there are problems with this line of thinking. First, to proclaim that the war was unnecessary requires an analysis of the relevant counterfactuals. For any historical event, the ability to construct counterfactuals is always easier with the benefit of hindsight. Second, by accepting the premise that the war was unnecessary, it frees the researcher from examining the incentives to go to war. For example, if the war was unnecessary, then there should have been little incentive to go to war. This therefore begs the question as to how the McKinley and the United States would end up at war. The researcher is naturally led to an examination of McKinley himself and the role of outside pressures.

In this paper, I approach the question from a different perspective. I focus on the incentives to go to war. This requires thinking about the war in terms of the ex ante estimates of the benefits of a successful war with Spain and the ex ante cost estimates of such a conflict. The United States had attempted to purchase Cuba from the Spanish and had made it an official policy that the control of Cuba would either rest in the hands of Spain or the United States. The rebellion in Cuba created unique problems for the United States. If the Cubans successfully expelled the Spanish, what role would the United States play? How would a Cuban victory affect US business interests in Cuba? Furthermore, how long would a prolonged Cuban rebellion against Spain affect the capital investment of US firms operating in Cuba? At the same time, the Spanish were nearly gone from the Western Hemisphere. If the United States went to war with Spain and won, the United States could potentially remove Spanish interests in Cuba and Puerto Rico and thereby establish the stronger role in the Western Hemisphere – an important goal of US foreign policy since the outline of the Monroe Doctrine.

When viewed in this context, it is easy to see why President McKinley might see potentially large benefits from a successful war with Spain. Such a conflict would protect established trade relationships and capital investment in Cuba, expel the Spanish from the Western Hemisphere, and enhance the international standing and reputation of the United States and its military.

Against this backdrop, I argue that the best way to think about McKinley's decision to go to war is by thinking about his decision as an optimal timing problem. While McKinley had expressed a commitment to peace, he also promised to use force if necessary. If one is going to threaten the use of force on a potential adversary, there must be some threshold for reneging on the commitment to peace. Furthermore, this threshold should be one that puts the United States in a position of strength. Given the potential costs and benefits of a successful military conflict with Spain, I show how to derive this threshold. I then use simulations of the model to determine the probability of reneging.

What the model demonstrates is that the probability of reneging at any given point in time is a function of the perceived benefit-cost ratio. If the ex ante estimates of the benefits of military conflict with Spain are sufficiently high then the probability that McKinley would renege in his first term are sufficiently high. My paper therefore suggests that to understand why McKinley reneged on his commitment to peace so early in his presidency, one should begin by examining the magnitude of the perceived benefits of a successful war within the McKinley administration. Furthermore, I show that back-of-the-envelope estimates of the potential loss of trade and capital alone might be sufficiently large to understand why McKinley was willing to renege on his commitment to peace after only one year in office.

Finally, I should note that my paper does not prove an absence of outside influence in McKinley's decision-making. In fact, it is possible that outside influence might have either increased the benefits or reduced the political cost of going to war in the context of my model. Nonetheless, the point of my paper is to challenge these conventional narratives. One can think of my model as an attempt to examine the likelihood that McKinley would have gone to war if none of these outside influences was a factor. Judged by this metric, the model and the simulation results suggest that one need not rely on outside influence to explain McKinley's decision to go to war.

Acknowledgments This paper is the last paper that I ever discussed with John Murray. I mentioned the paper to John during our last, long lunch together. I was afraid that economists would think this was political science, political scientists would think I was trying to make a contribution to theory, and that historians would think I spent too much time on a model and didn't disprove their existing hypotheses. However, John really liked the idea and encouraged me to pursue it. He agreed that I might find it difficult to find the correct audience, but he thought that it was a compelling argument. As we departed that lunch, he told me to keep him posted on my progress. It therefore seems appropriate to include it here.

References

Beard C, Beard M (1934) The rise of American civilization. Macmillan, New York

Edwards RD (2014) U.S. War costs: two parts temporary, one part permanent. J Public Econ 113:54–66

Fordham BO (2004) A very sharp sword: the influence of military capabilities on American decisions to use force. J Confl Resolut 48(5):632–656

Gould L (1982) The Spanish-American war and president McKinley. University Press of Kansas, Lawrence

Hendrickson JR, Salter AW (2016) A theory of why the ruthless revolt. *Economics & Politics* 28(3):296–316

Kapur N (2011) William McKinley's values and the origins of the Spanish-American War. Pres Stud Quart 41(1):18–38

Kugler JJ, Organski AFK, Fox DJ (1980) Deterrence and the arms race: the impotence of power. Int Secur 4(4):105–138

Most BA, Starr H (1989) Inquiry, logic, and international politics. University of South Carolina Press, Columbia

Offner JL (1992) The unwanted war. University of North Carolina Press, Chapel Hill

Offner JL (2004) President McKinley and the Spanish-American war. Pres Stud Quart 34:50–61

Rockoff H (2012) America's way of war: war and the US Economy from the Spanish-American war to the Persian Gulf war. Cambridge University Press, Cambridge

Singer JD (1987) Reconstructing the correlates of war dataset on material capabilities of states, 1816–1985. Int Interact 14:115–132

Singer JD, Bremer S, Stuckey J (1972) Capability distribution, uncertainty, and major power war, 1820–1965. In: Russell B (ed) Peace, war, and numbers. Sage Publishing, Beverly Hills, pp 19–48

Williams WA (1972) The tragedy of American diplomacy. Dell Publishing Company, New York

Wisan JE (1934) The Cuban crisis as reflected in the New York Press (1895–1898). Columbia University Press, New York, NY

Chapter 20
Capitalism and the Good Society: The Original Case for and Against Commerce

Daniel Cullen

Abstract The contemporary debate over the morality of capitalism would benefit from attention to eighteenth-century philosophical arguments for and against commercial life. Well before Karl Marx, Jean-Jacques Rousseau condemned the emerging commercial society as incompatible with equality, freedom, and virtue. And well before Milton Friedman, Adam Smith defended commerce as a system of natural liberty that indeed fostered considerable inequality but only in the course of dramatically improving the condition of the poor. Smith shared many of Rousseau's concerns about the negative effects of commerce and directly addressed them in his major works. Smith concluded that the benefits of commercial life outweighed the risks and contributed substantially to human progress—a possibility Rousseau vigorously denied.

Keywords *Amour-propre* · Capitalism · Commerce · Dependence/Independence · Division of Labor · Equality/Inequality · Invisible Hand · System of Natural Liberty

One of the pleasures of teaching in a liberal arts college is the opportunity to cross the boundaries ordinarily separating philosophy, politics, and economics, and to discover colleagues keen to seize it. John Murray was such a one and this essay is inspired by several conversations I had with John about the philosophical foundations of commercial society. The assumption that capitalism is immoral and that any good society must replace commercial values with "humane" ones, functions as an article of faith in contemporary intellectual culture. But the philosophical spokesmen for the emergent commercial republic of the eighteenth century defended its moral as well its economic superiority to traditional conceptions of virtue *qua* self-renunciation. Hume argued that the good society did not require a passion for the public good characteristic of a military camp. Citizens animated with "a spirit of

D. Cullen (✉)
Rhodes College, Memphis, TN, USA
e-mail: cullen@rhodes.edu

P. Gray et al. (eds.), *Standard of Living*, Studies in Economic History,
https://doi.org/10.1007/978-3-031-06477-7_20

avarice and industry, art and luxury" would indirectly serve the public good (Hume 1997, p. 263). Society could unify and prosper better by allowing the natural desire to better one's condition to follow its course. No one acts for the sake of society, but without their intending it the self-interested behavior of individuals makes others better off than they would be without it.

The encouragement of commerce could be justified by its utilitarian effects alone, but Adam Smith argued that commerce also promoted freedom and virtue. Jean-Jacques Rousseau famously denied every part of that complex proposition. Perhaps because of his own research on how the Shakers managed the tension of communitarian and commercial values, John was fascinated by the Rousseauian critique, and especially by the discovery that Smith's argument can be read as a reply to it. We discussed developing a course that would use this Enlightenment dialogue (carried out one-sidedly by Smith) to deepen reflection on the continuing argument about the morality of capitalism. My essay merely sketches some of the philosophical questions that arise in reading Smith and Rousseau together. But I hope that it conveys some sense of the dialogue with a superb teacher, scholar, and friend that, sadly, I must now continue one-sidedly.

*

Capitalist society faces a crisis today, but it is not the inevitability of overproduction predicted by Marx. It is rather a moral critique older than capitalism itself, and more profound than the objection that capitalism systematically fails the many while it benefits the few. That objection is belied by the empirical evidence, marshaled by economic historians like Deidre McCloskey, that the market system of production, exchange and, above all, innovation has improved the material condition of human beings—not at the same rate, nor to the same degree, but dramatically (McCloskey 2010). Failed experiments with central planning confirm that there is no serious economic alternative to the market mechanism (suitably regulated) if our goal is material improvement. But here indeed is a case where "ought" does not follow from "is." The fact that capitalism makes the poor better off than any realistic alternative notwithstanding, the conviction persists that it fails the test of morality insofar as it not only tolerates but exacerbates inequality.

Now the case for capitalism concedes that in a commercial society people will prosper at different rates and that the gap between the condition of the poorest and the richest may be vast. The defense is that while the rich get richer, the poor get richer too and, in any case, the social problem is not the gap between rich and poor per se but the fact that some do not have enough (Frankfurt 2015). Distinguishing between poverty and inequality is crucial, for two reasons: first, capitalism necessarily engenders inequality as a by-product of prosperity; second, and more importantly, a free society will necessarily be unequal, and an equal society will necessarily be unfree. Different talents, opportunities, and luck will produce different results, and coercion would be required to reimpose the egalitarian pattern continuously disrupted by "capitalist acts between consenting adults."[1] As cogent as this defense may be, the identification of "social justice" with equality persists, fortified perhaps by a related belief that unequal success in the market is "unfair" since winners often do not deserve their gains, nor losers their losses. This objection assumes that capitalism is a system that aims to reward merit. Former president Barack Obama liked to say that our implicit social promise is: "if you're willing to work hard and play by the rules, you should be able to get ahead." The most astute defense of capitalism insists, however, that the market does not, indeed *cannot*, reward merit. Market success is a token not of the moral virtue of producers but the value created for, and measured by, consumers (Hayek 1960, pp. 86–88, 93–99; Nozick 1974, 160–64).

To these moral intuitions about equality and merit we must add a third hurdle faced by the proponents of capitalism: its reliance on the profit motive. However facile the identification may be, moral virtue is frequently associated with altruism, and capitalism rests on the insight that the free play of self-interest is a more reliable human motive and a greater contributor to the general welfare than benevolence. The deepest critique of the goodness of capitalist society, the one that lingers despite the great enrichment underscored by McCloskey, has less to do with equality than with virtue.

So far I have discussed "capitalism," a term popularized by Marx, its most famous critic, rather than Adam Smith, its most famous defender. Smith refers to "commercial society" and, more fundamentally, to "the system of natural liberty." Smith remains significant to us because his overarching concern was to demonstrate the morality of commercial society by explaining its systematic conversion of self-seeking behavior into virtue, or at least into a virtuous result (Cropsey 1977, p. 85). The case for the goodness of commercial society could be justified on utilitarian grounds alone, but Smith proposed that commerce also encouraged freedom and virtue. It was this proposition that Jean-Jacques Rousseau explicitly and vigorously denied.

*

The "great principle" unifying Rousseau's diverse works is that "nature made man happy and good, and that society depraves him and makes him miserable" (Rousseau 1990, p. 213). In his seminal philosophic work, the *Discourse on the Origin and Foundations of Inequality Among Men*, published in 1755, Rousseau argued that "social man" is a corruption of natural man and that the former's contemporary incarnation, the bourgeois, is a self painfully divided between inclination and duty. Social life, Rousseau thought, forces upon the individual a psychologically damaging contradiction between being and seeming that transforms his natural and benign self-love (*amour de soi*) into *amour-propre*, a self-centeredness fixated on comparisons with others.

[1] The clever phrase is of course Robert Nozick's.

The *Discourse* offers a conjectural account of the modifications to man's original and solitary condition that "make a being evil while making him sociable," and "bring the world and man to the point where we see them" (Rousseau 1964, p. 140). The individual we observe now has become dependent on others for the satisfaction of his needs, but in clinging to the spirit of his lost independence he remains separated from those with whom he ought to be united. This tension between the objective dependence of social man and his subjective independence leaves him in a state of profound alienation. His *amour-propre* craves the recognition of his equally self-centered fellows, a zero-sum game he can never win. As memorably described by Allan Bloom, social man, the bourgeois, "is the man who, when dealing with others, thinks only of himself, and on the other hand, in his understanding of himself, thinks only of others" (Bloom 1979, p. 5).

Rousseau presents humanity's social development as coeval with the loss of natural independence: "From the moment one man needed the help of another, as soon as they observed that it was useful for a single person to have provisions for two, equality disappeared, property was introduced, labor became necessary; and vast forests were changed into smiling fields which had to be watered with the sweat of men, and in which slavery and misery were soon seen to germinate and grow with the crops" (Rousseau 1964, pp. 151–52).[2] The dependency coincident with commercial society is uniquely soul-distorting, impinging on the individual in a way the challenges of self-preservation in the natural condition did not. *Amour-propre* fuels the desire to be preferred to the other people on whom one now depends for the satisfaction of expanded needs. In the social condition, those needs "bring us together in proportion as our passions divide us, and the more we become enemies of our fellow men, the less we can do without them" (Rousseau 1978, p. 158). Man as nature formed him was, Rousseau imagines, "a being acting always by fixed and invariable principles," but social man's relations lack consistency and regularity and "he can never be sure of being the same for two moments in his life. Peace and happiness are only momentary for him; nothing is permanent except the misery that results from all these vicissitudes" (Rousseau 1964, p. 91, 1978, p. 158).

In a resonant passage, Rousseau asserts that "savage man and civilized man differ so much in the bottom of their hearts and inclinations that what constitutes the supreme happiness of one would reduce the other to despair" (Rousseau 1964, pp. 178–79). In the course of economic progress, however, civilized man actually forfeits his happiness, and this conviction underlies Rousseau's sweeping dissent against the Enlightenment project as a whole:

> All our writers regard the crowning achievement of our century's politics to be the sciences, the arts, luxury, commerce, laws, and all the other bonds which, by tightening the social ties among men through self-interest, place them all in a position of mutual dependence, impose on them mutual needs and common interests, and oblige everyone to contribute to everyone else's happiness in order to secure their own. … What a wonderful thing, then, to have put men in a position where they can only live together by obstructing, supplanting, deceiving, betraying, destroying one another! From now on we must take care never to let ourselves be

[2] Smith translates this passage in his "Letter to the Edinburgh Review."

> seen as we are: because for every two men whose interests coincide, perhaps a hundred thousand oppose them, and the only way to succeed is either to deceive or ruin all those people. (Rousseau 1997b, p. 100)

Rousseau's response to the malaise of commercial life was an argument for a *political* economy, a vision of civic equality, but one removed from both the redistributive economics and the liberal politics of our time.[3] If the human predicament originates in the socialization of natural man, restoring equality and independence requires a second transformation of social man into a citizen. The cause of unhappiness is the contradiction between our inclinations and our duties, between our nature and the requirements of social life. If it is the dividedness of existence that makes it unbearable, the solution is to reunify the individual on the plane of political society. Rousseau reasons as follows: "Natural man is entirely for himself. He is numerical unity, the absolute whole which is relative only to itself or its kind." "Civil man" can only be only "a fractional unity dependent on the denominator; his value … determined by his relation to the whole, which is the social body." Only through a republican dedication to a common good could a unified existence be restored to human beings who are "swept along in contrary routes," forced to divide themselves between contrary impulses that render them neither good for themselves nor for others (Rousseau, 1979, pp. 39–41). Rousseau's conception of citizenship involves an extraordinary transformation in the individual's mode of being, replacing, as it were, his absolute existence with a relative one that "transports the I into the common unity, with the result that each individual believes himself no longer one but a part of the unity and no longer feels except within the whole" (Rousseau 1979, pp. 39–40, 1978, Social Contract 1.6.1).

In no way did Rousseau supposes that identification with the social whole was natural—it is profoundly unnatural; but a corrupt social condition having emerged out of a healthy natural order, both must now give way to a reformed political order. Rousseau speculated that the tangled web of interpersonal dependency characteristic of commercial society might be transcended in a new dependence of each on all. Equal subordination to law, in Rousseau's view, avoids the problem of personal dependence and approximates the dependence on things characteristic of the natural condition. Social man is the individual who by suffering the contradictions of the social state is no longer an individual. In becoming divided he has become a double being, an impossible human model. Rousseau could not subscribe to the sophisticated logic of deriving unity from the very private interest that divides society's members. He proposed in favor of a positive bond that unites individuals not by their self-love, but by the love of their civic union, but the entire rationale of the latter is to protect the individual from dependence on another's will.[4]

*

[3] I draw from Ignatieff (1984, pp. 114–15).

[4] I paraphrase the analysis of Manent (1977, p. 204).

A new consensus has taken hold among scholars of eighteenth-century thought that Adam Smith took Jean-Jacques Rousseau seriously, if not literally. Not literally, because in his *Letter to the Edinburgh Review* heralding Rousseau's *Discourse on Inequality*, Smith (1980, p. 251) remarks that Rousseau's account of the solitary condition of natural man and his transition from nature to society was deliberately rhetorical and therefore defied analysis. Smith translated three passages from the *Discourse* and presented them without further comment, but the selections reveal great penetration and the evidence is compelling that Smith subsequently took both Rousseau's philosophical anthropology and his rhetoric very seriously indeed. In some of the most incisive passages in *The Theory of Moral Sentiments* and the *Wealth of Nations*, Smith uses the *Discourse* as a whetstone.[5] As a new wave of scholarship has shown, Smith shared Rousseau's concern for equality, liberty, and virtue and harbored his own ambivalence about commercial society; but, while accepting much of Rousseau's diagnosis of its ills, Smith believed that commercial life could generate its own cure.[6]

The *Letter's* first excerpt highlights Rousseau's claim that, from the moment one man needed the assistance of another, equality disappeared, property was introduced, and labor became necessary. The second describes the disjuncture of seeming and being following fast upon the new needs that divest natural man of his independence. The final passage fittingly quotes Rousseau's peroration on the inversely proportional happiness and misery of natural and social man and the irony that, "in the midst of so much philosophy, so much humanity, so much politeness, and so many sublime maxims we have nothing but a dreadful and frivolous exterior; honour without virtue, reason without wisdom, and pleasure without happiness" (Smith 1980, p. 254).

At various points in *Theory of Moral Sentiments* and *Wealth of Nations*, Smith revisits the Rousseauian themes he highlighted in the *Letter*. In the first passage, Rousseau had emphasized that as long as primitive individuals could supply their needs by their own productive efforts, they could live "free, healthy, humane and happy (Smith 1980, p. 252)."[7] He describes incipient sociality, intriguingly, as "*un commerce independent*," a phrase Smith translates as "an independent society," which is faithful to Rousseau's evocation of a condition prior to relations of buying and selling. Yet, Rousseau continues, from the moment one man needed the help of another, as soon as they observed "that it was useful (*utile*) for one person to have provisions for two," labor (*travail*) became necessary to satisfy inflated needs. Surprisingly, Rousseau does not regard the activities of sewing skins, improving bows and arrows, and carving canoes as *labor*. His reason is that these tasks or arts

[5] Smith wrote his review within a year of the *Discourse*'s publication and only four years before the appearance of *Theory of Moral Sentiments*.

[6] For a careful analysis of Smith's treatment of Rousseau from which I have benefited, see Rasmussen (2008, pp. 59–71). See also Hanley (2008, pp. 137–58).

[7] The latter proviso is intriguing. Does Rousseau mean that the contentedness of the first human beings was fragile and liable to disruption? Or does he mean that their happiness was as limited as they were, as primitive as their rustic dwellings?

did not require "the cooperation of several hands." Properly speaking, labor is coeval with the division of labor that destroys the independence original man enjoyed so long as his "subjection" to nature remained unmediated by other men.[8] For a time, nascent social man continued to enjoy the equilibrium of power and desire that made solitary or independent existence possible. As Rousseau elaborated in his contemporaneous *Essay on the Origin of Languages*, in the primitive social state, "no one knew or desired anything but what was ready to hand; [man's] needs, far from drawing him closer to those like himself, draw him away from them (Rousseau 1997a, p. 269)." Need, Rousseau maintains, establishes nothing beyond a solitary relation of the individual to nature (Manent 1977, p. 200).

For his part, in the *Wealth of Nations* Smith associates the division of labor with the exponential increase of productive power that makes the great improvement of primitive life possible. He agrees with Rousseau that, once established, the division of labor decisively changes our mode of being. Only a fraction of our needs or wants can be supplied by our own activity, and "[e]very man thus lives by exchanging, or becomes in some measure a merchant, and the society itself grows to be what is properly a commercial society (Smith 1981, 1.4.1)." Smith departs sharply from Rousseau, however, in celebrating the numerous advantages and "general opulence," occasioned by the division of labor. In Smith's view there is nothing ennobling or redemptive about poverty, and a rising standard of living makes individual and family life more secure and humane (Berry 1997, 122). But no human intentionality is responsible for or foresees these positive effects. "It is," rather, "the necessary, though very slow and gradual consequence of a certain propensity in human nature ... to truck, barter and exchange one thing for another." Where Rousseau imagined individuals casually improving their bows or amusedly adorning themselves with shells, Smith imagines *exchanging* bows for shells and vice versa. Where Rousseau sees the division of labor transforming a condition of independence into dependence, Smith sees the reverse:

> In civilised society [man] stands at all times in need of the cooperation and assistance of great multitudes, while his whole life is scarce sufficient to gain the friendship of a few persons. ... [M]an has almost constant occasion for the help of his brethren, and it is in vain for him to expect it from their benevolence only. He will be more likely to prevail if he can interest their self-love in his favour, and show them that it is for their own advantage to do for him what he requires of them. ... It is not from the benevolence of the butcher, the brewer, or the baker that we expect our dinner, but from their regard to their own interest. We address ourselves, not to their humanity but to their self-love, and never talk to them of our own necessities but of their advantages. Nobody but a beggar chooses to depend chiefly upon the benevolence of his fellow-citizens. Even a beggar does not depend upon it entirely (Smith 1981, 1.2.2).

The gravamen of this celebrated argument is that, unlike benevolent interest, the relations of commercial society are impersonal, like the relations among strangers, and this quality has both a utilitarian and a moral advantage. The first is that we need not depend on the kindness of strangers if we can appeal to their self-interest;

[8] I owe this insight to Florence Khodoss (1987, pp. 153–54).

whereas friends willing to come to our aid will always be few, innumerable providers stand ready to meet our needs—and without condescension. A second and more indirect benefit of impersonal relations is the cultivation of a sense of strict justice. Whereas relations of love are notoriously forgiving, dependence on strangers requires confidence in their regularity. Commercial contracts subject to the rule of law instill the habit of law-abidingness that reinforces the social trust on which a society of strangers depends. The very risk of reliance on strangers makes reliability a genuine, if modest, virtue.[9]

Smith was as troubled as Rousseau by the moral effects of dependency, especially in circumstances of one-sided dominance like masters and slaves; but he saw the division of labor as its solution rather than its cause: "Nothing tends so much to corrupt and enervate the mind as dependency, and nothing gives such noble and generous notions of probity as freedom and independency. Commerce is one great preventive of this custom."[10] The division of labor means specialization, but in a modern economy an occupation need not be a destiny. For Smith the real moral problem of the progressive specialization and narrowing of tasks was its stultifying effect on the worker's mind, including its capacity for sympathy (Smith 1981, V.i.f.50).

Rousseau regarded the division of labor as the precursor of the divided self. Dependence on others for one's preservation triggers the fatal dialectic described in the second highlighted passage of the *Letter*. As human faculties develop and need multiply, the "independent commerce" of the first times is succeeded by an endemic competition for prestige. Before the onset of *amour-propre*, the individual regarded himself as "the sole spectator to observe him, as the sole being in the universe to take an interest in him, and as the sole judge of his merit" (Rousseau 1964, note O, p. 222). But the social condition prompts individuals to flaunt their qualities because rank depends on their recognition. So begins, from Rousseau's point of view, man's *unnatural* desire to better his condition. To rise, one must either have or affect the socially advantageous qualities, with the result that being and seeming become indistinguishable. Eventually,

> Man, from being free and independent, [becomes] by a multitude of new necessities subjected in a manner, to all nature, and above all to his fellow creatures, whose slave he is in one sense even while he becomes their master; rich, he has occasion for their services; poor, he stands in need of their assistance; and even mediocrity does not enable him to live without them. He is obliged therefore to endeavour to interest them in his situation, and to make them find, either in reality or in appearance, their advantage in labouring for his (Smith 1980, p. 252).

We are reminded that Smith found a formula for the *preservation* of independence in this very process of enlisting the self-love of others in one's own objectives. He even discovered an emergent virtue in this prudent calculation, for in appealing to the other's self-interest, we acknowledge the universality of self-love and this

[9] See the elaboration of this point in Berry (1997, pp. 129–33).

[10] Quoted in Griswold (1999, p. 294 n.61).

awareness moderates our partiality. In other words, the mechanism of sympathy is automatically at work in commercial relations. Where Rousseau finds only an invidious competition, Smith detects a necessary collaboration. Commerce has an essential sociality that can be developed rightly as well as wrongly (Cropsey 1977, p. 78).

Smith characterizes the inner logic of commercial society as a "system of natural liberty" in which "[e]very man, as long as he does not violate the laws of justice, is left perfectly free to pursue his own interest his own way, and to bring both his industry and capital into competition with those of any other man, or order of men (Smith 1981, IV.ix)."[11] This liberty is natural, it appears, because the desire to better one's condition is natural. Whether or not it is folly to exert oneself to acquire provisions for two when one has a sufficiency, the ubiquity of that desire is self-evident. Smith does not dispute Rousseau's explanation of the psychological dynamics at work in commercial life; he grants that "the toil and bustle" of the world, "the avarice and ambition," the pursuit of wealth and power and preeminence is not to supply "the necessities of nature," and he is well aware of the operation of *amour-propre* or vanity at its center:

> From whence, then, arises that emulation which runs through all the different ranks of men, and what are the advantages which we propose by that great purpose of human life which we call bettering our condition? To be observed, to be attended to, to be taken notice of with sympathy, complacency and approbation, are all the advantages which we can propose to derive from it. It is the vanity, not the ease, or the pleasure, which interests us (Smith 1982, 1.3.2).

What remains unclear is whether the natural desire to better one's condition is primarily a desire for greater comfort and convenience or for the positional good of superiority. The individual pursuit of utility, Smith has shown, generates economic benefits for others; but the consequences for the social bond of a vain desire for preeminence are surely more ominous.[12] The pursuit of a private good need not be at the expense of others; but it depends on the nature of the good being pursued. There is also an important question to ask about the mentality, the soul, of the individual bent on bettering his condition when that improvement is hostage to an unlimited imagination.

Smith addresses both matters in his first invocation of the invisible hand in *Theory of Moral Sentiments*. Regarding the motive of acquisitiveness, he writes:

> The rich ... consume little more than the poor, and in spite of their natural selfishness and rapacity, though they mean only their own conveniency, though the sole end which they propose from the labours of all the thousands whom they employ, be the gratification of their own vain and insatiable desires, they divide with the poor the produce of all their improvements. They are led by an invisible hand to make nearly the same distribution of the

---

[11] The passage continues: "The sovereign is completely discharged from a duty, in the attempting to perform which he must always be exposed to innumerable delusions, and for the proper performance of which no human wisdom or knowledge could ever be sufficient; the duty of superintending the industry of private people, and of directing it towards the employments most suitable to the interest of the society."

[12] On this matter see Manent (1998, pp. 88–89).

> necessaries of life, which would have been made, had the earth been divided into equal portions among all its inhabitants, and thus without intending it, without knowing it, advance the interest of the society, and afford means to the multiplication of the species. When Providence divided the earth among a few lordly masters, it neither forgot nor abandoned those who seemed to have been left out in the partition. These last too enjoy their share of all that it produces. In what constitutes the real happiness of human life, they are in no respect inferior to those who would seem so much above them. In ease of body and peace of mind, all the different ranks of life are nearly upon a level, and the beggar, who suns himself by the side of the highway, possesses that security which kings are fighting for (Smith, 4.1.10).

The taste for luxury, Smith acknowledges, is indeed fueled by vanity more than a desire for comfort. But the vice of the rich is more cupidity than rapacity and its upshot remains the unintended advancement of the general good. But in what sense is the *individual* driven by the most powerful natural desire free? Or moral?

*

This brings us to the last of Smith's excerpts from the *Discourse* and to the status of freedom and virtue in the system of natural liberty. The culmination of the *Discourse* is the contrast between the savage "who breathes nothing but liberty and repose" and the miserable commercial man who "toils, bestirs and torments himself without end, to obtain employments which are still more laborious" (Smith 1980, p. 253). Smith surely has this passage in mind in his parable of the poor man's son, "whom heaven in its anger has visited with ambition" and who blindly admires the condition of the rich:

> He thinks if he had attained [their comforts], he would sit still contentedly, and be quiet, enjoying himself in the thought of the happiness and tranquillity of his situation. He is enchanted with the distant idea of this felicity[,] … he devotes himself for ever to the pursuit of wealth and greatness. To obtain the conveniencies which these afford, he submits … to more fatigue of body and more uneasiness of mind, than he could have suffered through the whole of his life from the want of them. … If we consider the real satisfaction which all these things are capable of affording, by itself and separated from the beauty of that arrangement which is fitted to promote it, it will always appear in the highest degree contemptible and trifling. But we rarely view it in this abstract and philosophical light. We naturally confound it in our imagination with the order, the regular and harmonious movement of the system, the machine or economy by means of which it is produced. The pleasures of wealth and greatness, when considered in this complex view, strike the imagination as something grand, and beautiful, and noble, of which the attainment is well worth all the toil and anxiety which we are so apt to bestow upon it (Smith 1982, 4.1.8).

As noted above, it is our expansive imagination that perpetrates this dreadful deceit. But Smith's conclusion is startling: "And it is well that nature imposes on us in this manner. It is this deception which arouses and keeps in continual motion the industry of mankind" (Smith 1982, 4.1.8). The prodigious achievements of civilization depend on an illusion, on the cunning of the invisible hand.

In alerting readers to the enchanting rhetoric of the *Discourse on Inequality*, Smith remarked that Rousseau's portrait of natural man also betrays the addition of "a little philosophical chemistry" to give the sublimity of Platonic morality. The same might be said of Smith's account of the invisible hand. In an acute analysis of Smith's understanding of nature, Joseph Cropsey remarks that "the invisible hand is not a metaphor for a power by which nature compels men to perform acts." It *is* a metaphor that presupposes "that something called nature transforms the ugliness and bondage of man into a true human good." Smith's conception of nature is thus a construction. "No one has ever seen nature; what we see is the world, and from it we go on to arrive at nature, which is an explanation of the world." The point is that there can be no account of the world "as nature" that does not add something to the phenomena to make the world *intelligible*. Smith, Cropsey suggests, "added compulsion and benevolent purpose to the world in order to arrive at nature. Man in nature is the subject of a benevolent despotism that, added to the world, makes it intelligible and, incidentally, good" (Cropsey 1977, p. 84). The irony remains that the individual pursues an illusory good and his freedom, while uncoerced in a practical sense, hardly appears to be a matter of self-direction in any moral sense. Smith's philosophical chemistry is the addition of the philosopher's panoramic perspective that subsumes the individual within the mechanism of nature and recognizes the sublimity of the *common* good.[13]

I dwell on this "constructive" aspect of Smith's philosophy because he is justifiably credited with an empiricism that manifestly contrasts with Rousseau's conjectural history. But as Pierre Manent has indicated, the powerful role played by the imagination in Smith's theory cries out for a history of the imagination, an empirical record of its plastic power and the variety of ways it puts human beings to work.[14]

The elusive character of Smith's concept of nature casts a shadow on the system of natural liberty. The strong suggestion of *nature's* agency implies a troubling determinism in that unimpeded human behavior remains unwilled or unintended. Is natural liberty anything more than following desire where *it* leads or does it include a particular stance toward desire that raises the individual above the realm of necessity? Ryan Hanley argues powerfully for the view that the system of natural liberty does not dispense with virtue: prudence is the cure for the restlessness and distractedness of vanity; magnanimity is the antidote to the mediocrity of materialism; and beneficence (not to be confused with benevolence) is the necessary counterweight to individualism's tendency to social indifference (Hanley 2009, p. 93). Self-interested individuals motivated by the desire for recognition are amenable to an education that directs their vanity to worthy objects. The propensity to truck and barter, and to better one's condition is not our exclusive natural impulse; also natural is the desire for approbation, and Smith describes how this more obviously social inclination can be encouraged toward moderation and self-command.

Smith is keenly aware that our opinion of the propriety of our own conduct is infected with partiality. He remarks that this self-deceit is "the source of half the disorders of human life." But unlike Rousseau, he concludes that nature has not left

---

[13] For another careful analyis of Smith's conception of nature, see Griswold (1999, pp. 311–17).

[14] Manent (1998, pp. 97–102). For a different interpretation of the role of the imagination in the pursuit of happiness, see Griswold (1999, pp. 302–03).

us without a remedy: "Our continual observations upon the conduct of others, insensibly lead us to form to ourselves certain general rules concerning what is fit and proper either to be done or to be avoided" (Smith 1982, 3.4.5–6). And it is not nature alone that responds. "Man naturally desires, not only to be loved, but to be lovely; or to be that thing which is the natural and proper object of love. He naturally dreads, not only to be hated, but to be hateful; or to be that thing which is the natural and proper object of hatred" (Smith 1982, 3.2.1). Here, one may say, is Smith's reply to Rousseau's fatalism about the power of *amour-propre* to corrupt the individual's very self-consciousness. The concern for reputation, he counters, leads to a certain self-detachment that allows for self-examination. To the extent that this detachment involves alienation it is, *pace* Rousseau, good for oneself and for others.

This brings us back to the question with which we began: what is the foundational justification of our way of life? As Cropsey incisively puts it, "Smith advocated capitalism because it makes freedom possible, not because it is freedom." It makes freedom possible by encouraging people toward self-restraint and law-abidingness and thus toward an ordered social life by way of their own capacity for self-command rather than the state's capacity for coercion. Commercial society releases the "freedom of the individual from the restraint of an implausible virtue into the custody of his own natural impulses," but it also "directs" the appetites, rather than merely unleashing them (Cropsey 1957, pp. x, 70). Smith worried as much as Rousseau about the disintegrative effects of a consumer society that would be nothing more than "a deceitful and frivolous exterior; honour without virtue, reason without wisdom, and pleasure without happiness" (Smith 1980, pp. 253–54). In the final analysis, there is a virtue in both the system of natural liberty and the individuals who compose it. In the same way that capitalism isn't freedom, commerce isn't virtue; but commerce is hardly antithetical to morality and it gives the virtues an arena in which to develop.

References

Berry C (1997) Social theory of the Scottish enlightenment. Edinburgh University Press, Edinburgh
Bloom A (1979) Introduction Jean-Jacques Rousseau, Emile. University of Chicago Press, Chicago
Cropsey J (1957) Polity and economy: an interpretation of the principles of Adam Smith. Greenwood Press, Westport
Cropsey J (1977) Political philosophy and the issues of politics. University of Chicago Press, Chicago
Frankfurt H (2015) On inequality. Princeton University Press, Princeton
Griswold CL Jr (1999) Adam Smith and the virtues of enlightenment. Cambridge University Press, Cambridge
Hanley RA (2008) Commerce and corruption: Rousseau's diagnosis and Adam Smith's cure. Eur J Soc Polit Theor 7:137–158
Hanley RA (2009) Adam Smith and the character of virtue. Cambridge University Press, Cambridge
Hayek FA (1960) The constitution of liberty. Gateway, Chicago
Hume D (1997) Of commerce. In: Miller EF (ed) Essays: moral, political and literary. Liberty Classics, Indianapolis

Ignatieff M (1984) The needs of strangers. Penguin, New York
Khodoss F (1987) Discours sur l'origine et les fondements de l'inegalite parmi les hommes. Bordas, Paris
Manent P (1977) Naissances de la politique moderne. Payot, Paris
Manent P (1998) The city of man. Translated by LePain MA. Princeton University Press, Princeton
McCloskey DN (2010) Bourgeois dignity: why economics can't explain the modern world. University of Chicago Press, Chicago
Nozick R (1974) Anarchy, state, and utopia. Basic Books, New York
Rasmussen DC (2008) The problems and promise of commercial society: Adam's Smith's response to Rousseau. Pennsylvania University Press, University Park
Rousseau J (1964) Discourse on the origin and foundations of inequality among men. In: Masters RD, Masters JR (trans) The first and second discourses. St. Martin's Press, New York
Rousseau J (1978) On the social contract. In: Masters RD, Masters JR (Trans) On the social contract with Geneva manuscript and political economy. St. Martin's Press, New York
Rousseau J (1979) Emile. Bloom A (trans). Basic Books, New York
Rousseau J (1990) Rousseau, judge of Jean-Jacques: dialogues. In: Masters RD, Kelly C (eds) Bush JR, Masters RD, Kelly C (trans) Collected writings of Rousseau, vol. 1. University Press of New Hampshire, Hanover
Rousseau J (1997a) Essay on the origins of language. In: Gourevitch V (trans, ed) The discourses and other early political writings. Cambridge University Press, Cambridge, pp 247–99
Rousseau J (1997b) Preface to Naricissus. In: Gourevitch V (trans, ed) The discourses and other early political writings. Cambridge University Press, Cambridge, pp 92–106
Smith A (1980) Letter to the Edinburgh review. In: Wightman W, Bryce J, Ross I (eds) Essays on philosophical subjects. Liberty Fund Press, Indianapolis, pp 242–256
Smith A (1981) In: Campbell R, Skinner A (eds) An inquiry into the nature and causes of the wealth of nations. Liberty Fund Press, Indianapolis. [Cited by book, part, chapter, and paragraph.]
Smith A (1982) The theory of moral sentiments. MacFie A, Raphael D (eds) Liberty Fund Press, Indianapolis [Cited by part, chapter, and paragraph.]

Chapter 21
Situating Southern Influences in James M. Buchanan and Modern Public Choice Economics

Art Carden, Vincent Geloso, and Phillip W. Magness

Abstract In her 2017 book *Democracy in Chains*, historian Nancy MacLean identifies John C. Calhoun as the "lodestar" of public choice theory and argues that the conservative Southern Agrarian poets (Donald Davidson, Allen Tate, Robert Penn Warren, and others) were influential in the formation of 1986 Nobel Laureate James M. Buchanan's worldview. We test this argument with reference to the scholars cited in Buchanan's collected works and elsewhere. The evidence for any direct or even indirect influence of Calhoun and the Agrarians is very scant, and we conclude that Buchanan's intellectual program was shaped far more by Knut Wicksell, Frank Knight, and the Italian public finance tradition than by Calhoun or early twentieth-century segregationists.

Keywords James M. Buchanan · Segregation · South · Public choice · Constitutional political economy · John C. Calhoun · Southern Agrarians

21.1 Introduction

Are free market capitalism and the classical liberal intellectual tradition stained by associations with defenders of slavery and segregation? A steady stream of books has linked American capitalism to chattel slavery, often describing it as

A. Carden (✉)
Samford University, Birmingham, AL, USA
e-mail: wcarden@samford.edu

V. Geloso
George Mason University, Fairfax, VA, USA
e-mail: vgeloso@gmu.edu

P. W. Magness
American Institute for Economic Research, Great Barrington, MA, USA
e-mail: phil.magness@aier.org

P. Gray et al. (eds.), *Standard of Living*, Studies in Economic History,
https://doi.org/10.1007/978-3-031-06477-7_21

"indispensable" and in other, similar language (e.g., Beckert 2014; Baptist 2014; Johnson 2013; Schermerhorn 2015, 2018).[1] These arguments have been vigorously criticized and, we believe, refuted decisively by economic historians.[2] In 2017, Duke University historian Nancy MacLean made waves with her book *Democracy in Chains: The Deep History of the Radical Right's Stealth Plan for America.* In it, she argues that 1986 Nobel laureate James M. Buchanan is the man behind the scenes writing the playbook for Charles Koch and other right-wing plutocrats.

MacLean tries to place Buchanan within a southern segregationist intellectual tradition, specifically arguing that he was an intellectual heir of pro-slavery South Carolina firebrand and former US Vice President John C. Calhoun. Calhoun, she claims, is the "intellectual lodestar" of public choice economics. MacLean goes further, though, by connecting Buchanan to the Vanderbilt Agrarians, a group of literary figures in the 1920s and 1930s based at Vanderbilt University who celebrated and romanticized Thomas Jefferson's ideal of the independent yeoman farmer. They also defended segregation. She writes specifically that poet Donald Davidson was "the Nashville writer who seemed most decisive in Buchanan's emerging intellectual system." Calhoun, Davidson, and the racial dimensions of their work are lurking in the background of MacLean's depiction of Buchanan's work at the University of Virginia between 1956 and 1968, particularly his purported involvement in Virginia's "Massive Resistance" to school desegregation.

Democracy in Chains was not the only Buchanan-centered volume to appear in 2017, however. Buchanan's former student, colleague, and collaborator Richard Wagner published *James M. Buchanan and Liberal Political Economy: A Rational Reconstruction.* He notes, with reference to urban theorist Jane Jacobs: "So far as I know, Buchanan was not familiar with the work of Jane Jacobs. I say this based on her absence from the index of names in the twentieth volume of Buchanan's Collected Works" (Wagner 2017). We adopt a similar principle in attempting to locate Buchanan within the political tradition of Calhoun and find essentially no evidence to support MacLean's claim that the southern intellectual tradition influenced the development of Public Choice Theory. From Buchanan's work, it is apparent that his influences and motivations lay elsewhere. In asking "What Should Economists Do?" as Buchanan (1964) did in his famous presidential address to the Southern Economic Association—and in actually doing economics—Buchanan was drawing directly from a body of influences that, as far as his oeuvre suggests, included little if anything from John C. Calhoun, the Southern Agrarians, or other southern intellectuals.[3]

[1] Each of these provide representative contribution, with Beckert, Baptist, and Johnson's books constituting a "Big Three" of sorts.

[2] For more information see the collection of reviews in 75(3) of the *Journal of Economic History* by John E. Murray, Alan L. Olmstead, Trevon D. Logan, and Jonathan B. Pritchett (Murray et al. 2015). See also Engerman (2018), Hilt (2017), Olmstead and Rhode (2018), Margo (2018), and Wright (2020).

[3] See Magness (2020) for further discussion of anti-discrimination in the public choice tradition.

21.2 John C. Calhoun Was Not the Public Choice "Lodestar"

The reader of *Democracy in Chains* would come away with the impression that Buchanan was an intellectual descendent of South Carolina politician and former US Vice President John C. Calhoun, a thinker MacLean calls the "intellectual lodestar" of the public choice movement based on Tabarrok and Cowen's (1992) discussion of Calhoun as a "precursor" to public choice who discussed similar themes but who differed mightily in his methodological and normative commitments. There are parallels between Calhoun's concern with unrestrained majorities and Buchanan's concern with the same, but there is nothing to suggest that Buchanan owes a particular intellectual debt to Calhoun or that Calhoun even minimally influenced Buchanan's constitutional political economy.

While the suggestion of a connection between Buchanan and Calhoun predates MacLean's work, it also substantially postdates the most plausible parallel, Buchanan and Gordon Tullock's *Calculus of Consent* (1962). In 1975 political scientist Douglas Rae attempted to classify the "new political economy" of Buchanan and Tullock within a lineage of political consensus doctrines that flowed through the contributions to political theory stretching from John Locke, William Godwin, John Stuart Mill, and particularly Calhoun (Rae 1975).

Tullock answered that Rae was mistaken in his intellectual genealogy when it came to Calhoun. The *Calculus,* he explained, came from a "quite disparate" line of technical reasoning that followed the work of European economists Vilfredo Pareto and Knut Wicksell. Similarities "between their position and that of certain earlier political philosophers" were important but coincidental as the ideas had developed independently. Furthermore, Tullock was unaware of this alleged lineage, having "never read so much as one page of Calhoun and hav[ing] no desire to do so." He knew Calhoun only from a secondary literature and presumed his work to have been prompted by "a desire to protect slavery" separate from the optimality conditions of a Paretian decision rule. According to Tullock, Buchanan was "totally ignorant of the original text of Calhoun's work" (Tullock 1975).

A handful of scholars have nonetheless suggested similarities between the *Calculus* and Calhoun's *Disquisition on Government,* in particular as both respectively explore the use of decision rules to constrain simple majoritarian outcomes in governance. Works in this vein include Aranson (1991), Ordeshook (1992), Tabarrok and Cowen (1992), and Salter (2015), and while they interpret various parallels, none asserts the genealogical claim found in MacLean. The observed parallels in these works as well as in Rae, we believe, come from the fact that both Buchanan and Tullock and Calhoun were independently responding to the constitutional thinking of James Madison. In this sense they drank from the same well, but Buchanan wasn't drinking from Calhoun's cup.

Buchanan's written work provides further evidence for Tullock's assertion of Calhoun's lack of influence on their collaboration. If Calhoun were an influential presence, we would expect to see his name figure prominently in Buchanan's

Collected Works (Buchanan 1999–2002). Calhoun does not appear in the indexes to the Collected Works, the index to *Better Than Plowing*, or the index to his normative vision *Why I, Too, Am Not a Conservative*. Nor does Calhoun appear in the index to the *Selected Works of Gordon Tullock*, and the mentions of Calhoun that appear in a search of the online Library of Economics and Liberty do not support the thesis that he was an important intellectual influence on Buchanan's constitutional thinking.

Furthermore, there are no entries on Calhoun in standard Public Choice reference texts, such as the Charles Rowley-edited *Encyclopedia of Public Choice* or the Michael Reksulak, Laura Razzolini, and William Shughart-edited *Elgar Companion to Public Choice* (Reksulak et al. 2013). Calhoun does not warrant an article or even a mention, apparently, in the *International Encyclopedia of Political Science*.

The earliest utilization of Calhoun's work from within the broader Public Choice tradition that we were able to locate is a 1978 article by William A. Niskanen exploring the implications of adopting a "nullification" principle as a state veto mechanism at the constitutional level. Niskanen acknowledged the concept's mixed constitutional history as both a device to deflect constitutionally dubious legislation (the Alien and Sedition Acts, or in a lesser known case, the veto of the Fugitive Slave Act by the legislature of Wisconsin) and, in Calhoun's arguing, a mechanism to defend slavery. But these were matters largely settled by the Civil War and thus, in Niskanen's telling, primarily illustrative as early operational derivatives of Madison's "compound republic" (Niskanen et al. 1978 [172]).

Further explorations of Calhoun from within the Public Choice tradition are confined to the four aforementioned papers: Aranson (1991), Ordeshook (1992), Tabarrok and Cowen (1992), and Salter (2015). Two other works, McGuire and Van Cott (2003) and Magness (2009), substantively engage Calhoun as a historical figure in Public Choice interpretations of nineteenth-century tariff legislation and another, Grynaviski and Munger (2014), does the same with regard to a Public Choice interpretation of slavery. All other references to Calhoun in the scholarly journals *Public Choice* and *Constitutional Political Economy* are tangential and minor.[4] Taken in sum, Calhoun's connection to the larger Public Choice tradition in the time since Buchanan and Tullock is at best a niche topic of peripheral interest. It is certainly true that a thinker can be influential without being cited or discussed prominently—Karl Marx's influence in the twentieth century comes to mind—but the literature's silence on Calhoun's influence in political science and Public Choice is, we think, deafening.

[4] We counted a total of 13 tangential references to Calhoun between these two journals from their respective founding to January 2018. For comparison, the word "Calhoun" was almost as likely to appear in connection to a geographic place name.

21.3 Donald C. Davidson and the Southern Agrarians Did Not Shape Buchanan's Vision

H.L. Mencken's jibe about "The Sahara of the Bozart" notwithstanding, the South has a venerable literary tradition. Among the leaders of the Southern literary tradition in the 1930s were the writers and poets based at Vanderbilt University that came to be known as the Southern Agrarians (or Nashville Agrarians, or Tennessee Agrarians) and who wrote the famous "Twelve Southerners" essay collection *I'll Take My Stand*, published in 1930. In *I'll Take My Stand* and elsewhere, they fired passionate salvos against what they saw as the enemy: industrial society.[5]

Citing Buchanan's reference to the Southern Agrarians on page 126 of *Better than Plowing*, Buchanan's 1992 collection of autobiographical essays, MacLean (2017 [32]) writes:

> Vanderbilt University, in Nashville, loomed large in the family's vision for Jim's future, its stature as the state's top private university no doubt a draw. Vanderbilt was also the site of a cultural project that attracted James Buchanan—one that stamped his vision of the good society and the just state. The university was the home of the Southern Agrarians, the literary men who in 1930 published a manifesto for southern rural life, *I'll Take My Stand*. The "Twelve Southerners," the collective authors on the spine, were mainly literary men, novelists and poets, remembered still for their call to preserve humane rural values from corruption by creeping industrialism and materialism. But their version of those values was racially exclusive, and their mission was profoundly political.

Buchanan, it seems from this passage, had his worldview shaped by the Agrarians' vision. MacLean continues (2017 [32]):

> The Nashville writer who seemed most decisive in Jim Buchanan's emerging intellectual system was Donald Davidson, the Agrarians' ringleader, who portrayed the growth of the federal government since the Progressive Era as a move toward "the totalitarian state" that was destroying regional folkways. It was Davidson who also named the enemy: Leviathan.

While acknowledging that Thomas Hobbes used the term, she credits Davidson with interpreting it a new way and insinuates [33–34] that Buchanan's project was explicitly Davidsonian: "Leviathan was 'the subtlest and most dangerous foe of humanity—the tyranny that wears the mask of humanitarianism and benevolence.' Buchanan would devote the first part of his career to tearing off what he called the 'romantic' mask, and the last part to enchaining the beast behind it." One presumes that Buchanan would have been an avid participant in the Agrarian program had he attended Vanderbilt and not Middle Tennessee State Teachers College, where he ultimately graduated with degrees in literature, mathematics, and economics.

In discussing Buchanan's move to New York for World War II in 1941, MacLean writes that Buchanan "seemed to see through lenses wholly crafted by Donald Davidson" [34]. In discussing Buchanan's encounter with discrimination based on his humble southern roots, she recounts his "Davidson-like framing of the problem

---

[5] For more information on this see Richard Weaver's essay "The Tennessee Agrarians," especially pages 8–10. The essay appears as the first chapter in Curtis and Thompson (1987).

in regional terms that missed the most egregious impact of bigotry: on Catholics, Jews, Mexican Americans, working-class white men, and, above all, African Americans" [34] and claims that he did not "sympathize with the plight of black Americans." This is, perhaps, what we should expect from someone who saw the world through "lenses wholly crafted by Donald Davidson."

But alas, this is not what Buchanan saw. Furthermore, there is no evidence in Buchanan's work to suggest that he was looking through Davidsonian lenses. First, MacLean's discussion of Buchanan's response to discrimination quotes from page four of *Better Than Plowing*, and the text immediately after it is conspicuously missing from an account in which she suggests Buchanan did not "***sympathize*** with the plight of black Americans" (MacLean 2017 [35], emphasis added). But here is Buchanan immediately after the text she quotes: "This sobering experience made me forever ***sympathetic*** to those who suffer discriminatory treatment, and it forestalled any desire to be a part of any eastern establishment institution" (emphasis added) (Buchanan 1992 [4]).

Second, we think it is reasonable to expect that influence from the Southern literary tradition generally, the Agrarians specifically, and Davidson in particular should be reflected in Buchanan's citations as reflected, for example, in the Indexes to his Collected Works and his autobiographical collection *Better Than Plowing*.

The hypothesis that Buchanan's intellectual system was influenced by the Agrarians does not fare well. Buchanan does not cite or discuss Davidson. Nor, for that matter, does he cite or discuss any of the other contributors to *I'll Take My Stand*. Buchanan mentions, for example, his and Frank Knight's mutual affinity for the poetry of Thomas Hardy, but the major contributors to the Southern literary tradition are essentially absent from Buchanan's work and recollections. Of the authors represented in *The Literature of the American South: A Norton Anthology*, the only two names appearing in Buchanan's *Collected Works* and *Better Than Plowing* are Thomas Jefferson and Martin Luther King, Jr.: Jefferson in several places because of his thinking on the institutions of governance, King in a section in which Buchanan points out that "(t)he local [segregation] statutes that were violated by the restaurant sit-ins of the early 1960's were 'Southern' laws, of course, and properly and universally condemned as 'unjust'" (Buchanan 1968 [668]).[6]

If anything, this is evidence against the thesis that Buchanan's worldview was formed by the Agrarians. Davidson and the Agrarians may have influenced today's conservative movement (as distinct from the libertarian movement) through, for example, thinkers like Russell Kirk and Richard Weaver, but there is nothing to suggest that he had an influence on Buchanan even through Kirk and Weaver. Buchanan does not cite Kirk, and his only reference to Weaver is a footnote in volume 7 of the *Collected Works* in which he mentions the title of Weaver's *Ideas Have Consequences* in a discussion of Keynes and institutions.

Buchanan did mention the Agrarians on page 126 of *Better Than Plowing*, but only in pointing out that they too had discussed "Jefferson's ideal polity of yeoman

[6]More information can be found in the reprinted volume 16 of the *Collected Works*.

farmers," part of a "country aesthetic" he had come to appreciate in his later years. In light of the available evidence, we do not think this is sufficient to establish a meaningful intellectual link between Buchanan and the Agrarians.

21.4 So Who Influenced Buchanan?

Buchanan was a man of letters, the only American economist other than James Heckman known to the economist and polymath Deirdre McCloskey to read the *Times Literary Supplement* (McCloskey 2000 [27]). Throughout his work, he left a considerable record of his intellectual influences. His work suggests that they were not Calhoun and the Southern Agrarians. Rather, they included the thinkers of the enlightenment, the economists Frank Knight and Knut Wicksell, the American founders, and Italian public finance scholars. Over time, Thomas Hobbes "moved to center stage as the political philosopher to be pondered" whereas his "work had seemed only peripherally relevant to [Buchanan] in 1960" (Buchanan 1992 [100–101] cf. McCloskey 2000 [26]).

Hobbes' place among Buchanan's intellectual influences is itself another mark against the Davidson theory. Whereas MacLean specifically credits Davidson as a likely candidate for instilling the Leviathan concept in Buchanan's work, this claim is not simply without evidence but also in direct conflict with the term's actual Hobbesian source. As Buchanan recounted in the same passage [101–102], his interest in Hobbes surged shortly after his move to Virginia Polytechnic Institute in 1969 thanks in large part to the work of his colleague Winston Bush, integrating Hobbesian thought into the emerging field of public choice. The earliest use of the Leviathan metaphor that we could locate in Buchanan's works dates to his 1973 essay "America's Third Century in Perspective" in the inaugural issue of the *Atlantic Economic Journal*. It quickly became a mainstay in Buchanan's lexicon in his 1975 book *The Limits of Liberty* (dedicated to Bush, who died in a car accident as the work was being prepared) and provided a name for his famous model for conceptualizing taxation in 1980s *The Power to Tax,* coauthored with Geoffrey Brennan. Combined with Buchanan's recollections, these patterns point to an unambiguous Hobbesian origin of Buchanan's use of the term. Davidson's Leviathan, by contrast, is nowhere to be found.

While these measures are imperfect, we can get an idea as to Buchanan's influences by looking at the scholars he cites and the ideas he discusses. Calhoun, Davidson, and the Agrarians are conspicuously absent while Knight, Wicksell, a number of Italian public finance economists, a host of prominent political economists from the English-speaking and German-speaking traditions of the late nineteenth and early twentieth centuries, and the most prominent thinkers of the Enlightenment and the American founding are cited extensively.

Buchanan's 2007 update of *Better Than Plowing*, titled *Economics from the Outside In*, offers an explicit list of the influences on his academic life and thought in Chap. 15, titled "Influences on My Academic Life and Thought." He discusses

Frank H. Knight, Knut Wicksell, Kenneth J. Arrow, Antonio de Viti de Marco, Rutledge Vining, Gordon Tullock, John von Neumann and Oskar Morgenstern, F.A. Hayek, and Adam Smith. In Chap. 9 of *Better Than Plowing*, Buchanan offers us a unique insight into the thinkers who influenced him. The chapter contains a loosely-arranged collection of quotes he had written "in three small black notebooks." For Buchanan (1992 [127]),

> [I]t is worthy of note here that the selections are not taken primarily from writings within my own discipline, economics, and only a few of the ideas expressed are relevant for this discipline's scientific enterprise. Most of the ideas are methodological, philosophical, or moral—relevant to the development and reinforcement of a generalizable personal philosophy for someone who just happens to have been trained professionally as an economist.

In this chapter, we get a look into the ideas that shaped Buchanan's worldview. It is perhaps reasonable to expect that, had they left important impressions on Buchanan's mind, Calhoun and Davidson would be represented among those quoted. They are not, which suggests to us that their influence was of, at best, minimal importance. The quotes are loosely organized into several sections: "Analysis, Abstraction, and Education," "Choice, Imagination, Reality, and Time," "Constitutional Rules, Politics, and the Law," "Ethics," "Intellectuals," "Motive, Power, and Influence," and "The Utility of Composition." Buchanan draws from a wide array of literary figures and philosophers, which makes the absence of Calhoun and Davidson that much more conspicuous. The writers Buchanan quotes and the frequency with which they are quoted appear in Table 21.1.

Table 21.1 Writers quoted in Chap. 9 of Buchanan, *Better Than Plowing*

Name	Quotes	Name	Quotes	Name	Quotes
Friedrich Nietzche	7	Luigi Einaudi	1	Thucydides	1
Lord Acton	3	Michael Polanyi	1	Adam Ferguson	1
Frank Knight	3	Immanuel Kant	1	David Hume	1
A. Geoffrey Woodhead	2	Herbert Spencer	1	John Adams	1
F. Scott Fitzgerald	2	G.L.S. Shackle	1	Raymond Aron	1
T.H. Huxley	2	Thomas Sutcliffe	1	R.G. Ross	1
George Orwell	2	Alfred Schutz	1	Henry Thomas Buckle	1
Samuel Johnson	2	Edwin Land	1	Jeremy Bentham	1
James Joyce	2	Irving Babbitt	1	Aldous Huxley	1
W.A. Orton	2	Wilhelm Ropke	1	Johann Goethe	1
Jose Ortega y Gasset	1	Robert Louis Stevenson	1	David McCord Wright	1
John Donne	1	Adam Smith	1	Karl Popper	1
Jean Piaget	1	Richard McKeon	1	Georg Hegel	1
Plato	1	Walter Kauffman	1	Thomas Hobbes	1
Moira Roberts	1	Shirley Robin Letwin	1	Iris Murdoch	1
Albert Camus	1	Joseph Conrad	1	Jakob Burckhardt	1
Norbert Weiner	1	John Updike	1	St. Augustine	1
Arnold Schoenberg	1	*John C. Calhoun*	*0*	*Donald Davidson*	*0*

Of the writers mentioned in Chap. 9 of *Better Than Plowing*, the only one with a meaningful "southern" connection was the economist David McCord Wright, who spent parts of his career at the University of Virginia and the University of Georgia. None of the literary figures mentioned were "southern." W.A. Orton was an economist at Smith College, and R.G. Ross was a philosopher at Queen's College in New York. We found nothing to connect Moira Roberts to the southern tradition. Taken in sum, there is exceedingly little evidence that a distinctive "southern-ness" even registered upon Buchanan's thought or those he identified as his primary influences.

We caution readers not to over-interpret this exercise as there are several omissions one might expect to see if it were an exhaustive list of Buchanan's influences (James Madison and Thomas Jefferson, for example). However, the variety of political thinkers and literary figures represented here makes the absence of Calhoun, Davidson, or any of the Southern Agrarians conspicuous given their prominence in *Democracy in Chains* and their supposed importance for modern public choice. The available evidence suggests a stronger filiation with classical liberal thinkers.

21.5 Conclusion

Buchanan is a fascinating character for his contributions to philosophy, politics, and economics, but he is also fascinating given his rural southern upbringing and his defiant rejection of what he called "the establishment." Attempts to situate him within the pantheon of twentieth-century thinkers and contributors to a Southern tradition specifically are very interesting; however, the evidence suggests that Buchanan's formative intellectual influences came from the European Enlightenment, the American founding, early- and mid-twentieth-century Italian public finance, and two economists in particular: Frank Knight and Knut Wicksell.

MacLean's effort to situate Buchanan within the segregationist-conservative tradition in Tennessee and Virginia, while interesting, runs aground on the evidence contained within Buchanan's corpus. We note that some of Buchanan's papers are still being processed and made available for research, thus we cannot completely preclude new discoveries that would alter our findings. We consider this unlikely, though, given the conspicuous absence of distinctively southern intellectual traditions in his voluminous known works.

As things stand right now, there is little in the documentary record to connect him to the Southern Agrarians and other Southern conservatives. After reviewing Buchanan's intellectual output and influences, we find no evidence to sustain MacLean's depiction of Buchanan's intellectual lineage or placement within the context of southern conservatism. Further dissimilarities between Buchanan's political economy and these claimed southern intellectual influences are both unaccounted for in MacLean's telling. In the case of Calhoun, readily available evidence that MacLean overlooked directly refutes the connections she claims to have discovered.

Acknowledgements We are grateful to scholars and commentators inside and outside our professional circles who have been sources of stimulating conversation and insights about Buchanan's intellectual context. These include but are not limited to Jonathan Adler, David Bernstein, Steven G. Horwitz, Edward J. Lopez, Michael C. Munger, and Daniel J. Smith. In addition to John Murray, we also take this opportunity to mourn the passing of Steven G. Horwitz. All three authors are or have been affiliated with organizations that receive funding from the Charles Koch Foundation.

Appendix: Carden on Murray

John Murray and I were colleagues at Rhodes College in 2011–2012. He was an inspiring scholar and a dedicated teacher who took economics and history very seriously. He was also an excellent colleague who was unafraid to wrestle with the biggest of the big questions both on and off the clock. I gave a presentation on the subject of this paper (and a companion paper (Magness et al. 2019) at Rhodes College a week before John Murray passed away; it was, to the best of my knowledge, the last "academic" event John attended. It is fitting that this paper found a home in a volume dedicated to his memory. We understand the world better because of his scholarship, but more importantly, those of us who knew him are better people because of it.

References

Aranson PH (1991) Calhoun's constitutional economics. Consti Pol Econ 2:31–52

Baptist EE (2014) The half has never been told: slavery and the making of American capitalism. Basic Books, New York

Beckert S (2014) Empire of cotton: a global history. Alfred A. Knopf, New York

Buchanan JM (1964) What should economists do? South Econ J 30:213–222

Buchanan JM (1968) Student revolts, academic liberalism, and constitutional attitudes. Soc Res 35:666–680

Buchanan JM (1973) America's third century in perspective. Atl Econ J 1:3–12

Buchanan JM (1992) Better than plowing and other personal essays. University of Chicago Press, Chicago

Buchanan JM (1999–2002) The collected works of James M. Buchanan. 20 vols. Liberty Fund, Indianapolis

Buchanan JM (2007) Economics from the outside. In: "Better than plowing" and beyond. Texas A&M University Press, College Station

Curtis GM III, Thompson JJ Jr (1987) The southern essays of Richard M. Weaver. Liberty Press, Indianapolis

Engerman SL (2018) Review of the business of slavery and the rise of American capitalism, 1815-1860 by Calvin Schermerhorn and the half has never been told: slavery and the making of American capitalism by Edward E. Baptist. J Econ Lit 55:637–643

Grynaviski JD, Munger M (2014) Did southerners favor slavery? Inferences from an analysis of prices in New Orleans, 1805-1860. Public Choice 159:341–361

Hilt E (2017) Economic history, historical analysis, and the 'new history of capitalism'. J Econ Hist 77:511–536

Johnson W (2013) River of dark dreams: slavery and empire in the cotton kingdom. Belknap Press of Harvard University Press, Cambridge

MacLean N (2017) Democracy in chains: the deep history of the radical right's stealth plan for America. Viking, New York

Magness PW (2009) Constitutional tariffs, incidental protection, and the Laffer relationship in the early United States. Consti Pol Econ 20:177–192

Magness PW (2020) The anti-discriminatory tradition in Virginia school public choice theory. Public Choice 183:417–441

Magness PW, Carden A, Geloso V (2019) James M. Buchanan and the political economy of desegregation. South Econ J 85:715–741

Margo RA (2018) The integration of economic history into economics. Cliometrica 12:377–406

McCloskey DN (2000) How to be human (though an economist). University of Michigan Press, Ann Arbor

McGuire RA, Van Cott TN (2003) A supply and demand exposition of a constitutional tax loophole: the case of tariff symmetry. Consti Pol Econ 14:39–45

Murray JE, Olmstead AL, Logan TD, Pritchett JB, Rousseau PL (2015) Reviews of the half has never been told: slavery and the making of American capitalism, by Edward E. Baptist. J Econ Hist 75:919–931

Niskanen W, Martin B, Tollison RD (1978) The Prospect for Liberal Democracy, in Buchanan JM, Wagner RE, eds Fiscal responsibility in constitutional democracy. Springer, New York, pp. 157–180

Olmstead AL, Rhode PW (2018) Cotton, slavery, and the new history of capitalism. Explor Econ Hist 67:1–17

Ordeshook PC (1992) Constitutional stability. Consti Pol Econ 3:137–175

Rae DW (1975) The limits of consensual decision. Am Pol Sci Rev 69:1270–1294

Reksulak M, Razzolini L, Shughart W (2013) The Elgar companion to public choice. Edward Elgar, Cheltenham

Salter AW (2015) Calhoun's concurrent majority as a generality norm. Consti Pol Econ 26:375–390

Schermerhorn C (2015) The business of slavery and the rise of American capitalism, 1815-1860. Yale University Press, New Haven

Schermerhorn C (2018) Unrequited toil: a history of United States slavery. Cambridge University Press, Cambridge

Tabarrok A, Cowen T (1992) The public choice theory of John C. Calhoun. J Inst Theor Econ 148:655–674

Tullock G (1975) Comment on Rae's 'the limits of consensual decision'. Am Pol Sci Rev 69:1295–1297

Twelve Southerners (1930 [1977]) I'll take my stand. Louisiana State University Press, Baton Rouge

Wagner R (2017) James M. Buchanan and liberal political economy: a rational reconstruction. Lexington Books, Lanham

Wright G (2020) Slavery and Anglo-American capitalism revisited. Econ Hist Rev 73:353–383

Chapter 22
John Murray: A Teacher, a Mentor, and a Friend

Joshua R. Hendrickson

Abstract Upon starting my undergraduate education, I did not have a clear idea of what I wanted to do. I was really interested in learning history and so I decided that I would major in history. As a history major, I was required to take some core economics courses. I really enjoyed them and I wanted to learn more. I thought that a background in history *and* economics might be useful. When I contacted the economics department, I was told that the person to talk to was the undergraduate adviser, John Murray. I had no idea that this fateful meeting would have such a big influence on my life.

Keywords John Murray · Teach · Mentor

Upon starting my undergraduate education, I did not have a clear idea of what I wanted to do. I was really interested in learning history and so I decided that I would major in history. As a history major, I was required to take some core economics courses. I really enjoyed them and I wanted to learn more. I thought that a background in history *and* economics might be useful. When I contacted the economics department, I was told that the person to talk to was the undergraduate adviser, John Murray. I had no idea that this fateful meeting would have such a big influence on my life.

I remember showing up to John's office. When I walked in, it was everything that you would expect from a professor's office. Bookshelves lined every wall. They were all full. In fact, there were stacks of books on the bookshelf in front of the other books. There were stacks of books on his desk and on the floor. He pointed to one particular pile of books that I subsequently recognized was disguising a chair and instructed me to sit down. I told him that I was interested in adding economics either as a minor or another major. He asked my current major. I told him that it was

J. R. Hendrickson (✉)
University of Mississippi, Oxford, MS, USA
e-mail: jrhendr1@olemiss.edu

P. Gray et al. (eds.), *Standard of Living*, Studies in Economic History,
https://doi.org/10.1007/978-3-031-06477-7_22

history and his face seemed to light up. I had no idea that there was even such a thing as economic history at the time, let alone that it was his field.

I ended up deciding to minor in economics and then pursue my Master's degree in the same department. This meant that John was my teacher on several occasions along the way. The main courses I remember are Mathematical Economics and American Economic History.

John was a great teacher. He loved ideas and he loved to share those ideas. His course on American Economic History opened my eyes to a new way of thinking about historical events. John really loved to demonstrate how basic economic concepts could help explain historical events. Whenever he knew of some paper or book that made an interesting argument about a particular topic, he seemed so excited to discuss it. I realize now that this is because he loved to learn and he loved to share what he had learned.

John was also very funny. He always had a dry sense of humor and he loved to sneak in little funny or sarcastic remarks when he could. His deadpan delivery of sarcasm was an inspiration. It was not always clear to me that the other students got the jokes, but I loved them – and I loved the way that they were delivered, without any attempt to acknowledge a joke was being told. He loved to joke, but he also loved to laugh. This was especially the case if you could execute your own dry jokes with the same deadpan delivery.

My appreciation for his teaching has grown over the years as I now have experience of my own. Reflecting back, his comfort level was one characteristic of his teaching that I never would have recognized without the experience of teaching. He was so comfortable as a teacher. As weird as it sounds, one thing I remember about John's classes is silence. John was so comfortable with silence. He was content to let students sit with an idea or a question and think about it.

For me, silence was the most difficult thing to deal with when I started teaching. I assumed that silence must mean that students did not understand the question, or worse, the material. Faced with silence, I would immediately and instinctively have to repeat the question or offer the answer. Not John. He was content to let us think – and he always seemed to know the optimal amount of time to give us to think.

John supervised my Master's thesis, which I wrote on the political motivations of New Deal spending. Working with him really helped me to understand how to do research. Our conversations were incredibly helpful. I could always tell that this part of the job was not work to him. He genuinely enjoyed just sitting and talking about this stuff. He always had questions and he always wanted to know what I thought. When I finished the thesis, he told me that he thought it was really good and that I should try to polish it up and get it published.

The following year when I started my Ph.D. program, I did just that. Shortly thereafter I received some referee reports. They were very negative. I had no idea at the time how frequently one is subjected to negative and cantankerous reviews nor did I consider that the paper might have warranted such reviews. I was really discouraged. The first thing I did was reach out to John to tell him and talk to him about it. He told me not to take it personally, that reviewers could be mean, and that I should stick with it. Although I got busy with the Ph.D. program and never continued with the paper, that advice turned out to be really important when I became an assistant professor. I always kept that advice in the back of my head.

During my Ph.D. program, John and I kept in touch via email. He would always ask what I was working on and was eager to read whatever I sent. After I became a Ph.D. candidate, I asked to see if we could invite John to present in our seminar series. He was working on a paper on maternity insurance and our department had some health economists who I thought might be interested. The seminar went really well and he received some good comments on his paper. He was really happy with how helpful the seminar had been, mentioning it to me several times, even years later. However, the thing that he most wanted to talk about was me. In fact, he apparently spent his visit asking the faculty about me.

When it became apparent that I was going to get done writing my dissertation early, I decided to look for a visiting job during my final year of graduate school. My wife and I already had one child and another on the way. The prospect of having something other than a graduate stipend as my financial contribution to the relationship was important to me. As luck would have it, the University of Toledo was looking for a visitor to come in and teach. My office was right down the hall from John's. It was nice to have regular, face-to-face conversations again. He loved to ask me what kind of research that I was working on and to talk about it with me.

When I accepted the job at Ole Miss, I was in my office. I started going around telling people about the job, but John was not in his office that afternoon and I sent him an email. John was so excited. He described my new job as a "big, big deal." He later stopped by my office to congratulate me and to tell me that he was moving to Rhodes College, in Memphis. He could not believe that we would both be moving and still only be an hour away from one another. We agreed to make sure to meet up on a regular basis.

After the move, John and I would meet about twice a year to have lunch together. Sometimes this included one of us giving a talk. However, most of the time, we just had lunch. These were some of the longest and best lunches of my life. We would sit for hours and talk. We would talk about what was going on in our respective departments and universities. We would talk about our families.[1] We would talk about projects we were working on. My favorite part of these conversations was when we talked about some of our crazier ideas that would be fun to research, but that we had no real plans to pursue.

Although my field of specialization is macroeconomics, I started to be drawn to other topics. Most of those other topics were historical. When I started working on these papers, John was always so excited to talk about them. He wanted to know every detail. He wanted to challenge me to convince him of my argument. John always asked insightful questions. Oftentimes, I could not answer some of his

[1] Here is another example of how our lives were intertwined in unexpected ways. When John had to have neck surgery, he was sent to recover in the neurological unit. My wife is a nurse and worked in that unit. When he arrived, she was assigned to be his nurse. When he was sent home, John made sure to contact me and tell me that my wife did an excellent job during his stay. In fact, he would frequently remind me of this during our visits.

questions, but that was a great benefit because it always made the paper better. In many ways, I think that he felt like I had come full circle. He first met me as a history major who wanted to learn more about economics, and now I was starting to write about historical topics. I never saw more excitement on his face than when I told him about a new historical topic I was working on. He was always just so eager to read it and talk about it.

I knew John my entire adult life. In many ways, John saw me grow up. He was always there along the way, first as a teacher, then as mentor, but ultimately as a friend. John taught me a great deal, both inside and outside the classroom. I miss him, especially in October and March when we would normally meet for our long lunches. He helped me every step of the way, and for that I will always be grateful.

The manufacturer's authorised representative in the EU is Springer
Nature Customer Service Centre GmbH, Europaplatz 3, 69115 Heidelberg,
Germany. If you have any concerns regarding our products, please
contact ProductSafety@springernature.com

Printed and bound by CPI Group (UK) Ltd, Croydon, CR0 4YY
30/09/2026
02225493-0017